OXFORD ENGLISH DR
General Editor: MICHAEL COI
Associate General Editors: PETER HOLLAND

THE ROARING GIRL
AND OTHER CITY COMEDIES

THE growth of London in the late sixteenth and early seventeenth centuries inspired the writers of the period across a range of forms, but nowhere so powerfully as in the theatre, where Londoners saw their lives represented, dissected, and debated in history plays, tragedies, and, most extensively, in comedies. A novel genre even arose: City Comedy. The plays in this volume show how City Comedy engaged with contemporary debates about London and its impact on the wider nation, from those who regarded the city as Sodom-on-Thames, to those who depicted it as a new Troy or Jerusalem, and those who revelled in its diversity, complexity, and transgressiveness. Each of the plays explores different facets of London life, including the impact of capitalism, colonialism, and overseas trade, and especially its effect on relations between the sexes and conceptions of gender roles and identity. They show the different ways in which London was represented in the early modern period, and how contemporaries explored a rapidly changing and expanding world and one that challenged many of the political and sexual certainties of the era.

JAMES KNOWLES teaches English at the University of Stirling. He has written widely on the Jacobean masque and has edited *Shakespeare's Late Plays: New Essays* (with Jenny Richards). He is currently editing the entertainments and selected masques for the forthcoming *Cambridge Edition of the Works of Ben Jonson*.

EUGENE GIDDENS is a Research Associate in the Faculty of English, University of Cambridge, working on the forthcoming *Cambridge Edition of the Works of Ben Jonson*.

MICHAEL CORDNER is Ken Dixon Professor of Drama at the University of York. He has edited George Farquhar's *The Beaux' Stratagem*, the *Complete Plays* of Sir George Etherege, *Four Comedies* of Sir John Vanbrugh, and, for Oxford English Drama, *Four Restoration Marriage Plays* and Sheridan's *The School for Scandal and Other Plays*. He is writing books on *The Comedy of Marriage* and *Shakespeare and the Actor*.

PETER HOLLAND is McMeel Family Professor in Shakespeare Studies at the University of Notre Dame.

MARTIN WIGGINS is a Fellow of the Shakespeare Institute and Lecturer in English at the University of Birmingham.

OXFORD ENGLISH DRAMA

OXFORD WORLD'S CLASSICS

The Roaring Girl
and Other City Comedies

THOMAS DEKKER
The Shoemaker's Holiday

GEORGE CHAPMAN, BEN JONSON, and
JOHN MARSTON
Eastward Ho

BEN JONSON
Every Man In His Humour

THOMAS DEKKER and THOMAS MIDDLETON
The Roaring Girl

Edited with an Introduction by
JAMES KNOWLES

Notes and Glossary by
EUGENE GIDDENS

OXFORD
UNIVERSITY PRESS

OXFORD
UNIVERSITY PRESS

Great Clarendon Street, Oxford OX2 6DP

Oxford University Press is a department of the University of Oxford.
It furthers the University's objective of excellence in research, scholarship,
and education by publishing worldwide in

Oxford New York

Athens Auckland Bangkok Bogotá Buenos Aires Cape Town
Chennai Dar es Salaam Delhi Florence Hong Kong Istanbul Karachi
Kolkata Kuala Lumpur Madrid Melbourne Mexico City Mumbai Nairobi
Paris São Paulo Shanghai Singapore Taipei Tokyo Toronto Warsaw

with associated companies in Berlin Ibadan

Oxford is a registered trade mark of Oxford University Press
in the UK and in certain other countries

Published in the United States
by Oxford University Press Inc., New York

Introduction © James Knowles 2001; Notes and Glossary © Eugene Giddens 2001

The moral rights of the author have been asserted

Database right Oxford University Press (maker)

First published as an Oxford World's Classics paperback 2001
Reissued 2008

British Library Cataloguing in Publication Data

Data available

Library of Congress Cataloging in Publication Data

The roaring girl and other city comedies / edited with an introduction by James Knowles
notes and glossary by Eugene Giddens.
(Oxford English drama) (Oxford world's classics)
Includes bibliographical references.
Contents: The shoemaker's holiday / Thomas Dekker—Eastward ho / George
Chapman, Ben Jonson, and John Marston—Every man in his humour / Ben Jonson—
The roaring girl / Thomas Dekker and Thomas Middleton.
1. English drama—17th century. 2. City and town life—Drama. 3. English drama
(Comedy). I. Knowles, James. II. Dekker, Thomas, ca. 1572–1632. III. Chapman,
George, 1559?–1634. Eastward ho. IV. Jonson, Ben, 1573?–1637. Every man in his
humour. V. Series. VI. Oxford world's classics (Oxford University Press)
PR1265.5 .R63 2001   822'.05230803—dc21   2001034363

ISBN 978–0–19–954010–5

14

Typeset in Ehrhardt by
RefineCatch Limited, Bungay, Suffolk
Printed in Great Britain by
Clays Ltd, Elcograf S.p.A.

CONTENTS

ACKNOWLEDGEMENTS

I would like to thank my general editor, Dr Martin Wiggins, for his eagle-eyed reading of this edition and his many helpful suggestions and criticisms. Also, Roberta Barker for her meticulous checking of the texts. Both have saved me from many errors. I am also indebted to Judith Luna and Elizabeth Stratford of OUP for their care and patience with this edition, and the series General Editor, Michael Cordner, for his forbearance during its protracted gestation.

Many individuals have helped with specific points and in various ways: Jerome de Groot, Erica Fudge, Tom and Margaret Healy, Jan Hewitt, Philip Jones, Gordon McMullan, and Lois Potter. Most of all I'd like to thank someone who isn't here anymore, Malcolm Edwards (1947–90). Malcolm was a teacher, director, and friend and I still treasure the evenings spent with him in the theatre which were both a pleasure and an education.

JK

My greatest debt is to Martin Wiggins for his thorough advice and encouragement with all stages of this work. Paul Edmondson provided useful comments on an early draft of the *Roaring Girl* notes; Coral Lancaster and Richard Partridge gave help with early music and instruments. Working on the *Cambridge Edition of the Works of Ben Jonson* under David Bevington, Martin Butler, and Ian Donaldson has taught me much about editorial practice, to the general benefit of the notes here. Judith Luna at Oxford University Press has been helpful and timely with her assistance, and Elizabeth Stratford has saved me from many embarrassing errors. Any that remain are, of course, my own.

EG

INTRODUCTION

The four City comedies presented in this volume are heterogeneous in their content and style, their writers, their audiences, and in the theatrical traditions they employ, but they are united by their presentation of London life. As London grew into a city of 250,000 inhabitants, the complexity and variety of the urban experience increased, and the plays in this volume, along with other City comedies, sought to interpret the novel phenomena of mass urban living and culture. Writing in 1612, the preacher Thomas Adams compared London to a 'perspective' picture 'that represent[s] to divers beholders, at divers stations, divers forms'. Perspectives, or anamorphic pictures, alter depending on how they are viewed (perhaps showing a portrait from one angle and a death's head from another as a *memento mori*), and Adams uses this image to represent the contradictoriness of London:

Looking one way you see a beautiful virgin; another way, some deformed monster. Cast an eye upon her profession, she is a well-graced creature; turn it upon her conversation, she is a misshapen stigmatic. View her peace, she is fairer than the daughters of men; view her pride, the children of the Hittites and Amorites are beauteous to her. Think of her good works; then, 'Blessed art thou of the Lord'; number her sins, then 'How is that faithful city become an harlot!' To tell of her charity, and how many hundreds she feeds in a year, you will say with Paul, 'In this I praise her.' To tell of her oppressions and how many thousands she undoes in a year, you will say with Paul, 'In this I praise her not.' Behold her like a nurse, drawing her breasts and giving her milk to orphans; you wish her cup to run over with fullness. Behold her like a horse-leech, sucking the blood of the Church, to feed her sacriligious avarice; you will say her cup is too full.[1]

Thus, London might either epitomize trading and industrial wealth, the centre of a civilized, ordered, and stable society, the reincarnation of ancient Rome or Troy, or it might suggest a new Sodom, the sink of all sin, danger, and disorder, whose commercial hegemony drained rather benefited the nation and whose political structures and culture threatened national security.

If London's population was the expression of, and also created by,

---

[1] *Eirenopolis: The City of Peace* (1612), cited in L. Manley (ed.), *London in the Age of Shakespeare: An Anthology* (1986), 108.

the City's economic dominance, its populousness caused much concern amongst the early modern ruling classes, who feared the City's potential for social unrest (especially amongst its poor immigrant workers and 'idle and masterless men') as much as they excoriated but sought to control the metropolitan culture which developed during the late sixteenth and early seventeenth centuries. Another preacher, Robert Milles, merges these concerns when he attacked the 'mimical comedians and apish actors' who typified the 'idleness' of the City. Milles warns that the 'licentious poet and player together are grown to such impudency' that:

they teach nobility, knighthood, grave matrons and civil citizens,—and like country dogs snatch at every passenger's heels. Yea, plays are grown nowadays into such high request as that some profane persons affirm they can learn as much both for example and edifying at a play, as at a sermon . . . Tremble thou earth, blush ye heavens, and speak O head, if any Sodomite uttered such blasphemy within thy gates . . . To compare a lascivious stage to this sacred pulpit and oracle of truth? To compare a silken counterfeit to a prophet . . . And to compare the idle and scurrile invention of an illiterate bricklayer, to the holy, pure and powerful word of God, which is the food of our souls to eternal salvation. Lord forgive them, they know not what they say.[2]

Milles's sermon typifies many of the social and cultural concerns that grew out of London's population expansion: social mobility, the transgression of class boundaries and decorum, the challenge to authority and religion. Perhaps the most interesting feature of his account lies, however, in his recognition of the 'high request', the popularity of London theatre, appealing to a broad audience, from 'nobility' to 'civil citizens'.

This popularity, the ability to appeal to a large audience from a broad range of social backgrounds, means that the plays in this volume offer modern readers a different perspective on early modern culture. These plays (predominantly) depict the life of the middling sort and urban culture and, significantly, include many elements from the overlapping cultures of the middling and plebeian sorts—what we might call 'popular' culture.[3] These heterogeneous groups and cultures, encompassing both literate and oral traditions, in effect formed the first mass audience, and London's theatrical companies set out, calculatedly, to appeal to their tastes, drawing upon popular traditions to

    [2] R. Milles, *Abraham's Suit to Sodom* (1612), cited in *London*, ed. Manley, 106.
    [3] R. Williams, *Keywords: A Vocabulary of Culture and Society* (1983), 236–8, considers shifts in the meaning of 'popular'.

explore the urban culture which shaped the lives of the working people of the city.[4] So, whereas most modern historical and literary scholarship concentrates on court politics and court culture, that is, on the intellectual and cultural production of a tiny minority (perhaps 2 per cent) of early modern society, these plays offer an important corrective, providing images of sections of society largely ignored in many studies of early modern culture. Frequently this bias reflects the exigencies of survival, as written texts deposited in aristocratic collections have survived with greater frequency than the chapbooks, almanacs, ballads, and jigs of the 'middling sort' and the oral traditions of the poor, which have vanished or survive only in later mediations; but it also reflects critical blindness and partiality.[5] Although the plays in this volume are not wholly disconnected from the court and its politics, either in their subject-matter (*Eastward Ho* illustrates the interaction of court and City politics), or in their auspices (*The Shoemaker's Holiday*, *Eastward Ho*, and *Every Man In His Humour* were all performed at court), their vitality and variety as plays addressed to the first urban mass audience illustrate the shortcomings of such elite-centred approaches.[6]

Scurrile Inventions and Illiterate Bricklayers: London and Popular Theatre

The difference of London from other English cities of this period cannot be overstated. During the period in which the plays in this volume were written (*c.*1600–15) London's population (about 250,000 inhabitants) represented almost 6 per cent of the total population of the country of just over 4 million, while its growth far outstripped the national rate.[7] The next largest city, Norwich, only boasted a

[4] A. Leggatt, *Jacobean Public Theatre* (1992), 28–45, succinctly explores the connections between theatre and popular culture.

[5] See B. Reay, 'Popular Culture in Early Modern England', in B. Reay (ed.), *Popular Culture in Seventeenth-Century England* (1985), 1–30, and T. Harris, 'Problematising Popular Culture', in *Popular Culture in England, c. 1500–1850* (1995), 1–27, esp. 1–5.

[6] Given the (largely) popular origins of early modern theatre, the very elements which so concerned Milles and his fellow moralists, it is inexplicable why critics continue to elevate its elite connections. For a stimulating recent example of such criticism, see A. Kernan, *Shakespeare, the King's Playwright: Theater in the Stuart Court, 1603–1613* (New Haven, 1995).

[7] By 1650 London had a population of 400,000, while the national population had only grown to 5 million.

population of about 15,000.[8] This demographic dominance was matched by commercial hegemony. London was the centre of English commerce, both inland and overseas, as well as the main centre for most forms of manufacturing. The large numbers of tradesfolk, shop-keepers, artisans, and other middling folk were joined by a substantial professional class (lawyers, scriveners, clerics, and schoolmasters), along with the gentry and greater merchants, who either resided in the capital or flocked there to do business during the legal terms. All of these required large numbers of servants and apprentices, and below this class there existed yet another stratum of the labouring poor, the 'day labourers, poor husbandmen, artificers and servants' mentioned in Thomas Harrison's *Description of England* (1577). In addition, London, with its rich potential for employment, became a magnet for the poor and unemployed, the idle and masterless men who so exercised civic and national authorities.

London's population was not only heterogeneous, it was also dis-tinctive. The economic importance of the import and export trades supported a large number of merchants and small tradesmen, while the growing leisure industry of the period generated a new commercial culture which some have seen as the forerunner of consumerism or of the modern service sector. Certainly, the size of London allowed for the creation of distinct sub-cultural groups, such as the apprentices, with their own dress codes, jargon, social rituals, and literature. In general, groups like the apprentices originated from a wide variety of social backgrounds (as exemplified by Golding and Quicksilver in *Eastward Ho*), and had a greater degree of literacy than other social groups.[9] The presence of such significant cultural blocs within early modern London, especially those with greater than average literacy, provided an important sector of the theatre audience, facilitating the complex cultural interactions which typified London culture.

London's theatre industry grew up to cater to the demands of this urban population for entertainment. Theatres were carefully sited to avoid regulation by the civic authorities, while being close enough to their audiences for easy access. Some of the first theatres (the Theatre

---

[8] E. A. Wrigley, 'Urban Growth and Agricultural Change: England and the Contin-ent in the Early Modern Period', in P. Borsay (ed.), *The Eighteenth Century Town: A Reader in English Urban History, 1688–1820* (1990), 39–82, Table 1 (p. 42).

[9] S. R. Smith, 'The London Apprentices as Seventeenth-Century Adolescents', *Past and Present*, 61 (1973), 149–61, and L. S. O'Connell, 'The Elizabethan Bourgeois Hero-Tale: Aspects of an Adolescent Social Consciousness', in B. C. Malament (ed.), *After the Reformation: Essays in Honour of J. H. Hexter* (Manchester, 1980), 267–90.

and Curtain, built in 1576 and 1577 respectively) were built in the northern suburbs, while the next generation capitalized on the freedom offered by the south bank of the Thames (the Rose and the Globe, constructed in 1587 and 1599 respectively). The Bankside area was the equivalent of a modern entertainment district, with theatres, bear-baiting and fencing-display arenas, taverns, bath-houses, and brothels all jostled together. The crowds which attended concerned the City authorities, fearing the lapse of church attendance, the spread of plague, and, worse, 'evil practices of great incontinency in great inns, having chambers and secret places adjoining to their open stages and galleries, inveigling and alluring of maids, specially orphans and good citizen's children to privy and unmeet contracts'.[10]

In his study of *Playgoing in Shakespeare's London*, Andrew Gurr has calculated that approximately 52 million playhouse visits occurred during the period 1574–1642. The industry which served this demand was complexly organized, but flexible in the way it could respond to commercial pressures.[11] It is no surprise, therefore, that Middleton's Epistle to *The Roaring Girl* compares play-making and the fashion industry:

The fashion of play-making I can properly compare to nothing so naturally as the alteration in apparel: for, in the time of your great crop-doublet your huge bombasted plays, quilted with mighty words to lean purpose, was only then in fashion; and, as the doublet fell, neater inventions began to set up. Now in the time of spruceness, our plays follow the neatness of our garments—single plots, quaint conceits, lecherous jests, dressed up in hanging-sleeves—and those are fit for the times and the termers. Such a kind of light-colour summer stuff, mingled with diverse colours, you shall find this published comedy . . . (Appendix, lines 1–10).

To increase their audiences, certainly until the 1620s, the players sought to appeal to as wide an audience as possible, altering their 'product' on a regular basis. As a matter of course the companies played up to six different plays each week, seeking to attract audiences with novelty and maximize their profits, since new plays were the most profitable. During 1594–5 the Admiral's Men staged seventeen new plays, seven in 1595–6 and five in 1596–7 (that is, given the playing seasons, about one a fortnight), although in the 1610s and 1620s this

---

[10] Act of the Common Council of London, 6 Dec. 1574, cited in E. K. Chambers, *The Elizabethan Stage*, 4 vols. (Oxford, 1923), iv. 273.

[11] R. L. Knutson, *The Repertory of Shakespeare's Company, 1594–1613* (Fayetteville, 1991). I have drawn heavily on this book in what follows.

declined to about three or four new plays per year.[12] In order to meet this demand for new texts plays were often written by collaborative teams, speeding up the rate of composition and sometimes capitalizing on the reputations of recognized dramatists. Companies used what we would now recognize as standard marketing techniques, such as mounting sequels (*1 and 2 Henry IV*), staging connected plays (such as *Every Man Out Of His Humour* (1599) to follow *Every Man In His Humour*) or commissioning plays which deliberately imitated the success of other companies' hits, and revivals—usually with revisions—of old successes (such as *The Spanish Tragedy*, *Dr Faustus*, *The Jew of Malta*, and *Mucedorus*).[13] A good example of these commercial tactics would be the fashion for humour plays which began with Chapman's *An Humorous Day's Mirth* (Admiral's, 1597), and then spread, taking in *The Merry Wives of Windsor* (1597), *Every Man In His Humour* (1598), and *Every Man Out Of His Humour* (1599; all Chamberlain's Men), while the Admiral's men probably hit back with *The Fount of New Fashions* and *The London Florentine, Part Two* (both lost plays).[14]

The economic structure of this industry was not quite the unrestrained market that this might suggest. Internally, the companies were organized partly like guilds, whose hierarchy of sharers, hired men, and apprentices mirrors the freeman, journeyman, apprentice structure of trade guilds, although the sharer system itself was more like a form of early capitalist co-operativism.[15] Beyond this, some companies relied upon the householders (the owners of the theatre), combined with the sharers for their capital, while others required an entrepreneur, such as Henslowe, to supply their capital, usually in the form of loans. At the other extreme, most of the boy companies were managed by consortia of owners and speculators, such as Robert Keysar, and the boys were either impressed (under royal warrant) or all-but purchased from their parents. Moreover, the companies operated between a market-driven commercial system and a patronage economy, as they relied upon aristocratic sponsorship and protection

[12] A. Gurr, *The Shakespearean Playing Companies* (Oxford, 1996), 101.

[13] D. J. Lake, 'Three Seventeenth-Century Revisions: *Thomas of Woodstock*, *The Jew of Malta* and *Faustus B*', *Notes and Queries*, 228 (1983), 133–43.

[14] Knutson, *The Repertory of Shakespeare's Company*, 43 and 75. Knutson also includes Jonson's *The Case Is Altered* (Pembroke's Men, 1597). In the case of the lost plays *The Fount of New Fashions* and *The London Florentine, Part Two* it is difficult to be certain of their topics, although they both sound like 'humour' texts.

[15] W. Cohen, *Drama of a Nation: Public Theatre in Renaissance England and Spain* (Ithaca, 1985), ch. 3.

xii

(hence the names of the companies), and a portion of their revenue derived from performances at court and in private aristocratic houses.[16] This complex situation between economic systems partly accounts for the political and ideological diversity of London's early modern theatre.

The impact of the market is illuminating if we are seeking to understand how theatre appealed to a mass audience. One of the most revealing descriptions of this audience and the kind of interactions that the market fostered can be found in Dekker's spoof courtesy-manual, *The Gull's Horn-Book* (1609):

> The theatre is your poet's Royal Exchange upon which thrive their Muses—that are now turned to merchants—meeting, barter away that light commodity for a lighter ware than words—plaudits . . . Players are their factors who put away the stuff and make the best of it they possibly can. . . . Your gallant, your courtier and your captain had wont to be the soundest paymasters . . . when your groundling and gallery commoner buys his sport by the penny and like a haggler is glad to utter it again by retailing.[17]

This passage shows the social heterogeneity of the audience in early modern theatre, and also how the shift from elite patronage and markets ('paymasters') to a more plebeian commercialism was recognized. What is striking in the passage is the awareness of the fluidity of the social and cultural interaction that occurs, making theatre a 'Royal Exchange' parallel to Gresham's Royal Exchange in Cornhill Street. This ability to 'exchange' makes theatre one of the most important institutions in early modern London, combining economic forces with a range of cultural and social transactions. Dekker's final sentence captures this, as what had once been an elite product is exchanged with the 'gallery commoner' and 'groundling', who themselves then 'utter' (sell) the sport (the play) by selling it retail.

'Retailing' has a secondary meaning in this period which opens up the other, central reason for theatre's significance within urban culture. To 'retail' was not just to sell (*OED*, s.v. 1) it was also to retell (s.v. 2), a verbal quibble which suggests the complex ways in which cultures are purchased, appropriated, sold on, and circulated through both oral and literate transmissions. The most important exchange which London theatre effected was between elite, written cultures and other cultural groups, especially those used to oral cultures. Theatre,

---

[16] K. McLuskie, 'The Poets' Royal Exchange: Patronage and Commerce in Early Modern Drama', *Yearbook of English Studies*, 21 (1991), 53–62.

[17] Cited ibid. 53.

although it depended on the skills of writing and reading, operated at the boundaries of written and spoken cultures, and thus it was open to a wide audience, who could listen to what they could not have read. Thus, social groups likely to be less literate, including some apprentices and women but especially the labouring poor, could gain access to a whole range of ideas through theatre. Yet, equally, the implication of the exchange and market metaphors suggests that theatre also operated as a real exchange, with goods and ideas passing in both directions. Drama also had to embody the 'sport' of the plebeian classes if it was to succeed, and, therefore, popular elements were incorporated, not solely to appeal to a 'groundling' class (a somewhat pejorative term) but to create as well an accessible theatre which deployed elements of traditions recognized by all social classes. Early modern writers, in so far as they ever theorized about audiences and their participation, seem to have used a slightly different set of terms, describing how plays appealed to both 'auditors' and 'spectators', including both verbal and visual dimensions. Most importantly, however, given the oral medium the illiterate or sub-literate could partake in both aspects of the performance.[18] Theatre, no matter how socially exclusive due to its pricing structure, is an inherently inclusive medium.

Whilst theatre is generally an inclusive form, large markets such as that in which the early modern metropolitan theatre operated tend towards, and, indeed, encourage specialization. Yet, although over the long-term the complex audience demographics of London theatre may show a gradual division of audiences, broadly speaking during this period the London theatre audience was highly diverse, with different classes and social groups frequently interacting in the playhouse. Even in the Caroline period (after 1625), when some differentiation in audiences did exist, London theatre retained a vigorous popular tradition which still attracted a substantial cross-class audience.[19] During the earlier Jacobean period (1603–25) the major—and most familiar—division of theatres into the 'public' amphitheatres and the 'private' hall-theatres, reveals more about the class pretensions of

---

[18] A. Gurr, *Playgoing in Shakespeare's London*, 2nd ed. (Cambridge, 1996), 86.

[19] In addition to the evidence amassed in Gurr's *Playgoing*, the notion of 'privileged playgoers' is challenged in M. Butler, *Theatre and Crisis 1632–1642* (Cambridge, 1984), ch. 8 and app. II, which establishes the heterogeneity of audiences throughout the period, providing evidence for a 'third, alternative [popular] tradition of theatre in Caroline London running concurrently with the private court stage and the elite professional theatres' (pp. 182–3).

the audiences than about real social differences.[20] Certainly the amphi-theatres, which had a capacity of about 3,500 (Globe) and 2,000 people (Fortune), catered for a socially diverse audience since their admission prices were 1*d.* entry into the yard and a further 1*d.* entry into the galleries (hence *Roaring Girl*, Scene 10, line 260 refers to 'twopenny' galleries).[21] Thus records of 'public' theatre going suggest a highly diverse audience, ranging from ambassadors to apprentices. In contrast, the hall-playhouses catered for a more socially exclusive audience (Blackfriars seating about 750 spectators), with prices starting at 6*d.* (for the upper gallery) and rising from 1*s.* 6*d.* for a bench-seat in the pit to 2*s.* 6*d.* for seats in the boxes.[22] Even so, it was not unknown for apprentices to frequent the Blackfriars.

Even more problematic has been the manner in which, all too often, the little evidence that exists for the separation of elite and popular theatres has been translated straightforwardly into taste and repertoire differences. Wealthier audiences do not necessarily have 'elite' tastes. Much of the popular fare of the Jacobean stage appears to have appealed to the relatively well-heeled, as in the case of *The Roaring Girl*, which, in its published text at least, specifically invokes the 'termers' and those able to afford a 'gallery-room at the play-house and [a] chamber-room' at their lodgings (Appendix, Epistle, lines 16, 17). 'Termers' were the elite classes who flocked to London during the law terms which formed the nascent London social season, while privacy, either in playhouse or lodging house, was also the pre-serve of a wealthier elite. Moreover, the repertoire circulated between different theatres and audiences. Plays such as *Every Man In His Humour* started life in the amphitheatre but ended in the Blackfriars in the 1630s, and Marston's *The Malcontent* (1603–4) played first at the Blackfriars, with boy performers, and then at the Globe with adults, while the court selected plays from the amphitheatre as much as from the hall-theatre repertoire. Indeed, after 1608, when the King's Men resumed playing at the Blackfriars, at least a certain proportion of their repertoire was adaptable to performances in both places.[23] So, in reading these plays it is important not to homogenize the audience's

---

[20] Gurr, *Playgoing*, 13.

[21] Ibid. 20–1 and A. Gurr, *The Shakespearean Stage, 1574–1642*, 3rd edn. (Cambridge, 1992), 134–5.

[22] Gurr, *Playgoing*, 27 and *The Shakespearean Stage*, 157–9.

[23] A. Gurr, 'Money or Audiences: The Impact of Shakespeare's Globe', *Theatre Notebook*, 42 (1988), 3–13, explores the financial crisis which led to the construction of the Globe and its impact upon the repertoire.

potential reactions, either in class terms or, indeed, in gender terms, nor to assume that there can be a singular 'audience' for a particular text. As Edmund Gayton commented in 1654, 'men come not to study at a playhouse, but love such expressions and passages which with ease insinuate themselves into their capacities'.[24] This is not merely a cry for pleasure rather than (intellectual) profit, but a recognition, too, of the variety of 'capacities' which any audience might contain.

Gayton's 'expressions and passages which with ease insinuate themselves' suggests some of the strategies by which playing companies could engage their audience—by using familiar (and thus, easy) forms or styles.[25] Indeed, throughout this period playwrights readily borrowed the varied vocabularies of popular culture, weaving them into the textures of their works to attract as wide an audience as possible. Recognizable plot patterns were repeated, often drawing upon biblical or homiletic sources or upon popular literary forms, all familiar either from the visual culture (especially wall paintings, emblems, and prints), from oral teaching, or even from the traditional festive calendar. Thus morality-patterned plays such as *The Contention Between Liberality and Prodigality* survived in the repertoire into the seventeenth century, while *The London Prodigal* was only written for the King's Men in 1604. Narratives based on popular figures might also be used, such as Dick Whittington (mentioned in *Eastward Ho*, 4.2.65), who appeared in numerous ballads and in a Prince's (Admiral's) Men play of 1605. The familiarity of the narratives may have helped make the play more marketable, just as other plays exploited the audience's prior knowledge of 'historical' events to make plays more palatable.

More contemporary, newsworthy events might also be dramatized, especially for their capacity to shock and titillate. Sensational murders provided good copy for the popular pamphlet writers, and many of these tabloid-like news-flashes were translated to the stage, in plays such as *The Lamentable Tragedy of Page of Plymouth* (Dekker and Jonson).[26] Although most of the best-known examples of this

---

[24] E. Gayton, *Pleasant Notes on Don Quixote* (1654), cited in A. Leggatt, *Jacobean Public Theatre* (1992), 33.

[25] Gayton's 'ease', probably refers to the fashion of the mid-century for witty, elegant, and metrically poised forms.

[26] On these pamphlets, see P. Lake, 'Deeds against Nature: Cheap Print, Protestantism and Murder in Early Seventeenth Century England', in K. Sharpe and P. Lake (eds.), *Culture and Politics in Early Stuart England* (1994), 257–84.

form, such as *Arden of Faversham* (anon; 1591?) or Heywood's *A Woman Killed With Kindness* (1603), focus on regional murders and monstrosities, several, such as *The Late Murder in Whitchapel, or Keep the Widow Waking* (1624), dealt with London events, and there is every reason to think that such plays were both numerous and a staple of the theatrical repertoire of this period.[27] Popular playwrights often adapted material from the widely disseminated forms of cheap print, such as ballads and pamphlets, texts which they had often themselves supplied, as in Dekker's use (with Middleton) of his own canting pamphlets in *The Roaring Girl*. The aim was to appeal to a broad audience by using sensationalist tactics, linking the theatre into the news culture of early modern England, and drawing upon popular religious discourses which emphasized human punishment and divine retribution for aberrations.

Although many of the ballads and tracts revelled in the novelty and monstrosity of the events they depicted, this was only one aspect of the ways in which London theatre interacted with cheap print forms. Another important facet was the dramatization of quasi-historical events, often of symbolic significance in the London civic calendar or mythology, which might be commemorated, either through the individuals involved (Gresham and Whittington often being evoked) or through buildings or monuments erected to memorialize them, such as the Royal Exchange.[28] The appearance of the King, almost certainly meant to be Henry V, in Dekker's *Shoemaker's Holiday*, to bless the foundation of Leadenhall deploys this technique, and draws upon a long popular tradition exemplified in such plays as *The Famous Victories of Henry the Fifth* (printed 1598, but probably originally staged 1586–7). This play, which celebrated the role of John Cobbler and his humble neighbours in national history and myth, is echoed in a wide range of other popular history plays of the period, such as Heywood's *Edward IV* (1599) and the anonymous *Jack Straw* (1591?),

---

[27] C. J. Sisson, *Lost Plays of Shakespeare's Age* (Cambridge, 1936), 80–124. The (lost) play written by Dekker, Rowley, Ford, and Webster drew upon the ballad version of a contemporary murder (pp. 120–1), while the same consortium (minus Webster) were responsible for the *Witch of Edmonton* (1621, pub. 1658), set in a village 7 miles north of London, a witchcraft play based on *The wonderful discoverie of Elizabeth Sawyer, a Witch* (1621).

[28] The growth of London comedy in the 1590s matches the emerging 'civic consciousness' of the period, best embodied in John Stow's *Survey of London* (1598), ed. H. B. Wheatley and V. Pearl (1987).

which linked the very survival of the monarchy with the patriotic loyalty of London's citizenry.[29]

The Shoemaker's Holiday, based upon Thomas Deloney's popular prose fiction,[30] shows how such strategies aimed to draw in as large an audience as possible, connecting the play to motifs, persons, places, forms, and styles that spectators might recognize from the wider popular cultures of the City and thus to *popularize* them, that is, make them accessible to a diversity of auditors, spectators, and readers.[31] The Shoemaker's Holiday exploits ideas of festivity, not only in its title and in the mythical account it gives of the foundation of the apprentices' Shrove Tuesday feast, but also in the way that it dramatizes the life story of one of the heroes of London and transforms his workshop into a festive space. Similarly, The Roaring Girl utilizes the story of a well-known London figure, Moll Frith, which also echoes many ballads about cross-dressing heroines, such as Long Meg of Westminster.[32] Both plays are shot through with references to ballads, popular songs, jigs, and dances. So, in The Shoemaker's Holiday, Scene 13, the action moves between the spoken word and song choruses, while in Scene 11 a tabor and pipe (instruments often associated with clowns and popular entertainment) are heard, followed by the shoemakers dancing a morris (Scene 11, lines 48 f.).[33] The Three-Man's Songs exemplify this use of popular music in the play, drawing upon folk motifs in their words, the use of commonplace refrains, and also in their musical

[29] M. Heinemann, 'Political Drama', in A. R. Braunmuller and M. Hattaway (eds.), *Cambridge Companion to Renaissance Drama* (Cambridge, 1990), 161–206, provides a fascinating overview of this material. *The Famous Victories* can be found in *The Narrative and Dramatic Sources of Shakespeare, Vol. IV: Later English History Plays*, ed. G. Bullough (1962).

[30] T. Deloney, *The Gentle Craft*, in two parts (c.1597–8), in F. O. Mann (ed.), *The Works of Thomas Deloney* (Oxford, 1912). The printing of Dekker's play in the medium of popular fiction, black-letter type, a form associated with the lowest levels of literacy, singles this play out as targeted at the broadest possible audience. On black-letter, see K. Thomas, 'Literacy in Early Modern England', in G. Baumann (ed.), *The Written Word: Literacy in Transition* (Oxford, 1986), 97–131, esp. 99.

[31] J. Barry, 'Literacy and Literature in Popular Culture', in *Popular Culture in England*, 69–94, esp. 78–9, explores the strategies for popularization in a wide range of printed texts from this period.

[32] See *Roaring Girl*, Scene 10, line 2 and note on Long Meg of Westminster, and B. Capp, 'Popular Literature', in *Popular Culture in Seventeenth-Century England*, 198–243, esp. 208 and 211.

[33] See esp. the CD by The Mvsicians of Swanne Alley, *In The Streets and Theatres of London: Elizabethan Ballads and Theatre Music* (Virgin Classics, 1989 [0777 7595342 8]), and tunes such as 'Mother Watkins' Ale' for examples of popular music.

style, since they were almost certainly set to jigs, possibly even to a specific jig tune known as 'The Cobbler's Jig'.[34]

The Roaring Girl also uses music and words to appeal to a broad audience, but deliberately stages a genre popular amongst Londoners of the middling sort, making it accessible to an even larger audience. The canting scene (Scene 10) recycles Dekker's own prose tracts, *The Bellman of London* (1608) and *Lanthorn and Candlelight, or the Bellman's Second Night's Walk* (1608)—containing 'The Canter's Dictionary'—which in turn draw upon earlier canting literature such as Thomas Harman's *A Caveat for Common Cursitors* (1566). Such underworld literature was hugely popular.[35] In this case the scene is carefully staged to use canting terms familiar to many of the audience, and not to exclude anyone, since many of the unusual usages are carefully glossed or translated. Part of the purpose may be to allow audience members who recognized the language to feel 'streetwise' (and to some extent identify with Moll's superior knowledge of London underworld). The underworld chic of this scene (and, indeed, the whole of *The Roaring Girl*) prefigures the fascination with London gangster figures such as the Kray twins in the 1960s, reinforcing the sense of exciting transgressiveness which fuelled the play's popularity.

The most extended use of familiar and popular linguistic forms can be seen in the frequent repetition of proverbs and moral tags in all four of these plays. In Dekker's *Shoemaker's Holiday* the collective culture of the workshop and its labour practices are defined by the exchange of proverbial and quasi-proverbial tags, especially in Scene 4, with its emphasis on drinking and working ('drink you mad Greeks, and work like true Trojans'). The combination of these phrases with nicknames (Madge Mumblecrust, Cicely Bumtrinket, Dame Clapperdudgeon) and images of appetite (Gargantua) drawn from popular culture, combined with Eyre's linguistic inventiveness, shape our perception of the festivity and collectivity of the workshop.[36] Conversely, in *Eastward Ho*

---

[34] It is instructive to compare the use of music in *Eastward Ho*, where much of the music dramatizes Gertrude's courtly aspirations, although most of the tunes are actually popular and the words she uses over-sexualized and inappropriate. See L. P. Austern, *Music In English Children's Drama of the Later Renaissance* (Philadelphia, 1992), 146, 158, and 205.

[35] *Lanthorn and Candlelight* went through seven editions before 1640. See A. V. Judges, *The Elizabethan Underworld: A Collection of Tudor and Early Stuart Tracts* (1930).

[36] *Shoemaker's Holiday*, Scene 4, line 103. See also lines 13 and 111.

Touchstone's tedious proverbs come to symbolize the emptiness of City culture as the collective culture becomes an oppressive tool. The constant injunction to 'work upon that now' (almost 'put that in your pipe and smoke it!') neatly signals a sneering one-upmanship and self-righteousness, while reminding the audience of a harsh work ethic.

Every Man In His Humour often satirizes such verbal tics, along with fashionable speech affections and vulgarisms. The constant repetition of phrases such as 'I protest' (1.2.76 and 80), 'resolve so' (1.4.39), 'peremptory-beautiful' (1.4.74), 'accommodate' (1.4.111), 'cam'rades' (2.1.147), the affected use of foreign terms, such as Bobadill's duelling phrases (1.4.96–101, 130, 137), or misplaced, misquoted, and misunderstood tags and Latinisms, all foreground the importance of language as a marker of social (and moral) status. Of course such verbal fashions change meaning over time, and it is possible that when the play was first presented (in an earlier version, set in Italy) before audiences at the Curtain, Theatre, or Globe (the theatres in which the early version may have appeared during 1598–1600) such attention to speech-patterns may well have operated only partly as satire and partly like the canting terms of *The Roaring Girl*, fostering the recognition of a shared subcultural language which establishes group solidarity. By the time *Every Man In His Humour* was played at the Globe or Blackfriars (perhaps *c.*1610) and again at the Blackfriars (1631), such linguistic patterns had shifted, and thus the gallants' jargon may have acquired far more overtly satirical implications, emphasizing the dated quality of some of the City's would-be bravos, like Stephen or Matthew.

The use of comic catchphrases complements another element of the popular tradition which these plays drew upon: clowning. For example, Cob's long speech (*Every Man In His Humour*, 1.3) to his ancestors, the pickled herrings, derives from the European clown tradition which used fish names as the source of humour.[37] Different clowns probably used different styles, some drawing more on verbal wit and others on physical humour, both appealing in slightly different ways to both auditors and spectators. In the earliest performances of *Every Man In His Humour* Cob was played by William Kemp, a wit-based clown, while it seems highly likely that Firk in *The Shoemaker's Holiday* was played by John Singer, a much more physical and, probably, bawdy actor.[38] The differences these clowns represented are

---

[37] C. R. Baskervill, *The Elizabethan Jig and Related Song Drama* (Chicago, 1929), 93.
[38] Chambers, *The Elizabethan Stage*, ii. 325–7 and 339–40, gives brief biographies.

articulated by David Wiles, who argues that: 'While Singer may best be likened to a modern farce actor concerned to force the pace, Kemp seems closer to music hall: the audience's pleasure lies in seeing how the actor, with nothing but a bare stage, and expanse of time, and his personality, can conjure up pleasurable ways of filling the vacuum.'[39] So although the use of the clown appeals to a wide range of tastes, and the repetition of his routines makes the play accessible to many levels of understanding; the particular inflection of clown styles belongs to the world of commercial competition. The farcical clowning of Firk, with a marked emphasis upon sexual jokes, puns, and presumably a great deal of improvised stage business (for example, the end of Scene 4) and mimicry for the Admiral's Men is placed in competition with the King's Men's clowning style, which favoured a more reflective and witty approach. Whatever the differences, no doubt accentuated as part of commercial rivalry, the importance of these clowns is the accessibility and familiarity their routines and catchphrases created. In particular, at the end of the plays they would dance and sing their most famous routines, such as 'Singing Simpkin', Kemp's best-known jig.[40] Many of these jigs were extemporized, either around the play or around contemporary events and personalities, offering many opportunities for bawdiness. Theatres like the Fortune were often attacked by both satirists and the civic authorities for their 'lewde jigges songes and daunces', although such material probably only heightened the popularity of the theatres, contributing the exciting sense of transgression associated with theatre going.[41]

The reliance on the popular tradition in these plays extends beyond performance styles. The core of both *The Shoemaker's Holiday* and *The Roaring Girl* are the urban myths of social mobility, and the glorification of the City and its citizens through their association with heroic, often chivalric deeds and tales.[42] In *The Shoemaker's Holiday* the utilization of heroic material is most obvious in the treatment of Ralph as a civic Hercules or Prince Arthur (Scene 1, lines 164, 165). These myths had a potent force in early modern metropolitan culture,

[39] D. Wiles, *Shakespeare's Clown: Actor and Text in the Elizabethan Playhouse* (Cambridge, 1987), 105.

[40] Gurr, *The Shakespearean Stage*, 174

[41] Comments of the Middlesex magistrates (1612), cited in ibid. 175.

[42] A whole genre of heroic apprentice ballads developed, such as W.V., *The Honourable Apprentice* (1616), while plays such as Thomas Heywood's *Four Prentices of London* (c.1600) depicted apprentices participating in the Crusades. See Capp, 'Popular Literature', 207–9.

since chivalric romance was one of the main staples of the market in cheap print and, indeed, many civic pageants and rituals used the Arthurian myths and the popular historical tradition.[43] This civic chivalry combined with the popular discourses of City heroism and tales of fabulous social advancement (such as Dick Whittington) or the 'valiant apprentice' genre of ballads to create a world of fantasy for the lower and middling classes.[44] Combined with tales of love and courtship, magical disguises (as in *Shoemaker's Holiday*, especially Scenes 3 and 6), and chivalric motifs, these ballads and plays create fantasy narratives which provided escape from a brutal everyday reality, but which also embodied behavioural models to be emulated. Indeed, these narratives often show the older generation outwitted by the wily young, venial masters outmanoeuvred by clever servants, or dubious foreigners outsmarted by patriotic and Protestant Londoners. These elements would have a strong appeal both to the youth market and to a broader strain of national and civic pride associated with much of the metropolitan populace.

The interest in narratives of social aspiration also embodies more serious tensions which inform the plays in this volume and which account for some very different emphases. In *Eastward Ho*, Golding's insistence on the honour of his position against Quicksilver's consciousness that apprenticeship demeans his gentility articulates some of the tensions and debates surrounding apprenticeship in this era.[45] More explicitly, the series of journeys which dominate the plot of *Eastward Ho* symbolizes the potential dangers of the uncontrollable social mobility associated with urbanization. In particular, Gertrude and Sir Petronel Flash combine the instability apparently encouraged in civic chivalric romance with the worst aspects of the new, unstable (landless) courtier class. Even Golding, who might have appeared as an idealistic figure in a citizen hero-tale, emerges as a dull, self-important

---

[43] Members of civic guilds, such as the Fellowship of Prince Arthur's Knights, regularly held Arthurian pageants, and their 1587 show, which involved elaborate processions and target-shooting for some 300 participants (described in John Nichols, *The Progresses and Public Processions of Elizabeth I*, 3 vols. (1789–1805), iii. 210*), displayed a strongly patriotic emphasis. Many other writers celebrated civic valour in a chivalric frame, for example Dekker's *The artillery garden: A poem dedicated to all those gentlemen who (there) practize military discipline* (1616).

[44] Capp, 'Popular Literature', 204–12 and Barry, 'Literacy and Literature in Popular Culture', 74 and 84.

[45] E. Bolton, *The Cities Advocate* (1629), emphasizes the gentility of obedient apprentices (sig. A2v), or 'Schollars, and Disciples in Citie-Artes' as he called them (A2r), against the 'irregular frie' (ibid) of the City.

figure whose meteoric, not to say fantastic, rise to civic office epitomizes the failings of middling culture and the delusory wish-fulfilment of citizen genres.

Eastward Ho's final act is constructed around a pointed critique of these citizen genres and the popular piety they embody, with Quicksilver playing the part of the penitent sinner: 'He can tell you almost all the stories of the *Book of Martyrs*, and speak you all the *Sick Man's Salve* without book' (5.2.48–9). Although the scene allows some doubt to remain as to whether Quicksilver has genuinely converted, the implications of his name (he is, forever, quicksilver) might undermine such possibilities, especially as in Quicksilver's hands two of the keystones of popular Protestantism are turned to use, the penitent reformed sinner becoming a role he has learned to recite 'without book'.[46] Similarly, Quicksilver's prison ballad appropriates the 'Repentance' and 'Last Farewell' (5.3.51–2) genre of ballads—here an adaptation of 'Mannington's Repentance' (5.5.36–7), the most famous of all conversion ballads—possibly signalled by the combination of metrical awkwardness and glib rhymes which renders the whole song comic rather than serious.[47] Quicksilver's version of this ballad, originally printed in 1576 and sung to 'Labandala Shot', a well-known tune, neatly illustrates the ways in which popular culture crossed over onto more 'elite' stages, since the scene depends both on the audience's recognition of the tune and then upon a secondary reaction which comprehends the parody. While some of the audience might simply enjoy the well-known tune and the variant words, a more sophisticated playgoer might be expected to grasp the joke. Touchstone's gullibility ('I am ravished . . . and could stand here a whole prenticeship') in accepting the 'Repentance' at face value becomes an indictment of the failure, not only of his claim to ascertain truth and falsity (embodied in his name), but also of the whole culture he represents. It is a quintessentially Jonsonian moment, as the inability to appreciate poetry or, in this case, recognize insincere doggerel, symbolizes moral failure.

Divergences over the impact of citizen social aspiration and the implications of civic narratives expose a broader division amongst these plays, between those that celebrate the community and heterocosm of the City, and those that regard community and heterocosm as incompatible, the one depending on social stability, the other tending

---

[46] In his 'Repentance' (in 5.5) Quicksilver plays a part in the moral drama of vice against virtue, becoming Virtue's highwayman.

[47] The point is reinforced in Security's verses which follow in 5.5.133–40.

to social fragmentation. *The Shoemaker's Holiday* embodies the loyal, patriotic City community through the image of the final feast, drawing together Court and City, with civic pride accentuated but balanced by proper reverence for the status quo (Scene 21, 160 ff.). *The Roaring Girl*, in particular, celebrates the ability of the civic body to encompass a wide variety of types, displaying the basic honesty of the outlaws such as Moll, and the capacity of the City to self-regulate. In contrast, in *Every Man In His Humour* the instrument of plot resolution, the merry Justice Clement, is the representative of royal law and order rather than the civic authorities. More ambiguously still, in *Eastward Ho* the supposedly reformed Quicksilver dominates the end of the play, and his manipulation of the citizens on stage and the citizen audience imagined in the Epilogue conveys the inability of the City to control its irregular members.

City Monsters and Suburb Humours: The City Staged

As the sermons by Adams and Milles cited earlier show, these inter-linked issues of the audience and social control were at the heart of much of the concern about London and its theatre. Not everyone in the early modern period regarded London's growth and its shifting populace as a cause for celebration, and considerable debate raged about the place and function of London within the nation. Theatre mediated this debate but was also its medium, as a tool of official propaganda in the Lord Mayor's pageants and as a widely available form of popular entertainment. Indeed, the plays in this volume respond not only to the availability of a mass market by utilizing the forms and traditions of popular culture; they also debate the place and impact of the City. This is achieved through the exploration of a linked series of ideas, centred upon monstrosity, the role of women, spectacle, and the 'humours'. Indeed, gender in particular, both in the direct role of women in the plays but also through the gendering of City space, becomes a crucial part of the debate.

Pro-City writers, such as the chronicler and antiquary John Stow or the poets employed as City chronologers (the official City propagand-ist) or as pageant writers for the Lord Mayor's inauguration, stressed the integration of the City, both into the fabric of national life and also internally, bringing together its diverse populations, binding them into a proper civic hierarchy. Thus the mayoral pageants, in particular, combine celebrations of the trading wealth of the City with insistence upon its dispersal amongst both London's population and the nation.

Dekker's *Troia-Nova Triumphans or London's Triumphing* (1612) re-
creates London as a New Troy (which is the title also afforded to
Rome in *Virgil's Aeneid*), even using the form of a Roman triumph as a
model for the pageant, while celebrating the charitable unity of the
City. Thus, for Dekker, the Lord Mayor must

> Shelter with spread arms, the poorest Citizen . . .
> Set Plenty at thy table, at thy gate
> Bounty and hospitality: he's most ingrate
> Into whose lap the public weal having poured
> Her golden showers, from Her his wealth should hoard.[48]

This emphasis upon the beneficent use of wealth answered critics who
regarded London's wealth as damaging national prosperity, assuaged
those who considered the extremes of civic poverty and wealth as
divisive, and created a mythology of urban charitable civility. Time
and again in the pageants London is figured as classical temple, an
exchange of wealth, a noble household, and, often, as a garden. In 1619
Thomas Middleton celebrated the installation of the mayor with a
pageant of a civic Orpheus who civilized the beasts of City, nation, and
overseas.[49]

These positive images provided a mythology which operated both
within and outside the City, urging a vision of the City as a unified and
unifying place which benefited its inhabitants and the wider nation.
This broader address was important because often London was seen as
over-mighty and, potentially, as destabilizing the nation. Its olig-
archical government could be seen as dangerously near-democratic
(although it was no such thing), so civic propagandists often recalled
the role of London in supporting the monarchy and the status quo in
times of unrest. Indeed, civic writers often personified London as a
woman, drawing on iconographical traditions which depicted Truth
(especially Protestant truth) as female.[50] Such feminization of the City
enabled the civic propagandists to stress the subordinate and subservi-
ent position of London (wives were supposed unquestioningly to obey
their husbands), and to connect London with ideas of natural plenty
and prosperity through classical figures such as Flora.

---

[48] T. Dekker, *Troia-Nova Triumphans. London Triumphing* . . . (1612), sig. B3v.

[49] T. Middleton, *The Triumphs of Love and Antiquity* (1619).

[50] L. Manley, 'From Matron to Monster: Tudor and Stuart London and the
Languages of Urban Description', in H. Dubrow and R. Strier (eds.), *The Historical
Renaissance* (Chicago, 1988), 347–74, at 349.

Yet other writers expressed contrary views. Politicians and econo-
mists attacked the damage caused to the rest of the country by London's mercantile dominance: James I described London as 'the spleen
... which in measure as it overgrows, the body wastes'.[51] Moralists
and preachers equated the City with Babylon and Sodom, citing, in
particular, civic extravagance and greed:

you give glozingly, illiberally, too late; not a window you have erected, but
must bear your names ... It is not seasonable, nor reasonable charity, to undo
whole towns by your usuries, enclosings, oppressions, impropriations; and for
a kind of expiation, to give three or four the yearly pension of twenty marks
... he is but poorly charitable, that having made a hundred beggars, relieves
two.[52]

An extensive genre of anti-metropolitan satires developed, retelling
the sins of the city, dwelling upon its vices to such an extent as to
appear dangerously voyeuristic to modern readers. These satires con-
centrated not only upon the sexual licence of London, but on the
associated vices of excessive consumption, epitomized by the role of
women in London's growing consumer culture. Thus James I attacked
women as a major cause of London's overcrowding, through their
desire to shop and amuse themselves during the social season which
had developed during the law terms of the early seventeenth century,
while the fashionableness of Cheapside's 'gay daughters' with 'a pow-
dered frizzle, a painted hide shadowed with a fan not more painted,
breasts displayed, and a loose lock erring wantonly over her shoulder
betwixt a painted cloth, and skin', created a 'mixture in nature' which
is nothing less than 'a monster'.[53] Indeed, London was herself often
associated with, and depicted as, a monstrous woman, more whore of
Babylon than 'well-graced' nurse. In Thomas Nashe's *Pierce Penniless*
(1592), London's trading is imagined as prostitution and London herself is depicted as a decrepit old whore, Madame Troynovant, a
'Grandmother of Corporations' whose 'aged mothers of iniquity will
have their deformities new plastered over, and wear nosegays of yellow
hair on their foreheads, when age hath written "No God be here" on
their bald burnt parchments'.[54]

Whether represented as the New Jerusalem/Troynovant, or as

---

[51] James VI and I, 'Speech in Star Chamber' (1616), in *The Political Works of James I*,
ed. C. H. McIlwain (Cambridge, Mass., 1916), 343.

[52] Thomas Adams, *The White Devil* (1613), in *London*, ed. Manley, 108.

[53] John Hall, *The Righteous Mammon* (1618), ibid. 110.

[54] Cited ibid. 277–8.

Sodom or Babylon, the striking feature of civic discourse lies in the gendering of the City. For pro-civic writers London might stand as a chaste and obedient wife, nursing the nation, while for anti-civic writers it was, like all women, a leaky vessel, its commercial transactions akin to prostitution, its essential nature fallen. Such gendering of the City encapsulates much of the anxiety which surrounded London, and in part explains the concerns of many City plays with the role and position of women. Such prominence for women not only responded to their significance in the social fabric and in the theatrical audience; it also became a discourse through which the urban experience could be framed and shaped. Thus the variousness of the metropolitan experience, the capacity of the City to offer great beauty and great danger, could be explained through an already familiar series of binarisms and discursive patterns. It is no accident that when Thomas Adams depicts London as an anamorphic picture, he immediately imagines a woman, fair one way, but transformed into a 'misshapen stigmatic' when viewed again.

The association of the City with women, and the gendering of the City as female, explains how quickly the discourse around London slides into images of monstrosity and sexual ambiguity. The association of the female body with uncontrolled humours and passions, with an inherent monstrosity in need of corrective male authority, derives from a variety of sources, including scientific theory, although it permeated both literate and oral cultures. As Gail Paster has argued:

This discourse inscribes women as leaky vessels by isolating one element of the female body's material expressiveness—its production of fluids—as excessive, hence either disturbing or shameful. It also characteristically links this liquid expressiveness to excessive verbal fluency. In both formations, the issue is women's bodily self-control or, more precisely, the representation of a particular kind of uncontrol as a function of gender.[55]

Female 'uncontrol' was seen as the product of the physical female body, but it also shaped behaviour and the position of women. Women were regarded as being subject to greater physical flux than men, and thus to be in need of greater, masculine and rational, control. A whole range of medico-social theories, from reproduction to state-formation, imagined women as incomplete or uncontrolled without men, and this 'natural' state of the female body (its weaker, leakier, less controlled

[55] G. K. Paster, *The Body Embarrassed: Drama and the Disciplines of Shame in Early Modern England* (Ithaca, 1993), 25.

qualities) 'justified' the need for male dominance in both the family and the state. Indeed, discourses about bodies, families, and state structure often operated using the same gender-based analogies, making male domination a natural product of his natural bodily and mental superiority. Thus, just as the male seed overcame the female in reproduction (at least of a man), so men should control and regulate women (as Adam had done Eve, she being the product of his lower rib), so men should rule the family and thus control the state, and cities—gendered as female—should be subordinate to the male control of the monarch. Disordered cities and disordered women were, by implication, similar entities, in need of proper male domination to control their inherently unstable bodies and to suppress their potential for monstrosity.[56]

Perhaps the most extreme expression of London's monstrosity is found in Jonson's 'On the Famous Voyage', printed in his *Epigrams*, in which two would-be 'knight-adventurers' attempt in heroic style to navigate the River Fleet (or Fleet Ditch), formerly a river but by the time of the poem's composition (*c*.1610) a choked sewer, full of rubbish, offal, dead animals, and excrement.[57] The explorers navigate the river, and traverse a hellish landscape, reaching a 'Stygian pool' inhabited by ghostly farts, crossing towards the Fleet Prison through Fleet Lane, and the 'furies and hot cooks | That with still-scalding steams make the place hell' (143–4). This 'hell' is filled with the souls of the unworthy dead transmuted into feral cats, and fed by an ever-running stream of rubbish:

> The sinks ran grease, and hair of measled hogs,
> The heads, houghs, entrails, and the hides of dogs . . .
>
> (lines 145–6)

The poem continues this image of City waste choking its sewers, and indeed, amongst the monsters that these knight-adventurers must slay is 'Mud':

> which when their oars did once stir,
> Belched forth an air as hot as the muster
> Of all your night tubs, when the carts do cluster,

---

[56] 2 *Esdras* 5 makes the linkage of women and monstrosity explicit: 'menstrous women shall bring forth monsters.' See L. Dasten and K. Park, *Wonders and the Order of Nature, 1150–1750* (New York, 1998), 180.

[57] 'On the Famous Voyage', in *Ben Jonson*, ed. I. Donaldson (Oxford, 1985).

Who shall discharge first his merd-urinous load . . .

(lines 61–5)

The poem envisages the City built upon and sinking back into mud, almost engulfed by the foul smells and effluvia which it produces. The banks of the ditch, moreover, are peopled by mythical monsters, 'ugly centaurs . . . | Gorgonian scolds and harpies, while over all | Hung stench, diseases, and old filth their mother' (lines 68–70). This maternal image ('old filth' is the 'mother' of the diseased City) is extended to the cityscape itself, as Bridewell Dock, where the Fleet Ditch entered the Thames, is described as the 'womb' which the explorers penetrate, almost as if the City were a monstrous, diseased female body, producing the endless supply of bodily fluids which early modern medicine associated with women.

Jonson's poem depicts the City as both constipated and overflowing with endless sewage, a nightmare landscape closer to hell than the New Jerusalem or refounded (or reformed) Rome of pro-City texts; and in choosing the mock-romance form for the poem, he satirizes both a genre he disliked and its potential readers (London citizens). This mock-heroic poem denies any romance to the City, and its hellish, disgusting landscape contrasts with the pastoral images used by City propagandists, emphasizing instead the inherent monstrosity of the City and its inhabitants. Throughout, this monstrosity is continuously associated with women, from the image of the City as a grotesque female body, through the depiction of its inhabitants as furies, gorgons, and harpies; even its tutelary deity is 'Madam Caesar, great Proserpina' (line 180). For Jonson, London is a stark underworld 'peopled' by creatures half-human and half-beast, and presided over by a brothel madam.

Although the City comedies of this volume are less coruscating in their representations of London, many of the ideas in Jonson's poem are implicit in their depiction of urban life. Even Dekker's *The Shoemaker's Holiday*, produced for a citizen audience, is suffused with the language of the humours, potentially grotesque bodies, and images of civic festivity and consumption, but presented in an overwhelmingly positive light. Against this, *Eastward Ho*, written for a more socially exclusive theatre, depicts the City as a snakepit of deceit and cozenage (cheating).

The Shoemaker's Holiday: Festive Capitalisms

In Dekker's play the issues of the City and social control are presented through the idealized vision of the workshop and the civic festivity. As the title suggests, holiday, and its associations with acceptable liberty from labour, dominates. Because the Elizabethan punctuation (or lack of it) renders the title ambiguous (how many shoemakers are on holiday is a moot point), the play can be seen to celebrate both Eyre's institution of an important civic event and the festive culture of a whole trade. The play does both, transforming Eyre into a City hero in the mould of Dick Whittington or Sir Thomas Gresham and providing a mythology for the foundation of Leadenhall and its associated trading privileges while, crucially, framing them within an overarching ideal of social concern. The ringing of the pancake bell (Scene 18) marks the proper regulation of time (holiday and labour are carefully designated and provided for), giving the apprentices, the lowest rung of the City hierarchy, their proper rights.[58] Indeed, the play goes further by conflating work and holiday in the image of the workshop. Although Eyre's household is carefully ordered, with himself at its head and the proper trade hierarchy observed (master craftsmen, foremen, journeymen, and apprentices), labour is depicted as carnivalesque. Thus, in Scene 4 we see Eyre buying drink for his workman (even his sleight of hand in paying for fewer beers than ordered is regarded as canny management), while in Scene 13 Firk and the other workmen sing as they work, their joking exchanges translating labour into pleasure. Indeed, in its celebration of Eyre's workshop, his rapid rise to wealth, and his generosity, the play creates a 'festive capitalism' which overrides the concerns about Eyre's business methods or the class conflict depicted in the clash of the Lord Mayor and the Earl of Lincoln.

The play, however, is not simply festive. Its events are set against a background of war and its casualties, class conflict surfaces, and simmering social disorder (especially between the apprentices and Hammon's servants) threatens to erupt. Yet, significantly, the play resolves these tensions, especially in the final scenes of feasting, where civic wealth is employed to generate social cohesion, while the loyalty of the citizens is stressed (Scenes 18 and 20). In these scenes, what critics regarded as civic extravagance is transformed into an urban equivalent

---

[58] This stands against ballads such as *The Cries of the Dead* (*c.*1625), which told of the murderous cruelty of one master towards his apprentices (repr. in *London*, ed. Manley, 147–50).

of the Land of Cockaigne, where it was supposed to rain food and drink: 'O, my brethren! There's cheer for the heavens—venison pasties walk up and down piping hot like sergeants, beef and brewis comes marching in dry vats, fritters and pancakes come trolling in in wheelbarrows . . .' (Scene 18, lines 194–7). These ideas coalesce in the foundation of Leadenhall, which is given a spurious Roman history (harking back towards the idea of London as the New Troy or Rome), while the trading privileges associated with its markets are shown as gifts of the royal prerogative, and so beyond question, as rewards for civic loyalty (Scene 21).

In this vision of civic benevolence the characters of Eyre and his wife are central, not simply as surrogate parents in the urban family, but as figures of how the potential excesses of City life are properly regulated. Mistress Eyre, for instance, is associated with female grotesquery ('Madge Mumblecrust' and 'Dame Clapperdudgeon' are two of Eyre's affectionate terms of abuse for her), while her malapropisms further emphasize her association with uncontrolled female garrulity. Yet, unlike the gross female bodies of Jonson's 'Famous Voyage', Margery is controlled, both through the constant puncturing of her social climbing (especially in Scene 10) and in Eyre's domination. She is the 'midriff' (Scene 1, line 135) while he is clearly her 'head' (Scene 1, line 158). This image of the potentially disruptive and excessive female body controlled by citizen authority extends the social control exercised throughout the play, and even includes Eyre himself. For although he is depicted as 'mad' and 'humorous', potentially full of the dangerous imbalances of the City body, his humorousness is contained, balanced by his 'airy' qualities. Thus, Eyre's own festive humour, rather than endangering social order, is regulated, and furthermore also controls his men and apprentices so that their riotous energy is channelled into productivity by him: 'frolic free-booters' (Scene 20, line 55) are made into proper shoemakers.[59] Again, these connections between the body, the control of its humours, and social control and the obedience of the City to the Crown are brought together in the interactions between Eyre and the King. In Scene 21 Eyre not only displays and excuses his 'rude manner' which is the result of his recognized status as 'handicraftsman' (which allows him

---

[59] The various names Eyre uses for his workers, 'Babylonian knaves' (Scene 10, line 139), 'dapper Assyrian lads' (Scene 17, line 46), and so on makes them sound like potential roaring boys, but they are also subordinated to his authority and rendered 'gentle'.

to stress his lack of deceit or 'craft'), but also his loyalty (lines 23–4) and the relation between the festive body and productivity. Asked his age, Eyre replies: 'My liege, I am six-and-fifty year old . . . Mark this old wench, my King. I danced the shaking of the sheets with her six-and-thirty years ago, and yet I hope to get two or three young Lord Mayors ere I die. I am lusty still . . .' (lines 26–30). Eyre's 'lusty' qualities (his liveliness and, implicitly, his potency) represent an urban vigour which is seen as natural, productive, and above all at the service of society. The lines are partly a demonstration of the romantic implications of Eyre's 'gentle craft', but they also focus an image implicit throughout the play, of Eyre and Margery as originary parents (here of a dynasty of gentlemen shoemakers). Indeed, through its representation of the workshop as family, with the Eyres as model parents showing proper male control and female submissiveness, the Eyres almost embody the proper relations of City (female) and State/Crown (male). At times *The Shoemaker's Holiday* appears to be an urban Genesis—but without a fall, and with the aristocratic snake firmly suppressed.

Eastward Ho: 'nothing but stone-fruit'

In contrast, *Eastward Ho* depicts the City less as paradise than wilderness, stressing the deceit and greed of its inhabitants, concentrating not upon a necessary urban industry, shoemaking, but on goldsmithing, a symbol of the luxury consumer industries which were developing in the capital. Whereas *The Shoemaker's Holiday* adapts the conventions of romance to urban life, the disguisings of *Eastward Ho* are all to deceive rather than relieve; its love affairs are shown to be less romantic than economic, both in personal terms (Mildred and Golding make a good match for money's sake), and in wider terms, as the City loves money more than anything else. In Dekker's play Eyre's dubious dealings with the Dutch ship-master and his enormous profits are glossed over, but in *Eastward Ho* the dominant citizen figures are Touchstone, the mean-spirited, moralizing goldsmith, and Security the usurer, who is so keen to cheat others that he ends up organizing his own wife's adultery. Both the City's social aspirations and morality are depicted as disordered, and, most importantly, romance, the form which in *The Shoemaker's Holiday* ennobles the City, is translated into delusion. Thus the journeys *Eastward Ho* depicts are profit-motivated escapes from creditors (the Virginia voyage) or deluded fantasies of self-aggrandisement, such as Lady Flash's 'vagary' (3.2.181) to her (non-existent) Eastwards castle rather than romantic quest narratives of deeds of derring-do. Indeed, *Eastward Ho* uses the escapist, fantastic world of romance to suggest that the City women, in particular, inhabit a fantasy world:

The knighthood nowadays are nothing like the knighthood of old time. They rid a-horseback, ours go afoot. They went attended by their squires, ours by their lackeys. They went buckled in their armour, ours muffled in their cloaks. They travelled wildernesses, and deserts, ours dare scarce walk the streets. They were still pressed to engage their honour, ours still ready to pawn their clothes. They would gallop on at sight of a monster, ours run away from the sight of a sergeant. They would help poor ladies, ours make poor ladies . . . (5.1.29–37)

Romance as an appropriate urban mode is not only undercut, but is seen as a dangerous delusion, such as the fantasy that Gertrude and Sindefy will recover their fortunes by finding a lost jewel, and a symbol of the dangerous imaginings which City life produces: 'pretty waking dreams' (5.1.80).

Indeed, the only 'monsters' encountered in the City are its women. *Eastward Ho* constantly links femininity and monstrosity, either through their dress and manners, which transform them into half-beasts, or in their uncontrolled sexual appetites which suggest their bestial natures. Thus in Act 1, Scene 2, where Gertrude insists 'I must be a lady' (lines 4 and 14), she also disports herself in courtier's clothes accompanied by her pet monkey. The clothes themselves are imitated from court fashion, and suggest immodest, sexualized dress (such as the 'close' fitting Scotch farthingale or the French headdress), which Gertrude sees as in keeping with the 'boldness' (line 72) required of the court, against the excessive City modesty (lines 69–70). Once dressed, Gertrude 'trips about the stage' as the bawdy tailor comments, '[N]ow you are in the lady-fashion, you must do all things light. Tread light, light. Ay and fall so: that's the court-amble . . .' (1.2.57–9). The court 'amble' suggests a mincing, sexualized step (which Gertrude mistakes for chic), while the subsequent lines, which call her walk 'a trot' and a 'false gallop' (1.2.60–1), stress the sexual and animal dimensions of her behaviour. Indeed, the pet monkey, as well as literally aping the court fashions for such pets, through the lewd and profane gestures it probably performed, emphasizes Gertrude's uncontrolled sexual imaginings. It is no accident that almost all of her song snatches are bawdy, while her constant spoken innuendo (especially in her exchanges with Quicksilver in Act 3, Scene 2) articulates her sexual obsession. As she departs for her coach, another symbol of potential sexual transgression, her cry that she will faint without it embodies disordered, uncontrolled female desires and humours.[60] Indeed, in many ways Gertrude parallels the women in Jonson's *Epicene* (1609), especially Mrs Otter and Lady Centaur, whose names announce their half-human, half-bestial natures.[61]

Eastward Ho presents the City as inhabited by monsters. The women, like Gertrude, are man-eaters or destroyers, compared to sirens, hyenas, crocodiles, and wolves (5.4.31–2), while the men are themselves beasts, either through their excesses or through their cuckoldry, which renders them either 'turnspit dogs' (2.2.250) desperate to satisfy their insatiable womenfolk, or 'horned beasts' (3.2.259). These images particularly dominate Act 4, Scene 1, where Slitgut's 'dishonest satire' imagines the whole City 'horned' in various ways, from 'headsman' to 'huntsman'.[62] This presents the City as a grotesque wilderness or forest, in which the chase follows women or money, using whatever means of cheating and crime are available, a place where the law is embodied by Wolf (the keeper of the Counter prison), and the result is not the paradisal garden of the City panegyrists, but a 'horn tree, that bearest nothing but stone-fruit' (4.1.267–8). This grotesque image of excessive sexual appetite, leading to disease and sterility comes far closer to the disgust of Jonson's 'On the Famous Voyage' than any of the other plays in this volume. Indeed, *Eastward Ho* culminates in Act 4, Scene 1, rather than in its final (and possibly ironic repentances), because on the coast of the Isle of Dogs, another highly symbolic, dreary, marginal location, the real nature of the City and its inhabitants is exposed. We see the City in prospect, and Slitgut's speech presents a verbal panorama or anatomy (as his name suggests) of its nature, while the arrival of the pathetic Sir Petronel, the incompetent Seagull, the Frenchified gentry, the petty criminal Quicksilver, and the serpentine Security provides a parade of its types. Even the only sympathetic figures, Winifred and the Drawer, stress the deceit of the City, as Winifred regains her place by tricking her husband into believing her lies. This is an urban Genesis writ large— complete with tree and snake.

[60] Cf. Quicksilver's vision of her humours in 2.2.243–54.

[61] Otters lived in two elements and were supposedly bisexual, while centaurs were mythological half-human, half-horses of lustful savagery: see Ben Jonson, *Epicoene*, ed. R.V. Holdsworth (1979), 4–5.

[62] The passage is full of sexual reference, so the 'horn of pleasure' is both a hunting horn and an erect penis. The hunt metaphor may deliberately parody the pretensions of *The Shoemaker's Holiday* and its use of hunting (esp. Scene 6).

The Roaring Girl: 'the fantasticalest girl'

The Shoemaker's Holiday and *Eastward Ho*, in different ways, present
the two extremes of contemporary discourses about London, one a
romanticized view, the other a cynical satire of a City built upon
dishonesty and bestiality. In contrast, Dekker and Middleton's *The
Roaring Girl* draws upon elements from both of these discourses, not
simply to create a balance, but rather to suggest, and celebrate, the
variety of the City. Thus, although this play also presents a bestial
world (the Dappers, Goshawk, Neatfoot) inhabited by the characters
whose names, at least, suggest sexual inadequacy or ambiguity
(Laxton, Sir Beauteous Ganymede), suffused with an animalistic sexual language directed especially towards the women, yet those women
manage to outwit their would-be sexual predators. Moreover, the
younger generation of Sebastian Wengrave and Mary Fitzallard manage to outsmart the corrupt behaviours and imaginings of the older
generation, as does Jack Dapper in a lesser way. The agency in the
generational conflict lies with the figure who is also seen as the most
monstrous: Moll. She collaborates in the deceiving of Sir Alexander
Wengrave; assists Jack Dapper to escape the ambush laid by the sergeants set on by his father, Sir Davy; and most of all, her duel with
Laxton frames the attitude towards rapacious male sexuality in the
play. In Scene 5 Laxton assumes that he can treat all women as sexually available, using sexually derogatory terms (he refers to women as
'jades'), and offering to entice Moll for a coach-ride to the Three
Pigeons at Brentford (a notorious spot for illicit liaisons). Moll first
destroys him verbally and then fights him, and her speech frames an
entirely different attitude to women and female sexuality:

> Thou'rt one of those
> That thinks each woman thy fond flexible whore,
> If she but cast a liberal eye upon thee,
> Turn back her head, she's thine; or, amongst company,
> By chance drink first to thee, then she's quite gone,
> There's no means to help her; nay, for a need
> Wilt swear unto thy credulous fellow lechers
> That thou art more in favour with a lady
> At first sight than her monkey all her lifetime.
> How many of our sex, by such as thou
> Have their good thoughts paid with a blasted name
> That never deserved loosely or did trip

In path of whoredom beyond cup and lip?
But for the stain of conscience and of soul,
Better had women fall into the hands
Of an act silent than a bragging nothing,
There's no mercy in't. What durst move you, sir,
To think me whorish?—A name which I'd tear out
From the high German's throat if it lay ledger there
To dispatch privy slanders against me.
In thee I defy all men, their worst hates
And their best flatteries, all their golden witchcrafts,
With which they entangle the poor spirits of fools:
Distressed needlewomen and trade-fallen wives—
Fish that needs must bite or themselves be bitten—
Such hungry things as these may soon be took
With worm fastened on a golden hook:
Those are the lecher's food, his prey. He watches
For quarrelling wedlocks and poor shifting sisters,
'Tis the best fish he takes. But why, good fisherman,
Am I thought meat for you, that never yet
Had angling rod cast towards me? 'Cause, you'll say,
I'm given to sport, I'm often merry, jest:
Had mirth no kindred in the world but lust?
O, shame take all her friends then! But howe'er
Thou and the baser world censure my life,
I'll send 'em word by thee, and write so much
Upon thy breast, 'cause thou shalt bear't in mind:
Tell them 'twere base to yield where I have conquered.
I scorn to prostitute myself to a man,
I that can prostitute a man to me!

(Scene 5, lines 67–107)

Moll's speech reverses the language and assumptions of the men of the play about women, answers for them point for point, just as she then defeats Laxton with her sword-point to prove his unmanliness. The power of the speech lies in the way Moll refuses to accept male discourse, moving the focus away from victim to victimizer. Thus 'the best fish' are seen as innocent victims of the 'good fisherman' (an ironic term), while men's slanders of women, which treat them as loose even before they have consented, are rejected as the empty words of impotent men: 'I scorn to prostitute myself to a man, | I that can prostitute a man to me!'

The Roaring Girl also deploys the discourse of monstrosity to evoke more complex responses, playing between horror, pleasure, and repugnance.[63] On one hand figures such as Sir Alexander Wengrave and Sir Adam depict Moll as a monster, 'A creature . . . nature hath brought forth | To mock the sex of woman . . . a thing | One knows not how to name' (Scene 2, lines 127–9), but against this lies a discourse which regards Moll as the most 'fantasticalest girl' (Scene 3, line 186). Although Goshawk uses these terms in a sexual sense, his language suggests another response beyond horror and repugnance: pleasure and fascination. 'Fantastical' carries associations of the grotesque and bizarre, but without the opprobrium of Sir Alexander's medico-moral language of prodigy, inhumanity, and pollution.[64] Moll may be seen as a violator of norms, but the description of her as 'mad' perhaps recalls the merry madness of Eyre. Moll's treatment as hermaphroditic thus seems to draw less upon ideas of nature's prodigies than on Neoplatonic ideals of the hermaphrodite as a perfect union of male and female souls and bodies.[65] Yet, most importantly, her actions make her a heroic figure in the play. She not only turns the language of monstrosity back upon men (it is, after all, Goshawk, Laxton, and Sir Beauteous Ganymede who manifest kinds of 'deviant' sexuality), but her active role is endowed with a positive force rather than negative associations. This active involvement in the plot and her positive role in facilitating Mary and Sebastian's union means that she stands outside the norms without being seen as dangerously violating them.

Moll can be presented in this positive way because the play provides different responses to spectacle, monstrosity, and the urban environment. Although the city-space of *The Roaring Girl* does carry moral associations (notably in Marylebone Park and the extra-mural journeys to Brentford and Ware), the moralized landscape typical of *The Shoemaker's Holiday* or *Eastward Ho* is much reduced. In fact, Sir Alexander Wengrave's attempt to read moral significance into his son's journey in Scene 11 is treated as comic. The City landscape is, instead, shown in a more ambiguous fashion, open to its varieties and pleasures, which are celebrated rather than eschewed. Some of this complexity can be glimpsed in Sir Davy Dapper's description of the

---

[63] On these overlapping reactions to monsters and monstrosity, see Dasten and Park, *Wonders*, 176.

[64] Wengrave, in Scene 2, line 134, compares her to a 'blazing star', often interpreted as an apocalyptic warning from nature of impending doom.

[65] Cheney, 'Moll Cutpurse as Hermaphrodite in Dekker and Middleton's *The Roaring Girl*', *Renaissance et Réforme*, 7 (1983), 120–34.

City as full of 'Roaring boys . . . fencers and ningles— | Beasts Adam ne'er gave name to . . . ' (Scene 7, lines 61–2). On one hand this situates the City as a perverted paradise, yet because the audience recognizes this as part of Sir Davy's own imaginings (his son is a harmless gull rather than the dissolute prodigal of his father's paranoia), his sense of civic monstrosity is undermined. Indeed, when his son later describes his escape from the planned ambush, he describes the Counter as 'a park in which all the wild beasts of the city run by head' (Scene 10, lines 42–3), and although the lines mock his foolish bravado, they also suggest a fundamentally different attitude in which the dangers of the City are contained, almost as if in a menagerie.

The Roaring Girl develops the City as a spectacle, full of dangers, pleasures, monsters, and prodigies. As a 'park' rather than a 'wilderness', it contains and displays all parts of the City. Thus a careful distinction is made between honest knaves and truly dangerous thieves in Scene 10 (the canting scene). The combination of song, the fascinating canting terms, and the sense of a social order at work even within marginalized groups, turns the gipsy-thieves into objects of wonder, amusement, and pleasure rather than simply danger. In effect, the City is translated from wilderness into *Wunderkammer*, a cabinet of human curiosities which stimulates different responses, and even educates the audience. Cabinets of curiosities, often containing a vast array of objects, from rare stuffed animals through to rare minerals, ethnographic materials, and weird objects such as bizarrely shaped vegetables, were major tourist attractions in this period (the Strand home of Sir Walter Cope boasted one which was particularly famous), and are often seen as the forerunners of modern museums. Here the City's 'curiosities' are shown to the audience, but also different cultures and languages are offered, goods are displayed (especially in the shop scenes which might have resembled a cabinet of curiosities), and commerce celebrated, while the places and pastimes of the City are also memorialized. In this wondrous place, however, social norms and values are reversed. The officers of the law are shown to be rapacious (Scene 7, lines 132–8), fathers betray their children, and the outsider figure, Moll, a mannish woman, acts as an agent for good, even instilling order. Disorder stems not from the City and its marginalized groups but, rather, from the older, supposedly respectable City gentry.

In this respect the different auspices of *The Roaring Girl* are significant. Written for the Fortune, with its lower-class audience, the play produces a more complex social analysis which, rather than utilizing a pro/anti-civic binary, opens up some of the social differences within the City and amongst citizens. Thus the older generation of wealthy citizen-gentry are associated with a withdrawal from proper civic concerns, symbolized through their withdrawal into private architectural space. In Scene 2 Sir Alexander Wengrave offers his guests an opulent gallery to rival that in any aristocratic house, but it is a scene which has echoes in City drama, harking back to the 'gallery' scene in Heywood's *If You Know Not Me, You Know Nobody, Part 2* (1606), in which the Dean of St Paul's displays his collection of portraits of London worthies (including Dick Whittington) as a reminder of the charitable deeds of the City and to persuade two feuding merchants, Sir Thomas Gresham and Sir Thomas Ramsey, to heal the breach for the benefit of the City and its charities. In contrast to these civic worthies, Sir Alexander's gallery offers nothing but a prospect and private comfort for his guests and an expression of wealth (it cost 'many a fair grey groat') rather than civic charity.[66] The contrast between the proper civic charity which benefits all and the privatization which these City-gents embody is pointed up by the description of the galleries, which are actually those of the Fortune, filled not with portraits but with the City audience. This image works in a double manner, partly as a critique of the withdrawal of the City's mercantile class from charity, but also as a celebration of the City itself, or rather the city-dwellers, both citizens and others, as a theatrical spectacle. Moreover, this audience is not simply the privileged few but the whole social range of the City.

In its celebration of all parts of London society, the critique it offers of the City merchants who behave more like the aristocrats of *The Shoemaker's Holiday*, and its encouragement of the marginalized city dwellers (younger sons, mannish women) who use the kind of 'gentle craft' espoused by mercantile heroes like Eyre, *The Roaring Girl* implicitly invokes ideas of the City as commonwealth. A commonwealth allows for the heterogeneity of London society, but binds all together in a shared ('common') state ('weal' or 'wealth'). This political model was well known in the early modern period, especially amongst the more politically radical (often Protestant) sections of society with whom both the authors, Dekker and Middleton, were connected.[67] It treated society not as a natural or divine hierarchy or monarchy, but

---

[66] *The Roaring Girl*, Scene 2, line 12.

[67] On the idea of the 'commonweal', see D. Norbrook, *Poetry and Politics in the English Renaissance* (1984), 49 and 95. For Dekker's politics, see J. Gaspar, *The Dragon and the Dove: The Plays of Thomas Dekker* (Oxford, 1990), and on Middleton's radical connections, M. Heinemann, *Puritanism and Theatre* (Cambridge, 1980).

rather stressed the collective, artificial creation of a society through human agency. This politically radical potential in *The Roaring Girl* may also be related to the attitude towards the female body in the play, and marks a development from Dekker's position in *The Shoemaker's Holiday*. In that play, the idea of the state as body is explored in the description of Margery's position as 'stomach' to Simon Eyre's 'head,' and the female body is shown to require male regulation; but in *The Roaring Girl*, the male control of the female body is at the very least questioned, in that it is shown to be male sexual attitudes which denigrate women, treating them as 'common dame[s]' (Scene 5, line 131). Moll's behaviour not only questions this depiction of women as a male construct, but her own hermaphroditic body draws on an idea of equalized balance of male and female elements which differentiates it from hierarchical views of the body. Given the propensity of this period to think through such analogies as that of body and state, and given the frequent use of the female body as a figure for the City and Moll's own identification with the City throughout the play, it seems possible that her role and the representation of her body acts as a new, inclusive, non-hierarchical model for City politics.

Every Man In His Humour: Or, The Fountain of Self-Love

Perhaps the most instructive contrast here lies with Jonson's *Every Man In His Humour*, where the City is also depicted as peopled with monsters and prodigies. These range from the 'accomplished monster' Stephen, to the monstrosity implied by Bobadill's dress and behaviour. Notably, this City does not regulate itself, but requires the intervention of the 'merry' magistrate, Justice Clement. Clement is, of course, a royal appointee, and his function in resolving the plot, exposing Matthew's literary monstrosity, and puncturing the monstrous imaginings of Kitely and even Knowell Senior, firmly subordinates the City to royal prerogative. The connections between cultural and political deformity are registered in Act 5, Scene 1, where Matthew's plagiarism is revealed:

JUSTICE CLEMENT [*to the servants*] Yes, yes, search him for a taste of his vein.

[*The Servants search Matthew and discover sheets of poems*]

WELLBRED You must not deny the Queen's Justice, sir, under a writ o'rebellion.

[*The Servants give the papers to Justice Clement*]

JUSTICE CLEMENT What! All this verse? Body o'me, he carries a whole

realm, a commonwealth of paper, in's hose! Let's see some of his
subjects!

(5.1.219–25)

Failure to submit to royal writ in both political and cultural matters is
not only aligned with 'rebellion', but Matthew's poetry is imagined as
a 'realm, a commonwealth' with its own 'subjects' (topics, but also
citizens). In this paper kingdom, deformity and literary theft, which
renders the original ridiculous, debases the verbal currency. The
choice of the term 'commonwealth' exploits the City commonwealth
(see above p. xxix), but equates it with plagiarism and theft rather
than an ideal social order of shared benefit and mutuality, a point
which is reinforced by Matthew's depiction as 'the town gull'. Indeed,
Clement even calls poetlings like Matthew 'paper-peddlers', dealers in
paper, while also punning on 'pedlars', sellers of cheap, tawdry goods.
This establishes an important link between popular culture, low-level
commerce, and the debasement of literary culture. On the one hand,
Matthew's association with the City (he is from the 'town') positions
him as a figure of civic culture, while his 'trade' in poetry parodies
commerce, suggesting that all forms of commerce are debased and
close to, if not actually, theft. Here implicitly, as explicitly in the passage from Dekker's *Gull's Horn Book* (cited above, p. xiii), Jonson
links 'retailing' and 'retelling', making the commercialization of
theatre and literary texts a debasement.

This idea runs throughout *Every Man In His Humour*, where the
ability to appreciate poetry and and the capacity to produce the right
style are associated with moral uprightness, from Wellbred's letter
through to Matthew and Bobadill's outmoded recitation of Kyd's
Spanish Tragedy and their inane literary criticism (1.4.44–63).
Matthew's pose as a literary melancholic and his facile literary
invention are associated with a lack of control which echoes the
depiction of women as leaky vessels:

MATTHEW O, it's your only fine humour, sir; your true melancholy breeds
your perfect fine wit, sir. I am melancholy myself divers times, sir, and then
do I no more but take pen and paper presently and overflow you half a
score or a dozen of sonnets at a sitting.
EDWARD (*aside*) Sure he utters them then by the gross.

(3.1.75–9)

This poetic incontinence (he 'overflows') renders Matthew 'effemin-
ate' as he becomes like a woman in his inability to control his bodily
and poetic humours. This fails to meet Jonson's own standard, the

pursuit of a 'virile style', 'strong to show the composition manly', which Jonson contrasts with the 'affected and preposterous' over-elaborate dress of gallants.[68] The sonnet, in particular, is associated with this uncontrolled humorousness (Matthew is called 'songs-and-sonnets' by Downright at 4.1.162), along with the poetry of Jonson's rival Daniel (his *Delia* is parodied in 5.1.226–7), but the key issue lies in the 'utter[ing]' of the poems, as Knowell puns not only on their production, but also on their selling.[69] Poems which should be the object of thought, care, and a manly style are reduced to commodities, sold by the 'gross' by such poetasters.

In Act 5, Scene 1, Clement's justice rejects 'commonwealth' ideals in favour of a social view which insists on the links between poetry and monarchy as well upon divine sanction: 'Nay, no speech or act of mine be drawn against such [poets] such as profess it [poetry] worthily. They are not born every year, as an alderman. There goes more to the making of a good poet, than a sheriff . . .' (5.1.239–42). This speech echoes a passage Jonson uses in *Timber or Discoveries*, which claims that 'Every beggarly corporation affords the state a mayor or two bailiffs yearly; but only poets and kings are not born every year'.[70] This passage not only glosses Clement's comment that he 'will do more reverence to him, when I meet him, than I will to the mayor, out of his year' (5.1.243–4), placing the poet firmly above the civic official, but it also confirms the contrast between commonwealths ('corporation', the term used in *Discoveries*, suggests the same idea) and divinely sanctioned hierarchy, of which the poet and king are the apex. The world propounded by Clement is not a republic of letters but a king-dom of poets.

Plagiarism and poetic incontinence are important manifestations of the humours and the loss of control which Jonson associated with civic culture, along with the unbridled commercialism which debases litera-ture. Clement's act of poetic justice in Act 5, Scene 1, denouncing and burning Matthew's parody-poetry, is also a purgation of the City, both of its false poets and the culture they embody: 'Cleanse the air. Here

---

[68] *Timber or Discoveries*, lines 592–3, in *Ben Jonson*, ed. Donaldson, and Parker, 'Virile Style', in L. Fradenburg and C. Freccero (eds.), *Premodern Sexualities* (1996), 201–22, esp. 207.

[69] Downright also calls Matthew a 'ballad-singer' and refers to 'poets' and 'potlings' (4.1.131 and 129) as examples of debased poets.

[70] *Discoveries*, lines 2454–7. Jonson's text cites the passage in Latin, '*solus rex, aut poeta, non quotannis nascitur*', and misattributes it to Petronius, when it comes from Florus, *Of the Qualities of Life*.

xlii

was enough to have infected the whole City, if it has not been taken in time' (5.1.233–4). This image of the poetlings infecting the City like some poetic plague (which was also associated with the idea of airborne miasma or infection thought to be dispelled by the burning of herbs) may seem to overstate the influence of poetry, but Jonson's point is about the broader issue of imitation. Just as poets were supposed to learn their craft through the imitation of poetic models, a process which was to be carefully differentiated from plagiarism, so society was also supposed to operate through imitation. Thus the faulty imitation of false models, be they social or poetic, endangered society as they corrupted through their debased content, but also through the destruction of a central social process.

In *Every Man In His Humour* urban culture is seen to encourage the witless imitation of foolish and dangerous social models, so that the would-be gallant's behaviour, as with Stephen in Act 1, Scene 1 in pursuit of a hunting manual or the homoeroticized fencing lesson of Act 1, Scene 4, illustrates a failure of self- and social control. Jonson clarifies this relation between false social and poetic models and the imitative process in the Epistle added to the 1616 text of *Cynthia's Revels*, which called the court 'the special fountain of manners' and the 'mirror' in which 'the whole kingdom dresseth itself', warning 'Beware, then thou render men's figures truly and teach them no less to hate their deformities, than to love their forms'.[71] In many ways *Every Man In His Humour* treats London in the same way, as a 'fountain of self-love' which deforms culture, and the play, in its concentration upon the City gallants rather than the citizens, insists upon the complicity of the gentry in this debasement. In this respect *Every Man In His Humour* alters the emphasis seen in plays such as *The Shoemaker's Holiday*, where the gentry are all knaves and the citizens honest, suggesting that true gentility lies not in the enjoyment of 'town' pleasures, the consumerist paradise offered by the City, but in proper self control. Every man, especially the gentry should be *within* their humour, controlled and measured like Edward Knowell, rather than seen *in* their humour.

The complicity of the gentry in the urban debasement of culture is the central subject of the Prologue, added to the text sometime after 1611. This Prologue, with its well-known attacks on popular theatrical conventions such as exotic and multiple locations, creaking stage

---

[71] *The Fountain of Self-Love, or Cynthia's Revels*, Epistle, lines 7–10, in vol. 4 of *Ben Jonson*, ed. C. H. Herford, P. Simpson, and E. Simpson, 11 vols. (Oxford, 1925–52).

descents, thunder, and the 'long jars' of martial and historical plays, uses the imagery of monstrosity to connect the urban deformation of taste with its debased society. Jonson ends the Prologue wishing that 'You, that have so graced monsters, may like men' (line 30), probably glancing both at *The Tempest*, but also more broadly at the deformed taste represented by the older history and mythological plays which he had condemned earlier, as well as the preference for romances (which were undergoing something of a revival in 1610).[72] These tastes are seen as manifestations of 'popular errors' (line 26), common faults, but also errors created by the urban populace, which if treated individually, can be dismissed as 'follies', but if seen as markers of broader social decay, must be treated as 'crimes' (line 24). Thus literary discrimination becomes a marker of true gentility and the failure to reform taste marks social failure, rapidly slipping from venial folly into social crime.

This Prologue belongs to the defence of poetry which Jonson undertook at the outset of the 1616 folio edition of his *Works* (a defence which encompasses the dedication of *Every Man In His Humour* to his teacher, the historian Camden), and marks his determination to establish poetry, even in the form of plays, as a socially educative and morally and politically reformatory tool. The image which Clement uses of kings and poets, as both born gifted with divine sanction and power, marks Jonson's sense of the significance and seriousness of poets and poetry, against those who would describe his plays as the 'scurrile invention of an illiterate bricklayer' (see above, p. viii). Yet even as Jonson published his plays as *Works*, he sought to distance himself from the commercial theatrical world, reshaping them to emphasize their classical affinities; and indeed, this determined disengagement from his origins as a popular dramatist continues throughout Jonson's career, the 'not so loved . . . stage' (Prologue, line 3) becoming 'loathèd' by the end of his career.[73] In part, this reshaping of his own narrative as well as the text of his plays was stimulated by his absorption into the Jacobean establishment (no matter what awkwardness and uncertainties his works may reveal) as the main masque poet and propagandist-in-chief for the court.[74] The ordering of the

---

[72] *Mucedorus*, the most popular romance of the Elizabethan era, was reissued in 1610.

[73] 'Come leave the loathèd stage' ('On *The New Inn* Ode. To Himself'), in *Ben Jonson*, ed. Donaldson, 502. We should always remember that Jonson began his career as a hack playwright, and even collaborated with Dekker on *Page of Plymouth*.

[74] The best brief account of Jonson's relations with the court remains Norbrook's *Poetry and Politics*, ch. 7.

texts within the *Works* further shows this process, as the volume opens with *Every Man In His Humour*, an Elizabethan play, which looks back to an age of proper royal justice (Clement) controlling social disorder, and ends with the last text of the volume, the masque, *The Golden Age Restored*. This masque, which transferred the myth of the return of Astraea the goddess of justice (and the dominant symbol of Elizabeth I's reign) to the Jacobean court, represents a conscious conclusion to the volume in which, through the royal patronage of the masque, the 'ill customs of the age' will be reformed. The agents of this reform will be poet and king.

Thus the choice of *Every Man In His Humour*, in its revised form, to head Jonson's new *Works* represents a conscious and careful self-presentation. It was neither his first play (this was probably an early, lost, collaborative work), nor his first success (*The Case Is Altered*), but it was his poetic manifesto, his attempt to establish himself as an author with poetic authority. It belongs to Jonson's self-description of himself as a laureate poet, and his careful self-reformulation which stressed the continuity of his career, glossing over 'unworthy' texts, and his self-censorship. From this self-created Jonson has emerged the critical tradition which celebrates his erudition and his self-announced position as the Jacobean Horace.[75] Yet no matter how much Jonson rejected—and how much Jonsonian criticism has ignored—what he later called 'the concupiscence of dances and antics', Jonson's origins, and much of his most powerful theatrical work, remains rooted in the traditions of popular theatre.[76] Even as he erased the traces of his collaborative endeavours (excluded from the *Works*) and allowed his civic pageants to fade away quietly while preserving much aristocratic ephemera, the longevity of plays like *Every Man In His Humour*, and their accessibility to a wide variety of audiences, belie the attempt at self-revision. Interestingly, for all his rejection of the City, Jonson continued to pay his dues as a guild-member of the Bricklayers Company, while his City comedies testify to a complex, fascinating, and productive engagement with metropolitan popular culture and popular theatre.

[75] R. Helgerson, *Self-Crowned Laureates: Spenser, Jonson, Milton and the Literary System* (Berkeley, 1983), ch. 3.

[76] 'To the Reader', *The Alchemist*, line 5, in vol. 6 of *Ben Jonson*, ed. Herford and P. and E. Simpson.

NOTE ON THE TEXTS

Despite the considerable uncertainty over the precise dating of the revised *Every Man In His Humour*, this volume orders texts by the dates of performance, placing the bulk of the revision of *Every Man In His Humour* in 1608–9. The plays are thus ordered: *The Shoemaker's Holiday* (1599), *Eastward Ho* (1605), *Every Man In His Humour* (1608–9), and *The Roaring Girl* (1611). Each of the plays has been edited afresh from the original quartos (or, in the case of Jonson, the folio), and modernized in accordance with the principles outlined in *Modernizing Shakespeare's Spelling* (Oxford, 1979) and *Re-editing Shakespeare for the Modern Reader* by Stanley Wells (Oxford, 1984), although, in general, the edition is conservative in its preservation of forms (especially where they alter the metre), the treatment of names, and dialect or comic linguistic effects. Stage directions marked in square brackets are editorial additions. In particular, where rhyme would be altered by modernization (as in the grieve/Shrieve rhyme in *The Shoemaker's Holiday*, Scene 10, lines 111–12) the text retains the early modern forms.

Although two of these plays are collaborations (*Eastward Ho* and *The Roaring Girl*), I have omitted discussion of the author's shares and matters of planning as irrelevant to the plays in performance. These issues are covered at length in the Revels and New Mermaid editions of both plays (see below).

The Shoemaker's Holiday

Printed in black-letter in 1600 (Q1), the play went through numerous editions (six by 1657). The black-letter print and the longevity of the multiple editions testify to the play's popularity. Q1 has been used as the basis of this edition although, in line with previous editions, emendations from the contemporary quartos have been adopted. In fact, the Q1 text requires considerable emendation, especially of speech-headings for the Lord Mayor (here Oatley) and Lacy, who is often referred to as Hans (after Scene 7). Many of the emendations proposed by earlier editors (notably 'beckons' Scene 1, line 97, tawsoone, Scene 1, line 160) have been silently adopted.[1] Q1 is not divided into either acts or scenes, but I have followed the Elizabethan practice of printing plays with scenes but without act divisions (Bowers and others insert acts and scenes).[2]

There is one substantial change in this text from previous editions: the treatment of the Prologue. The Prologue, designed for a court performance on 1 January 1600, has been relegated to the status of an Additional Passage. It was presumably only performed the once, and does not reflect the continuing performance practice for the text, which may well have had another prologue, but not this one.

The other controversial matter is the placing of the two 'Three-Man's' songs placed at the front of Q (between the Epistle and the Prologue on sigs. A3v and A4v). There has been much debate about the placing of these songs and it is tempting to locate them in the text. In particular, the 1st Song, with its theme of maying, complements the pastoral tone of Scene 11, and it is plausible that the performance of Scene 11, which already requires a taborer for the morris, would include further songs. The 2nd Song is more problematic, but as a drinking song it might help establish the festivity of Scene 20, although this quality is a feature of many scenes within the play. Given the lack of evidence as to where they might have been performed (which is presumably why they were printed separately in Q) they have been removed to the Additional Passages. The text has, however, been altered to give the chorus in full twice and the stage direction 'Singing close with the tenor boy' has been moved to provide a more plausible performance strategy.

The Dutch of the play is treated in a slightly different fashion from that recommended in Wells *Re-editing Shakespeare*, in that it seems that Lacy's speeches as Hans are not Dutch in any meaningful linguistic sense, but approximations, a kind of comic stage 'Dutch'. Thus spelling has been regularized but the phonetic effects have been retained wherever possible. This is closer to the actual editorial practice in the 1979 Smallwood and Wells Revels edition.[3]

---

[1] See J. George, 'Four Notes on the Text of Dekker's "Shoemaker's Holiday"', *Notes and Queries*, 194 (1949), 192.

[2] *The Dramatic Works of Thomas Dekker*, ed. F. Bowers, 4 vols. (Cambridge, 1953–61), i.

[3] *The Shoemaker's Holiday*, ed. R. Smallwood and S. Wells (Manchester, 1979).

Eastward Ho

Eastward Ho was printed in three editions in 1605 (Q1–3). The rapid succession of editions suggests the notoriety and popularity of the play, and the controversy that caused two of the authors to be imprisoned and the play heavily, if erratically, censored.[4] Most importantly, Q1 survives in two issues, a(i) and a(ii), both of which have been censored.

This edition follows the a(i) text throughout. As a result several substantial emendations are required, notably in 3.1 where the speech-prefixes are confused. This text follows Van Fossen and substitutes Seagull (for Q's 'Spoyl').[5] In 3.2 in the stage direction 'Por' (23 f.) is emended to 'Potkin' on grounds of economy. Generally accepted emendations from earlier editions (Herford and P. and E. Simpson, Petter, Van Fossen) are silently adopted. Punctuation follows Q and has been kept as simple as possible.

Censorship and Revision

The single extant copy of a(i), BL Ashley 371, preserves two leaves, E3 and E4 (end of 3.2 and opening of 3.3), which contained a substantial portion of the satirical material excised during the revision, although the Dyce Collection, Victoria and Albert Museum, copy of a(ii) also contains the *cancellandum* (the removed leaf), along with the *cancellans* that replaced them. In addition to this major evidence in the text for censorship several other anomalies have been pointed out as further instances of tampering:

(1) Sig. A4v (1.2, opening SD): in Q1 these lines are lineated as verse, taking up a large amount of space. It may be that the monkey brought in by the ghost character Beatrice performed some kind of obscene or satirical jest or jig at this point, possibly part of the satire on the Scots in the scene.[6] Herford and P. and E. Simpson calculate that as much as nine lines may be omitted.

(2) Sigs. C1v–C2r (2.2.51–110): these leaves are markedly 'white'

---

[4] E. K. Chambers, *The Elizabethan Stage*, 4 vols. (Oxford, 1923), iii. 254–6, provides a useful survey of the problems, along with *Ben Jonson*, ed. C. H. Herford and P. and E. Simpson, 11 vols. (Oxford, 1925–52), iv. 489–512. The best discussions are supplied in *Eastward Ho!*, ed. C. G. Petter (1973) and *Eastward Ho*, ed. R. W. Van Fossen (Manchester, 1979).

[5] *Eastward Ho*, ed. Van Fossen.

[6] J. Q. Adams, '*Eastward Hoe* and Its Satire Against the Scots', *Studies in Philology*, 28 (1931), 689–701.

(that is, there are a lot of gaps) which seems to suggest material has been excised. In particular, the catchword between C1r and C1v does not match, so that a speech-prefix is signalled at the bottom of C1v ('Quick.') whereas what follows is a speech ('Your place maintained before . . .'). Also, further down the same sheet the spacing runs awry, and both Petter and Herford and P. and E. Simpson argue that lines about the Scots gentlemen of the bedchamber have been removed (2.2.72–80).

(3) Sig. E3r–E4v: these are the leaves removed in the second issue and reset and replaced (see above). An anti-Scottish jibe (3.3.36–42) is cut, a line altered (3.3.45 where 'Nobleman' is replaced by 'any other officer'), and three lines added (after 3.3.47). These rather lame lines seem to have acted as a filler to cover for the removed material, and read: 'Besides there we shall no more law than conscience, and not too much either; serve God enough, eat and drink enough, and enough is as good as a feast.'

When listed thus the alterations appear to produce a clear pattern whereby systematic removal of offending anti-Scots material was attempted, but the situation is complicated by the survival of xenophobic jokes at 1.2.47 and 2.2.264, and the parody of Scottish accents in 4.1.156–7. Moreover, the *cancellandum* leaves in their first state (that is in a(i)), show evidence of *earlier* tampering, before the wholesale excision occurred, perhaps suggesting that there were several stages of revision or censorship.

Much of the problem arises because we are uncertain of the precise cause of the offence, whether it was the production or the publication that triggered intervention.[7] Furthermore, scholars are divided about the general workings of Jacobean censorship and how they might have influenced the case. Jonson and Chapman suggest (in a series of letters written by Chapman and Jonson to various court grandees from prison, preserved in Folger Library, MS V.a.321, fos. 88r–93r) that 'but two clauses' caused offence and that they were not theirs.[8] This could be evidence that the players were responsible and their improvisation had somehow got into print, or that Marston (who does not appear to have been imprisoned) was responsible. In Jonson's later discussion of the case with Drummond of Hawthornden, recorded in

[7] R. Dutton, *Mastering the Revels: The Regulation and Censorship of English Renaissance Drama* (Basingstoke, 1991), esp. ch. 7.

[8] A. R. Braunmuller, *A Seventeenth-Century Letter-Book: A Facsimile Edition of Folger Library, MS V.a.321, With Transcript, Annotations and Commentary* (Newark, 1983).

the *Conversations*, he mentions that the play was 'delated' (that is, denounced) to the King by a member of his Scottish entourage, Sir James Murray, brother of a powerful member of James's bedchamber staff, Sir John Murray, who may have taken umbrage at 2.2.72–80 and whatever was removed.[9] This would appear to relate to the publication, and might explain why there appears to have been a rather half-hearted attempt at alteration (Dutton, in *Mastering the Revels*, argues for last-minute nerves on the printer's part).

The situation was compounded by the position of the Children of the Queen's Revels, who operated under the control of Queen Anne's household and, initially, through her own Master of the Revels, Samuel Daniel. Daniel, after having caused offence with *Philotas* (1604), appears to have been removed, but the question of who took over responsibility for the licensing of this company apparently remained unresolved, possibly with James's Lord Chamberlain, the earl of Suffolk, taking over. His absence with the court on its summer progress in 1605 explains the lack of his approval.

It would, on balance, appear that the Children of the Queen's Revels operated with a greater degree of permissiveness than other companies because of their association with the court. Possibly this was actually a matter of policy on Anne's part. Certainly, the company seems to have exploited this liberty for commercial advantage, and constantly pressed the boundaries of their permission. The censorship of *Eastward Ho*, and the complex negotiations and threats surrounding it, may have arisen for a multiplicity of reasons, not least of which was the uncertain status of the company and divided control over its activities.

Every Man In His Humour

Text

There are two texts of this play: Q1 (1601), a single-text copy with an Italian setting and names, and F1 (1616), in the collected *Works*. The latter text, with its London setting, has been used as the basis of this edition.

The folio text is consciously literary in its use of act and scene divisions, massed entries, and the relegation of stage directions to the

---

[9] *Conversations with Drummond*, in *Ben Jonson*, ed. I. Donaldson (Oxford, 1985), lines 225–9.

1

margin. Scene divisions have been silently emended in line with the practice of earlier editors, massed entries have been distributed, and the marginal stage directions have been restored to the body of the text, supplemented by more detailed stage directions drawn from Q1 where applicable.

Date of Revision

Although there is little doubt about the 1598 date for the first version of *Every Man In His Humour*, no such certainty accompanies the revision which produced the second redaction, although most scholars place it some time after 1604.[10] The play was certainly staged at court in 1605, but apart from this there is no evidence of performances until 1631.[11] It has often been suggested that the revision may have preceded the 1605 court performance, or that revision sought to capitalize on the success of *The Alchemist* in 1610. Yet, although the Prologue can be dated securely to *c*.1611–12, and appears to belong to a Blackfriars revival, no evidence for any such performances exist.[12] In this situation scholars are forced to rely upon circumstantial and subjective internal evidence, susceptible to varying interpretation.

In fact there are three main dates with which the revision might be associated: early (*c*.1604–5), late (after 1610, but *c*.1611–12 and perhaps as late as 1615), and intermediate (*c*.1606–9).

Early revision (c.1604–5)

The Candlemas Eve court performance in 1605 would appear a natural occasion for revision to occur, yet the other plays presented in this season were all revivals, and the King's Men appear to have been rifling their back-catalogue to produce suitably entertaining texts. The text also presents some problems for this hypothesis. For instance, much of the revision removes classical allusions which would have appealed to James VI and I. It has often been suggested that the

---

[10] *Every Man In His Humour: A Parallel-Text Edition of the 1601 Quarto and the 1616 Folio*, ed. J. W. Lever (Lincoln, Nebr., 1971), and Herford and P. and E. Simpson, *Ben Jonson*, i. 373–89, iii. 193–403, and ix. 168–85 and 331–94 consider the dating issue. The best discussion of these matters is found in *Every Man In His Humour*, ed. G. B. Jackson (New Haven, 1969), 221–39. I have drawn heavily on Professor Jackson's work in what follows.

[11] See Chambers, *The Elizabethan Stage*, i. 359–60 and R. L. Knutson, *The Repertory of Shakespeare's Company, 1594–1613* (Fayetteville, 1991), 75–7 and 183–4.

[12] It is just possible that an allusion to a Jonson performance in 1613 may not refer to *Eastward Ho*, but to *Every Man In His Humour*.

cleansing of the text might assuage a royal distaste for blasphemous stage plays; however, while the play tones down some oaths it still retains many phrases which might be regarded as indelicate or indecorous.[13] (In fact, there is little evidence to support the idea of royal squeamishness, and much to the contrary which suggests that James, especially when in the company of his bedchamber favourites, enjoyed the bawdy body-tradition of Scots culture.) The revision anyway pre-dates the 1606 legislation against oaths by a year, and that legislation was less the product of royal pressure than of a moral clique within parliament. Indeed, none of the circumstantial evidence adduced proves the case for revision in 1604–5 in anticipation of the 1605 performance.[14]

Late revision (c.1611–15)

If 1605 cannot be established as a date for revision, neither can the late-revision hypothesis, based on performances following *The Alchemist*. The primary evidence for the late date concerns the Prologue, yet there is no actual proof of performance at this time, and the dating evidence only supports a date *after c.*1611–12, so that any date between 1612 and mid-1615 might be possible, especially if we accept recent bibliographical studies which argue that Jonson was revising the folio texts until early 1616.[15] Indeed, it is quite feasible that the Prologue, which has many programmatic features which link it with other prefatory materials for the 1616 folio, may not have performance origins, but rather belong to the literary self-construction which characterizes much of the *Works*.[16]

Intermediate revision (c.1606–9)

Even if doubt can be cast upon the performance provenance of the folio Prologue, it would seem most likely that Jonson revised *Every Man*'s main text for performance rather than simply for literary ends. Without hard external evidence to locate the revision more precisely within the broadly accepted parameters of 1604–15, we must fall back

[13] Indeed, 'serving of God' (3.2.251–2), probably a euphemism for 'swearing of God', is added in the folio.

[14] For instance, Bobadill's reference to the siege of Strigonium (3.1.99) as ten years since is as unreliable as its speaker.

[15] J. A. Riddell, 'The Printing of the Plays in the Jonson Folio of 1616', *Studies in Bibliography*, 49 (1996), 149–68, shows that the final quires of *Every Man In His Humour* were printed after the *Epigrams* (see pp. 149, 157, and 161).

[16] See Introduction, pp. xliii–xliv above.

upon circumstantial evidence, particularly that of the chronology of Jonson's career, looking for likely points when a revision might practically have been undertaken.

Most scholars accept that a date between 1606 and 1609 offers the most likely opportunities without contradicting the shards of circumstantial evidence which can be excavated from the text.[17] The year 1604 and 1605 are seen as too busy to permit the revision: Jonson produced two entertainments, one masque, (lost) speeches for a mayoral triumph, numerous poems, and spent some time in prison. The year 1606 is perhaps too close to the anti-swearing legislation to allow the kinds of slippage on oaths which the text retains. Later dates are ruled out due to heavy commitments (1610 and 1611 include *The Alchemist, Catiline*, two masques, one tilting pageant, and (probably) a lost pastoral) and absence in France (spring 1612–13). These considerations perhaps reduce the parameters to a revision *c*.1607–1609, possibly with a further tidying after 1612–13 for publication purposes, and possibly including the addition of the Prologue (all some time before 1615).

Some features of the text suggest that the period 1607–9 presents the most likely dates, and within that range later rather than earlier. After 1608 the King's Men had moved into the Blackfriars, which might necessitate the revision of old texts, including the addition of act breaks (to allow for candle changes and so on) and possibly the reshaping of the play to appeal to a socially slightly different audience.[18] Indeed, the retention of some oaths might appeal to the taste of that audience for the mildly titillating and transgressive. Some of the potential allusions to the anniversary of Strigonium and the Gunpowder Plot would be still within medium-term memory and Jonson had time to undertake the work. During late 1608 and most of 1609 actual performance would be blocked by the plague, but this would provide leisure for rewriting.

Some internal evidence supports this hypothesis. The allusion to the Artillery Company (3.2.330–1), revived in 1610 (and celebrated in Dekker's *Artillery Garden*), might point towards the date. As discussions of the reformation of this company had occurred earlier in

---

[17] This chronology is based on the provisional chronology prepared by the general editors (Professors Bevington, Butler, and Donaldson) for the new *Cambridge Edition of the Works of Ben Jonson*.

[18] G. Taylor, 'The Structure of Performance: Act Intervals in the London Theatres, 1576–1642', in G. Taylor and J. Jowett (eds.), *Shakespeare Re-shaped, 1606–1623* (Oxford, 1993), 3–50.

1609, so a 1609–10 date is possible. Moreover, during 1608 and 1609 the relationship of poetics and spectacle were central to Jonson's thinking following the long sequence of entertainments produced in collaboration with Inigo Jones for the Cecil family, and the court masques of the period 1606–9. This might account for the scornful use (in a passage added to the F text) of the term 'architect' in 3.2.223, which Jonson later used to pillory Inigo Jones. Indeed, as part of his Cecilian comissions Jonson's attention had been drawn to the importance of London's trade and its civic culture through his involvement in *The Entertainment at Britain's Burse* (1609), and especially the development of consumerism, fashion, and the role of women, which he then satirized in *Epicene* (1609–10). The revised text of *Every Man In His Humour* manifests similar concerns, especially around the culture of fashionable City gallants. On balance—and very tentatively—it would seem that the evidence favours 1608–9 as the likely date for revisions of the main text, although whether they precede or follow *Epicene* is a matter which cannot be resolved. Given that in 1608 Jonson only wrote two masques (*Beauty* and *Haddington*), it might be that 1608–9 offers the most plausible point for revision.

The Roaring Girl

This edition follows Q1 throughout, and thus, unlike in previous editions, act and scene divisions are not inserted. The 'Act. I. Scæ. i.' heading at the start of the text is the only evidence of any attempt to subdivide the play and, more generally, the Fortune seems to have been slow to adopt act divisions.[19]

The important press-variants noted by Paul Mulholland in the Princeton exemplar are incorporated (see Scene 3, lines 365–81).[20] There was clearly some confusion over speech prefixes in this section of the scene, so that in most copies of Q the speakers are Tiltyard, Mistress Gallipot, Tiltyard, Gallipot, Mistress Gallipot, Gallipot, Mistress Gallipot, Gallipot, Gallipot, Mistress Openwork, Gallipot. The Princeton copy preserves a corrected state of Q1 which expunges the obvious error in giving Gallipot two consecutive speeches (at 369–71), and which also makes more dramatic sense (for instance, Mistress

[19] Taylor, 'The Structure of Performance', 34 and *The Roaring Girl*, ed. P. A. Mulholland (Manchester, 1987).

[20] '*The Roaring Girl*: New Readings and Further Notes', *Studies in Bibliography*, 37 (1984), 159–70.

Openwork answers the question as to her husband's whereabouts (366), rather than Mistress Gallipot. Many of the emendations proposed in Mulholland's excellent Revels edition are also adopted.[21] The alternation between verse and prose is especially fluid in this play but, in general, this edition accepts many of the changes in lineation proposed by earlier editors, especially those suggested by Mulholland (his Appendix A provides a collation of changes in lineation).

One controversial Q reading has been retained which requires comment. In Scene 9 (line 284) 'Get-feathers' is preferred over emendations, such as Mulholland's '*Gelt feathers*' (his edition, 4.2.291) or the more frequently chosen 'gilt'. Although the *OED* lists 'gelt' (gelt, *sb.* 2) as 'perhaps a pseudo-archaism for gold', as Mulholland notes 'Get-feathers' might mean 'booty to feather one's nest' on the analogy of words such as 'get-penny'.

For the treatment of the Dutch, see the note on Dekker's *The Shoemaker's Holiday* above, p. xlvii.

[21] See also vol. 3 of *The Dramatic Works of Thomas Dekker*, ed. Bowers, and *The Roaring Girl*, ed. A. Gomme (1976).

SELECT BIBLIOGRAPHY

Approaches to City comedy either seek to define the form or locate the plays within their social and political contexts. Generic studies tend to be less succesful due to the hybrid nature of these plays, but the most useful are B. Gibbons's *Jacobean City Comedy*, 2nd edn., (London, 1980), and H. Levin's 'Notes towards a Definition of City Comedy', in B. K. Lewalski (ed.), *Renaissance Genres: Essays on Theory, History and Interpretation* (Cambridge, Mass., 1986), 126–46. Lorna Hutson examines the interaction between the plays' classical sources and early modern economics ('The Displacement of the Market in Jacobean City Comedy', *The London Journal*, 14 (1989), 3–16) while A. Leggatt's *Citizen Comedy in the Age of Shakespeare* (Toronto, 1973) explores other dramatic influences. T. B. Leinwand, *The City Staged: Jacobean Comedy, 1603–13* (Madison, 1986), also surveys a range of plays looking at typical figures.

The originary contextual study by L. C. Knights, *Drama and Society in the Age of Jonson* (1930), relates Jonson's texts to changing attitudes towards finance and 'capitalism', while others update the historical context, notably D. Bruster's *Drama and the Market in the Age of Shakespeare* (Cambridge, 1992) and S. Wells, 'Jacobean City Comedy and the Ideology of the City', *English Literary Renaissance*, 48 (1981), 37–60. The most stimulating studies, A. Barton's 'London Comedy and the Ethos of the City', *The London Journal*, 4 (1978), 158–70 and L. Manley's *Literature and Culture in Early Modern London* (Cambridge, 1995), ch. 8, synthesize historical and generic approaches.

Many historians have written fine studies of London history and culture which help to explicate these plays. Particularly useful as a general study is I. W. Archer's, *The Pursuit of Stability: Social Relations in Elizabethan London* (Cambridge, 1991). More specialist studies of population, trade, medicine, and other social issues are covered in A. L. Beier and R. Finlay (eds.), *London 1500–1700: The Making of the Modern Metropolis* (Harlow, 1994) and V. Harding, 'Early Modern London, 1550–1700', *The London Journal*, 20 (1995), 34–45. Material on civic pageantry, often written by public theatre dramatists such as Dekker and Middleton, also illuminates the social context of these works, especially D. Bergeron, *English Civic Pageantry, 1558–1642*

(London, 1971); M. Berlin, 'Civic Ceremony in Early Modern London', *Urban History Yearbook 1986*, 15–27; and B. Klein, '"Between the Bums and Bellies of the Multitude": Civic Pageantry and the Problem of the Audience in Late Stuart London', *The London Journal*, 17 (1992), 18–26. The best introduction to the context of these plays remains, however, the contemporary historian John Stow. His *Survey of London (1598)*, ed. H. B. Wheatley and V. Pearl (1987), is a classic and may be usefully supplemented with the extracts given in L. Manley's *London in the Age of Shakespeare: An Anthology* (Beckenham, 1986).

London's popular culture is surveyed in P. Earle, 'The Middling Sort in London', in J. Barry and C. Brooks (eds.), *The Middling Sort of People: Culture, Society and Politics in England, 1550–1800* (1994), 141–58; R. Ashton, 'Popular Entertainment and Social Control in Later Elizabethan and Early Stuart London', *The London Journal*, 9 (1983), 3–19; and P. Burke, 'Popular Culture in Seventeenth-Century London', in B. Reay (ed.), *Popular Culture in Seventeenth-Century England* (Beckenham, 1985), 31–58. Some of the definitional problems of the term 'popular' are discussed in T. Harris, 'Problematising Popular Culture', in Harris (ed.), *Popular Culture in England, c. 1500–1850* (1995), 1–27, and R. Scribner, 'Is a History of Popular Culture Possible?', *History of European Ideas*, 10 (1989), 175–91. Particular discussions, with special relevance to early modern theatre and these plays, can be found in C. R. Baskervill, *The Elizabethan Jig* (Chicago, 1929); B. Capp, 'Popular Literature', in Reay (ed.), *Popular Culture in Seventeenth-Century England*, 198–243; L. S. O'Connell, 'The Elizabethan Bourgeois Hero-Tale: Aspects of an Adolescent Social Consciousness', in B. Malament (ed.), *After the Reformation* (Philadelphia, 1980), 267–87; and T. Watt, *Cheap Print and Popular Piety, 1550–1640* (Cambridge, 1991). Again, contemporary sources are the most illuminating, and two CDs give a particularly rich sense of the popular performance culture of the period: The City Waites, *The Musitians of Grope Lane: Music of Brothels and Bawdy Houses of Purcell's England* (Musica Oscura CD, 1996 [070969]) and The Mvsicians of Swanne Alley, *In The Streets and Theatres of London: Elizabethan Ballads and Theatre Music* (Virgin Classics CD, 1989 [0777 7595342 8]).

Studies of the individual plays in this volume are numerous. For *The Shoemaker's Holiday* critics have often debated how far the play simply celebrates Eyre and his 'capitalism', or how far it presents a critical perspective. Three articles in particular have shaped this debate: J. P. Kaplan, 'Virtue's Holiday: Thomas Dekker and Simon

Eyre', *Renaissance Drama*, NS 2 (1969), 103–22; P. Mortensen, 'The Economics of Joy in *The Shoemaker's Holiday*', *Studies in English Literature*, 16 (1976), 241–52; and D. Kastan, 'Workshop and/as Playhouse: Comedy and Commerce in *The Shoemaker's Holiday*', *Studies in Philology*, 84 (1987), 324–37, repr. in D. Kastan and P. Stallybrass, *Staging the Renaissance: Interpretations of Elizabethan and Jacobean Drama* (1991), 151–63. In 'Thomas Dekker's *The Shoemaker's Holiday*: The Artisanal World', in *The Theatrical City: Culture, Theatre and Politics, 1576–1649* (Cambridge, 1995), 87–100, the historian Paul Seaver uses his unrivalled knowledge of London's artisan class to contextualize the play.

In contrast, most studies of *Eastward Ho* neglect critical issues to concentrate on the problems of censorship, the text, and politics (see Note on the Texts). R. A. Cohen's, 'The Function of Setting in *Eastward Ho*', *Renaissance Papers 1973*, (1974), 83–96, considers the play's use of London landscape, while C. Leech explores the commercial rivalries between the companies who mounted *Westward Ho* (1605), *Eastward Ho,* and *Northward Ho* (1605) in 'Three Times *Ho* and a Brace of Widows: Some Plays for the Private Theatre', in D. Galloway (ed.), *The Elizabethan Theatre III* (Hamden, 1973), 14–32. Some of the best critical discussions of the play are found in the New Mermaid edition (ed. Petter, 1973) and the Revels text (ed. Van Fossen, 1979).

The popularity of Jonson's *Every Man In His Humour* on stage during the nineteenth century (Dickens played a notable Bobadill), and the play's continued presence in the repertoire (there was an influential Royal Shakespeare Company production in 1986), is augmented by the massive Jonsonian critical industry. Three important studies have sections on the play: J. Barish, *Ben Jonson and the Language of Prose Comedy* (Cambridge, Mass., 1962); A. Barton, *Ben Jonson, Dramatist* (Cambridge, 1984); and P. Womack, *Ben Jonson* (Oxford, 1986). Womack, in particular, approaches the play from a lively, Bakhtinian position, exploring the interaction of class and language, an issue which is at the heart of Jonathan Haynes's new historicist *The Social Relations of Jonson's Theatre* (Cambridge, 1992). R. A. Cohen has also considered the landscape of this play in 'The Importance of Setting in the Revision of *Every Man in his Humour*', *English Literary Renaissance*, 8 (1978), 183–96. Much of the current debate about Jonson's political allegiances have passed this play by, but even though D. Norbrook's *Poetry and Politics in the English Renaissance* (1984) does not deal directly with the plays (beyond *Volpone* and *The*

Alchemist in passing), his account of Jonson's affiliations with the Jacobean establishment has much to illuminate this play. An alternative view, largely based on the later plays, by Julie Sanders (*Ben Jonson's Theatrical Republics* (Basingstoke, 1998)) argues for a more radical view of Jonson.

The Roaring Girl is a play which has become much more prominent following the growth of feminist studies of Jacobean drama in the 1980s and a succesful Royal Shakespeare Company production in 1983. Earlier criticism is summarized in Mulholland's excellent Revels edition (1987), but most of the current debate centres upon the impact of Moll, the precise meaning of her 'transvestism', and its implications for gender and class politics in Jacobean London. The most stimulating essays are: M. Garber, 'The Logic of the Transvestite', in Kastan and Stallybrass, *Staging the Renaissance*, 221–34; J. Howard, 'Sex and Social Conflict: The Erotics of *The Roaring Girl*', in S. Zimmerman (ed.), *Erotic Politics: Desire on the Renaissance Stage* (1992), 170–90; K. McLuskie, *Dekker and Heywood: Professional Dramatists* (Basingstoke, 1994); S. Orgel, 'The Subtexts of *The Roaring Girl*', in *Erotic Politics*, 12–26; and M. B. Rose, 'Women in Men's Clothing: Apparel and Social Stability in *The Roaring Girl*', *English Literary Renaissance*, 14 (1984), 367–91. Professor McLuskie's book is particularly useful for its synthesis of social history, theatrical context, and feminist ideas.

A CHRONOLOGY OF JACOBEAN
CITY COMEDIES

This is a highly selective list which includes only plays with a London setting or a strong London affiliation (some critics would include plays such as *Volpone* as City comedies). Only a limited number of pre-Jacobean plays are included.

THE SHOEMAKER'S HOLIDAY
OR
THE GENTLE CRAFT

THOMAS DEKKER

THE PERSONS OF THE PLAY

Simon Eyre,° *a master shoemaker*
Mistress Eyre, *his wife*
Roger or Hodge,° *his foreman*
Ralph Damport, *Eyre's journeyman*° } *shoemakers*
Jane, *his wife*
Firk,° *Eyre's journeyman*
A Boy, *Eyre's apprentice*

Sir Roger Oatley, *Lord Mayor of London*
Rose, *his daughter*
Sybil, *her maid*
Master Hammon, *a rich citizen* } *citizens*
Master Warner, *Hammon's brother-in-law*
Master Scott, *a friend of Sir Roger Oatley*

Hugh Lacy, *the Earl of Lincoln*
Rowland Lacy, *his nephew, later disguised as Hans
    Meulter*
Askew, *Lacy's cousin* } *courtiers*
Cornwall
Lovell
Dodger,° *the Earl of Lincoln's parasite*

The King°

A Dutch Skipper
A Boy, *with the hunters*
A Prentice, *Oatley's servant*
A Servingman, *working for Hammon*

Nobles
Soldiers
Huntsmen
Shoemakers
Apprentices
Servants

[Scene 1]

Enter [Sir Roger Oatley, the] Lord Mayor [, and the Earl of]
Lincoln

LINCOLN My Lord Mayor, you have sundry times
    Feasted myself and many courtiers more.
    Seldom or never can we be so kind
    To make requital of your courtesy.
    But leaving this, I hear my cousin° Lacy   5
    Is much affected° to your daughter Rose.
OATLEY True, my good lord, and she loves him so well
    That I mislike her boldness in the chase.
LINCOLN Why, my Lord Mayor, think you it then a
      shame,
    To join a Lacy with an Oatley's name?   10
OATLEY Too mean° is my poor girl for his high birth,
    Poor citizens must not with courtiers wed,
    Who will in silks and gay apparel spend
    More in one year than I am worth by far.
    Therefore your honour need not doubt° my girl.   15
LINCOLN Take heed, my lord, advise you what you do,
    A verier unthrift lives not in the world
    Than is my cousin, for I'll tell you what,
    'Tis now almost a year since he requested
    To travel countries for experience.   20
    I furnished him with coin, bills of exchange,°
    Letters of credit, men to wait on him,
    Solicited my friends in Italy
    Well to respect him. But to see the end:
    Scant had he journeyed through half Germany   25
    But all his coin was spent, his men cast off,
    His bills embezzled,° and my jolly coz,
    Ashamed to show his bankrupt presence here,
    Became a shoemaker in Wittenberg—
    A goodly science for a gentleman   30
    Of such descent. Now judge the rest by this.
    Suppose your daughter have a thousand pound,
    He did consume me more in one half-year,
    And make him heir to all the wealth you have,

One twelve-month's rioting° will waste it all,   35
Then seek, my lord, some honest citizen
To wed your daughter to.
OATLEY   I thank your lordship—
[*Aside*] Well, fox, I understand your subtlety—
[*To Lincoln*] As for your nephew, let your lordship's eye
But watch his actions, and you need not fear,   40
For I have sent my daughter far enough.
And yet your cousin Rowland might do well
Now he hath learned an occupation.
[*Aside*] And yet I scorn to call him son-in-law.
LINCOLN Ay, but I have a better trade for him.   45
I thank his Grace° he hath appointed him,
Chief colonel of all those companies
Mustered° in London and the shires about,
To serve his Highness in those wars of France:
See where he comes.   50
        Enter Lovell, Lacy, and Askew
                Lovell, what news with you?
LOVELL My Lord of Lincoln, 'tis his Highness' will,
That presently your cousin ship for France
With all his powers.° He would not for a million
But they should land at Dieppe within four days.
LINCOLN Go certify his Grace it shall be done: 55
    Exit Lovell
Now, cousin Lacy, in what forwardness°
Are all your companies?
LACY   All well prepared,
The men of Hertfordshire lie at Mile End;°
Suffolk and Essex train in Tothill Fields;°
The Londoners, and those of Middlesex,   60
All gallantly prepared in Finsbury,°
With frolic spirits long for their parting hour.
OATLEY They have their imprest,° coats, and furniture,°
And if it please your cousin Lacy come
To the Guildhall,° he shall receive his pay,   65
And twenty pounds besides my brethren°
Will freely give him, to approve° our loves
We bear unto my lord your uncle here.
LACY I thank your honour.
LINCOLN   Thanks, my good Lord Mayor.

OATLEY At the Guildhall we will expect your coming.   70
    Exit [Oatley]
LINCOLN *[aside]* To approve your loves to me? No, subtlety—
    [Aloud] Nephew, that twenty pound he doth bestow,
    For joy to rid you from his daughter Rose:
    But cousins both, now here are none but friends,
    I would not have you cast an amorous eye   75
    Upon so mean a project as the love
    Of a gay, wanton, painted° citizen.
    I know this churl, even in the height of scorn,
    Doth hate the mixture of his blood with thine,
    I pray thee do thou so. Remember, coz,   80
    What honourable fortunes wait on thee.
    Increase the King's love which so brightly shines
    And gilds thy hopes. I have no heir but thee—
    And yet not thee if, with a wayward spirit,
    Thou start from the true bias° of my love.   85
LACY My lord, I will for honour, not desire
    Of land or livings, or to be your heir,
    So guide my actions in pursuit of France,
    As shall add glory to the Lacys' name.
LINCOLN *[giving out money]* Coz, for those words here's thirty
    portagues,   90
    And nephew Askew, there's a few for you.
    Fair honour in her loftiest eminence
    Stays in France for you till you fetch her thence.
    Then, nephews, clap swift wings on your designs—
    Begone, begone, make haste to the Guildhall,   95
    There presently I'll meet you. Do not stay:
    Where honour beckons, shame attends delay.
    Exit Lincoln
ASKEW How gladly would your uncle have you gone!
LACY True, coz, but I'll o'er-reach his policies.°
    I have some serious business for three days,   100
    Which nothing but my presence can dispatch.
    You, therefore, cousin, with the companies
    Shall haste to Dover. There I'll meet with you,
    Or if I stay past my prefixèd time
    Away for France—we'll meet in Normandy.   105
    The twenty pounds my Lord Mayor gives to me
    You shall receive, and these ten portagues,

Part of mine uncle's thirty. Gentle coz,
Have care to our great charge. I know your wisdom
Hath tried itself in higher consequence.° 110
ASKEW Coz, all myself am yours, yet have this care,
To lodge in London with all secrecy.
Our uncle Lincoln hath, besides his own,
Many a jealous° eye that in your face
Stares only to watch means for your disgrace. 115
LACY Stay, cousin, who be these?
Enter Simon Eyre, Mistress Eyre, Hodge, Firk, Jane, and Ralph
with a piece° [and carrying a pair of shoes]
EYRE Leave whining, leave whining, away with this whimpering, this
puling, these blubbering tears, and these wet eyes. I'll get thy hus-
band discharged, I warrant thee, sweet Jane! Go to!°
HODGE Master, here be the captains. 120
EYRE Peace, Hodge, husht ye knave, husht.
FIRK Here be the cavaliers° and the colonels, master.
EYRE Peace, Firk, peace, my fine Firk. Stand by with your pishery-
pashery,° away, I am a man of the best presence, I'll speak to them
an they were popes. [*To Lacy and Askew*] Gentlemen, captains, col- 125
onels, commanders, brave men, brave leaders, may it please you to
give me audience. I am Simon Eyre, the mad° shoemaker of Tower
Street.° This wench with the mealy mouth that will never tire, is
my wife, I can tell you; here's Hodge, my man, and my foreman;
here's Firk my fine firking° journeyman—and this is blubbered 130
Jane. All we come to be suitors for this honest Ralph. Keep him at
home, and as I am a true shoemaker, and a gentleman of the Gentle
Craft, buy spurs yourself and I'll find ye boots these seven years.
MISTRESS EYRE Seven years, husband?
EYRE Peace, midriff,° peace, I know what I do, peace. 135
FIRK Truly, Master Cormorant,° you shall do God good service to let
Ralph and his wife stay together. She's a young new-married
woman, if you take her husband away from her a-night, you undo°
her; she may beg in the daytime; for he's as good a workman at a
prick and an awl,° as any is in our trade. 140
JANE O, let him stay, else I shall be undone.°
FIRK Ay, truly, she shall be laid at one side like a pair of old shoes else,
and be occupied° for no use.
LACY Truly, my friends, it lies not in my power.
The Londoners are pressed,° paid and set forth 145
By the Lord Mayor.° I cannot change a man.

HODGE Why, then, you were as good be a corporal as a colonel, if you
cannot discharge one good fellow. And I will tell you true, I think
you do more than you can answer, to press a man within a year and
a day of his marriage.°   150

EYRE Well said, melancholy° Hodge. Gramercy, my fine foreman.

MISTRESS EYRE Truly, gentlemen, it were ill done, for such as you to
stand so stiffly against° a poor young wife, considering her case. She
is new married, but let that pass: I pray, deal not roughly with her,
her husband is a young man and but newly entered—but let that   155
pass.

EYRE Away with your pishery-pashery, your pols and your edepols.°
Peace, midriff, silence Cicely Bumtrinket,° let your head° speak.

FIRK Yea, and the horns° too, master.

EYRE Tawsoone,° my fine Firk, tawsoone! Peace, scoundrels! See   160
you this man, captains? You will not release him, well let him
go, he's a proper shot, let him vanish. Peace, Jane, dry up thy
tears, they'll make his powder dankish. Take him brave men. Hec-
tor° of Troy was a hackney to him, Hercules and Termagent°
scoundrels, Prince Arthur's round table, by the Lord of Ludgate,°   165
ne'er fed such a tall, such a dapper swordsman, by the life of
Pharaoh, a brave resolute swordsman. Peace Jane. I say no more,
mad knaves.

FIRK See, see, Hodge, how my master raves in commendation of
Ralph.   170

HODGE Ralph, thou'rt a gull by this hand, an thou goest not.

ASKEW I am glad, good Master Eyre, it is my hap
To meet so resolute a soldier.
Trust me, for your report and love to him,
A common slight regard shall not respect him.°   175

LACY Is thy name Ralph?

RALPH   Yes, sir.

LACY   Give me thy hand.
Thou shalt not want, as I am a gentleman:
[To Jane] Woman, be patient. God, no doubt, will send
Thy husband safe again, but he must go.
His country's quarrel says it shall be so.   180

HODGE Thou'rt a gull, by my stirrup, if thou dost not go. I will not
have thee strike thy gimlet° into these weak vessels,° prick thine
enemies, Ralph.

            Enter Dodger

DODGER My lord, your uncle on the Tower Hill°

Stays° with the Lord Mayor and the Aldermen,   185
And doth request you with all speed you may
To hasten thither.

ASKEW   Cousin, let's go.

LACY Dodger, run you before, tell them we come—
          Exit Dodger
This Dodger is mine uncle's parasite,°
The arrant'st varlet that e'er breathed on earth,   190
He sets more discord in a noble house,
By one day's broaching of his pickthank tales,
Than can be salved again in twenty years—
And he, I fear, shall go with us to France,
To pry into our actions.

ASKEW   Therefore, coz,   195
It shall behove you to be circumspect.

LACY Fear not, good cousin. Ralph, hie to your colours.°
          [*Exeunt Lacy and Askew*]

RALPH I must because there's no remedy,
But, gentle master and my loving dame,
As you have always been a friend to me,   200
So in mine absence think upon my wife.

JANE Alas, my Ralph.

MISTRESS EYRE   She cannot speak for weeping.

EYRE Peace, you cracked groats,° you mustard tokens,° disquiet not
the brave soldier. Go thy ways, Ralph.

JANE Ay, ay, you bid him go, what shall I do when he is gone?   205

FIRK Why, be doing with me, or my fellow Hodge, be not idle.

EYRE Let me see thy hand, Jane—[*taking her hand*] this fine hand, this
white hand, these pretty fingers must spin, must card, must work,
work, you bombast-cotton-candle-quean,° work for your living with
a pox to you. [*Giving Ralph money*] Hold thee, Ralph, here's five   210
sixpences° for thee. Fight for the honour of the Gentle Craft, for the
gentleman shoemakers, the courageous cordwainers, the flower of
Saint Martin's,° the mad knaves of Bedlam,° Fleet Street, Tower
Street, and Whitechapel.° Crack me the crowns° of the French
knaves, a pox on them, crack them. Fight, by the Lord of Ludgate,   215
fight, my fine boy.

FIRK [*giving Ralph coins*] Here Ralph, here's three twopences: two
carry into France, the third shall wash our souls at parting, for
sorrow is dry.° For my sake, firk the *baisez-mon-culs*.°

HODGE Ralph, I am heavy at parting, [*giving him money*] but here's a 220

shilling for thee. God send thee to cram thy slops with French
crowns,° and thy enemies' bellies with bullets.

RALPH I thank thee, master, and I thank you all:
Now, gentle wife, my loving lovely Jane,
Rich men at parting give their wives rich gifts,   225
Jewels and rings, to grace their lily hands.
Thou knowest our trade makes rings for women's heels:
    [*He presents Jane with the shoes*]
Here take this pair of shoes cut out by Hodge,
Stitched by my fellow, Firk, seamed by myself,
Made up and pinked,° with letters for thy name.   230
Wear them, my dear Jane, for thy husband's sake,
And every morning, when thou pull'st them on,
Remember me, and pray for my return.
Make much of them, for I have made them so,
That I can know them from a thousand moe.°   235
    Sound drum, enter [Sir Roger Oatley] the Lord Mayor, Lincoln,
    Lacy, Askew, Dodger, and soldiers, they pass over° the stage,
    Ralph falls in amongst them, Firk and the rest cry 'farewell',
    etc. and so exeunt

[Scene 2]

Enter Rose alone, making a garland

ROSE Here sit thou down upon this flow'ry bank
And make a garland for thy Lacy's head.
These pinks, these roses, and these violets,
These blushing gillyflowers,° these marigolds,
The fair embroidery of his coronet,°   5
Carry not half such beauty in their cheeks,
As the sweet countenance of my Lacy doth.
O, my most unkind father! O, my stars!
Why loured you so at° my nativity,
To make me love, yet live robbed of my love?   10
Here as a thief am I imprisonèd,
For my dear Lacy's sake, within those walls,
Which by my father's cost were builded up
For better purposes. Here must I languish
For him that doth as much lament, I know,   15

Mine absence, as for him I pine in woe.
 Enter Sybil
SYBIL Good morrow, young mistress. I am sure you make that gar-
 land for me, against° I shall be Lady of the Harvest.°
ROSE Sybil, what news at London?
SYBIL None but good! My Lord Mayor, your father, and Master 20
 Philpot, your uncle, and Master Scott, your cousin, and Mistress
 Frigbottom by Doctors' Commons,° do all, by my troth, send you
 most hearty commendations!
ROSE Did Lacy send kind greetings to his love?
SYBIL O, yes, out of cry.° By my troth, I scant knew him. Here a wore° a 25
 scarf° and here a scarf, here a bunch of feathers, and here precious
 stones and jewels, and a pair of garters: O, monstrous! Like one of
 our yellow silk curtains at home here in Old Ford° House, here in
 Master Bellymount's chamber. I stood at our door in Cornhill,°
 looked at him, he at me indeed, spake to him, but he not to me, not 30
 a word. 'Marry, gup,'° thought I, 'with a wanion!' He passed by me
 as proud—'marry, foh, are you grown humorous?',° thought I—and
 so shut the door, and in I came.
ROSE O, Sybil, how dost thou my Lacy wrong!
 My Rowland is as gentle as a lamb,° 35
 No dove was ever half so mild as he.
SYBIL Mild? Yea, as a bushel of stamped crabs,° he looked upon me as
 sour as verjuice.° 'Go thy ways,'° thought I, 'thou mayest be much in
 my gaskins, but nothing in my netherstocks.'° This is your fault,
 mistress, to love him that loves not you, he thinks scorn to do as 40
 he's done to, but if I were as you, I'd cry, 'Go by, Hieronimo,° go by!'
 I'd set mine old debts against my new driblets,
 And the hare's foot against the goose giblets;°
 For if ever I sigh when sleep I should take,
 Pray God I may lose my maidenhead when I wake. 45
ROSE Will my love leave me then and go to France?
SYBIL I know not that, but I am sure I see° him stalk before the
 soldiers. By my troth, he is a proper° man, but he is proper that
 proper doth. Let him go snick up,° young mistress.
ROSE Get thee to London, and learn perfectly, 50
 Whether my Lacy go to France or no:
 Do this, and I will give thee for thy pains
 My cambric apron, and my Romish° gloves,
 My purple stockings, and a stomacher.
 Say, wilt thou do this Sybil, for my sake? 55

SYBIL Will I, quoth-a? At whose suit?° By my troth yes, I'll go. A
cambric apron, gloves, a pair of purple stockings, and a stomacher?
I'll sweat in purple,° mistress, for you. I'll take anything that comes
o' God's name.° O, rich, a cambric apron. Faith, then, have at uptails
all,° I'll go jiggy-joggy° to London, and be here in a trice, young   60
mistress.
 Exit [Sybil]
ROSE Do so, good Sybil. Meantime wretched I
Will sit and sigh for his lost company.
 Exit

[Scene 3]

 Enter Lacy like [Hans] a Dutch shoemaker°
LACY How many shapes have gods and kings devised,
 Thereby to compass their desirèd loves?°
 It is no shame for Rowland Lacy then
 To clothe his cunning with the Gentle Craft,
 That, thus disguised, I may unknown possess   5
 The only happy presence° of my Rose.
 For her have I forsook my charge in France,
 Incurred the King's displeasure, and stirred up
 Rough hatred in mine uncle Lincoln's breast.
 O, love, how powerful art thou, that canst change   10
 High birth to bareness,° and a noble mind,
 To the mean semblance of a shoemaker.
 But thus it must be: for her cruel father,
 Hating the single union of our souls,
 Hath secretly conveyed my Rose from London   15
 To bar me of her presence—but I trust
 Fortune and this disguise will further me
 Once more to view her beauty, gain her sight.
 Here in Tower Street, with Eyre the shoemaker,
 Mean I a while to work. I know the trade,   20
 I learned it when I was in Wittenberg.
 Then cheer thy hoping sprites, be not dismayed,
 Thou canst not want, do Fortune what she can,
 The Gentle Craft is living for a man.
 Exit

[Scene 4]

Enter Eyre making himself ready°

EYRE Where be these boys, these girls, these drabs, these scoundrels?
They wallow in the fat brewis of my bounty, and lick up the crumbs
of my table, yet will not rise to see my walks cleansed! Come out,
you powder-beef° queans! What, Nan! What, Madge Mumblecrust!°
Come out, you fat midriff-swag-belly° whores, and sweep me these   5
kennels,° that the noisome stench offend not the nose of my neighbours. What, Firk, I say! What, Hodge! Open my shop windows!°
What, Firk, I say!

Enter Firk

FIRK O, master, is't you that speak bandog and bedlam° this morning?
I was in a dream and mused what mad man was got into the street   10
so early. Have you drunk this morning that your throat is so clear?

EYRE Ah, well said Firk, well said, Firk. To work, my fine knave, to
work. Wash thy face and thou'lt be more blessed.

FIRK Let them wash my face that will eat it. Good master, send for a
souse-wife,° if you'll have my face cleaner.   15

Enter Hodge

EYRE Away sloven, avaunt scoundrel! Good morrow, Hodge, good
morrow, my fine foreman.

HODGE O, master, good morrow, you're an early stirrer. Here's a fair
morning. Good morrow, Firk. I could have slept this hour. Here's a
brave day towards.°   20

EYRE O, haste to work, my fine foreman, haste to work.

FIRK Master, I am as dry as dust° to hear my fine fellow Roger talk of
fair weather. Let us pray for good leather, and let clowns° and
ploughboys, and those that work in the fields, pray for brave days.
We work in a dry shop, what care I if it rain?   25

Enter Mistress Eyre

EYRE How now, Dame Margery, can you see to rise?° Trip and go,° call
up the drabs your maids.

MISTRESS EYRE See to rise? I hope 'tis time enough, 'tis early enough
for any woman to be seen abroad. I marvel° how many wives in
Tower Street are up so soon. God's me, 'tis not noon. Here's a   30
yawling.

EYRE Peace, Margery, peace. Where's Cicely Bumtrinket your maid?
She has a privy° fault: she farts in her sleep. Call the quean up; if
my men want° shoe-thread, I'll swinge her in° a stirrup.

FIRK Yet that's but a dry beating,° here's still a sign of drought.   35
     Enter Lacy [dressed as Hans], singing

LACY
       Der was een boor van Gelderland,
         Frolick sie byen.
       He was als dronck he could niet stand,
         Upsee al sie byen.
       Tap eens de cannikin   40
       Drincke, schone mannikin.°

FIRK Master, for my life, yonder's a brother of the Gentle Craft! If he
bear not Saint Hugh's bones,° I'll forfeit my bones. He's some
uplandish° workman. Hire him, good master, that I may learn some
gibble-gabble.° 'Twill make us work the faster.   45
EYRE Peace, Firk. A hard world,° let him pass, let him vanish. We have
journeymen enough. Peace, my fine Firk.
MISTRESS EYRE Nay, nay, you're best follow your man's counsel. You
shall see what will come on't. We have not men enough, but we
must entertain every butter-box°—but let that pass.   50
HODGE Dame, 'fore God, if my master follow your counsel, he'll
consume little beef. He shall be glad of men an he can catch them.
FIRK Ay, that he shall.
HODGE 'Fore God, a proper man, and I warrant a fine workman.
Master, farewell. Dame, adieu. If such a man as he cannot find   55
work, Hodge is not for you.
     [Hodge] offer[s] to go
EYRE Stay, my fine Hodge.
FIRK Faith, an your foreman go, Dame, you must take a journey to
seek a new journeyman. If Roger remove, Firk follows. If Saint
Hugh's bones shall not be set a-work, I may prick mine awl in the   60
walls, and go play.° Fare ye well, Master. Goodbye, Dame.
EYRE Tarry, my fine Hodge, my brisk foreman. Stay, Firk. Peace,
pudding broth,° by the Lord of Ludgate, I love my men as my life.
Peace, you gallimaufry.° Hodge, if he want work, I'll hire him. One
of you to him°—stay, he comes to us.   65
LACY *Goeden dach, meester, end you fro, auch.*°
FIRK 'Nails, if I should speak after him without drinking, I should
choke. And you friend Oak, are you of the Gentle Craft?
LACY *Yaw, yaw, ik bin den skomawker.*°
FIRK '*Den skomawker*', quoth-a. And hark you, '*skomawker*', have you   70
all your tools, a good rubbing-pin,° a good stopper,° a good
dresser,° your four sorts of awls, and your two balls of wax,° your

paring-knife, your hand and thumb-leathers,° and good Saint
Hugh's bones to smooth up your work?

LACY *Yaw, yaw, be niet vorveard. Ik hab all die dingen voour mack skoes*   75
groot end klene.°

FIRK Ha, ha! Good master, hire him. He'll make me laugh so that I
shall work more in mirth, than I can in earnest.

EYRE Hear ye friend, have ye any skill in the mystery° of cordwainers?

LACY *Ik weet niet wat yow seg, ik verstaw you niet.*°   80

FIRK Why thus, man! [*He mimes shoemaking*] '*Ik verste you niet*', quoth a.

LACY *Yaw, yaw, yaw, ik can dat wel doen.*°

FIRK '*Yaw, yaw!*' He speaks yawing like a jackdaw that gapes to be fed
with cheese curds. O, he'll give a villainous pull at a can of double°
beer, but Hodge and I have the vantage, we must drink first,   85
because we are the eldest journeymen.

EYRE What is thy name?

LACY Hans, Hans Meulter.

EYRE Give me thy hand, thou'rt welcome. Hodge entertain him, Firk
bid him welcome. Come Hans. Run wife, bid your maids, your   90
trullibubs,° make ready my fine men's breakfasts. — To him, Hodge.

HODGE Hans, thou'rt welcome, use thyself° friendly for we are good
fellows, if not thou shalt be fought with, wert thou bigger than a
giant.

FIRK Yea and drunk with, wert thou Gargantua.° My master keeps no   95
cowards, I tell thee.

> *Enter Boy*

Ho, boy, bring him an heelblock.° Here's a new journeyman.

LACY *O, ik verstaw yow. Ik moet een halve dossen cans betaelen.* Here
boy, *nempt dis skilling, tap eens freelick.*°

> [*Lacy gives the Boy money.*] *Exit Boy*

EYRE Quick, snipper-snapper,° away. Firk, scour thy throat, thou shalt   100
wash it with Castilian liquor. Come, my last of the fives.°

> *Enter Boy* [*with tankards of beer*]

Give me a can. [*Handing out the beer*] Have° to thee, Hans! Here,
Hodge, here, Firk. Drink you mad Greeks,° and work like true
Trojans,° and pray for Simon Eyre the shoemaker. Here, Hans, and
thou'rt welcome.   105

FIRK Lo, Dame, you would have lost a good fellow that will teach us
to laugh. This beer came hopping in well.

MISTRESS EYRE Simon, it is almost seven.

EYRE Is't so, Dame Clapper-dudgeon?° Is't seven o'clock and my
men's breakfast not ready? Trip and go, you soused conger,° away.   110

Come, you mad Hyperboreans.° Follow me, Hodge! Follow me,
Hans! Come after, my fine Firk. To work, to work a while, and then
to breakfast.

    Exit [Eyre]

FIRK Soft, yaw, yaw, good Hans. Though my master have no more wit
but to call you afore me, I am not so foolish to go behind you, I 115
being the elder journeyman.

    Exeunt

[Scene 5]

    Halloaing within. Enter Warner and Hammon, [dressed] like
    hunters

HAMMON Cousin, beat every brake,° the game's not far,
  This way with wingèd feet he fled from death
  Whilst the pursuing hounds, scenting his steps,
  Find out his highway to destruction.
  Besides, the miller's boy told me even now,   5
  He saw him take soil,° and he halloaed him,
  Affirming him so embossed°
  That long he could not hold.

WARNER   If it be so,
  'Tis best we trace° these meadows by Old Ford.

    A noise of hunters within. Enter a Boy

HAMMON How now, boy, where's the deer? Speak, sawst thou him? 10

BOY O, yea, I saw him leap through a hedge, and then over a ditch,
then at my Lord Mayor's pale.° Over he skipped me° and in he went
me, and 'Halloa' the hunters cried, and 'There boy, there boy',° but
there he is, o' mine honesty.

HAMMON Boy, God-a-mercy. Cousin, let's away,   15
  I hope we shall find better sport today.

    Exeunt

[Scene 6]

    Hunting within,° enter Rose and Sybil

ROSE Why, Sybil, wilt thou prove° a forester?

SYBIL Upon some,° no! Forester, go by!° No, faith, mistress, the deer

came running into the barn through the orchard and over the pale.
I wot well I looked as pale as a new cheese to see him, but 'Whip!'
says Goodman Pinclose, up with his flail, and our Nick with a   5
prong, and down he fell, and they upon him, and I upon them. By
my troth, we had such sport, and in the end we ended him, his
throat we cut, flayed him, unhorned him, and my Lord Mayor shall
eat of him anon when he comes.
    Horns sound within
ROSE Hark, hark, the hunters come!—You're best take heed: 10
    They'll have a saying to you° for this deed.
    Enter Hammon, Warner, Huntsmen, and Boy
HAMMON God save you, fair ladies.
SYBIL   'Ladies?' O, gross!°
WARNER Came not a buck this way?
ROSE   No, but two does.°
HAMMON And which way went they? Faith, we'll hunt at
    those.
SYBIL At those? Upon some, no. When, can you tell?°   15
WARNER Upon some, ay.
SYBIL   Good Lord!
WARNER   'Wounds, then farewell.
HAMMON Boy, which way went he?
BOY   This way, sir, he ran.
HAMMON This way he ran, indeed. Fair Mistress Rose,
    Our game was lately in your orchard seen.
WARNER Can you advise which way he took his flight?   20
SYBIL Follow your nose,° his horns will guide you right.°
WARNER Thou'rt a mad wench.
SYBIL   O, rich!
ROSE   Trust me, not I.
    It is not like° the wild forest deer
    Would come so near to places of resort.
    You are deceived, he fled some other way.   25
WARNER Which way, my sugar-candy, can you show?
SYBIL Come up,° good honey-sops.° Upon some, no.
ROSE Why do you stay, and not pursue your game?
SYBIL I'll hold my life their hunting nags be lame.
HAMMON A deer more dear is found within this place.   30
ROSE But not the deer, sir, which you had in chase.
HAMMON I chased the deer, but this dear chaseth me.
ROSE The strangest hunting that ever I see,

But where's your park?
> *She offers to go away*

HAMMON   'Tis here: O, stay.

ROSE Impale me,° and then I will not stray.   35

WARNER They wrangle, wench. We are more kind than they.

SYBIL What kind of hart is that, dear heart, you seek?

WARNER A hart, dear heart.

SYBIL   Whoever saw the like?

ROSE To lose your hart, is't possible you can?

HAMMON My heart is lost.

ROSE   Alack, good gentleman.   40

HAMMON This poor lost heart would I wish you might find.

ROSE You by such luck might prove your hart a hind.°

HAMMON Why, luck had horns,° so I have heard some say.

ROSE Now God, an't be his will, send luck° into your way.

> *Enter [Sir Roger Oatley, the] Lord Mayor, and Servants*

OATLEY What, Master Hammon, welcome to Old Ford.   45

SYBIL God's pitikins,° hands off,° sir, here's my Lord.

OATLEY I hear you had ill luck, and lost your game.

HAMMON 'Tis true, my lord.

OATLEY   I am sorry for the same.

What gentleman is this?

HAMMON   My brother-in-law.

OATLEY You're welcome both. Sith Fortune offers you   50
Into my hands, you shall not part from hence,
Until you have refreshed your wearied limbs.
Go, Sybil, cover the board. You shall be guest
To no good cheer, but even a hunters' feast.°

HAMMON I thank your Lordship. [*Aside*] Cousin, on my life   55
For our lost venison, I shall find a wife.

> *Exeunt [all except Lord Mayor]*

OATLEY In, gentlemen. I'll not be absent long.
This Hammon is a proper gentleman,
A citizen by birth, fairly allied,
How fit an husband were he for my girl?   60
Well, I will in, and do the best I can,
To match my daughter to this gentleman.

> *Exit*

[Scene 7]

Enter Lacy [as Hans], Skipper, Hodge and Firk

SKIPPER *Ik sal yow wat seggen Hans; dis skip dat comen from Candy is al fol, by Got's sacrament, van sugar, civet, almonds, cambric end alle dingen, towsand, towsand ding. Nempt it, Hans, nempt it vor your meester. Daer be de bills van laden. Your meester Simon Eyre sal ha' good copen, wat seggen yow, Hans?*°   5

FIRK *Wat seggen de reggen de copen, slopen.*° Laugh, Hodge, laugh.

LACY *Mine liever broder Firk, bringt Meester Eyre tot den signe van swannekin. Daer sal yow find dis skipper end me. Wat seggen yow, broder Firk? Doot it, Hodge.*° Come, skipper!

Exeunt [Lacy and the Skipper]

FIRK 'Bring him', quoth you? Here's no knavery, to bring my master   10
to buy a ship, worth the lading of° two or three hundred thousand pounds.° Alas, that's nothing, a trifle, a bauble, Hodge.

HODGE The truth is, Firk, that the merchant owner of the ship dares not show his head,° and therefore this skipper that deals for him, for the love he bears to Hans, offers my master Eyre a   15
bargain in the commodities. He shall have a reasonable day of payment.° He may sell the wares by that time, and be a huge gainer himself.

FIRK Yea, but can my fellow Hans lend my master twenty porpentines° as an earnest-penny?°   20

HODGE 'Portagues' thou wouldst say. Here they be, Firk. Hark, they jingle in my pocket like Saint Mary Overy's° bells.

Enter Eyre and Mistress Eyre [and a Boy]

FIRK Mum, here comes my dame and my master. She'll scold on my life for loitering this Monday. But all's one. Let them all say what they can, Monday's our holiday.°   25

MISTRESS EYRE You sing, Sir Sauce,° but I beshrew° your heart, I fear for this your singing we shall smart.

FIRK Smart for me, dame? Why, dame, why?

HODGE Master, I hope you'll not suffer my dame to take down° your journeymen?   30

FIRK If she take me down, I'll take her up—yea and take her down, too, a buttonhole lower.°

EYRE Peace, Firk. Not I, Hodge. By the life of Pharaoh, by the Lord of Ludgate, by this beard, every hair whereof I value at a king's ransom, she shall not meddle with° you. Peace, you bombast-cotton-   35

candle quean, away, Queen of Clubs,° quarrel not with me and my
men, with me and my fine Firk. I'll firk you if you do.

MISTRESS EYRE Yea, yea, man, you may use me as you please: but let
that pass.

EYRE Let it pass, let it vanish away. Peace, am I not Simon Eyre? Are   40
not these my brave men, brave shoemakers, all gentlemen of the
Gentle Craft? Prince am I none, yet am I nobly born, as being the
sole son of a shoemaker.° Away rubbish, vanish, melt, melt like
kitchen-stuff.°

MISTRESS EYRE Yea, yea, 'tis well, I must be called rubbish, kitchen-   45
stuff, for a sort° of knaves.

FIRK Nay, dame, you shall not weep and wail in woe for me. Master,
I'll stay no longer. Here's a venentory° of my shop tools. Adieu,
master. Hodge, farewell.

HODGE Nay, stay, Firk, thou shalt not go alone.   50

MISTRESS EYRE I pray, let them go. There be more maids than Malkin,° more men than Hodge, and more fools than Firk.

FIRK Fools? 'Nails, if I tarry now, I would my guts might be turned to
shoe-thread.

HODGE And if I stay, I pray God I may be turned to a Turk° and set in   55
Finsbury° for boys to shoot at. Come, Firk.

EYRE Stay, my fine knaves, you arms of my trade, you pillars of
my profession. What, shall a tittle-tattle's words make you forsake Simon Eyre? Avaunt kitchen-stuff! Rip,° you brown-bread
Tannikin,° out of my sight! Move me not. Have not I ta'en you   60
from selling tripes in Eastcheap,° and set you in my shop, and made
you hail-fellow with Simon Eyre the shoemaker? And now do you
deal thus with my journeymen? Look, you powder-beef quean, on
the face of Hodge. Here's a face for a lord.

FIRK And here's a face for any lady of Christendom.   65

EYRE Rip, you chitterling,° avaunt! Boy, bid the tapster of the Boar's
Head° fill me a dozen cans of beer for my journeymen.

FIRK A dozen cans? O, brave Hodge! Now I'll stay.

EYRE [aside to Boy] And the knave fills any more than two, he pays for
them.   70

[Exit Boy]

A dozen cans of beer for my journeymen!

[Enter Boy with two cans of beer. Exit Boy]

[Drinking] Here, you mad Mesopotamians, wash your livers with
this liquor. Where be the odd ten? No more, Madge, no more.° Well
said,° drink and to work. What work dost thou Hodge? What work?

HODGE I am making a pair of shoes for my Lord Mayor's daughter, 75
Mistress Rose.

FIRK And I a pair of shoes for Sybil, my lord's maid. I deal with her.

EYRE Sybil? Fie, defile not thy fine workmanly fingers with the feet of
kitchen-stuff and basting-ladles. Ladies of the Court, fine ladies,
my lads, commit their feet to our apparelling. Put gross work to 80
Hans. Yerk° and seam, yerk and seam.

FIRK For yerking and seaming let me alone, an I come to't.

HODGE Well, master, all this is from the bias. Do you remember the
ship my fellow Hans told you of? The Skipper and he are both
drinking at the Swan. Here be the portagues to give earnest.° If you 85
go through with it, you cannot choose but be a lord at least.

FIRK Nay, dame, if my master prove not a lord and you a lady, hang me.

MISTRESS EYRE Yea, like enough, if you may loiter and tipple thus.

FIRK Tipple, dame? No, we have been bargaining with Skellum-
Skanderbag-can-you-Dutch-spreaken° for a ship of silk cypress, 90
laden with sugar candy.°

EYRE Peace, Firk. Silence, tittle-tattle. Hodge, I'll go through with it.
Here's a seal ring, and I have sent for a guarded gown and a damask
cassock.°

Enter the Boy with a velvet coat and an alderman's gown

See where it comes. Look here, Madgy. Help me, Firk. Apparel me, 95
Hodge.

Eyre puts the gown on

Silk and satin, you mad Philistines, silk and satin.

FIRK Ha, ha! My master will be as proud as a dog in a doublet,° all in
beaten damask and velvet.

EYRE Softly, Firk, for rearing of° the nap and wearing threadbare my 100
garments. How dost thou like me, Firk? How do I look, my fine
Hodge?

HODGE Why, now you look like yourself, master. I warrant you,
there's few in the City but will give you the wall° and come upon°
you with the 'Right Worshipful'.° 105

FIRK 'Nails, my master looks like a threadbare cloak new turned and
dressed.° Lord, Lord, to see what good raiment doth! Dame, dame,
are you not enamoured?

EYRE How sayst thou, Madgy, am I not brisk? Am I not fine?

MISTRESS EYRE Fine? By my troth, sweetheart, very fine. By my troth, 110
I never liked thee so well in my life, sweetheart. But let that pass. I
warrant there be many women in the City have not such handsome
husbands, but only for° their apparel. But let that pass too.

Enter [Lacy as] Hans and Skipper

LACY Godden day, meester; dis be de skipper dat heb de skip van march-
andise. De commodity ben good. Nempt it, meester, nempt it.°   115

EYRE God-a-mercy, Hans. Welcome, Skipper. Where lies this ship of
merchandise?

SKIPPER *De skip ben in revere. Dor be van sugar, civet, almonds, cambric,
and a towsand towsand tings, Got's sacrament. Nempt it, meester, yo
shal heb good copen.*°   120

FIRK To him, master. O, sweet master. O, sweet wares. Prunes,
almonds, sugar-candy, carrot-roots, turnips. O, brave° fatting meat.°
Let not a man buy a nutmeg but yourself.

EYRE Peace, Firk. Come, Skipper, I'll go aboard with you. Hans, have
you made him drink?°   125

SKIPPER *Yaw, yaw, ik heb veal gedrunk.*°

EYRE Come, Hans. Follow me, Skipper. Thou shalt have my counten-
ance° in the City.

Exeunt [Eyre, Skipper, Lacy as Hans]

FIRK 'Yaw, heb veal gedrunck', quotha! They may well be called
butter-boxes when they drink fat veal,° and thick beer too. But   130
come, dame, I hope you'll chide us no more?

MISTRESS EYRE No, 'faith, Firk. No, perdie, Hodge. I do feel honour
creep upon me, and which is more, a certain rising in my flesh: but
let that pass.

FIRK Rising in your flesh do you feel, say you? Ay, you may be with   135
child. But why should not my master feel a rising in his flesh having
a gown and a gold ring on?° But you are such a shrew, you'll soon
pull him down!°

MISTRESS EYRE Ha, ha! Prithee, peace, thou makest my worship°
laugh: but let that pass. Come, I'll go in. Hodge, prithee go before   140
me. Firk, follow me.

FIRK Firk doth follow. Hodge, pass out in state.°

Exeunt

[Scene 8]

Enter Lincoln and Dodger

LINCOLN How now, good Dodger, what's the news in France?

DODGER My lord, upon the eighteen° day of May,
The French and the English were prepared to fight,

Each side with eager fury gave the sign
Of a most hot encounter. Five long hours   5
Both armies fought together: at the length
The lot of victory fell on our sides.
Twelve thousand of the Frenchmen that day died,
Four thousand English, and no man of name°
But Captain Hyam and young Ardington.°   10
LINCOLN Two gallant gentlemen: I knew them well.
   But, Dodger, prithee tell me in this fight
   How did my cousin Lacy bear himself?
DODGER My lord, your cousin Lacy was not there.
LINCOLN Not there?
DODGER   No, my good lord.
LINCOLN   Sure thou mistakest?   15
   I saw him shipped, and a thousand eyes beside
   Were witness to the farewells which he gave
   When I with weeping eyes bid him adieu.
   Dodger, take heed.
DODGER   My lord, I am advised°
   That what I spake is true. To prove it so,   20
   His cousin Askew, that supplied his place,
   Sent me for him from France° that secretly
   He might convey himself thither.
LINCOLN   Is't even so?
   Dares he so carelessly venture his life
   Upon the indignation of a King?   25
   Hath he despised my love, and spurned those favours,
   Which I, with prodigal hand, poured on his head?
   He shall repent his rashness with his soul.
   Since of my love he makes no estimate,°
   I'll make him wish he had not known my hate.   30
   Thou hast no other news?
DODGER   None else, my lord.
LINCOLN None worse I know thou hast. Procure the King
   To crown his giddy brows with ample honours,
   Send him chief colonel, and all my hope
   Thus to be dashed? But 'tis in vain to grieve,   35
   One evil cannot a worse relieve.
   Upon my life, I have found out his plot.
   That old dog love that fawned upon him so,
   Love to that puling girl, his fair-cheeked Rose,

The Lord Mayor's daughter, hath distracted him,   40
And in the fire of that love's lunacy,
Hath he burnt up himself, consumed his credit,°
Lost the King's love, yea and I fear, his life,
Only to get a wanton to his° wife.
Dodger, it is so.

DODGER   I fear so, my good lord.

LINCOLN It is so. Nay, sure it cannot be?   45
I am at my wit's end. Dodger—

DODGER   Yea, my lord?

LINCOLN Thou art acquainted with my nephew's haunts.
Spend this gold for thy pains. Go seek him out.
Watch at my Lord Mayor's. There if he live,   50
Dodger, thou shalt be sure to meet with him:
Prithee, be diligent. Lacy, thy name
Lived once in honour, now dead in shame.
Be circumspect.
          Exit [Lincoln]

DODGER   I warrant you, my lord.
          Exit

[Scene 9]

Enter [Sir Roger Oatley, the] Lord Mayor, and Master Scott

OATLEY Good Master Scott, I have been bold with you
To be a witness to a wedding knot,°
Betwixt young Master Hammon and my daughter.
O, stand aside, see where the lovers come.
          [Oatley and Master Scott stand aside, concealing themselves]
          Enter Hammon and Rose

ROSE Can it be possible you love me so?   5
No, no, within those eyeballs I espy
Apparent likelihoods of flattery.
Pray now, let go my hand.

HAMMON   Sweet Mistress Rose,
Misconstrue not my words, nor misconceive
Of my affection, whose devoted soul   10
Swears that I love thee dearer than my heart.

ROSE As dear as your own heart? I judge it right.

Men love their hearts best when they're out of sight.
HAMMON I love you, by this hand.
ROSE   Yet hands off now:
  If flesh be frail,° how weak and frail's your vow?   15
HAMMON Then by my life I swear.
ROSE   Then do not brawl,°
  One quarrel loseth wife and life and all.
  Is not your meaning thus?
HAMMON   In faith, you jest.
ROSE Love loves to sport;° therefore leave love, you're best.
OATLEY [aside, to Master Scott] What, square° they, Master Scott?
SCOTT [aside, to Oatley]   Sir, never doubt,   20
  Lovers are quickly in, and quickly out.
HAMMON Sweet Rose, be not so strange in fancying° me,
  Nay never turn aside. Shun not my sight.
  I am not grown so fond, to fond my love°
  On any that shall quit° it with disdain.   25
  If you will love me, so; if not, farewell.
OATLEY [aloud, coming forward] Why, how now, lovers, are you
      both agreed?
HAMMON Yes, faith, my lord.
OATLEY   'Tis well. Give me your hand.
  Give me yours, daughter. How now, both pull back?
  What means this, girl?
ROSE   I mean to live a maid.   30
HAMMON [aside] But not to die one. Pause 'ere that be said.°
OATLEY Will you still cross me? Still be obstinate?
HAMMON Nay chide her not, my lord, for doing well,
  If she can live an happy virgin's life,
  'Tis far more blessèd than to be a wife.   35
ROSE Say, sir, I cannot. I have made a vow,
  Whoever be my husband, 'tis not you.
OATLEY Your tongue is quick. But, Master Hammon, know
  I bade you welcome to another end.°
HAMMON What, would you have me pule, and pine, and pray,   40
  With 'lovely lady', 'mistress of my heart',
  'Pardon your servant', and the rhymer play,
  Railing on Cupid, and his tyrant's dart?
  Or shall I undertake some martial spoil,°
  Wearing your glove° at tourney° and at tilt,   45
  And tell how many gallants I unhorsed?

Sweet, will this pleasure you?

ROSE   Yea, when wilt begin?
  What, love-rhymes, man? Fie on that deadly sin!

OATLEY If you will have her, I'll make her agree.

HAMMON Enforcèd love is worse than hate to me.   50
  [*Aside*] There is a wench keeps shop in th' Old Change,°
  To her will I, it is not wealth I seek,
  I have enough, and will prefer her love
  Before the world. [*To Oatley*] My good Lord Mayor, adieu,
  Old love for me, I have no luck with new.   55
         Exit [Hammon]

OATLEY Now, mammet,° you have well behaved yourself,
  But you shall curse your coyness° if I live.
  Who's within there?
         [*Enter a Servant*]
                         See you convey your mistress
  Straight to the Old Ford—[*to Rose*] I'll keep you strait°
      enough!
  'Fore God, I would have sworn the puling girl   60
  Would willingly accepted Hammon's love.
  But banish him my thoughts. Go, minion, in!
         Exeunt Rose [and Servant]
  Now tell me, Master Scott, would you have thought
  That Master Simon Eyre, the shoemaker,
  Had been of wealth to buy such merchandise?   65

SCOTT 'Twas well, my lord, your honour and myself
  Grew partners with him, for your bills of lading
  Show that Eyre's gains in one commodity
  Rise at the least to full three thousand pound,
  Besides like gain in other merchandise.   70

OATLEY Well, he shall spend some of his thousands now
  For I have sent for him to the Guildhall—
         Enter Eyre
  See where he comes. Good morrow, Master Eyre.

EYRE Poor Simon Eyre, my lord, your shoemaker.

OATLEY Well, well, it likes yourself° to term you so.   75
         Enter Dodger
  Now, Master Dodger, what's the news with you?

DODGER I'll gladly speak in private to your honour.

OATLEY You shall, you shall. Master Eyre and Master Scott,
  I have some business with this gentleman,

25

I pray let me entreat you to walk before   80
To the Guildhall, I'll follow presently.
Master Eyre, I hope 'ere noon to call you sheriff.°
EYRE I would not care, my lord, if you might call me King of Spain.
Come, Master Scott.
    [Exeunt Eyre and Scott]
OATLEY Now, Master Dodger, what's the news you bring?
DODGER The Earl of Lincoln by me greets your lordship   85
And earnestly requests you, if you can,
Inform him where his nephew Lacy keeps.°
OATLEY Is not his nephew Lacy now in France?
DODGER No, I assure your Lordship, but disguised
Lurks here in London.
OATLEY   London? Is't even so?   90
It may be, but upon my faith and soul
I know not where he lives, or whether he lives.
So tell my Lord of Lincoln. Lurk in London?
Well, Master Dodger, you perhaps may start him.°
Be but the means to rid him into France,   95
I'll give thee a dozen angels for your pains,
So much I love his honour, hate his nephew,
And, prithee, so inform thy lord from me.
DODGER I take my leave.
    Exit Dodger
OATLEY   Farewell, good Master Dodger.
Lacy in London? I dare pawn my life   100
My daughter knows thereof, and for that cause,
Denied young Master Hammon in his love.
Well, I am glad I sent her to Old Ford.
God's Lord, 'tis late!—To Guildhall I must hie.
I know my brethren stay my company.   105
    Exit

[Scene 10]

Enter Firk, [Eyre's] Wife, [Lacy as] Hans, and Hodge
MISTRESS EYRE Thou goest too fast for me, Roger. O, Firk.
FIRK Ay, forsooth.
MISTRESS EYRE I pray thee, run—do you hear—run to Guildhall,

and learn if my husband Master Eyre, will take that worshipful
vocation of Master Sheriff upon him. Hie thee, good Firk.   5

FIRK Take it? Well, I go. An he should not take it, Firk swears to
forswear° him. Yes, forsooth, I go to Guildhall.

MISTRESS EYRE Nay, when?° Thou art too compendious° and tedious.

FIRK O, rare, your excellence is full of eloquence! [*Aside*] How like a
new cart-wheel° my dame speaks, and she looks like an old musty   10
ale-bottle° going to scalding.

MISTRESS EYRE Nay, when? Thou wilt make me melancholy.

FIRK God forbid your worship should fall into that humour. I run.

Exit [Firk]

MISTRESS EYRE Let me see now, Roger and Hans.

HODGE Ay, forsooth, dame°—mistress I should say—but the old term   15
so sticks to the roof of my mouth I can hardly lick it off.

MISTRESS EYRE Even what thou wilt, good Roger. Dame is a fair name
for any honest Christian: but let that pass. How dost thou, Hans?

LACY *Me tank you, fro.*°

MISTRESS EYRE Well, Hans and Roger, you see God hath blest your   20
master and, perdie, if he ever comes to be Master Sheriff of London, as we are all mortal, you shall see I will have some odd thing or
other in a corner for you. I will not be your back friend.°—But let
that pass. Hans, pray thee, tie my shoe.

LACY [*tying her shoe*] *Yaw, ik sal fro.*°   25

MISTRESS EYRE Roger, thou knowst the length of my foot,° as it is none
of the biggest, so I thank God it is handsome enough. Prithee, let me
have a pair of shoes made, cork, good Roger, wooden heel,° too.

HODGE You shall.

MISTRESS EYRE Art thou acquainted with never a farthingale-maker,°   30
nor a French-hood-maker?° I must enlarge my bum. Ha, ha! How
shall I look in a hood, I wonder? Perdie, oddly, I think.

HODGE [*aside*] As a cat out° of a pillory. [*To her*] Very well, I warrant
you, mistress.

MISTRESS EYRE Indeed, all flesh is grass,°—and, Roger, canst thou tell   35
where I may buy a good hair?°

HODGE Yes, forsooth, at the poulterer's° in Gracious Street.°

MISTRESS EYRE Thou art an ungracious wag. Perdie, I mean a false
hair for my periwig.

HODGE Why, mistress, the next time I cut my beard, you shall have   40
the shavings of it, but they are all true hairs.

MISTRESS EYRE It is very hot, I must get me a fan or else a mask.°

HODGE [*aside*] So you had need, to hide your wicked face.

MISTRESS EYRE Fie upon it, how costly this world's calling° is. Perdie,
but that is one of the wonderful works of God, I would not deal   45
with it. Is not Firk come yet? Hans, be not so sad, let it pass and
vanish, as my husband's worship says.

LACY *Ik bin frolick, lot see yow so.*°

HODGE Mistress, will you drink° a pipe of tobacco?°

MISTRESS EYRE O, fie upon it, Roger! Perdie, these filthy tobacco   50
pipes are the most idle° slavering baubles° that ever I felt. Out upon
it! God bless us, men look not like men that use them.

> *Enter Ralph, being lame*

HODGE What, fellow Ralph? Mistress, look here, Jane's husband.
Why, how now, lame? Hans, make much of him, he's a brother of
our trade, a good workman, and a tall° soldier.   55

LACY You be welcome, *broder.*°

MISTRESS EYRE Perdie, I knew him not. How dost, good Ralph? I am
glad to see thee well.

RALPH I would God you saw me, dame, as well
As when I went from London into France.   60

MISTRESS EYRE Trust me, I am sorry Ralph to see thee impotent.°
Lord, how the wars have made him sunburnt.° The left leg is not
well. 'Twas a fair gift of God the infirmity took not hold a little
higher, considering thou camest from France:° but let that pass.

RALPH I am glad to see you well, and I rejoice   65
To hear that God hath blessed my master so
Since my departure.

MISTRESS EYRE Yea, truly, Ralph, I thank my maker.—But let that pass.

HODGE And, sirrah Ralph, what news, what news in France?

RALPH Tell me, good Roger, first, what news in England?   70
How does my Jane? When didst thou see my wife?
Where lives my poor heart? She'll be poor indeed
Now I want limbs to get whereon to feed.

HODGE Limbs? Hast thou not hands, man? Thou shalt never see a
shoemaker want bread, though he have but three fingers on a hand.   75

RALPH Yet all this while I hear not of my Jane.

MISTRESS EYRE O, Ralph, your wife! Perdie, we know not what's
become of her. She was here a while, and because she was married
grew more stately° than became her. I checked° her and so forth.
Away she flung, never returned, nor said bye nor bah. And, Ralph,   80
you know: ka me, ka thee.° And so as I tell ye. Roger, is not Firk yet
come?

HODGE No, forsooth.

MISTRESS EYRE And so, indeed, we heard not of her. But I hear she
lives in London—but let that pass. If she had wanted, she might   85
have opened her case° to me, or my husband, or to any of my men. I
am sure there's not any of them, perdie, but would have done her
good to his power. Hans, look if Firk be come.

LACY *Yaw, ik sal, fro.*°

    Exit [Lacy as] Hans

MISTRESS EYRE And so as I said. But, Ralph, why dost thou weep?   90
Thou knowest that naked we came out of our mother's womb, and
naked we must return, and therefore thank God for all things.°

HODGE No, faith, Jane is a stranger here. But, Ralph, pull up a good
heart,° I know thou hast one. Thy wife, man, is in London; one told
me he saw her a while ago very brave° and neat. We'll ferret her out,   95
an London hold her.

MISTRESS EYRE Alas, poor soul, he's overcome with sorrow. He does
but as I do, weep for the loss of any good thing. But, Ralph, get thee
in, call for some meat and drink. Thou shalt find me worshipful°
towards thee.   100

RALPH I thank you, dame. Since I want limbs and lands,
I'll to God, my good friends, and to these my hands.

    Exit [Ralph]
    Enter [Lacy as] Hans, and Firk running

FIRK Run, good Hans! O, Hodge! O, Mistress! Hodge, heave up thine
ears. Mistress, smug° up your looks, on with your best apparel. My
master is chosen, my master is called, nay condemned,° by the cry   105
of the country, to be sheriff of the City for this famous year now to
come and time now being. A great many men in black gowns were
asked for their voices° and their hands, and my master had all their
fists about his ears° presently, and they cried 'ay, ay, ay, ay', and so I
came away.   110
Wherefore without all other grieve
I do salute° you, Mistress Shrieve.

LACY *Yaw, my meester is de groot man, de shrieve.*°

HODGE Did not I tell you, mistress? Now may I boldly say 'Good
morrow to your worship'.   115

MISTRESS EYRE Good morrow, good Roger. I thank you, my good
people all. Firk, hold up thy hand, here's a threepenny piece for thy
tidings.

    [She gives Firk money]

FIRK 'Tis but three halfpence, I think: yes, 'tis three pence, I smell the
rose.°   120

HODGE But, mistress, be ruled by me and do not speak so pulingly.

FIRK 'Tis her worship speaks so, and not she. No, 'faith, mistress, speak me in the old key: 'To it, Firk', 'There, good Firk', 'Ply your business, Hodge',—'Hodge', with a full mouth,° 'I'll fill your bellies with good cheer till they cry twang'.° 125

Enter Eyre wearing a gold chain° [*and carrying a French hood*]

LACY *See, myn leiver broder, heer compt my meester.*°

MISTRESS EYRE Welcome home, Master Sheriff. I pray God continue you in health and wealth.

EYRE See here, my Maggy, a chain, a gold chain for Simon Eyre. I shall make thee a lady—here's a French hood for thee. 130

[*Eyre gives her the hood and Mistress Eyre puts it on*]

On with it, on with it. Dress thy brows with this flap of a shoulder of mutton° to make thee look lovely. Where be my fine men? Roger, I'll make over my shop and tools to thee. Firk, thou shalt be the foreman. Hans, thou shalt have an hundred for twenty.° Be as mad 135 knaves as your master Simon Eyre hath been, and you shall live to be sheriffs of London. How dost thou like me, Margery? Prince am I none, yet am I princely born. Firk, Hodge, and Hans.

ALL THREE Ay, forsooth, what says your worship, Master Sheriff?

EYRE Worship and honour, you Babylonian knaves, for the Gentle Craft. But I forget myself. I am bidden by my Lord Mayor to 140 dinner to Old Ford. He's gone before, I must after. Come, Madge, on with your trinkets. Now, my true Trojans, my fine Firk, my dapper Hodge, my honest Hans, some device, some odd crochets,° some morris or such like, for the honour of the gentle° shoemakers. Meet me at Old Ford, you know my mind. 145 Come, Madge, away. Shut up the shop, knaves, and make holiday!

Exeunt [*Eyre and Mistress Eyre*]

FIRK O, rare, O, brave! Come, Hodge. Follow me, Hans: We'll be with them for a morris dance.

Exeunt

[Scene 11]

Enter [*Sir Roger Oatley the*] *Lord Mayor, Eyre, his Wife in a French hood,* [*Rose*], *Sybil, and other Servants*

OATLEY Trust me, you are as welcome to Old Ford as I myself.

MISTRESS EYRE Truly, I thank your lordship.

OATLEY Would our bad cheer were worth the thanks you give.

EYRE Good cheer, my Lord Mayor, fine cheer, a fine house, fine walls,
    all fine and neat.   5

OATLEY Now, by my troth, I'll tell thee, Master Eyre,
    It does me good, and all my brethren,
    That such a madcap fellow as thyself
    Is entered into our society.

MISTRESS EYRE Ay, but my lord, he must learn now to put on   10
    gravity.

EYRE Peace, Maggy, a fig for gravity!° When I go to Guildhall in my
    scarlet° gown, I'll look as demurely as a saint, and speak as gravely
    as a justice of the peace, but now I am here at Old Ford, at my good
    Lord Mayor's house, let it go by, vanish! Maggy, I'll be merry. Away   15
    with flip-flap,° these fooleries, these gulleries! What, honey? Prince
    am I none, yet am I princely born. What says my Lord Mayor?

OATLEY Ha, ha, ha! I had rather than a thousand pound
    I had an heart but half so light as yours.

EYRE Why, what should I do, my lord? A pound of care pays not a   20
    dram of debt.° Hum, let's be merry whiles we are young. Old age,
    sack and sugar° will steal upon us ere we be aware.

OATLEY It is well done. Mistress Eyre, pray give good counsel to my
    daughter.

MISTRESS EYRE I hope Mistress Rose will have the grace to take   25
    nothing that's bad.

OATLEY Pray God she do! For, i'faith, Mistress Eyre,
    I would bestow upon that peevish girl
    A thousand marks° more than I mean to give her,
    Upon condition she'd be ruled by me.   30
    The ape° still crosseth me. There came of late
    A proper gentleman of fair revenues,
    Whom gladly I would call son-in-law,
    But my fine cockney° would have none of him.
    [*To Rose*] You'll prove a coxcomb for it ere you die,   35
    A courtier or no man must please your eye.

EYRE Be ruled, sweet Rose, thou'rt ripe for a man. Marry not with a
    boy that has no more hair on his face then thou hast on thy cheeks.
    A courtier? Wash,° go by. Stand not upon pishery-pashery. Those
    silken fellows are but painted images, outsides, outsides, Rose, their   40
    inner linings are torn. No, my fine mouse, marry me° with a gentle-
    man grocer like my Lord Mayor your father. A grocer is a sweet

trade: plums, plums! Had I a son or daughter should marry out of
the generation and blood of the shoemakers, he should pack.° What,
the Gentle Trade is a living for a man through Europe, through the   45
world.

    A noise within of a tabor and a pipe°

OATLEY What noise is this?

EYRE O, my Lord Mayor, a crew of good fellows that for love to your
honour are come hither with a morris dance. Come in, my Mesopotamians, cheerly.   50

    Enter Hodge, [Lacy as] Hans, Ralph, Firk, and other
    Shoemakers in a morris. After a little dancing [Sir Roger
    Oatley, the] Lord Mayor speaks

OATLEY Master Eyre, are all these shoemakers?

EYRE All cordwainers, my good Lord Mayor.

ROSE [*aside*] How like my Lacy looks yond shoemaker.

LACY [*aside*] O, that I durst but speak unto my love!

OATLEY Sybil, go fetch some wine to make these drink.   55

    [*Exit Sybil*]

You are all welcome.

ALL We thank your lordship.

    [*Enter Sybil with wine.*] *Rose takes a cup of wine and goes to*
    [*Lacy as*] *Hans*

ROSE For his sake whose fair shape thou represent'st,°
Good friend, I drink to thee.

LACY *Ik be danke, good frister.*°   60

MISTRESS EYRE I see, Mistress Rose, you do not want° judgement, you
have drunk to the properest man I keep.

FIRK Here be some have done their parts to be as proper as he.

OATLEY Well, urgent business calls me back to London:
Good fellows, first go in and taste our cheer,   65
And to make merry as you homeward go,
Spend these two angels in beer at Stratford Bow.°

    [*Oatley gives the Shoemakers money*]

EYRE To these two, my mad lads, Sim Eyre adds another. [*Giving
money*] Then cheerly, Firk, tickle it,° Hans, and all for the honour of
shoemakers.   70

    All [the Shoemakers] go dancing out

OATLEY Come, Master Eyre, let's have your company.

    Exeunt [Lord Mayor, and Eyre with Mistress Eyre]

ROSE Sybil, what shall I do?

SYBIL Why, what's the matter?

ROSE   That Hans the shoemaker is my love Lacy
    Disguised in that attire to find me out.   75
    How should I find the means to speak with him?

SYBIL   What, mistress, never fear, I dare venture my maidenhead to
    nothing, and that's great odds, that Hans the Dutchman, when we
    come to London, shall not only see and speak with you, but in spite
    of your father's policies, steal you away and marry you. Will not   80
    this please you?

ROSE   Do this, and ever be assured of my love.

SYBIL   Away then, and follow your father to London, lest your
    absence cause him to suspect something.
    Tomorrow, if my counsel be obeyed,   85
    I'll bind you prentice to the Gentle Trade.
      [*Exeunt*]

[Scene 12]

Enter Jane in a sempster's shop,° working, and Hammon,
muffled,° at another door. He stands aloof

HAMMON   Yonder's the shop, and there my fair love sits.
    She's fair and lovely but she is not mine.
    O, would she were. Thrice have I courted her,
    Thrice hath my hand been moistened with her hand,
    Whilst my poor famished eyes do feed on that   5
    Which made them famish. I am unfortunate,
    I still love one,° yet nobody loves me.
    I muse in other men what women see
    That I so want? Fine Mistress Rose was coy,
    And this too curious.° O, no, she is chaste,   10
    And for she thinks me wanton, she denies
    To cheer my cold heart with her sunny eyes.
    How prettily she works. O, pretty hand!
    O, happy work!° It doth me good to stand
    Unseen to see her. Thus I oft have stood   15
    In frosty evenings, a light burning by her,
    Enduring biting cold, only to eye her,
    One only look hath seemed as rich to me
    As a king's crown, such is love's lunacy.
    Muffled I'll pass along, and by that try   20

33

Whether she know me.

JANE   Sir, what is't you buy?
What is't you lack,° sir? Calico, or lawn,
Fine cambric shirts, or bands,° what will you buy?

HAMMON [aside] That which thou wilt not sell. Faith yet I'll try.
[To her] How° do you sell this handkercher?

JANE   Good cheap.   25

HAMMON And how these ruffs?

JANE   Cheap, too.

HAMMON   And how this band?

JANE Cheap, too.

HAMMON   All cheap. How sell you then this hand?

JANE My hands are not to be sold.

HAMMON   To be given, then.
Nay, 'faith, I come to buy.

JANE   But none knows when.°

HAMMON Good sweet, leave work a little while, let's play.   30

JANE I cannot live by keeping holiday.

HAMMON I'll pay you for the time which shall be lost.

JANE With me you shall not be at so much cost.

HAMMON Look how° you wound this cloth,° so you wound me.

JANE It may be so.

HAMMON   'Tis so.

JANE   What remedy?   35

HAMMON Nay, 'faith, you are too coy.

JANE   Let go my hand.

HAMMON I will do any task at your command,
I would let go this beauty, were I not
Enjoined to disobey you by a power
That controls kings: I love you.

JANE   So, now part.   40

HAMMON With hands I may, but never with my heart.
In faith, I love you.

JANE   I believe you do.

HAMMON Shall a true love in me breed hate in you?

JANE I hate you not.

HAMMON   Then you must love.

JANE   I do.
What are you better now? I love not you.   45

HAMMON All this I hope is but a woman's fray,°
That means, 'Come to me!', when she cries, 'Away!'

34

In earnest, mistress, I do not jest,
A true chaste love hath entered in my breast,
I love you dearly as I love my life,   50
I love you as a husband loves a wife.
That, and no other love, my love requires,
Thy wealth I know is little, my desires
Thirst not for gold. Sweet, beauteous Jane, what's mine
Shall, if thou make myself thine,° all be thine.   55
Say, judge, what is thy sentence, life or death?
Mercy or cruelty lies in thy breath.

JANE Good sir, I do believe you love me well.
For 'tis a silly conquest, silly pride,
For one like you (I mean a gentleman)   60
To boast that by his love tricks he hath brought
Such and such women to his amorous lure.
I think you do not so, yet many do,
And make it even a very trade to woo.
I could be coy, as many women be,   65
Feed you with sunshine smiles, and wanton looks,
But I detest witchcraft. Say that I
Do constantly believe you constant have—

HAMMON Why dost thou not believe me?

JANE   I believe you.
But yet, good sir, because I will not grieve you   70
With hopes to taste fruit which will never fall,
In simple truth this is the sum of all:
My husband lives—at least I hope he lives—
Pressed was he to these bitter wars in France.
Bitter they are to me by wanting° him.   75
I have but one heart, and that heart's his due.
How can I then bestow the same on you?
Whilst he lives, his I live, be it ne'er so poor,
And rather be his wife than a king's whore.

HAMMON Chaste and dear woman, I will not abuse thee,   80
Although it cost my life if thou refuse me.
Thy husband pressed for France, what was his name?

JANE Ralph Damport.

HAMMON   Damport? Here's a letter sent
From France to me, from a dear friend of mine,
A gentleman of place.° Here he doth write   85
Their names that have been slain in every fight.

35

[*Hammon produces a letter*]

JANE I hope death's scroll contains not my love's name.

HAMMON Cannot you read?

JANE   I can.

HAMMON   Peruse the same.
　　To my remembrance such a name I read
　　Amongst the rest—see, here.
　　　　　[*Jane reads the letter*]

JANE   Ay me, he's dead!   90
　　He's dead! If this be true, my dear heart's slain.

HAMMON Have patience, dear love.

JANE   Hence, hence!

HAMMON   Nay, sweet Jane,
　　Make not poor sorrow proud with these rich tears,
　　I mourn thy husband's death because thou mournest.

JANE That bill° is forged. 'Tis signed by forgery.   95

HAMMON I'll bring thee letters sent besides to many
　　Carrying the like report. Jane 'tis too true.
　　Come, weep not: mourning though it rise from love
　　Helps not the mourned, yet hurts them that mourn.°

JANE For God's sake, leave me.

HAMMON   Whither dost thou turn?   100
　　Forget the dead, love them that are alive,
　　His love is faded, try how mine will thrive.

JANE 'Tis now no time for me to think on love.

HAMMON 'Tis now best time for you to think on love,
　　Because your love lives not.

JANE   Though he be dead,   105
　　My love for him shall not be burièd:
　　For God's sake, leave me to myself alone.

HAMMON 'Twould kill my soul to leave thee drowned in moan.°
　　Answer me to my suit and I am gone:
　　Say to me, yea, or no.

JANE   No!

HAMMON   Then, farewell.   110
　　One farewell will not serve, I come again.
　　Come, dry these wet cheeks. Tell me faith sweet Jane,
　　Yea or no, once more.

JANE   Once more I say no.
　　Once more, be gone, I pray, else will I go.

HAMMON Nay, then, I will grow rude° by this white hand   115

Until you change that cold no, here I'll stand
Till by your hard heart—
JANE   Nay, for God's love, peace!
My sorrows by your presence more increase,
Not that you thus are present,° but all grief
Desires to be alone. Therefore in brief   120
Thus much I say, and saying bid adieu,
If ever I wed man it shall be you.
HAMMON O, blessèd voice. Dear Jane, I'll urge no more,
Thy breath hath made me rich.
JANE   Death makes me poor.

    Exeunt

[Scene 13]

    Enter Hodge at his shop board,° Ralph, Firk, [Lacy as] Hans,
    and a Boy at work

ALL [*singing*] Hey, down, a–down, down–derry.°
HODGE Well said,° my hearts. Ply your work today, we loitered yester-
    day. To it, pell-mell, that we may live to be lord mayors or aldermen
    at least.
FIRK [*singing*] Hey down a–down derry.   5
HODGE Well said, i'faith. How sayest thou, Hans, doth not Firk tickle it?
LACY *Yaw, meester.*°
FIRK Not so, neither. My organ pipe squeaks this morning for want of
    liquoring. [*Singing*] Hey down a–down derry.
LACY *Forware Firk, tow beest un jolly yongster. Hort I, mester, ik bid you*   10
    cut me un pair vampies vor Meester Jeffrey's boots.°
HODGE Thou shalt, Hans.
FIRK Master.
HODGE How now, boy?
FIRK Pray, now you are in the cutting vein,° cut me out a pair of   15
    counterfeits,° or else my work will not pass current.° [*Singing*] Hey
    down a–down.
HODGE Tell me, sirs, are my cousin Mistress Priscilla's shoes done?
FIRK Your cousin? No, master, one of your aunts.° Hang her, let them
    alone.   20
RALPH I am in hand with° them. She gave charge that none but I
    should do them for her.

FIRK Thou do for her? Then 'twill be a lame doing° and that she loves
  not. Ralph, thou mightest have sent her to me, in faith, I would
  have yerked° and firked your Priscilla. [*Singing*] Hey down a-down   25
  derry.—This gear will not hold.°

HODGE How sayest thou Firk? Were we not merry at Old Ford?

FIRK How merry? Why our buttocks went jiggy-jiggy like a quagmire.
  Well, Sir Roger Oatmeal,° if I thought all meal of that nature,° I
  would eat nothing but bag-puddings.°   30

RALPH Of all good fortunes, my fellow Hans had the best.

FIRK 'Tis true, because Mistress Rose drank to him.

HODGE Well, well, work apace. They say seven of the Aldermen be
  dead, or very sick.

FIRK I care not, I'll be none.   35

RALPH No, nor I, but then my Master Eyre will come quickly to be
  Lord Mayor.

        Enter Sybil

FIRK Whoop, yonder comes Sybil.

HODGE Sybil, welcome, i'faith. And how dost thou, mad wench?

FIRK Syb-whore,° welcome to London.   40

SYBIL God-a-mercy, sweet Firk. Good Lord, Hodge, what a delicious
  shop you have got, you tickle it, i'faith.

RALPH God-a-mercy, Sybil, for our good cheer at Old Ford.

SYBIL That you shall have,° Ralph.

FIRK Nay, by the mass, we had tickling cheer Sybil. And how the   45
  plague dost thou and Mistress Rose, and my Lord Mayor? I put the
  women in first.°

SYBIL Well, God-a-mercy. But God's me,° I forget myself—where's
  Hans the Fleming?

FIRK Hark, butter-box, now you must yelp out some sprecken.   50

LACY *Wat begaey you, vat vod you, frister?*°

SYBIL Marry, you must come to my young mistress, to pull on° her
  shoes you made last.

LACY *Ware ben your edle fro, vare ben your mistress?*°

SYBIL Marry, here at our London house in Cornwall.°   55

FIRK Will nobody serve her turn but Hans?

SYBIL No, sir. Come, Hans, I stand upon needles.°

HODGE Why then, Sybil, take heed of pricking.

SYBIL For that, let me alone! I have a trick in my budget.° Come,
  Hans.   60

LACY *Yaw, yaw, ik sal mit you gane.*°

        Exit [Lacy as] Hans and Sybil

HODGE Go, Hans, make haste again. Come, who lacks work?
FIRK I, master, for I lack my breakfast—'tis munching time, and past.
HODGE Is't so? Why then leave work, Ralph. To breakfast. Boy, look
    to the tools. Come, Ralph. Come, Firk.   65
    Exeunt

[Scene 14]

    Enter a Servingman [carrying a shoe]
SERVINGMAN Let me see now, the sign of the last° in Tower Street.
    Mass, yonder's the house. What haw, who's within?
    Enter Ralph
RALPH Who calls there? What want you, sir?
SERVINGMAN Marry, I would have a pair of shoes made for a
    gentlewoman against° tomorrow morning. What, can you do   5
    them?
RALPH Yes sir, you shall have them,—but what length's her foot?
SERVINGMAN [*handing Ralph the shoe*] Why, you must make them in
    all parts like this shoe, but at any hand° fail not to do them, for the
    gentlewoman is to be married very early in the morning.   10
RALPH How? By this shoe must it be made? By this? Are you sure, sir?
    By this?
SERVINGMAN How, 'by this', 'am I sure', 'by this'? Art thou in thy
    wits? I tell thee I must have a pair of shoes, dost thou mark me? A
    pair of shoes, two shoes, made by this very shoe, this same shoe,   15
    against tomorrow morning by four o'clock. Dost understand me?
    Canst thou do't?
RALPH Yes, sir, yes. Ay, ay, I can do't. By this shoe, you say? I should
    know this shoe. Yes, sir, yes, by this shoe, I can do't. Four o'clock.
    Well, whither shall I bring them?   20
SERVINGMAN To the sign of the Golden Ball° in Watling Street.°
    Enquire for one Master Hammon, a gentleman, my master.
RALPH Yea, sir. By this shoe, you say?
SERVINGMAN I say Master Hammon at the Golden Ball. He's the
    bridegroom, and those shoes are for his bride.   25
RALPH They shall be done by this shoe. Well, well, Master Hammon
    at the Golden Shoe—I would say the Golden Ball—very well,
    very well. But I pray you, sir, where must Master Hammon be
    married?

SERVINGMAN At Saint Faith's° Church under Paul's. But what's that   30
   to thee? Prithee, dispatch those shoes, and so farewell.
     Exit [Servingman]

RALPH By this shoe, said he. How am I amazed
   At this strange accident? Upon my life,
   This was the very shoe I gave my wife
   When I was pressed for France, since when, alas,   35
   I never could hear of her. It is the same,
   And Hammon's bride no other but my Jane.
     Enter Firk

FIRK 'Snails, Ralph, thou hast lost thy part of three pots a country-
   man° of mine gave me to breakfast.

RALPH I care not. I have found a better thing.   40

FIRK A thing? Away, is it a man's thing or a woman's thing?°

RALPH *[showing the shoe]* Firk, dost thou know this shoe?

FIRK No, by my troth, neither doth that know me. I have no acquaintance with it, 'tis a mere° stranger to me.

RALPH Why, then, I do. This shoe, I durst be sworn,   45
   Once covered the instep of my Jane:
   This is her size, her breadth, thus trod my love,
   These true-love knots I pricked,° I hold my life.
   By this old shoe I shall find out my wife.

FIRK Ha, ha. Old shoe, that wert new. How o' murrain came this   50
   ague-fit of foolishness upon thee?

RALPH Thus, Firk. Even now here came a servingman,
   By this shoe would he have a new pair made
   Against tomorrow morning for his mistress,
   That's to be married to a gentleman.   55
   And why may not this be my sweet Jane?

FIRK And why mayest not thou be my sweet ass? Ha, ha.

RALPH Well, laugh and spare not: but the truth is this,
   Against tomorrow morning I'll provide
   A lusty crew of honest shoemakers   60
   To watch the going of the bride to church.
   If she prove Jane, I'll take her in despite
   From Hammon and the devil, were he by.
   If it be not my Jane, what remedy?
   Hereof am I sure, I shall live till I die,   65
   Although I never with a woman lie.
     Exit [Ralph]

FIRK Thou lie with a woman to build nothing but Cripple-gates!°

Well, God sends fools fortune,° and it may be he may light upon his
matrimony by such a device, for wedding and hanging goes by
destiny.°   70
    Exit

[Scene 15]

    Enter [Lacy as] Hans and Rose, arm in arm
LACY [*speaking as himself*] How happy am I by embracing thee.
  O, I did fear such cross° mishaps did reign
  That I should never see my Rose again.
ROSE Sweet Lacy, since fair Opportunity
  Offers herself to further our escape,   5
  Let not too over-fond esteem of me°
  Hinder that happy hour. Invent the means,
  And Rose will follow thee through all the world.
LACY O, how I surfeit with excess of joy,
  Made happy by thy rich perfection!   10
  But since thou payest sweet interest to my hopes,
  Redoubling love on love, let me once more,
  Like to a bold-faced debtor, crave of thee
  This night to steal abroad, and at Eyre's house,
  Who now by death of certain aldermen,   15
  Is Mayor of London, and my master once,
  Meet thou thy Lacy, where, in spite of chance,
  Your father's anger, and mine uncle's hate,
  Our happy nuptials will we consummate.
    Enter Sybil
SYBIL O, God, what will you do, mistress? Shift for yourself, your   20
  father is at hand, he's coming, he's coming! Master Lacy, hide
  yourself. In, my mistress, for God's sake, shift for yourselves!
LACY Your father come, sweet Rose, what shall I do?
  Where shall I hide me? How shall I escape?
ROSE A man and want° wit in extremity?   25
  Come, come, be Hans still, play the shoemaker,
  Pull on my shoe.
    Enter [Sir Roger Oatley, the former] Lord Mayor
LACY [*aside*]   Mass, and that's well remembered.
SYBIL Here comes your father.

41

LACY [*as Hans*] *Forware, metress, 'tis un good skoe, it sal vel dute, or ye*
    sal neit betaelen.°   30
ROSE O, God, it pincheth me. [*Aside to Lacy*] What will you do?
LACY [*aside as himself*] Your father's presence pincheth, not the shoe.
OATLEY Well done. Fit my daughter well,° and she shall please thee
    well.
LACY [*as Hans*] Yaw, yaw, ik weit dat well. *Forware, 'tis un good skoe,*   35
    'tis gi-mait van neats leather, se ever, mine heer.°
          Enter a Prentice
OATLEY I do believe it. [*To the Prentice*] What's the news with you?
PRENTICE Please you, the Earl of Lincoln at the gate
    Is newly lighted,° and would speak with you.
OATLEY The Earl of Lincoln come to speak with me?   40
    Well, well, I know his errand. Daughter Rose,
    Send hence your shoemaker. [*To Lacy*] Dispatch, have done.
    Sib, make things handsome. Sir boy, follow me.
          Exit [*Lord Mayor, Sybil and the Prentice*]
LACY [*as himself*] Mine uncle come. O, what may this portend?
    Sweet Rose, this of our love threatens an end.   45
ROSE Be not dismayed at this. Whate'er befall,
    Rose is thine own. To witness I speak truth,
    Where thou appoints the place I'll meet with thee,
    I will not fix a day to follow thee,
    But presently° steal hence. Do not reply.   50
    Love which gave strength to bear my father's hate,
    Shall now add wings to further our escape.
          Exeunt

[Scene 16]

        Enter [*Sir Roger Oatley, the former*] *Lord Mayor and Lincoln*
OATLEY Believe me, on my credit I speak truth,
    Since first your nephew Lacy went to France,
    I have not seen him. It seemed strange to me
    When Dodger told me that he stayed behind,
    Neglecting the high charge that the King imposed.   5
LINCOLN Trust me, Sir Roger Oatley, I did think
    Your counsel had given head to° this attempt,
    Drawn to it by the love he bears your child.

Here I did hope to find him in your house,
But now I see mine error and confess   10
My judgement wronged you by conceiving so.

OATLEY Lodge in my house, say you? Trust me, my lord,
I love your nephew Lacy too too dearly
So much to wrong his honour, and he hath done so,
That° first gave him advice to stay from France.   15
To witness I speak truth, I let you know
How careful I have been to keep my daughter
Free from all conference or speech of° him.
Not that I scorn your nephew, but in love
I bear your honour, lest your noble blood   20
Should by my mean worth be dishonourèd.

LINCOLN [aside] How far the churl's tongue wanders from his heart.
[To him] Well, well, Sir Roger Oatley I believe you,
With more than many thanks for the kind love,
So much you seem to bear me. But my Lord,   25
Let me request your help to seek my nephew,
Whom if I find, I'll straight embark for France.
So shall your Rose be free, my thoughts at rest,
And much care die which now lives in my breast.

      Enter Sybil

SYBIL O, Lord, help, for God's sake! My mistress, O, my young   30
mistress!

OATLEY Where is thy mistress? What's become of her?

SYBIL She's gone, she's fled.

OATLEY Gone? Whither is she fled?

SYBIL I know not, forsooth. She's fled out of doors with Hans the   35
shoemaker. I saw them scud, scud, scud, apace, apace.

OATLEY Which way? What, John! Where be my men? Which way?

SYBIL I know not, an it please your worship.

OATLEY Fled with a shoemaker! Can this be true?

SYBIL O, Lord, sir, as true as God's in heaven.°   40

LINCOLN [aside] Her love turned shoemaker? I am glad of this.

OATLEY A Fleming butter-box, a shoemaker!
Will she forget her birth? Requite my care
With such ingratitude? Scorned she young Hammon
To love a honnikin,° a needy knave?   45
Well, let her fly, I'll not fly after her,
Let her starve if she will, she's none of mine.

LINCOLN Be not so cruel, sir.

Enter Firk with shoes

SYBIL [*aside*] I am glad she's 'scaped.

OATLEY I'll not account of her as of my child: 50
    Was there no better object for her eyes
    But a foul drunken lubber, swill-belly,
    A shoemaker? That's brave!

FIRK Yea, forsooth, 'tis a very brave shoe, and as fit as a pudding.°

OATLEY How now, what knave is this? From whence comest thou?   55

FIRK No knave, sir. I am Firk the shoemaker, lusty Roger's chief lusty
    journeyman, and I come hither to take up the pretty leg of sweet
    Mistress Rose, and thus hoping your worship is in as good health as
    I was at the making hereof, I bid you farewell. Yours, Firk.°

OATLEY Stay, stay, sir knave.   60

LINCOLN Come hither, shoemaker.

FIRK 'Tis happy the knave is put before the shoemaker,° or else I
    would not have vouchsafed to come back to you. I am moved, for I
    stir.°

OATLEY My Lord, this villain calls us knaves by craft.   65

FIRK Then 'tis by the Gentle Craft, and to call one knave gently is no
    harm. Sit your worship merry.° [*Aside*] Sib, your young mistress—
    I'll so bob them, now my master, Master Eyre, is Lord Mayor of
    London.

OATLEY Tell me, sirrah, whose man are you?   70

FIRK I am glad to see your worship so merry. I have no maw to this
    gear,° no stomach as yet to a red petticoat (*pointing to Sybil*).

LINCOLN He means not, sir, to woo you to his maid,
    But only to demand whose man you are.

FIRK I sing now to the tune of Rogero.° Roger, my fellow, is now my   75
    master.

LINCOLN Sirrah, knowst thou one Hans, a shoemaker?

FIRK Hans shoemaker? O, yes—stay—yes, I have him.° I tell you
    what—I speak it in secret—Mistress Rose and he are by this
    time—no, not so—but shortly are to come over one another with   80
    'Can you dance the shaking of the sheets?'° It is that Hans? [*Aside*]
    I'll so gull these diggers.°

OATLEY Knowest thou then where he is?

FIRK Yes, forsooth, yea, marry.

LINCOLN Canst° thou in sadness?°   85

FIRK No, forsooth. No, marry.

OATLEY Tell me, good honest fellow, where he is,
    And thou shalt see what I'll bestow of thee.

FIRK Honest fellow? No, sir, not so, sir. My profession is the Gentle
Craft. I care not for seeing, I love feeling.° Let me feel it here, *aurium* 90
tenus, ten pieces of gold, *genuum tenus*,° ten pieces of silver, and then
Firk is your man in a new pair of stretchers.°

OATLEY [*showing a coin*] Here is an angel, part of thy reward,
Which I will give thee. Tell me where he is.

FIRK No point.° Shall I betray my brother? No. Shall I prove Judas to 95
Hans? No. Shall I cry treason to my corporation?° No. I shall be
firked and yerked then. But give me your angel,—your angel shall
tell you.

    [*Oatley gives Firk the money*]

LINCOLN Do so, good fellow. 'Tis no hurt to thee.

FIRK Send simpering Sib away.

OATLEY Hussy, get you in. 100

    Exit Sybil

FIRK Pitchers have ears° and maids have wide mouths. But for Hauns
Prauns, upon my word, tomorrow morning, he and young Mistress
Rose go to this gear:° they shall be married together, by this rush.° Or
else turn Firk to a firkin of butter to tan leather withal. 105

OATLEY But art thou sure of this?

FIRK Am I sure that Paul's steeple is a handful higher than London
Stone?° Or that the Pissing Conduit° leaks nothing but pure Mother
Bunch?° Am I sure I am lusty Firk? God's nails, do you think I am so
base to gull you? 110

LINCOLN Where are they married? Dost thou know the church?

FIRK I never go to church, but I know the name of it. It is a swearing
church°—stay awhile—'tis, 'Ay, by the mass', no, no, 'tis 'Ay, by my
troth', no, nor that, 'tis 'Ay, by my faith',—that, that, 'tis 'Ay, by my
Faith's' Church under Paul's Cross. There they shall be knit like a 115
pair of stockings in matrimony. There they'll be incony.°

LINCOLN Upon my life, my nephew Lacy walks
In the disguise of this Dutch shoemaker.

FIRK Yes, forsooth.

LINCOLN Doth he not, honest fellow? 120

FIRK No, forsooth, I think Hans is nobody but Hans, no spirit.

OATLEY My mind misgives me now, 'tis so indeed.

LINCOLN My cousin speaks the language, knows the trade.

OATLEY Let me request your company, my lord,
Your honourable presence may, no doubt, 125
Refrain° their headstrong rashness, when myself
Going alone perchance may be o'erborne.

Shall I request this favour?

LINCOLN   This or what else?°

FIRK Then you must rise betimes, for they mean to fall to their 'hey
    pass, and repass'° pindy-pandy° 'which hand will you have?' very   130
    early.

OATLEY My care shall every way equal their haste.
    This night accept your lodging in my house,
    The earlier shall we stir, and at Saint Faith's,
    Prevent this giddy, hare-brained nuptial.   135
    This traffic of hot love shall yield cold gains,
    They ban° our loves and we'll forbid their banns.

            Exit [Oatley]

LINCOLN At Saint Faith's church, thou sayest?

FIRK Yes, by their troth.

LINCOLN Be secret, on thy life.   140

        [Exit Lincoln]

FIRK Yes, when I kiss your wife. Ha, ha. Here's no craft in the Gentle
    Craft. I came hither of purpose with shoes to Sir Roger's worship,
    whilst Rose his daughter be coney-catched° by Hans. Soft now,
    these two gulls will be at Saint Faith's church tomorrow morning
    to take master bridegroom and mistress bride napping, and they in   145
    the meantime shall chop up the matter° at the Savoy.° But the best
    sport is, Sir Roger Oatley will find my fellow, lame Ralph's wife,
    going to marry a gentleman, and then he'll stop her instead of his
    daughter. O, brave, there will be fine tickling sport. Soft now, what
    have I to do? O, I know. Now a mess of shoemakers meet at the   150
    Woolsack° in Ivy Lane, to cozen my gentlemen of lame Ralph's wife,
    that's true.
            Alack, alack
            Girls, hold out tack,°
            For now smocks° for this jumbling°   155
            Shall go to wrack.
        Exit

[Scene 17]

Enter Eyre, his Wife, [Lacy as] Hans, and Rose

EYRE This is the morning then, say, my bully, my honest Hans, is it
    not?

LACY This is the morning that must make us two
Happy or miserable, therefore, if you—

EYRE Away with these ifs and ans, Hans, and these etceteras. By mine   5
honour, Rowland Lacy, none but the king shall wrong thee. Come,
fear nothing. Am not I Sim Eyre? Is not Sim Eyre Lord Mayor of
London? Fear nothing, Rose, let them all say what they can. [*Singing*] 'Dainty come thou to me'.° Laughest thou?

MISTRESS EYRE Good my lord, stand° her friend in what thing you   10
may.

EYRE Why, my sweet Lady Madgy, think you Simon Eyre can forget
his fine Dutch journeyman? No, vah! Fie, I scorn it! It shall never
be cast in my teeth° that I was unthankful. Lady Madgy, thou hadst
never covered thy Saracen's head° with this French flap, nor loaden   15
thy bum with this farthingale,—'tis trash, trumpery, vanity—
Simon Eyre had never walked in a red petticoat,° nor wore a chain of
gold, but for my fine journeyman's portagues. And shall I leave
him? No. Prince am I none, yet bear a princely mind.

LACY My lord, 'tis time for us to part from hence.   20

EYRE Lady Madgy, Lady Madgy, take two or three of my pie-crust
eaters, my buff-jerkin varlets,° that do walk in black gowns at Simon
Eyre's heels, take them good Lady Madgy. Trip and go, my brown°
queen of periwigs, with my delicate Rose and my jolly Rowland to
the Savoy, see them linked, countenance° the marriage, and when it   25
is done, cling, cling together, you Hamburg° turtle-doves. I'll bear
you out. Come to Simon Eyre, come dwell with me, Hans, thou
shalt eat minced pies, and marchpane. Rose, away cricket. Trip and
go, my Lady Madgy, to the Savoy. Hans, wed and to bed, kiss and
away, go, vanish.   30

MISTRESS EYRE Farewell, my lord.

ROSE Make haste, sweet love.

MISTRESS EYRE   She'd fain the deed were done.

LACY Come, my sweet Rose, faster than deer we'll run.
      Exeunt [Mistress Eyre, Lacy (as Hans), and Rose]

EYRE Go, vanish, vanish, avaunt, I say! By the Lord of Ludgate, it's a
mad life to be a Lord Mayor. It's a stirring life, a fine life, a velvet   35
life, a careful life. Well, Simon Eyre, yet set a good face on it, in the
honour of Saint Hugh. Soft, the King this day comes to dine with
me, to see my new buildings.° His Majesty is welcome, he shall have
good cheer, delicate cheer, princely cheer. This day my fellow prentices of London come to dine with me too. They shall have fine   40
cheer, gentleman-like cheer. I promised the mad Cappidoceans,°

when we all served at the Conduit° together, that if ever I came to be
Mayor of London, I would feast them all. And I'll do't, I'll do't, by
the life of Pharaoh, by this beard, Sim Eyre will be no flincher.
Besides, I have procured that upon every Shrove Tuesday, at the   45
sound of the pancake bell,° my fine dapper Assyrian lads shall clap
up their shop-windows and away. This is the day, and this day they
shall do't, they shall do't.
          Boys, that day are you free: let masters care,
          And prentices shall pray for Simon Eyre.   50
   Exit

[Scene 18]

*Enter Hodge, Firk, Ralph, and five or six Shoemakers, all with
cudgels, or such weapons*

HODGE Come, Ralph. Stand to it, Firk. My masters, as we are the
brave bloods° of shoemakers, heirs apparent to Saint Hugh, and
perpetual benefactors to all good fellows, thou shalt have no wrong.
Were Hammon a king of spades,° he should not delve in thy close°
without thy sufferance.° But tell me Ralph, art thou sure 'tis thy   5
wife?

RALPH Am I sure this is Firk? This morning, when I stroked on her
shoes, I looked upon her, and she upon me, and sighed, asked me if
ever I knew one Ralph. 'Yes', said I. 'For his sake', said she, tears
standing in her eyes, 'and for thou art somewhat like him, spend   10
this piece of gold.'
   [Ralph shows a gold coin]
I took it. My lame leg and my travel beyond the sea made me
unknown. All is one for that. I know she's mine.

FIRK Did she give thee this gold? O, glorious glittering gold! She's
thine own. 'Tis thy wife and she loves thee. For I'll stand to't,   15
there's no woman will give gold to any man but she thinks better of
him than she thinks of them she gives silver to. And for Hammon,
neither Hammon nor hangman° shall wrong thee in London. Is not
our old master, Eyre, Lord Mayor? Speak, my hearts.

ALL THE SHOEMAKERS Yes, and Hammon shall know it to his cost.   20
   *Enter Hammon, his [Serving]man, Jane [in wedding clothes and
   masked], and others°*

HODGE Peace my bullies, yonder they come.

RALPH Stand to't, my hearts. Firk, let me speak first.

HODGE No, Ralph, let me. Hammon, whither away so early?

HAMMON Unmannerly rude slave, what's that to thee?

FIRK To him, sir? Yes, sir, and to me, and others. Good morrow, Jane, 25
how dost thou? Good Lord, how the world is changed with you,
God be thanked.

HAMMON Villains, hands off! How dare you touch my love?

ALL THE SHOEMAKERS Villains? Down with them! Cry 'Clubs° for
prentices'! 30

HODGE Hold, my hearts. Touch her Hammon? Yea, and more than
that, we'll carry her away with us. My masters and gentlemen,
never draw your bird-spits,° shoemakers are steel to the back,° men
every inch of them, all spirit.

ALL OF HAMMON'S SIDE Well, and what of all this? 35

HODGE I'll show you. Jane, dost thou know this man? 'Tis Ralph, I
can tell thee. Nay, 'tis he, in faith, though he be lamed by the wars.
Yet look not strange,° but run to him, fold him about the neck and
kiss him.

JANE Lives then my husband? O God, let me go, 40
Let me embrace my Ralph.

HAMMON   What means my Jane?

JANE Nay, what meant you to tell me he was slain?

HAMMON Pardon me, dear love, for being misled.
[To Ralph] 'Twas rumoured here in London thou wert dead.

FIRK Thou seest he lives. Lass, go, pack° home with him. Now, Master 45
Hammon, where's your mistress, your wife?

SERVINGMAN 'Swounds, master, fight for her! Will you thus lose?

ALL THE SHOEMAKERS Down with that creature! Clubs! Down with
him!

HODGE Hold! Hold! 50

HAMMON [to Servingman] Hold, fool! [To the Shoemakers] Sirs, he
shall do no wrong.
Will my Jane leave me thus, and break her faith?

FIRK Yea, sir, she must sir, she shall sir. What then? Mend it.

HODGE Hark, fellow Ralph, follow my counsel. Set the wench in the 55
midst, and let her choose her man, and let her be his woman.

JANE Whom should I choose? Whom should my thoughts affect°
But him whom heaven hath made to be my love?
[To Ralph] Thou art my husband and these humble weeds
Makes thee more beautiful than all his wealth. 60
Therefore I will but put off his attire,°

49

    Returning it into the owner's hand,
    And after ever be thy constant wife.

HODGE Not a rag, Jane. The law's on our side. He that sows in another
man's ground forfeits his harvest. Get thee home, Ralph. Follow   65
him, Jane. He shall not have so much as a busk-point° from thee.

FIRK Stand to that, Ralph. Thy appurtenances° are thine own. Hammon, look not at her.

SERVINGMAN O, 'swounds, no!

FIRK Bluecoat,° be quiet. We'll give you a new livery else! We'll make   70
Shrove Tuesday Saint George's day° for you. Look not, Hammon,
leer not,—I'll firk you. For° thy head now, one glance, one sheep's
eye,° anything at her. Touch not a rag, lest I and my brethren beat
you to clouts.

SERVINGMAN Come, Master Hammon, there's no striving° here.   75

HAMMON Good fellows, hear me speak. And honest Ralph,
    Whom I have injured most by loving Jane,
    Mark what I offer thee. [*Takes out purse*] Here in fair gold
    Is twenty pound. I'll give it for thy Jane.
    If this content thee not, thou shalt have more.   80

HODGE Sell not thy wife, Ralph. Make her not a whore.

HAMMON Say, wilt thou freely cease thy claim in her,
    And let her be my wife?

ALL THE SHOEMAKERS No, do not, Ralph!

RALPH Sirrah Hammon, Hammon, dost thou think a shoemaker   85
is so base to be a bawd to his own wife for commodity?° Take thy
gold, choke with it! Were I not lame, I would make thee eat thy
words.

FIRK A shoemaker sell his flesh and blood, O, indignity!

HODGE Sirrah, take up your pelf° and be packing.   90

HAMMON I will not touch one penny, but in lieu
    Of that great wrong I offerèd thy Jane,
    To Jane and thee I give that twenty pound.
    [*Throwing down the purse*] Since I have failed of her, during my life
    I vow no woman else shall be my wife.   95
    Farewell, good fellows of the Gentle Trade,
    Your morning's mirth my mourning day hath made.
        Exeunt [*Hammon, Servingman and others*]

FIRK [*to Servingman as he exits*] Touch the gold, creature, if you dare.
You're best be trudging. [*Picking up the purse and giving it to Jane*]
Here Jane, take thou it, now let's home my hearts.   100

HODGE Stay, who comes here? Jane, on again with thy mask.°

Enter Lincoln, [Sir Roger Oatley, the former] Lord Mayor, and
   Servants

LINCOLN Yonder's the lying varlet mocked us so.

OATLEY Come hither, sirrah.

FIRK I, sir? I am 'sirrah'? You mean me, do you not?

LINCOLN Where is my nephew married?   105

FIRK Is he married? God give him joy, I am glad of it. They have a fair
   day, and the sign is in a good planet, Mars in Venus.°

OATLEY Villain, thou toldst me that my daughter Rose
   This morning should be married at Saint Faith's.
   We have watched there these three hours at the least   110
   Yet see we no such thing.

FIRK Truly, I am sorry for't. A bride's a pretty thing.

HODGE Come to the purpose. Yonder's the bride and bridegroom you
   look for, I hope. Though you be lords, you are not to bar by your
   authority men from women, are you?   115

OATLEY See, see, my daughter's masked.

LINCOLN   True, and my nephew,
   To hide his guilt, counterfeits him lame.

FIRK Yea, truly, God help the poor couple, they are lame and blind.

OATLEY I'll ease her blindness.

LINCOLN   I'll his lameness cure.°

FIRK [*to shoemakers*] Lie down, sirs, and laugh!° My fellow Ralph is   120
   taken for Rowland Lacy and Jane for Mistress Damask° Rose. This
   is all my knavery.

OATLEY What, have I found you, minion?

LINCOLN [*to Ralph*]   O, base wretch!
   Nay hide thy face, the horror of thy guilt
   Can hardly be washed off. Where are thy powers?°   125
   What battles have you made? O, yes, I see
   Thou foughtest with Shame, and Shame hath conquered thee.
   This lameness will not serve.

OATLEY [*to Jane*]   Unmask yourself.

LINCOLN [*to Oatley*] Lead home your daughter.

OATLEY [*to Lincoln*]   Take your nephew hence.

RALPH Hence? 'Swounds, what mean you? Are you mad? I hope you   130
   cannot enforce my wife from me. Where's Hammon?

OATLEY Your wife?

LINCOLN What Hammon?

RALPH Yea, my wife, and therefore the proudest of you that lays
   hands on her first, I'll lay my crutch across his pate.   135

51

FIRK To him, lame Ralph! Here's brave sport!

RALPH Rose, call you her? Why, her name is Jane. Look here else,
[*unmasks Jane*] do you know her now?

LINCOLN Is this your daughter?

OATLEY   No, nor this your nephew.
My Lord of Lincoln, we are both abused   140
By this base crafty varlet.

FIRK Yea, forsooth, no 'varlet', forsooth, no 'base', forsooth, I am but
mean.° No 'crafty' neither, but of the Gentle Craft.

OATLEY Where is my daughter Rose? Where is my child?

LINCOLN Where is my nephew Lacy married?   145

FIRK Why, here is good laced mutton,° as I promised you.

LINCOLN Villain, I'll have thee punished for this wrong.

FIRK Punish the journeyman villain,° but not the journeyman
shoemaker.

              Enter Dodger

DODGER My lord, I come to bring unwelcome news.   150
Your nephew Lacy and [*to Oatley*] your daughter Rose,
Early this morning wedded at the Savoy,
None being present but the Lady Mayoress.
Besides, I learned among the officers°
The Lord Mayor vows to stand in their defence   155
'Gainst any that shall seek to cross the match.

LINCOLN Dares Eyre the shoemaker uphold the deed?

FIRK Yes, sir, shoemakers dare stand° in a woman's quarrel, I warrant
you, as deep as another, and deeper too.

DODGER Besides, his Grace° today dines with the Mayor,   160
Who on his knees humbly intends to fall
And beg pardon for your nephew's fault.

LINCOLN But I'll prevent him. Come, Sir Roger Oatley,
The King will do us justice in this cause:
Howe'er their hands have made them man and wife,   165
I will disjoin the match or lose my life.

              Exit [*Lincoln, Oatley, and Dodger*]

FIRK Adieu, monsieur Dodger. Farewell, fools. Ha ha! O, if they
had stayed I would have so lammed them with flouts.° O, heart,
my codpiece point° is ready to fly in pieces every time I think
upon the Mistress Rose!—But let that pass, as my Lady Mayor-   170
ess says.

HODGE This matter is answered.° Come, Ralph, home with thy wife.
Come, my fine shoemakers, let's to our master's the new Lord

Mayor and there swagger this Shrove Tuesday. I'll promise you
wine enough, for Madge° keeps the cellar.   175
ALL THE SHOEMAKERS O, rare! Madge is a good wench!
FIRK And I'll promise you meat° enough, for simpering Susan keeps
the larder. I'll lead you to victuals my brave soldiers. Follow your
captain! O, brave!

    Bell rings

Hark, hark!   180
ALL THE SHOEMAKERS The pancake bell rings! The pancake bell!
Trill-lill, my hearts!
FIRK O, brave! O, sweet bell! O, delicate pancakes! Open the doors,
my hearts, and shut up the windows. Keep in° the house, let out the
pancakes. O, rare, my hearts. Let's march together for the honour   185
of Saint Hugh to the great new hall in Gracious Street corner,
which our master the new Lord Mayor hath built.
RALPH O, the crew of good fellows that will dine at my Lord Mayor's
cost today!
HODGE By the Lord, my Lord Mayor is a most brave° man. How shall   190
prentices be bound to pray for him and the honour of the gentlemen shoemakers! Let's feed and be fat with my lord's bounty.
FIRK O, musical bell still! O, Hodge, O my brethren! There's cheer for
the heavens: venison pasties walk up and down piping hot like
sergeants, beef and brewis comes° marching in dry vats,° fritters and 195
pancakes comes trolling in wheelbarrows, hens and oranges hopping in porter's baskets, collops and eggs in scuttles,° and tarts and
custards comes quavering in malt shovels.°

    Enter more Prentices°

ALL THE PRENTICES Whoop, look here, look here!
HODGE How now, mad lads, whither away so fast?   200
1ST PRENTICE Whither? Why to the great new hall. Know you not
why? The Lord Mayor hath bidden all the prentices in London to
breakfast this morning.
ALL THE PRENTICES O, brave shoemaker! O, brave lord of incompre-
hensible° good fellowship! Whoop! Hark you? The pancake bell   205
rings!

    [They] cast up [their] caps

FIRK Nay, more my hearts. Every Shrove Tuesday is our year of jubilee,° and when the pancake bell rings, we are as free as my Lord
Mayor. We may shut up our shops and make holiday. I'll have it
called Saint Hugh's holiday.   210
ALL THE PRENTICES Agreed, agreed. Saint Hugh's holiday!

HODGE And this shall continue forever.
ALL THE PRENTICES O, brave! Come, come my hearts, away, away.
FIRK O, eternal credit to us of the Gentle Craft. March fair, my
hearts. O, rare!
        Exeunt

[Scene 19]

Enter King and his train [pass] over the stage°
KING Is our Lord Mayor of London such a gallant?
NOBLEMAN One of the merriest madcaps in your land.
Your Grace will think when you behold the man,
He's rather a wild ruffian than a Mayor.
Yet thus much I'll ensure your Majesty: 5
In all his actions that concern his state,°
He is as serious, provident, and wise,
As full of gravity amongst the grave,
As any Mayor hath been these many years.
KING I am with child° till I behold this huff cap.°   10
But all my doubt is,° when we come in presence,
His madness will be dashed clean out of countenance.
NOBLEMAN It may be so, my liege.
KING   Which to prevent
Let someone give him notice 'tis our pleasure
That he will put on his wonted merriment: 15
Set forward.
ALL THE NOBLES On afore!
        Exeunt

[Scene 20]

*Enter Eyre, Hodge, Firk, Ralph, and other Shoemakers, all with
napkins on their shoulders°*
EYRE Come, my fine Hodge, my jolly gentlemen shoemakers. Soft,
where be those cannibals,° these varlets, my officers? Let them all
walk and wait on my brethren; for my meaning is that none but
shoemakers, none but the livery of my company° shall in their satin
hoods wait upon the trencher of my sovereign.   5

FIRK O, my lord, it will be rare.

EYRE No more, Firk. Come, lively! Let your fellow prentices want no
cheer, let wine be plentiful as beer, and beer as water. Hang these
penny-pinching fathers that cram wealth in innocent lamb-skins.°
Rip,° knaves, avaunt! Look to my guests.   10

HODGE My lord, we are at our wits' end for room, those hundred
tables will not feast the fourth part of them.

EYRE Then cover me those hundred tables again, and again, till all my
jolly prentices be seated. Avoid,° Hodge! Run, Ralph! Firk about,
my nimble Firk! Carouse me fathom healths° to the honour of the   15
shoemakers. Do they drink lively, Hodge? Do they tickle it, Firk?

FIRK Tickle it? Some of them have taken their liquor standing so
long that they can stand no longer. But for meat,° they would eat it
an they had it.

EYRE Want they meat? Where's this swag-belly, this greasy kitchen- 20
stuff cook? Call the varlet to me! Want meat! Firk, Hodge, lame
Ralph, run, my tall men, beleaguer the shambles,° beggar all Eastcheap, serve me whole oxen in chargers,° and let sheep whine upon
the table like pigs for want of good fellows to eat them. Want meat!
Vanish, Firk! Avaunt, Hodge!   25

HODGE Your lordship mistakes my man Firk. He means that their
bellies want meat, not the boards; for they have drunk so much they
can eat nothing.

　　　　Enter [Lacy as] Hans, Rose, and Mistress Eyre

MISTRESS EYRE Where is my lord?

EYRE How now, Lady Madgy?   30

MISTRESS EYRE The King's most excellent Majesty is new come; he
sends me for thy honour. One of his most worshipful peers bade me
tell thou must be merry, and so forth: but let that pass.

EYRE Is my sovereign come? Vanish my tall shoemakers, my nimble
brethren, look to my guests the prentices. Yet, stay a little. How   35
now, Hans, how looks my little Rose?

LACY Let me request you to remember me.
I know your honour easily may obtain
Free pardon of the King for me and Rose,
And reconcile me to my uncle's grace.°   40

EYRE Have done, my good Hans, my honest journeyman. Look
cheerly! I'll fall upon both my knees till they be as hard as horn but
I'll get thy pardon.

MISTRESS EYRE Good my lord, have a care what you speak to his
Grace.   45

EYRE Away, you Islington whitepot!° Hence, you hopper-arse,° you
barley-pudding° full of maggots, you broiled carbonado.° Avaunt,
avaunt! Avoid Mephistophilus!° Shall Sim Eyre leave to speak of
you, Lady Madgy? Vanish, Mother Miniver-Cap.° Vanish! Go, trip
and go, meddle with your partlets and your pishery-pashery, your   50
flews° and your whirligigs! Go, rub, out of mine alley. Sim Eyre
knows how to speak to a pope, to Sultan Soliman, to Tamburlaine°
an he were here. And shall I melt, shall I droop before my sovereign? No! Come, my Lady Madgy. Follow me, Hans. About your
business, my frolic free-booters.° Firk, frisk about, and about,   55
and about, for the honour of mad Simon Eyre, Lord Mayor of
London.

FIRK Hey for the honour of the shoemakers!
       Exeunt

[Scene 21]

*A long flourish or two. Enter King, Nobles, Eyre, Mistress Eyre,
Lacy [undisguised], Rose. Lacy and Rose kneel*

KING Well, Lacy, though the fact° was very foul
Of your revolting from our kingly love
And your own duty, yet we pardon you.
Rise both, and Mistress Lacy, thank my Lord Mayor
For your young bridegroom here.   5

EYRE So, my dear liege, Sim Eyre and my brethren, the gentlemen
shoemakers, shall set your sweet Majesty's image cheek by jowl by
Saint Hugh for this honour you have done poor Simon Eyre. I
beseech your Grace pardon my rude behaviour, I am a handicraftsman, yet my heart is without craft.° I would be sorry at my   10
soul that my boldness should offend my King.

KING Nay, I pray thee, good Lord Mayor, be even as merry
As if thou wert among thy shoemakers.
It does me good to see thee in this humour.

EYRE Sayest thou me so, my sweet Diocletian?° Then, hump!° Prince   15
am I none, yet am I princely born. By the Lord of Ludgate, my
liege, I'll be as merry as a pie.°

KING Tell me, in faith, mad Eyre, how old thou art.

EYRE My liege, a very boy, a stripling, a younker. You see not a white
hair on my head, not a grey in this beard. Every hair, I assure thy   20

Majesty, that sticks in this beard, Sim Eyre values at the King of
Babylon's ransom.° Tamar Cham's beard° was a rubbing-brush to't.
Yet I'll shave it off and stuff tennis balls with it to please my bully
King.

KING But all this while I do not know your age.   25

EYRE My liege, I am six-and-fifty year old, yet I can cry 'hump' with a
sound heart for the honour of Saint Hugh. Mark this old wench,
my King, I danced the shaking of the sheets with her six-and-thirty
years ago, and yet I hope to get° two or three young Lord Mayors ere
I die. I am lusty still, Sim Eyre still. Care and cold lodgings brings   30
white hairs. My sweet Majesty, let care vanish. Cast it upon thy
nobles. It will make thee look always young, like Apollo,° and cry
'Hump!' Prince am I none, yet am I princely born.

KING [laughing] Ha, ha. Say, Cornwall, didst thou ever see his like?

NOBLEMAN Not I, my lord.

     Enter Lincoln and [Sir Roger Oatley, the former] Lord Mayor

KING   Lincoln, what news with you?   35

LINCOLN My gracious lord, have care unto yourself,
  For there are traitors here.

ALL   Traitors? Where? Who?

EYRE Traitors in my house? God forbid! Where be my officers? I'll
spend° my soul ere my King shall feel harm.

KING Where is the traitor, Lincoln?

LINCOLN [pointing to Lacy]   Here he stands.   40

KING Cornwall, lay hold on Lacy. Lincoln, speak:
  What canst thou lay unto thy nephew's charge?

LINCOLN This, my dear liege. Your Grace, to do me honour,
  Heaped on the head of this degenerous° boy,
  Desertless favours. You made choice of him   45
  To be commander over powers in France,
  But he—

KING   Good Lincoln, prithee, pause awhile.
  Even in thine eyes I read what thou wouldst speak.
  I know how Lacy did neglect our love,
  Ran himself deeply, in the highest degree,   50
  Into vile treason.

LINCOLN   Is he not a traitor?

KING Lincoln, he was: now have we pardoned him.
  'Twas not a base want° of true valour's fire
  That held him out of France, but love's desire.

LINCOLN I will not bear his shame upon my back.   55

KING Nor shalt thou, Lincoln. I forgive you both.

LINCOLN Then, good my liege, forbid the boy to wed
  One whose mean birth will much disgrace his bed.

KING Are they not married?

LINCOLN   No, my liege.

LACY AND ROSE   We are.

KING Shall I divorce them then? O, be it far   60
  That any hand on earth should dare untie
  The sacred knot knit by God's majesty.
  I would not for my crown disjoin their hands
  That are conjoined in holy nuptial bands.°
  How sayest thou Lacy, wouldst thou lose thy Rose?   65

LACY Not for all India's wealth, my sovereign.

KING But Rose, I am sure, her Lacy would forgo?

ROSE If Rose were asked that question, she'd say no.

KING You hear them, Lincoln?

LINCOLN   Yea, my liege, I do.

KING Yet canst thou find i'the heart to part these two?   70
  Who seeks, besides you to divorce these lovers?

OATLEY I do, my gracious lord. I am her father.

KING Sir Roger Oatley, our last Lord Mayor, I think.

NOBLEMAN The same, my liege.

KING   Would you offend love's laws?
  Well, you shall have your wills. You sue to me   75
  To prohibit the match. Soft, let me see,
  You both are married, Lacy, are you not?

LACY I am, dread sovereign.

KING   Then, upon thy life,
  I charge thee, not to call this woman wife.

OATLEY I thank your Grace.

ROSE (kneel[ing])   O, my most gracious lord!   80

KING Nay, Rose, never woo me. I tell you true,
  Although as yet I am a bachelor,
  Yet I believe I shall not marry you.

ROSE Can you divide the body from the soul,
  Yet make the body live?

KING   Yea, so profound?   85
  I cannot, Rose, but you I must divide:
  Fair maid, this bridegroom cannot be your bride.°
  Are you pleased, Lincoln? Oatley, are you pleased?

OATLEY AND LINCOLN Yes, my lord.

KING   Then must my heart be eased.
  For credit me, my conscience lives in pain,   90
  Till these whom I divorced be joined again.
  Lacy, give me thy hand. Rose, lend me thine.
  Be what you would be. Kiss now. So, that's fine.
  At night, lovers, to bed. Now, let me see,
  Which of you all mislikes this harmony?   95
OATLEY Will you then take from me my child perforce?
KING Why, tell me, Oatley, shines not Lacy's name
  As bright in the world's eye as the gay beams
  Of any citizen?
LINCOLN   Yea, but my gracious lord,
  I do mislike the match far more than he.   100
  Her blood is too too base.
KING   Lincoln, no more,
  Dost thou not know that love respects no blood,°
  Cares not for difference of birth or state?
  The maid is young, well-born, fair, virtuous,
  A worthy bride for any gentleman.   105
  Besides, your nephew for her sake did stoop
  To bare necessity and, as I hear,
  Forgetting honours and all courtly pleasures,
  To gain her love became a shoemaker.
  As for the honour which he lost in France,   110
  Thus I redeem it: Lacy, kneel thee down.
  Arise, Sir Rowland Lacy. Tell me now,
  Tell me in earnest, Oatley, canst thou chide,
  Seeing thy Rose a lady and a bride?
OATLEY I am content with what your Grace hath done.   115
LINCOLN And I, my liege, since there's no remedy.
KING Come on then, all shake hands, I'll have you friends:
  Where there is much love, all discord ends.
  What says my mad Lord Mayor to all this love?
EYRE O, my liege, this honour you have done to my fine journeyman   120
  here, Rowland Lacy, and all these favours which you have shown to
  me this day in my poor house, will make Simon Eyre live longer by
  one dozen of warm summers more than he should.
KING Nay, my mad Lord Mayor, that shall be thy name
  If any grace of mine can length thy life,   125
  One honour more I'll do thee. That new building
  Which at thy cost in Cornhill is erected

Shall take a name from us. We'll have it called
The Leaden Hall,° because in digging it
You found the lead that covereth the same.   130

EYRE I thank your Majesty.

MISTRESS EYRE   God bless your Grace.

KING Lincoln, a word with you.

    Enter Hodge, Firk, Ralph and more Shoemakers

EYRE How now my mad knaves? Peace, speak softly,
  Yonder is the King.

KING With the old troop which there we keep in pay   135
  We will incorporate a new supply.
  Before one summer more pass o'er my head,
  France shall repent England was injurèd.
  What are all those?

LACY   All shoemakers, my liege,
  Sometimes° my fellows. In their companies   140
  I lived as merry as an emperor.°

KING My mad Lord Mayor, are all these shoemakers?

EYRE All shoemakers, my liege, all gentlemen of the Gentle Craft,
  true Trojans, courageous cordwainers. They all kneel to the shrine
  of holy Saint Hugh.   145

ALL THE SHOEMAKERS God save your Majesty, all shoemaker[s]!

KING Mad Simon, would they anything with us?

EYRE [*to the Shoemakers*] Mum, mad knaves, not a word. I'll do't, I
  warrant you. [*To the King*] They are all beggars, my liege, all for
  themselves, and I for them all on both my knees do entreat that for   150
  the honour of poor Simon Eyre, and the good of his brethren, these
  mad knaves, your Grace would vouchsafe some privilege to my new
  Leaden Hall, that it may be lawful for us to buy and sell leather
  there two days a week.

KING Mad Sim, I grant your suit. You shall have patent   155
  To hold two market days in Leaden Hall,
  Mondays and Fridays, those shall be the times.
  Will this content you?

ALL THE SHOEMAKERS Jesus bless your Grace!

EYRE In the name of these my poor brethren shoemakers, I most
  humbly thank your Grace. But before I rise, seeing you are in the   160
  giving vein, and we in the begging, grant Sim Eyre one boon more.

KING What is it, my Lord Mayor?

EYRE Vouchsafe to taste of a poor banquet° that stands sweetly waiting
  for your sweet presence.

KING I shall undo thee, Eyre, only with feasts,   165
    Already have I been too troublesome,
    Say, have I not?
EYRE O, my dear King, Sim Eyre was taken unawares upon a day of
    shroving which I promised° long ago to the prentices of London.
    For, an't please your Highness, in time past   170
    I bare the water tankard, and my coat
    Sits not a whit the worse upon my back.°
    And then upon a morning some mad boys, —
    It was Shrove Tuesday even as 'tis now, —
    gave me my breakfast, and I swore then by the stopple of my   175
    tankard, if ever I came to be Lord Mayor of London, I would feast
    all the prentices. This day, my liege, I did it, and the slaves had an
    hundred tables five times covered. They are gone home and
    vanished.
    Yet add more honour to the Gentle Trade,   180
    Taste of Eyre's banquet, Simon's happy made.
KING Eyre, I will taste of thy banquet, and will say
    I have not met more pleasure on a day.
    Friends of the Gentle Craft, thanks to you all.
    Thanks, my kind Lady Mayoress, for our cheer.   185
    Come lords, a while let's revel it at home.
    When all our sports and banquetings are done,
    Wars must right wrongs which Frenchmen have begun.
       Exeunt

ADDITIONAL PASSAGES

Of the two additional passages printed here, the Prologue was written for a court performance on 1 January 1600, and it may have replaced another, more everyday Prologue used for repertory performances. The two songs were clearly key parts of the performances but, unfortunately, the text affords no certain indications of their placing. A discussion of their likely positions can be found in the Note On the Texts.

A. PROLOGUE

[*Enter the Prologue*]

PROLOGUE As wretches in a storm, expecting day,
    With trembling hands and eyes cast up to heaven
    Make prayers the anchor of their conquered hopes,
    So we, dear goddess,° wonder of all eyes,
    Your meanest vassals, through mistrust and fear   5
    To sink into the bottom of disgrace
    By our imperfect pastimes, prostrate thus
    On bended knees our sails of hope do strike,°
    Dreading the bitter storms of your dislike.

    Since, then, unhappy men, our hap is such   10
    That to ourselves our selves no hope can bring,
    But needs must perish if your saint-like ears,
    Locking the temple where all mercy sits,
    Refuse the tribute of our begging tongues.
    O grant, bright mirror of true chastity,°   15
    From those life-breathing° stars your sun-like eyes
    One gracious smile, for your celestial breath
    Must send us life, or sentence us to death.
       [*Exit*]

B. SONGS

The First Three-Man's Song

O, the month of May, the merry month of May,
  So frolic, so gay, and so green, so green, so green:
O, and then did I unto my true love say,
  'Sweet Peg, thou shalt be my summer's queen'.

Now the nightingale, the pretty nightingale,   5
  The sweetest singer in all the forest's choir,
Entreats thee, sweet Peggy, to hear thy true love's tale—
  Lo, yonder she sitteth, her breast against a briar.°

But, O, I spy the cuckoo,° the cuckoo, the cuckoo,
  See where she sitteth,—come away my joy.   10
Come away, I prithee, I do not like the cuckoo
  Should sing where my Peggy and I kiss and toy.

O, the month of May, the merry month of May,
  So frolic, so gay, and so green, so green, so green:
And then did I unto my true love say,   15
  'Sweet Peg, thou shalt be my summer's queen'.

The Second Three-Man's Song
(This is to be sung at the latter end°)

Cold's the wind, and wet's the rain
  Saint Hugh° be our good speed,
Ill is the weather that bringeth no gain
  Nor helps good hearts in need.   5

Troll the bowl,° the jolly nut-brown° bowl,
  And here, kind mate to thee,
Let's sing a dirge for St Hugh's soul,
  And down it merrily.
Down-a-down, hey, down-a-down,   10
  Hey derry, derry, down-a-down
[*Singing*] (*close with the tenor boy*°)
  Ho, well done, to me let come,
  Ring compass,° gentle joy.

Troll the bowl, the jolly nut-brown bowl,
  And here, kind mate to thee,   15

Let's sing a dirge for St Hugh's soul,
    And down it merrily.
Down-a-down, hey, down-a-down,
    Hey derry, derry, down-a-down.
[*Singing*] (*close with the tenor boy*)
    Ho, well done, to me let come,   20
        Ring compass, gentle joy.

They repeat the chorus as often as there are men to drink and at last when all have drunk, they sing this verse

Cold's the wind, and wet's the rain
    Saint Hugh be our good speed,
Ill is the weather that bringeth no gain
    Nor helps good hearts in need.   25

Appendix

[THE EPISTLE]

to all good fellows, professors° of the Gentle Craft,° of
what degree soever.

Kind gentlemen and honest boon companions, I present you here with
a merry conceited° comedy called *The Shoemaker's Holiday*, acted by   5
my Lord Admiral's Players° this present Christmas before the Queen's
most excellent majesty; for the mirth and pleasant matter, by her
Highness graciously accepted, being indeed no way offensive. The
argument° of the play I will set down in this epistle. Sir Hugh Lacy,
Earl of Lincoln, had a young gentleman of his own name, his near   10
kinsman, that loved the Lord Mayor's daughter of London; to prevent
and cross which love the Earl caused his kinsman to be sent colonel of
a company into France, who resigned his place to another gentleman,
his friend, and came disguised like a Dutch shoemaker to the house of
Simon Eyre in Tower Street, who served the Mayor and his household   15
with shoes; the merriments that passed in Eyre's house, his coming to
be Mayor of London, Lacy's getting his love, and other accidents,°
with two merry three-man's songs.° Take all in good worth that is well
intended, for nothing is purposed but mirth. Mirth lengtheneth long
life,° which, with all other blessings, I heartily wish you.   20

Farewell.

EASTWARD HO

GEORGE CHAPMAN, BEN JONSON, *and* JOHN MARSTON

THE PERSONS OF THE PLAY

Master William Touchstone,° *a goldsmith*
Mistress Touchstone, *his wife*
Francis Quicksilver° ⎱ *his apprentices*
Golding ⎰
Gertrude ⎱
Mildred ⎰ *Touchstone's daughters*
Beatrice

Sir Petronel Flash,° *a knight*
Security,° *an old usurer*
Winifred, *his wife*
Sindefy,° *Quicksilver's mistress*
Bramble,° *a lawyer*
Seagull, *a sea captain*
Scapethrift ⎱ *Virginian adventurers*
Spendall ⎰

Poldavy,° *a tailor*
Hamlet,° *a footman*
Potkin,° *a tankard-bearer*
Mistress Fond ⎱ *City wives*
Mistress Gazer ⎰
Slitgut, *a butcher's apprentice*
Wolf ⎱ *jailers at the Counter*
Holdfast ⎰

Scrivener
Coachman
Sir Petronel's Page
Drawer from the Blue Anchor Tavern
Messenger
Gentlemen
Prisoners
Prisoners' Friend

Prologue

PROLOGUE

[*Enter the Prologue*]
[PROLOGUE] Not out of envy, for there's no effect
 Where there's no cause; nor out of imitation
 For we have evermore been imitated;
 Nor out of our contention to do better
 Than that which is opposed to ours in title,°   5
 For that was good, and better cannot be;
 And for the title, if it seem affected,
 We might as well have called it, 'God you good even',°
 Only that eastward, westwards still exceeds:
 Honour the sun's fair rising, not his setting.   10
 Nor is our title utterly enforced,°
 As by the points we touch at, you shall see.
 Bear with our willing pains, if dull or witty—
 We only dedicate it to the City.
  [*Exit*]

1.1

Enter Master Touchstone and Quicksilver at several° doors,
Quicksilver with his hat, pumps, short sword, and dagger, and a
racket trussed° up under his cloak. At the middle door, enter
Golding discovering° a goldsmith's shop, and walking short turns
before it

TOUCHSTONE And whither with you° now? What loose action are you
bound for? Come, what comrades are you to meet withal? Where's
the supper? Where's the rendezvous?

QUICKSILVER Indeed, and in very good sober truth, sir—

TOUCHSTONE 'Indeed, and in very good sober truth, sir'? Behind my   5
back thou wilt swear faster than a French footboy, and talk more
bawdily than a common midwife, and now, 'Indeed, and in very
good sober truth, sir'. But, if a privy search should be made, with
what furniture° are you rigged now? Sirrah, I tell thee, I am thy
master, William Touchstone, goldsmith, and thou my prentice,   10
Francis Quicksilver, and I will see whither you are running. Work
upon that now!°

QUICKSILVER Why, sir, I hope a man may use his recreation with° his
master's profit.

TOUCHSTONE Prentices' recreations are seldom with their master's   15
profit. Work upon that now! You shall give up your cloak, though
you be no alderman.°

> *Touchstone uncloaks Quicksilver* [*and reveals his sword, pumps,*
> *and racket*]

Heyday, Ruffians' Hall.° Sword, pumps, here's a racket,° indeed.

QUICKSILVER Work upon that now.

TOUCHSTONE Thou shameless varlet, dost thou jest at thy lawful   20
master contrary to thy indentures?°

QUICKSILVER Why, 'sblood, sir, my mother's a gentlewoman, and my
father a justice of peace, and of quorum,° and though I am a younger
brother and a prentice, yet I hope I am my father's son and, by
God's lid,° 'tis for your worship and for your commodity° that I keep   25
company. I am entertained among gallants, true: they call me
'Cousin Frank', right; I lend them monies, good, they spend it,
well. But when they are spent, must not they strive to get more?
Must not their land fly?° And to whom? Shall not your worship ha'
the refusal?° Well, I am a good member of the City if I were well   30

considered. How would merchants thrive if gentlemen would not
be unthrifts? How could gentlemen be unthrifts, if their humours°
were not fed? How should their humours be fed but by white-meat
and cunning secondings?° Well, the City might consider us. I am
going° to an ordinary° now; the gallants fall to play; I carry some light   35
gold° with me; the gallants call 'Cousin Frank, some gold for silver';
I change, gain by it, the gallants lose the gold; and then call 'Cousin
Frank, lend me some silver'. Why—

TOUCHSTONE Why? I cannot tell, seven score pound art thou out in
the cash, but look to it, I will not be gallanted out of my monies.   40
And as for my rising by other men's fall, God shield me! Did I gain
my wealth by ordinaries? No. By exchanging of gold? No. By keeping of gallants' company? No. I hired me a little shop, bought low,
took small gain, kept no debt book, garnished my shop for want of
plate, with good wholesome thrifty sentences, as° 'Touchstone, keep   45
thy shop and thy shop will keep thee.'° 'Light gains make heavy
purses.'° ''Tis good to be merry and wise.'° And when I was wived,
having something to stick to, I had the horn of suretyship° ever
before my eyes. You all know the device of the horn, where the
young fellow slips in at the butt end, and comes squeezed out at the   50
buccal,° and I grew up, and I praise providence, I bear my brows
now as high° as the best of my neighbours, but thou—well look to
the accounts—your father's bond° lies° for you. Seven score pound is
yet in the rear.°

QUICKSILVER Why, 'slid, sir, I have as good, as proper, gallants' words   55
for it as any are in London, gentlemen of good phrase, perfect
language, passingly behaved, gallants that wear socks° and clean
linen, and call me 'kind cousin Frank', 'good cousin Frank', for they
know my father; and by God's lid, shall not I trust 'em? Not trust?

Enter a Page as enquiring for Touchstone's shop

GOLDING [*to the Page*] What do ye lack, sir?° What is't you'll buy, sir?   60
TOUCHSTONE Ay, marry, sir, there's a youth of another piece. There's
thy fellow prentice, as good a gentleman born as thou art: nay, and
better meaned.° But does he pump it,° or racket it? Well, if he thrive
not, if he outlast not a hundred such crackling bavins° as thou art,
God and men neglect industry.   65
GOLDING [*to the Page*] It is his shop, and here my master walks.
TOUCHSTONE [*to the Page*] With me, boy?
PAGE My master, Sir Petronel Flash, recommends his love to you, and
will instantly visit you.
TOUCHSTONE To make up the match with my eldest daughter, my   70

wife's dilling, whom she longs to call madam. He shall find me unwillingly ready, boy.

Exit Page

There's another affliction, too. As I have two prentices, the one of a boundless prodigality, the other of a most hopeful industry, so have I only two daughters—the eldest, of a proud ambition and nice° 75
wantonness, the other of a modest humility and comely soberness. The one must be ladyfied, forsooth, and be attired just to the court-cut, and long tail.° So far is she ill-natured° to the place and means of my preferment and fortune that she throws all the contempt and despite hatred itself can cast upon it. Well, a piece of land she has, 80
'twas her grandmother's gift—let her, and her Sir Petronel, flash out that. But as for my substance, she that scorns me, as I am a citizen and tradesman, shall never pamper her pride with my industry, shall never use me as men do foxes, keep themselves warm in the skin and throw the body that bare it to the dunghill. I must 85
go entertain this Sir Petronel. Golding, my utmost care's for thee, and only trust in thee, look to the shop. As for you, Master Quicksilver, think of husks, for thy course is running directly to the prodigal's hogs' trough. Husks, sirrah! Work upon that now.

Exit Touchstone

QUICKSILVER Marry, foh,° goodman flatcap!° 'Sfoot, though I am a 90
prentice I can give arms,° and my father's a justice o' peace by descent! And, 'sblood—

GOLDING Fie, how you swear.

QUICKSILVER 'Sfoot, man, I am a gentleman, and may swear by my pedigree, God's my life. Sirrah Golding, wilt be ruled by a fool? 95
Turn goodfellow,° turn swaggering gallant, and 'let the welkin roar, and Erebus also'.° Look not westward to the fall of Don Phoebus,° but to the east. Eastward ho!

'Where radiant beams of lusty Sol appear,
And bright Eos° makes the welkin clear.' 100

We are both gentlemen, and therefore should be no coxcombs. Let's be no longer fools to this flat-cap Touchstone. Eastward, bully!° This satin-belly and canvas-backed° Touchstone,—'slife, man, his father was a maltman, and his mother sold gingerbread° in Christ Church.°

GOLDING What would ye ha' me do? 105

QUICKSILVER Why, do nothing, be like a gentleman, be idle, the curse of man is labour. Wipe thy bum with testons, and make ducks and drakes with shillings.° What, Eastward ho! Wilt thou cry, 'What is't

ye lack?' Stand with a bare pate° and a dropping nose, under a
wooden penthouse,° and art a gentleman? Wilt thou bear tankards,°   110
and mayst bear arms? Be ruled,° turn gallant. Eastward ho, ta ly re,
ly re, ro!° 'Who calls Hieronimo? Speak, here I am.'° God's so, how
like a sheep thou look'st. O' my conscience, some cowherd begot
thee, thou Golding of Golding Hall, ha, boy?

GOLDING Go, ye are a prodigal coxcomb. I, a cowherd's son, because   115
I turn not a drunk whore–hunting rakehell like thyself?

QUICKSILVER Rakehell? Rakehell?

> *Offers to draw [his sword], and Golding trips up his heels and
> holds him*

GOLDING Pish, in soft terms,° ye are a cowardly bragging boy. I'll ha'
you whipped.

QUICKSILVER Whipped, that's good i'faith. Untruss me.°   120

GOLDING No, thou wilt undo° thyself. Alas, I behold thee with pity,
not with anger, thou common shot-clog,° gull of all companies.
Methinks I see thee already walking in Moorfields,° without a cloak,
with half a hat, without a band,° a doublet with three buttons,° without a girdle, a hose with one point° and no garter, with a cudgel°   125
under thine arm, borrowing and begging threepence.

QUICKSILVER Nay, 'slife, take this and take all!° As I am a gentleman
born, I'll be drunk, grow valiant, and beat thee.

> *Exit Quicksilver*

GOLDING Go, thou most madly vain, whom nothing can recover° but
that which reclaims atheists, and makes great persons sometimes   130
religious: calamity. As for my place and life, thus I have read—

> 'Whate'er some vainer youth may term disgrace,
> The gain of honest pains is never base:
> From trades, from arts, from valour honour springs,
> These three are founts of gentry, yea, of kings.'   135
> *[Exit]*

[1.2]

> *Enter Gertrude, Mildred, Beatrice, and Poldavy a tailor,
> Poldavy with a fair gown, Scotch farthingale, and French fall in
> his arms, Gertrude in a French head attire° and citizen's gown;
> Mildred sewing, and Beatrice leading a monkey° after her*

GERTRUDE For the passion of patience, look if Sir Petronel approach—that sweet, that fine, that delicate, that—for love's sake, tell me if he come. O, sister Mil, though my father be a low-capped tradesman, yet I must be a lady: and I praise God, my mother must call me medam.° Does he come? 5

    [*Gertrude removes her citizen's gown and starts to put on the other dress*]

Off with this gown, for shame's sake, off with this gown! Let not my knight take me in the City cut° in any hand!° Tear't, pax° on't! Does he come? Tear't off! [*Singing*] 'Thus whilst she sleeps I sorrow, for her sake.'°

MILDRED Lord, sister, with what an immodest impatiency and dis- 10
graceful scorn do you put off your City tire.° I am sorry to think you imagine to right yourself, in wronging that° which hath made both you and us.

GERTRUDE I tell you, I cannot endure it, I must be a lady! Do you wear your coif with a London licket,° your stammel petticoat with 15
two guards,° the buffin° gown with the tuftaffety° cape, and the velvet lace. I must be a lady, and I will be a lady! I like some humours° of the City dames well, to eat cherries only at an angel° a pound, good, to dye rich scarlet° black, pretty, to line a grogram° gown clean through with velvet, tolerable, their pure° linen, their smocks° of 20
three pounds a smock are to be borne withal. But your mincing niceries,° taffeta pipkins,° durance° petticoats, and silver bodkins°— God's my life, as I shall be a lady I cannot endure it. Is he come yet? Lord, what a long° knight 'tis! [*Singing*] 'And ever she cried shout home',° and yet I knew one longer,° 'and ever she cried shout 25
home, fa, la, ly, re, lo, la'.

MILDRED Well, sister, those that scorn their nest oft fly with a sick wing.°

GERTRUDE Bow-bell.°

MILDRED Where titles presume to thrust before fit means to second 30
them, wealth and respect often grow sullen and will not follow. For sure in this, I would for your sake I spake not truth. 'Where ambition of place goes before fitness of birth, contempt and disgrace follow.' I heard a scholar once say that Ulysses, when he counter-feited himself mad, yoked cats and foxes and dogs° together to draw 35
his plough, whilst he followed and sowed salt, but sure I judge them truly mad that yoke citizens and courtiers, tradesmen and soldiers, a goldsmith's daughter and a knight. Well, sister, pray God my father sow not salt too.

GERTRUDE Alas, poor Mil, when I am a lady I'll pray for thee yet,   40
i'faith. Nay, and I'll vouchsafe to call thee sister Mil still, for though
thou art not like° to be a lady as I am, yet sure thou art a creature of
God's making, and mayest, peradventure, to be saved as soon as I.
Does he come? [*Singing*] 'And ever and anon she doubled° in her
song.'   45

    [*The monkey dances and gestures*]

Now, Lady's° my comfort, what a profane ape's° here! Tailor,
Poldavis, prithee fit it, fit it: is this a right Scot?° Does it clip close?
And bear up round?°

    [*Poldavy helps Gertrude fit the farthingale*]

POLDAVY Fine and stiffly, i'faith! 'Twill keep your thighs so cool and
make your waist so small. Here was a fault in your body, but I have   50
supplied the defect with the effect of my steel instrument,° which
though it have but one eye, can see to rectify the imperfection of the
proportion.

GERTRUDE Most edifying tailor! I protest you tailors are most sancti-
fied members,° and make many crooked thing go upright.° How   55
must I bear my hands? Light?° Light?

POLDAVY O, ay, now you are in the lady-fashion, you must do all
things light.° Tread light, light. Ay, and fall so: that's the court-
amble.

    She trips about° the stage

GERTRUDE Has the court ne'er a trot?   60

POLDAVY No, but a false gallop,° lady.

GERTRUDE [*singing*] 'And if she will not go to bed—'

BEATRICE The knight's come, forsooth.

    Enter Sir Petronel, Touchstone, [Golding,] and Mistress
    Touchstone

GERTRUDE Is my knight come? O, the Lord, my band?° Sister, do
my cheeks look well? Give me a little box o'the ear that I may   65
seem to blush: [*slapping herself*] now, now. So, there, there, there!
Here he is. O, my dearest delight, Lord, Lord, and how does my
knight?

TOUCHSTONE Fie, with more modesty.

GERTRUDE Modesty! Why, I am no citizen now. Modesty? Am I   70
not to be married? You're best to keep me modest now I am to be a
lady.

SIR PETRONEL Boldness is good fashion and courtlike.

GERTRUDE Ay, in a country lady° I hope it is, as I shall be. And how
chance ye came no sooner, knight?   75

SIR PETRONEL Faith, I was so entertained in the progress° with one
Count Epernoum, a Welsh knight. We had a match at balloon,° too,
with my Lord Whachum, for four crowns.°

GERTRUDE At baboon?° Jesu! You and I will play at baboon in the
country, knight!   80

SIR PETRONEL O, sweet lady, 'tis a strong play with the arm.

GERTRUDE With arm, or leg, or any other member, if it be a court-
sport. And when shall's be married, my knight?

SIR PETRONEL I come now to consummate it, and your father may
call a poor knight, son-in-law.   85

TOUCHSTONE Sir, ye are come, what is not mine to keep I must not
be sorry to forgo. A hundred pound land° her grandmother left her,
'tis yours. Herself, as her mother's gift, is yours. But if you expect
aught from me, know, my hand and mine eyes open together. I do
not give blindly: work upon that now.   90

SIR PETRONEL Sir, you mistrust not my means? I am a knight.

TOUCHSTONE Sir, sir, what I know not, you will give me leave to say I
am ignorant of.

MISTRESS TOUCHSTONE Yes, that he is a knight! I know where he
had money to pay the gentleman ushers and heralds their fees.° Ay,   95
that he is a knight!—And so might you have been too, if you had
been aught else than an ass, as well as some of your neighbours.
And° I thought you would not ha' been knighted, as I am an honest
woman, I would ha' dubbed you° myself. I praise God I have
wherewithal! But as for you, daughter—   100

GERTRUDE Ay, mother, I must be a lady tomorrow and, by your leave,
mother, I speak it not without my duty, but only in the right of my
husband, I must take place° of you, mother.

MISTRESS TOUCHSTONE That you shall, lady-daughter, and have a
coach as well as I, too.   105

GERTRUDE Yes, mother. But, by your leave mother, I speak it not
without my duty, but only in my husband's right, my coach-horses
must take the wall° of your coach-horses.

TOUCHSTONE Come, come, the day grows low, 'tis supper time. Use
my house—the wedding solemnity° is at my wife's cost, thank me   110
for nothing but my willing blessing, for, I cannot feign, my hopes
are faint. And, sir, respect my daughter,—she has refused for you
wealthy and honest matches, known good men, well-moneyed,
better-traded,° best-reputed.

GERTRUDE Body o' truth,° Chitizens,° Chitizens! Sweet knight, as soon   115
as ever we are married, take me to thy mercy out of this miserable

Chity! Presently carry me out of the scent of Newcastle coal,° and
the hearing of Bow-bell! I beseech thee, down with me,° for God's
sake.

TOUCHSTONE Well, daughter, I have read that old wit sings: 120

    'The greatest rivers flow from little springs.°
    Though thou art full, scorn not thy means at first,
    He that's most drunk may soonest be athirst.'°

Work upon that now.
All but Master Touchstone, Mildred, and Golding depart
[*Aside*] No, no: yond stand my hopes. [*Aloud*] Mildred, come hither   125
daughter. And how approve you your sister's fashion? How do you
fancy her choice? What dost thou think?

MILDRED I hope as a sister, well.

TOUCHSTONE Nay but, nay but, how dost thou like her behaviour
and humour? Speak freely.   130

MILDRED I am loath to speak ill and, yet—I am sorry of this—I
cannot speak well.

TOUCHSTONE Well, very good. As I would wish: a modest answer.
Golding, come hither! Hither, Golding! How dost thou like the
knight, Sir Flash? Does he not look big?° How lik'st thou the ele-   135
phant? He says he has a castle in the country.

GOLDING Pray heaven, the elephant carry not his castle° on his back.

TOUCHSTONE 'Fore heaven, very well! But seriously, how dost repute
him?

GOLDING The best I can say of him is, I know him not.   140

TOUCHSTONE Ha, Golding? I commend thee, I approve thee, and
will make it appear my affection is strong to thee. My wife has her
humour, and I will ha' mine. Dost thou see my daughter here? She
is not fair, well-favoured or so, indifferent,° which modest measure
of beauty shall not make it thy only work to watch her, nor suf-   145
ficient mischance to suspect her.° Thou art towardly,° she is modest,
thou art provident, she is careful. [*Taking Golding's hand*] She's
now mine: give me thy hand, she's now thine.° Work upon that now.

GOLDING Sir, as your son, I honour you, and as your servant, obey
you.   150

TOUCHSTONE Sayest thou so? Come hither, Mildred! Do you see
yond fellow? He is a gentleman, though my prentice, and has
somewhat to take to,°—a youth of good hope, well-friended, well-
parted.° [*Taking Mildred's hand*] Are you mine? [*He gives Mildred's
hand to Golding*] You are his. Work you upon that now.   155

77

MILDRED Sir, I am all yours. Your body gave me life, your care and
love happiness of life, let your virtue still direct it, for to your
wisdom I wholly dispose myself.

TOUCHSTONE Say'st thou so? Be you two better acquainted. Lip° her,
lip her, knave.   160

    [Golding kisses Mildred]

So, shut up shop! In! We must make holiday.

    Exeunt Golding and Mildred

This match shall on, for I intend to prove
Which thrives the best, the mean° or lofty love.
Whether fit wedlock vowed 'twixt like and like,
Or prouder hopes, which daringly o'erstrike   165
Their place and means: 'tis honest Time's expense,°
When seeming lightness° bears a moral sense.
Work upon that now.

    Exit

[2.1]

*[Enter] Touchstone [to] Golding and Mildred sitting on either
side of the stall°*

TOUCHSTONE Quicksilver! Master Francis Quicksilver! Master
Quicksilver!

Enter Quicksilver

QUICKSILVER Here, sir. *[Hiccups, aside]* Ump!°

TOUCHSTONE So, sir, nothing but flat Master Quicksilver, without any familiar addition,° will fetch you? Will you truss my   5
points,° sir?

QUICKSILVER Ay, forsooth. *[Hiccups]* Ump!

TOUCHSTONE How now, sir? The drunken hiccup, so soon this
morning?

QUICKSILVER 'Tis but the coldness of my stomach, forsooth.   10

TOUCHSTONE What? Have you the cause natural° for it? You're a very
learned drunkard! I believe I shall miss some of my silver spoons
with your learning. The nuptial night will not moisten your throat
sufficiently, but the morning likewise must rain her dews into your
gluttonous weasand.   15

QUICKSILVER An't please you sir, we did but drink—*[hiccups]*
ump!—to the coming off of the knightly bridegroom.

TOUCHSTONE To the coming off on him?

QUICKSILVER Ay, forsooth. We drunk to his coming on°—*[hiccups]*
ump!—when we went to bed, and now we are up, we must drink to   20
his coming off—for that's the chief honour of a soldier,° sir, and
therefore we must drink so much the more to it, forsooth. *[Hiccups]*
Ump!

TOUCHSTONE A very capital reason. So that you go to bed late, and
rise early to commit drunkenness? You fulfil the scripture° very   25
sufficient wickedly, forsooth.

QUICKSILVER The knight's men, forsooth, be still o' their knees° at
it—*[hiccups]* ump!—and because 'tis for your credit, sir, I would be
loath to flinch.

TOUCHSTONE I pray, sir, e'en to 'em again then! You're one of the   30
separated crew,° one of my wife's faction, and my young lady's, with
whom and with their great match, I will have nothing to do.

QUICKSILVER So, sir, now I will go keep my—*[hiccups]* ump!—credit
with 'em, an't please you, sir.

TOUCHSTONE In any case, sir, lay up one cup of sack more o' your   35
cold stomach, I beseech you.

QUICKSILVER Yes, forsooth.

Exit Quicksilver

TOUCHSTONE This is for my credit? Servants ever maintain drunkenness in their master's house for their master's credit. A good, idle
serving-man's reason. I thank Time the night is past! I ne'er waked°   40
to such cost! I think we have stowed more sorts of flesh in our
bellies than ever Noah's Ark received and, for wine, why my house
turns giddy with it, and more noise in it than at a conduit!° Ay me,
even beasts condemn our gluttony. Well, 'tis our City's fault, which
because we commit seldom, we commit the more sinfully, we lose   45
no time in our sensuality, but we make amends for it.°—O, that we
would do so in virtue and religious negligences. But see, here° are all
the sober parcels° my house can show. I'll eavesdrop, hear what
thoughts they utter this morning.

[*Touchstone withdraws to one side, and Golding and Mildred
come forward*]

GOLDING But is it possible that you, seeing your sister preferred° to   50
the bed of a knight, should contain your affections in the arms of a
prentice?

MILDRED I had rather make up the garment of my affections in some
of the same piece than, like a fool, wear gowns of two colours,° or
mix sackcloth with satin.   55

GOLDING And do the costly garments, the title and fame of a lady, the
fashion, observation,° and reverence proper to such preferment, no
more inflame you than such convenience° as my poor means and
industry can offer to your virtues?

MILDRED I have observed that the bridle given to those violent flat-   60
teries of fortune is seldom recovered, they bear one headlong in
desire from one novelty to another and, where those ranging
appetites reign, there is ever more passion than reason, no stay,°
and so no happiness. These hasty advancements are not natural:
Nature hath given us legs to go° to our objects, not wings to fly to   65
them.

GOLDING How dear an object you are to my desires I cannot express,
whose fruition, would my master's absolute consent and yours
vouchsafe me, I should be absolutely happy. And though it were a
grace so far beyond my merit, that I should blush with unworthi-   70
ness to receive it, yet thus far both my love and my means shall
assure your requital. You shall want nothing fit for your birth and

education. What increase of wealth and advancement the honest
and orderly industry and skill of our trade will afford in any, I doubt
not will be aspired by me. I will ever make your contentment the   75
end of my endeavours, I will love you above all, and only your grief
shall be my misery, and your delight my felicity.

TOUCHSTONE [*aside*] Work upon that now. By my hopes, he woos
honestly and orderly. He shall be anchor of my hopes. Look, see the
ill-yoked° monster his fellow!   80

> Enter Quicksilver unlaced,° a towel about his neck, in his flat
> cap, drunk

QUICKSILVER Eastward ho! 'Holla, ye pampered jades of Asia!'°

TOUCHSTONE [*aside*] Drunk now downright, o' my fidelity.

QUICKSILVER [*hiccups*] Ump!—Pulldo, pulldo!° Showse,° quoth the
caliver!

GOLDING Fie, fellow Quicksilver, what a pickle° are you in?   85

QUICKSILVER Pickle? Pickle in thy throat!° Zounds, pickle! Wahahowe!° Good morrow, Knight Petronel, morrow, Lady Goldsmith.
Come off, knight, with a counterbuff,° for the honour of
knighthood!

GOLDING Why, how now, sir? Do ye know where ye are?   90

QUICKSILVER Where I am? Why, 'sblood, you jolthead,° where I am.

GOLDING Go to,° go to, for shame go to bed, and sleep out this
immodesty! Thou shamest both my master and his house.

QUICKSILVER Shame? What shame? I thought thou wouldst show thy
bringing up: an thou wert a gentleman as I am, thou wouldst think   95
it no shame to be drunk. Lend me some money, save my credit,° I
must dine with the servingmen and their wives, and their wives,
sirrah.

GOLDING E'en who you will, I'll not lend thee three pence.

QUICKSILVER 'Sfoot, lend me some money—'Hast thou not Hiren   100
here?'°

TOUCHSTONE [*to Quicksilver*] Why, how now, sirrah? What vein's
this,° ha?

QUICKSILVER 'Who cries on murder? Lady was it you?'° How does our
master? Pray thee, cry 'Eastward ho!'   105

TOUCHSTONE Sirrah, sirrah, you're past your hiccup now, I see
you're drunk.

QUICKSILVER 'Tis for your credit, master.

TOUCHSTONE And hear you keep a whore in town.

QUICKSILVER 'Tis for your credit, master.   110

TOUCHSTONE And what you are out° in cash, I know.

QUICKSILVER So do I. My father's a gentleman—work upon that
now! Eastward ho!

TOUCHSTONE Sir, 'Eastward ho!' will make you go westward ho.° I
will no longer dishonest° my house, nor endanger my stock,° with   115
your licence.° [*Handing over the indenture*] There, sir, there's your
indenture. All your apparel—that I must know—is on your back,
and from this time my door is shut to you. From me, be free—but
for other freedom, and the monies you have wasted, 'Eastward ho!'
shall not serve you.   120

QUICKSILVER Am I free o' my fetters? Rent!°—Fly with a duck in thy
mouth!° And now I tell thee, Touchstone—

TOUCHSTONE Good, sir.

QUICKSILVER 'When this eternal substance of my soul'—

TOUCHSTONE Well said! Change your gold ends for your play   125
ends.°

QUICKSILVER 'Did live imprisoned in my wanton flesh'—

TOUCHSTONE What then, sir?

QUICKSILVER 'I was a courtier in the Spanish court,
And Don Andrea was my name.'°   130

TOUCHSTONE Good Master Don Andrea, will you march?

QUICKSILVER Sweet Touchstone, will you lend me two shillings?

TOUCHSTONE Not a penny.

QUICKSILVER Not a penny? I have friends and I have acquaintance. I
will piss at thy shop posts and throw rotten eggs at thy sign. Work   135
upon that now.

    Exit [*Quicksilver*] *staggering*

TOUCHSTONE [*to Golding*] Now, sirrah, you. Hear you? You shall
serve me no more neither, not an hour longer.

GOLDING What mean you, sir?

TOUCHSTONE I mean to give thee thy freedom, and with thy free-   140
dom, my daughter, and with my daughter, a father's love. And with
all these such a portion° as shall make Knight Petronel himself envy
thee. You're both agreed, are ye not?

GOLDING AND MILDRED With all submission both of thanks and
duty.   145

TOUCHSTONE Well then, the great power of heaven bless and confirm
you. And, Golding, that my love to thee may not show less than my
wife's love to my eldest daughter, thy marriage feast shall equal the
knight's and hers.

GOLDING Let me beseech you no, sir. The superfluity and cold meat   150
left at their nuptials will with bounty furnish ours, the grossest

prodigality is superfluous cost of the belly. Nor would I wish any invitement of states° or friends, only your reverent° presence and witness shall sufficiently grace and confirm us.

TOUCHSTONE Son to my own bosom, take her and my blessing. The 155 nice fondling,° my Lady Sir-reverence,° that I must not now presume to call daughter, is so ravished with desire to handsel° her new coach, and see her knight's Eastward Castle, that the next morning will sweat with her busy setting forth. Away will she and her mother, and while their preparation is making, ourselves with 160 some two or three other friends will consummate the humble match we have in God's name concluded.

[*Exeunt Golding and Mildred*]
    'Tis to my wish, for I have often read,
    Fit birth, fit age, keeps long a quiet bed.
    'Tis to my wish, for tradesmen, well 'tis known, 165
    Get with more ease than gentry keeps his own.
Exit

[2.2]

[*Enter*] *Security, alone*
SECURITY My privy guest, lusty Quicksilver, has drunk too deep of the bride-bowl,° but with a little sleep he is much recovered, and I think he is making himself ready to be drunk in a gallanter likeness.° My house is, as 'twere, the cave where the young outlaw hoards the stolen vails° of his occupation, and here when he will revel it in his 5 prodigal similitude,° he retires to his trunks, and (I may say softly) his punks. He dares trust me with the keeping of both—for I am security itself. My name is Security, the famous usurer.
    *Enter Quicksilver in his prentice's coat and cap, his gallant
    breeches and stockings, gartering himself*
QUICKSILVER Come, old Security, thou father of destruction: th'indented sheepskin° is burned wherein I was wrapped, and I am 10 now loose to get more children of perdition into thy usurious bonds. Thou feed'st my lechery, and I thy covetousness. Thou art pander to me for my wench, and I to thee for thy cozenages: 'ka me, ka thee'° runs through Court and country.
SECURITY Well said, my subtle Quicksilver, these K's° ope the doors 15 to all this world's felicity: the dullest forehead sees it. Let not

83

Master Courtier think he carries all the knavery on his shoulders.
I have known poor Hob° in the country that has worn hobnails°
on's shoes have as much villainy in's head as he that wears gold
buttons in's cap.   20

QUICKSILVER Why, man, 'tis the London highway to thrift,° if virtue
be used, 'tis but as a scrap° to the net of villainy. They that use it
simply, thrive simply,° I warrant. Weight and fashion makes
goldsmiths cuckolds.°

    Enter Sindefy, with Quicksilver's doublet, cloak, rapier, and
    dagger

SINDEFY Here, sir, put off the other half of your prenticeship.   25
    [*Quicksilver puts on his doublet, cloak, rapier, and dagger*]

QUICKSILVER Well said, sweet Sin: bring forth my bravery.°
  Now let my trunks° shoot forth their silks concealed,
  I now am free, and now will justify
  My trunks and punks. Avaunt dull flat-cap, then,
  Via,° the curtain that shadowed Borgia;°   30
  There lie, thou husk of my envassalled state.
  I, Samson now, have burst the Philistines' bands,
  And in thy lap, my lovely Dalida,°
  I'll lie and snore out my enfranchised state.
    [*Quicksilver sings*]

      When Samson was a tall young man   35
      His power and strength increasèd then,°
      He sold no more nor cup, nor can,
      But did them all despise.
      Old Touchstone, now write to thy friends
      For one to sell thy base gold ends,   40
      Quicksilver now no more attends
      Thee, Touchstone.

But, Dad,° hast thou seen my running gelding dressed° today?

SECURITY That I have, Frank. The ostler o'the Cock° dressed him for
a breakfast.°   45

QUICKSILVER What, did he eat him?

SECURITY No, but he ate his breakfast for dressing him: and so
dressed him for breakfast.

QUICKSILVER O, witty age, where age is young in wit,
  And all youth's words have greybeards full of it!   50

SINDEFY But, alas, Frank, how will all this° be maintained now? Your
place maintained it before.

QUICKSILVER Why, and I maintained my place. I'll to the Court, another manner of place for maintenance I hope than the silly City. I heard my father say, I heard my mother sing a noble song and a true: 'Thou art a she fool, and know'st not what belongs to our male wisdom.' I shall be a merchant forsooth: trust my estate in a wooden trough as he does? What are these ships but tennis balls° for the winds to play withal? Tossed from one wave to another, now under-line,° now over the house,° sometimes brick-walled° against a rock, so that the guts° fly out again, sometimes struck under the wide hazard,° and farewell Master Merchant.   55   60

SINDEFY Well, Frank, well. The seas, you say, are uncertain, but he that sails in your Court seas shall find 'em ten times fuller of hazard wherein to see what is to be seen is torment more than a free spirit can endure—but when you come to suffer, how many injuries swallow you? What care and devotion must you use to humour an imperious lord? Proportion your looks to his looks? Smiles to his smiles? Fit your sails to the wind of his breath?   65

QUICKSILVER Tush, he's no journeyman in his craft that cannot do that.   70

SINDEFY But he's worse than a prentice that does it, not only humouring the lord, but every trencher-bearer,° every groom that by indulgence and intelligence° crept into his favour, and by panderism into his chamber, he rules the roost.° And when my honourable lord says it shall be thus, my worshipful rascal—the groom of his close stool°—says it shall not be thus, claps the door after him, and who dares enter? A prentice, quoth you? 'Tis but to learn to live, and does that disgrace a man? He that rises hardly, stands firmly: but he that rises with ease, alas, falls as easily.   75   80

QUICKSILVER A pox on you, who taught you this morality?

SECURITY 'Tis long of° this witty age, Master Francis. But indeed, Mistress Sindefy, all trades complain of inconvenience, and therefore 'tis best to have none. The merchant, he complains, and says traffic is subject to much uncertainty and loss: let 'em keep their goods on dry land with a vengeance, and not expose other men's substances to the mercy of the winds, under protection of a wooden wall° (as Master Francis says), and all for greedy desire to enrich themselves with unconscionable gain, two for one, or so. Where I and such other honest men as live by lending money are content with moderate profit—thirty or forty i'th' hundred°—so we may have it with quietness, and out of the peril of wind and weather, rather than run those dangerous courses of trading, as they do.   85   90

QUICKSILVER Ay, Dad, thou mayst well be called Security, for thou
takest the safest course.   95

SECURITY Faith, the quieter and the more contented and, out of
doubt, the more godly. For merchants in their courses are never
pleased, but ever repining against heaven. One prays for a westerly
wind to carry his ship forth, another for an easterly to bring his ship
home, and at every shaking of a leaf he falls into an agony, to think   100
what danger his ship is in on such a coast, and so forth. The farmer,
he is ever at odds with the weather, sometimes the clouds have been
too barren, sometimes the heavens forget themselves,° their harvests
answer not their hopes, sometimes the season falls out° too fruitful,
corn will bear no price, and so forth. Th'artificer, he's all for a   105
stirring world—if his trade be too full and fall short of his expectation, then falls he out of joint.° Where° we, that trade nothing but
money, are free from all this, we are pleased with all weathers, let it
rain or hold up, be calm or windy, let the season be whatsoever, let
trade go how it will, we take all in good part—e'en what please the   110
heavens to send us—so° the sun stand not still and the moon keep
her usual returns and make up days, months, and years.

QUICKSILVER And you have good security?

SECURITY Ay, marry, Frank, that's the special point.

QUICKSILVER And yet, forsooth, we must have trades to live withal   115
for we cannot stand without legs, nor fly without wings,° and a
number of such scurvy phrases.° No, I say still: he that has wit, let
him live by his wit—he that has none, let him be a tradesman.

SECURITY Witty Master Francis! 'Tis pity any trade should dull that
quick brain of yours. Do but bring Knight Petronel into my   120
parchment toils once, and you shall never need to toil in any trade,
'o my credit. You know his wife's land?

QUICKSILVER Even to a foot, sir. I have been often there: a pretty fine
seat, good land, all entire° within itself.

SECURITY Well wooded?   125

QUICKSILVER Two hundred pounds worth of wood ready to fell. And
a fine sweet house that stands just in the midst on't, like a prick° in
the midst of a circle. Would I were your farmer,° for a hundred
pound a year.

SECURITY Excellent Master Francis, how I do long to do thee good!   130
How I do hunger and thirst to have the honour to enrich thee. Ay,
even to die, that thou mightest inherit my living, even hunger and
thirst, for o' my religion, Master Francis—and so tell Knight
Petronel—I do it to do him a pleasure.

QUICKSILVER Marry, Dad, his horses are now coming up to bear   135
down his lady, wilt thou lend him thy stable to set 'em in?

SECURITY Faith, Master Francis, I would be loath to lend my stable
out of doors.° In a greater matter I will pleasure him, but not in this.

QUICKSILVER A pox of your hunger and thirst. Well, Dad, let him
have money: all he could any way get is bestowed on a ship, now   140
bound for Virginia, the frame° of which voyage is so closely° conveyed that his new lady nor any of her friends know it. Notwith-
standing, as soon as his lady's hand is gotten to the sale of her
inheritance, and you have furnished him with money, he will
instantly hoist sail, and away.   145

SECURITY Now a frank° gale of a wind go with him, Master Frank. We
have too few such knight adventurers. Who would not sell away
competent° certainties to purchase, with any danger, excellent
uncertainties? Your true knight venturer ever does it. Let his wife
seal° today, he shall have his money today.   150

QUICKSILVER Tomorrow she shall, Dad, before she goes into the
country—to work her to which action, with more engines,° I purpose presently to prefer my sweet Sin here to the place of her
gentlewoman, whom you, for the more credit, shall present as your
friend's daughter, a gentlewoman of the country, new come up with   155
a will for a while to learn fashions, forsooth, and be toward° some
lady. And she shall buzz pretty devices° into her lady's ear, feeding
her humours so serviceable, as the manner of such as she is, you
know.

SECURITY True, good Master Francis.   160

QUICKSILVER That she shall keep her port open to anything she
commends to her.

SECURITY O' my religion, a most fashionable° project—as good she
spoil the lady, as the lady spoil her,° for 'tis three to one° of one side.
Sweet Mistress Sin, how are you bound to Master Francis. I do not   165
doubt to see you shortly wed one of the head men of our city!

SINDEFY But, sweet Frank, when shall my father Security present
me?

QUICKSILVER With all festination.° I have broken the ice to it° already
and will presently to the knight's house, whither, my good old Dad,   170
let me pray thee with all formality to man° her.

SECURITY Command me, Master Francis! I do hunger and thirst to
do thee service. Come, sweet Mistress Sin, take leave of my Winifred, and we will instantly meet frank Master Francis at your lady's.

Enter Winifred, above

87

WINIFRED Where is my Cu° there? Cu?   175
SECURITY Ay, Winnie.
WINIFRED Wilt thou come in, sweet Cu?
SECURITY Ay, Winnie, presently.
      Exeunt [all except Quicksilver]
QUICKSILVER 'Ay, Winnie', quod he? That's all he can do,° poor man,
    he may well cut off her name at Winnie. O, 'tis an egregious pander.   180
    What will not an usurous knave be, so he may be rich? O, 'tis a
    notable Jew's trump!° I hope to live to see dog's meat made of the
    old usurer's flesh, dice of his bones, and indentures of his skin, and
    yet his skin is too thick to make parchment, 'twould make good
    boots for a peterman to catch salmon in. Your only smooth skin to   185
    make fine vellum is your Puritan's skin—they be the smoothest and
    slickest knaves in a country.
      Enter Sir Petronel in boots with a riding wand°
SIR PETRONEL I'll out of this wicked town as fast as my horse can
    trot. Here's now no good action for a man to spend his time in.
    Taverns grow dead, ordinaries° are blown up,° plays are at a stand,°   190
    houses of hospitality° at a fall, not a feather waving nor a spur°
    jingling anywhere. I'll away instantly.
QUICKSILVER You'd best take some crowns in your purse, knight, or
    else your eastward castle will smoke but miserably.
SIR PETRONEL O, Frank. My castle? Alas, all the castles I have are   195
    built with air,° thou know'st.
QUICKSILVER I know it, knight, and therefore wonder whither your
    lady is going.
SIR PETRONEL Faith, to seek her fortune, I think. I said I had a castle
    and land eastward, and eastward she will, without contradiction!   200
    Her coach and the coach of the sun must meet full butt,° and the
    sun, being outshined with her ladyship's glory, she fears he goes
    westward to hang himself.
QUICKSILVER And, I fear, when her enchanted castle becomes invis-
    ible, her ladyship will return and follow his example.   205
SIR PETRONEL O, that she would have the grace, for I shall never be
    able to pacify her, when she sees herself deceived so.
QUICKSILVER As easily as can be. Tell her she mistook your direc-
    tions, and that shortly yourself will down with her to approve° it,
    and then, clothe but her crupper° in a new gown, and you may drive   210
    her any way you list: for these women, sir, are like Essex calves,
    you must wriggle 'em on by the tail still, or they will never drive
    orderly.

SIR PETRONEL But, alas, sweet Frank, thou know'st my ability° will
not furnish her blood° with those costly humours.° 215

QUICKSILVER Cast that cost on me, sir. I have spoken to my old
pander, Security, for money or commodity,° and commodity, if you
will, I know he will procure you.

SIR PETRONEL Commodity. Alas, what commodity?

QUICKSILVER Why, sir, what say you to figs and raisins? 220

SIR PETRONEL A plague of figs and raisins, and all such frail° commodities! We shall make nothing of 'em.

QUICKSILVER Why, then, sir, what say you to forty pound° in roasted
beef?

SIR PETRONEL Out upon't, I have less stomach to° that than to the figs 225
and raisins. I'll out of town, though I sojourn with a friend of mine,
for stay here I must not. My creditors have laid° to arrest me, and I
have no friend under heaven but my sword to bail me.

QUICKSILVER God's me, knight, put 'em in sufficient sureties,° rather
than let your sword bail you. Let 'em take their choice, either the 230
King's Bench, or the Fleet, or which of the two Counters° they like
best, for, by the Lord, I like none of 'em.

SIR PETRONEL Well, Frank, there is no jesting with my earnest necessity. Thou know'st if I make not present money° to further my
voyage begun, all's lost, and all I have laid out about it. 235

QUICKSILVER Why then, sir, in earnest,° if you can get your wise lady
to set her hand to the sale of her inheritance, the bloodhound
Security will smell out ready money for you instantly.

SIR PETRONEL There spake an angel.° To bring her to which conform-
ity, I must feign myself extremely amorous, and alleging urgent 240
excuses for my stay behind, part with her as passionately as she
would from her foisting° hound.

QUICKSILVER You have the sow by the right ear,° sir. I warrant there
was never a child longed more to ride a cock-horse, or wear his new
coat, than she longs to ride in her new coach. She would long° for 245
everything when she was a maid, and now she will run mad for 'em.
I lay my life she will have every year four children, and what charge
and change of humour° you must endure while she is with child, and
how she will tie you to your tackling° till she be with child,—a dog
would not endure! Nay, there is no turnspit dog° bound to his wheel 250
more servilely than you shall be to her wheel,° for as that dog can
never climb the top of his wheel but when the top comes under
him, so shall you never climb to the top of her contentment but
when she is under you.

SIR PETRONEL 'Slight, how thou terrifiest me.   255

QUICKSILVER Nay, hark you, sir! What nurses, what midwives, what
    fools, what physicians, what cunning women° must be sought for—
    fearing sometimes she is bewitched, sometimes in a consumption—
    to tell her tales, to talk bawdy to her, to make her laugh, to give her
    clysters, to let her blood° under the tongue, and betwixt the toes.   260
    How she will revile and kiss you, spit in your face, lick it off again,
    and how she will vaunt you are her creature! She made you of
    nothing. How she could have had thousand-mark° jointures, she
    could have been made a lady by a Scotch knight°—and never ha'
    married him°—she could have had poinados° in her bed every morn-   265
    ing. How she set you up, and how she will pull you down°—you'll
    never be able to stand of your legs to endure it!

SIR PETRONEL Out of° my fortune, what a death is my life bound face-
    to-face to? The best is, a large° time-fitted° conscience is bound to
    nothing: marriage is but a form° in the school of policy, to which   270
    scholars sit fastened only with painted° chains. Old Security's young
    wife is ne'er the further off with me.°

QUICKSILVER Thereby lies a tale,° sir. The old usurer will be here
    instantly, with my punk Sindefy, whom you know your lady has
    promised me entertain for° her gentlewoman: and he, with a pur-   275
    pose to feed on you, invites you most solemnly by me to supper.

SIR PETRONEL It falls out excellently fitly. I see desire of gain makes
    jealousy venturous.

        Enter Gertrude

    See, Frank, here comes my lady. Lord, how she views thee, she
    knows thee not I think, in this bravery.°   280

GERTRUDE How now? Who be you, I pray?

QUICKSILVER One Master Francis Quicksilver, an't please your
    ladyship.

GERTRUDE God's my dignity. As I am a lady, if he did not make me
    blush so that mine eyes stood a-water, would I were unmarried   285
    again.

        Enter Security and Sindefy

    Where's my woman, I pray?

QUICKSILVER See, madam, she now comes to attend you.

SECURITY [*removing his hat*] God save my honourable knight, and
    his worshipful lady.   290

GERTRUDE You're very welcome. You must not put on your hat yet.°

SECURITY No, madam. Till I know your ladyship's further pleasure, I
    will not presume.

GERTRUDE And is this a gentleman's daughter new come out of the
country?   295

SECURITY She is, madam, and one that her father hath a special care
to bestow in some honourable lady's service, to put her out of her
honest humours,° forsooth,—for she had a great desire to be a nun,
an't please you.

GERTRUDE A nun? What nun? A nun substantive?° Or a nun adjective?   300

SECURITY A nun substantive, madam, I hope, if a nun be a noun. But,
I mean, lady, a vowed maid of that order.°

GERTRUDE I'll teach her to be a maid of the order I warrant you. [*To
Sindefy*] And can you do any work that belongs to a lady's chamber?

SINDEFY What I cannot do, madam, I would be glad to learn.   305

GERTRUDE Well said, hold up then, hold up your head,° I say. Come
hither a little.

SINDEFY I thank your ladyship.

GERTRUDE And hark you—[*to Security*] goodman, you may put on
your hat now, I do not look on you—I must have you of my faction   310
now, not of my knight's, maid.

SINDEFY No, forsooth, madam, of yours.

GERTRUDE And draw all my servants in my bow,° and keep my counsel, and tell me tales, and put me riddles,° and read on a book
sometimes when I am busy, and laugh at country gentlewomen, and   315
command anything in the house for my retainers, and care not
what you spend, for it is all mine, and in any case, be still a maid
whatsoever you do, or whatsoever any man can do unto you.

SECURITY I warrant your ladyship for that.

GERTRUDE Very well, you shall ride in my coach with me into the   320
country tomorrow morning. Come, knight, pray thee let's make a
short supper, and to bed presently.

SECURITY Nay, good madam, this night I have a short supper at home
waits on his worship's acceptation.

GERTRUDE By my faith, but he shall not go, sir!—I shall swoon an he 325
sup from me.

SIR PETRONEL Pray thee, forbear. Shall he lose his provision?

GERTRUDE Ay, by'r Lady, sir, rather than I lose my longing. Come in,
I say: as I am a lady you shall not go.

QUICKSILVER [*aside to Security*] I told him what a burr° he had gotten. 330

SECURITY If you will not sup from your knight, madam, let me
entreat your ladyship to sup at my house with him.

GERTRUDE No, by my faith, sir, then we cannot be abed soon enough,
after supper.

SIR PETRONEL What a medicine° is this? Well, Master Security, you 335
are new married as well as I—I hope you are bound as well. We
must honour our young wives you know.

QUICKSILVER [*aside to Security*] In policy, Dad, till tomorrow she has
sealed.°

SECURITY I hope in the morning yet your knighthood will breakfast 340
with me.

SIR PETRONEL As early as you will, sir.

SECURITY Thank your good worship! I do hunger and thirst to do
you good, sir.

GERTRUDE Come, sweet knight, come, I do hunger and thirst to be 345
abed with thee.

  Exeunt

[3.1]

Enter Sir Petronel, Quicksilver, Security, Bramble, and Winifred

SIR PETRONEL Thanks for our feast-like breakfast, good Master
Security. I am sorry, by reason of my instant haste to so long a
voyage as Virginia, I am without means by any kind amends° to
show how affectionately I take your kindness, and to confirm by
some worthy ceremony a perpetual league of friendship betwixt us. 5

SECURITY Excellent knight, let this be a token betwixt us of inviolable
friendship. I am new married to this fair gentlewoman, you know,
and by my hope to make her fruitful, though I be something in
years. I vow faithfully unto you to make you godfather, though in
your absence, to the first child I am blest withal. And henceforth, 10
call me gossip,° I beseech you, if you please to accept it.

SIR PETRONEL In the highest degree of gratitude, my most worthy
gossip, for confirmation of which friendly title, let me entreat my
fair gossip your wife here, to accept this diamond, and keep it as
my gift to her first child, wheresoever my fortune in event° of my 15
voyage shall bestow me.

[Sir Petronel offers Winifred a diamond. She refuses his offer]

SECURITY How now, my coy wedlock!° Make you strange of° so noble a
favour? Take it, I charge you, with all affection, and, by way of
taking your leave, present boldly your lips to our honourable gossip.

QUICKSILVER *[aside]* How venturous he is to him, and how jealous to 20
others!

[Sir Petronel gives Winifred the diamond and kisses her]

SIR PETRONEL Long may this kind touch of our lips print in our
hearts all the forms of affection. And now, my good gossip, if the
writings be ready to which my wife should seal, let them be brought
this morning before she takes coach into the country, and my 25
kindness shall work her to dispatch it.

SECURITY The writings are ready, sir. My learned counsel here, Master Bramble the lawyer, hath perused them, and within this hour I
will bring the scrivener with them to your worshipful lady.

SIR PETRONEL Good Master Bramble, I will here take my leave of 30
you then. God send you fortunate pleas, sir, and contentious
clients.

BRAMBLE And you foreright° winds, sir, and a fortunate voyage.

Exit [Bramble]

Enter a Messenger

MESSENGER Sir Petronel, here are three or four gentlemen desire to
    speak with you.   35
SIR PETRONEL What are they?
MESSENGER They are your followers in this voyage, knight, Captain
    Seagull and his associates. I met them this morning, and told them
    you would be here.
SIR PETRONEL Let them enter, I pray you. I know they long to be   40
    gone, for their stay is dangerous.°
    Enter Seagull, Scapethrift, and Spendall
SEAGULL God save my honourable colonel.°
SIR PETRONEL Welcome, good Captain Seagull, and worthy gentle-
    men! If you will meet my friend Frank here, and me, at the Blue
    Anchor Tavern by Billingsgate° this evening, we will there drink to   45
    our happy voyage, be merry, and take boat to our ship with all
    expedition.°
SPENDALL Defer it no longer, I beseech you, sir, but as your voyage is
    hitherto carried closely,° and in another knight's name, so for your
    own safety and ours, let it be continued, our meeting and speedy   50
    purpose of departing known to as few as possible, lest your ship and
    goods be attached.°
QUICKSILVER Well advised, captain. Our colonel shall have money
    this morning to dispatch all our departures. Bring those gentlemen
    at night to the place appointed, and with our skins full of vintage   55
    we'll take occasion by the vantage,° and away.
SPENDALL We will not fail but be there, sir.
SIR PETRONEL Good morrow, good captain, and my worthy associ-
    ates. Health and all sovereignty to my beautiful gossip. For you, sir,
    we shall see you presently with the writings.   60
SECURITY With writings and crowns° to my honourable gossip! I do
    hunger and thirst to do you good, sir.
    Exeunt

[3.2]

Enter a Coachman in haste, in his frock [coat], feeding°

COACHMAN Here's a stir, when citizens ride out of town, indeed, as if
    all the house were afire. 'Slight, they will not give a man leave to
    eat's breakfast afore he rises.

Enter Hamlet, a footman, in haste

HAMLET What, coachman! My lady's coach, for shame! Her ladyship's ready to come down!   5

Enter Potkin, a tankard-bearer° [carrying his tankard]

POTKIN 'Sfoot, Hamlet, are you mad? Whither run you now, you
should brush up my old mistress?°

Enter Sindefy

SINDEFY What, Potkin? You must put off your tankard, and put on your
blue coat° and wait upon Mistress Touchstone into the country.

Exit [Sindefy]

POTKIN I will, forsooth, presently.   10

Exit [Potkin]. Enter Mistress Fond and Mistress Gazer

MISTRESS FOND Come, sweet Mistress Gazer, let's watch here and
see my Lady Flash take coach.

MISTRESS GAZER O' my word, here's a most fine place to stand in.
Did you see the new ship launched last day,° Mistress Fond?

MISTRESS FOND O, God, an we citizens should lose such a sight!   15

MISTRESS GAZER I warrant here will be double as many people to see
her take coach as there were to see it take water.

MISTRESS FOND O, she's married to a most fine castle i'th' country,
they say.

MISTRESS GAZER But there are no giants in the castle, are there?   20

MISTRESS FOND O, no. They say her knight killed 'em all, and therefore he was knighted.

MISTRESS GAZER Would to God her ladyship would come away.°

*Enter Gertrude, Mistress Touchstone, Sindefy, Hamlet, [and]
Potkin*

MISTRESS FOND She comes, she comes, she comes.

MISTRESS FOND [AND] MISTRESS GAZER Pray heaven bless your   25
ladyship.

GERTRUDE Thank you, good people. My coach for the love of heaven,
my coach? In good truth, I shall swoon else.

HAMLET Coach! Coach, my lady's coach!

Exit [Hamlet]

GERTRUDE As I am a lady, I think I am with child already, I long°   30
for a coach so. May one be with child afore they are married,°
mother?

MISTRESS TOUCHSTONE Ay, by'r Lady, madam, a little thing does
that. I have seen a little prick° no bigger than a pin's head swell
bigger and bigger, till it has come to an ancome,° and e'en so 'tis in 35
these cases.°

Enter Hamlet

HAMLET Your coach is coming, madam.

GERTRUDE That's well said. Now, heaven, methinks I am e'en up to the knees in preferment! [*Sings*]

> *But a little higher, but a little higher, but a little higher,*   40
> *There, there, there lies Cupid's fire.*°

MISTRESS TOUCHSTONE But must this young man, an't please you, madam, run by your coach all the way afoot?

GERTRUDE Ay, by my faith, I warrant him. He gives no other milk,° as I have another servant does.   45

MISTRESS TOUCHSTONE Alas! 'Tis e'en pity, methinks. For God's sake, madam, buy him but a hobby horse, let the poor youth have something betwixt his legs to ease° 'em. Alas! We must do as we would be done to.

GERTRUDE Go to, hold your peace, dame! You talk like an old fool, I   50
tell you.

Enter Sir Petronel and Quicksilver

SIR PETRONEL Wilt thou be gone, sweet honeysuckle, before I can go with thee?

GERTRUDE I pray thee, sweet knight, let me. I do long to dress up thy castle afore thou com'st. But I mar'l how my modest sister occupies   55
herself this morning, that she cannot wait on me to my coach, as well as her mother!

QUICKSILVER Marry, madam, she's married by this time to prentice Golding. Your father, and some one more, stole to church with 'em, in all the haste° that the cold meat left at your wedding might serve   60
to furnish their nuptial table.°

GERTRUDE There's no base fellow, my father, now! But he's e'en fit to father such a daughter. He must call me daughter no more now, but 'madam', and 'please you madam'; and 'please your worship, madam', indeed. Out upon him! Marry his daughter to a base   65
prentice?

MISTRESS TOUCHSTONE What should one do? Is there no law for one that marries a woman's daughter against her will? How shall we punish him, madam?

GERTRUDE As I am a lady, an't would snow, we'd so pebble 'em with   70
snowballs as they come from church! But, sirrah, Frank Quicksilver—

QUICKSILVER Ay, madam.

GERTRUDE Dost remember since thou and I clapped what-d'ye-call'ts° in the garret?

QUICKSILVER I know not what you mean, madam.

GERTRUDE [*singing*]

> *His head as white as milk,*
> *All flaxen was his hair:*
> *But now he is dead,*
> *And laid in his bed,*
> *And never will come again.*

God be at your labour.°

SIR PETRONEL [*aside*] Was there ever such a lady?

Enter Touchstone, Golding, [and] Mildred with rosemary°

QUICKSILVER See, madam, the bride and bridegroom.

GERTRUDE God's my precious!° God give you joy, Mistress What-lack-you?° Now, out upon thee, baggage! My sister married in a taffeta hat?° Marry, hang you! Westward with a wanion t' ye! Nay, I have done wi' ye, minion, then. I'faith, never look to have my countenance° any more, nor anything I can do for thee. Thou ride in my coach? Or come down to my castle? Fie upon thee! I charge thee, in my ladyship's name, call me sister no more.

TOUCHSTONE An't please your worship, this is not your sister, this is my daughter, and she calls me father, and so does not your ladyship,—an't please your worship, madam.

MISTRESS TOUCHSTONE No, nor she must not call thee father by heraldry,° because thou mak'st thy prentice thy son as well as she. Ah, thou misproud° prentice, dar'st thou to presume to marry a lady's sister?

GOLDING It pleased my master, forsooth, to embolden me with his favour. And, though I confess myself far unworthy so worthy a wife, being in part her servant as I am your prentice, yet (since I may say it without boasting) I am born a gentleman and, by the trade I have learned of my master (which I trust taints not my blood), able with mine own industry and portion to maintain your daughter. My hope is heaven will so bless our humble beginning that in the end I shall be no disgrace to the grace with which my master hath bound me his double prentice.

TOUCHSTONE Master me° no more, son, if thou think'st me worthy to be thy father.

GERTRUDE Sun? Now, good Lord, how he shines an you mark him! He's a gentleman.

97

GOLDING Ay, indeed, madam, a gentleman born.

SIR PETRONEL Never stand o' your gentry,° master bridegroom: if
your legs be no better than your arms,° you'll be able to stand upon
neither shortly.   115

TOUCHSTONE An't please your good worship, sir, there are two sorts
of gentlemen.

SIR PETRONEL What mean you, sir?

TOUCHSTONE Bold to put off my hat to your worship—

SIR PETRONEL Nay, pray forbear, sir, and then forth with your two   120
sorts of gentlemen.

TOUCHSTONE If your worship will have it so. I say there are two sorts
of gentlemen. There is a gentleman artificial, and a gentleman natural; now, though, your worship be a gentleman natural.° Work
upon that now!   125

QUICKSILVER Well said, old Touchstone. I am proud to hear thee
enter a set° speech, i'faith. Forth, I beseech thee.

TOUCHSTONE Cry you mercy,° sir, your worship's a gentleman I do
not know. If you be one of my acquaintance you're very much
disguised, sir.   130

QUICKSILVER Go to, old quipper! Forth with thy speech I say.

TOUCHSTONE What, sir, my speeches were ever in vain to your gracious worship, and therefore, till I speak to you gallantry indeed,° I
will save my breath for my broth° anon. Come, my poor son and
daughter, let us hide ourselves in our poor humility and live safe: 135
ambition consumes itself, with the very show. Work upon that now.

    [*Exeunt Touchstone, Golding, and Mildred*]

GERTRUDE Let him go, let him go, for God's sake! Let him make his
prentice his son, for God's sake! Give away his daughter, for God's
sake!—And when they come a-begging to us, for God's sake, let's
laugh at their good husbandry, for God's sake! Farewell, sweet   140
knight, pray thee make haste after.

SIR PETRONEL What shall I say? I would not have thee go.

QUICKSILVER [*singing*]

> *Now, O now, I must depart;*
> *Parting though it absence move.°*

This ditty, knight, do I see in thy looks in capital letters.° [*Sings again*] 145

> *What a grief 'tis to depart,*
> *And leave the flower that has my heart?*
> *My sweet lady, and alack for woe,*
> *Why should we part so?*

Tell truth, knight, and shame all dissembling lovers. Does not your   150
pain lie on that side?°

SIR PETRONEL If it do, canst thou tell me how I may cure it?

QUICKSILVER Excellent easily. Divide yourself in two halves, just by
the girdlestead,°—send one half with your lady, and keep the
other to yourself—or else do as all true lovers do, part with your   155
heart and leave your body behind. I have seen't done a hundred
times. 'Tis as easy a matter for a lover to part without a heart
from his sweetheart, and he ne'er the worse, as for a mouse to get
from a trap and leave her tail behind her. See, here comes the
writings.   160

Enter Security with a Scrivener

SECURITY Good morrow to my worshipful lady. I present your
ladyship with this writing, to which, if you please to set your hand°
with your knight's, a velvet gown shall attend your journey, o' my
credit.

GERTRUDE What writing is it, knight?   165

SIR PETRONEL The sale, sweetheart, of the poor tenement I told thee
of, only to make a little money to send thee down furniture for my
castle, to which my hand shall lead thee.

GERTRUDE Very well. Now give me your pen, I pray.

QUICKSILVER [*aside*] It goes down without chewing,° i'faith.   170

SECURITY Your worships deliver this as your deed?

SIR PETRONEL AND GERTRUDE We do.

GERTRUDE So now, knight, farewell till I see thee.

SIR PETRONEL All farewell to my sweetheart.

MISTRESS TOUCHSTONE God b' w' ye, son knight.   175

SIR PETRONEL Farewell, my good mother.

GERTRUDE Farewell, Frank, I would fain take thee down° if I could.

QUICKSILVER I thank your good ladyship. Farewell, Mistress
Sindefy.

Exeunt [all, except Sir Petronel, Quicksilver, and Security]

SIR PETRONEL O, tedious voyage, whereof there is no end! What will   180
they think of me?

QUICKSILVER Think what they list!—They longed for a vagary° into
the country, and now they are fitted: so a woman marry to ride in a
coach, she cares not if she rides to her ruin. 'Tis the great end of
many marriages. This is not the first time a lady has rid a false   185
journey in her coach,° I hope.

SIR PETRONEL Nay, 'tis no matter, I care little what they think: he
that weighs men's thoughts has his hands full of nothing. A man in

the course of this world should be like a surgeon's instrument,
work in the wounds of others and feel nothing himself. The   190
sharper, and subtler, the better.

QUICKSILVER As it falls out now, knight, you shall not need to devise
excuses or endure her outcries when she returns, we shall now be
gone before where they cannot reach us.

SIR PETRONEL Well, my kind compeer,° you have now th'assurance   195
We both can make you. Let me now entreat you
The money we agreed may be brought
To the Blue Anchor near to Billingsgate,
By six o'clock, where I and my chief friends
Bound for this voyage will with feasts attend you.   200

SECURITY The money, my most honourable compeer,
Shall without fail observe your appointed hour.

SIR PETRONEL Thanks, my dear gossip. I must now impart
To your approved love, a loving secret,
As one on whom my life doth more rely   205
In friendly trust than any man alive.
Nor shall you be the chosen secretary°
Of my affections for affection only;
For I protest, if God bless my return,
To make you partner in my action's gain   210
As deeply as if you had ventured with me
Half my expenses. Know, then, honest gossip,
I have enjoyed with such divine contentment
A gentlewoman's bed, whom you well know,
That I shall ne'er enjoy this tedious voyage,   215
Nor live the least part of the time it asketh,
Without her presence, so I 'thirst and hunger'
To taste the dear feast of her company.
And if the 'hunger' and the 'thirst' you vow,
As my sworn gossip, to my wishèd good   220
Be, as I know it is, unfeigned and firm,
Do me an easy favour in your power.

SECURITY Be sure, brave gossip, all that I can do
To my best nerve° is wholly at your service.
Who is the woman, first, that is your friend?°   225

SIR PETRONEL The woman is your learned counsel's wife,
The lawyer, Master Bramble,—whom would you
Bring out this even, in honest neighbourhood,°
To take his leave with you of me, your gossip,—

I, in the meantime, will send this my friend   230
Home to his house, to bring his wife disguised
Before his face into our company:
For love hath made her look for such a wile,
To free her from his tyrannous jealousy.
And I would take this course before another   235
In stealing her away to make us sport,
And to gull his circumspection the more grossly.
And I am sure that no man like yourself
Hath credit with him to entice his jealousy
To so long stay abroad, as may give time   240
To her enlargement,° in such safe disguise.

SECURITY A pretty, pithy,° and most pleasant project!
Who would not strain a point of neighbourhood
For such a point-device,° that as the ship
Of famous Draco,° went about the world,   245
Will wind about the lawyer, compassing
The world° himself,° he hath it° in his arms:
And that's enough, for him, without his wife.
A lawyer is ambitious, and his head
Cannot be praised, nor raised too high,   250
With any fork° of highest knavery.
I'll go fetch him straight.
        Exit Security

SIR PETRONEL So, so. Now, Frank, go thou home to his house,
Stead of his lawyer's, and bring his wife hither;
Who just like the lawyer's wife, is prisoned   255
With his stern usurious jealousy; which could never
Be over-reached° thus, but with over-reaching.°
        Enter Security

SECURITY And, Master Francis, watch you th'instant time
To enter with his exit.° 'Twill be rare,
Two fine horned beasts, a camel and a lawyer!   260
        Exit [Security]

QUICKSILVER How the old villain joys in villainy!
        Enter Security

SECURITY And hark you, gossip, when you have her here,
Have your boat ready, ship her to your ship
With utmost haste, lest Master Bramble stay you.
To o'er reach that head that outreacheth° all heads?   265
'Tis a trick rampant,° 'tis a very quiblin!°

I hope this harvest to pitch cart with lawyers,°
Their heads will be so forked. This sly touch
Will get apes° to invent a number such!
    Exit [*Security*]

QUICKSILVER Was ever a rascal honeyed° so with poison?   270

      'He that delights in slavish avarice
      Is apt to joy in every sort of vice.'

Well, I'll go fetch his wife, whilst he the lawyer.

SIR PETRONEL But stay, Frank, let's think how we may disguise her
  Upon this sudden.°

QUICKSILVER   God's me, there's the mischief!   275
  But hark you, here's an excellent device—
  'Fore God, a rare one—I will carry her
  A sailor's gown and cap, and cover her—
  And a player's beard.

SIR PETRONEL   And what upon her head?

QUICKSILVER I tell you, a sailor's cap! 'Slight, God forgive me,   280
  What kind of figent° memory have you?

SIR PETRONEL Nay then, what kind of figent wit hast thou?
  A sailor's cap? How shall she put it off
  When thou present'st her to our company?

QUICKSILVER Tush, man, for that, make her a saucy sailor.   285

SIR PETRONEL Tush, tush, 'tis no fit sauce for such sweet mutton!°
  I know not what t'advise.
    Enter Security with his wife's gown

SECURITY   Knight, knight, a rare device!

SIR PETRONEL [*aside to Quicksilver*] 'Swounds, yet again.

QUICKSILVER   What stratagem have you now?

SECURITY The best that ever. You talked of disguising?

SIR PETRONEL Ay, marry, gossip, that's our present care.   290

SECURITY Cast care away,° then; here's the best device
  For plain Security (for I am no better)
  I think that ever lived. Here's my wife's gown,
  Which you may put upon the lawyer's wife,
  And which I brought you sir, for two great reasons;   295
  One is, that Master Bramble may take hold
  Of some suspicion that it is my wife,
  And gird° me so, perhaps with his law wit;
  The other, which is policy° indeed,
  Is that my wife may now be tied at home,   300

Having no more but her old gown abroad,°
And not show me a quirk,° while I firk° others.
Is not this rare?
SIR PETRONEL AND QUICKSILVER The best that ever was.
SECURITY Am I not born to furnish,° gentlemen?
SIR PETRONEL O, my dear gossip.
SECURITY   Well, hold, Master Francis,   305
Watch when the lawyer's out, and put it in.
And now I will go fetch him.
          Exit [Security]
QUICKSILVER   O, my Dad!
He goes as 'twere the devil to fetch the lawyer,°
And devil shall he be, if horns will make him.
          [Enter Security]
SIR PETRONEL Why, how now, gossip, why stay you there musing?   310
SECURITY A toy,° a toy runs through my head, i'faith.
QUICKSILVER *[aside to Sir Petronel]* A pox of that head, is there more
     toys yet?
SIR PETRONEL What is it, pray thee, gossip?
SECURITY   Why, sir, what if you
Should slip away now with my wife's best gown,
I having no security for it?
QUICKSILVER   For that, I hope, Dad, you will take our words.   315
SECURITY Ay, by th' mass, your word, that's a proper staff,
For wise Security to lean upon!
But 'tis no matter, once I'll trust my name
On your cracked° credits, let it take no shame.
Fetch the wench, Frank.
          Exit [Security]
QUICKSILVER   I'll wait upon you, sir.   320
And fetch you over, you were ne'er so fetched.°
Go, to the tavern, knight, your followers
Dare not be drunk, I think, before their captain.
          Exit [Quicksilver]
SIR PETRONEL Would I might lead them to no hotter service
Till our Virginian gold were in our purses.   325
          Exit

[3.3]

Enter Seagull, Spendall, and Scapethrift in the tavern,° with a Drawer°

SEAGULL Come drawer, pierce your neatest hogsheads,° and let's have cheer, not fit for your Billingsgate tavern, but for our Virginian colonel. He will be here instantly.

DRAWER You shall have all things fit, sir. Please you have any more wine?   5

SPENDALL More wine, slave? Whether we drink it or no, spill it and draw more.

SCAPETHRIFT Fill all the pots in your house with all sorts of liquor, and let 'em wait on us here like soldiers in their pewter coats.° And though we do not employ them now, yet we will maintain 'em till we do.   10

DRAWER Said like an honourable captain. You shall have all you can command, sir.

Exit Drawer

SEAGULL Come boys, Virginia longs till we share the rest of her maidenhead.°

SPENDALL Why, is she inhabited already with any English?   15

SEAGULL A whole country of English is there man, bred of those that were left there in '79. They have married with the Indians and make 'em bring forth as beautiful faces as any we have in England. And therefore the Indians are so in love with 'em, that all the treasure they have they lay at their feet.°   20

SCAPETHRIFT But is there such treasure there, Captain, as I have heard?

SEAGULL I tell thee, gold is more plentiful there than copper is with us; and for as much red copper as I can bring, I'll have thrice the weight in gold. Why man, all their dripping pans° and their cham-   25
berpots are pure gold, and all the chains with which they chain up the streets° are massy gold, all the prisoners they take are fettered in gold, and for rubies and diamonds they go forth on holidays and gather 'em by the seashore to hang on their children's coats, and stick in their caps, as commonly as our children wear saffron gilt°   30
brooches, and groats with holes in 'em.

SCAPETHRIFT And is it a pleasant country withal?

SEAGULL As ever the sun shined on: temperate and full of all sorts of excellent viands. Wild boar is as common there as our tamest bacon is here, venison as mutton. And then you shall live freely there,   35 without sergeants, or courtiers, or lawyers, or intelligencers,° only a few industrious Scots perhaps, who indeed are dispersed over the face of the whole earth. But as for them, there are no greater friends to Englishmen and England, when they are out on't, in the world, than they are. And for my part, I would a hundred thousand of 'em were there, for we are all one countrymen now, ye know; and we should find ten times more comfort of them there, than we do here. Then for your means to advancement, there, it is simple, and not preposterously° mixed: you may be an alderman there and never be a scavenger;° you may be a nobleman, and never be a slave; you may come to preferment enough, and never be a pander; to riches and fortune enough and have never the more villainy, nor the less wit.

SCAPETHRIFT God's me! And how far is it thither?

SEAGULL Some six week's sail, no more, with any indifferent° good wind. And if I get to any part of the coast of Africa I'll sail thither with any wind. Or, when I come to Cape Finisterre,° there's a fore-right wind continually wafts us till we come again at Virginia. See, our colonel's come.

    Enter Sir Petronel

SIR PETRONEL Well met, good Captain Seagull, and my noble gentlemen! Now the sweet hour of our freedom is at hand. Come drawer, fill us some carouses, and prepare us for the mirth that will be occasioned presently. Here will be a pretty wench, gentlemen, that will bear us company all the voyage!

SEAGULL Whatsoever she be, here's to her health, noble colonel, both with cap and knee.°

SIR PETRONEL Thanks, kind Captain Seagull, she's one I love dearly, and must not be known till we be free from all that know us. And so, gentlemen, here's to her health!

SPENDALL [AND] SCAPETHRIFT Let it come, worthy colonel—we do hunger and thirst for it.

SIR PETRONEL Afore heaven, you have hit the phrase of one° that her presence will touch, from the foot to the forehead,° if ye knew it.

SPENDALL Why then, we will join his forehead with her health, sir: and captain Scapethrift, here's to 'em both.

    [*They kneel and drink a toast.*] *Enter Security and*
    Bramble

SECURITY See, see, Master Bramble! 'Fore heaven their voyage cannot but prosper, they are o'their knees for success to it!

BRAMBLE And they pray to god Bacchus.

SECURITY God save my brave colonel with all his tall° captains and

corporals! See, sir, my worshipful, learned counsel Master Bramble, is come to take his leave of you.   75

SIR PETRONEL Worshipful Master Bramble, how far do you draw us
into the sweet briar of your kindness? Come, Captain Seagull,
another health to this rare Bramble, that hath never a prick° about
him.

SEAGULL I pledge his most smooth disposition, sir. Come, Master   80
Security, bend your supporters° and pledge this notorious° health
here.

SECURITY Bend you yours likewise, Master Bramble, for it is you
shall pledge me.

SEAGULL Not so, Master Security, he must not pledge his own health.   85

SECURITY No, Master Captain?

    Enter Quicksilver with Winifred disguised

Why then, here's one is fitly come to do him that honour.

QUICKSILVER Here's the gentlewoman your cousin, sir, whom with
much entreaty I have brought to take her leave of you in a tavern,
ashamed whereof, you must pardon her if she put not off her mask.°   90

SIR PETRONEL Pardon me, sweet cousin, my kind desire to see you
before I went made me so importunate to entreat your presence
here.

SECURITY How now, Master Francis? Have you honoured this
presence with a fair gentlewoman?   95

QUICKSILVER Pray sir, take you no notice of her, for she will not be
known to you.

SECURITY But my learned counsel, Master Bramble here, I hope may
know her.

QUICKSILVER No more than you, sir, at this time. His learning° must   100
pardon her.

SECURITY Well, God pardon her, for my part, an I do I'll be sworn.—
And so, Master Francis, here's to all that are going eastward tonight
towards Cuckold's Haven,° and so, to the health of Master Bramble.

QUICKSILVER [*kneeling*] I pledge it, sir. Hath it gone round,° captains?   105

SEAGULL It has, sweet Frank, and the round closes with thee.

QUICKSILVER Well, sir, here's to all eastward and toward° cuckold's,
and so to famous Cuckold's Haven, so fatally° remembered.

    He rises

SIR PETRONEL [*to Winifred*] Nay, pray thee, coz, weep not. Gossip
Security—   110

SECURITY Ay, my brave gossip.

SIR PETRONEL A word, I beseech you, sir. Our friend, Mistress

Bramble here, is so dissolved in tears that she drowns the whole
mirth of our meeting. Sweet gossip, take her aside and comfort her.

SECURITY Pity of all true love, Mistress Bramble, what weep you to   115
enjoy your love? What's the cause, lady? Is't because your husband
is so near, and your heart earns,° to have a little abused° him? Alas,
alas, the offence is too common to be respected.° So great a grace
hath seldom chanced to so unthankful a woman—to be rid of an old
jealous dotard, to enjoy the arms of a loving young knight that,   120
when your prick-less Bramble is withered° with grief of your loss,
will make you flourish afresh in the bed of a lady.

    Enter Drawer

DRAWER Sir Petronel, here's one of your watermen° come to tell you it
will be flood these three hours,° and that t'will be dangerous going
against the tide, for the sky is overcast, and there was a porpoise   125
even now seen at London Bridge, which is always the messenger of
tempests, he says.

SIR PETRONEL A porpoise? What's that to the purpose? Charge him
if he love his life to attend us. Can we not reach Blackwall,° where
my ship lies, against the tide, and in spite of tempests? Captains and   130
gentlemen, we'll begin a new ceremony at the beginning of our
voyage, which I believe will be followed of all° future adventurers.

SEAGULL What's that, good colonel?

SIR PETRONEL This, Captain Seagull—we'll have our provided supper brought aboard Sir Francis Drake's ship,° that hath compassed   135
the world, where, with full cups and banquets,° we will do sacrifice
for a prosperous voyage. My mind gives me° that some good spirits
of the waters should haunt the desert ribs of her° and be auspicious
to all that honour her memory, and will with like orgies° enter their
voyages.   140

SEAGULL Rarely conceited!° One health more to this motion and
aboard to perform it. He that will not this night be drunk, may he
never be sober.

    They compass in° Winifred, dance the drunken round, and drink
    carouses

BRAMBLE Sir Petronel, and his honourable captains in these young
services, we old servitors may be spared: we only came to take our   145
leaves, and with one health to you all, I'll be bold to do so. Here,
neighbour Security, to the health of Sir Petronel, and all his
captains.

SECURITY You must bend then, Master Bramble, [*they kneel*]—so,
now I am for you—I have one corner of my brain, I hope, fit to bear   150

one carouse more. Here lady, to you that are encompassed there, and are ashamed of our company. Ha, ha, ha, by my troth, my learned counsel Master Bramble, my mind runs so of Cuckold's Haven tonight that my head runs over with admiration.°

BRAMBLE But is that not your wife, neighbour?   155

SECURITY No, by my troth, Master Bramble. Ha, ha, ha! A pox of all Cuckold's Havens, I say!

BRAMBLE O' my faith, her garments are exceeding like your wife's.

SECURITY *Cucullus non facit monachum,*° my learned counsel.—All are not cuckolds that seem so, nor all seem not that are so. Give me   160
your hand, my learned counsel, you and I will sup somewhere else than at Sir Francis Drake's ship tonight. Adieu, my noble gossip.

BRAMBLE Good fortune, brave captains. Fair skies, God send ye.

ALL Farewell, my hearts, farewell.

SIR PETRONEL Gossip, laugh no more at Cuckold's Haven, gossip.   165

SECURITY I have done, I have done, sir, will you lead, Master Bramble? Ha, ha, ha.

SIR PETRONEL Captain Seagull, charge° a boat.

ALL A boat, a boat, a boat!

Exeunt [all except the Drawer]

DRAWER You're in a proper taking° indeed, to take a boat, especially at   170
this time of night, and against tide and tempest. They say yet, drunken men never take harm°—this night will try the truth of that proverb.

Exit

[3.4]

Enter Security

SECURITY What, Winnie? Wife, I say? Out of doors at this time! Where should I seek the gadfly?° Billingsgate, Billingsgate, Billingsgate! She's gone with the knight, she's gone with the knight! Woe be to thee, Billingsgate! A boat, a boat, a boat, a full hundred marks for a boat!°   5

Exit

Enter Slitgut, with a pair of ox horns,° discovering Cuckold's
Haven above°

SLITGUT All hail, fair haven of married men only, for there are none
but married men cuckolds. For my part, I presume not to arrive
here but in my master's behalf, a poor butcher° of East Cheap,° who
sends me to set up (in honour of Saint Luke°) these necessary
ensigns° of his homage. And up I got this morning, thus early, to get   5
up to the top of this famous tree,° that is all fruit and no leaves,° to
advance this crest of my master's occupation.° Up then!° Heaven and
Saint Luke bless me, that I be not blown into the Thames as I
climb, with this furious tempest. 'Slight, I think the devil be
abroad, in likeness of a storm, to rob me of my horns. Hark how he   10
roars. Lord! What a coil° the Thames keeps! She bears some unjust°
burden, I believe, that she kicks and curvets° thus to cast it. Heaven
bless all honest passengers that are upon her back now, for the bit is
out of her mouth I see, and she will run away with 'em. So, so, I
think I have made it look the right way, it runs against° London   15
Bridge, as it were, even full butt. And now, let me discover from
this lofty prospect what pranks the rude Thames plays in her desperate lunacy. O, me, here's a boat been cast away hard by. Alas,
alas! See one of her passengers, labouring for his life, to land at this
haven here—pray heaven he may recover° it. His next° land is even   20
just under me,—hold out yet a little, whatsoever thou art, pray,—
and take a good heart to thee! 'Tis a man; take a man's heart to thee;
yet a little further, get up o'thy legs, man! Now 'tis shallow enough.
So, so, so! Alas, he's down again! Hold up thy wind,° father—'tis a
man in a nightcap. So! Now he's got up again; now he's past the   25
worst. Yet thanks be to heaven, he comes toward me pretty and
strongly.

Enter Security without his hat, in a nightcap [and] wet band,° etc.

SECURITY Heaven, I beseech thee, how have I offended thee! Where
am I cast ashore now that I may go a righter way home by land? Let
me see. O, I am scarce able to look about me! Where is any sea-mark°   30
that I am acquainted withal?

SLITGUT Look up, father. Are you acquainted with this mark?

SECURITY What! Landed at Cuckold's Haven? Hell and damnation! I
will run back and drown myself.

He falls down

SLITGUT Poor man, how weak he is! The weak water has washed away   35
his strength.

SECURITY Landed at Cuckold's Haven? If it had not been to die
twenty times alive, I should never have 'scaped death. I will never
arise more. I will grovel here and eat dirt till I be choked. I will
make the gentle earth do that which the cruel water has denied me.   40

SLITGUT Alas, good father, be not so desperate! Rise, man. If you will,
I'll come presently and lead you home.

SECURITY Home? Shall I make any know my home that has known
me thus abroad? How low shall I crouch away, that no eye may see
me? I will creep on the earth while I live, and never look heaven in   45
the face more.

Exit [Security] creep[ing]

SLITGUT What young planet reigns now trow, that old men are so
foolish? What desperate young swaggerer would have been abroad
such a weather as this, upon the water? Ay me, see another remnant
of this unfortunate shipwreck! Or some other. A woman! I'faith, a   50
woman. Though it almost be at Saint Katherine's,° I discern it to be
a woman, for all her body is above the water, and her clothes swim
about her most handsomely. O, they bear her up most bravely!° Has
not a woman reason to love the taking up of her clothes° the better
while she lives, for this? Alas, how busy the rude Thames is about   55
her! A pox of° that wave. It will drown her, 'ifaith, 'twill drown her.
Cry God mercy,° she has 'scaped it! I thank heaven she has 'scaped
it. O, how she swims like a mermaid! Some vigilant body look out,
and save her! That's well said,° just where the priest fell in,° there's
one sets down a ladder, and goes to take her up. God's blessing o'   60
thy heart boy, now take her up in thy arms and to bed with her.
She's up, she's up! She's a beautiful woman, I warrant her, the
billows durst not devour her.

Enter the Drawer in the tavern before,° with Winifred

DRAWER How fare you now, lady?

WINIFRED Much better, my good friend, than I wish; as one desper-   65
ate of my fame,° now my life is preserved.

DRAWER Comfort yourself. That power that preserved you from
death can likewise defend you from infamy, howsoever you deserve
it. Were not you one that took boat, late this night, with a knight
and other gentlemen at Billingsgate?   70

WINIFRED Unhappy that I am, I was.

DRAWER I am glad it was my good hap to come down thus far after

you, to a house of my friend's here in Saint Katherine's, since I am
now happily made a mean to your rescue from the ruthless tempest,
which, when you took boat, was so extreme, and the gentleman that   75
brought you forth so desperate and unsober, that I feared long ere
this I should hear of your shipwreck, and therefore, with little other
reason, made thus far this way. And this I must tell you, since
perhaps you may make use of it, there was left behind you at our
tavern brought by a porter, hired by the young gentleman that   80
brought you, a gentlewoman's gown, hat, stockings, and shoes,
which if they be yours, and you please to shift you,° taking hard bed
here in this house of my friend, I will presently go fetch you.

WINIFRED Thanks, my good friend, for your more than good news.
The gown with all things bound with it are mine which, if you   85
please to fetch as you have promised, I will boldly receive the kind
favour you have offered, till your return,—entreating you,—by all
the good you have done in preserving me hitherto,—to let none
take knowledge of what favour you do me, or where such a one as I
am bestowed, lest you procure me much more damage in my fame   90
than you have done me pleasure in preserving my life.

DRAWER Come in, lady, and shift yourself; resolve,° that nothing, but
your own pleasure, shall be used in your discovery.°

WINIFRED Thank you, good friend. The time may come I shall requite
you.   95
    Exeunt [Winifred and Drawer]

SLITGUT See, see, see! I hold° my life, there's some other a-taking up°
at Wapping,° now! Look, what a sort° of people cluster about the
gallows° there! In good troth it is so. O, me! A fine young gentleman!
What? And taken up at the gallows? Heaven grant he be not one
day taken down° there: 'o my life it is ominous. Well, he is delivered   100
for the time, I see the people have all left him, yet I will keep my
prospect awhile, to see if any more have been shipwrecked.
    Enter Quicksilver bareheaded

QUICKSILVER Accursed that ever I was saved or born.
How fatal° is my sad arrival here?
As if the stars and providence spake to me,   105
And said, 'The drift of all unlawful courses,
Whatever end they dare propose themselves,
In frame of° their licentious policies,
In the firm order of just Destiny,
They are the ready highways to our ruins.'   110
I know not what to do, my wicked hopes

Are, with this tempest, torn up by the roots.
O, which way shall I bend my desperate steps,
In which unsufferable shame and misery
Will not attend them? I will walk this bank   115
And see if I can meet the other relics
Of our poor shipwrecked crew, or hear of them.
The knight, alas, was so far gone with wine,
And th'other three, that I refused their boat,
And took the hapless woman in another,   120
Who cannot but be sunk, whatever Fortune
Hath wrought upon the others' desperate lives.
          [*Exit Quicksilver.*] *Enter Sir Petronel, and Seagull,*
          bareheaded

SIR PETRONEL Zounds, Captain, I tell thee, we are cast up o'the coast
of France. 'Sfoot, I am not drunk still, I hope? Dost remember
where we were last night?   125

SEAGULL No, by my troth, knight, not I, but methinks we have been a
horrible while upon the water and in the water.

SIR PETRONEL Ay me, we are undone forever. Hast any money about
thee?

SEAGULL Not a penny, by heaven.   130

SIR PETRONEL Not a penny betwixt us, and cast ashore in France?

SEAGULL Faith, I cannot tell that. My brains nor mine eyes are not
my own, yet.
          Enter two Gentlemen

SIR PETRONEL 'Sfoot, wilt not believe me? I know by the elevation of
the pole,° and by the altitude and latitude of the climate.° See! Here   135
comes a couple of French gentlemen. I knew we were in France:
dost thou think our Englishmen are so Frenchified,° that a man
knows not whether he be in France or in England when he sees
'em? What shall we do? We must e'en to 'em, and entreat some
relief of 'em. Life is sweet, and we have no other means to relieve   140
our lives now, but their charities.

SEAGULL Pray you, do you beg on 'em then,—you can speak French.

SIR PETRONEL *Monsieur, plaist-il d'avoir pitié de notre grand infor-*
tunes? Je suis un pauvre chevalier d'Angleterre, qui a souffrit l'infortune
de naufrage.°   145

1ST GENTLEMAN *Un pauvre chevalier d'Angleterre?*

SIR PETRONEL *Oui, monsieur, il est trop vrai, mais vous savez bien nous*
sommes tous subject a fortune.°

2ND GENTLEMAN A poor knight of England? A poor knight of

Windsor,° are you not? Why speak you this broken French, when   150
you're a whole Englishman? On what coast are you, think you?

SIR PETRONEL On the coast of France, sir.

1ST GENTLEMAN On the coast of Dogs, sir. You're i'th' Isle o' Dogs,° I
tell you. I see you've been washed in the Thames here, and I believe
ye were drowned in a tavern before, or else you would never have   155
took boat in such a dawning as this was. Farewell, farewell! We will
not know you for shaming of you. I ken the man weel,° he's one of
my thirty pound knights.°

2ND GENTLEMAN No, no, this is he that stole his knighthood o'the
grand day,° for four pound, giving to a page° all the money in's purse,   160
I wot well.

        Exeunt [Gentlemen]

SEAGULL 'Sdeath, colonel, I knew you were overshot.°

SIR PETRONEL Sure, I think now indeed, Captain Seagull, we were
something overshot.

        Enter Quicksilver

What! My sweet Frank Quicksilver! Dost thou survive to rejoice   165
me? But what? Nobody at thy heels, Frank? Ay me, what is become
of poor Mistress Security?

QUICKSILVER Faith, gone quite from her name, as she is from her
fame, I think. I left her to the mercy of the water.

SEAGULL Let her go, let her go: let us go to our ship at Blackwall and   170
shift us.°

SIR PETRONEL Nay, by my troth, let our clothes rot upon us, and let
us rot in them: twenty to one our ship is attached° by this time. If we
set her not under sail by this last tide, I never looked for any other.
Woe, woe is me, what shall become of us? The last money we could   175
make, the greedy Thames has devoured, and if our ship be
attached, there is no hope can relieve us.

QUICKSILVER 'Sfoot, knight, what an unknightly faintness transports
thee? Let our ship sink,° and all the world that's without us be taken
from us, I hope I have some tricks in this brain of mine shall not let   180
us perish.

SEAGULL Well said, Frank, i'faith. O, my nimble-spirited Quicksilver.
'Fore God, would thou hadst been our colonel.

SIR PETRONEL I like his spirit rarely, but I see no means he has to
support that spirit.   185

QUICKSILVER Go to, knight, I have more means than thou art aware
of. I have not lived amongst goldsmiths and gold-makers all this
while, but I have learned something worthy of my time with 'em.

And, not to let thee stink where thou stand'st, knight, I'll let thee
know some of my skill presently.   190

SEAGULL Do, good Frank, I beseech thee.

QUICKSILVER I will blanch copper° so cunningly, that it shall endure
all proofs, but the test.° It shall endure malleation,° it shall have the
ponderosity of Luna,° and the tenacity° of Luna, by no means friable.°

SIR PETRONEL 'Slight, where learn'st thou these terms, trow?   195

QUICKSILVER Tush, knight, the terms of this art every ignorant
quacksalver is perfect in. But I'll tell you how yourself shall blanch
copper thus cunningly. Take arsenic, otherwise called realga°
(which, indeed, is plain ratsbane). Sublime° 'em three or four times,
then take the sublimate of this realga, and put 'em into a glass, into   200
chymia,° and let 'em have a convenient decoction natural,° four and
twenty hours, and he will become perfectly fixed.° Then take this
fixed powder, and project him upon well-purged copper,° *et habebis
magisterium.*°

SIR PETRONEL AND SEAGULL Excellent Frank, let us hug thee.   205

QUICKSILVER Nay, this I will do besides. I'll take you off twelve pence
from every angel, with a kind of aquafortis, and never deface any
part of the image.

SIR PETRONEL But then it will want° weight?

QUICKSILVER You shall restore that thus: take your *sal alchyme°* pre-   210
pared, and your distilled urine, and let your angels lie in it but four
and twenty hours, and they shall have their perfect weight again.
Come, on now, I hope this is enough to put some spirit into the
livers of you, I'll infuse more another time. We have saluted the
proud air long enough with our bare sconces,° now will I have you to   215
a wench's house of mine at London, there make shift to shift us,
and after take such fortunes as the stars shall assign us.

SIR PETRONEL AND SEAGULL Notable Frank, we will ever adore
thee!

> *Exeunt [Quicksilver, Sir Petronel, and Seagull]. Enter Drawer*
> *with Winifred, new attired*

WINIFRED Now, sweet friend, you have brought me near enough your   220
tavern, which I desired that I might with some colour° be seen near,
enquiring for my husband, who I must tell you stole thither last
night with my wet gown we have left at your friends, which,—to
continue your former honest kindness,—let me pray you to keep
close from the knowledge of any. And so, with all vow of your   225
requital, let me now entreat you to leave me to my woman's wit and
fortune.

DRAWER All shall be done you desire. And so, all the fortune you can
wish for, attend you.

Exit Drawer. Enter Security

SECURITY I will once more to this unhappy tavern before I shift one   230
rag of me more, that I may there know what is left behind, and
what news of their passengers. I have brought me a hat and band
with the little money I had about me, and made the streets a little
leave staring at my nightcap.

WINIFRED O, my dear husband! Where have you been tonight? All   235
night abroad at taverns? Rob me of my garments? And fare as one
run away from me? Alas! Is this seemly for a man of your credit? Of
your age? And affection to your wife?

SECURITY What should I say? How miraculously sorts this?° Was not I
at home, and called thee last night?   240

WINIFRED Yes, sir, the harmless sleep you broke, and my answer to
you would have witnessed it, if you had had the patience to have
stayed and answered me, but your so sudden retreat made me
imagine you were gone to Master Bramble's, and so rested patient,
and hopeful of your coming again, till this your unbelieved° absence   245
brought me abroad with no less than wonder to seek you, where the
false knight had carried you.

SECURITY Villain, and monster that I was, how have I abused thee!
I was suddenly gone, indeed! For my sudden jealousy trans-
ferred° me. I will say no more but this, dear wife: I suspected   250
thee.

WINIFRED Did you suspect me?

SECURITY Talk not of it, I beseech thee, I am ashamed to imagine it. I
will home, I will home, and every morning, on my knees, ask thee
heartily forgiveness.   255

Exeunt [Security and Winifred]

[SLITGUT] Now will I descend my honourable prospect, the farthest
seeing sea-mark of the world—no marvel then if I could see two
miles about me. I hope the rude tempest's anger be now over-
blown, which sure I think heaven sent as a punishment, for pro-
faning holy Saint Luke's memory with so ridiculous a custom.   260
Thou dishonest satire,° farewell to honest married men. Farewell
to all sorts and degrees of thee. Farewell, thou horn of hunger,°
that call'st the Inns of Court° to their manger.° Farewell, thou
horn of abundance,° that adornest the headsmen° of the commonwealth. Farewell, thou horn of direction, that is the city   265
lantern. Farewell, thou horn of pleasure,° the ensign of the

huntsman. Farewell, thou horn of destiny,° th' ensign of the
married man. Farewell, thou horn tree that bearest nothing but
stone fruit.°

Exit

[4.2]

Enter Touchstone

TOUCHSTONE Ha, sirrah! Thinks my knight adventurer we can° no
point of our compass? Do we not know north-north-east? North-
east-and-by-east? East-and-by-north? Nor plain eastward? Ha?
Have we never heard of Virginia? Nor the *cavallaria*?° Nor the
colonoria?° Can we discover no discoveries? Well, mine errant Sir   5
Flash, and my runagate Quicksilver, you may drink drunk, crack°
cans, hurl away a brown° dozen of Monmouth caps° or so, in sea-
ceremony to your *boon voyage*, but for reaching any coast save the
coast of Kent or Essex, with this tide, or with this fleet, I'll be your
warrant for a Gravesend° toast. There's that gone afore will stay   10
your admiral,° and vice-admiral, and rear admiral, were they all (as
they are) but one pinnace, and under sail, as well as a remora,° doubt
it not; and from this sconce,° without either powder or shot. Work
upon that now. Nay, and° you'll show tricks, we'll vie° with you a
little. My daughter, his lady, was sent eastward, by land, to a castle   15
of his, i'th' air (in what region° I know not) and, as I hear, was glad
to take up her lodging in her coach, she and her two waiting-
women, her maid and her mother, like three snails in a shell, and
the coachman atop 'em, I think. Since, they have all found the way
back again by weeping cross.° But I'll not see 'em. And for two of   20
'em, madam and her malkin,° they are like to bite of the bridle° for
William,° as the poor horses have done all this while that hurried
'em, or else go graze o'the common.°—So should my Dame Touchstone too, but she has been my cross these thirty years, and I'll now
keep her, to fright away sprites,° i'faith. I wonder I hear no news of   25
my son Golding? He was sent for to the Guildhall,° this morning
betimes, and I marvel° at the matter. If I had not laid up comfort,
and hope in him, I should grow desperate of all. See, he is come
i'my thought!° How now, son? What news at the Court of
Aldermen?°   30

Enter Golding

GOLDING Troth, sir, an accident somewhat strange, else it hath little
in it worth reporting.

TOUCHSTONE What? It is not borrowing of money then?

GOLDING No, sir, it hath pleased the worshipful commoners° of the
City to take me one i' their number at presentation of the inquest.°   35

TOUCHSTONE Ha!

GOLDING And the alderman of the ward wherein I dwell to appoint
me his deputy—

TOUCHSTONE How!

GOLDING In which place, I have had an oath ministered me since I   40
went.

TOUCHSTONE Now my dear and happy son! Let me kiss thy new
worship, and a little boast mine own happiness in thee. What a
fortune was it (or rather my judgement, indeed) for me, first to see
that in his disposition, which a whole city so conspires° to second?   45
Ta'en into the livery° of his company, the first day of his freedom?°
Now, not a week married, chosen commoner? And alderman's deputy in a day? Note but the reward of thy thrifty course. The wonder
of his time! Well, I will honour Master Alderman for this act, as
becomes me, and shall think the better of the Common Council's   50
wisdom and worship° while I live, for thus meeting, or but coming
after me in the opinion of his desert. Forward, my sufficient° son,
and as this is the first, so esteem it the least step to that high and
prime honour that expects° thee.

GOLDING Sir, as I was not ambitious of this, so I covet no higher   55
place.—It hath dignity enough, if it will but save me from
contempt. And I had rather had my bearing in this, or any
other office, should add worth to it, than the place give the least
opinion° of me.

TOUCHSTONE Excellently spoken: this modest answer of thine   60
blushes, as if it said, I will wear scarlet° shortly. Worshipful son! I
cannot contain myself! I must tell thee, I hope to see thee one o'the
monuments° of our City, and reckoned among her worthies, to be
remembered the same day with the Lady Ramsey,° and grave
Gresham,° when the famous fable of Whittington and his puss°   65
shall be forgotten, and thou and thy acts become the posies° for
hospitals, when thy name shall be written on conduits, and thy
deeds played i'thy lifetime by the best company of actors, and be
called their get-penny.° This I divine. This I prophesy.

GOLDING Sir, engage not your expectation farther than my abilities   70
will answer. I that know mine own strengths, fear 'em, and there is

so seldom a loss in promising the least, that commonly it brings
with it a welcome deceit. I have other news for you, sir.

TOUCHSTONE None more welcome, I am sure!

GOLDING They have their degrees of welcome, I dare affirm. The   75
colonel and all his company, this morning putting forth drunk from
Billingsgate, had like to have been cast away o' this side Greenwich;
and (as I have intelligence, by a false brother°) are come dropping to
town, like so many masterless men,° i' their doublets and hose,
without hat or cloak or any other—   80

TOUCHSTONE A miracle! The justice of heaven! Where are they?
Let's go presently and lay° for 'em.

GOLDING I have done that already, sir, both by constables, and other
officers, who shall take 'em at their old Anchor,°—and with less
tumult or suspicion than if yourself were seen in't—under colour°   85
of a great press° that is now abroad, and they shall here be brought
afore me.

TOUCHSTONE Prudent and politic son! Disgrace 'em all that ever
thou canst; their ship I have already arrested.° How to my wish it
falls out that thou hast the place of a justicer upon 'em! I am partly   90
glad of the injury done to me, that thou mayest punish it. Be severe
i' thy place, like a new officer o' the first quarter,° unreflected.° You
hear how our lady is come back with her train, from the invisible
castle?

GOLDING No, where is she?   95

TOUCHSTONE Within, but I have not seen her yet, nor her mother, who
now begins to wish her daughter undubbed,° they say, and that she
had walked a foot-pace° with her sister. Here they come, stand back.

Enter Mistress Touchstone, Gertrude, Mildred, [and] Sindefy
God save your ladyship! 'Save your good ladyship! Your ladyship is
welcome from your enchanted castle; so are your beauteous retinue.   100
I hear your knight errant is travelled on strange adventures. Surely,
in my mind, your ladyship hath fished fair, and caught a frog,°—as
the saying is.

MISTRESS TOUCHSTONE Speak to your father, madam, and kneel
down.   105

GERTRUDE Kneel? I hope I am not brought so low yet. Though my
knight be run away, and has sold my land, I am a lady still.

TOUCHSTONE Your ladyship says true, madam, and it is fitter and a
greater decorum that I should curtsey to you, that are a knight's
wife, and a lady, than you be brought o' your knees to me, who am a   110
poor cullion and your father.

GERTRUDE Law!° My father knows his duty.

MISTRESS TOUCHSTONE O, child!

TOUCHSTONE And therefore I do desire your ladyship, my good
Lady Flash, in all humility, to depart my obscure cottage, and   115
return in quest of your bright and most transparent castle, how
ever presently concealed to mortal eyes. And as for one poor
woman of your train here, I will take that order, she shall no longer
be a charge unto you, nor help to spend your ladyship. She shall
stay at home with me, and not go abroad, not put you to the   120
pawning of an odd coach-horse, or three wheels, but take part with
the Touchstone. If we lack, we will not complain to your ladyship.
And so, good madam, with your damsel here, please you let us see
your straight backs, in equipage.°—For truly, here is no roost for
such chickens as you are, or birds o' your feather,° if it like your   125
ladyship.

GERTRUDE Marry, fist° o' your kindness. I thought as much. Come
away, Sin, we shall as soon get a fart from a dead man,° as a farthing
of courtesy here.

MILDRED O, good sister!   130

GERTRUDE Sister, sir reverence? Come away, I say! Hunger drops out
at his nose.°

GOLDING O, madam, fair words never hurt the tongue!°

GERTRUDE How say you by that? You come out with your gold-ends°
now!   135

MISTRESS TOUCHSTONE Stay lady-daughter: good husband—

TOUCHSTONE Wife, no man loves his fetters, be they be made of
gold:° I list not° ha' my head fastened under my child's girdle.° As
she has brewed, so let her drink.° O' God's name, she went witless
to wedding,° now she may go wisely a-begging. It's but honeymoon   140
yet with her ladyship.° She has coach-horses, apparel, jewels yet
left, she needs care for no friends, nor take knowledge of father,
mother, brother, sister, or anybody. When those are pawned, or
spent, perhaps we shall return into the list of her acquaintance.

GERTRUDE I scorn it, i' faith. Come Sin.   145

　　　　Exit Gertrude [and Sindefy]

MISTRESS TOUCHSTONE O, madam, why do you thus provoke your
father, thus?

TOUCHSTONE Nay, nay, e'en let pride go afore, shame will follow
after,° I warrant you. Come, why dost thou weep now? Thou art not
the first good cow hast had an ill calf,° I trust.   150

　　　　Enter Constable

What's the news, with that fellow?

GOLDING Sir, the knight and your man Quicksilver are without.° Will
you ha 'em brought in?

TOUCHSTONE O, by any means.°

[*Exit Constable*]

And, son, here's a chair. Appear terrible unto 'em, on the first   155
interview. Let them behold the melancholy° of a magistrate and
taste the fury of a citizen in office!

GOLDING Why, sir, I can do nothing to 'em, except you charge 'em
with somewhat.

TOUCHSTONE I will charge 'em, and recharge 'em, rather than   160
authority should want foil° to set it off.

[*He offers Golding a chair*]

GOLDING No, good sir, I will not.

TOUCHSTONE Son, it is your place, by any means.

GOLDING Believe it, I will not, sir.

Enter Sir Petronel, Quicksilver, Constable, [and] Officers

SIR PETRONEL How misfortune pursues us still in our misery!   165

QUICKSILVER Would it had been my fortune to have been trussed up°
at Wapping, rather than ever ha' come here.

SIR PETRONEL Or mine, to have famished in the island.

QUICKSILVER Must Golding sit upon us?

CONSTABLE You must carry an 'M' under your girdle° to Master   170
Deputy's worship.

GOLDING What are those, Master Constable?

CONSTABLE An't please your worship, a couple of masterless men I
pressed for the Low Countries,° sir.

GOLDING Why do you not carry 'em to Bridewell,° according to your   175
order, they° may be shipped away?

CONSTABLE An't please your worship, one of 'em says he is a knight,
and we thought good to show him to your worship for our
discharge.°

GOLDING Which is he?   180

CONSTABLE This, sir.

GOLDING And what's the other?

CONSTABLE A knight's fellow, sir, an't please you.

GOLDING What? A knight and his fellow thus accoutred? Where are
their hats and feathers, and their rapiers and their cloaks?   185

QUICKSILVER O, they mock us.

CONSTABLE Nay, truly, sir, they had cast both their feathers and their
hats too, before we see° 'em. Here's all their furniture,° an't please

you, that we found. They say, knights are now to be known without
feathers, like cockerels by their spurs,° sir.   190
GOLDING What are their names, say they?
TOUCHSTONE [aside] Very well this. He should not take knowledge of
'em in his place, indeed.
CONSTABLE This is Sir Petronel Flash.
TOUCHSTONE How!   195
CONSTABLE And this, Francis Quicksilver.
TOUCHSTONE Is't possible? I thought your worship had been gone
for Virginia, sir. You are welcome home, sir. Your worship has made
a quick return, it seems, and no doubt a good voyage. Nay, pray
you, be covered,° sir. How did your biscuit° hold out, sir? Methought 200
I had seen this gentleman afore. Good Master Quicksilver! How a
degree to the southward° has changed you.
GOLDING Do you know 'em, father? [To Quicksilver and Petronel]
Forbear your offers° a little, you shall be heard anon.
TOUCHSTONE Yes, Master Deputy: I had a small venture with them 205
in the voyage, a thing called a son-in-law or so. Officers, you may let
'em stand alone, they will not run away—I'll give my word for
them. A couple of very honest gentlemen. One of them was my
prentice, Master Quicksilver here, and when he had two year to
serve, kept his whore and his hunting nag, would play his hundred 210
pound at gresco° or primero,° as familiarly, and all o' my purse, as any
bright piece of crimson° on 'em all; had his changeable trunks of
apparel,° standing at livery° with his mare, his chest of perfumed
linen, and his bathing tubs, which when I told him off why he—he
was a gentleman, and I a poor Cheapside groom. The remedy was 215
we must part. Since when he hath had the gift of gathering up some
small parcels° of mine, to the value of five hundred pound dispersed
among my customers, to furnish this his Virginian venture;
wherein this knight was the chief, Sir Flash—one that married a
daughter of mine, ladyfied her, turned two thousand pounds worth 220
of good land of hers into cash, within the first week, brought her a
new gown and a coach, sent her to seek her fortune by land, whilst
himself prepared for his fortune by sea, took in fresh flesh° at Billingsgate, for his own diet, to serve him the whole voyage,—the wife
of a certain usurer, called Security, who hath been broker for 'em in 225
all this business. Please, Master Deputy, work upon that now.
GOLDING If my worshipful father have ended?
TOUCHSTONE I have, it shall please Master Deputy.
GOLDING Well then, under correction°—

TOUCHSTONE [*aside to Golding*] Now son, come over 'em with some   230
    fine gird,° as thus: 'Knight, you shall be encountered', that is, to the
    Counter; or, 'Quicksilver, I will put you into a crucible', or so.

GOLDING Sir Petronel Flash, I am sorry to see such flashes° as these
    proceed from a gentleman of your quality and rank. For mine own
    part, I could wish I could say I could not see them: but such is the   235
    misery of magistrates, and men in place,° that they must not wink at°
    offenders. [*To Officers*] Take him aside, I will hear you anon, sir.

TOUCHSTONE I like this well, yet; there's some grace i' the knight
    left. He cries.

GOLDING Francis Quicksilver, would God thou hadst turned quack-   240
    salver, rather than run into these dissolute and lewd courses. It is a
    great pity. Thou art a proper° young man, of an honest and clean
    face, somewhat near a good one—God hath done his part in thee°—
    but thou hast made too much, and been too proud of that face, with
    the rest of thy body, for maintenance of which,—in neat° and garish   245
    attire, only to be looked upon by some light housewives,—thou hast
    prodigally consumed much of thy master's estate. And being by
    him greatly admonished, at several times, hast returned° thyself
    haughty, and rebellious, in thine answers, thundering out uncivil
    comparisons, requiting all his kindness with a coarse and harsh   250
    behaviour, never returning thanks for any one benefit, but receiving
    all, as if they had been debts to thee, and no courtesies. I must tell
    thee, Francis, these are manifest signs of an ill nature, and God
    doth often punish such pride and *outrecuidance*° with scorn and
    infamy, which is the worst of misfortune. My worshipful father,   255
    what do you please to charge them withal? From the press I will
    free 'em, Master Constable.

CONSTABLE Then I'll leave your worship, sir.

GOLDING No, you may stay, there will be other matters against 'em.

TOUCHSTONE Sir, I do charge this gallant, Master Quicksilver, on   260
    suspicion of felony, and the knight as being accessory in the receipt
    of my goods.

QUICKSILVER O, God, sir!

TOUCHSTONE Hold thy peace, impudent varlet, hold thy peace. With
    what forehead° or face dost thou offer to chop logic° with me, having   265
    run such a race of riot as thou hast done? Does not the sight of this
    worshipful man's fortune and temper confound thee, that was thy
    younger fellow in household, and now come to have the place of a
    judge upon thee? Dost not observe this? Which of all thy gallants
    and gamesters, thy swearers and thy swaggerers, will come now to   270

moan thy misfortune or pity thy penury? They'll look out a window, as thou rid'st in triumph to Tyburn, and cry, 'Yonder goes
honest Frank, mad Quicksilver'. 'He was a free boon companion,°
when he had money', says one! 'Hang him, fool,' says another! 'He
could not keep it when he had it!' 'A pox o' the cullion his master,'   275
says a third, 'he has brought him to this'—when their pox° of pleasure, and their piles° of perdition, would have been better bestowed
upon thee, that hast ventured for 'em with the best, and by the clew°
of thy knavery brought thyself weeping, to the cart of calamity.°
QUICKSILVER Worshipful master!   280
TOUCHSTONE Offer not to speak, crocodile,° I will not hear a sound
  come from thee. Thou hast learnt to whine at the play yonder.
  Master deputy, pray you commit 'em both to safe custody till I be
  able farther to charge 'em.
QUICKSILVER O, me, what an unfortunate thing am I!   285
SIR PETRONEL Will you not take security,° sir?
TOUCHSTONE Yes, marry will I, Sir Flash, if I can find him, and
  charge him as deep as the best on you. He has been the plotter of all
  this: he is your engineer,° I hear. Master Deputy, you'll dispose of
  these? In the meantime, I'll to my Lord Mayor and get his warrant   290
  to seize that serpent Security into my hands, and seal up both
  house and goods to the King's use, or my satisfaction.
GOLDING Officers, take 'em to the Counter.
QUICKSILVER [AND] SIR PETRONEL O, God.
TOUCHSTONE Nay on, on: you see the issue of your sloth. Of sloth   295
  cometh pleasure, of pleasure cometh riot, of riot comes whoring, of
  whoring comes spending, of spending comes want, of want comes
  theft, of theft comes hanging, and there is my Quicksilver fixed.
      Exeunt

[5.1]

Enter Gertrude [and] Sindefy

GERTRUDE Ah, Sin! Hast thou ever read i' the chronicle of any lady
and her waiting woman driven to that extremity that we are, Sin?

SINDEFY Not I, truly madam, and if I had, it were but cold comfort°
should come out of books, now.

GERTRUDE Why, good faith Sin, I could dine with a lamentable story, 5
now. O, hone, hone, O, no nero.° Canst thou tell ne'er a one, Sin?

SINDEFY None but mine own, madam, which is lamentable enough.
First to be stolen from my friends, which were worshipful and of
good account, by a prentice in the habit and disguise of a gentleman, and here brought up to London, and promised marriage, and 10
now likely to be forsaken, for he is in possibility to be hanged—

[Sindefy starts to weep]

GERTRUDE Nay, weep not, good Sin. My Petronel is in as good possibility as he. Thy miseries are nothing to mine, Sin. I was more than
promised marriage, Sin—I had it, Sin, and was made a lady, and by
a knight, Sin, which is now as good as no knight, Sin! And I was 15
born in London, which is more than brought up, Sin. And already
forsaken, which is past likelihood, Sin. And instead of land i' the
country, all my knight's living lies i' the Counter, Sin.—There's his
castle now!

SINDEFY Which he cannot be forced out of, madam. 20

GERTRUDE Yes, if he would live hungry a week, or two. Hunger, they
say, breaks stone walls.° But he is e'en well enough served, Sin, that
so soon as ever he had got my hand to the sale of my inheritance,
run away from me, an° I had been his punk, God bless us! Would the
Knight o' the Sun° or Palmerin of England° have used their ladies so, 25
Sin? Or Sir Lancelot? Or Sir Tristram?°

SINDEFY I do not know, madam.

GERTRUDE Then thou know'st nothing, Sin. Thou art a fool, Sin.
The knighthood nowadays are nothing like the knighthood of old
time. They rid a-horseback, ours go afoot. They went attended by 30
their squires, ours by their lackeys. They went buckled in their
armour, ours muffled in their cloaks. They travelled wildernesses
and deserts, ours dare scarce walk the streets. They were still
pressed to engage their honour, ours still° ready to pawn their
clothes. They would gallop on at sight of a monster, ours run away 35

at the sight of a sergeant. They would help poor ladies, ours make poor ladies.

SINDEFY Ay, madam, they were the knights of the Round Table at Winchester,° that sought adventures, but these of the square table at ordinaries, that sit at hazard.°

GERTRUDE True, Sin, let him vanish. And tell me what shall we pawn next?

SINDEFY Ay, marry, madam, a timely consideration, for our hostess, profane woman, has sworn by bread and salt° she will not trust us another meal.

GERTRUDE Let it stink in her hand then. I'll not be beholding° to her. Let me see, my jewels be gone, and my gowns, and my red velvet petticoat that I was married in, and my wedding silk-stockings, and all thy best apparel, poor Sin. Good faith, rather than thou shouldst pawn a rag more, I'd lay my ladyship in lavender,° if I knew where.

SINDEFY Alas, madam, your ladyship?

GERTRUDE Ay, why? You do not scorn my ladyship, though it is in a waistcoat?° God's my life, you are a peat° indeed! Do I offer to mortgage my ladyship, for you, and for your avail,° and do you turn the lip° and the alas to my ladyship?

SINDEFY No, madam, but I make question who will lend anything upon it?

GERTRUDE Who? Marry enough, I warrant you, if you'll seek 'em out. I'm sure I remember the time when I would have given a thousand pound, if I had had it, to have been a lady. And I hope I was not bred and born with the appetite alone,—some other gentle-born o'the City have the same longing I trust. And for my part, I would afford 'em a pennorth,° my ladyship is little the worse for the wearing,° and yet I would bate° a good deal of the sum. I would lend it, let me see, for forty pound in hand, Sin, that would apparel us; and ten pound a year, that would keep me, and you Sin, with our needles,° and we should never need to be beholding to our scurvy parents. Good Lord, that there are no fairies° nowadays, Sin.

SINDEFY Why, madam?

GERTRUDE To do miracles, and bring ladies money. Sure, if we lay in a cleanly house they would haunt it, Sin? I'll try. I'll sweep the chamber soon° at night, and set a dish of water o' the hearth. A fairy may come and bring a pearl or a diamond. We do not know, Sin. Or, there may be a pot of gold hid o' the backside,° if we had tools to dig for't. Why may not we two rise early i' the morning, Sin, afore anybody is up, and find a jewel in the streets worth a hundred pounds? May not some great court lady, as she comes from the revels at midnight, look out of her coach, as 'tis running, and lose such a jewel, and we find it? Ha?

SINDEFY They are pretty waking dreams, these.   80

GERTRUDE Or may not some old usurer be drunk over night, with a bag of money, and leave it behind him on a stall? For God's sake, Sin, let's rise tomorrow by break of day, and see. I protest, law, if I had as much money as an alderman, I would scatter some on't° i'the streets, for poor ladies to find when their knights were laid up.° And,   85 now I remember my song of the golden shower,° why may not I have such a fortune? I'll sing it, and try what luck I shall have after it.

    [*Singing*]

       Fond fables tell of old
       How Jove in Danaë's lap
       Fell in a shower of gold,
       By which she caught a clap;°   90
       O, had it been my hap,°
       (How'er the blow° *doth threaten)*
       So well I like the play,
       That I could wish all day   95
       And night to be so beaten.

    Enter Mistress Touchstone

O, here's my mother! Good luck, I hope. Ha' you brought any money, mother? Pray you, mother, your blessing. Nay, sweet mother, do not weep.

MISTRESS TOUCHSTONE [*weeping*] God bless you. I would I were in   100 my grave!

GERTRUDE Nay, dear mother, can you steal no more money from my father? Dry your eyes, and comfort me. Alas, it is my knight's fault, and not mine that I am in a waistcoat and attired thus simply.

MISTRESS TOUCHSTONE Simply? 'Tis better than thou deserv'st.   105 Never whimper for the matter. Thou should have looked before thou had'st leaped.° Thou wert afire to be a lady, and now your ladyship and you may both blow at the coal,° for aught I know. Self do, self have.° The hasty person never wants woe,° they say.

GERTRUDE Nay then, mother, you should ha' looked to it! A body   110 would think you were the older: I did but my kind, I.° He was a knight, and I was fit to be a lady. 'Tis not lack of liking, but lack of living,° that severs us. And you talk like yourself and a cittiner° in this, i'faith. You show what husband you come on,° iwis. You smell

o'the Touchstone. He that will do more for his daughter that he has   115
married a scurvy gold-end man, and his prentice, than he will for
his tother° daughter that has wedded a knight, and his customer. By
this light, I think he is not my legitimate father.

SINDEFY O, good madam, do not take up° your mother so.

MISTRESS TOUCHSTONE Nay, nay, let her e'en alone. Let her lady-   120
ship grieve me still with her bitter taunts and terms. I have not dole°
enough to see her in this miserable case, I? Without her velvet
gowns, without ribbons, without jewels, without French-wires,° or
cheat-bread,° or quails, or a little dog, or a gentleman usher, or
anything indeed that's fit for a lady—   125

SINDEFY Except her tongue.

MISTRESS TOUCHSTONE And I not able to relieve her neither, being
kept so short by my husband. Well, God knows my heart. I did
little think that ever she should have had need of her sister Golding.

GERTRUDE Why, mother, I ha' not yet. Alas, good mother, be not   130
intoxicate° for me, I am well enough. I would not change husbands
with my sister, I. The leg of a lark is better than the body of a kite.°

MISTRESS TOUCHSTONE I know that. But—

GERTRUDE What, sweet mother, what?

MISTRESS TOUCHSTONE It's but ill food when nothing's left but the   135
claw.

GERTRUDE That's true, mother. Aye me!

MISTRESS TOUCHSTONE Nay, sweet lady bird,° sigh not. Child,
madam. Why do you weep thus? Be of good cheer. I shall die, if you
cry and mar your complexion, thus.   140

GERTRUDE Alas, mother, what should I do?

MISTRESS TOUCHSTONE Go to thy sister's, child, she'll be proud thy
ladyship will come under her roof. She'll win thy father to release
thy knight, and redeem thy gowns, and thy coach, and thy horses,
and set thee up again.   145

GERTRUDE But will she get him to set my knight up, too?

MISTRESS TOUCHSTONE That she will, or anything else thou'lt ask her.

GERTRUDE I will begin to love her, if I thought she would do this.

MISTRESS TOUCHSTONE Try her, good chuck,° I warrant thee.

GERTRUDE Dost think she'll do't?   150

SINDEFY Ay, madam, and be glad you will receive it.

MISTRESS TOUCHSTONE That's a good maiden, she tells you true.
Come, I'll take order for° your debts i'th' ale-house.

GERTRUDE Go, Sin, and pray for thy Frank, as I will, for my Pet.

[Exeunt]

[5.2]

Enter Touchstone, Golding, [and] Wolf

TOUCHSTONE I will receive no letters, Master Wolf, you shall pardon me.

GOLDING Good father, let me entreat you.

TOUCHSTONE Son Golding, I will not be tempted. I find° mine own easy nature and know not what a well-penned subtle letter may work upon it. There may be tricks, packing,° do you see? Return with your packet, sir.

WOLF Believe it, sir, you need fear no packing here. These are but letters of submission, all.

TOUCHSTONE Sir, I do look for no submission. I will bear myself in this like blind justice.° Work upon that now. When the Sessions come, they shall hear from me

GOLDING From whom come your letters, Master Wolf?

WOLF An't please you, sir. One from Sir Petronel. Another from Master Francis Quicksilver. And a third, from old Security who is almost mad in prison. There are two to your worship: one from Master Francis, sir. Another from the knight.

TOUCHSTONE I do wonder, Master Wolf, why you should travail thus, in a business so contrary to kind,° or the nature o' your place! That you, being the keeper of a prison, should labour the release of your prisoners! Whereas methinks, it were far more natural and kindly in you to be ranging about for more, and not let these scape you have already under the tooth. But they say, you wolves, when you ha' sucked the blood once, that° they are dry, you ha' done.

WOLF Sir, your worship may descant° as you please o' my name, but I protest I was never so mortified° with any men's discourse, or behaviour in prison; yet I have had of all sorts of men i'the kingdom under my keys and almost all religions i'the land, as Papist,° Protestant, Puritan, Brownist,° Anabaptist,° Millenary,° Family o' Love,° Jew, Turk, Infidel, Atheist, Good-fellow,° etcetera.

GOLDING And which of all these, thinks Master Wolf, was the best religion?

WOLF Troth, Master Deputy, they that pay fees° best. We never examine their consciences farther.

GOLDING I believe you, Master Wolf. Good faith, sir, here's a great deal of humility i' these letters.

WOLF Humility, sir? Aye, were your worship an eyewitness of it, you would say so. The knight will i'the Knight's Ward,° do what we can, sir, and Master Quicksilver would be i'the Hole,° if we would let him. I never knew or saw prisoners more penitent, or more devout. They will sit you up all night singing of psalms, and edifying the whole prison. Only, Security sings a note too high, sometimes, because he lies i' the Two-penny Ward,° far off, and cannot take° his tune. The neighbours cannot rest for° him, but come every morning to ask what godly prisoners we have.

TOUCHSTONE Which on 'em is't is so devout, the knight or the tother?

WOLF Both, sir. But the young man especially! I never heard his like! He has cut his hair,° too. He is so well given° and has such good gifts! He can tell you almost all the stories of the *Book of Martyrs*,° and speak you all the *Sick-Man's Salve*° without book.°

TOUCHSTONE Ay, if he had had grace, he was brought up where it grew, iwis. On, Master Wolf.

WOLF And he has converted one Fangs, a sergeant, a fellow could neither write, nor read. He was called the bandog° o'the Counter, and he has brought him already to pare his nails, and say his prayers, and 'tis hoped he will sell his place shortly and become an intelligencer.°

TOUCHSTONE No more, I am coming° already. If I should give any farther ear, I were taken. Adieu, good Master Wolf. Son, I do feel mine own weakness, do not importune me. Pity is a rheum° that I am subject to, but I will resist it. Master Wolf, fish is cast away that is cast in dry pools.° Tell hypocrisy, it will not do—I have touched and tried° too often. I am yet proof,° and I will remain so. When the Sessions come, they shall hear from me. In the meantime, to all suits, to all entreaties, to all letters, to all tricks, I will be deaf as an adder,° and blind as a beetle,° lay mine ear to the ground, and lock mine eyes i' my hand, against all temptations.

Exit [*Touchstone*]

GOLDING You see, Master Wolf, how inexorable he is. There is no hope to recover° him. Pray you commend me to my brother knight, and my fellow Francis, present 'em with this small token of my love [*giving him money*]. Tell 'em I wish I could do 'em any worthier office, but in this,° 'tis desperate. Yet I will not fail to try the uttermost of my power for 'em. And, sir, as far as I have any credit with you, pray you let 'em want nothing: though I am not ambitious° they should know so much.

WOLF Sir, both your actions and your words speak you to be a true gentleman. They shall know only what is fit, and no more.

Exeunt

[5.3]

Enter Holdfast, [and] Bramble

HOLDFAST Who would you speak with, sir?

BRAMBLE I would speak with one Security that is prisoner here.

HOLDFAST You are very welcome, sir. Stay there, I'll call him to you.
Master Security.

[Security appears at the grate°]

SECURITY Who calls?   5

HOLDFAST Here's a gentleman would speak with you.

SECURITY What is he? Is't one that grafts my forehead° now I am in
prison, and comes to see how the horns shoot up and prosper?

HOLDFAST You must pardon him, sir, the old man is a little crazed
with his imprisonment.   10

SECURITY What say you to me, sir? Look you here. My learned counsel, Master Bramble! Cry you mercy, sir, when saw you my wife?

BRAMBLE She is now at my house, sir, and desired me that I would
come to visit you, and enquire of your case, that we might work
some means to get you forth.   15

SECURITY My case, Master Bramble, is stone walls, and iron grates.
You see it: this is the weakest part on't. And, for getting me forth,
no means but hang myself, and so be carried forth, from which they
have here bound me in intolerable bands.

BRAMBLE Why, but what is't you are in for, sir?   20

SECURITY For my sins, for my sins, sir, whereof marriage is the greatest. O, had I never married, I had never known this purgatory, to
which hell is a kind of cool bath in respect.° My wife's confederacy,
sir, with old Touchstone, that she might keep her *Jubilae,*° and the
feast of her new-moon.° Do you understand me, sir?   25

Enter Quicksilver

QUICKSILVER Good sir, go in and talk with him. The light does him
harm, and his example will be hurtful to the weak prisoners. Fie,
Father Security, that you'll be still so profane. Will nothing humble
you?

[As they depart] enter two Prisoners, with a Friend

FRIEND What's he?   30

1ST PRISONER O, he is a rare young man. Do you not know him?

FRIEND Not I. I never saw him, I can remember.

2ND PRISONER Why, it is he that was the gallant prentice of London,
Master Touchstone's man.

FRIEND Who, Quicksilver?   35
1ST PRISONER Ay, this is he.
FRIEND Is this he? They say he has been a gallant indeed.
[2ND] PRISONER O, the royallest fellow that ever was bred up i'the
City. He would play you° his thousand pound a night at dice; keep
knights and lords company; go with them to bawdy houses; had his   40
six men in livery;° kept a stable of hunting horses; and his wench in
her velvet gown, and her cloth of silver.° Here's one knight with him
here in prison.
FRIEND And how miserably he is changed!
1ST PRISONER O, that's voluntary in him. He gave away all his rich   45
clothes, as soon as ever he came in here, among the prisoners—and
will eat o'the basket,° for humility.
FRIEND Why will he do so?
[1ST] PRISONER Alas, he has no hope of life. He mortifies himself. He
does but linger on, till the Sessions.   50
2ND PRISONER O, he has penned the best thing, that he calls his
Repentance, or his *Last Farewell*, that ever you heard. He is a pretty
poet, and for prose.—You would wonder° how many prisoners he has
helped out, with penning petitions for 'em, and not take a penny.
Look, this is the knight, in the rug gown.° Stand by.   55
        Enter Sir Petronel, Bramble, [and] Quicksilver
BRAMBLE Sir, for Security's case, I have told him. Say he should be
condemned to be carted° or whipped, for a bawd, or so, why I'll lay
an execution on him o' two hundred pounds;° let him acknowledge a
judgement, he shall do it in half an hour; they shall not fetch him
out, without paying the execution, o'my word—   60
SIR PETRONEL But can we not be bailed, Master Bramble?
BRAMBLE Hardly, there are none of the judges in town, else you
should remove yourself in spite of him with a *habeas corpus*.° But if
you have a friend to deliver your tale sensibly° to some justice o'the
town, that he may have feeling of it—do you see?—you may be   65
bailed. For as I understand the case, 'tis only done *in terrorem*,° and
you shall have an action of false imprisonment against him when
you come out, and perhaps a thousand pound costs—
        Enter Master Wolf
QUICKSILVER How now, Master Wolf? What news? What return?°
WOLF Faith, bad all. Yonder will be no letters received. He says the   70
Sessions shall determine it. Only Master Deputy Golding commends him to you, and with this token [*giving him money*] wishes he
could do you other good.

QUICKSILVER I thank him. Good Master Bramble, trouble our quiet
   no more. Do not molest us in prison thus, with your winding   75
   devices.° Pray you, depart. For my part, I commit my cause to him
   that can succour me,—let God work his will. [*Giving money*] Master Wolf, I pray you let this be distributed among the prisoners, and
   desire 'em to pray for us.
WOLF It shall be done, Master Francis.
       [*Exit Quicksilver*]
1ST PRISONER An excellent temper!   80
2ND PRISONER Now God send him good luck.
       Exeunt [*Prisoners, Friend and Bramble*]
SIR PETRONEL But what said my father-in-law, Master Wolf?
       Enter Holdfast
HOLDFAST [*to Wolf*] Here's one would speak with you, sir.
WOLF I'll tell you anon, Sir Petronel.
       [*Exit Sir Petronel*]
   Who is't?   85
HOLDFAST A gentleman, sir, that will not be seen.
       Enter Golding
WOLF Where is he? Master Deputy! Your worship is welcome—
GOLDING Peace!
WOLF Away, sirrah.
       [*Exit Holdfast*]
GOLDING Good faith, Master Wolf, the estate° of these gentlemen, for   90
   whom you were so late and willing a suitor, does much affect me,
   and because I am desirous to do them some fair office, and find
   there is no means to make my father relent, so likely, as to bring him
   to be a spectator of their miseries, I have ventured on a device,
   which is, to make my self your prisoner—entreating, you will pres-   95
   ently go report it to my father, and, feigning an action, at suit of
   some third person, pray him by this token, [*gives him a ring*] that he
   will presently, and with all secrecy, come hither for my bail,—
   which train,° if any, I know will bring him abroad,° and then, having
   him here, I doubt not but we shall be all fortunate, in the event.°   100
WOLF Sir, I will put on my best speed to effect it. Please you come in.
GOLDING Yes. And let me rest concealed, I pray you.
       [*Exit Golding*]
WOLF See here a benefit, truly done, when it is done timely, freely,
   and to no ambition.
       Exit

[5.4]

Enter Touchstone, Mistress Touchstone, daughters [Gertrude and Mildred], Sindefy, [and] Winifred

TOUCHSTONE I will sail by you, and not hear° you, like the wise Ulysses.°

MILDRED Dear father—

MISTRESS TOUCHSTONE Husband—

GERTRUDE Father—

WINIFRED AND SINDEFY Master Touchstone—   5

TOUCHSTONE Away, sirens! I will immure myself against your cries and lock myself up to your lamentations!

MISTRESS TOUCHSTONE Gentle husband, hear me.

GERTRUDE Father, it is I, father, my Lady Flash. My sister and I am   10
friends.

MILDRED Good father.

WINIFRED Be not hardened, good Master Touchstone.

SINDEFY I pray you, sir, be merciful.

TOUCHSTONE I am deaf, I do not hear you. I have stopped mine ears   15
with shoemaker's wax,° and drunk Lethe,° and mandragora° to forget
you. All you speak to me I commit to the air.
        [Exit Touchstone.] Enter Wolf

MILDRED How now, Master Wolf?

WOLF Where's Master Touchstone? I must speak with him presently!
I have lost my breath for haste.   20

MILDRED What's the matter, sir? Pray all be well.

WOLF Master Deputy Golding is arrested upon an execution, and
desires him presently to come to him, forthwith.

MILDRED Ay me, do you hear, father?

TOUCHSTONE [*within*] Tricks, tricks, confederacy tricks, I have 'em   25
in my nose, I scent 'em.

WOLF Who's that? Master Touchstone?

MISTRESS TOUCHSTONE Why, it is Master Wolf himself, husband.

MILDRED Father.

TOUCHSTONE [*within*] I am deaf still, I say: I will neither yield to   30
the song of the siren, nor the voice of the hyena,° the tears of the
crocodile, nor the howling o' the wolf. Avoid my habitation,
monsters!

WOLF Why, you are not mad, sir? I pray you look forth, and see the
token I have brought you, sir.   35

[*Enter Touchstone*]

TOUCHSTONE Ha! What token is it?

WOLF Do you know it, sir?

TOUCHSTONE My son Golding's ring! Are you in earnest, Master Wolf?

WOLF Ay, by my faith, sir. He is in prison and required° me to use all   40
speed and secrecy to you.

TOUCHSTONE [*calling within*] My cloak there! [*To Wolf*] Pray you be
patient. I am plagued for my austerity. [*Calling within*] My cloak!
At whose suit, Master Wolf?

WOLF I'll tell you as we go, sir.   45

    Exeunt

[5.5]

Enter Friend [and] Prisoners

FRIEND Why, but is his offence such as he cannot hope of life?

1ST PRISONER Troth, it should seem so.—And 'tis great pity, for he
is exceeding penitent.

FRIEND They say he is charged but on suspicion of felony, yet.

2ND PRISONER Ay, but his master is a shrewd° fellow. He'll prove   5
great matter against him.

FRIEND I'd as lief as anything I could see his *Farewell*.

1ST PRISONER O, 'tis rarely written. Why, Toby° may get him to sing
it to you—he's not curious° to anybody.

2ND PRISONER O, no. He would that all the world should take know-   10
ledge of his *Repentance*, and he thinks he merits in't, the more
shame he suffers.

1ST PRISONER Pray thee, try what thou canst do.

2ND PRISONER I warrant you, he will not deny it—if he be not hoarse
with the often repeating of it.   15

    Exit [2nd Prisoner]

1ST PRISONER You never saw a more courteous creature than he is,
and the knight, too. The poorest prisoner of the house may command 'em. You shall hear a thing admirably penned.

FRIEND Is the knight any scholar too?

1ST PRISONER No, but he will speak very well, and discourse admir-   20
ably of running horses, and Whitefriars,° and against bawds, and of
cocks, and talk as loud as a hunter, but is none.

Enter Wolf and Touchstone

WOLF Please you stay here, sir, I'll call his worship down to you.

[*Exit Wolf.*] *Enter Quicksilver, Sir Petronel, and [2nd Prisoner]*

1ST PRISONER See, he has brought him, and the knight, too. Salute him, I pray. Sir, this gentleman, upon our report, is very desirous to   25
hear some piece of your *Repentance.*

QUICKSILVER Sir, with all my heart, and as I told Master Toby, I shall be glad to have any man a witness of it. And the more openly I profess it, I hope it will appear the heartier and the more unfeigned.

Enter Wolf and Golding

TOUCHSTONE Who is this? My man, Francis? And my son-in-law?   30

QUICKSILVER Sir, it is all the testimony I shall leave behind me to the world and my master that I have so offended.

FRIEND Good sir.

QUICKSILVER I writ it when my spirits were oppressed.

SIR PETRONEL Ay, I'll be sworn for you, Francis.   35

QUICKSILVER It is in imitation of Mannington's°—he that was hanged at Cambridge, that cut off the horse's head at a blow.

FRIEND So, sir.

QUICKSILVER To the tune of 'I wail in woe, I plunge in pain'.°

SIR PETRONEL An excellent ditty it is, and worthy of a new tune.   40

QUICKSILVER [*singing*]

> *In Cheapside famous for gold and plate,*
> *Quicksilver I did dwell of late:*
> *I had a master good and kind,*
> *That would have wrought me to his mind.*
> *He bade me still, work upon that,*   45
> *But alas I wrought I knew not what.*
> *He was a Touchstone black° but true:*
> *And told me still, what would ensue,*
> *Yet, woe is me, I would not learn,*
> *I saw, alas, but could not discern.*   50

FRIEND Excellent, excellent well.

GOLDING O, let him° alone, he° is taken already.

QUICKSILVER [*singing*]

> *I cast my coat and cap away,*
> *I went in silks and satins gay,*
> *False metal of good manners° I*   55

135

> *Did daily coin unlawfully.*
> *I scorned my master, being drunk.*
> *I kept my gelding, and my punk,*
> *And with a knight, Sir Flash by name,*
> *(Who now is sorry for the same).*   60

SIR PETRONEL I thank you, Francis.
[QUICKSILVER] [*singing*]

> *I thought by sea to run away,*
> *But Thames, and tempest, did me stay.*

TOUCHSTONE This cannot be feigned, sure. Heaven pardon my
severity—the ragged colt may prove a good horse.°   65
GOLDING [*aside*] How he listens! And is transported! He has forgot
me.
QUICKSILVER [*singing*]

> *Still 'Eastward Ho!' was all my word,*
> *But Westward I had no regard.*
> *Nor never thought what would come after,*   70
> *As did alas his youngest daughter.*
> *At last the black ox trod o'my foot,°*
> *And I saw then what 'longed° unto't.*
> *Now cry I, Touchstone, touch me still,°*
> *And make me current° by thy skill.*   75

TOUCHSTONE And I will do it, Francis.
WOLF Stay him,° Master Deputy, now is the time, we shall lose the
song else.
FRIEND I protest it is the best that ever I heard.
QUICKSILVER How like you it, gentlemen?   80
ALL O, admirable, sir!
QUICKSILVER This stanza now following alludes to the story of Man-
nington, from whence I took my project° for my invention.
FRIEND Pray you go on, sir.
QUICKSILVER [*singing*]

> *O, Mannington thy stories show,*   85
> *Thou cutt'st a horse-head off at a blow.*
> *But I confess, I have not the force*
> *For to cut off the head of a horse,*
> *Yet I desire this grace to win,*
> *That I may cut off the horse-head of sin,*   90

> *And leave his body in the dust*
> *Of sin's highway and bogs of lust,*
> *Whereby I may take Virtue's purse,*
> *And live with her for better, for worse.*

FRIEND Admirable sir, and excellently conceited.°   95
QUICKSILVER Alas, sir.
TOUCHSTONE Son Golding and Master Wolf, I thank you: the deceit
 is welcome, especially from thee, whose charitable soul in this hath
 shown a high point of wisdom and honesty. Listen. I am ravished
 with his *Repentance*, and could stand here a whole prenticeship° to   100
 hear him.
FRIEND Forth,° good sir.
QUICKSILVER And this is the last, and the *Farewell*.
   [*He sings*]

> *Farewell Cheapside, farewell sweet trade*
> *Of goldsmiths all, that never shall fade.*   105
> *Farewell, dear fellow prentices all,*
> *And be you warned by my fall:*
> *Shun usurers, bawds and dice, and drabs,°*
> *Avoid them as you would French scabs.°*
> *Seek not to go beyond your tether,*   110
> *But cut your thongs unto your leather,°*
> *So shall you thrive by little and little,*
> *Scape Tyburn, Counters, and the Spital.°*

TOUCHSTONE And scape them shalt thou, my penitent and dear
 Francis.   115
QUICKSILVER Master!
SIR PETRONEL Father!
TOUCHSTONE I can no longer forbear to do your humility right.
 Arise, and let me honour your *Repentance*, with the hearty and
 joyful embraces of a father, and friend's love. Quicksilver, thou hast 120
 eat into my breast, Quicksilver, with the drops of thy sorrow, and
 killed the desperate° opinion I had of thy reclaim.°
QUICKSILVER O, sir, I am not worthy to see your worshipful face.
SIR PETRONEL Forgive me, father.
TOUCHSTONE Speak no more, all former passages° are forgotten and 125
 here my word shall release you. Thank this worthy brother and
 kind friend, Francis.—Master Wolf, I am their bail.
   A shout° in the prison. [*Security appears at the grate*]

SECURITY Master Touchstone? Master Touchstone?

TOUCHSTONE Who's that?

WOLF Security, sir.   130

SECURITY Pray you, sir, if you'll be won with a song, hear my lamentable tune, too:
>   [*He sings*]

>   *O, Master Touchstone,*
>   *My heart is full of woe;*
>   *Alas, I am cuckold:*   135
>   *And why should it be so?*
>   *Because I was a usurer*
>   *And bawd, as all you know,*
>   *For which, again I tell you,*
>   *My heart is full of woe.*   140

TOUCHSTONE Bring him forth, Master Wolf, and release his bands.
>   [*Wolf unlocks the door. Enter Security*]
This day shall be sacred to mercy, and the mirth of this encounter
in the Counter. See, we are encountered with more suitors.
>   *Enter Mistress Touchstone, Gertrude, Mildred, Sindefy, [and]*
>   *Winifred*
Save your breath, save your breath! All things have succeeded to
your wishes, and we are heartily satisfied in their events.   145

GERTRUDE Ah, runaway, runaway! Have I caught you? And how has
my poor knight done all this while?

SIR PETRONEL Dear lady-wife, forgive me.

GERTRUDE As heartily, as I would be forgiven, knight. Dear father,
give me your blessing and forgive me too. I have been proud, and   150
lascivious, father—and a fool, father—and being raised to the state
of a wanton coy thing, called a lady, father, have scorned you,
father, and my sister, and my sister's velvet cap, too, and would
make a mouth at° the City, as I rid through it, and stop mine ears at
Bow-bell. I have said your beard was a base one, father, and that you   155
looked like Twierpipe,° the taborer, and that my mother was but my
midwife.

MISTRESS TOUCHSTONE Now God forgi' you, child-madam.

TOUCHSTONE No more repetitions. What else is wanting, to make
our harmony full?   160

GOLDING Only this, sir. That my fellow Francis make amends to
Mistress Sindefy with marriage.

QUICKSILVER With all my heart.

GOLDING And Security give her a dower, which shall be all the resti-
tution he shall make of that huge mass he hath so unlawfully   165
gotten.

TOUCHSTONE Excellently devised! A good motion! What says Master
Security?

SECURITY I say anything sir, what you'll ha' me say. Would I were no
cuckold.   170

WINIFRED Cuckold, husband? Why, I think this wearing yellow° has
infected you.

TOUCHSTONE Why, Master Security, that should rather be a comfort
to you than a corrosive.° If you be a cuckold, it's an argument you
have a beautiful woman to your wife; then, you shall be made much   175
of; you shall have store of friends; never want money; you shall be
eased of much of your wedlock pain:° others will take it for you.
Besides, you being a usurer, and likely to go to Hell, the devils will
never torment you—they'll take you for one of their own race.°
Again, if you be a cuckold, and know it, you are an innocent. If you   180
know it, and endure it, a true martyr.

SECURITY I am resolved,° sir. Come hither, Winny.

TOUCHSTONE Well then, all are pleased, or shall be anon. Master
Wolf, you look hungry, methinks. Have you no apparel to lend
Francis to shift him?   185

QUICKSILVER No, sir, nor I desire none, but here make it my suit that
I may go home, through the streets, in these, as a spectacle, or
rather an example, to the children of Cheapside.

TOUCHSTONE Thou hast thy wish. Now London, look about,
And in this moral, see thy glass° run out: 190
Behold the careful father, thrifty son,
The solemn deeds, which each of us have done,
The usurer punished, and from fall so steep
The prodigal child reclaimed, and the lost sheep.

EPILOGUE

[QUICKSILVER] Stay, sir, I perceive the multitude are gathered
together to view our coming out at the Counter. See, if the streets
and the fronts of the houses be not stuck° with people, and the
windows filled with ladies,° as on the solemn day of the pageant!°
> [*To audience*]
>> O, may you find in this our pageant, here,   5
>> The same contentment, which you came to seek;
>> And as that show but draws you once a year,
>> May this attract you hither once a week.°

[*Exeunt*]

EVERY MAN IN HIS HUMOUR

BEN JONSON

THE PERSONS OF THE PLAY

Knowell,° *an old gentleman*
Edward Knowell, *his son*
Brainworm,° *the father's man,*° [*later disguised as Fitzsword*]
Master Stephen, *a country gull*°
Downright, *a plain squire*°
Wellbred, *his half brother*

Kitely, *a merchant*
Dame Kitely, *his wife*
Mistress Bridget, *his sister*
Master Matthew, *the town gull*
Thomas Cash, *Kitely's man*

Cob,° *a water-bearer*°
Tib,° *his wife*
Captain Bobadill, *a Paul's man*°

Justice Clement, *an old merry magistrate*
Roger Formal, *his clerk*
[Pages and Servants]

[Prologue]

   THE SCENE
      London

PROLOGUE

[*Enter the Prologue*]

PROLOGUE Though need make many poets, and some such
As art and nature have not bettered much;
Yet ours, for want, hath not so loved the stage
As he dare serve th'ill customs of the age,°
Or purchase your delight at such a rate,   5
As, for it, he himself must justly hate.
To make a child, now swaddled, to proceed
Man, and then shoot up, in one beard and weed,
Past threescore years;° or, with three rusty swords,
And help of some few foot-and-half-foot words,°   10
Fight over York and Lancaster's long jars,°
And in the tiring-house° bring wounds to scars.
He rather prays you will be pleased to see
One such, today, as other plays should be.
Where neither Chorus wafts you o'er the seas;   15
Nor creaking throne comes down, the boys to please;
Nor nimble squib is seen, to make afeared
The gentlewomen; nor rolled bullet heard
To say it thunders; nor tempestuous drum
Rumbles, to tell you when the storm doth come;°   20
But deeds, and language, such as men do use;
And persons, such as Comedy would choose,
When she would show an image of the times,
And sport with human follies, not with crimes,
Except we make 'em such by loving still   25
Our popular errors, when we know they're ill.°
I mean such errors, as you'll all confess
By laughing at them, they deserve no less;
Which when you heartily do, there's hope left, then,
You, that have so graced monsters,° may like men.   30

[*Exit*]

1.1

Enter Knowell [and] Brainworm

KNOWELL A goodly day toward° and a fresh morning! Brainworm,
  Call up your young master, bid him rise, sir:
  Tell him I have some business to employ him.

BRAINWORM I will, sir, presently.

KNOWELL   But hear you, sirrah,
  If he be at his book,° disturb him not.

BRAINWORM   Well, sir.   5

  [Exit Brainworm]

KNOWELL How happy yet should I esteem myself
  Could I, by any practice, wean the boy
  From one vain course of study he affects.
  He is a scholar, if a man may trust
  The liberal voice of fame in her report,   10
  Of good account in both our universities,°
  Either of which hath favoured him with graces.°
  But their indulgence must not spring in me
  A fond° opinion that he cannot err.
  Myself was once a student and, indeed,   15
  Fed with the self-same humour he is now,
  Dreaming on nought but idle poetry,
  That fruitless and unprofitable art,
  Good unto none, but least to the professors,°
  Which, then, I thought the mistress of° all knowledge: 20
  But since, time and the truth have waked my judgement,
  And reason taught me better to distinguish
  The vain from th'useful learnings.

  [Enter Stephen]

                                    Cousin Stephen!
  What news with you that you are here so early?

STEPHEN Nothing, but e'en come to see how you do, uncle.   25

KNOWELL That's kindly done, you are welcome, coz.

STEPHEN Ay, I know that sir, I would not ha' come else.
  How do my cousin Edward, uncle?

KNOWELL O, well, coz, go in and see; I doubt° he be scarce stirring yet.

STEPHEN Uncle, afore I go in can you tell me an he have e'er a° book of   30
  the sciences of hawking and hunting? I would fain borrow it.

KNOWELL Why, I hope you will not a-hawking now, will you?

STEPHEN No wusse,° but I'll practice against° next year uncle. I have
    brought me a hawk, and a hood and bells° and all; I lack nothing but
    a book to keep it by.°   35

KNOWELL O, most ridiculous.

STEPHEN Nay, look you now, you are angry, uncle. Why you know,
    an a man have not skill in the hawking and hunting languages
    nowadays, I'll not give a rush° for him. They are more studied than
    the Greek or the Latin. He is for no° gallants' company without   40
    'em. And by God's lid,° I scorn it, I, so I do, to be a consort for
    every humdrum,° hang'em scrolls, there's nothing in 'em i'the
    world. What do you talk on it? Because I dwell at Hogsden° I shall
    keep company with none but the archers of Finsbury?° Or the
    citizens that come a-ducking° to Islington ponds?° A fine jest,   45
    i'faith! 'Slid, a gentleman mun show himself like a gentleman.
    Uncle, I pray you be not angry, I know what I have to do, I trow, I
    am no novice.

KNOWELL You are a prodigal absurd coxcomb—go to.°
    Nay, never look at me,° it's I that speak.   50
    Take't as you will, sir, I'll not flatter you.
    Ha' you not yet found means enough to waste
    That which your friends have left you, but you must
    Go cast away your money on a kite,°
    And know not how to keep it when you ha' done?   55
    O, it's comely! This will make you a gentleman?
    Well, cousin, well. I see you are e'en past hope
    Of all reclaim. Ay, so, now you are told on° it,
    You look another way.

STEPHEN   What would you ha' me do?

KNOWELL What would I have you do? I'll tell you, kinsman: 60
    Learn to be wise, and practise how to thrive,
    That would I have you do; and not to spend
    Your coin on every bauble that you fancy,
    Or every foolish brain° that humours you.
    I would not have you to invade each place   65
    Nor thrust yourself on all societies,
    Till men's affections, or your own desert,°
    Should worthily invite you to your rank.
    He, that is so respectless in his courses,
    Oft sells his reputation at cheap market.   70
    Nor would I° you should melt away yourself

In flashing bravery, lest while you affect
To make a blaze of gentry° to the world,
A little puff of scorn extinguish it,
And you be left, like an unsavoury snuff   75
Whose property° is only to offend.
I'd ha' you sober and contain yourself;
Not that your sail be bigger than your boat,°
But moderate your expenses now, at first,
As you may keep the same proportion still.   80
Nor stand so much on your gentility,°
Which is an airy and mere borrowed thing,
From dead men's dust and bones, and none of yours
Except you make, or hold it. Who comes here?
    [*Enter a*] *Servant*
SERVANT Save you,° gentlemen.   85
STEPHEN Nay, we don't stand much on our gentility, friend; yet, you
    are welcome, and I assure you mine uncle here is a man of a thou-
    sand a year, Middlesex land;° he has but one son in all the world, I
    am his next heir (at the common law), Master Stephen, as simple° as
    I stand here. If my cousin die, as there's hope he will, I have a   90
    pretty° living o'mine own too, beside, hard by° here.
SERVANT In good time, sir.°
STEPHEN In good time, sir? Why, and in very good time, sir! You do
    not flout, friend, do you?
SERVANT Not I, sir.   95
STEPHEN Not you, sir? You were not best,° sir. An you should, here be
    them that can perceive it, and that quickly, too—go to. And they
    can give it again soundly too, an need be.
SERVANT Why, sir, let this satisfy you. Good faith, I had no such
    intent.   100
STEPHEN Sir, an I thought you had, I would talk with you, and that
    presently.
SERVANT Good Master Stephen, so you may, sir, at your pleasure.
STEPHEN And so I would, sir, good my saucy companion!° An you
    were out o'mine uncle's ground,° I can tell you; though I do not   105
    stand upon my gentility° neither in't.
KNOWELL Cousin! Cousin! Will this ne'er be left?
STEPHEN Whoreson base fellow! A mechanical serving man! By this
    cudgel, an't were not for shame, I would—
KNOWELL What would you do, you peremptory gull?°   110
    If you cannot be quiet, get you hence.

You see the honest man demeans° himself
Modestly to'ards you, giving no reply
To your unseasoned,° quarrelling, rude fashion—
And still you huff it, with a kind of carriage°   115
As void of wit as of humanity.
Go, get you in. 'Fore heaven, I am ashamed
Thou hast a kinsman's interest in me.
          [*Exit Stephen*]
SERVANT [*removing his hat*] I pray you, sir, is this Master Knowell's
     house?   120
KNOWELL Yes, marry, is it sir.
SERVANT I should enquire for a gentleman here, one Master Edward
     Knowell. Do you know any such, sir, I pray you?
KNOWELL I should forget myself else, sir.
SERVANT Are you the gentleman? Cry you mercy,° sir, I was required   125
     by a gentleman i'the City,° as I rode out at this end o' the town, to
     deliver you this letter, sir.
          [*The Servant gives Knowell a letter*]
KNOWELL To me, sir! What do you mean? Pray you, remember your
     courts'y.°
          [*The Servant replaces his hat*]
     [*Reads*]. 'To his most selected friend, Master Edward Knowell.'   130
     What might the gentleman's name be, sir, that sent it? Nay, pray
     you be covered.
SERVANT One Master Wellbred, sir.
KNOWELL Master Wellbred! A young gentleman, is he not?
SERVANT The same, sir. Master Kitely married his sister, the rich   135
     merchant i'the old Jewry.°
KNOWELL You say very true. Brainworm!
          [*Enter*] Brainworm
BRAINWORM Sir?
KNOWELL Make this honest friend drink here; [*to Servant*] pray you
     go in.   140
          [*Exeunt Brainworm and Servant*]
     This letter is directed to my son,
     Yet I am Edward Knowell too, and may
     With the safe conscience of good manners, use
     The fellow's error to my satisfaction.
     Well, I will break it ope (old men are curious),   145
     Be it but for the style's sake and the phrase,
     To see if both do answer° my son's praises

147

Who is, almost, grown the idolater
Of this young Wellbred. What have we here? What's this?
    [*Knowell reads*] *the letter*
'Why, Ned, I beseech thee, hast thou foresworn all thy friends i'the   150
Old Jewry? Or dost thou think us all Jews that inhabit there yet?°
If thou dost, come over and but see our frippery,° change an old
shirt for a whole smock° with us. Do not conceive° that antipathy
between us and Hogsden as was between Jews and hog's flesh.
Leave thy vigilant father alone to number over° his green apricots   155
evening and morning o' the northwest wall. An I had been his son
I had saved him the labour long since, if taking in all the young
wenches that pass by at the back door and coddling every kernel of
the fruit° for 'em, would ha' served. But, prithee, come over to me
quickly this morning, I have such a present for thee (our Turkey   160
Company° never sent the like to the Grand Signor). One is a
rhymer, sir, o' your own batch, your own leaven,° but doth think
himself Poet-Mayor° o' the town, willing to be shown and worthy
to be seen. The other—I will not venture his description with
you till you come because I would ha' you make hither with an   165
appetite. If the worst of 'em be not worth your journey, draw your
bill of charges as unconscionable as any Guildhall verdict° will
give it you, and you shall be allowed your *viaticum.*° From the
Windmill°—'
From the bordello it might come as well,   170
The Spital, or Pict-hatch!° Is this the man
My son hath sung so for the happiest° wit,
The choicest° brain, the times hath sent us forth?
I know not what he may be in the arts,
Nor what in schools, but surely, for his manners,   175
I judge him a profane and dissolute wretch—
Worse, by possession of such great good gifts,
Being the master of so loose a spirit.
Why, what unhallowed ruffian would have writ
In such a scurrilous manner to a friend?   180
Why should he think I tell my apricots,
Or play th' Hesperian dragon° with my fruit
To watch it? Well, my son, I had thought
You'd more judgement, t' have made election
Of your companions, t' have ta'en on trust   185
Such petulant, jeering gamesters, that can spare
No argument or subject from their jest.

But I perceive, affection makes a fool
Of any man, too much the father. Brainworm!
    [*Enter Brainworm*]
BRAINWORM Sir?   190
KNOWELL Is the fellow gone that brought this letter?
BRAINWORM Yes, sir, a pretty while since.
KNOWELL And where's your young master?
BRAINWORM In his chamber, sir.
KNOWELL He spake not with the fellow, did he?   195
BRAINWORM No, sir, he saw him not.
KNOWELL Take you this letter and deliver it my son, but with no
    notice that I have opened it, on your life.
BRAINWORM O, lord, sir, that were a jest indeed!°
    [*Exit Brainworm*]
KNOWELL I am resolved. I will not stop his journey   200
  Nor practice any violent mean to stay°
  The unbridled course of youth in him, for that
  Restrained, grows more impatient, and in kind
  Like to the eager but the generous° greyhound,
  Who, ne'er so little from his game withheld,°   205
  Turns head and leaps up at his holder's throat.
  There is a way of winning more by love,
  And urging of the modesty, than fear:
  Force works on servile natures, not the free.
  He that's compelled to goodness may be good   210
  But 'tis but for that fit,° where others, drawn
  By softness and example, get a habit.
  Then, if they stray, but warn 'em: and, the same
  They should for virtue have done, they'll do for shame.
    [*Exit*]

1.[2]

    Enter Edward [*and*] *Brainworm*
EDWARD Did he open it, sayest thou?
BRAINWORM Yes, o' my word, sir, and read the contents.
EDWARD That scarce contents me. What countenance, prithee, made
  he i'the reading of it? Was he angry or pleased?

BRAINWORM Nay, sir, I saw him not read it, nor open it, I assure your   5
worship.

EDWARD No? How know'st thou, then, that he did either?

BRAINWORM Marry sir, because he charged me, on my life, to tell
nobody that he opened it; which, unless he had done, he would
never fear to have it revealed.   10

EDWARD That's true. Well, I thank thee, Brainworm.

    [Enter] Stephen

STEPHEN O, Brainworm, didst thou not see a fellow here in a what-
sha'-call-him doublet?° He brought mine uncle a letter e'en now.

BRAINWORM Yes, Master Stephen, what of him?

STEPHEN O, I ha' such a mind° to beat him. Where is he? Canst thou   15
tell?

BRAINWORM 'Faith, he is not of that mind. He is gone, Master
Stephen.

STEPHEN Gone? Which way? When went he? How long since?

BRAINWORM He is rid hence. He took horse at the street door.   20

STEPHEN And I stayed i'the fields.° Whoreson scanderbag rogue! O,
that I had but a horse to fetch him back again.

BRAINWORM Why, you may ha' my master's gelding to save your
longing, sir.

STEPHEN But I ha' no boots, that's the spite on't.   25

BRAINWORM Why, a fine wisp of hay rolled hard,° Master Stephen.

STEPHEN No, 'faith, it's no boot° to follow him now; let him e'en go
and hang. Pray thee, help to truss me a little. He does so vex me—

BRAINWORM You'll be worse vexed when you are trussed,° Master
Stephen. Best keep unbraced° and walk yourself till you be cold—   30
your choler° may founder you else.

STEPHEN By my faith, and so I will, now thou tell'st me on't. How
dost thou like my leg, Brainworm?

BRAINWORM A very good leg, Master Stephen! But the woollen
stocking does not commend it so well.   35

STEPHEN Foh, the stockings be good enough, now summer is coming
on, for the dust! I'll have a pair of silk again' winter, that I go to
dwell i'the town. I think my leg would show in a silk-hose.

BRAINWORM Believe me, Master Stephen, rarely well.

STEPHEN In sadness,° I think it would: I have a reasonable good leg.   40

BRAINWORM You have an excellent good leg, Master Stephen, but I
cannot stay to praise it longer now, and I am very sorry for't.

STEPHEN Another time will serve, Brainworm. Gramercy for this.

    [Exit Brainworm]

    [*Edward*] *laughs having read the letter*

EDWARD Ha, ha, ha!

STEPHEN 'Slid, I hope he laughs not at me, an he do—   45

EDWARD Here was a letter, indeed, to be intercepted by a man's father
    and do him good with him! He cannot but think most virtuously,
    both of me and the sender, sure, that make the careful coster-
    monger of him in our familiar epistles.° Well, if he read this with
    patience, I'll be gelt° and troll ballads for Master John Trundle°   50
    yonder, the rest of my mortality. It is true, and likely, my father may
    have as much patience as another man, for he takes much physic,
    and oft taking physic makes a man very patient. But would your
    packet, Master Wellbred, had arrived at him in such a minute of his
    patience, then we had known the end of it, which now is doubtful   55
    and threatens. [*Noticing Stephen*] What, my wise cousin! Nay, then,
    I'll furnish our feast with one gull more to'ard the mess. He writes
    to me of a brace, and here's one, that's three. O, for a fourth!
    Fortune,° if ever thou'lt use thine eyes, I entreat thee—

STEPHEN O, now I see who he laughed at—he laughed at somebody   60
    in that letter. By this good light, an he had laughed at me—

EDWARD How now, cousin Stephen, melancholy?

STEPHEN Yes, a little. I thought you had laughed at me, cousin.

EDWARD Why, what an I had, coz, what would you ha' done?

STEPHEN By this light, I would ha' told mine uncle.   65

EDWARD Nay, if you would ha' told your uncle, I did laugh at you,
    coz.

STEPHEN Did you indeed?

EDWARD Yes, indeed.

STEPHEN Why, then—   70

EDWARD What then?

STEPHEN I am satisfied, it is sufficient.

EDWARD Why, be so, gentle coz. And, I pray you, let me entreat a
    courtesy of you. I am sent for this morning by a friend i'the Old
    Jewry to come to him. It's but crossing over the fields to Moorgate.°   75
    Will you bear me company? I protest, it is not to draw you into
    bond,° or any plot against the state, coz.

STEPHEN Sir, that's all one, an 'twere.° You shall command me twice
    so far as Moorgate to do you good in such a matter. Do you think I
    would leave you? I protest—   80

EDWARD No, no, you shall not protest, coz.

STEPHEN By my fackins,° but I will, by your leave. I'll protest more to
    my friend than I'll speak of at this time.

EDWARD You speak very well, coz.

STEPHEN Nay, not so neither, you shall pardon me; but I speak to   85
serve my turn.°

EDWARD Your turn, coz? Do you know what you say? A gentleman of
your sort, parts, carriage, and estimation, to talk o' your turn i' this
company, and to me, alone, like a tankard-bearer at a conduit. Fie!
A wight° that, hitherto, his every step hath left the stamp of a great   90
foot behind him, as every word the savour° of a strong spirit! And
he, this man, so graced, gilded, or—to use a more fit metaphor—so
tinfoiled by nature, as not ten housewives' pewter again' a good
time,° shows more bright to the world then he! And he,—as I said
last, so I say again and still shall say it—this man, to conceal such   95
real ornaments as these, and shadow their glory as a milliner's wife
does her wrought stomacher, with a smoky lawn° or a black cypress?°
O, coz! It cannot be answered;° go not about it. Drake's old ship at
Deptford° may sooner circle the world again. Come, wrong not the
quality of your desert with looking downward, coz, but hold up   100
your head, so, and let the *Idea* of what you are be portrayed i' your
face, that men may read i' your physiognomy°—'Here, within this
place is to be seen the true, rare, and accomplished monster, or
miracle of nature'—which is all one. What think you of this, coz?

STEPHEN Why, I do think of it, and I will be more proud, and melan-   105
choly,° and gentleman-like than I have been, I'll ensure you.

EDWARD Why, that's resolute, Master Stephen! [*Aside*] Now, if I can
but hold him up to his height,° as it is happily begun, it will do well
for a suburb-humour.° We may hap have a match with the City° and
play him° for forty pound. [*To Stephen*] Come, coz.   110

STEPHEN I'll follow you.

EDWARD Follow me? You must go before.°

STEPHEN Nay, an I must, I will. Pray you, show me, good cousin.

[*Exeunt*]

1.[3]

[*Enter*] Matthew [*carrying a book*]

MATTHEW I think this be the house. What, ho?

COB [*within*] Who's there?

[*Enter Cob*]

O, Master Matthew, gi'° your worship good morrow.

MATTHEW What, Cob! How dost thou, good Cob? Dost thou inhabit
here, Cob?   5

COB Ay, sir, I and my lineage ha' kept a poor house here, in our days.

MATTHEW Thy lineage, Monsieur Cob, what lineage? What lineage?

COB Why, sir, an ancient lineage and a princely. Mine ancestry came
from a king's belly, no worse man, and yet no man neither (by your
worship's leave, I did lie in that) but Herring the King of Fish,°   10
from his belly I proceed. One of the monarchs o'the world, I assure
you. The first red herring that was broiled in Adam and Eve's
kitchen do I fetch my pedigree from, by the heralds'° books. His cob
was my great-great-mighty-great grandfather.

MATTHEW Why mighty? Why mighty, I pray thee?   15

COB O, it was a mighty while ago, sir, and a mighty great cob.

MATTHEW How knowst thou that?

COB How know I? Why, I smell his ghost ever and anon.

MATTHEW Smell a ghost? O, unsavoury jest, and the ghost of a
herring, Cob!   20

COB Ay, sir, with a favour of your worship's nose, Master Matthew,
why not the ghost of a herring-cob as well as the ghost of rasher
bacon?

MATTHEW Roger Bacon,° thou wouldst say?

COB I say rasher bacon. They were both broiled o' the coals and a man   25
may smell broiled meat, I hope? You are a scholar, upsolve me that
now.

MATTHEW O, raw° ignorance! Cob, canst thou show me of a gentleman, one Captain Bobadill, where his lodging is?

COB O, my guest, sir, you mean.   30

MATTHEW Thy guest! Alas! Ha, ha!

COB Why do you laugh, sir, do you not mean Captain Bobadill?

MATTHEW Cob, pray thee, advise thyself well; do not wrong the
gentleman and thyself, too. I dare be sworn he scorns thy house.
He! He lodge in such a base, obscure place as thy house? Tut,   35
I know his disposition so well, he would not lie in thy bed if
thou'ldst gi' it him.

COB I will not give it him, though, sir. Mass, I thought somewhat was
in't,° we could not get him to bed all night! Well, sir, though he lie
not o' my bed he lies o' my bench. An't please you to go up, sir, you   40
shall find him with two cushions under his head, and his cloak
wrapped about him, as though he had neither won nor lost,° and yet
I warrant he ne'er cast° better in his life than he has done tonight.

MATTHEW Why, was he drunk?

COB Drunk, sir? You hear not me say so. Perhaps he swallowed a   45
tavern token° or some such device, sir; I have nothing to do withal. I
deal with water, and not with wine. [*Calls offstage to Tib*] Gi' me my
tankard there, ho! God b'w'you, sir. It's six o'clock, I should
ha' carried two turns° by this. [*Calls offstage again*] What, ho? My
stopple? Come!   50
            [*Enter Tib with tankard and stopple*]
MATTHEW Lie in a water-bearer's house? A gentleman of his havings!
Well, I'll tell him my mind.
COB What, Tib, show this gentleman up to the Captain.
            [*Exit Tib and Matthew*]
[*To audience*] O, an my house were The Brazen Head now! 'Faith, it
would e'en speak: 'mo' fools yet.' You should ha' some now would   55
take this Master Matthew to be a gentleman, at the least. His
father's an honest man, a worshipful° fishmonger and so forth; and
now does he creep and wriggle into acquaintance with all the brave
gallants about the town, such as my guest is—O, my guest is a fine
man,—and they flout him invincibly.° He useth every day to a   60
merchant's house, where I serve water, one Master Kitely's, i'the
Old Jewry, and here's the jest: he is in love with my master's sister,
Mistress Bridget, and calls her mistress, and there he will sit you a
whole afternoon sometimes, reading o' these same abominable,
vile—a pox on 'em, I cannot abide them—rascally verses, 'poyetry,   65
poyetry', and speaking of interludes: 'twill make a man burst to
hear him. And the wenches they do so jeer and tee-hee at him—
well, should they do so much to me, I'd forswear them all, by the
foot of Pharaoh. There's an oath! How many water-bearers shall
you hear swear such an oath? O, I have a guest—he teaches me—he   70
does swear the legiblest of any man christened. 'By Saint George',
'the foot of Pharaoh', 'the body of me', 'as I am gentleman and a
soldier'—such dainty oaths! And withal, he does take this same
filthy roguish tobacco, the finest and cleanliest! It would do a man
good to see the fume come forth at's tunnels.° Well, he owes me   75
forty shillings° my wife lent him out her purse by sixpence a time,
besides his lodging: I would I had it. I shall ha'it, he says, the next
'*Action*'.° Helter-skelter, hang sorrow, care'll kill a cat, up-tails all
and a louse for the hangman.°
            [*Exit*]

1.[4]

Bobadill is discovered° lying on a bench

BOBADILL Hostess, hostess!

[*Enter*] *Tib*

TIB What say you, sir?

BOBADILL A cup o' thy small beer,° sweet hostess.

TIB Sir, there's a gentleman below would speak with you.

BOBADILL A gentleman! 'Ods so, I am not within.   5

TIB My husband told him you were, sir.

BOBADILL What! A plague!—what meant he?

MATTHEW [*within*] Captain Bobadill?

BOBADILL Who's there? Take away the basin, good hostess. Come up,
sir.   10

TIB [*to Matthew within*] He would desire you to come up, sir. You
come into a cleanly house here.

[*Enter*] *Matthew* [*carrying a book*]

MATTHEW 'Save you, sir. 'Save you, Captain.

BOBADILL Gentle Master Matthew, is't you, sir? Please you sit down.

MATTHEW Thank you, good Captain; you may see I am somewhat   15
audacious.°

BOBADILL Not so, sir. I was requested to supper last night by a sort° of
gallants, where you were wished for, and drunk to, I assure you.

MATTHEW Vouchsafe me, by whom, good Captain?

BOBADILL Marry, by young Wellbred and others. Why, hostess, a   20
stool here for this gentleman.

MATTHEW No haste, sir, 'tis very well.

BOBADILL Body of me! It was so late ere we parted last night, I can
scarce open my eyes yet; I was but new risen as you came. How
passes the day abroad, sir? You can tell.   25

MATTHEW 'Faith, some half hour to seven. Now trust me, you have
an exceeding fine lodging here, very neat and private!

BOBADILL Ay, sir. Sit down, I pray you. Master Matthew, in any case,°
possess no gentlemen of our acquaintance with notice of my
lodging.   30

MATTHEW Who? I, sir? No.

BOBADILL Not that I need to care who know it, for the cabin° is
convenient, but in regard I would not be too popular and generally
visited, as some are.

MATTHEW True, Captain; I conceive° you.   35

BOBADILL For, do you see, sir, by the heart of valour in me, except it
be to some peculiar and choice spirits, to whom I am extraordinar-
ily engaged, as yourself or so, I could not extend thus far.°

MATTHEW O, Lord, sir, I resolve° so.

BOBADILL I confess, I love a cleanly and quiet privacy above all the   40
tumult and roar of fortune. What new book ha' you there? What,
'Go by Hieronimo!'°

MATTHEW Ay, did you ever see it acted? Is't not well penned?

BOBADILL Well penned? I would fain see all the poets of these times
pen such another play as that was! They'll prate and swagger, and   45
keep a stir of art and devices, when, as I am a gentleman, read 'em,
they are the most shallow, pitiful, barren fellows that live upon the
face of the earth again.

MATTHEW Indeed, here are a number of fine speeches in this book.
[*He reads*] 'O, eyes, no eyes, but fountains fraught with tears!'—   50
There's conceit! Fountains fraught with tears. 'O, life, no life, but
lively form of death!'—Another! 'O, world, no world, but mass of
public wrongs!'—A third! 'Confused and filled with murder, and
misdeeds!'—A fourth! O, the Muses! Is't not excellent, is't not
simply the best that ever you heard, Captain? Ha? How do you like   55
it?

BOBADILL 'Tis good.

MATTHEW [*reading*] 'To thee, the purest object to my sense,
The most refinèd essence heaven covers,
Send I these lines, wherein I do commence   60
The happy state of turtle-billing° lovers.
If they prove rough, unpolished, harsh, and rude,
Haste made the waste. Thus, mildly, I conclude.'
    Bobadill is making him ready° all this while

BOBADILL Nay, proceed, proceed. Where's this?°

MATTHEW This, sir? A toy o' mine own in my nonage, the infancy of   65
my muses. But when will you come and see my study? Good faith, I
can show you some very good things I have done of late. That boot
becomes your leg passing well, Captain, methinks.

BOBADILL So, so. It's the fashion gentlemen now use.

MATTHEW Troth, Captain, an now you speak o' the fashion, Master   70
Wellbred's elder brother and I are fallen out exceedingly. This
other day I happened to enter into some discourse of a hanger,
which I assure you, both for fashion and workmanship, was most
peremptory-beautiful and gentleman-like. Yet he condemned it
and cried it down for the most pied° and ridiculous that ever he saw!   75

BOBADILL Squire Downright, the half-brother, was't not?

MATTHEW Ay, sir, he.

BOBADILL Hang him, rook,° he! Why, he has no more judgement than
a malt-horse. By Saint George, I wonder you'd lose a thought upon
such an animal. The most peremptory absurd clown of Christendom   80
this day, he is holden.° I protest to you, as I am a gentleman and a
soldier, I ne'er changed words with his like. By his discourse he
should eat nothing but hay. He was born for the manger, pannier, or
pack-saddle! He has not so much as a good phrase in his belly, but
all old iron and rusty proverbs—a good commodity for some smith   85
to make hobnails° of.

MATTHEW Ay, and he thinks to carry it away with his manhood° still,
where he comes. He brags he will gi' me the *bastinado*, as I hear.

BOBADILL How? He, the *bastinado*? How came he by that word, trow?

MATTHEW Nay, indeed, he said cudgel me; I termed it so for my more   90
grace.

BOBADILL That may be; for I was sure it was none of his word. But
when, when said he so?

MATTHEW 'Faith, yesterday, they say. A young gallant, a friend of
mine, told me so.   95

BOBADILL By the foot of Pharaoh, an't were my case now, I should
send him a *chartel* presently. The *bastinado*! A most proper and
sufficient *dependence*,° warranted by the great Caranza.° Come
hither. You shall *chartel* him. I'll show you a trick or two you
shall kill him with at pleasure: the first *stoccata*, if you will, by this   100
air.

MATTHEW Indeed, you have absolute knowledge i'the mystery,° I have
heard, sir.

BOBADILL Of whom? Of whom ha' you heard it, I beseech
you?   105

MATTHEW Troth, I have heard it spoken of divers° that you have very
rare and un-in-one-breath-utterable skill, sir.

BOBADILL By heaven, no, not I; no skill i' the earth: some small
rudiments i' the science as to know my time, distance,° or so. I have
professed it more for noblemen and gentlemen's use than mine own   110
practice, I assure you. Hostess, accommodate us with another
bedstaff here, quickly!

[*Enter Tib*]

Lend us another bedstaff.°

[*Exit Tib*]

The woman does not understand the words of action. Look you,

sir, exalt not your point° above this state at any hand,° and let your   115
poniard° maintain your defence, thus.
    [*Tib enters with a bedstaff*]
Give it the gentleman and leave us.
    [*Exit Tib*]
So, sir.
    [*Bobadill stands on guard ready to fence with the bedstaff.*
    Matthew imitates his movements]
Come on. O, twine your body more about, that you may fall to a
more sweet, comely, gentleman-like guard. So, indifferent. Hollow   120
your body more, sir, thus. Now, stand fast o' your left leg, note your
distance, keep your due proportion of time—O, you disorder your
point most irregularly!

MATTHEW   How is the bearing of it now, sir?

BOBADILL   O, out of measure° ill! A well-experienced hand would pass   125
upon you at pleasure.

MATTHEW   How mean you, sir, pass upon me?

BOBADILL   Why, thus sir. Make a thrust at me, come in, upon the
answer control your point and make full career at° the body. The
best practised gallants of the time name it the *passada*, a most   130
desperate thrust, believe it!

MATTHEW   Well, come, sir.

BOBADILL   Why, you do not manage your weapon with any facility or
grace to invite me; I have no spirit to play with you. Your dearth of
judgement renders you tedious.   135

MATTHEW   But one *venue*,° sir.

BOBADILL   *Venue*! Fie! Most gross denomination as ever I heard. O,
the *stoccata*, while you live, sir. Note that. Come, put on your cloak,
and we'll go to some private place where you are acquainted, some
tavern or so, and have a bit. I'll send for one of these fencers, and he   140
shall breathe you° by my direction; and, then, I will teach you your
trick. You shall kill him with it at the first, if you please. Why, I will
learn you by the true judgement of the eye, hand, and foot to
control any enemy's point i'the world. Should your adversary con-
front you with a pistol, 'twere nothing! By this hand, you should,   145
by the same rule, control his bullet in a line—except it were hail-
shot, and spread. What money ha' you about you, Master
Matthew?

MATTHEW   'Faith, I ha' not past a two shillings or so.

BOBADILL   'Tis somewhat with the least;° but, come. We will have a   150
bunch of radish and salt, to taste° our wine, and a pipe of tobacco to

close the orifice of the stomach, and then we'll call upon young
Wellbred. Perhaps we shall meet the Corydon,° his brother, there
and put him to the question.

    [*Exeunt*]

2.1

[Enter] Kitely, Cash, and Downright

KITELY Thomas, come hither.
There lies a note within, upon my desk;
Here, take my key; it is no matter, neither.
Where is the boy?
CASH   Within, sir, i' the warehouse.
KITELY Let him tell over° straight that Spanish gold,   5
And weigh it, with th' pieces of eight.° Do you
See the delivery of those silver stuffs
To Master Lucar.° Tell him, if he will,
He shall ha' the grograns at the rate I told him,
And I will meet him on the Exchange° anon.   10
CASH Good, sir.
          [Exit Cash]
KITELY Do you see that fellow, brother Downright?
DOWNRIGHT Ay, what of him?
KITELY   He is a jewel, brother.
I took him of° a child, up at my door,
And christened him, gave him mine own name,
    Thomas;   15
Since bred him at the Hospital;° where proving
A toward imp,° I called him home and taught him
So much, as I have made him my cashier,
And given him, who had none, a surname, Cash—
And find him, in his place, so full of faith   20
That I durst trust my life into his hands.
DOWNRIGHT So would not I in any bastard's, brother,
As it is like he is, although I knew
Myself his father. But you said you'd somewhat
To tell me, gentle brother. What is't? What is't?   25
KITELY 'Faith, I am very loath to utter it,
As fearing it may hurt your patience;
But that I know your judgement is of strength
Against the nearness of affection—
DOWNRIGHT What need this circumstance? Pray you, be direct.   30
KITELY I will not say how much I do ascribe
Unto your friendship; nor in what regard

160

I hold your love, but let my past behaviour
And usage of your sister but confirm
How well I've been affected to your—   35
DOWNRIGHT You are too tedious, come to the matter: the matter.
KITELY Then, without further ceremony, thus.
My brother° Wellbred, sir, I know not how,
Of late is much declined in what he was,
And greatly altered in his disposition.   40
When he came first to lodge here in my house,
Ne'er trust me, if I were not proud of him.
Methought he bare himself in such a fashion
So full of man and sweetness in his carriage
And, what was chief, it showed not borrowed in him,   45
But all he did became him as his own,
And seemed as perfect, proper, and possessed
As breath with life, or colour with the blood.
But now, his course is so irregular,
So loose, affected, and deprived of grace,   50
And he himself withal so far fall'n off
From that first place, as scarce no note remains
To tell men's judgements where he lately stood.
He's grown a stranger to all due respect,
Forgetful of his friends and, not content   55
To stale himself in all societies,°
He makes my house here common as a mart,
A theatre, a public receptacle
For giddy humour and diseased riot.
And here, as in a tavern or a stews,   60
He and his wild associates spend their hours
In repetition of lascivious jests,
Swear, leap,° drink, dance, and revel night by night,
Control my servants, and—indeed—what not?
DOWNRIGHT 'Sdines, I know not what I should say to him, i' the   65
whole world. He values me at a cracked three-farthings° for aught I
see. It will never out o' the flesh that's bred i' the bone.° I have told
him 'enough', one would think, if that would serve; but counsel to
him is as good as a shoulder of mutton to a sick horse.° Well, he
knows what to trust to, 'fore George!° Let him spend, and spend,   70
and domineer till his heart ache; an he think to be relieved by me
when he is got into one o' your City pounds, the Counters, he has
the wrong sow by the ear, i'faith, and claps his dish at the wrong

man's door. I'll lay my hand o' my halfpenny ere I part with't° to
fetch him out, I'll assure him.   75
KITELY Nay, good brother, let it not trouble you thus.
DOWNRIGHT 'Sdeath, he mads me, I could eat my very spur-leathers
    for anger! But why are you so tame? Why do not you speak to him,
    and tell him how he disquiets your house?
KITELY O, there are divers reasons to dissuade, brother.   80
    But, would yourself vouchsafe to travail in it,°
    Though but with plain and easy circumstance,°
    It would both come much better to his sense,
    And savour less of stomach° or of passion.
    You are his elder brother, and that title   85
    Both gives and warrants° you authority
    Which, by your presence seconded,° must breed
    A kind of duty in him and regard;
    Whereas, if I should intimate the least,
    It would but add contempt to his neglect,   90
    Heap worse on ill, make up a pile of hatred,
    That in the rearing would come tott'ring down
    And in the ruin bury all our love.
    Nay, more than this, brother; if I should speak
    He would be ready from his heat of humour°   95
    And over-flowing of the vapour in him
    To blow the ears of his familiars°
    With the false breath of telling what disgraces
    And low disparagements I had put upon him.
    Whilst they, sir, to relieve him in the fable,°   100
    Make their loose comments upon every word,
    Gesture, or look I use; mock me all over
    From my flat cap unto my shining shoes;°
    And, out of their impetuous rioting fant'sies
    Beget some slander that shall dwell with me.   105
    And what would that be, think you? Marry, this.
    They would give out, because my wife is fair,
    Myself but lately married, and my sister
    Here sojourning a virgin in my house,
    That I were jealous! Nay, as sure as death,°   110
    That they would say. And how that I had quarrelled°
    My brother purposely, thereby to find
    An apt pretext to banish them my house.
DOWNRIGHT Mass, perhaps so; they are like° enough to do it.

KITELY Brother, they would, believe it. So should I,   115
    Like one of these penurious quacksalvers,
    But set the bills up to mine own disgrace
    And try experiments upon myself;
    Lend scorn and envy opportunity
    To stab my reputation and good name—   120
        [*Enter*] *Matthew* [*and*] *Bobadill*
MATTHEW I will speak to him—
BOBADILL Speak to him? Away, by the foot of Pharaoh, you shall not.
    You shall not do him that grace! [*To Kitely*] The time of day to you,
    gentleman o' the house. Is Master Wellbred stirring?
DOWNRIGHT How then?° What should he do?   125
BOBADILL [*to Kitely*] Gentleman of the house, it is to you. Is he
    within, sir?
KITELY He came not to his lodging tonight, sir, I assure you.
DOWNRIGHT [*to Bobadill*] Why, do you hear? You?
BOBADILL The gentleman-citizen hath satisfied me, I'll talk to no   130
    scavenger.°
        [*Exeunt Bobadill and Matthew*]
DOWNRIGHT How, scavenger? Stay, sir, stay!
KITELY Nay, brother Downright.
DOWNRIGHT 'Heart! Stand you away, an you love me.
KITELY You shall not follow him now, I pray you, brother. Good faith,   135
    you shall not. I will over-rule you.
DOWNRIGHT Ha! Scavenger? Well, go to, I say little: but by this good
    day—God forgive me I should swear—if I put it up° so, say I am the
    rankest° cow that ever pissed. 'Sdines, an I swallow this, I'll ne'er
    draw my sword in the sight of Fleet Street° again, while I live. I'll sit   140
    in a barn with madge howlet° and catch mice first! Scavenger!
    'Heart, and I'll go near to fill that huge tumbrel slop of yours with
    somewhat,° an I have good luck; your Garagantua breech cannot
    carry it away° so.
KITELY O, do not fret yourself thus; never think on't.   145
DOWNRIGHT These are my brother's consorts, these! These are his
    cam'rades, his walking mates! He's a gallant, a *cavaliero* too, right
    hangman cut!° Let me not live, an I could not find in my heart to
    swinge the whole ging of 'em, one after another, and begin with
    him first. I am grieved it should be said he is my brother, and take   150
    these courses. Well, as he brews, so shall he drink,° 'fore George,
    again! Yet he shall hear on't, and that tightly° too, an I live, i'faith.
KITELY But brother, let your reprehension,° then,

Run in an easy current, not o'er high
Carried with rashness or devouring choler;   155
But rather use the soft persuading way,
Whose powers will work more gently, and compose
Th'imperfect thoughts you labour to reclaim;°
More winning than enforcing the consent.

DOWNRIGHT Ay, ay, let me alone for° that, I warrant you.   160
          [*A*] *bell rings*

KITELY How now? O, the bell rings to breakfast.
Brother, I pray you go in and bear my wife
Company till I come; I'll but give order
For some dispatch of business to my servants—
          [*Exit Downright.*] [*Enter*] *Cob. He passes by with his water*
          tankard
What, Cob? Our maids will have you by the back°   165
I'faith, for coming so late this morning.

COB Perhaps so, sir. Take heed somebody have not them by the belly°
for walking so late in the evening.
          [*Exit Cob*]

KITELY Well, yet my troubled spirit's somewhat eased,
Though not reposed in that security   170
As I could wish. But I must be content.
Howe'er I set a face on't to the world,°
Would I had lost this finger at a venture,
So Wellbred had ne'er lodged within my house.
Why't cannot be, where there is such resort   175
Of wanton gallants and young revellers,
That any woman should be honest long.
Is't like that factious° beauty will preserve
The public weal of chastity unshaken,
When such strong motives muster and make head°   180
Against her single peace? No, no. Beware
When mutual appetite doth meet to treat,°
And spirits of one kind and quality
Come once to parley° in the pride of blood:
It is no slow conspiracy° that follows.   185
Well, to be plain, if I but thought the time
Had answered their affections, all the world
Should not persuade me but I were a cuckold.
Marry, I hope they ha' not got that start;
For opportunity hath balked 'em yet,   190

And shall do still, while I have eyes and ears
To attend the impositions of my heart.
My presence shall be as an iron bar
'Twixt the conspiring motions of desire;
Yea, every look or glance mine eye ejects   195
Shall check occasion, as one doth his slave
When he forgets the limits of prescription.
          [*Enter*] *Dame Kitely and* [*Bridget*]
DAME KITELY Sister Bridget, pray you fetch down the rosewater
     above in the closet.
          [*Exit Bridget*]
     Sweetheart, will you come in to breakfast?   200
KITELY [*aside*] An she have overheard me now?
DAME KITELY I pray thee, good muss,° we stay for you.
KITELY [*aside*] By heaven, I would not for a thousand angels.°
DAME KITELY What ail you, sweetheart? Are you not well? Speak,
     good muss.   205
KITELY Troth, my head aches extremely, on a sudden.
DAME KITELY [*feeling his forehead*] O, the Lord!
KITELY How now? What?
DAME KITELY Alas, how it burns! Muss, keep you warm; good truth,
     it is this new disease! There's a number are troubled withal. For   210
     love's sake, sweetheart, come in out of the air.
KITELY [*aside*] How simple, and how subtle, are her answers!
     A new disease, and many troubled with it!
     Why, true, she heard me, all the world to nothing.°
DAME KITELY I pray thee, good sweetheart, come in; the air will do   215
     you harm, in troth.
KITELY [*aside*] The air?° She has me i' the wind!° [*Aloud*] Sweetheart,
     I'll come to you presently; 'twill away, I hope.
DAME KITELY Pray heaven it do.
          [*Exit Dame Kitely*]
KITELY A new disease? I know not, new or old,   220
     But it may well be called poor mortal's plague;
     For like a pestilence it doth infect
     The houses of the brain.° First, it begins
     Solely to work upon the fantasy,
     Filling her seat with such pestiferous air   225
     As soon corrupts the judgement; and from thence
     Sends like° contagion to the memory,
     Still each to other giving the infection,

Which, as a subtle vapour, spreads itself
Confusedly through every sensive part,   230
Till not a thought or motion in the mind
Be free from the black poison of suspect.
Ah, but what mis'ry is it to know this,
Or knowing it, to want the mind's erection°
In such extremes? Well, I will once more strive,   235
In spite of this black cloud, myself to be,
And shake the fever off that thus shakes me.
      [*Exit*]

2.[2]

[Enter] Brainworm [disguised as Fitzsword, a soldier]

BRAINWORM 'Slid, I cannot choose but laugh to see myself translated
      thus from a poor creature to a creator; for now must I create an
      intolerable sort of lies or my present profession loses the grace°—
      and yet the lie to a man of my coat is as ominous a fruit as the *fico*.°
      O, sir, it holds for good policy ever, to have° that outwardly in vilest   5
      estimation that inwardly is most dear to us. So much for my bor-
      rowed shape. Well, the troth is, my old master intends to follow my
      young, dryfoot° over Moorfields to London this morning. Now I,
      knowing of this hunting match,° or rather conspiracy, and to insinu-
      ate° with my young master—for so must we that are blue-waiters,   10
      and men of hope and service do, or perhaps we may wear motley at
      the year's end,° and who wears motley,° you know—have got me
      afore, in this disguise, determining here to lie in *ambuscado*, and
      intercept him in the midway. If I can but get his cloak, his purse, his
      hat, nay, anything to cut him off, that is, to stay his journey, *veni,*   15
      vidi, vici,° I may say with Captain Caesar; I am made forever, i'faith.
      Well, now must I practice to get the true garb of one of these lance-
      knights; my arm here,° and my—
            [Enter] Edward [and] Stephen
      [*aside*] young master! And his cousin, Master Stephen, as I am true
      counterfeit man of war, and no soldier.   20
            [Brainworm conceals himself]
EDWARD So, sir, and how then, coz?
STEPHEN 'Sfoot, I have lost my purse, I think.
EDWARD How, lost your purse? Where? When had you it?

STEPHEN I cannot tell. Stay!

BRAINWORM [*aside*] 'Slid, I am afeared they will know me; would I   25
could get by them.

EDWARD What? Ha' you it?

STEPHEN No; I think I was bewitched, I—
          [*Stephen starts to cry*]

EDWARD Nay, do not weep the loss; hang it, let it go.

STEPHEN O, it's here. No, an it had been lost, I had not cared, but for   30
a jet° ring Mistress Mary sent me.

EDWARD A jet ring? O, the posy, the posy?

STEPHEN Fine, i'faith!—'*Though fancy sleep, my love is deep.*'
Meaning that, though I did not fancy her, yet she loved me dearly.

EDWARD Most excellent!   35

STEPHEN And then, I sent her another, and my posy was: '*The deeper
the sweeter,*° *I'll be judged by Saint Peter.*'

EDWARD How, by Saint Peter? I do not conceive that.

STEPHEN Marry, Saint Peter, to make up the metre.

EDWARD Well, there the saint was your good patron, he helped you at   40
your need. Thank him, thank him!
          [*Brainworm*] *come*[*s*] *back*

BRAINWORM [*aside*] I cannot take leave on 'em so; I will venture°
come what will. [*To Edward and Stephen*] Gentlemen, please you
change a few crowns° for a very excellent good blade here? I am a
poor gentleman, a soldier, one that in the better state of my for-   45
tunes scorned so mean a refuge, but now it is the humour of necessity to have it so. You seem to be gentlemen, well affected to martial
men, else I should rather die with silence than live with shame;
however, vouchsafe to remember it is my want speaks, not myself.
This condition agrees not with my spirit—   50

EDWARD Where hast thou served?

BRAINWORM May it please you, sir, in all the late wars of Bohemia,
Hungaria, Dalmatia, Poland, where not, sir? I have been a poor
servitor by sea and land, anytime this fourteen years, and followed
the fortunes of the best commanders in Christendom. I was twice   55
shot at the taking of Aleppo, once at the relief of Vienna; I have
been at Marseilles, Naples, and the Adriatic Gulf;° a gentleman slave
in the galleys,° thrice, where I was most dangerously shot in the
head, through both the thighs, and yet, being thus maimed, I am
void of maintenance, nothing left me but my scars, the noted marks   60
of my resolution.

STEPHEN How° will you sell this rapier,° friend?

BRAINWORM Generous sir, I refer it to your own judgement. You are
a gentleman, give me what you please.

STEPHEN True, I am a gentleman, I know that friend—but what   65
though? I pray you say, what would you ask?

BRAINWORM I assure you the blade may become the side, or thigh, of
the best prince in Europe.

EDWARD Ay, with a velvet scabbard,° I think.

STEPHEN Nay, an't be mine, it shall have a velvet scabbard, coz, that's   70
flat°—I'd not wear it as 'tis, an you would give me an angel.

BRAINWORM At your worship's pleasure, sir; nay, 'tis a most pure
Toledo.°

STEPHEN I had rather it were a Spaniard! But tell me, what shall I
give you for it? An it had a silver hilt—   75

EDWARD Come, come, you shall not buy it; hold, there's a shilling,
fellow; take thy rapier.

STEPHEN Why, but I will buy it now, because you say so, and there's
another shilling, fellow. I scorn to be out-bidden. What, shall I walk
with a cudgel like Higgenbottom?° And may have a rapier for   80
money?

EDWARD You may buy one in the City.

STEPHEN Tut, I'll buy this i' the field, so I will; I have a mind to't,
because 'tis a field rapier.° Tell me your lowest price.

EDWARD You shall not buy it, I say.   85

STEPHEN By this money, but I will, though I give more than 'tis
worth.

EDWARD Come away, you are a fool.

STEPHEN Friend, I am a fool, that's granted; but I'll have it, for that
word's sake. [To Brainworm] Follow me for your money.   90

BRAINWORM At your service, sir.

[Exeunt]

2.[3]

[Enter] Knowell

KNOWELL I cannot lose the thought yet of this letter
Sent to my son, nor leave t'admire° the change
Of manners and the breeding of our youth
Within the kingdom, since myself was one.
When I was young, he lived not in the stews   5

Durst have conceived a scorn and uttered it
On a grey head;° age was authority
Against a buffoon, and a man had, then,
A certain reverence paid unto his years
That had none due unto his life. So much   10
The sanctity of some prevailed for others.
But now we all are fall'n; youth from their fear,
And age from that which bred it,° good example.
Nay, would ourselves were not the first, even° parents,
That did destroy the hopes in our own children,   15
Or they not learned our vices in their cradles,
And sucked in our ill customs with their milk.
Ere all their teeth be born, or they can speak,
We make their palates cunning! The first words
We form their tongues with are licentious jests!   20
Can it call, 'whore'? Cry, 'bastard'? O, then, kiss it;
A witty child. Can 't swear? The father's darling!
Give it two plums. Nay, rather than 't shall learn
No bawdy song, the mother herself will teach it!
But this is in the infancy; the days   25
Of the long coat;° when it puts on the breeches
It will put off all this. Ay, it is like,°
When it is gone into the bone already.
No, no: this die goes deeper than the coat,
Or shirt or skin. It stains unto the liver   30
And heart, in some. And, rather than it should not,
Note what we fathers do! Look how we live!
What mistresses we keep! At what expense
In our sons' eyes, where they may handle our gifts,
Hear our lascivious courtships, see our dalliance,   35
Taste of the same provoking meats with us,
To ruin of our states! Nay, when our own
Portion is fled, to prey on their remainder,°
We call them into fellowship of vice!
Bait 'em with the young chambermaid to seal,°   40
And teach 'em all bad ways to buy affection!°
This is one path; but there are millions more
In which we spoil our own with leading them.
Well, I thank heaven I never yet was he
That travelled with my son, before sixteen,   45
To show him the Venetian courtesans;°

Nor read the grammar of cheating I had made
To my sharp boy at twelve, repeating still
The rule: 'Get money'; still, 'Get money, boy;
No matter by what means; money will do   50
More, boy, than my lord's letter'.° Neither have I
Dressed snails or mushrooms curiously° before him,
Perfumed my sauces and taught him to make 'em;
Preceding° still with my grey gluttony
At all the ordinaries;° and only feared   55
His palate should degenerate, not his manners.
These are the trade of fathers now! However,
My son, I hope, hath met within my threshold
None of these household precedents, which are strong
And swift to rape youth to their precipice.°   60
But, let the house at home be ne'er so clean—
Swept, or kept sweet from filth, nay, dust and cobwebs,
If he will live abroad with his companions
In dung and leystalls, it is worth a fear.
Nor is the danger of conversing° less   65
Than all that I have mentioned of example.°
        [*Enter*] Brainworm [*as Fitzsword*]

BRAINWORM [*aside*] My master? Nay, faith, have at you: I am fleshed
   now, I have sped so well.° [*To Knowell*] Worshipful sir, I beseech
   you, respect the estate of a poor soldier. I am ashamed of this base
   course of life, God's my comfort, but extremity provokes me to't,   70
   what remedy?

KNOWELL I have not for you now.

BRAINWORM By the faith I bear unto truth, gentleman, it is no ordinary custom in me, but only to preserve manhood. I protest to you, a
   man I have been, a man I may be, by your sweet bounty.   75

KNOWELL Pray thee, good friend, be satisfied.

BRAINWORM Good sir, by that hand, you may do the part of a kind
   gentleman, in lending a poor soldier the price of two cans of beer, a
   matter of small value. The king of heaven shall pay you, and I shall
   rest thankful; sweet worship—   80

KNOWELL Nay, an you be so importunate—

BRAINWORM O, tender sir, need will have his course; I was not made
   to this vile use! Well, the edge° of the enemy could not have abated
   me so much. It's hard when a man hath served his prince's cause,
   and be thus. (*He weeps*)—Honourable worship, let me derive a   85
   small piece of silver from you, it shall not be given in the course of

time,° by this good ground, I was fain to pawn my rapier last night
for a poor supper, I had sucked° the hilts long before, I am a pagan
else; sweet honour.

KNOWELL Believe me, I am taken with some wonder,   90
To think a fellow of thy outward presence
Should, in the frame and fashion of his mind,
Be so degenerate and sordid-base!
Art thou a man? And sham'st thou not to beg?
To practise such a servile kind of life?   95
Why, were thy education ne'er so mean,
Having thy limbs, a thousand fairer courses
Offer themselves to thy election.
Either the wars might still supply thy wants,
Or service of some virtuous gentleman,   100
Or honest labour: nay, what can I name,
But would become thee better than to beg?
But men of thy condition feed on sloth,
As doth the beetle on the dung she breeds in,
Not caring how the metal° of your minds   105
Is eaten with the rust of idleness.
Now, afore me,° what e'er he be that should
Relieve a person of thy quality,
While thou insists in this loose desperate course,
I would esteem the sin not thine, but his.   110

BRAINWORM 'Faith, sir, I would gladly find some other course, if
so—

KNOWELL Ay, you'd gladly find it, but you will not seek it.

BRAINWORM Alas, sir, where should a man seek? In the wars there's
no ascent by desert these days, but—and for service, would it were   115
as soon purchased° as wished for; the air's my comfort. I know what
I would say—

KNOWELL What's thy name?

BRAINWORM Please you, Fitzsword,° sir.

KNOWELL Fitzsword?   120
Say that a man should entertain° thee now,
Wouldst thou be honest, humble, just, and true?

BRAINWORM Sir, by the place and honour of a soldier—

KNOWELL Nay, nay, I like not those affected oaths;
Speak plainly, man—what thinkst thou of my words?   125

BRAINWORM Nothing, sir, but wish my fortunes were as happy as my
service should be honest.

171

KNOWELL   Well, follow me; I'll prove° thee if thy deeds
   Will carry a proportion to thy words.
BRAINWORM   Yes, sir, straight, I'll but garter my hose.   130
        [*Exit Knowell*]
   O, that my belly were hooped now, for I am ready to burst with
   laughing. Never was bottle or bagpipe fuller. 'Slid, was there ever
   seen a fox in years° to betray himself thus? Now shall I be possessed
   of all his counsels, and by that conduit, my young master.° Well, he
   is resolved to prove my honesty, 'faith, and I am resolved to prove   135
   his patience. O, I shall abuse him intolerably! This small piece of
   service will bring him clean out of love with the soldier forever. He
   will never come within the sign of it, the sight of a cassock, or a
   musket-rest,° again. He will hate the musters at Mile End° for it to
   his dying day. It's no matter, let the world think me a bad counter- 140
   feit, if I cannot give him the slip at an instant; why, this is better
   than to have stayed his journey! Well, I'll follow him. O, how I long
   to be employed!
        [*Exit*]

3.1

[*Enter*] *Matthew, Wellbred,* [*and*] *Bobadill*

MATTHEW Yes, 'faith, sir, we were at your lodging to seek you, too.

WELLBRED O, I came not there tonight.

BOBADILL Your brother delivered us° as much.

WELLBRED Who? My brother Downright?

BOBADILL He. Master Wellbred, I know not in what kind you hold   5
me but let me say to you this: as sure as honour, I esteem it so much
out of the sunshine of reputation to throw the least beam of regard
upon such a—

WELLBRED Sir, I must hear no ill words of my brother.

BOBADILL I protest to you, as I have a thing to be saved° about me, I   10
never saw any gentleman-like part°—

WELLBRED Good Captain, faces about:° to some other discourse.

BOBADILL With your leave, sir, an there were no more men living
upon the face of the earth, I should not fancy him, by Saint George.

MATTHEW Troth, nor I; he is of a rustical cut,° I know not how; he   15
doth not carry himself like a gentleman of fashion—

WELLBRED O, Master Matthew, that's a grace peculiar but to a few:
quos aequus amavit Jupiter.°

MATTHEW I understand you, sir.

WELLBRED No question you do or you do not, sir.   20

[*Edward*] *Knowell enters* [*and Stephen*]

Ned Knowell! By my soul, welcome. How dost thou, sweet spirit,
my genius?° 'Slid, I shall love Apollo and the mad Thespian girls°
the better, while I live, for this. My dear fury,° now I see there's
some love in thee! Sirrah, these be the two I writ to thee of—nay,
what a drowsy humour is this now? Why dost thou not speak?   25

EDWARD O, you are a fine gallant, you sent me a rare letter!

WELLBRED Why, was't not rare?°

EDWARD Yes, I'll be sworn, I was ne'er guilty of reading the like;
match it in all Pliny° or Symmachus'° epistles, and I'll have my
judgement burned in the ear for a rogue.° Make much of thy vein,°   30
for it is inimitable. But I mar'l what camel° it was that had the
carriage of it? For doubtless, he was no ordinary° beast that brought
it.

WELLBRED Why?

EDWARD Why, sayest thou? Why, dost thou think that any reasonable   35

173

creature, especially in the morning, the sober time of the day too,
could have mista'en my father for me?

WELLBRED 'Slid, you jest, I hope?

EDWARD Indeed, the best use we can turn it to, is to make a jest on't
now; but I'll assure you my father had the full view o' your flourish-   40
ing° style some hour before I saw it.

WELLBRED What a dull slave was this! But, sirrah, what said he to it,
i'faith?

EDWARD Nay, I know not what he said; but I have a shrewd guess
what he thought.   45

WELLBRED What? What?

EDWARD Marry, that thou art some strange, dissolute young fellow,
and I a grain or two better, for keeping thee company.

WELLBRED Tut, that thought is like the moon in her last quarter,
'twill change shortly. But, sirrah, I pray thee be acquainted with my   50
two hang-bys here; thou wilt take exceeding pleasure in 'em if thou
hear'st 'em once go; my wind instruments. I'll wind° 'em up—but
what strange piece of silence is this? The sign of the Dumb Man?°

EDWARD O, sir, a kinsman of mine; one that may make your music the
fuller, an he please; he has his humour, sir.   55

WELLBRED O, what is't? What is't?

EDWARD Nay, I'll neither do your judgement nor his folly that wrong,
as to prepare your apprehension. I'll leave him to the mercy o' your
search; if you can take him, so.°

WELLBRED Well, Captain Bobadill, Master Matthew, pray you know   60
this gentleman here, he is a friend of mine and one that will deserve
your affection. (*To Stephen*) I know not your name, sir, but I shall be
glad of any occasion to render me more familiar to you.

STEPHEN My name is Master Stephen, sir; I am this gentleman's own
cousin, sir; his father is mine uncle, sir; I am somewhat melancholy,   65
but you shall command me, sir, in whatsoever is incident to a
gentleman.

BOBADILL (*to [Edward] Knowell*) Sir, I must tell you this, I am no
general man;° but for Master Wellbred's sake, you may embrace it
at what height of favour you please, I do communicate with you   70
and conceive you to be a gentleman of some parts. I love few words.

EDWARD And I fewer, sir. I have scarce enough to thank you.

MATTHEW (*to Stephen*) But are you indeed, sir, so given to it?

STEPHEN Ay, truly, sir, I am mightily given to melancholy.°

MATTHEW O, it's your only fine° humour, sir; your true melancholy   75
breeds your perfect fine wit, sir. I am melancholy myself divers

times, sir, and then do I no more but take pen and paper presently
and overflow you half a score or a dozen of sonnets at a sitting.

EDWARD (*aside*) Sure he utters° them then by the gross.°

STEPHEN Truly, sir, and I love such things out of measure.°   80

EDWARD [*aside*] I'faith, better than in measure,° I'll undertake.

MATTHEW Why, I pray you, sir, make use of my study; it's at your
service.

STEPHEN I thank you, sir; I shall be bold, I warrant you; have you a
stool there, to be melancholy upon?   85

MATTHEW That I have, sir, and some papers there of mine own doing
at idle hours, that you'll say there's some sparks of wit in 'em, when
you see them.

WELLBRED Would the sparks would kindle once and become a fire
amongst 'em; I might see self-love burnt for her heresy.   90

STEPHEN Cousin, is it well? Am I melancholy enough?

EDWARD O, ay, excellent!

WELLBRED Captain Bobadill, why muse you so?

EDWARD [*aside*] He is melancholy, too.

BOBADILL 'Faith, sir, I was thinking of a most honourable piece of   95
service was performed tomorrow, being Saint Mark's Day,° shall be
some ten years now.

EDWARD In what place, Captain?

BOBADILL Why, at the beleag'ring of Strigonium,° where, in less than
two hours, seven hundred resolute gentlemen as any were in   100
Europe lost their lives upon the breach.° I'll tell you, gentlemen, it
was the first, but the best, leaguer that ever I beheld with these
eyes, except the taking in of—what do you call it?—last year by the
Genoese;° but that of all other was the most fatal and dangerous
exploit that ever I was ranged° in, since I first bore arms before the   105
face of the enemy, as I am a gentleman and soldier.

STEPHEN [*aside*] 'So, I had as lief as an angel I could swear as well as
that gentleman!°

EDWARD Then you were a servitor° at both, it seems. At Strigonium,
and what do you call't?   110

BOBADILL O, Lord, sir! By Saint George, I was the first man that
entered the breach; and, had I not effected it with resolution, I had
been slain if I had had a million of lives.

EDWARD [*aside*] 'Twas pity you had not ten; a cat's and your own,
i'faith. [*To Bobadill*] But was it possible?   115

MATTHEW (*aside to Stephen*) Pray you, mark this discourse, sir.

STEPHEN [*aside to Matthew*] So I do.

BOBADILL I assure you, upon my reputation, 'tis true, and yourself
shall confess.

EDWARD You must bring me to the rack° first.   120

BOBADILL Observe me judicially, sweet sir; they had planted me°
three demi-culverins just in the mouth of the breach; now, sir, as we
were to give on,° their master gunner—a man of no mean skill and
mark, you must think—confronts me with his linstock ready to give
fire. I, spying his intendment, discharged my petronel in his bosom,   125
and with these single° arms, my poor rapier, ran violently upon the
Moors that guarded the ordnance° and put 'em pell-mell to the
sword.

WELLBRED To the sword? To the rapier,° Captain?

EDWARD O, it was a good figure observed, sir! But did you all this,   130
Captain, without hurting your blade.

BOBADILL Without any impeach° o' the earth; you shall perceive, sir.
It is the most fortunate weapon that ever rid on poor gentleman's
thigh: shall I tell you, sir? You talk of Morglay, Excalibur,
Durindana,° or so? Tut, I lend no credit to that is fabled of 'em; I   135
know the virtue of mine own and therefore I dare the boldlier
maintain it.

STEPHEN I mar'l whether it be a Toledo or no?

BOBADILL A most perfect Toledo, I assure you, sir.

STEPHEN I have a countryman of his here.   140

    [Draws his rapier]

MATTHEW Pray you, let's see, sir. Yes, faith, it is!

BOBADILL This a Toledo? Pish!

STEPHEN Why do you 'pish', Captain?

BOBADILL A Fleming,° by heaven, I'll buy them for a guilder° apiece,
an I would have a thousand of them.   145

EDWARD How say you, cousin? I told you thus much.

WELLBRED Where bought you it, Master Stephen?

STEPHEN Of a scurvy rogue soldier—a hundred of lice go with
him—he swore it was a Toledo.

BOBADILL A poor provant° rapier, no better.   150

MATTHEW Mass, I think it be, indeed, now I look on't better.

EDWARD Nay, the longer you look on't, the worse. Put it up,° put it up.

STEPHEN Well, I will put it up, but by—I ha' forgot the Captain's
oath, I had thought to ha' sworn by it—an ere I meet him—

WELLBRED O, it is past help now, sir; you must have patience.   155

STEPHEN Whoreson coney-catching rascal! I could eat the very hilts
for anger.

EDWARD A sign of good digestion! You have an ostrich stomach,°
cousin.

STEPHEN A stomach?° Would I had him here, you should see, an I had   160
a stomach.

WELLBRED It's better as 'tis.° Come, gentlemen, shall we go?
  [*Enter*] *Brainworm* [*as Fitzsword*]

EDWARD A miracle, cousin, look here! Look here!

STEPHEN O, God's 'lid, by your leave, do you know me, sir?

BRAINWORM Ay, sir, I know you by sight.   165

STEPHEN You sold me a rapier, did you not?

BRAINWORM Yes, marry, did I, sir

STEPHEN You said it was a Toledo, ha?

BRAINWORM True, I did so.

STEPHEN But it is none.   170

BRAINWORM No, sir, I confess it, it is none.

STEPHEN Do you confess it? Gentlemen, bear witness, he has
confessed it. By God's will, an you had not confessed it—

EDWARD O, cousin, forbear, forbear.

STEPHEN Nay, I have done, cousin.   175

WELLBRED Why, you have done like a gentleman. He has confessed
it, what would you more?

STEPHEN Yet, by his leave, he is a rascal; under his favour,° do you see?

EDWARD [*aside to Wellbred*] Ay, by his leave, he is, and under favour;
a pretty piece of civility! Sirrah, how dost thou like him?   180

WELLBRED [*aside to Edward*] O, it's a most precious fool, make much
on him.° I can compare him to nothing more happily° than a drum;
for everyone may play upon him.

EDWARD [*aside to Wellbred*] No, no, a child's whistle were far the
fitter.   185

BRAINWORM [*to Edward*] Sir, shall I entreat a word with you?

EDWARD With me, sir? You have not another Toledo to sell, ha' you?

BRAINWORM You are conceited,° sir; [*draws him aside*] your name is
Master Knowell, as I take it?

EDWARD You are i'the right. You mean not to proceed in the   190
catechism,° do you?

BRAINWORM No, sir, I am none of that coat.°

EDWARD Of as bare a coat, though. Well, say, sir.

BRAINWORM 'Faith, sir, I am but servant to the drum extraordinary;°
and, indeed, this smoky varnish being washed off and three or four   195
patches removed, I appear your worship's in reversion, after the
decease of your good father, Brainworm.

EDWARD Brainworm! 'Slight, what breath of a conjurer hath blown
    thee hither in this shape?
BRAINWORM The breath o' your letter, sir, this morning—the same   200
    that blew you to the Windmill, and your father after you.
EDWARD My father?
BRAINWORM Nay, never start, 'tis true; he has followed you over the
    fields by the foot, as you would do a hare i' the snow.
EDWARD Sirrah Wellbred, what shall we do, sirrah? My father is come   205
    over after me.
WELLBRED Thy father? Where is he?
BRAINWORM At Justice Clement's house here, in Coleman Street,
    where he but stays° my return; and then—
WELLBRED Who's this? Brainworm?   210
BRAINWORM The same, sir.
WELLBRED Why, how, i' the name of wit, com'st thou transmuted thus?
BRAINWORM 'Faith, a device,° a device! Nay, for the love of reason,
    gentlemen, and avoiding the danger, stand not here—withdraw,
    and I'll tell you all.   215
WELLBRED But art thou sure he will stay thy return?
BRAINWORM Do I live, sir? What a question is that?
WELLBRED We'll prorogue his expectation° then a little. Brainworm,
    thou shalt go with us. Come on, gentlemen! Nay, I pray thee, sweet
    Ned, droop not: 'heart, an our wits be so wretchedly dull that one   220
    old plodding brain can outstrip us all, would we were e'en pressed
    to make porters° of, and serve out the remnant of our days in
    Thames Street or at Custom House Quay,° in a civil war against the
    carmen.°
BRAINWORM Amen, amen, amen, say I.   225
    [*Exeunt*]

3.[2]

[*Enter*] *Kitely* [*and*] *Cash*

KITELY What says he, Thomas? Did you speak with him?
CASH He will expect you, sir, within this half hour.
KITELY Has he the money ready, can you tell?
CASH Yes, sir, the money was brought in last night.
KITELY O, that's well: fetch me my cloak, my cloak!   5
    [*Exit Cash*]

Stay, let me see, an hour, to go and come,
Ay, that will be the least: and then 'twill be
An hour before I can dispatch with him,
Or very near: well, I will say two hours.
Two hours? Ha? Things never dreamt of yet   10
May be contrived, ay, and effected too
In two hours' absence: well, I will not go.
Two hours; no, fleering opportunity,
I will not give your subtlety that scope.
Who will not judge him worthy to be robbed   15
That sets his doors wide open to a thief
And shows the felon where his treasure lies?
Again, what earthy spirit but will attempt
To taste the fruit of beauty's golden tree
When leaden sleep seals up the dragon's eyes?°   20
I will not go. Business, go by, for once.
No, beauty, no,—you are of too good caract,
To be left so, without a guard, or open.
Your lustre too'll enflame, at any distance,
Draw courtship to you, as a jet° doth straws,   25
Put motion in a stone, strike fire from ice,°
Nay, make a porter leap° you with his burden!
You must be then kept up, close and well-watched,
For, give you opportunity, no quicksand
Devours or swallows swifter! He that lends   30
His wife (if she be fair) or time,° or place,
Compels her to be false. I will not go.
The dangers are too many. And, then, the dressing
Is a most main attractive!° Our great heads°
Within the City never were in safety,   35
Since our wives wore these little caps: I'll change 'em,
I'll change 'em, straight,° in mine. Mine shall no more
Wear three-piled acorns,° to make my horns° ache.
Nor will I go: I am resolved for that.
        [*Enter Cash with cloak*]
Carry in my cloak again. Yet, stay. Yet, do too.   40
I will defer going, on all occasions.
CASH Sir, Snare, your scrivener, will be there with th' bonds.
KITELY That's true. Fool on me! I had clean forgot it:
    I must go. What's o'clock?
        [*Kitely puts on the cloak*]

CASH	Exchange time,° sir.
KITELY [*aside*]	'Heart, then will Wellbred presently be here too,

With one or other of his loose consorts.
I am a knave, if I know what to say,
What course to take, or which way to resolve.
My brain, methinks, is like an hour-glass,
Wherein my 'maginations run like sands,
Filling up time, but then are turned, and turned,
So that I know not what to stay upon,°
And less to put in act.° It shall be so.
Nay, I dare build upon° his secrecy,
He knows not to deceive me. Thomas?

CASH   Sir.

KITELY [*aside*] Yet now, I have bethought me, too, I will not.
[*Aloud*] Thomas, is Cob within?

CASH   I think he be, sir.

KITELY [*aside*] But he'll prate too, there's no speech of him.°
No, there were no man o' the earth to Thomas,°
If I durst trust him, there is all the doubt.
But should he have a chink° in him, I were gone,
Lost i' my fame for ever; talk for th' Exchange.
The manner he hath stood with, till this present,
Doth promise no such change. What should I fear then?
Well, come what will, I'll tempt my fortune, once.
[*To Cash*] Thomas, you may deceive me, but I hope
Your love to me is more—

CASH   Sir, if a servant's
Duty, with faith may be called love, you are
More than in hope; you are possessed of it.

KITELY I thank you, heartily, Thomas; gi' me your hand:
With all my heart, good Thomas. I have, Thomas,
A secret to impart unto you—but
When once you have it, I must seal your lips up.
So far I tell you, Thomas—

CASH   Sir, for that—

KITELY Nay, hear me out. Think, I esteem you, Thomas,
When I will let you in, thus, to my private.°
It is a thing sits nearer to my crest°
Than thou art 'ware of, Thomas. If thou should'st
Reveal it, but—

CASH   How? I reveal it?

KITELY   Nay,
  I do not think thou wouldst; but if thou shouldst,   80
  'Twere a great weakness.
CASH   A great treachery.
  Give it no other name.
KITELY   Thou wilt not do't, then?
CASH Sir, if I do, mankind disclaim° me ever.
KITELY [aside] He will not swear, he has some reservation,
  Some concealed purpose, and close meaning, sure;   85
  Else, being urged so much, how should he choose
  But lend an oath to all this protestation?
  He's no precisian,° that I am certain of,
  Nor rigid Roman Catholic. He'll play
  At fayles and tick-tack,° I have heard him swear.   90
  What should I think of it? Urge him again,
  And by some other way? I will do so.
  [To Cash] Well, Thomas, thou hast sworn not to disclose;
  Yes, you did swear?
CASH   Not yet, sir, but I will.
  Please you—
KITELY   No, Thomas, I dare take thy word.   95
  But, if thou wilt swear, do, as thou think'st good;
  I am resolved without it; at thy pleasure.
CASH By my soul's safety then, sir, I protest.°
  My tongue shall ne'er take knowledge of a word,
  Delivered me in nature of your trust.   100
KITELY It's too much, these ceremonies need not;°
  I know thy faith to be as firm as rock.
  Thomas, come hither, near: we cannot be
  Too private in this business. So it is,—
  (Aside) Now he has sworn, I dare the safelier venture.   105
  [To Cash] I have of late, by divers observations—
  (Aside) But whether his oath can bind him, yea or no,
  Being not taken lawfully. Ha? Say you?°
  I will ask counsel ere I do proceed:—
  [To Cash] Thomas, it will be now too long to stay,   110
  I'll spy some fitter time soon, or tomorrow.
CASH Sir, at your pleasure.
KITELY   I will think. And, Thomas,
  I pray you search the books 'gainst my return,
  For the receipts 'twixt me and Traps.

CASH   I will, sir.

KITELY And, hear you, if your mistress' brother, Wellbred,   115
  Chance to bring hither any gentlemen,
  Ere I come back, let one straight bring me word.

CASH Very well, sir.

KITELY   To the Exchange, do you hear?
  Or here, in Coleman Street, to Justice Clement's.
  Forget it not, nor be not out of the way.°   120

CASH I will not, sir.

KITELY   I pray you have a care on't.
  Or whether he come or no, if any other,
  Stranger or else, fail not to send me word.

CASH I shall not, sir.

KITELY   Be't your special business
  Now, to remember it.

CASH   Sir, I warrant you.   125

KITELY But, Thomas, this is not the secret, Thomas,
  I told you of.

CASH   No, sir, I do suppose it.

KITELY Believe me, it is not.

CASH   Sir, I do believe you.

KITELY By heaven, it is not, that's enough. But, Thomas,
  I would not you should utter it, do you see,   130
  To any creature living. Yet, I care not.
  Well, I must hence. Thomas, conceive thus much:
  It was a trial of you, when I meant°
  So deep a secret to you, I mean not this,
  But that I have to tell you; this is nothing, this.   135
  But, Thomas, keep this from my wife, I charge you,
  Locked up in silence, midnight,° buried here.°
  No greater hell, than to be slave to fear.
      [Exit Kitely]

CASH 'Locked up in silence, midnight, buried here?'
  Whence should this flood of passion, trow, take head?° Ha?   140
  Best dream no longer of this running humour,°
  For fear I sink! The violence of the stream
  Already hath transported me so far,
  That I can feel no ground at all! But soft.
      [Enter] Cob
  O, 'tis our water-bearer—somewhat has crossed him now.   145

COB Fasting days?° What tell you me of fasting days? 'Slid, would they

were all on a light fire° for me. They say the whole world shall be
consumed with fire one day, but would I had these ember weeks°
and villainous Fridays burnt in the meantime, and then—

CASH Why, how now, Cob, what moves thee to this choler? Ha? 150

COB Collar, Master Thomas? I scorn your collar. I, sir, I am none o'
your carthorse, though I carry and draw water. An you offer to ride°
me, with your collar, or halter either, I may hap show you a jade's
trick,° sir.

CASH O, you'll slip your head out of the collar? Why, goodman Cob, 155
you mistake me.

COB Nay, I have my rheum,° and I can be angry as well as another,
sir.

CASH Thy rheum, Cob? Thy humour, thy humour? Thou mistak'st.

COB Humour? Mack,° I think it be so, indeed: what is that humour? 160
Some rare thing, I warrant.

CASH Marry, I'll tell thee, Cob. It is a gentleman-like monster, bred in
the special gallantry of our time, by affectation; and fed by folly.

COB How? Must it be fed?

CASH O, ay, humour is nothing, if it be not fed. Didst thou never hear 165
that? It's a common phrase, 'Feed my humour'.°

COB I'll none on it. Humour, avaunt, I know you not, begone! Let
who will make hungry meals for your monstership,° it shall not be I.
Feed you, quoth he? 'Slid, I ha' much ado to feed myself; especially
on these lean rascally° days, too; an't had been any other day but a 170
fasting day (a plague on them all for me) by this light, one might
have done the commonwealth good service, and have drowned
them all i' the flood, two or three hundred thousand years ago. O, I
do stomach° them hugely! I have a maw now, an't were for Sir Bevis,
his horse, against 'em.° 175

CASH I pray thee, good Cob, what makes thee so out of love with
fasting days?

COB Marry, that which will make any man out of love with 'em, I
think: their bad conditions, an you will needs know.° First, they are
of a Flemish° breed, I am sure on't, for they ravin up° more butter 180
than all the days of the week beside; next, they stink of fish and
leek-porridge miserably; thirdly, they'll keep a man devoutly hungry all day and at night send him supperless to bed.

CASH Indeed, these are faults, Cob.

COB Nay, an this were all, 'twere something, but they are the only 185
known enemies to my generation.° A fasting day no sooner comes,
but my lineage goes to rack, poor cobs they smoke for it, they are

made martyrs o' the gridiron, they melt in passion;° and your maids
too know this, and yet would have me turn Hannibal,° and eat my
own fish and blood. (*He pulls out a red herring*) My princely coz,   190
fear nothing; I have not the heart to devour you, an I might be made
as rich as King Cophetua.° O, that I had room for my tears, I could
weep salt-water enough now to preserve the lives of ten thousand
of my kin. But I may curse none but these filthy almanacs,° for an't
were not for them, these days of persecution would ne'er be known.   195
I'll be hanged, an some fishmonger's son do not make of 'em; and
puts in more fasting days than he should do, because he would utter°
his father's dried stockfish and stinking conger.

CASH 'Slight, peace, thou'lt be beaten like a stockfish else.

　　　[Exit Cob]

Here is Master Matthew. Now must I look out for a messenger to   200
my master.

　　　[Exit Cash.] [Enter] Wellbred, [Edward] Knowell, Brainworm,
　　　Bobadill, Matthew [, and] Stephen

WELLBRED Beshrew me, but it was° an absolute good jest, and exceedingly well carried!°

EDWARD Ay, and our ignorance maintained it as well, did it not?

WELLBRED Yes, 'faith; but was't possible thou shouldst not know   205
him? I forgive Master Stephen, for he is stupidity itself.

EDWARD 'Fore God, not I, an I might have been joined patent with
one of the seven wise masters,° for knowing him. He had so writhen
himself into the habit° of one of your poor infantry, your decayed,
ruinous, worm-eaten gentlemen of the round;° such as have vowed   210
to sit on the skirts of the City, let your provost° and his half-dozen
of halberdiers° do what they can; and have translated begging out
of old hackney-pace° to a fine easy amble, and made it run as
smooth of the tongue as a shove-groat shilling.° Into the likeness of
one of these *reformados*° had he moulded himself so perfectly,   215
observing every trick of their action, as varying the accent, swearing with an emphasis, indeed all, with so special and exquisite a
grace, that (hadst thou seen him) thou wouldst have sworn he
might have been sergeant-major, if not a lieutenant-colonel to the
regiment.   220

WELLBRED Why, Brainworm, who would have thought thou hadst
been such an artificer?°

EDWARD An artificer? An architect! Except a man had studied begging all his lifetime, and been a weaver of language from his infancy,
for the clothing of it,° I never saw his rival!   225

WELLBRED Where got'st thou this coat, I mar'l?

BRAINWORM Of a Houndsditch° man, sir. One of the devil's near kinsmen, a broker.

WELLBRED That cannot be, if the proverb hold; for, 'a crafty knave needs no broker'.   230

BRAINWORM True, sir, but I did need a broker, *ergo*—

WELLBRED [*aside*] Well put off!—No crafty knave, you'll say?

EDWARD Tut, he has more of these shifts.°

BRAINWORM And yet where I have one, the broker has ten, sir.

            [*Enter Cash*]

CASH Francis! Martin!° Ne'er a one to be found now. What a spite's°   235
this?

WELLBRED How now, Thomas? Is my brother Kitely within?

CASH No, sir, my master went forth e'en now—but Master Downright is within. Cob! What, Cob! Is he gone too?

WELLBRED Whither went your master? Thomas, canst thou tell?   240

CASH I know not. To Justice Clement's, I think, sir. Cob!

            [*Exit Cash*]

EDWARD Justice Clement, what's he?

WELLBRED Why, dost thou not know him? He is a City magistrate, a Justice here, an excellent good lawyer and a great scholar: but the only mad,° merry, old fellow in Europe! I showed him you, the other   245
day.

EDWARD O, is that he? I remember him now. Good faith, and he has a very strange presence, methinks; it shows as if he stood out of the rank from other men. I have heard many of his jests i' university. They say he will commit a man for taking the wall° of his horse.   250

WELLBRED Ay, or wearing a cloak off one shoulder, or serving of God; anything indeed if it come in the way of his humour.

            [*Cash*] *goes in and out calling*

CASH Gasper, Martin, Cob! 'Heart, where should they be, trow?

BOBADILL Master Kitely's man, pray thee vouchsafe us the lighting of this match.°   255

            [*Bobadill hands Cash a match*]

CASH Fire on° your match, no time but now to vouchsafe? Francis! Cob!

            [*Exit Cash*]

BOBADILL [*taking out tobacco and filling his pipe*] Body of me! Here's the remainder of seven pound, since yesterday was seven-night.° 'Tis your right *Trinidado!*° Did you never take any, Master   260
Stephen?

STEPHEN No, truly, sir; but I'll learn to take it now, since you commend it so.
BOBADILL [*passing the tobacco to Matthew who starts to fill his pipe*] Sir,
   believe me, upon my relation, for what I tell you the world shall not   265
   reprove.° I have been in the Indies, where this herb grows, where
   neither myself nor a dozen gentlemen more, of my knowledge, have
   received the taste of any other nutriment, in the world, for the
   space of one and twenty weeks, but the fume of this simple° only.
   Therefore, it cannot be, but 'tis most divine! Further, take it in the   270
   nature,° in the true kind so, it makes an antidote that, had you taken
   the most deadly poisonous plant in all Italy,° it should expel it, and
   clarify you, with as much ease as I speak. And for your green°
   wound, your Balsamum and your Saint John's wort are all mere
   gulleries and trash to it, especially your *Trinidado*—your *Nicotian*°   275
   is good, too. I could say what I know of the virtue of it, for the
   expulsion of rheums,° raw humours, crudities,° obstructions, with
   a thousand of this kind, but I profess myself no quacksalver. Only,
   thus much, by Hercules, I do hold it, and will affirm it, before any
   prince in Europe, to be the most sovereign and precious weed that   280
   ever the earth tendered to the use of man.
EDWARD This speech would ha' done decently in a tobacco trader's
   mouth!
   [*Enter Cash with Cob*]
CASH At Justice Clement's he is: in the middle of Coleman Street.
COB O, O?   285
BOBADILL Where's the match I gave thee, Master Kitely's man?
CASH [*aside*] Would his match, and he, and pipe, and all were at San
   Domingo!° [*Aloud*] I had forgot it.
   [*Exit Cash*]
COB By God's me, I mar'l what pleasure or felicity they have in taking
   of this roguish tobacco!° It's good for nothing but to choke a man,   290
   and fill him full of smoke and embers: there were four died out of
   one house last week, with taking of it, and two more the bell° went
   for, yesternight; one of them, they say, will ne'er scape it—he
   voided° a bushel of soot yesterday, upward and downward. By the
   stocks, an there were no wiser men than I, I'd have it present°   295
   whipping, man or woman, that should but deal with a tobacco pipe.
   Why, it will stifle them all in the end, as many as use it; it's little
   better than ratsbane or rosaker.
   Bobadill beats [*Cob*] *with a cudgel*
ALL O, good Captain, hold, hold!

186

BOBADILL You base cullion, you.   300
    [*Enter Cash with a lighted match*]
CASH Sir, here's your match. Come, thou must needs be talking, too,
    thou'rt well enough served.
COB Nay, he will not meddle with his match,° I warrant you. Well, it
    shall be a dear beating, an I live.
BOBADILL [*lighting his pipe and passing the match to Matthew*] Do you   305
    prate? Do you murmur?
EDWARD Nay, good Captain, will you regard the humour of a fool?
    Away, knave.
WELLBRED Thomas, get him away.
    [*Exeunt Cash and Cob*]
BOBADILL A whoreson filthy slave, a dungworm, an excrement! Body   310
    o' Caesar, but that I scorn to let forth so mean a spirit, I'd ha'
    stabbed him to the earth.
WELLBRED Marry, the law forbid, sir.
BOBADILL By Pharaoh's foot, I would have done it.
STEPHEN O, he swears admirably! 'By Pharaoh's foot', 'body of   315
    Caesar', I shall never do it, sure, upon mine honour, and by Saint
    George, no, I ha' not the right grace.
MATTHEW [*offering Stephen his pipe*] Master Stephen, will you any?
    By this air, the most divine tobacco that ever I drunk!°
STEPHEN None, I thank you, sir.   320
    [*Exeunt Bobadill and Matthew*]
    O, this gentleman does it rarely, too, but nothing like the other!
    (*Stephen is practising to the post*°) 'By this air', 'as I am a gentleman',
    'by—
BRAINWORM [*aside*] Master, glance,° glance! Master Wellbred!
STEPHEN [*to the post*] As I have somewhat to be saved, I protest—   325
WELLBRED You are a fool; it needs no affidavit.
EDWARD Cousin, will you any tobacco?
STEPHEN I, sir! Upon my reputation—
EDWARD How now, cousin?
STEPHEN I protest, as I am a gentleman, but no soldier, indeed—   330
WELLBRED No, Master Stephen? As I remember, your name is
    entered in the Artillery Garden.°
STEPHEN Ay, sir, that's true. Cousin, may I swear, 'as I am a soldier'
    by that?
EDWARD O, yes, that you may. It's all you have for your money.   335
STEPHEN Then, as I am a gentleman, and a soldier, it is divine
    tobacco!

WELLBRED But soft,° where's Master Matthew? Gone?

BRAINWORM No, sir, they went in here.

WELLBRED O, let's follow them—Master Matthew is gone to salute   340
his mistress, in verse. We shall ha' the happiness to hear some of his
poetry now. He never comes unfurnished. Brainworm?

STEPHEN Brainworm? Where? Is this Brainworm?

EDWARD Ay, cousin, no words of it, upon your gentility.

STEPHEN Not I, body of me, by this air, Saint George and the foot of   345
Pharaoh.

WELLBRED Rare! Your cousin's discourse is simply drawn out° with
oaths!

EDWARD 'Tis larded° with 'em. A kind of French dressing, if you love it.

[*Exeunt*]

3.[3]

[*Enter*] *Kitely* [*and*] *Cob*

KITELY Ha? How many are there, sayest thou?

COB Marry, sir, your brother, Master Wellbred—

KITELY Tut, beside him: what strangers are there, man?

COB Strangers? Let me see, one, two; mass, I know not well, there are
so many.   5

KITELY How? So many?

COB Ay, there's some five, or six of them, at the most.

KITELY [*aside*] A swarm, a swarm. Spite of the devil, how they sting
my head—
[*Making horns with his fingers above his head*]
With forkèd stings thus wide and large!° [*Aloud*] But, Cob,   10
How long hast thou been coming hither, Cob?

COB A little while, sir.

KITELY Didst thou come running?

COB No, sir.

KITELY [*aside*] Nay, then I am familiar with thy haste!   15
Bane° to my fortunes! What meant I to marry?
I, that before was ranked° in such content,
My mind at rest too, in so soft a peace,
Being free master of mine own free thoughts,
And now become a slave? What? Never sigh,   20
Be of good cheer, man: for thou art a cuckold,

'Tis done, 'tis done! Nay, when such flowing store,°
Plenty itself, falls in my wife's lap,
The *cornucopiae*° will be mine, I know. [*Aloud*] But Cob,
What entertainment° had they? I am sure   25
My sister and my wife would bid them welcome! Ha?
COB Like enough, sir, yet, I heard not a word of it.
KITELY [*aside*] No: their lips were sealed with kisses, and the voice
Drowned in a flood of joy, at their arrival,
Had lost her motion,° state,° and faculty.°   30
[*Aloud*] Cob, which of them was't, that first kissed my wife?
My sister, I should say. My wife, alas,
I fear not her. Ha? Who was it, say'st thou?
COB By my troth, sir, will you have the truth of it?
KITELY O, ay, good Cob; I pray thee, heartily.   35
COB Then, I am a vagabond, and fitter for Bridewell° than your wor-
ship's company, if I saw anybody to be kissed, unless they would
have kissed the post° in the middle of the warehouse; for there I left
them all, at their tobacco, with a pox.°
KITELY How? Were they not gone in, then, ere thou cam'st?   40
COB O, no, sir.
KITELY Spite of the devil! What do I stay here, then? Cob, follow me.
        [*Exit*] *Kitely*
COB Nay, soft and fair, I have eggs on the spit;° I cannot go yet, sir.
Now am I for some five and fifty reasons hammering, hammering
revenge. O, for three or four gallons of vinegar to sharpen my wits!   45
Revenge! Vinegar, revenge! Vinegar and mustard, revenge!° Nay, an
he had not lain in my house, 'twould never have grieved me, but
being my guest, one that, I'll be sworn, my wife has lent him her
smock off her back, while his one shirt has been at washing;
pawned her neckerchers for clean bands° for him; sold almost all my   50
platters to buy him tobacco; and he to turn monster of ingratitude,
and strike his lawful host!° Well, I hope to raise up an host of fury
for't: here comes Justice Clement.
        [*Enter Justice*] *Clement, Knowell,* [*and*] *Formal*
JUSTICE CLEMENT What's Master Kitely gone? Roger?
FORMAL Ay, sir.   55
JUSTICE CLEMENT Heart of me! What made him leave us so
abruptly? [*To Cob*] How now, sirrah? What make you here? What
would you have, ha?
COB An't please your worship, I am a poor neighbour of your
worship's—   60

JUSTICE CLEMENT A poor neighbour of mine? Why, speak, poor
  neighbour.
COB I dwell, sir, at the sign of the water-tankard,° hard by the Green
  Lattice.° I have paid scot and lot° there, any time this eighteen years.
JUSTICE CLEMENT To the Green Lattice?   65
COB No, sir, to the parish—marry, I have seldom 'scaped scot-free, at
  the Lattice.
JUSTICE CLEMENT O, well! What business has my poor neighbour
  with me?
COB An't like your worship, I am come to crave the peace° of your   70
  worship.
JUSTICE CLEMENT Of me, knave? Peace of me, knave? Did I e'er hurt
  thee? Or threaten thee? Or wrong thee? Ha?
COB No, sir, but your worship's warrant, for one that has wronged
  me, sir; his arms are at too much liberty, I would fain have them   75
  bound to a treaty of peace, an my credit could compass it° with your
  worship.
JUSTICE CLEMENT Thou goest far enough about° for't, I'm sure.
KNOWELL Why, dost thou go in danger of thy life for him, friend?
COB No, sir; but I go in danger of my death, every hour, by his means.   80
  An I die within a twelve-month and a day,° I may swear by the law of
  the land, that he killed me.
JUSTICE CLEMENT How? How, knave? Swear he killed thee? And by
  the law? What pretence? What colour° hast thou for that?
COB Marry, an't please your worship, both black and blue; colour   85
  enough, I warrant you. I have it here, to show your worship.
    [Displays his bruises]
JUSTICE CLEMENT What is he that gave you this, sirrah?
COB A gentleman, and a soldier, he says he is, o' the City here.
JUSTICE CLEMENT A soldier o' the City? What call you him?
COB Captain Bobadill.   90
JUSTICE CLEMENT Bobadill? And why did he bob° and beat you, sir-
  rah? How began the quarrel betwixt you? Ha? Speak truly, knave, I
  advise you.
COB Marry, indeed, an please your worship, only because I spake
  against their vagrant° tobacco, as I came by 'em when they were   95
  taking on't, for nothing else.
JUSTICE CLEMENT Ha? You speak against tobacco? Formal, his
  name.
FORMAL What's your name, sirrah?
COB Oliver, sir, Oliver Cob, sir.   100

JUSTICE CLEMENT Tell Oliver Cob, he shall go to the jail, Formal.

FORMAL Oliver Cob, my master Justice Clement says, you shall go to the jail.

COB O, I beseech your worship, for God's sake, dear Master Justice.

JUSTICE CLEMENT Nay, God's precious:° an such drunkards, and 105
tankards° as you are, come to dispute of tobacco once—I have done!°
Away with him!

COB O, good Master Justice, sweet old gentleman.

KNOWELL Sweet Oliver,° would I could do thee any good. Justice
Clement, let me entreat you, sir.   110

JUSTICE CLEMENT What? A threadbare rascal! A beggar! A slave that
never drunk out of better than piss-pot metal° in his life! And he to
deprave and abuse the virtue of an herb, so generally received in the
courts of princes, the chambers of nobles, the bowers of sweet
ladies, the cabins of soldiers! Roger, away with him, by God's 115
precious—I say, go to.

COB Dear Master Justice; let me be beaten again, I have deserved
it,—but not the prison, I beseech you.

KNOWELL Alas, poor Oliver!

JUSTICE CLEMENT Roger, make him a warrant—he shall not go—I 120
but fear° the knave.

FORMAL Do not stink,° sweet Oliver, you shall not go, my master will
give you a warrant.

COB O, the Lord maintain his worship, his worthy worship.

JUSTICE CLEMENT Away, dispatch him.   125

    [*Exeunt Cob and Formal*]

How now, Master Knowell? In dumps?° In dumps? Come, this
becomes not.

KNOWELL Sir, would I could not feel my cares—

JUSTICE CLEMENT Your cares are nothing! They are like my cap,
soon put on, and as soon put off. What? Your son is old enough to 130
govern himself—let him run his course, it's the only way to make
him a staid° man. If he were an unthrift,° a ruffian, a drunkard, a
licentious liver, then you had reason; you had reason to take care:
but, being none of these, mirth's my witness, an I had twice so
many cares as you have, I'd drown them all in a cup of sack. Come, 135
come, let's try it.—I muse,° your parcel° of a soldier returns not all
this while.

    [*Exeunt*]

4.1

[Enter] Downright [and] Dame Kitely

DOWNRIGHT Well, sister, I tell you true; and you'll find it so in the
end.

DAME KITELY Alas, brother, what would you have me do? I cannot
help it; you see my brother brings 'em in here, they are his friends.

DOWNRIGHT His friends? His fiends. 'Slud, they do nothing but 5
haunt him up and down like a sort of unlucky sprites,° and tempt
him to all manner of villainy that can be thought of. Well, by this
light, a little thing would make me play the devil° with some of 'em;
an't were not more for your husband's sake than anything else, I'd
make the house too hot for the best on 'em: they should say, and 10
swear, hell were broken loose ere they went hence. But, by God's
will, 'tis nobody's fault but yours; for an you had done as you might
have done, they should have been parboiled,° and baked too, every
mother's son, ere they should ha' come in, e'er a one of 'em.

DAME KITELY God's my life!° Did you ever hear the like? What a 15
strange man is this! Could I keep out all them, think you? I should
put myself against half a dozen men, should I? Good faith, you'd
mad the patientest body in the world, to hear you talk so, without
any sense or reason!

[Enter] Bridget, Master Matthew, Stephen, [and] Bobadill, [to
them, followed by] Edward, Wellbred, [and] Brainworm.
[Edward, Wellbred, and Brainworm stand aside to observe the
action]

BRIDGET *[to Matthew]* Servant,° in troth, you are too prodigal 20
Of your wit's treasure, thus to pour it forth
Upon so mean a subject as my worth.

MATTHEW You say well, mistress; and I mean as well.

DOWNRIGHT *[aside]* Hey-day,° here is stuff!°

WELLBRED *[aside to Edward]* O, now stand close;° pray heaven, she 25
can get him to read—he should do it of his own natural impudency.

[Edward, Wellbred, and Brainworm move closer]

BRIDGET *[to Matthew]* Servant, what is this same, I pray you?

MATTHEW Marry, an elegy, an elegy, an odd toy°—

DOWNRIGHT *[aside]* To mock an ape° withal. O, I could sew up his
mouth now. 30

DAME KITELY Sister, I pray you, let's hear it.

DOWNRIGHT Are you rhyme-given,° too?

MATTHEW Mistress, I'll read it, if you please.

BRIDGET Pray you do, servant.

DOWNRIGHT O, here's no foppery!° Death,° I can endure the stocks   35
better!

    [Exit Downright]

EDWARD *[aside to Wellbred]* What ails thy brother, can he not hold his
water° at reading of a ballad?

WELLBRED *[aside to Edward]* O, no: a rhyme to him is worse than
cheese or a bagpipe.° But mark, you lose the protestation.°   40

    [Edward, Wellbred, and Brainworm move closer again]

MATTHEW 'Faith, I did it in an humour; I know not how it is;° but
please you come near, sir. This gentleman has judgement, he knows
how to censure of a—. *[To Stephen]* Pray you, sir, you can judge.

STEPHEN Not I, sir; upon my reputation, and by the foot of Pharaoh.

WELLBRED *[aside to Edward]* O, chide your cousin for swearing.   45

EDWARD *[aside to Wellbred]* Not I, so long as he does not forswear
himself.°

BOBADILL Master Matthew, you abuse the expectation of your dear
mistress and her fair sister. Fie, while you live, avoid this prolixity.

MATTHEW I shall, sir. Well, *incipere dulce*.°   50

EDWARD *[aside to Wellbred]* How! *Insipere*° dulce? A sweet thing to be a
fool, indeed.

WELLBRED *[aside to Edward]* What, do you take *incipere* in that sense?

EDWARD *[aside to Wellbred]* You do not? You? This was your villainy,
to gull him with a *mot*.°   55

WELLBRED *[aside to Edward]* O, the benchers' phrase: *pauca verba,
pauca verba*.°

MATTHEW *[loudly]*

    'Rare creature, let me speak without offence,
    Would God my rude words had the influence,
    To rule thy thoughts, as thy fair looks do mine,   60
    Then shouldst thou be his prisoner, who is thine.'

EDWARD *[aside to Wellbred]* This is in *Hero and Leander*.°

WELLBRED *[aside to Edward]* O, ay. Peace, we shall have more of this.

MATTHEW

    'Be not unkind, and fair, misshapen stuff
    Is of behaviour boisterous and rough.'   65

WELLBRED *[to Stephen]* How like you that, sir?

Master Stephen answers with shaking his head

EDWARD [*aside to Wellbred*] 'Slight, he shakes his head like a bottle, to feel an there be any brain in it!

MATTHEW But observe the catastrophe° now,

> 'And I in duty will exceed all other,   70
> As you in beauty do excel Love's mother.'

EDWARD [*aside to Wellbred*] Well, I'll have him free of the wit-brokers,° for he utters nothing but stolen remnants.

WELLBRED [*aside to Edward*] O, forgive it him.

EDWARD [*aside to Wellbred*] A filching rogue? Hang him!° And from   75
the dead;° it's worse than sacrilege.

[*Wellbred comes forward and breaks into the group*]

WELLBRED Sister, what ha' you here? Verses? Pray you, let's see.

[*Bridget hands Wellbred the verses*]

Who made these verses? They are excellent good!

MATTHEW O, Master Wellbred, 'tis your disposition to say so, sir.
They were good i'the morning;° I made 'em, *extempore*, this   80
morning.

WELLBRED How, *extempore*?

MATTHEW I would I might be hanged else—ask Captain Bobadill. He
saw me write them at the—pox on it—the Star,° yonder.

BRAINWORM [*aside to Edward*] Can he find in his heart to curse the   85
stars so?

EDWARD [*aside to Brainworm*] 'Faith, his are even with him—they ha'
cursed him enough already.°

STEPHEN [*to Edward*] Cousin, how do you like this gentleman's
verses?   90

EDWARD O, admirable! The best that ever I heard, coz!

STEPHEN Body o' Caesar, they are admirable! The best that ever I
heard, as I am a soldier!

[*Enter Downright*]

DOWNRIGHT I am vexed, I can hold ne'er a bone of me° still! Heart, I
think they mean to build and breed° here!   95

WELLBRED [*to Bridget*] Sister, you have a simple servant here, that
crowns your beauty with such *encomions*° and devices. You may see
what it is to be the mistress of a wit that can make your perfections
so transparent that every bleary eye may look through them, and
see him drowned over head and ears, in the deep well of desire. [*To*   100
Mistress Kitely] Sister Kitely, I marvel you get you not a servant
that can rhyme, and do tricks,° too.

DOWNRIGHT O, monster! Impudence itself! Tricks?

DAME KITELY Tricks, brother? What tricks?

BRIDGET Nay, speak, I pray you; what tricks?   105

DAME KITELY Ay, never spare anybody here—but say, what tricks?

BRIDGET Passion of my heart! Do tricks?

WELLBRED 'Slight, here's a trick vied, and revied!° Why, you monkeys°
you, what a caterwauling do you keep? Has he not given you
rhymes, and verses, and tricks?   110

DOWNRIGHT O, the fiend!

WELLBRED Nay, you, lamp of virginity,° that take it in snuff° so! Come
and cherish this tame poetical fury° in your servant, you'll be
begged else shortly for a concealment°—go to, reward his muse. You
cannot give him less than a shilling, in conscience, for the book he   115
had it out of cost him a teston,° at least. How now, gallants? Master
Matthew? Captain? What, all sons of silence? No spirit?

DOWNRIGHT Come, you might practise your ruffian tricks somewhere else, and not here, I wusse;° this is no tavern, nor drinking-
school to vent your exploits in.   120

WELLBRED How now! Whose cow has calved?°

DOWNRIGHT Marry, that has mine, sir. Nay, boy, never look askance
at me for the matter; I'll tell you of it,° ay, sir, you, and your companions,° mend yourselves, when I ha' done.

WELLBRED My companions?   125

DOWNRIGHT Yes, sir, your companions, so I say. I am not afraid of
you, nor them neither, your hang-bys here. You must have your
poets and your potlings, your *soldados* and *foolados*,° to follow you up
and down the City, and here they must come to domineer and
swagger. [*To Matthew*] Sirrah, you, ballad-singer, and slops,° your   130
fellow there, get you out, get you home; [*drawing his sword*] or, by
this steel, I'll cut off your ears, and that presently.

WELLBRED [*drawing his sword*] 'Slight, stay, let's see what he dare do!
Cut off his ears? Cut a whetstone.° You are an ass, do you see?
Touch any man here, and by this hand, I'll run my rapier to the   135
hilts in you.

DOWNRIGHT Yea, that would I fain see, boy!

    [*Wellbred and Downright start to fight, and Matthew, Stephen
    and Bobadill all draw as if to join in*]

DAME KITELY O, Jesu! Murder! Thomas! Gaspar!

BRIDGET Help, help, Thomas!

    [*Cash*] and [*Kitely's servants*] make out [*from offstage*] to part
    them

EDWARD Gentleman, forbear, I pray you.   140

    [Cash and the other servants restrain Wellbred and Downright]

BOBADILL *[to Downright]* Well, sirrah, you, Holofernes:° by my hand,
  I will pink° your flesh full of holes with my rapier for this; I will, by
  this good heaven.

    *Downright [breaks free] and [Bobadill] offer[s]° to fight [with
    him]. [They] are parted [and restrained again by the servants]*

  Nay, let him come. Let him come, gentlemen. By the body of Saint
  George, I'll not kill him.   145

CASH Hold, hold, good gentlemen.

DOWNRIGHT *[to Bobadill]* You whoreson, bragging coistrel!

    [Enter] Kitely

KITELY Why, how now? What's the matter? What's the stir here?
  Whence springs the quarrel? Thomas! Where is he?
  Put up your weapons, and put off this rage.   150
  [Aside] My wife and sister, they are the cause of this.
  [Aloud] What, Thomas? Where is this knave?

CASH Here, sir.

WELLBRED *[to Edward]* Come, let's go. This is one of my brother's
  ancient° humours, this.   155

STEPHEN I am glad nobody was hurt by his ancient humour.

    *[Exeunt Wellbred, Stephen, Bobadill, Matthew, Edward and
    Brainworm]*

KITELY Why, how now, brother, who enforced this brawl?

DOWNRIGHT A sort of lewd rake-hells, that care neither for God nor
  the devil! And they must come here to read ballads, and roguery,
  and trash! I'll mar° the knot of 'em ere I sleep, perhaps—*[gesturing* 160
  offstage] especially Bob, there—he that's all manner of shapes!° And
  songs-and-sonnets,° his fellow.

BRIDGET Brother, indeed, you are too violent,
  Too sudden in your humour—and, you know
  My brother Wellbred's temper will not bear   165
  Any reproof, chiefly° in such a presence,
  Where every slight disgrace he should receive
  Might wound him in opinion and respect.

DOWNRIGHT Respect? What talk you of respect 'mong such,
  As ha' nor spark of manhood, nor good manners?   170
  'Sdines, I am ashamed to hear you! Respect?

    [Exit Downright]

BRIDGET Yes, there was one, a civil gentleman,
  And very worthily demeaned° himself.

KITELY O, that was some love of yours, sister.

BRIDGET A love of mine? I would it were no worse, brother!   175
You'd pay my portion° sooner than you think for.

DAME KITELY Indeed, he seemed to be a gentleman of exceeding fair
disposition, and of very excellent good parts.

[*Exeunt Dame Kitely and Bridget*]

KITELY [*aside*] Her love, by heaven! My wife's minion!°
Fair disposition? Excellent good parts?   180
Death, these phrases are intolerable!
Good parts? How should she know his parts?°
His parts? Well, well, well, well, well, well!
It is too plain, too clear: [*to Cash*] Thomas, come hither.
What, are they gone?

CASH   Ay, sir, they went in.   185
My mistress and your sister—

KITELY Are any of the gallants within?

CASH No, sir, they are all gone.

KITELY Art thou sure of it?

CASH I can assure you, sir.   190

KITELY What gentleman was that they praised so, Thomas?

CASH One, they call him Master Knowell, a handsome young
gentleman, sir.

KITELY Ay, I thought so: my mind gave me as much.
[*Aside*] I'll die, but they have° hid him i' the house   195
Somewhere; I'll go and search. [*To Cash*] Go with me, Thomas.
Be true to me, and thou shalt find me a master.

[*Exeunt*]

4.[2]

[*Enter*] Cob [*and*] Tib

COB [*knocking at the door*] What, Tib! Tib, I say!

TIB [*within*] How now, what cuckold is that knocks so hard?

[*Enter Tib*]

O, husband, is't you? What's the news?

COB Nay, you have stunned me, i'faith! You ha' given me a knock o'
the forehead, will stick by me!° Cuckold? 'Slid, cuckold?   5

TIB Away, you fool, did I know it was you that knocked? Come, come,
you may call me as bad when you list.°

COB May I? Tib, you are a whore.

TIB You lie in your throat,° husband!

COB How, the lie? And in my throat, too? Do you long to be stabbed,   10
ha?

TIB Why, you are no soldier, I hope?

COB O, must you be stabbed° by a soldier? Mass,° that's true! When was
Bobadill here? Your Captain? That rogue, that foist,° that fencing
Burgullian?° I'll tickle° him, i'faith.   15

TIB Why, what's the matter, trow?

COB O, he has basted° me rarely, sumptuously. But I have it here in
black and white;° for his black and blue shall pay him. O, the Justice!
The honestest old brave Trojan° in London! I do honour the very
flea of his dog. A plague on him, though; he put me once in a   20
villainous filthy fear; marry, it vanished away like the smoke of
tobacco; but I was smoked° soundly first. I thank the devil and his
good angel, my guest.° Well, wife, or Tib° (which you will), get you
in, and lock the door, I charge you, let nobody in to you,° wife, no
body into you: those are my words. Not Captain Bob himself, nor   25
the fiend in his likeness; you are a woman; you have flesh and blood
enough in you to be tempted: therefore, keep the door shut, upon
all comers.

TIB I warrant you, there shall no body enter here, without my consent.

COB Nor with your consent, sweet Tib, and so I leave you.   30

TIB It's more than you know, whether you leave me so.

COB How?

TIB Why, sweet.

COB Tut, sweet or sour, thou art a flower,
Keep close thy door, I ask no more.   35
    [*Exeunt*]

4.[3]

[*Enter*] *Edward, Wellbred, Stephen,* [*and*] *Brainworm* [*as
Fitzsword*]

EDWARD Well, Brainworm, perform this business happily, and thou
makest a purchase of my love forever.

WELLBRED I'faith, now let thy spirits use their best faculties. But, at
any hand, remember the message to my brother: for there's no
other means to start him.°   5

BRAINWORM I warrant you, sir, fear nothing; I have a nimble soul has
waked all forces of my fancy° by this time, and put 'em in true
motion. What you have possessed me withal,° I'll discharge it amply,
sir. Make it no question.

WELLBRED Forth, and prosper, Brainworm.   10

      [*Exit Brainworm*]

'Faith, Ned, how dost thou approve of my abilities in this
device?

EDWARD Troth, well, howsoever°—but it will come excellent, if it
take.

WELLBRED Take, man? Why, it cannot choose but take, if the circum-   15
stances miscarry not: but, tell me, ingenuously,° dost thou affect° my
sister Bridget, as thou pretendest?°

EDWARD Friend, am I worth belief?

WELLBRED Come, do not protest. In faith, she is a maid of good
ornament° and much modesty: and, except I conceived° very wor-   20
thily of her, thou shouldest not have her.

EDWARD Nay, that I am afraid will be a question yet, whether I shall
have her or no.

WELLBRED 'Slid, thou shalt have her; by this light, thou shalt.

EDWARD Nay, do not swear.   25

WELLBRED By this hand, thou shalt have her. I'll go fetch her, presently. 'Point° but where to meet, and as I am an honest man, I'll
bring her.

EDWARD Hold, hold, be temperate.

WELLBRED Why, by—what shall I swear by? Thou shalt have her, as I   30
am—

EDWARD Pray thee, be at peace, I am satisfied, and do believe thou
wilt omit no offered occasion to make my desires complete.

WELLBRED Thou shalt see, and know, I will not.

      [*Exeunt*]

4.[4]

      [*Enter*] *Formal* [*and*] *Knowell*

FORMAL Was your man a soldier, sir?

KNOWELL Ay, a knave, I took him begging o' the way,
This morning, as I came over Moorfields!°

      [*Enter Brainworm disguised as Fitzsword*]

O, here he is! [*To Brainworm*] You've made fair speed, believe me:
Where, i' the name o' sloth, could you be thus—   5

BRAINWORM Marry, peace be my comfort,° where I thought I should
have had little comfort of° your worship's service.

KNOWELL How so?

BRAINWORM O, sir! Your coming to the City, your entertainment° of
me, and your sending me to watch—indeed, all the circumstances   10
either of your charge, or my employment, are as open to your son as
to yourself!

KNOWELL How should that be? Unless that villain, Brainworm,
Have told him of the letter, and discovered°
All that I strictly charged him to conceal? 'Tis so!   15

BRAINWORM I am partly o' the faith 'tis so, indeed.

KNOWELL But how should he know thee to be my man?

BRAINWORM Nay, sir, I cannot tell; unless it be by the black art! Is not
your son a scholar,° sir?

KNOWELL Yes, but I hope his soul is not allied   20
Unto such hellish practice: if it were,
I had just cause to weep my part in him,
And curse the time of his creation.
But where didst thou find them, Fitzsword?

BRAINWORM You should rather ask where they found me, sir, for, I'll   25
be sworn I was going along in the street, thinking nothing, when
(of a sudden) a voice calls, 'Master Knowell's man', another cries
'soldier': and thus, half a dozen of 'em, till they had called me
within a house where I no sooner came, but they seemed men,°
and out flew all their rapiers at my bosom, with some three-or-four   30
score oaths to accompany 'em, and all to tell me, I was but a dead
man if I did not confess where you were, and how I was employed,
and about what; which, when they could not get out of me—as I
protest, they must ha' dissected and made an anatomy° o' me first,
and so I told 'em—they locked me up into a room i' the top of a   35
high house, whence, by great miracle (having a light heart°) I slid
down by a bottom of pack-thread° into the street, and so 'scaped.
But, sir, thus much I can assure you, for I heard it while I was
locked up, there were a great many rich merchants and brave citizens' wives with 'em at a feast, and your son, Master Edward,   40
withdrew with one of 'em, and has 'pointed to meet her anon, at
one Cob's house, a water-bearer, that dwells by the wall.° Now,
there your worship shall be sure to take him, for there he preys,
and fail he will not.

KNOWELL Nor will I fail to break his match,° I doubt not.   45
  Go thou along with Justice Clement's man,°
  And stay there for me. At one Cob's house, sayst thou?
BRAINWORM Ay, sir, there you shall have him.
        [*Exit*] *Knowell*
  [*Aside*] Yes? Invisible? Much wench, or much son!° 'Slight, when
  he has stayed there three or four hours, travelling with the expect-   50
  ation of wonders and at length be delivered of air: O, the sport that
  I should then take to look on him, if I durst!° But, now, I mean to
  appear no more afore him in this shape. I have another trick to act,
  yet. O, that I were so happy as to light on a nupson, now, of this
  Justice's novice.° Sir, I make you stay somewhat long.   55
FORMAL Not a whit, sir. Pray you, what do you mean, sir?
BRAINWORM I was putting up some papers—
FORMAL You ha' been lately in the wars, sir, it seems.
BRAINWORM Marry, have I, sir, to my loss and expense of all,
  almost—   60
FORMAL Troth, sir, I would be glad to bestow a pottle° of wine o' you,
  if it please you to accept it—
BRAINWORM O, sir—
FORMAL But, to hear the manner of your services and your devices in
  the wars, they say they be very strange, and not like those a man   65
  reads in the Roman histories,° or sees at Mile End.
BRAINWORM No, I assure you, sir, why, at any time when it please
  you, I shall be ready to discourse to you all I know—[*aside*] and
  more too, somewhat.
FORMAL No better time than now, sir; we'll go to the Windmill; there   70
  we shall have a cup of neat grist,° we call it. I pray you, sir, let me
  request you, to the Windmill.
BRAINWORM I'll follow you, sir,—[*aside*] and make grist o' you,° if I
  have good luck.
        [*Exeunt*]

4.[5]

[*Enter*] *Matthew, Edward, Bobadill,* [*and*] *Stephen*
MATTHEW Sir, did your eyes ever taste the like clown of him,° where
  we were today, Master Wellbred's half-brother? I think the whole
  earth cannot show his parallel, by this daylight.

201

EDWARD We were now speaking of him. Captain Bobadill tells me he
is fallen foul o' you, too.   5

MATTHEW O, ay, sir, he threatened me with the bastinado.

BOBADILL Ay, but I think I taught you prevention,° this morning, for
that—You shall kill him beyond question, if you be so generously°
minded.

MATTHEW Indeed, it is a most excellent trick!   10

BOBADILL [*practising at a post*] O, you do not give spirit enough to
your motion, you are too tardy, too heavy. O, it must be done like
lightning—[*making a showy sword thrust*] hai!°

MATTHEW Rare, Captain.

BOBADILL Tut, 'tis nothing, an't be not done in a [*making another   15
showy sword thrust*] punto!°

EDWARD Captain, did you ever prove yourself upon° any of our
masters of defence,° here?

MATTHEW O, good sir! Yes, I hope, he has!

BOBADILL I will tell you, sir. Upon my first coming to the City, after   20
my long travail° for knowledge (in that mystery° only), there came
three or four of 'em to me, at a gentleman's house, where it was my
chance to be resident at that time, to entreat my presence at their
schools, and withal so much importuned me that (I protest to you
as I am a gentleman) I was ashamed of their rude demeanour, out of   25
all measure.° Well, I told 'em, that to come to a public school, they
should pardon me, it was opposite (in diameter) to my humour, but,
if so they would give their attendance at my lodging, I protested to
do them what right or favour I could, as I was a gentleman, and so
forth.   30

EDWARD So, sir, then you tried their skill?

BOBADILL Alas, soon tried! You shall hear, sir. Within two or three
days after, they came; and, by honesty, fair sir, believe me I graced
them exceedingly, showed them some two or three tricks of prevention have purchased 'em since a credit,° to admiration! They cannot   35
deny this, and yet now they hate me, and why? Because I am
excellent, and for no other vile reason on the earth.

EDWARD This is strange and barbarous as ever I heard!

BOBADILL Nay, for a more° instance of their preposterous° natures, but
note, sir. They have assaulted me some three, four, five, six of them   40
together, as I have walked alone, in divers skirts° i' the town, as
Turnbull, Whitechapel, Shoreditch,° which were then my quarters,
and since upon the Exchange, at my lodging, and at my ordinary,°
where I have driven them afore me, the whole length of a street, in

the open view of all our gallants, pitying to hurt them, believe me.   45
Yet, all this lenity will not o'ercome their spleen: they will be doing
with the pismire, raising a hill a man may spurn abroad° with his
foot, at pleasure. By myself, I could have slain them all, but I
delight not in murder. I am loath to bear any other than this bastinado for 'em—yet, I hold it good policy not to go disarmed, for   50
though I be skilful, I may be oppressed with multitudes.

EDWARD Ay, believe me, may you sir—and (in my conceit°) our whole
nation should sustain the loss by it, if it were so.

BOBADILL Alas, no: what's a peculiar° man, to a nation? Not seen.

EDWARD O, but your skill, sir!   55

BOBADILL Indeed, that might be some loss; but who respects it? I
will tell you, sir, by the way of private, and under seal;° I am a
gentleman, and live here obscure, and to myself; but were I known
to Her Majesty and the Lords (observe me), I would undertake
(upon this poor head and life) for the public benefit of the state,   60
not only to spare the entire lives of her subjects in general, but to
save the one half, nay three parts of her yearly charge, in holding
war, and against what enemy soever. And how would I do it, think
you?

EDWARD Nay, I know not, nor can I conceive.   65

BOBADILL Why, thus, sir. I would select nineteen more, to myself,
throughout the land; gentlemen they should be of good spirit,
strong, and able constitution, I would choose them by an instinct, a
character,° that I have: and I would teach these nineteen the special
rules, as your *Punto*, your *Reverso*,° your *Stoccata*, your *Imbroccata*,°   70
your *Passada*, your *Montanto*,° till they could all play very near, or
altogether as well as myself. This done, say the enemy were forty
thousand strong, we twenty would come into the field, the tenth of
March, or thereabouts; and we would challenge twenty of the
enemy; they could not, in their honour, refuse us; well, we would   75
kill them; challenge twenty more, kill them; twenty more, kill
them; twenty more, kill them too; and thus, would we kill, every
man, his twenty a day, that's twenty score; twenty score, that's two
hundred;° two hundred a day, five days a thousand; forty thousand; forty times five, five times forty, two hundred days kills them   80
all up, by computation. And this will I venture my poor
gentleman-like carcass to perform (provided there be no treason
practised upon us) by fair and discreet manhood, that is, civilly by
the sword.

EDWARD Why, are you so sure of your hand, Captain, at all times?   85

BOBADILL Tut, never miss thrust, upon my reputation with you.

EDWARD I would not stand in Downright's state,° then, an you meet
him, for the wealth of any one street in London.

BOBADILL Why, sir, you mistake me! If he were here now, by this
welkin, I would not draw my weapon on him. Let this gentleman   90
do his mind°—but I will bastinado him (by the bright sun) wherever
I meet him.

MATTHEW 'Faith, and I'll have a fling at him, at my distance.

[Enter] Downright. [He] walks over the stage

EDWARD God's so, look where he is! Yonder he goes!

DOWNRIGHT What peevish luck have I, I cannot meet with these   95
bragging rascals.

[Exit Downright]

BOBADILL It's not he? Is it?

EDWARD Yes, 'faith, it is he.

MATTHEW I'll be hanged, then, if that were he.

EDWARD Sir, keep your hanging good° for some greater matter, for I   100
assure you, that was he.

STEPHEN Upon my reputation, it was he.

BOBADILL Had I thought it had been he, he must not have gone so,—
but I can hardly be induced to believe it was he, yet.

EDWARD That I think, sir. But see, he is come again!   105

[Enter Downright in his cloak]

DOWNRIGHT O, Pharaoh's foot,° have I found you? Come, draw, to
your tools:° draw, gipsy,° or I'll thrash you.

[Downright removes his cloak and draws his sword]

BOBADILL Gentleman of valour, I do believe in thee, hear me—

DOWNRIGHT Draw your weapon, then.

BOBADILL Tall° man, I never thought on it till now (body of me)—I   110
had a warrant of the peace served on me, even now, as I came along,
by a water-bearer; this gentleman saw it, Master Matthew.

DOWNRIGHT 'Sdeath, you will not draw, then?

Downright beats [Bobadill], and disarms him. Matthew runs away

BOBADILL Hold, hold, under thy favour, forbear.

DOWNRIGHT Prate again, as you like this,° you whoreson foist, you.   115
You'll control the point,° you? Your consort is gone? Had he stayed,
he had shared with you, sir.

[Exit Downright]

BOBADILL Well, gentlemen, bear witness, I was bound to the peace,
by this good day.

EDWARD No, 'faith, it's an ill day, Captain, never reckon it other—   120

but, say you were bound to the peace, the law allows you to defend
yourself, that'll prove but a poor excuse.

BOBADILL I cannot tell, sir. I desire good construction, in fair sort.° I
never sustained the like disgrace! By heaven, sure I was struck with
a planet° thence, for I had no power to touch my weapon.   125

EDWARD Ay, like enough, I have heard many that have been beaten
under a planet.° Go, get you to a surgeon.

            [*Exit Bobadill*]
'Slid, an these be your tricks, your *passadas* and your *mountantos*,
I'll none of them. O, manners! That this age should bring forth
such creatures! That Nature should be at leisure to make 'em!   130
Come, coz.

STEPHEN [*picking up Downright's cloak*] Mass, I'll ha' this cloak.

EDWARD God's will, 'tis Downright's.

STEPHEN Nay, it's mine now, another might have ta'en it up, as well as
I. I'll wear it, so I will.   135

EDWARD How, an he see it? He'll challenge° it, assure yourself.

STEPHEN Ay, but he shall not ha' it; I'll say I bought it.

EDWARD Take heed you buy it not too dear, coz.

            [*Exeunt*]

4.[6]

[*Enter*] Kitely, Wellbred, Dame Kitely, [*and*] Bridget

KITELY Now, trust me, brother, you were much to blame,
        T'incense his anger, and disturb the peace
        Of my poor house, where there are sentinels
        That every minute watch to give alarms
        Of civil war,° without adjection°   5
        Of your assistance, or occasion.°

WELLBRED No harm done, brother, I warrant you; since there is no
harm done. Anger costs a man nothing—and a tall man is never his
own man,° till he be angry. To keep his valour in obscurity is to keep
himself, as it were, in a cloak-bag. What's a musician, unless he   10
play? What's a tall man, unless he fight? For, indeed, all this, my
wise brother stands upon, absolutely,—and that made me fall in
with° him so resolutely.

DAME KITELY Ay, but what harm might have come of it, brother?

WELLBRED Might, sister? So might the good warm clothes your   15

husband wears be poisoned,° for anything he knows; or the whole-
some wine he drunk, even now, at the table—
KITELY [*aside*] No, God forbid! O, me! Now I remember,
  My wife drunk to me, last, and changed the cup;
  And bade me wear this cursed suit today.   20
  See, if heaven suffer murder° undiscovered!
  [*Aloud*] I feel me ill; give me some mithridate,
  Some mithridate and oil, good sister, fetch me;
  O, I am sick at heart!° I burn, I burn.
  If you will save my life, go, fetch it me.   25
WELLBRED O, strange humour! My very breath has° poisoned
  him.
BRIDGET [*to Kitely*] Good brother, be content, what do you mean?
  The strength of these extreme conceits° will kill you.
DAME KITELY Beshrew your heart-blood, brother Wellbred, now,   30
  For putting such a toy° into his head.
WELLBRED Is a fit simile, a toy? Will he be poisoned with a simile?
  Brother Kitely, what a strange and idle imagination is this? For
  shame, be wiser. O' my soul, there's no such matter.
KITELY Am I not sick? How am I, then, not poisoned?   35
  Am I not poisoned? How am I, then, so sick?
DAME KITELY If you be sick, your own thoughts make you sick.
WELLBRED His jealousy is the poison he has taken.
    [*Enter Brainworm*] *He comes disguised like* [*Formal,*] *Justice*
    Clement's man
BRAINWORM Master Kitely, my master, Justice Clement, salutes you;
  and desires to speak with you, with all possible speed.   40
KITELY No time, but now? When, I think, I am sick? Very sick! Well, I
  will wait upon his worship. Thomas! Cob! [*Aside*] I must seek them
  out, and set 'em sentinels, till I return. [*Aloud*] Thomas! Cob!
  Thomas!
    [*Exit Kitely*]
WELLBRED [*aside to Brainworm*] This is perfectly rare, Brainworm.   45
  But how got'st thou this apparel of the Justice's man?
BRAINWORM [*aside to Wellbred*] Marry, sir, my proper fine penman
  would needs bestow the grist o' me,° at the Windmill, to hear some
  martial discourse; where so I marshalled° him, that I made him
  drunk with admiration! And, because too much heat° was the cause   50
  of his distemper, I stripped him stark naked, as he lay along asleep,
  and borrowed his suit to deliver this counterfeit message in, leaving
  a rusty armour and an old brown bill° to watch him, till my return—

which shall be, when I ha' pawned his apparel, and spent the better
part o' the money, perhaps.   55

WELLBRED [*aside to Brainworm*] Well, thou art a successful, merry
knave, Brainworm, his absence will be a good subject for more mirth.
I pray thee, return to thy young master, and will him to meet me, and
my sister Bridget, at the Tower° instantly,—for, here, tell him, the
house is so stored with jealousy, there is no room for love to stand   60
upright° in. We must get our fortunes committed to° some larger
prison, say; and, than the Tower, I know no better air; nor where the
liberty° of the house may do us more present service. Away.

    [*Exit Brainworm.*] [*Enter Kitely and Cash*]

KITELY Come hither, Thomas! Now my secret's ripe,
And thou shalt have it—lay to both thine ears,°   65
Hark what I say to thee. I must go forth, Thomas.
Be careful of thy promise, keep good watch,
Note every gallant, and observe him well,
That enters in my absence, to thy mistress:
If she would show him rooms,° the jest is stale,°   70
Follow 'em, Thomas, or else hang on him,
And let him not go after;° mark their looks;
Note, if she offer but to see his band,
Or any other amorous toy,° about him;
But° praise his leg, or foot; or if she say,   75
The day is hot, and bid him feel her hand,
How hot it is,—O, that's a monstrous thing!
Note me all this, good Thomas, mark their sighs,
And if they do but whisper, break 'em off:
I'll bear thee out° in it. Wilt thou do this?   80
Wilt thou be true, my Thomas?

CASH   As truth's self, sir.°

KITELY Why, I believe thee: where is Cob, now? Cob!
    [*Exit Kitely*]

DAME KITELY He's ever calling for Cob! I wonder, how he employs
Cob so!

WELLBRED Indeed, sister, to ask how he employs Cob, is a necessary   85
question for you that are his wife, and a thing not very easy for you
to be satisfied in—but this I'll assure you, Cob's wife is an excellent
bawd, sister, and oftentimes your husband haunts her house, marry,
to what end I cannot altogether accuse him, imagine you what you
think convenient. But, I have known fair hides have foul hearts° ere   90
now, sister.

DAME KITELY Never said you truer than that, brother, so much I can
tell you for your learning. Thomas, fetch your cloak, and go with
me, I'll after him presently. I would to fortune I could take him
there,° i'faith! I'd return him his own,° I warrant him.   95
    [*Exit Dame Kitely with Cash*]

WELLBRED So, let 'em go—this may make sport anon. Now, my fair
sister-in-law, that you knew but how happy a thing it were to be fair,
and beautiful.

BRIDGET That touches not me,° brother.

WELLBRED That's true; that's even the fault of it: for, indeed, beauty   100
stands a woman in no stead, unless it procure her touching. But,
sister, whether it touch you or no, it touches your beauties; and I am
sure they will abide the touch;° an' they do not, a plague of all
ceruse,° say I: and it touches me too in part, though not in the—.°
Well, there's a dear and respected friend of mine, sister, stands very   105
strongly, and worthily affected towards you, and hath vowed to
inflame whole bonfires° of zeal, at his heart, in honour of your
perfections. I have already engaged my promise to bring you, where
you shall hear him confirm much more. Ned Knowell is the man,
sister. There's no exception against° the party. You are ripe for a   110
husband; and a minute's loss to such an occasion is a great trespass
in a wise beauty. What say you, sister? On my soul, he loves you.
Will you give him the meeting?

BRIDGET 'Faith, I had very little confidence in my own constancy,
brother, if I durst not meet a man,—but this motion of yours   115
savours of° an old knight-adventurer's servant, a little too much,
methinks.

WELLBRED What's that, sister?

BRIDGET Marry, of the squire.°

WELLBRED No matter if it did, I would be such an one for my   120
friend,—
    [*Enter Kitely*]
but see, who is returned to hinder us!

KITELY What villainy is this? Called out on a false message?
This was some plot! I was not sent for. Bridget,
Where's your sister?

BRIDGET   I think she be gone forth, sir.   125

KITELY How! Is my wife gone forth? Whither, for God's sake?

BRIDGET She's gone abroad with Thomas.

KITELY [*aside*] Abroad with Thomas? O, that villain dors° me.
He hath discovered° all unto my wife!

Beast that I was, to trust him. [*Aloud*] Whither, I pray you, went
she?   130
BRIDGET I know not, sir.
WELLBRED I'll tell you, brother, whither I suspect she's gone.
KITELY Whither, good brother?
WELLBRED To Cob's house, I believe; but, keep my counsel.
KITELY I will, I will. To Cob's house? Doth she haunt Cob's?   135
    She's gone o' purpose, now, to cuckold me,
    With that lewd rascal, who, to win her favour,
    Hath told her all.
        [*Exit Kitely*]
WELLBRED   Come, he's once more gone.
    Sister, let's lose no time; th'affair is worth it.
        [*Exeunt*]

4.[7]

[*Enter*] *Matthew* [*and*] *Bobadill*

MATTHEW I wonder, Captain, what they will say of my going away?
    Ha?
BOBADILL Why, what should they say? But as of a discreet gentle-
    man? Quick, wary, respectful of nature's fair lineaments:° and that's
    all.   5
MATTHEW Why, so! But what can they say of your beating?
BOBADILL A rude part,° a touch with soft wood,° a kind of gross
    battery used, laid on strongly, borne most patiently: and that's all.
MATTHEW Ay, but, would any man have offered it in Venice? As you
    say?   10
BOBADILL Tut, I assure you, no; you shall have there your *Nobilis*,°
    your *Gentilezza*° come in bravely upon your *reverse*, stand you close,
    stand you firm, stand you fair, save your *retricato*° with his° left leg,
    come to the *assalto*° with the right, thrust with brave steel, defy your
    base wood!° But, wherefore do I awake this remembrance? I was   15
    fascinated, by Jupiter, fascinated°—but I will be unwitched, and
    revenged, by law.
MATTHEW Do you hear? Is't not best to get a warrant, and have him
    arrested and brought before Justice Clement?
BOBADILL It were not amiss, would we had it.   20

MATTHEW Why, here comes his man, let's speak to him.

    [*Enter Brainworm disguised as Formal*]

BOBADILL Agreed, do you speak.

MATTHEW Save you, sir.

BRAINWORM With all my heart, sir.

MATTHEW Sir, there is one Downright, hath abused this gentleman,   25
    and myself, and we determine to make our amends by law; now, if
    you would do us the favour, to procure a warrant to bring him afore
    your master, you shall be well considered, I assure you, sir.

BRAINWORM Sir, you know my service is my living.° Such favours as
    these, gotten of my master, is his only preferment,° and therefore   30
    you must consider me, as I may make benefit of my place.

MATTHEW How is that, sir?

BRAINWORM 'Faith, sir, the thing is extraordinary, and the gentleman
    may be of great account°—yet, be what he will, if you will lay
    me down a brace of angels° in my hand, you shall have it, otherwise not.   35

MATTHEW How shall we do, Captain? He asks a brace of angels, you
    have no money?

BOBADILL Not a cross,° by fortune.

MATTHEW Nor I, as I am a gentleman, but two pence left of my two
    shillings in the morning for wine and radish—let's find him some   40
    pawn.

BOBADILL Pawn? We have none to the value of his demand.

MATTHEW O, yes. I'll pawn this jewel in my ear, and you may pawn
    your silk stockings, and pull up your boots, they will ne'er be
    missed: it must be done now.   45

BOBADILL Well, an there be no remedy, I'll step aside, and pull 'em
    off.

    [*Bobadill moves aside to remove his stockings*]

MATTHEW [*to Brainworm*] Do you hear, sir? We have no store of
    money at this time, but you shall have good pawns. [*Pointing to his
    earring*] Look you, sir, this jewel, and that gentleman's silk stock-   50
    ings, because we would have it dispatched ere we went to our
    chambers.

BRAINWORM I am content, sir. I will get you the warrant, presently;
    what's his name, say you? Downright?

MATTHEW Ay, ay, George Downright.   55

BRAINWORM What manner of man is he?

MATTHEW A tall big man, sir; he goes in a cloak, most commonly, of
    silk russet, laid about with russet° lace.

BRAINWORM 'Tis very good, sir.

MATTHEW [*giving Brainworm his earring*] Here, sir, here's my jewel.   60
BOBADILL [*giving Brainworm the stockings*] And, here, are stockings.
BRAINWORM Well, gentlemen, I'll procure you this warrant pres-
  ently, but, who will you have to serve it?
MATTHEW That's true, Captain. That must be considered.
BOBADILL Body o' me, I know not! 'Tis service of danger!   65
BRAINWORM Why, you were best to get one o' the varlets° o' the City,
  a sergeant. I'll appoint you one, if you please.
MATTHEW Will you, sir? Why, we can wish no better.
BOBADILL We'll leave it to you, sir.
    [*Exit Bobadill and Matthew*]
BRAINWORM This is rare! Now will I go pawn this cloak of the   70
  justice's man's at the brokers for a varlet's suit and be the varlet
  myself, and get either more pawns or more money of Downright
  for the arrest.
    [*Exit*]

4.[8]

[*Enter*] *Knowell*

KNOWELL O, here it is, I am glad: I have found it now.
  Ho? Who is within, here?
    [*Tib opens the door*]
TIB I am within, sir, what's your pleasure?
KNOWELL To know who is within, besides yourself?
TIB Why, sir, you are no constable, I hope.   5
KNOWELL O! Fear you the constable? Then, I doubt not
  You have some guests within deserve that fear—
  I'll fetch him straight.
TIB O'God's name,° sir.
KNOWELL Go to. Come, tell me, is not young Knowell here?   10
TIB Young Knowell? I know none such, sir, o' mine honesty.
KNOWELL Your honesty? Dame, it flies too lightly from you.
  There is no way but fetch the constable.
TIB The constable? The man is mad, I think.
    [*She claps to the door.*] [*Enter Dame Kitely and
    Cash*]
CASH Ho, who keeps house here?   15

KNOWELL [*aside*] O, this is the female copesmate° of my son!
  Now shall I meet him straight.
DAME KITELY   Knock, Thomas, hard.
CASH [*knocking*] Ho, good wife!
TIB [*within*]   Why, what's the matter with you?
DAME KITELY Why, woman, grieves it you to ope your door?
  Belike, you get something,° to keep it shut.   20
      [*Enter Tib*]
TIB What mean these questions, pray ye?
DAME KITELY So strange you make it? Is not my husband here?
KNOWELL [*aside*] Her husband!
DAME KITELY   My tried° husband, Master Kitely?
TIB I hope he needs not to be tried° here.
DAME KITELY No, dame: he does it not for need, but pleasure.   25
TIB Neither for need nor pleasure, is he here.
KNOWELL [*aside*] This is but a device° to balk me withal.
      [*Enter Kitely in his cloak*]
  Soft,° who is this? 'Tis not my son, disguised?
      [*Dame Kitely*] *spies her husband come, and runs to him*
DAME KITELY O, sir, have I forestalled your honest market?°
  Found your close° walks? You stand amazed, now, do you?   30
  I'faith, I am glad I have smoked you° yet at last!
  What is your jewel, trow? In: come, let's see her!
  [*To Tib*] Fetch forth your hussy,° dame. [*To Kitely*] If she be fairer,
  In any honest judgement, than myself,
  I'll be content with it—but, she is change,   35
  She feeds you fat, she soothes your appetite,
  And you are well? Your wife, an honest woman,
  Is meat twice sod° to you, sir? O, you treacher!°
KNOWELL She cannot counterfeit thus palpably.
KITELY Out on thy more than strumpet's impudence!   40
  Steal'st thou° thus to thy haunts? And, have I taken
  Thy bawd, and thee, and thy companion,
  (*Pointing to Knowell*) This hoary-headed lecher, this old goat,°
  Close at your villainy, and would'st thou 'scuse it,
  With this stale harlot's jest,° accusing me?   45
  (*To Knowell*) O, old incontinent,° dost not thou shame,
  When all thy powers' inchastity is spent,
  To have a mind so hot?° And to entice,
  And feed th'enticements of a lustful woman?
DAME KITELY Out, I defy thee, I, dissembling wretch!   50

KITELY Defy me, strumpet? Ask thy pander, here.

[*Pointing to Cash*] Can he deny it? Or that wicked elder?

KNOWELL Why, hear you,° sir!

KITELY   Tut, tut, tut: never speak—

Thy guilty conscience will discover thee.

KNOWELL What lunacy is this, that haunts this man?   55

KITELY Well, goodwife Bad, Cob's wife, and you

That make your husband such a hoddy-doddy;°

And you, young apple-squire;° and old cuckold-maker;

I'll ha' you every one before a Justice:

Nay, you shall answer it. [*To Knowell*] I charge you go.   60

KNOWELL Marry, with all my heart, sir: I go willingly.

Though I do taste this as a trick, put on me,

To punish my impertinent search—and justly,

And half forgive my son, for the device.

KITELY [*to Dame Kitely*] Come, will you go?

DAME KITELY   Go? To thy shame, believe it!   65

[*Enter Cob*]

COB Why, what's the matter here? What's here to do?

KITELY O, Cob, art thou come? I have been abused,

And i' thy house. Never was man so wronged!

COB 'Slid, in my house? My Master Kitely? Who wrongs you in my

house?   70

KITELY Marry, young lust in old and old in young here:

Thy wife's their bawd, here have I taken 'em.

COB How? Bawd? Is my house come to that? Am I preferred thither?°

Did I charge you to keep your doors shut, Is'bel?° And do you let

'em lie open for all comers?   75

[*Cob*] *falls upon*° *his wife and beats her*

KNOWELL Friend, know some cause, before thou beat'st thy wife,

This's madness in thee!

COB   Why? Is there no cause?

KITELY Yes, I'll show cause before the Justice, Cob.

Come, let her go with me.

COB   Nay, she shall go.

TIB Nay, I will go. I'll see, an you shall be allowed to make a bundle   80

o'hemp° o'your right and lawful wife thus, at every cuckoldly

knave's pleasure. Why do you not go?

KITELY A bitter quean.° Come, we'll ha' you tamed.

[*Exeunt*]

4.[9]

[*Enter*] *Brainworm* [*disguised as a sergeant, carrying a mace*]

BRAINWORM Well, of all my disguises yet, now am I most like myself, being in this sergeant's gown. A man of my present profession never counterfeits, till he lays hold upon a debtor, and says he 'rests° him, for then he brings him to all manner of unrest. A kind of little kings we are, bearing the diminutive of a mace,° made like° a young artichoke, that always carries pepper and salt in itself. Well, I know not what danger I undergo by this exploit; pray heaven I come well off.

[*Enter*] *Bobadill* [*and*] *Matthew*

MATTHEW See, I think yonder is the varlet, by his gown.

BOBADILL Let's go in quest of him.

MATTHEW [*to Brainworm*] 'Save you, friend, are not you here by appointment of Justice Clement's man?

BRAINWORM Yes, an't please you, sir. He told me two gentlemen had willed him to procure a warrant from his master (which I have about me) to be served on one Downright.

MATTHEW It is honestly done of you both; and see where the party comes, you must arrest.

[*Enter*] *Stephen* [*in Downright's cloak*]

Serve it upon him, quickly, afore he be aware!

BOBADILL Bear back,° Master Matthew.

BRAINWORM Master Downright, I arrest you, i'the Queen's name, and must carry you afore a Justice, by virtue of this warrant.

STEPHEN Me, friend? I am no Downright, I. I am Master Stephen, you do not well to arrest me, I tell you truly: I am in nobody's bonds, nor books,° I, would you should know it. A plague on you heartily, for making me thus afraid afore my time.

BRAINWORM Why, now are you deceived, gentlemen?

BOBADILL He wears such a cloak, and that deceived us—but see, here a comes, indeed! This is he, officer.

[*Enter Downright*]

DOWNRIGHT Why, how now, signor gull!° Are you turned filcher of late? Come, deliver my cloak!

STEPHEN Your cloak, sir? I bought it, even now, in open market.

BRAINWORM Master Downright, I have a warrant I must serve upon you, procured by these two gentlemen.

DOWNRIGHT These gentlemen? These rascals?

BRAINWORM [*raising his mace*] Keep the peace, I charge you, in Her   35
    Majesty's name!

DOWNRIGHT I obey thee. What must I do, officer?

BRAINWORM Go before Master Justice Clement, to answer what they
    can object against you, sir. I will use you kindly, sir.

MATTHEW Come, let's before, and make the Justice,° Captain—   40

BOBADILL The varlet's° a tall° man! Afore heaven!
        [*Exit Bobadill with Matthew*]

DOWNRIGHT Gull, you'll gi' me my cloak?

STEPHEN Sir, I bought it, and I'll keep it.

DOWNRIGHT You will?

STEPHEN Ay, that I will.   45

DOWNRIGHT [*giving money to Brainworm*] Officer, there's thy fee,
    arrest him!

BRAINWORM Master Stephen, I must arrest you.

STEPHEN Arrest me, I scorn it. There, take your cloak, I'll none on't.

DOWNRIGHT Nay, that shall not serve your turn now, sir. Officer, I'll   50
    go with thee to the Justice's: bring him along.

STEPHEN Why, is not here your cloak? What would you have?

DOWNRIGHT I'll ha' you answer it,° sir.

BRAINWORM Sir, I'll take your word; and this gentleman's, too, for
    his appearance.°   55

DOWNRIGHT I'll ha' no words taken. Bring him along.

BRAINWORM Sir, I may choose to do that: I may take bail.

DOWNRIGHT 'Tis true you may take bail and choose—at another
    time—but you shall not now, varlet. Bring him along, or I'll swinge°
    you.   60

BRAINWORM Sir, I pity the gentleman's case. Here's your money
    again.

DOWNRIGHT 'Sdines, tell me not of my money, bring him away, I say.

BRAINWORM I warrant you he will go with you of himself, sir.

DOWNRIGHT Yet more ado?   65

BRAINWORM [*aside*] I have made a fair mash° on't.

STEPHEN Must I go?

BRAINWORM I know no remedy, Master Stephen.

DOWNRIGHT Come along afore me here. I do not love your hanging
    look behind.°   70

STEPHEN Why, sir. I hope you cannot hang me for it. Can he, fellow?

BRAINWORM I think not, sir. It is but a whipping matter, sure!

STEPHEN Why, then, let him do his worst, I am resolute.
        [*Exeunt*]

5.1

Enter Justice Clement, Knowell, Kitely, Dame Kitely, Tib, Cob,
[and 1st] Servant

JUSTICE CLEMENT Nay, but stay, stay, give me leave—[*to 1st Servant*]
my chair, sirrah.

    [*The 1st Servant brings Justice Clement his chair*]
    [*Sitting*] You, Master Knowell, say you went thither to meet your
son?

KNOWELL Ay, sir. 5

JUSTICE CLEMENT But who directed you thither?

KNOWELL That did mine own man, sir.

JUSTICE CLEMENT Where is he?

KNOWELL Nay, I know not, now; I left him with your clerk, and
appointed him to stay here for me. 10

JUSTICE CLEMENT My clerk? About what time was this?

KNOWELL Marry, between one and two, as I take it.

JUSTICE CLEMENT And what time came my man with the false message to you, Master Kitely?

KITELY After two, sir. 15

JUSTICE CLEMENT Very good,—but, Mistress Kitely, how that you
were at Cob's? Ha?

DAME KITELY An please you, sir, I'll tell you. My brother, Wellbred,
told me that Cob's house was a suspected place—

JUSTICE CLEMENT So it appears, methinks—but, on. 20

DAME KITELY And that my husband used thither,° daily.

JUSTICE CLEMENT No matter, so he used° himself well, mistress.

DAME KITELY True, sir, but you know what grows by such haunts
oftentimes.

JUSTICE CLEMENT I see rank fruits of a jealous brain, Mistress 25
Kitely, but did you find your husband there, in that case, as you
suspected?

KITELY I found her there, sir.

JUSTICE CLEMENT Did you so? That alters the case. Who gave you
knowledge of your wife's being there? 30

KITELY Marry, that did my brother Wellbred.

JUSTICE CLEMENT How? Wellbred first tell her? Then tell you after?
Where is Wellbred?

KITELY Gone with my sister, sir, I know not whither.

JUSTICE CLEMENT Why, this is a mere trick, a device; you are gulled   35
    in this most grossly, all! Alas, poor wench, wert thou beaten for
    this?
TIB Yes, most pitifully, an't please you.
COB And worthily,° I hope—if it shall prove so.°
JUSTICE CLEMENT Ay, that's like, and a piece of a sentence.°   40
    [Enter 2nd Servant]
    How now, sir, what's the matter?
2ND SERVANT Sir, there's a gentleman, i'the court without, desires to
    speak with your worship.
JUSTICE CLEMENT A gentleman? What's he?
2ND SERVANT A soldier, sir, he says.   45
JUSTICE CLEMENT A soldier? Take down my armour, my sword,
    quickly! A soldier speak with me! [To Servants] Why, when,° knaves?
    Come on, come on! (He arms himself) [To 1st Servant] Hold my cap
    there, so. [To 2nd Servant] Give me my gorget,° my sword!° [To
    Knowell, the Kitelys, Cob, and Tib] Stand by, I will end your mat-   50
    ters, anon. Let the soldier enter—
    [Exit 2nd Servant.] [Enter] Bobadill [and] Matthew
    Now, sir, what ha' you to say to me?
BOBADILL By your worship's favour—
JUSTICE CLEMENT [to Matthew] Nay, keep out, sir, I know not your
    pretence. [To Bobadill] You send me word, sir, you are a soldier.—   55
    Why, sir, you shall be answered here, here be them have been
    amongst soldiers. Sir, your pleasure.
BOBADILL 'Faith, sir, so it is, this gentleman, and myself, have
    been most uncivilly wronged, and beaten, by one Downright, a
    coarse fellow about the town here, and for mine own part, I   60
    protest, being a man in no sort given to this filthy humour of
    quarrelling, he hath assaulted me in the way of my peace; despoiled
    me of mine honour; disarmed me of my weapons; and rudely laid
    me along° in the open streets, when I not so much as once offered
    to resist him.   65
JUSTICE CLEMENT O, God's precious! Is this the soldier? Here, take
    my armour off quickly, 'twill make him swoon, I fear; he is not fit to
    look on't, that will put up° a blow.
MATTHEW [coming forward] An't please your worship, he was bound
    to the peace.   70
JUSTICE CLEMENT Why, an he were, sir, his hands were not bound,
    were they?
    [Enter 2nd Servant]

2ND SERVANT There's one of the varlets of the City, sir, has brought
two gentlemen here, one upon your worship's warrant.

JUSTICE CLEMENT My warrant?   75

2ND SERVANT Yes, sir. The officer says, procured by these two.

JUSTICE CLEMENT Bid him come in. Set by this picture.°
        [*Exit 2nd Servant.*] [*Enter*] *Downright, Stephen,* [*and*]
        Brainworm [*disguised as a City Sergeant*]
    What, Master Downright! Are you brought in at Master Fresh-
    water's° suit, here!

DOWNRIGHT I'faith, sir. And here's another brought at my suit.°   80

JUSTICE CLEMENT What are you, sir?

STEPHEN A gentleman, sir. O, uncle!

JUSTICE CLEMENT Uncle? Who? Master Knowell?

KNOWELL Ay, sir! This is a wise kinsman of mine.

STEPHEN God's my witness, uncle, I am wronged here   85
    monstrously.—He charges me with stealing of his cloak, and would
    I might never stir if I did not find it° in the street, by chance.

DOWNRIGHT O, did you find it, now? You said you bought it
    erewhile.°

STEPHEN And you said I stole it; nay, now my uncle is here, I'll do   90
    well enough with you.

JUSTICE CLEMENT Well, let this breathe° awhile. You, that have cause
    to complain, there, stand forth. Had you my warrant for this
    gentleman's apprehension?

BOBADILL Ay, an't please your worship.   95

JUSTICE CLEMENT Nay, do not speak in passion° so: where had you it?

BOBADILL Of your clerk, sir.

JUSTICE CLEMENT That's well! An my clerk can make warrants,
    and my hand not at° 'em! Where is the warrant? Officer, have you it?

BRAINWORM No, sir, your worship's man, Master Formal, bid me do   100
    it, for these gentlemen, and he would be my discharge.°

JUSTICE CLEMENT Why, Master Downright, are you such a novice,
    to be served and never see the warrant?

DOWNRIGHT Sir. He did not serve it on me.

JUSTICE CLEMENT No? How then?   105

DOWNRIGHT Marry, sir, he came to me, and said he must serve it, and
    he would use me kindly, and so—

JUSTICE CLEMENT O, God's pity, was it so, sir? He must serve it? Give
    me my long sword there, and help me off;° so. Come on, sir varlet.
        ([*Justice Clement*] *flourishes over* [*Brainworm*] *with his long-*
        sword)

I must cut off your legs, sirrah. Nay, stand up, I'll use you kindly—I   110
   must cut off your legs, I say.
BRAINWORM [*kneeling*] O, good sir, I beseech you; nay, good Master
   Justice!
JUSTICE CLEMENT I must do it; there is no remedy. I must cut off
   your legs, sirrah, I must cut off your ears, you rascal, I must do it; I   115
   must cut off your nose, I must cut off your head.
BRAINWORM O, good your worship.
JUSTICE CLEMENT Well, rise, how dost thou do, now? Dost thou feel
   thyself well? Hast thou no harm?
BRAINWORM [*standing up*] No, I thank your good worship, sir.   120
JUSTICE CLEMENT Why, so! I said, I must cut off thy legs, and I must
   cut off thy arms, and I must cut off thy head, but I did not do it. So,
   you said, you must serve this gentleman with my warrant, but you
   did not serve him. You knave, you slave, you rogue, do you say you
   must? [*To 1st Servant*] Sirrah, away with him to the jail, I'll teach   125
   you a trick for your 'must', sir.
BRAINWORM Good sir, I beseech you, be good to me.
JUSTICE CLEMENT Tell him he shall to the jail, away with him, I say.
BRAINWORM Nay, sir, if you will commit me, it shall be for commit-
   ting more than this: I will not lose, by my travail, any grain of my   130
   fame certain.°
            [*Brainworm removes his disguise*]
JUSTICE CLEMENT How is this!
KNOWELL My man, Brainworm!
STEPHEN O, yes, uncle. Brainworm has been with my cousin Edward
   and I, all this day.   135
JUSTICE CLEMENT I told you all, there was some device.
BRAINWORM Nay, excellent Justice, since I have laid myself thus open
   to you; now, stand strong for me, both with your sword and your
   balance.°
JUSTICE CLEMENT Body o'me, a merry knave! [*To 1st Servant*] Give   140
   me a bowl of sack. If he belong to you, Master Knowell, I bespeak°
   your patience.
            [*1st Servant exits and then enters with drink*]
BRAINWORM That is it, I have most need of. Sir, if you'll pardon me
   only; I'll glory in all the rest of my exploits.
KNOWELL Sir, you know, I love not to have my favours come hard   145
   from me. You have your pardon,—though I suspect you shrewdly°
   for being of counsel with my son, against me.
BRAINWORM Yes, 'faith, I have, sir; though you retained me° doubly

this morning for yourself, first as Brainworm; after, as Fitzsword. I
was your reformed soldier, sir. 'Twas I sent you to Cob's, upon the   150
errand without end.

KNOWELL Is it possible? Or that thou should'st disguise thy language
so, as I should not know thee?

BRAINWORM O, sir, this has been the day of my metamorphosis! It is
not that shape alone that I have run through today. I brought this   155
gentleman, Master Kitely, a message too, in the form of Master
Justice's man here, to draw him out o' the way, as well as your
worship, while Master Wellbred might make a conveyance of
Mistress Bridget to my young master.

KITELY How! My sister stolen away?   160

KNOWELL My son is not married, I hope!

BRAINWORM 'Faith, sir, they are both as sure° as love, a priest, and
three thousand pound (which is her portion) can make 'em, and by
this time are ready to bespeak their wedding supper at the
Windmill,—except some friend here prevent 'em° and invite 'em   165
home.

JUSTICE CLEMENT Marry, that will I. I thank thee, for putting me in
mind on't. Sirrah, go you, and fetch 'em hither, upon my warrant.
    [Exit 1st Servant]
Neither's friends have cause to be sorry, if I know the young couple
aright. Here, I drink to thee, for thy good news. But, I pray thee,   170
what hast thou done with my man Formal?

BRAINWORM 'Faith, sir, after some ceremony passed, as making him
drunk, first with story and then with wine, but all in kindness, and
stripping him to his shirt,° I left him in that cool vein,° departed, sold
your worship's warrant to these two, pawned his livery for that   175
varlet's gown to serve it in; and thus have brought myself, by my
activity, to your worship's consideration.

JUSTICE CLEMENT And I will consider thee, in another cup of sack.
Here's to thee, which having drunk of, this is my sentence. Pledge
me.° Thou hast done, or assisted to nothing, in my judgement, but   180
deserves to be pardoned for the wit o'the offence. If thy master, or
any man here, be angry with thee, I shall suspect his ingine,° while I
know him for't.
    [A loud crash offstage]
How now? What noise is that?
    [Enter 2nd Servant]

2ND SERVANT Sir, it is Roger is come home.   185

JUSTICE CLEMENT Bring him in, bring him in.

[*Enter*] *Formal* [*in a suit of armour*]
What! Drunk in arms against me? Your reason, your reason for
this?

FORMAL I beseech your worship to pardon me; I happened into ill
company by chance, that cast me into a sleep, and stripped me of all   190
my clothes—

JUSTICE CLEMENT Well, tell him, I am Justice Clement, and do pardon him—but, what is this to your armour!° What may that signify?

FORMAL An't please you, sir, it hung up i'the room where I was
stripped; and I borrowed it of one of the drawers,° to come home in,   195
because I was loath to do penance through the street i'my shirt.°

JUSTICE CLEMENT Well, stand by awhile.

[*Enter*] *Edward, Wellbred,* [*and*] *Bridget* [*and 1st Servant*]
Who be these? O, the young company, welcome, welcome. Gi' you
joy. Nay, Mistress Bridget, blush not; you are not so fresh a bride,
but the news of it is come hither afore you. Master Bridegroom, I   200
ha' made your peace, give me your hand: so will I for all the rest, ere
you forsake my roof.

EDWARD We are the more bound° to your humanity, sir.

JUSTICE CLEMENT Only these two have so little of man in 'em, they
are no part of my care.   205

WELLBRED Yes, sir, let me pray you for this gentleman, he belongs to
my sister, the bride.

JUSTICE CLEMENT In what place,° sir?

WELLBRED Of her delight,° sir, below the stairs,° and in public, her
poet, sir.   210

JUSTICE CLEMENT A poet? I will challenge him myself, presently, at
extempore:

> Mount up thy Phlegon° muse, and testify,
> How Saturn,° sitting in a ebon° cloud,
> Disrobed his podex° white as ivory,°   215
> And through the welkin, thundered° all aloud.

WELLBRED He is not for *extempore*, sir. He is all for the pocket-muse.
Please you command a sight of it.

JUSTICE CLEMENT [*to the Servants*] Yes, yes, search him for a taste of
his vein.°   220

[*The Servants search Matthew and discover sheets of poems*]

WELLBRED You must not deny the Queen's Justice,° sir, under a writ
o'rebellion.°

[*The Servants give the papers to Justice Clement*]

221

JUSTICE CLEMENT What! All this verse? Body o'me, he carries a
whole realm,° a commonwealth of paper, in's hose! Let's see some of
his subjects!°   225
> [*Justice Clement reads the poems*]

> 'Unto the boundless Ocean of thy face,
> Runs this poor river charged with streams of eyes.'°

How? This is stolen!
EDWARD A parody! A parody!—With a kind of miraculous gift, to
make it absurder than it was.   230
JUSTICE CLEMENT [*to Matthew*] Is all the rest, of this batch?° [*To 1st
Servant*] Bring me a torch; lay it together and give fire.
> [*The 1st Servant exits and then enters with torch. The two
> Servants set fire to the papers*]

Cleanse the air! Here was enough to have infected° the whole City,
if it had not been taken in time! See, see, how our poet's glory
shines. Brighter, and brighter! Still it increases! O, now it's at the   235
highest and, now, it declines as fast! You may see. *Sic transit gloria
mundi.*°
KNOWELL There's an emblem° for you, son, and your studies!
JUSTICE CLEMENT Nay, no speech or act of mine be drawn against
such as profess it worthily.° They are not born every year, as an   240
alderman. There goes more to the making of a good poet than a
sheriff, Master Kitely. You look upon me! Though I live i'the City,
here amongst you, I will do more reverence to him, when I meet
him, than I will to the mayor, out of his year.° But, these paper-
peddlers! These ink dabblers! They cannot expect reprehension or   245
reproach. They will have it with the fact.°
EDWARD Sir, you have saved me the labour of a defence.
JUSTICE CLEMENT It shall be discourse for supper between your
father and me, if he dare undertake me. But, to dispatch away these,
you sign o' the soldier, and picture o' the poet (but both so false, I   250
will not ha' you hanged out at my door till midnight),° while we are
at supper you two shall penitently fast it out in my court, without;°
and, if you will, you may pray there, that we may be so merry
within as to forgive, or forget° you, when we come out. [*To Formal*]
Here's a third,° because we tender° your safety, shall watch you, he is   255
provided for the purpose.° Look to your charge, sir!
STEPHEN And what shall I do?
JUSTICE CLEMENT O, I had lost a sheep, an he had not bleated! Why,
sir, you shall give Master Downright his cloak, and I will entreat

him to take it. A trencher and a napkin you shall have, i' the buttery,° 260
and keep Cob and his wife company here—whom I will entreat first
to be reconciled—and you to endeavour with your wit, to keep 'em
so.

STEPHEN I'll do my best.

COB Why, now I see thou art honest, Tib, I receive thee as my dear 265
and mortal° wife again.

TIB And I you, as my loving and obedient husband.

JUSTICE CLEMENT Good complement!° It will be their bridal night,
too. They are married anew. Come, I conjure thee to rest, to put off
all discontent. You, Master Downright, your anger; you, Master 270
Knowell, your cares; Master Kitely and his wife, their jealousy.
For, I must tell you both, while that is fed,°
Horns i'th mind are worse than o'the head.

KITELY Sir, thus they go from me; kiss me, sweetheart.
[*Kitely kisses his wife*]

'See what a drove° of horns fly, in the air, 275
Winged with my cleansed, and my credulous breath!
Watch 'em, suspicious eyes, watch, where they fall.
See, see! On heads, that think they've none at all!
O, what a plenteous world of this will come,
When air rains horns, all may be sure of some!' 280

I ha' learned so much verse out of a jealous man's part in a play.

JUSTICE CLEMENT 'Tis well, 'tis well! This night we'll dedicate to
friendship, love, and laughter. Master bridegroom, take your bride
and lead; everyone, a fellow.° Here is my mistress, Brainworm! To
whom all my addresses of courtship shall have their reference.° 285
Whose adventures this day, when our grandchildren shall hear to be
made a fable, I doubt not but it shall find both spectators, and
applause.°
[*Exeunt*]

Appendix

SIR,
There are, no doubt, a supercilious race in the world, who will esteem
all office done you in this kind,° an injury: so solemn a vice it is with
them to use the authority of their ignorance to the crying down of
poetry,° or the professors.° But, my gratitude must not leave° to correct   10
their error; since I am none° of those that can suffer the benefits con-
ferred upon my youth to perish with my age. It is a frail memory that
remembers but present things. And, had the favour of the times so
conspired with my disposition, as it could have brought forth other, or
better, you had had the same proportion and number of the fruits, the   15
first.° Now, I pray you to accept this, such, wherein neither the confes-
sion° of my manners shall make you blush; nor of my studies, repent
you to have been the instructor. And, for the profession of my thankfulness,° I am sure, it° will, with good men, find either praise, or excuse.

                                        Your true lover,   20
                                        BEN. JONSON.

THE ROARING GIRL
OR
MOLL CUTPURSE

THOMAS MIDDLETON *and*

THOMAS DEKKER

THE PERSONS OF THE PLAY

Sir Alexander Wengrave
[Sebastian] Wengrave, [*his son*]
Sir Davy Dapper
Jack Dapper,° [*his son*]
Sir Adam Appleton
Lord Noland
Sir Beauteous Ganymede°
[Sir Thomas Long]
Laxton°
Goshawk°
Greenwit°

[Hippocrates] Gallipot,° [*an apothecary*]
[Mistress Prudence] Gallipot
Openwork, [*a sempster*]
[Mistress Rosamond] Openwork°
Tiltyard,° [*a feather-seller*]
[Mistress] Tiltyard

Citizens and Wives

Moll [Cutpurse], the Roaring Girl

Sir Guy Fitzallard
Mary Fitzallard, *his daughter*

Neatfoot [*Sir Alexander Wengrave's*] *man*
[Ralph] Trapdoor°
Gull, [*Jack Dapper's*] *page*
[Tearcat]°
Curtalax,° *a sergeant*
Hanger,° *his yeoman*

[Gentlemen]
[Sir Alexander's servingmen]
[Fellow with long rapier]
[Porter]
[Tailor]
[Coachman]
[Cutpurses]

[Prologue]

PROLOGUE

[Enter the Prologue]

PROLOGUE A play expected long makes the audience look
 For wonders, that each scene should be a book
 Composed to all perfection. Each one comes
 And brings a play in's head with him; up he sums
 What he would of a roaring girl have writ,   5
 If that he finds not here, he mews° at it.
 Only we entreat you think our scene
 Cannot speak high, the subject being but mean.°
 A roaring girl, whose notes till now never were,°
 Shall fill with laughter our vast theatre: 10
 That's all which I dare promise—tragic passion,
 And such grave stuff, is this day out of fashion.
 I see attention sets wide ope her gates
 Of hearing, and with covetous listening waits
 To know what girl this roaring girl should be,   15
 For of that tribe are many. One is she
 That roars at midnight in deep tavern bowls,°
 That beats the watch,° and constables controls;
 Another roars i'th' day-time, swears, stabs, gives braves,°
 Yet sells her soul of the lust of fools and slaves: 20
 Both these are suburb-roarers.° Then there's besides
 A civil, City-roaring girl, whose pride,
 Feasting, and riding, shakes her husband's state,
 And leaves him roaring through an iron grate.°
 None of these roaring girls is ours—she flies   25
 With wings more lofty. Thus her character° lies,
 Yet what need characters, when to give a guess
 Is better than the person to express?°
 But would you know who 'tis? Would you hear her name?
 She is called Mad Moll: her life our acts proclaim!   30
  [Exit]

[Scene 1]

*Enter Mary Fitzallard disguised like a sempster,° with a case
for bands,° and Neatfoot, a servingman, with her, with a
napkin on his shoulder, and a trencher in his hand, as from
table*

NEATFOOT The young gentleman, our young master, Sir Alexander's
son, is it into his ears, sweet damsel, emblem of fragility, you desire
to have a message transported, or to be transcendent?°

MARY A private word or two, sir, nothing else.

NEATFOOT You shall fructify in° that which you come for: your pleas-   5
ure shall be satisfied to your full contentation. I will, fairest tree of
generation,° watch when our young master is erected, that is to say
up, and deliver him to this your most white hand.

MARY Thanks, sir.

NEATFOOT And withal certify him, that I have culled out for him,   10
now his belly is replenished, a daintier bit or modicum than any lay
upon his trencher at dinner. Hath he notion of your name, I
beseech your chastity?

MARY One, sir, of whom he bespake falling bands.°

NEATFOOT Falling bands? It shall so be given him. If you had please   15
to venture your modesty in the hall, amongst a curl-pated° company
of rude servingmen, and take such as they can set before you, you
shall be most seriously and ingeniously welcome.

MARY I have dined indeed already, sir.

NEATFOOT Or will you vouchsafe to kiss the lip of a cup of rich   20
Orleans° in the buttery amongst our waiting-women?

MARY Not now, in truth, sir.

NEATFOOT Our young master shall then have a feeling of your being
here presently. It shall so be given him.

MARY I humbly thank you, sir.

Exit Neatfoot

                                    But that my bosom   25
Is full of bitter sorrows, I could smile
To see this formal ape° play antic tricks:
But in my breast a poisoned arrow sticks,
And smiles cannot become me. Love woven slightly,
Such as thy false heart makes, wears out as lightly,   30
But love being truly bred i'th soul (like mine)

228

Bleeds even to death, at the least wound it takes.
The more we quench this, the less it slakes. O, me!
    Enter Sebastian° with Neatfoot

SEBASTIAN A sempster speak with me, sayest thou?

NEATFOOT Yes sir, she's there, *viva voce*,° to deliver her auricular   35
confession.

SEBASTIAN With me, sweetheart. What is't?

MARY I have brought home your bands, sir.

SEBASTIAN Bands? Neatfoot!

NEATFOOT Sir?   40

SEBASTIAN Prithee, look in, for all the gentlemen are upon rising.°

NEATFOOT Yes, sir, a most methodical attendance shall be given.

SEBASTIAN And dost hear, if my father call for me, say I am busy with
a sempster.

NEATFOOT Yes, sir, he shall know it that you are busied with a   45
needlewoman.°

SEBASTIAN In's ear, good Neatfoot.

NEATFOOT It shall so be given him.
    Exit Neatfoot

SEBASTIAN Bands? You're mistaken, sweetheart, I bespake none.
When? Where, I prithee? What bands? Let me see them.   50

MARY Yes, sir, a bond fast sealed, with solemn oaths,°
Subscribed unto, as I thought, with your soul,
Delivered as your deed in sight of heaven.
Is this bond cancelled? Have you forgot me?

SEBASTIAN Ha! Life of my life, Sir Guy Fitzallard's daughter!   55
What has transformed my love to this strange shape?
Stay: make all sure [*checks both sides of stage*]—so. Now speak and
be brief,
Because the wolf's at door° that lies in wait
To prey upon us both. Albeit mine eyes   60
Are blest by thine, yet this so strange disguise
Holds me with fear and wonder.

MARY   Mine's a loathed sight,
Why from it are you banished else so long?

SEBASTIAN I must cut short my speech: in broken language,
Thus much, sweet Moll,° I must thy company shun,   65
I court another Moll, my thoughts must run,
As a horse runs, that's blind, round in a mill,
Out every step, yet keeping one path still.°

MARY Um! Must you shun my company? In one knot

Have both our hands by th' hands of heaven been tied,   70
Now to be broke? I thought me once your bride:
Our fathers did agree on the time when—
And must another bedfellow fill my room?

SEBASTIAN Sweet maid, let's lose no time. 'Tis in heaven's book
Set down that I must have thee: an oath we took,   75
To keep our vows; but when the knight your father
Was from mine parted, storms began to sit
Upon my covetous father's brow, which fell
From them on me. He reckoned up what gold
This marriage would draw from him, at which he swore   80
To lose so much blood could not grieve him more.
He then dissuades me from thee, called thee not fair,
And asked, 'What is she but a beggar's heir?'
He scorned thy dowry of five thousand marks.°
If such a sum of money could be found,   85
And I would match with that, he'd not undo it,
Provided his bags might add nothing to it,
But vowed, if I took thee, nay more did swear it,
Save birth from him, I nothing should inherit.

MARY What follows then, my shipwreck?

SEBASTIAN   Dearest, no: 90
Though wildly in a labyrinth I go,
My end is to meet thee: with a side wind
Must I now sail, else I no haven can find
But both must sink forever. There's a wench
Called Moll, mad Moll, or merry Moll, a creature   95
So strange in quality, a whole city takes
Note of her name and person. All that affection
I owe to thee, on her in counterfeit passion
I spend to mad my father. He believes
I dote upon this roaring girl, and grieves   100
As it becomes a father for a son
That could be so bewitched: yet I'll go on
This crookèd way, sigh still for her, feign dreams
In which I'll talk only of her. These streams
Shall, I hope, force my father to consent   105
That here I anchor rather than be rent
Upon a rock so dangerous! Art thou pleased,
Because thou seest we are waylaid, that I take
A path that's safe, though it be far about?

MARY My prayers with heaven guide thee!

SEBASTIAN   Then I will on.   110
  My father is at hand, kiss and be gone.
  Hours shall be watched for meetings. I must now,
  As men for fear, to a strange idol bow.

MARY Farewell.

SEBASTIAN   I'll guide thee forth. When next we meet,
  A story of Moll shall make our mirth more sweet.   115
    Exeunt

[Scene 2]

Enter Sir Alexander Wengrave, Sir Davy Dapper, Sir Adam
Appleton, Goshawk, Laxton, and Gentlemen

ALL Thanks, good Sir Alexander, for our bounteous cheer.

SIR ALEXANDER Fie, fie, in giving thanks you pay too dear.

SIR DAVY When bounty spreads the table, faith t'were sin,
  At going off, if thanks should not step in.

SIR ALEXANDER No more of thanks, no more. Ay, marry sir,   5
  Th'inner room was too close, how do you like
  This parlour, gentlemen?

ALL [GENTLEMEN]   O, passing well.

SIR ADAM What a sweet breath the air casts here, so cool!

GOSHAWK I like the prospect° best.

LAXTON   See how 'tis furnished.

SIR DAVY A very fair sweet room.

SIR ALEXANDER   Sir Davy Dapper,   10
  The furniture that doth adorn this room
  Cost many a fair grey groat ere it came here,
  But good things are most cheap, when they're most dear.°
  Nay, when you look into my galleries,°
  How bravely they are trimmed up,° you all shall swear   15
  You're highly pleased to see what's set down there:
  Stories of men and women, mixed together,
  Fair ones with foul, like sunshine in wet weather;
  Within one square a thousand heads° are laid
  So close that all of heads the room seems made;   20
  As many faces there, filled with blithe looks,
  Show like the promising titles of new books
  Writ merrily, the readers being their own eyes,

Which seem to move and to give plaudities.°
And here and there, whilst with obsequious ears,   25
Thronged heaps do listen, a cutpurse thrusts and leers
With hawk's eyes for his prey: I need not show him,
By a hanging villainous look yourselves may know him,
The face is drawn so rarely. Then, sir, below,
The very floor, as 'twere, waves to and fro,   30
And like a floating island seems to move,
Upon a sea bound in with shores above.

    Enter Sebastian and Master Greenwit

ALL These sights are excellent.
SIR ALEXANDER   I'll show you all;
  Since we are met, make our parting comical.°
SEBASTIAN This gentleman, my friend, will take his leave, sir.   35
SIR ALEXANDER Ha? Take his leave, Sebastian? Who?
SEBASTIAN   This gentleman.
SIR ALEXANDER [*to Greenwit*] Your love, sir, has already given me
    some time,
  And if you please to trust my age with more,
  It shall pay double interest. Good sir, stay.
GREENWIT I have been too bold.
SIR ALEXANDER   Not so, sir. A merry day   40
  'Mongst friends being spent, is better than gold saved.
  Some wine, some wine! Where be these knaves I keep?

    Enter three or four Servingmen [carrying wine], and Neatfoot

NEATFOOT At your worshipful elbow, sir.
SIR ALEXANDER You are kissing my maids, drinking, or fast asleep.
NEATFOOT Your worship has given it us right.
SIR ALEXANDER   You varlets, stir!   45
  Chairs, stools, and cushions!

    [*Servants bring in chairs, stools, cushions*]

                    Prithee, Sir Davy Dapper,
  Make that chair thine.
SIR DAVY   'Tis but an easy gift,°
  And yet I thank you for it, sir. I'll take it.
SIR ALEXANDER A chair for old Sir Adam Appleton.
NEATFOOT A back friend° to your worship.
SIR ADAM   Marry, good Neatfoot,   50
  I thank thee for it: back friends sometimes are good.
SIR ALEXANDER Pray make that stool your perch,° good Master
    Goshawk.

GOSHAWK I stoop to your lure,° sir.

SIR ALEXANDER   Son Sebastian,
   Take Master Greenwit to you.

SEBASTIAN   Sit, dear friend.

SIR ALEXANDER Nay, Master Laxton—[*to a Servant*] furnish Master
      Laxton   55
   With what he wants, a stone°—a stool I would say,
   A stool.

LAXTON I had rather stand,° sir.

SIR ALEXANDER I know you had, good Master Laxton. So, so—
            Exeunt [*Neatfoot and*] *Servants*
   Now here's a mess° of friends, and, gentlemen,
   Because time's glass shall not be running long,°   60
   I'll quicken it with a pretty tale.

SIR DAVY   Good tales do well
   In these bad days, where vice does so excel.

SIR ADAM Begin, Sir Alexander

SIR ALEXANDER   Last day I met
   An agèd man upon whose head was scored
   A debt of just so many years as these   65
   Which I owe to my grave:° the man you all know.

ALL [GENTLEMEN] His name, I pray you, sir?

SIR ALEXANDER   Nay, you shall pardon me,
   But when he saw me, with a sigh that brake,
   Or seemed to break his heart-strings, thus he spake:
   'O, my good knight,', says he, and then his eyes   70
   Were richer even by that which made them poor,
   They had spent so many tears, they had no more.
   'O, sir,' says he, 'you know it, for you ha' seen
   Blessings to rain upon mine house and me:
   Fortune, who slaves men, was my slave: her wheel   75
   Hath spun me golden threads,° for I thank heaven,
   I ne'er had but one cause to curse my stars.'
   I asked him then what that one cause might be.

ALL [GENTLEMEN] So, sir?

SIR ALEXANDER   He paused, and as we often see,
   A sea so much becalmed, there can be found   80
   No wrinkle on his brow, his waves being drowned
   In their own rage: but when th'imperious winds,
   Use strange invisible tyranny to shake
   Both heaven's and earth's foundation at their noise,

The seas swelling with wrath to part that fray,   85
Rise up, and are more wild, more mad, than they.
Even so this good old man was by my question
Stirred up to roughness. You might see his gall
Flow even in's eyes: then grew he fantastical.

SIR DAVY Fantastical? Ha, ha.

SIR ALEXANDER   Yes, and talked oddly.   90

SIR ADAM Pray sir, proceed. How did this old man end?

SIR ALEXANDER Marry, sir, thus.
He left his wild fit to read o'er his cards:°
Yet then, though age cast snow on all his hairs,
He joyed 'Because', says he, 'the god of gold   95
Has been to me no niggard. That disease,
Of which all old men sicken, avarice,
Never infected me—'

LAXTON [aside] He means not himself I'm sure.

SIR ALEXANDER   'For like a lamp,
Fed with continual oil, I spend and throw   100
My light to all that need it, yet have still
Enough to serve myself. O, but,' quoth he,
'Though heaven's dew fall thus on this aged tree,
I have a son that's like a wedge doth cleave
My very heart-root.'

SIR DAVY   Had he such a son?   105

SEBASTIAN [aside] Now I do smell a fox° strongly.

SIR ALEXANDER Let's see: no, Master Greenwit is not yet
So mellow in years° as he, but as like Sebastian,
Just like my son Sebastian, such another.

SEBASTIAN [aside] How finely, like a fencer, my father fetches his by-   110
blows to hit me, but if I beat you not at your own weapon of
subtlety—

SIR ALEXANDER 'This son,' saith he, 'that should be
The column and main arch unto my house,
The crutch unto my age, becomes a whirlwind   115
Shaking the firm foundation.'

SIR ADAM   'Tis some prodigal.

SEBASTIAN [aside] Well shot, old Adam Bell.°

SIR ALEXANDER No city monster neither, no prodigal,
But sparing, wary, civil, and, though wifeless,
An excellent husband, and such a traveller,   120
He has more tongues in his head than some have teeth.

SIR DAVY I have but two in mine.

GOSHAWK   So sparing and so wary.
    What then could vex his father so?

SIR ALEXANDER   O, a woman.

SEBASTIAN A flesh-fly,° that can vex any man.

SIR ALEXANDER A scurvy woman,   125
    On whom the passionate old man swore he° doted:
    A creature, saith he, nature hath brought forth
    To mock the sex of woman. It is a thing
    One knows not how to name, her birth began
    Ere she was all made.° 'Tis woman more than man,   130
    Man more than woman, and (which to none can hap)
    The sun gives her two shadows° to one shape;
    Nay more, let this strange thing walk, stand, or sit,
    No blazing star° draws more eyes after it.°

SIR DAVY A monster! 'Tis some monster!

SIR ALEXANDER   She's a varlet.   135

SEBASTIAN [aside] Now is my cue to bristle.°

SIR ALEXANDER A naughty pack.°

SEBASTIAN   'Tis false.

SIR ALEXANDER   Ha, boy?

SEBASTIAN   'Tis false.

SIR ALEXANDER What's false? I say she's naught.

SEBASTIAN   I say that tongue
    That dares speak so—but yours—sticks in the throat
    Of a rank villain.° Set yourself aside—   140
        [Sebastian and Sir Alexander move apart from the others]

SIR ALEXANDER [to Sebastian] So, sir, what then?

SEBASTIAN [to his father] Any here else had lied.
    [Aside] I think I shall fit you.

SIR ALEXANDER [aloud] Lie?

SEBASTIAN   Yes.

SIR DAVY   Does this concern him?

SIR ALEXANDER [aside to Sebastian]   Ah, sirrah boy,
    Is your blood heated? Boils it? Are you stung?   145
    I'll pierce you deeper yet!—[Aloud] O, my dear friends,
    I am that wretched father, this that son,
    That sees his ruin, yet headlong on doth run.

SIR ADAM Will you love such a poison?

SIR DAVY   Fie, fie!

SEBASTIAN   You're all mad.

SIR ALEXANDER Thou'rt sick at heart, yet feel'st it not. Of all these,   150
  What gentleman, but thou, knowing his disease
  Mortal, would shun the cure? O, Master Greenwit,
  Would you to such an idol bow?
GREENWIT   Not I, sir.
SIR ALEXANDER Here's Master Laxton. Has he mind to a woman
  As thou hast?
LAXTON No, not I sir.
SIR ALEXANDER   Sir, I know it.   155
LAXTON Their good parts are so rare, their bad so common,
  I will have nought° to do with any woman.
SIR DAVY 'Tis well done, Master Laxton.
SIR ALEXANDER   O, thou cruel boy,
  Thou wouldst with lust an old man's life destroy,
  Because thou seest I'm half way in my grave.   160
  Thou shovel'st dust upon me: would thou mightest have
  Thy wish, most wicked, most unnatural!
SIR DAVY Why, sir, 'tis thought Sir Guy Fitzallard's daughter
  Shall wed your son Sebastian.
SIR ALEXANDER   Sir Davy Dapper,
  I have upon my knees wooed this fond boy   165
  To take that virtuous maiden.
      [Sebastian draws Sir Alexander aside]
SEBASTIAN   Hark you, a word sir!
  You, on your knees, have cursed that virtuous maiden,
  And me for loving her; yet do you now
  Thus baffle° me to my face? Wear not your knees
  In such entreats. Give me Fitzallard's daughter.   170
SIR ALEXANDER I'll give thee ratsbane rather!
SEBASTIAN   Well, then, you know
  What dish I mean to feed upon.
SIR ALEXANDER *[to the others]*   Hark, gentlemen,
  He swears to have this cutpurse drab, to spite my gall.
ALL [GENTLEMEN] Master Sebastian!
SEBASTIAN   I am deaf to you all.
  I'm so bewitched, so bound to my desires,   175
  Tears, prayers, threats, nothing can quench out those fires
  That burn within me.
     Exit Sebastian
SIR ALEXANDER   Her blood shall quench it then!
  Lose him not: O, dissuade him, gentlemen!

SIR DAVY He shall be weaned, I warrant you.

SIR ALEXANDER   Before his eyes

Lay down his shame, my grief, his miseries.   180

ALL [GENTLEMEN] No more, no more! Away!

    Exeunt all but Sir Alexander

SIR ALEXANDER   I wash a negro,°

Losing both pains and cost—but take thy flight—

I'll be most near thee when I'm least in sight.

Wild buck, I'll hunt thee breathless. Thou shalt run on,

But I will turn thee° when I'm not thought upon.   185

    Enter Ralph Trapdoor [carrying a letter]

Now, sirrah, what are you? Leave your ape's tricks° and speak!

TRAPDOOR A letter from my captain to your worship.

SIR ALEXANDER O, O, now I remember, 'tis to prefer° thee into my
service.

TRAPDOOR To be a shifter under your worship's nose of a clean
trencher,° when there's a good bit upon't.   190

SIR ALEXANDER Troth, honest fellow—[*aside*] humh—ha—let me
see—

This knave shall be the axe to hew that down

At which I stumble—has a face that promiseth

Much of a villain. I will grind his wit,

And if the edge prove fine make use of it.   195

[*To Trapdoor*] Come hither, sirrah, canst thou be secret, ha?

TRAPDOOR As two crafty attorneys, plotting the undoing of their
clients.

SIR ALEXANDER Didst never, as thou hast walked about this town,

Hear of a wench called Moll, mad merry Moll?   200

TRAPDOOR Moll Cutpurse, sir?

SIR ALEXANDER The same. Dost thou know her then?

TRAPDOOR As well as I know 'twill rain on Simon and Jude's day°
next. I will sift all the taverns i'th' city, and drink half pots with all
the watermen° i'th' Bankside,° but if you will, sir, I'll find her out.   205

SIR ALEXANDER That task is easy—do't then. Hold thy hand up.
What's this? Is't burnt?°

TRAPDOOR No, sir, no—a little singed with making fireworks.

SIR ALEXANDER There's money—spend it. That being spent, fetch
more.   210

TRAPDOOR O, sir, that all the poor soldiers in England had such a
leader. For fetching, no water-spaniel is like me.

SIR ALEXANDER This wench we speak of strays so from her kind,

Nature repents she made her. 'Tis a mermaid°
Has tolled my son to shipwreck.   215

TRAPDOOR I'll cut her comb° for you.

SIR ALEXANDER I'll tell out gold for thee then! Hunt her forth,
Cast out a line hung full of silver hooks
To catch her to thy company. Deep spendings
May draw her that's most chaste to a man's bosom.   220

TRAPDOOR The jingling of golden bells° and a good fool with a hobby-
horse° will draw all the whores i'th' town to dance in a morris.

SIR ALEXANDER Or rather, for that's best—they say sometimes
She goes in breeches—follow her as her man.

TRAPDOOR And when her breeches are off, she shall follow° me!   225

SIR ALEXANDER Beat all thy brains° to serve her.

TRAPDOOR Zounds, sir, as country wenches beat cream—till butter
comes!°

SIR ALEXANDER Play thou the subtle spider, weave fine nets
To ensnare her very life.

TRAPDOOR   Her life?

SIR ALEXANDER   Yes, suck   230
Her heart-blood if thou canst. Twist thou but cords
To catch her, I'll find law to hang her up!

TRAPDOOR Spoke like a worshipful bencher!°

SIR ALEXANDER Trace all her steps. At this she-fox's den
Watch what lambs enter: let me play the shepherd   235
To save their throats from bleeding, and cut hers!

TRAPDOOR This is the goll shall do't.

SIR ALEXANDER   Be firm and gain me
Ever thine own. This done, I entertain thee.°
How is thy name?

TRAPDOOR My name, sir, is Ralph° Trapdoor. Honest Ralph.   240

SIR ALEXANDER Trapdoor, be like thy name, a dangerous step
For her to venture on, but unto me—

TRAPDOOR As fast as your sole to your boot or shoe, sir.

SIR ALEXANDER Hence then, be little seen here as thou cans't,
I'll still be at thine elbow.

TRAPDOOR   The trapdoor's set.   245
Moll, if you budge you're gone: this me shall crown—
A roaring boy the Roaring Girl puts down!

SIR ALEXANDER God-a-mercy, lose no time!

        Exeunt

[Scene 3]

*The three shops open in a rank:° the first an apothecary's shop, the
next a feather shop,° the third a sempster's shop. Mistress Gallipot
in the first, Mistress Tiltyard in the next, Master Openwork and his
wife in the third. To them enters Laxton, Goshawk, and Greenwit*

MISTRESS OPENWORK Gentlemen, what is't you lack?° What is't you
buy? See fine bands and ruffs, fine lawns, fine cambrics.° What is't
you lack, gentlemen, what is't you buy?

LAXTON [*pointing to apotherary's shop*] Yonder's the shop.

GOSHAWK Is that she? 5

LAXTON Peace!

GREENWIT She that minces tobacco?

LAXTON Ay: she's a gentlewoman born, I can tell you, though it be
her hard fortune now to shred Indian pot-herbs.°

GOSHAWK O, sir, 'tis many a good woman's fortune, when her hus- 10
band turns bankrupt, to begin with pipes° and set up again.

LAXTON And, indeed, the raising of the woman is the lifting up of the
man's head° at all times. If one flourish, t'other will bud as fast, I
warrant ye.

GOSHAWK Come, thou'rt familiarly acquainted there, I grope° that. 15

LAXTON An you grope no better i'th' dark you may chance lie i'th'
ditch° when you're drunk.

GOSHAWK Go, thou'rt a mystical° lecher!

LAXTON I will not deny but my credit may take up an ounce of pure
smoke. 20

GOSHAWK May take up an ell of pure smock!° Away, go! [*Aside*] 'Tis
the closest striker.° Life, I think he commits venery forty foot deep,
no man's aware on't. I, like a palpable smockster,° go to work so
openly, with the tricks of art, that I'm as apparently seen as a naked
boy in a vial;° and were it not for a gift of treachery that I have in me 25
to betray my friend when he puts most trust in me (mass, yonder he
is, too!) and by his injury to make good my access to her, I should
appear as defective in courting as a farmer's son the first day of his
feather,° that doth nothing at Court, but woo the hangings° and
glass windows for a month together, and some broken waiting- 30
woman for ever after. I find those imperfections in my venery that,
were't not for flattery and falsehood, I should want discourse and
impudence, and he that wants impudence among women is worthy
to be kicked out at bed's feet.—He shall not see me yet.

[*The gallants move to the apothecary's shop where Mistress
Gallipot is preparing a pipe of tobacco*]

GREENWIT Troth, this is finely shred.   35

LAXTON O, women are the best mincers.

MISTRESS GALLIPOT 'T had been a good phrase for a cook's wife, sir.

LAXTON But 'twill serve generally, like the front of a new almanac,° as
thus: 'Calculated for the meridian of cook's wives, but generally for
all Englishwomen.'   40

MISTRESS GALLIPOT Nay, you shall ha't, sir—I have filled it for you.
She puts it to the fire°

LAXTON The pipe's in a good hand, and I wish mine always so.°

GREENWIT But not to be used o' that fashion.°

LAXTON O, pardon me, sir, I understand no French.° I pray, be
covered.°—Jack,° a pipe of rich smoke?   45

GOSHAWK Rich smoke? That's six pence a pipe is't?

GREENWIT To me,° sweet lady.
[*Mistress Gallipot passes a pipe to Greenwit*]

MISTRESS GALLIPOT [*aside to Laxton*] Be not forgetful. Respect my
credit, seem strange.° Art and wit makes a fool of suspicion. Pray be
wary.   50

LAXTON [*aside to Mistress Gallipot*] Push,° I warrant you.—[*Aloud*]
Come, how is't, gallants?

GREENWIT Pure and excellent.

LAXTON I thought 'twas good, you were grown so silent. You are like
those that love not to talk at victuals, though they make a worse   55
noise i'the nose than a common fiddler's prentice and discourse the
whole supper with snuffling.—[*Aside to Mistress Gallipot*] I must
speak a word with you, anon.

MISTRESS GALLIPOT [*aside to Laxton*] Make your way wisely then.

GOSHAWK O, what else sir? He's perfection itself, full of manners, but   60
not an acre of ground belonging to them.

GREENWIT Ay, and full of form.° He's ne'er a good stool in's chamber.°

GOSHAWK But above all religious: he prayeth daily upon elder
brothers.

GREENWIT And valiant above measure: he's run three streets from a   65
sergeant!

LAXTON Pooh, pooh!°
He blows tobacco [smoke] in their faces

GREENWIT AND GOSHAWK O, pooh! Ho, ho!°
[*They move away*]

LAXTON So, so.

MISTRESS GALLIPOT What's the matter now, sir? 70

LAXTON I protest I'm in extreme want of money. If you can supply me now with any means, you do me the greatest pleasure, next to the bounty of your love, as ever poor gentleman tasted.

MISTRESS GALLIPOT What's the sum would please you, sir? Though you deserve nothing less at my hands.° 75

LAXTON Why 'tis but for want of opportunity thou know'st;—[aside] I put her off with opportunity still. By this light, I hate her, but for means to keep me in fashion with gallants; for what I take from her I spend on other wenches, bear her in hand° still. She has wit enough to rob her husband, and I ways enough to consume the 80 money. [To Goshawk and Greenwit] Why, how now? What, the chincough?

GOSHAWK Thou hast the cowardliest trick to come before a man's face and strangle him° 'ere he be aware. I could find it in my heart to make a quarrel in earnest. 85

LAXTON Pox, an thou dost! Thou know'st I never use to fight with my friends, thou'll but lose thy labour in't.
  Enter Jack Dapper and his man, Gull
Jack Dapper!

GREENWIT [bowing] Monsieur Dapper, I dive down to your ankles!

JACK DAPPER 'Save ye, gentlemen, all three in a peculiar salute. 90

GOSHAWK He were ill to make a lawyer: he dispatches three at once!

LAXTON So, well said.—[Taking a purse from Mistress Gallipot] But is this of the same tobacco, Mistress Gallipot?

MISTRESS GALLIPOT The same you had at first, sir.

LAXTON I wish it no better: this will serve to drink° at my chamber. 95

GOSHAWK Shall we taste a pipe on't?

LAXTON Not of this, by my troth, gentlemen, I have sworn before you.

GOSHAWK What, not Jack Dapper?

LAXTON Pardon me, sweet Jack, I'm sorry I made such a rash oath, but foolish oaths must stand. Where art going, Jack? 100

JACK DAPPER Faith,° to buy one feather.

LAXTON [aside] One feather? The fool's peculiar still!

JACK DAPPER Gull.

GULL Master?

JACK DAPPER [giving Gull money] Here's three halfpence for your 105 ordinary,° boy,—meet me a hour hence in Paul's.°

GULL How? Three single halfpence? Life, this will scarcely serve a man in sauce—a ha'p'orth° of mustard, a ha'p'orth of oil, a ha'p'orth of vinegar—what's left then for the pickle-herring? This

shows like small beer i'th morning after a great surfeit of wine   110
o'ernight. He could spend his three pound last night in a supper
amongst girls and brave bawdy-house boys—I thought his pockets
cackled not for nothing: [*showing coins*] these are the eggs° of three
pounds! I'll go sup 'em up presently.

 Exit Gull

LAXTON [*aside, counting his money*] Eight, nine, ten angels. Good   115
wench, i'faith, and one that loves darkness well! She puts out a
candle with the best tricks of any drugster's wife in England, but
that which mads her, I rail upon opportunity still, and take no
notice on't. The other night she would needs lead me into a room
with a candle in her hand to show me a naked picture,° where no   120
sooner entered, but the candle was sent of an errand; now I, not
intending to understand her, but like a puny° at the inns of venery,
called for another light innocently. Thus reward I all her cunning
with simple mistaking! I know she cozens her husband to keep me,
and I'll keep her honest, as long as I can, to make the poor man   125
some part of amends. An honest mind of a whoremaster! [*To Jack
Dapper and Goshawk*] How think you amongst you? What, a fresh
pipe? Draw in a third, man?°

GOSHAWK No, you're a hoarder, you engross both ounces

 At the feather shop now

JACK DAPPER Pooh, I like it not.

MISTRESS TILTYARD   What feather is't you'ld have, sir?   130
These are most worn and most in fashion
Amongst the beaver gallants,° the stone-riders°
The private stage's audience, the twelvepenny-stool gentlemen:°
I can inform you, 'tis the general feather!

JACK DAPPER And therefore I mislike it! Tell me of 'general'?   135
Now a continual Simon and Jude's rain
Beat all your feathers as flat down as pancakes!
Show me—a—spangled feather.

MISTRESS TILTYARD O, to go a-feasting with?
You'd have it for a hench-boy?°—You shall.   140

 At the sempster's shop now

OPENWORK Mass, I had quite forgot,
His honour's footman was here last night, wife:
Ha' you done with my lord's shirt?

MISTRESS OPENWORK What's that to you, sir?
I was this morning at his honour's lodging,   145
Ere such a snail° as you crept out of your shell.

OPENWORK O, 'twas well done, good wife.

MISTRESS OPENWORK   I hold it better, sir,
  Than if you had done't yourself.°

OPENWORK   Nay, so say I.
  But is the countess's smock almost done, mouse?

MISTRESS OPENWORK Here lies the cambric, sir, but wants I fear
  me.   150

OPENWORK I'll resolve you of that presently.

MISTRESS OPENWORK Heyday! O, audacious groom,
  Dare you presume to noblewomen's linen?
  Keep you your yard° to measure shepherd's holland°—
  I must confine you, I see that!   155
        At the tobacco shop now

GOSHAWK What say you to this gear?

LAXTON I dare the arrantest° critic in tobacco to lay one fault upon't.
        Enter Moll in a frieze jerkin° and a black safeguard°

GOSHAWK Life, yonder's Moll.

LAXTON Moll? Which Moll?

GOSHAWK Honest Moll.   160

LAXTON Prithee, let's call her.—Moll!

ALL [GALLANTS] Moll, Moll, pist, Moll!

MOLL How now, what's the matter?

GOSHAWK A pipe of good tobacco, Moll?

MOLL I cannot stay.   165

GOSHAWK Nay, Moll,—pooh—prithee hark, but one word, i'faith.

MOLL Well, what is't?

GREENWIT Prithee come hither, sirrah.

LAXTON [*aside*] Heart, I would give but too much money to be nib-
  bling with that wench. Life, sh' has the spirit of four great parishes, 170
  and a voice that will drown all the City. Methinks a brave captain
  might get° all his soldiers upon her, and ne'er be beholding to a
  company of Mile End milksops,° if he could come on and come off
  quick enough. Such a Moll were a marrowbone before an Italian:°
  he would cry *bona-roba*° till his ribs were nothing but bone. I'll lay 175
  hard siege to her—money is that aquafortis that eats into many a
  maidenhead. Where the walls are flesh and blood, I'll ever pierce
  through with a golden auger.

GOSHAWK Now thy judgement, Moll, is't not good?

MOLL Yes, faith, 'tis very good tobacco. How do you sell an ounce?° 180
  Farewell. God buy you, Mistress Gallipot.

GOSHAWK Why, Moll, Moll!

MOLL I cannot stay now i'faith, I am going to buy a shag ruff°—the
    shop will be shut in presently.

GOSHAWK 'Tis the maddest, fantasticalest girl:—I never knew so   185
    much flesh and so much nimbleness put together!

LAXTON She slips from one company to another like a fat eel between
    a Dutchman's fingers:°—[aside] I'll watch my time for her.

MISTRESS GALLIPOT Some will not stick to say she's a man, and
    some both man and woman.°   190

LAXTON That were excellent: she might first cuckold the husband
    and then make him do as much for the wife!

        The feather shop again

MOLL Save you. How does Mistress Tiltyard?

JACK DAPPER Moll.

MOLL Jack Dapper.   195

JACK DAPPER How dost, Moll?

MOLL I'll tell thee by and by, I go but to th' next shop.

JACK DAPPER Thou shalt find me here this hour about a feather.

MOLL Nay, an a feather hold you in play a whole hour, a goose will last
    you all the days of your life.   200

        [At] the sempster['s] shop

    [To Openwork] Let me see a good shag ruff.

OPENWORK Mistress Mary, that shalt thou, i'faith—and the best in
    the shop.

MISTRESS OPENWORK How now? Greetings, love terms, with a pox
    between you! Have I found out one of your haunts? I send you for   205
    hollands, and you're i'the Low Countries° with a mischief! I'm
    served with good ware by th'shift that makes it lie dead so long
    upon my hands! I were as good shut up shop, for when I open it I
    take nothing.°

OPENWORK Nay, an you fall a-ringing° once, the devil cannot stop   210
    you—I'll out of the belfry as fast as I can.—Moll.

        [Openwork retires inside the shop]

MISTRESS OPENWORK Get you from my shop!

MOLL I come to buy.

MISTRESS OPENWORK I'll sell ye nothing: I warn ye° my house and
    shop!   215

MOLL You, goody Openwork, you that prick out a poor living
    And sews many a bawdy skin-coat° together,
    Thou private pandress between shirt and smock,°
    I wish thee for a minute but a man:
    Thou shouldst never use more shapes;° but as thou'rt,   220

I pity my revenge. Now my spleen's up,
I would not mock it willingly—
  Enter a Fellow with a long rapier by his side
       Ha, be thankful,
Now I forgive thee.

MISTRESS OPENWORK Marry, hang thee, I never asked forgiveness in
 my life!
 [*Exit Mistress Openwork from the shop*]

MOLL [*to the Fellow*] You, goodman swine's face.   225

FELLOW What, will you murder me?

MOLL You remember, slave, how you abused me t'other night in a
 tavern?

FELLOW Not I, by this light.

MOLL No, but by candlelight you did. You have tricks to save your oaths, 230
 reservations have you, and I have reserved somewhat for you—[*hits
 him*] as you like that, call for more—you know the sign again.

FELLOW Pox on't! Had I brought any company along with me to have
 borne witness on't, 'twould ne'er have grieved me, but to be struck
 and nobody by,° 'tis my ill fortune still. Why, tread upon a worm, 235
 they say 'twill turn tail,° but indeed, a gentleman should have more
 manners.
  Exit Fellow

LAXTON Gallantly performed, i'faith, Moll, and manfully! I love thee
 forever for't. Base rogue, had he offered but the least counterbuff,
 by this hand, I was prepared for him.   240

MOLL You prepared for him? Why should you be prepared for him?
 Was he any more than a man?

LAXTON No, nor so much by a yard and a handful, London measure.°

MOLL Why do you speak this then? Do you think I cannot ride a
 stone-horse° unless one lead him by the snaffle?   245

LAXTON Yes, and sit him bravely, I know thou canst, Moll. 'Twas but
 an honest mistake through love, and I'll make amends for't any way.
 Prithee, sweet, plump Moll, when shall you and I go out o' town
 together?

MOLL Whither? To Tyburn,° prithee?   250

LAXTON Mass, that's out o' town, indeed! Thou hangest so many jests
 upon thy friends still—I mean honestly to Brentford, Staines, or
 Ware.°

MOLL What to do there?

LAXTON Nothing but be merry and lie together. I'll hire a coach with 255
 four horses.

MOLL I thought 'twould be a beastly journey! You may leave out one
well,—three horses will serve, if I play the jade myself.

LAXTON Nay, push, thou'rt such another kicking wench. Prithee be
kind and let's meet.   260

MOLL 'Tis hard but we shall meet, sir.

LAXTON Nay, but appoint the place then. [*Giving her a purse*] There's
ten angels in fair gold, Moll—you see I do not trifle with you—do
but say thou wilt meet me, and I'll have a coach ready for thee.

MOLL Why, here's my hand: I'll meet you, sir.   265

LAXTON [*aside*] O, good gold!—[*To her*] The place, sweet Moll?

MOLL It shall be your appointment.

LAXTON Somewhere near Holborn,° Moll.

MOLL In Gray's Inn Fields° then?

LAXTON A match.   270

MOLL I'll meet you there.

LAXTON The hour?

MOLL Three.

LAXTON That will be time enough to sup at Brentford.

> *Fall from them*° *to the* [*sempster's shop, where Openwork has
> returned*]

OPENWORK I am of such a nature, sir, I cannot endure the house   275
when she scolds, she's a tongue will be heard further in a still
morning than Saint Antling's° bell. She rails upon me for foreign
wenching, that I, being a freeman,° must needs keep a whore i'th'
suburbs, and seek to impoverish the liberties.° When we fall out, I
trouble you still to make all whole with my wife.   280

GOSHAWK No trouble at all, 'tis a pleasure to me to join things
together.

OPENWORK Go thy ways,—[*aside*] I do this but to try thy honesty,
Goshawk.

> [*Exit Master Openwork.*] [*At*] *the feather shop*

JACK DAPPER How lik'st thou this, Moll?   285

MOLL O, singularly, you're fitted now for a bunch. [*Aside*] He looks
for all the world with those spangled feathers like a nobleman's
bedpost.° The purity of your wench would I fain try, she seems like
Kent unconquered,° and I believe as many wiles are in her.—O, the
gallants of these times are shallow lechers, they put not their court-   290
ship home enough to a wench,—'tis impossible to know what
woman is thoroughly honest because she's ne'er thoroughly tried. I
am of that certain belief there are more queans in this town of their

own making than of any man's provoking. Where lies the slackness
then? Many a poor soul would down, and there's nobody will push 295
'em:

> Women are courted but ne'er soundly tried,
> As many walk in spurs that never ride.

[*At*] *the sempster's shop* [*where Mistress Openwork has returned*]

MISTRESS OPENWORK O, abominable!

GOSHAWK Nay, more I tell you in private, he keeps a whore i'th' 300
suburbs.

MISTRESS OPENWORK O, Spital dealing!° I came to him a gentlewoman born. I'll show you mine arms° when you please, sir.

GOSHAWK I had rather see your legs and begin that way.

MISTRESS OPENWORK 'Tis well known he took me from a lady's 305
service where I was well-beloved of the steward. I had my Latin
tongue and a spice of the French before I came to him, and now
doth he keep a suburbian whore under my nostrils.

GOSHAWK There's ways enough to cry quit with him. Hark in thine ear.°

> [*Whispers to Mistress Openwork*]

MISTRESS OPENWORK There's a friend worth a million. 310

MOLL [*aside*] I'll try one spear against your chastity, Mistress Tiltyard, though it prove too short by the burr.°

> *Enter Ralph Trapdoor*

TRAPDOOR [*aside*] Mass, here she is. I'm bound already to serve her,
though it be but a sluttish trick. [*To her*] Bless my hopeful young
mistress with long life and great limbs, send her the upper hand of 315
all bailiffs and their hungry adherents!

MOLL How now, what art thou?

TRAPDOOR A poor ebbing gentleman that would gladly wait for the
young flood of your service.

MOLL My service! What should move you to offer your service to me, 320
sir?

TRAPDOOR The love I bear to your heroic spirit and masculine
womanhood.

MOLL So, sir, put case° we should retain you to us, what parts are there
in you for a gentlewoman's service? 325

TRAPDOOR Of two kinds, right worshipful: movable and immovable.
Movable to run of errands and immovable to stand° when you have
occasion to use me.

MOLL What strength have you?

TRAPDOOR Strength, Mistress Moll? I have gone up into a steeple 330

and stayed the great bell as 't has been ringing, stopped a windmill
going.

MOLL And never struck down yourself?

TRAPDOOR Stood as upright as I do this present.

    Moll trips up his heels [and] he falls

MOLL Come, I pardon you for this, it shall be no disgrace to you. I   335
have struck up the heels of the high German's size° ere now.—
What, not stand?

TRAPDOOR I am of that nature where I love, I'll be at my mistress'
foot to do her service.

MOLL Why, well said. But say your mistress should receive injury,   340
have you the spirit of fighting in you? Durst you second her?

    [Moll helps Trapdoor up]

TRAPDOOR Life, I have kept° a bridge myself and drove seven at a time
before me.

MOLL Ay?

TRAPDOOR *(aside)* But they were all Lincolnshire bullocks, by my   345
troth.

MOLL Well, meet me in Gray's Inn Fields between three and four this
afternoon, and upon better consideration, we'll retain you.

TRAPDOOR I humbly thank your good mistress-ship. *[Aside]* I'll crack
your neck for this kindness!   350

    Exit Trapdoor. Moll meets Laxton

LAXTON Remember, three.

MOLL Nay, if I fail you, hang me.

LAXTON Good wench, i'faith.

    Then [Moll meets] Openwork [passing over the stage,
    muffled]

MOLL Who's this?

OPENWORK 'Tis I, Moll.   355

MOLL Prithee tend thy shop and prevent bastards.

OPENWORK We'll have a pint of the same wine,° i'faith, Moll.

    [Exit Openwork and Moll.] The bell° rings

GOSHAWK Hark, the bell rings—come, gentlemen. Jack Dapper,
where shall's all munch?

JACK DAPPER I am for Parker's Ordinary.°   360

LAXTON *[aside]* He's a good guest to'm, he deserves his board. He
draws all the gentlemen in a term time thither.—*[To Dapper]* We'll
be your followers, Jack: lead the way.—*[Aside]* Look you, by my
faith, the fool has feathered his nest well.

    Exeunt [Dapper, Goshawk, and Laxton]

Enter Master Gallipot, Master Tiltyard, and Servants, with
water-spaniels and a duck°

TILTYARD Come, shut up your shops! Where's Master Openwork?   365
[*The women start to shut up the shops*]

MISTRESS OPENWORK Nay, ask not me, Master Tiltyard.

GALLIPOT Where's his water-dog? Pooh—pist—hurr—hurr—pist!°

TILTYARD Come, wenches, come, we're going all to Hogsden.

MISTRESS GALLIPOT To Hogsden,° husband?

GALLIPOT Ay, to Hogsden, pigsney.   370

MISTRESS TILTYARD I'm not ready, husband.

TILTYARD Faith, that's well!

[*Tiltyard*] *spits in the dog's mouth°*
Hum—pist—pist.°

GALLIPOT Come, Mistress Openwork, you are so long.

MISTRESS OPENWORK I have no joy of my life, Master Gallipot.   375

GALLIPOT Push, let your boy lead his water-spaniel along and we'll
show you the bravest sport at Parlous Pond.° Hey, Trug,° hey Trug,
hey Trug! Here's the best duck in England, except my wife. Hey,
hey, hey! Fetch, fetch, fetch!
                    Come, let's away!   380
                    Of all the year, this is the sportfull'st day.

[*Exeunt*]

[Scene 4]

Enter Sebastian alone

SEBASTIAN If a man have a free will, where should the use
More perfect shine, than in his will to love?
All creatures have their liberty in that,
        Enter Sir Alexander [*who conceals himself and*] *listens to him*
Though else kept under servile yoke and fear,
The very bond-slave has his freedom there.   5
Amongst a world of creatures voiced and silent,
Must my desires wear fetters? [*Noticing Sir Alexander*]—Yea, are
    you
So near?—Then I must break with my heart's truth,
Meet grief at a back way. [*Aloud*]—Well: why, suppose
The two-leaved° tongues of slander or of truth   10

Pronounce Moll loathsome, if before my love
She appear fair, what injury have I?—
I have the thing I like. In all things else
Mine own eye guides me, and I find 'em prosper.
Life, what should ail it now? I know that man   15
Ne'er truly loves—if he gainsay'st he lies—
That winks and marries with his father's eyes.
I'll keep mine own wide open.
            Enter Moll and a Porter with a viol on his back
SIR ALEXANDER [*aside*]   Here's brave wilfulness.
    A made match!° Here she comes—they met o' purpose.
PORTER Must I carry this great fiddle to your chamber, Mistress   20
    Mary?
MOLL Fiddle, goodman hog-rubber?° Some of these porters bear so
    much for others, they have no time to carry wit for themselves.
PORTER To your own chamber, Mistress Mary?
MOLL Who'll hear an ass speak? Whither else, goodman pageant-   25
    bearer?° They're people of the worst memories!
            Exit Porter
SEBASTIAN Why, 'twere too great a burden, love, to have them carry
    things in their minds, and o'their backs together.
MOLL Pardon me, sir, I thought not you so near.
SIR ALEXANDER [*aside*] So, so, so.   30
SEBASTIAN I would be nearer to thee, and in that fashion,
    That makes the best part of all creatures honest.
    No otherwise I wish it.
MOLL Sir, I am so poor to requite you, you must look for nothing but
    thanks of me, I have no humour to marry. I love to lie o'both sides   35
    o'th'bed myself and again o'th' other side. A wife, you know, ought
    to be obedient, but I fear me I am too headstrong to obey, therefore
    I'll ne'er go about it. I love you so well, sir, for your good will, I'd be
    loath you should repent your bargain after, and therefore we'll ne'er
    come together at first.° I have the head now of myself, and am man   40
    enough for a woman: marriage is but a chopping and changing,°
    where a maiden loses one head,° and has a worse i'th' place.
SIR ALEXANDER [*aside*] The most comfortable answer from a roaring
        girl
    That ever mine ears drunk in.
SEBASTIAN   This were enough
    Now to affright a fool for ever from thee,   45
    When 'tis the music that I love thee for.

SIR ALEXANDER [*aside*] There's a boy spoils all again.

MOLL   Believe it, sir,
  I am not of that disdainful temper,
  But I could love you faithfully.

SIR ALEXANDER [*aside*]   A pox
  On you for that word. I like you not now,   50
  You're a cunning roarer, I see that already.

MOLL But sleep upon this once more, sir, you may chance shift a
  mind tomorrow: be not too hasty to wrong yourself. Never while
  you live, sir, take a wife running, many have run out at heels° that
  have done't. You see, sir, I speak against myself, and if every woman   55
  would deal with their suitor so honestly, poor younger brothers
  would not be so often gulled with old cozening widows° that turn
  o'er all their wealth in trust to some kinsman, and make the poor
  gentleman work hard for a pension. Fare you well, sir.

SEBASTIAN Nay, prithee one word more.   60

SIR ALEXANDER [*aside*] How do I wrong this girl, she puts him off
  still.

MOLL Think upon this in cold blood, sir. You make as much haste as
  if you were a-going upon a sturgeon voyage. Take deliberation, sir,
  never choose a wife as if you were going to Virginia.°

SEBASTIAN And so we parted, my too cursèd fate.   65
    [*Sebastian walks aside*]

SIR ALEXANDER [*aside*] She is but cunning, gives him longer time
  in't.

    Enter a Tailor

TAILOR Mistress Moll, Mistress Moll! So ho ho, so ho!°

MOLL There boy, there boy.° What, dost thou go a-hawking after me
  with a red clout° on thy finger?

TAILOR I forgot to take measure on you for your new breeches.   70

SIR ALEXANDER [*aside*] Hoyda, breeches! What, will he marry a monster with two trinkets?° What age is this? If the wife go in breeches,
  the man must wear long coats like a fool.

MOLL What fiddling's° here? Would not the old pattern have served
  your turn?   75

TAILOR You change the fashion—you say you'll have the great Dutch
  slop,° Mistress Mary?

MOLL Why, sir, I say so still.

TAILOR Your breeches then will take up a yard more.

MOLL Well, pray look it be put in then.   80

TAILOR It shall stand round and full, I warrant you.

MOLL Pray, make 'em easy enough.

TAILOR I know my fault now, t'other was somewhat stiff between the
legs, I'll make these open enough, I warrant you.

SIR ALEXANDER [*aside*] Here's good gear towards! I have brought up   85
my son to marry a Dutch slop, and a French doublet, a codpiece
daughter.

TAILOR So, I have gone as far as I can go.

MOLL Why, then, farewell.

TAILOR If you go presently to your chamber, Mistress Mary, pray   90
send me the measure of your thigh by some honest body.

MOLL Well, sir, I'll send it by a porter presently.

              Exit Moll

TAILOR So you had need, it is a lusty one. Both of them would make
any porter's back ache in England!

              Exit Tailor

SEBASTIAN [*stepping forward*] I have examined the best part of man,   95
Reason and judgement, and in love they tell me,
They leave me uncontrolled. He that is swayed
By an unfeeling blood, past heat of love
His springtime must needs err: his watch ne'er goes right
That sets his dial by a rusty clock.°   100

SIR ALEXANDER [*coming forward*] So, and which is that rusty clock,
        sir, you?

SEBASTIAN By the clock at Ludgate,° sir, it ne'er goes true.

SIR ALEXANDER But thou goest falser. Not thy father's cares
Can keep thee right, when that insensible work°
Obeys the workman's art, lets° off the hour,   105
And stops again when time is satisfied—
But thou run'st on, and judgement, thy main wheel,
Beats by all stops,° as if the work would break
Begun with long pains for a minute's ruin,
Much like a suffering man brought up with care,   110
At last bequeathed to shame and a short prayer.°

SEBASTIAN I taste you bitterer than I can deserve, sir.

SIR ALEXANDER Who has bewitched thee, son? What devil or drug
Hath wrought upon the weakness of thy blood,
And betrayed all her hopes to ruinous folly?   115
O, wake from drowsy and enchanted shame,
Wherein thy soul sits with a golden dream
Flattered and poisoned. I am old, my son,
O, let me prevail quickly,

For I have weightier business of mine own 120
Than to chide thee: I must not to my grave,
As a drunkard to his bed, whereon he lies
Only to sleep, and never cares to rise.
Let me dispatch in time, come no more near her.

SEBASTIAN Not honestly, not in the way of marriage? 125

SIR ALEXANDER What sayst thou? Marriage? In what place? The
sessions house?
And who shall give the bride, prithee? An indictment?

SEBASTIAN Sir, now ye take part with the world to wrong her.

SIR ALEXANDER Why, wouldst thou fain marry to be pointed at?
Alas, the number's great, do not o'erburden 't. 130
Why, as good marry a beacon on a hill,
Which all the country fix their eyes upon,
As her thy folly dotes on. If thou longest
To have the story of thy infamous fortunes,
Serve for discourse in ordinaries and taverns, 135
Thou'rt in the way. Or to confound thy name,
Keep on, thou canst not miss it. Or to strike
Thy wretched father to untimely coldness,
Keep the left hand still,° it will bring thee to't.
Yet if no tears wrung from thy father's eyes, 140
Nor sighs that fly in sparkles from his sorrows,
Had power to alter what is wilful in thee,
Methinks her very name should fright thee from her,
And never trouble me.

SEBASTIAN Why is the name of Moll so fatal, sir? 145

SIR ALEXANDER Many one, sir, where suspect is entered,
For seek all London from one end to t'other,
More whores of that name, than of any ten other.

SEBASTIAN What's that to her? Let those blush for themselves.
Can any guilt in others condemn her? 150
I've vowed to love her: let all storms oppose me,
That ever beat against the breast of man,
Nothing but death's black tempest shall divide us.

SIR ALEXANDER O, folly that can dote on nought but shame!

SEBASTIAN Put case a wanton itch runs through one name 155
More than another, is that name the worse,
Where honesty sits possessed in't? It should rather
Appear more excellent, and deserve more praise,
When through foul mists a brightness it can raise.

Why, there are of the devil's,° honest gentlemen,   160
And well descended, keep an open house,
And some o'th good man's° that are arrant knaves.
He hates unworthily, that by rote contemns,
For the name neither saves, nor yet condemns;
And for her honesty, I have made such proof on't,   165
In several forms, so nearly watched her ways,
I will maintain that strict, against an army,
Excepting you, my father. Here's her worst,
Sh' has a bold spirit that mingles with mankind,
But nothing else comes near it, and oftentimes   170
Through her apparel somewhat shames her birth,
But she is loose in nothing but in mirth:
Would all Molls were no worse.
SIR ALEXANDER This way I toil in vain and give but aim°
    To infamy and ruin. [*Aside*] He will fall,   175
My blessing cannot stay him. All my joys
Stand at the brink of a devouring flood
And will be wilfully swallowed, wilfully!
But why so vain let all these tears be lost?
I'll pursue her to shame, and so all's crossed.   180
    Exit Sir Alexander
SEBASTIAN He's gone with some strange purpose whose effect
    Will hurt me little if he shoot so wide,
To think I love so blindly. I but feed
His heart to this match, to draw on t'other
Wherein my joy sits with a full wish crowned,   185
Only his mood excepted, which must change
By opposite policies, courses indirect:
Plain dealing in this world takes no effect.
This mad girl I'll acquaint with my intent,
Get her assistance, make my fortunes known: 190
'Twixt lovers' hearts, she's a fit instrument,
And has the art to help them to their own.
By her advice, for in that craft she's wise,
My love and I may meet, spite of all spies.
    Exit

[Scene 5]

Enter Laxton in Gray's Inn Fields with the Coachman [carrying a whip]

LAXTON Coachman!

COACHMAN Here, sir.

LAXTON There's a tester° more. Prithee drive thy coach to the hither end of Marylebone Park—a fit place for Moll to get in.

COACHMAN Marylebone Park,° sir? 5

LAXTON Ay, it's in our way, thou knowest.

COACHMAN It shall be done, sir.

LAXTON Coachman.

COACHMAN Anon, sir.

LAXTON Are we fitted with good frampold jades? 10

COACHMAN The best in Smithfield,° I warrant you, sir.

LAXTON May we safely take the upper hand of any coached° velvet cap or tuftaffety° jacket? For they keep a vile swaggering in coaches nowadays, the highways are stopped with them.

COACHMAN My life for yours,° and baffle 'em too, sir!—Why, they are 15 the same jades, believe it sir, that have drawn all your famous whores to Ware.

LAXTON Nay, then they know their business, they need no more instructions.

COACHMAN They're so used to such journeys, sir, I never use whip to 20 'em, for if they catch but the scent of a wench once, they run like devils.

Exit Coachman

LAXTON Fine Cerberus! That rogue will have the start of a thousand ones, for whilst others trot afoot, he'll ride prancing to hell upon a coach-horse. Stay, 'tis now about the hour of her appointment, but 25 yet I see her not.

The clock strikes three

Hark, what's this? One, two, three. Three by the clock at Savoy. This is the hour, and Gray's Inn Fields the place she swore she'd meet me. Ha, yonder's two Inns-o'-Court men with one wench, but that's not she—they walk toward Islington out of my way. I see 30 none dressed like her, I must look for a shag ruff, a frieze jerkin, a short sword, and a safeguard or I get none. Why, Moll, prithee make haste or the coachman will curse us anon.

Enter Moll [dressed] like a man

MOLL [aside] O, here's my gentleman. If they would keep their days

as well with their mercers as their hours with their harlots, no   35
bankrupt would give seven score pound for a sergeant's place,° for
would you know a catchpole rightly derived,° the corruption of a
citizen is the generation of a sergeant. How his eye hawks for
venery!—[*To Laxton*] Come, are you ready, sir?

LAXTON Ready for what, sir?   40

MOLL Do you ask that now, sir? Why was this meeting 'pointed?

LAXTON I thought you mistook me, sir.
You seem to be some young barrister:
I have no suit in law—all my land's sold,
I praise heaven for't, t'has rid me of much trouble.   45

MOLL [*removing her hat*] Then I must wake you, sir. Where stands the
coach?

LAXTON Who's this? Moll? Honest Moll?

MOLL So young, and purblind? You're an old wanton in your eyes,° I
see that.   50

LAXTON Thou'rt admirably suited for the Three Pigeons° at Brentford. I'll swear I knew thee not.

MOLL I'll swear you did not: but you shall know me now.

LAXTON No, not here:° we shall be spied, i'faith!—The coach is better,
come.   55

MOLL Stay.

LAXTON What, wilt thou untruss a point,° Moll?
    She puts off her cloak and draws [her sword]

MOLL   Yes, here's a point°
That I untruss, 't has but one tag.° 'Twill serve, though,
To tie up a rogue's tongue!

LAXTON   How?

MOLL [*throwing down a purse*]   There's the gold
With which you hired your hackney, here's her pace:°   60
She racks° hard, and perhaps your bones will feel it.
Ten angels of mine own, I've put to thine,
Win 'em, and wear 'em.°

LAXTON   Hold, Moll! Mistress Mary!

MOLL Draw, or I'll serve an execution° on thee
Shall lay thee up till doomsday!   65

LAXTON Draw upon a woman? Why, what dost mean, Moll?

MOLL To teach thy base thoughts manners. Thou'rt one of those
That thinks each woman thy fond flexible whore,
If she but cast a liberal eye upon thee,
Turn back her head, she's thine; or, amongst company,   70

By chance drink first to thee, then she's quite gone,
There's no means to help her; nay, for a need
Wilt swear unto thy credulous fellow lechers
That thou art more in favour with a lady
At first sight than her monkey° all her lifetime. 75
How many of our sex, by such as thou
Have their good thoughts paid with a blasted name
That never deserved loosely or did trip
In path of whoredom beyond cup and lip?°
But for the stain of conscience and of soul, 80
Better had women fall into the hands
Of an act silent than a bragging nothing,
There's no mercy in't. What durst move you, sir,
To think me whorish?—A name which I'd tear out
From the high German's throat if it lay ledger° there 85
To dispatch privy slanders against me.
In thee I defy all men, their worst hates
And their best flatteries, all their golden witchcrafts,
With which they entangle the poor spirits of fools:
Distressed needlewomen and trade-fallen wives— 90
Fish that needs must bite or themselves be bitten—
Such hungry things as these may soon be took
With worm fastened on a golden hook:
Those are the lecher's food, his prey. He watches
For quarrelling wedlocks and poor shifting sisters,° 95
'Tis the best fish he takes. But why, good fisherman,
Am I thought meat for you, that never yet
Had angling rod cast towards me? 'Cause, you'll say,
I'm given to sport, I'm often merry, jest:
Had mirth no kindred in the world but lust? 100
O, shame take all her friends then! But howe'er
Thou and the baser world censure my life,
I'll send 'em word by thee, and write so much
Upon thy breast, 'cause thou shalt bear't in mind:
Tell them 'twere base to yield where I have conquered. 105
I scorn to prostitute myself to a man,
I that can prostitute a man to me!
And so I greet thee.
        [*Moll stabs at Laxton*]
LAXTON   Hear me!
MOLL   Would the spirits

Of all my slanderers were clasped in thine,
That I might vex an army at one time.   110
    [*Laxton draws his sword and*] *they fight*
LAXTON I do repent me! Hold!
    [*They pause*]
MOLL You'll die the better Christian then.
LAXTON I do confess I have wronged thee, Moll.
MOLL Confession is but poor amends for wrong,
    Unless a rope° would follow.
    [*Moll strikes again and they fight*]
LAXTON   I ask thee pardon.   115
MOLL I'm your hired whore, sir.
    [*Moll fights Laxton into submission*]
LAXTON   I yield both purse and body.
MOLL Both are mine and now at my disposing.
LAXTON [*kneeling*] Spare my life.
MOLL I scorn to strike thee basely.
LAXTON ·Spoke like a noble girl, i'faith. [*Aside*] Heart, I think I fight   120
    with a familiar,° or the ghost of a fencer! She's wounded me gal-
    lantly. Call you this a lecherous voyage? Here's blood would have
    served me this seven year in broken heads and cut fingers, and now
    it runs all out together. Pox o'the Three Pigeons, I would the coach
    were here now to carry me to the chirurgeons!   125
        Exit Laxton
MOLL If I could meet my enemies one by one thus,
    I might make pretty shift with 'em in time,
    And make 'em know, she that has wit and spirit
    May scorn to live beholding to her body for meat,
    Or for apparel like your common dame,   130
    That makes shame get her clothes to cover shame.
    Base is that mind that kneels unto her body
    As if a husband stood in awe on's wife.
    My spirit shall be mistress of this house,
    As long as I have time in't.
        Enter Trapdoor
                        O,   135
    Here comes my man that would be: 'tis his hour.
    Faith, a good well-set fellow, if his spirit
    Be answerable to his umbles.° He walks stiff,
    But whether he will stand to't stiffly,° there's the point.
    Has a good calf for't, and ye shall have many a woman   140

Choose him she means to make her head, by his calf;
I do not know their tricks in't. Faith, he seems
A man without; I'll try what he is within.

TRAPDOOR [*aside*] She told me Gray's Inn Fields 'twixt three and
    four.
    I'll fit her mistress-ship with a piece of service: 145
    I'm hired to rid the town of one mad girl.
        Moll jostles Trapdoor [*as she walks by*]
    [*To Moll*] What a pox ails you, sir?

MOLL He begins like a gentleman.

TRAPDOOR Heart, is the field so narrow, or your eyesight?
    Life, he comes back again!   150
        Moll comes towards Trapdoor

MOLL Was this spoke me, sir?

TRAPDOOR I cannot tell, sir.

MOLL Go, you're a coxcomb.

TRAPDOOR Coxcomb?

MOLL You're a slave.   155

TRAPDOOR I hope there's law for you, sir.

MOLL Yea, do you see, sir?
        Turn[s] his hat

TRAPDOOR Heart, this is no good dealing. Pray let me know what
    house you're of.

MOLL One of the Temple,° sir.   160
        Fillips him°

TRAPDOOR Mass, so methinks.

MOLL And yet sometime I lie about Chick Lane.°

TRAPDOOR I like you the worse because you shift your lodging so
    often; I'll not meddle with you for that trick, sir.

MOLL A good shift, but it shall not serve your turn.   165

TRAPDOOR You'll give me leave to pass about my business, sir?

MOLL Your business? I'll make you wait on me before I ha' done, and
    glad to serve me too!

TRAPDOOR How, sir, serve you? Not if there were no more men in
    England.   170

MOLL But if there were no more women in England,
    I hope you'd wait upon your mistress then.

TRAPDOOR Mistress!

MOLL O, you're a tried spirit, at a push, sir.

TRAPDOOR What would your worship have me do?   175

MOLL You a fighter?

TRAPDOOR No, I praise heaven, I had better grace and more manners.

MOLL As how, I pray, sir?

TRAPDOOR Life, 't had been a beastly part of me to have drawn my
    weapons upon my mistress, all the world would ha' cried shame of   180
    me for that.

MOLL Why, but you knew me not.

TRAPDOOR Do not say so, mistress. I knew you by your wide straddle,°
    as well as if I had been in your belly.

MOLL Well, we shall try you further, i'th' meantime we give you   185
    entertainment.°

TRAPDOOR Thank your good mistress-ship.

MOLL How many suits have you?

TRAPDOOR No more suits than backs, mistress.

MOLL Well, if you deserve, I cast off this next week,   190
    And you may creep into't.

TRAPDOOR   Thank your good worship.

MOLL Come, follow me to Saint Thomas Apostles°
    I'll put a livery cloak upon your back
    The first thing I do.

TRAPDOOR   I follow, my dear mistress.

    Exeunt

[Scene 6]

Enter Mistress Gallipot as from supper, her husband after her

GALLIPOT What, Prue! Nay, sweet Prudence!

MISTRESS GALLIPOT What a pru-ing° keep you! I think the baby
    would have a teat, it kyes° so. Pray, be not so fond of me, leave your
    city humours, I'm vexed at you to see how like a calf you come
    bleating after me.   5

GALLIPOT Nay, honey Prue, how does your rising up before all the
    table show? And flinging from my friends so uncivilly? Fie, Prue,
    fie, come.

MISTRESS GALLIPOT Then up and ride,° i'faith.

GALLIPOT Up and ride? Nay, my pretty Prue, that's far from my   10
    thought, duck.—Why, mouse, thy mind is nibbling at something.
    What is't? What lies upon thy stomach?

MISTRESS GALLIPOT Such an ass as you! Hoyda! You're best turn
    midwife, or physician;° you're a 'pothecary already, but I'm none of
    your drugs.   15

GALLIPOT Thou art a sweet drug, sweetest Prue, and the more thou
    art pounded, the more precious.

MISTRESS GALLIPOT Must you be prying into a woman's secrets: say
    ye?

GALLIPOT Woman's secrets?   20

MISTRESS GALLIPOT What? I cannot have a qualm come upon me
    but your teeth° waters, till your nose hang over it.

GALLIPOT It is my love, dear wife.

MISTRESS GALLIPOT Your love? Your love is all words; give me
    deeds, I cannot abide a man that's too fond over me, so cookish;°   25
    thou dost not know how to handle a woman in her kind.

GALLIPOT No, Prue? Why, I hope I have handled—

MISTRESS GALLIPOT Handle a fool's head° of your own! Fie! Fie!

GALLIPOT Ha, ha, 'tis such a wasp; it does me good now to have her
    sting me, little rogue.   30

MISTRESS GALLIPOT Now, fie, how you vex me, I cannot abide these
    apron husbands: such cotqueans, you overdo your things, they
    become you scurvily.

GALLIPOT [aside] Upon my life, she breeds.° Heaven knows how I
    have strained myself to please her, night and day: I wonder why we   35
    citizens should get children so fretful and untoward in the breed-
    ing, their fathers being for the most part as gentle as milch kine.°—
    [Aloud] Shall I leave thee, my Prue?

MISTRESS GALLIPOT Fie, fie, fie!

GALLIPOT Thou shalt not be vexed no more, pretty kind rogue, take   40
    no cold, sweet Prue.
        Exit Gallipot

MISTRESS GALLIPOT As your wit has done! [*Producing a letter*] Now,
    Master Laxton, show your head, what news from you? Would any
    husband suspect that a woman crying 'Buy any scurvy-grass?'°
    should bring love letters amongst her herbs to his wife? Pretty trick,   45
    fine conveyance! Had jealousy a thousand eyes, a silly woman with
    scurvy-grass blinds them all.
               Laxton, with bays
    Crown I thy wit for this, it deserves praise!
    This makes me affect thee more, this proves thee wise,   50
    'Lack, what poor shift is love forced to devise.
    To th'point!
        She reads the letter
    'O, sweet creature'—a sweet beginning—'pardon my long absence,
    for thou shalt shortly be possessed with my presence; though

Demophon was false to Phyllis,° I will be to thee as Pan-da-rus was   55
to Cres-sida:° though Aeneas made an ass of Dido,° I will die° to
thee 'ere I do so; O, sweetest creature, make much of me, for no
man beneath the silver moon shall make more of a woman than I do
of thee. Furnish me, therefore, with thirty pounds, you must do it
of necessity for me; I languish till I see some comfort come from   60
thee. Protesting not to die in thy debt, but rather to live so, as
hitherto I have and will.

                                              Thy true Laxton ever.'

Alas, poor gentleman! Troth, I pity him.
How shall I raise this money? Thirty pound?   65
'Tis thirty sure, a three before an O,
I know his threes too well. My childbed linen?°
Shall I pawn that for him? Then if my mark°
Be known, I am undone; it may be thought
My husband's bankrupt. Which way shall I turn?   70
Laxton, what with my own fears, and thy wants,
I'm like a needle 'twixt two adamants.
        Enter Gallipot hastily
GALLIPOT Nay, nay, wife, the women are all up. [*Aside*] Ha, how? Read-
    ing of letters? I smell a goose,° a couple of capons, and a gammon
    of bacon from her mother out of the country, I hold my life.   75
        [*He creeps up behind her*]
    Steal, steal°—
MISTRESS GALLIPOT O, beshrew your heart!
GALLIPOT What letter's that? I'll see't.
        She tears the letter
MISTRESS GALLIPOT O, would thou had'st no eyes to see
    The downfall of me and thyself: I'm for ever,   80
    For ever I'm undone.
GALLIPOT   What ails my Prue,
    What paper's that thou tear'st?
MISTRESS GALLIPOT   Would I could tear
    My very heart in pieces, for my soul
    Lies on the rack of shame that tortures me
    Beyond a woman's suffering.
GALLIPOT   What means this?   85
MISTRESS GALLIPOT Had you no other vengeance to throw down,
    But even in the height of all my joys?
GALLIPOT   Dear woman.

MISTRESS GALLIPOT When the full sea of pleasure and content
  Seemed to flow over me—
GALLIPOT   As thou desirest
  To keep me out of Bedlam,° tell what troubles thee! 90
  Is not thy child at nurse fallen sick, or dead?
MISTRESS GALLIPOT O, no!
GALLIPOT Heavens bless me, are my barns and houses
  Yonder at Hockley Hole° consumed with fire?
  I can build more, sweet Prue.
MISTRESS GALLIPOT 'Tis worse, 'tis worse! 95
GALLIPOT My factor° broke, or is the *Jonas*° sunk?
MISTRESS GALLIPOT Would we had all been swallowed in the waves,
  Rather than both should be the scorn of slaves.
GALLIPOT I'm at my wit's end!
MISTRESS GALLIPOT   O, my dear husband,
  Where once I thought myself a fixèd star, 100
  Placed only in the heaven of thine arms,
  I fear now I shall prove a wanderer.
  O, Laxton, Laxton, is it then my fate
  To be by thee o'erthrown?
GALLIPOT   Defend me, wisdom,
  From falling into frenzy. [*Kneeling*] On my knees, 105
  Sweet Prue, speak. What's that Laxton who so heavy
  Lies on thy bosom?
MISTRESS GALLIPOT I shall sure run mad.
GALLIPOT I shall run mad for company then! [*Rising*] Speak to me,
  I'm Gallipot thy husband!—Prue!—Why, Prue,
  Art sick in conscience for some villainous deed 110
  Thou wert about to act? Didst mean to rob me?
  Tush, I forgive thee. Hast thou on my bed
  Thrust my soft pillow under another's head?
  I'll wink at all faults, Prue; 'las, that's no more
  Than what some neighbours near thee have done before. 115
  Sweet honey Prue, what's that Laxton?
MISTRESS GALLIPOT   O!
GALLIPOT Out with him.
MISTRESS GALLIPOT   O, he's born to be my undoer!
  This hand which thou call'st thine, to him was given,
  To him was I made sure i'th' sight of heaven.
GALLIPOT I never heard this thunder.
MISTRESS GALLIPOT   Yes, yes, before 120

I was to thee contracted, to him I swore.°
Since last I saw him, twelve months three times told
The moon hath drawn through her light silver bow.
For o'er the seas he went, and it was said—
But Rumour lies—that he in France was dead.   125
But he's alive. O, he's alive. He sent
That letter to me, which in rage I rent,
Swearing with oaths most damnably to have me,
Or tear me from this bosom. O, heavens save me!

GALLIPOT My heart will break,—shamed and undone forever!   130

MISTRESS GALLIPOT So black a day, poor wretch, went o'er thee never.

GALLIPOT If thou shouldst wrestle with him at the law,
Thou'rt sure to fall—no odd sleight°—no prevention?—
I'll tell him thou'rt with child.

MISTRESS GALLIPOT   Um.

GALLIPOT   Or give out
One of my men was ta'en abed with thee.   135

MISTRESS GALLIPOT Um. Um.

GALLIPOT   Before I lose thee, my dear Prue,
I'll drive it to that push.

MISTRESS GALLIPOT   Worse, and worse still!
You embrace a mischief to prevent an ill.

GALLIPOT I'll buy thee of him, stop his mouth with gold.
Think'st thou 'twill do?

MISTRESS GALLIPOT   O me! Heavens grant it would!   140
Yet now my senses are set more in tune,
He writ, as I remember in his letter,
That he in riding up and down had spent,
Ere he could find me, thirty pounds. Send that—
Stand not on thirty with him.

GALLIPOT   Forty, Prue,   145
Say thou the word, 'tis done. We venture lives
For wealth, but must do more to keep our wives:
Thirty or forty, Prue?

MISTRESS GALLIPOT   Thirty, good sweet.
Of an ill bargain, let's save what we can.
I'll pay it him with my tears; he was a man,   150
When first I knew him of a meek spirit.
All goodness is not yet dried up, I hope.

GALLIPOT He shall have thirty pound. Let that stop all:
Love's sweets taste best, when we have drunk down gall.

Enter Tiltyard, and his wife, Goshawk, and Mistress Openwork

Gods-so, our friends! Come, come! Smooth your cheek—   155
After a storm the face of heaven looks sleek.

TILTYARD Did I not tell you these turtles were together?

MISTRESS TILTYARD How dost thou, sirrah?° Why, sister° Gallipot!

MISTRESS OPENWORK Lord, how she's changed!

GOSHAWK Is your wife ill, sir?   160

GALLIPOT Yes, indeed, la, sir, very ill, very ill, never worse.

MISTRESS TILTYARD How her head burns! Feel how her pulses work!

MISTRESS OPENWORK Sister, lie down a little—that always does me
good.

MISTRESS TILTYARD In good sadness,° I find best ease in that too.   165
Has she laid some hot thing to her stomach?

MISTRESS GALLIPOT No, but I will lay something anon.

TILTYARD Come, come, fools, you trouble her! Shall's go, Master
Goshawk?

GOSHAWK Yes, sweet Master Tiltyard.   170

        [*Goshawk talks apart with Mistress Openwork*]

Sirrah Rosamond, I hold my life, Gallipot hath vexed his wife.

MISTRESS OPENWORK She has a horrible high colour indeed.

GOSHAWK We shall have your face painted with the same red soon at
night, when your husband comes from his rubbers° in a false alley.
Thou wilt not believe me that his bowls run with a wrong bias?°   175

MISTRESS OPENWORK It cannot sink into me that he feeds upon stale
mutton abroad, having better and fresher at home.

GOSHAWK What if I bring thee where thou shalt see him stand at rack
and manger?°

MISTRESS OPENWORK I'll saddle him in's kind, and spur him till he   180
kick again!

GOSHAWK Shall thou and I ride our journey then?

MISTRESS OPENWORK Here's my hand.

GOSHAWK No more.—[*To Tiltyard*] Come, Master Tiltyard, shall we
leap into the stirrups with our women and amble home?   185

TILTYARD Yes, yes. Come, wife!

MISTRESS TILTYARD In troth, sister, I hope you will do well for all
this.

MISTRESS GALLIPOT I hope I shall. Farewell, good sister, sweet
Master Goshawk.   190

GALLIPOT Welcome, brother. Most kindly welcome, sir.

ALL [GUESTS] Thanks, sir, for our good cheer.

        Exeunt all but Gallipot and his wife

GALLIPOT It shall be so, because° a crafty knave
    Shall not outreach me, nor walk by my door
    With my wife arm in arm, as 'twere his whore.   195
    I'll give him a golden coxcomb. Thirty pound?
    Tush, Prue, what's thirty pound? Sweet duck, look
    cheerly.
MISTRESS GALLIPOT Thou art worthy of my heart, thou buy'st it
    dearly.
    Enter Laxton muffled
LAXTON [*aside*] Uds light, the tide's against me! A pox of your
    'pothecaryship! O, for some glister to set him going! 'Tis one of   200
    Hercules' labours, to tread° one of these city hens, because their
    cocks are still crowing over them. There's no turning tail here, I
    must on.
MISTRESS GALLIPOT O, husband see, he comes.
GALLIPOT   Let me deal with him.
LAXTON Bless you, sir.
GALLIPOT Be you blessed too, sir, if you come in peace.   205
LAXTON Have you any good pudding-tobacco,° sir?
MISTRESS GALLIPOT O, pick no quarrels, gentle sir. My husband
    Is not a man of weapon, as you are.
    He knows all, I have opened all before him,
    Concerning you.
LAXTON [*aside*]   Zounds, has she shown my letters?   210
MISTRESS GALLIPOT Suppose my case were yours, what would you
    do?
    At such a pinch, such batteries, such assaults,
    Of father, mother, kindred, to dissolve
    The knot you tied, and to be bound to him?
    How could you shift this storm off?
LAXTON   If I know, hang me.   215
MISTRESS GALLIPOT Besides, a story of your death was read
    Each minute to me.
LAXTON [*aside*]   What a pox means this riddling?
GALLIPOT Be wise, sir, let not you and I be tossed
    On lawyers' pens; they have sharp nibs and draw
    Men's very heart-blood from them. What need you, sir,   220
    To beat the drum of my wife's infamy,
    And call your friends together, sir, to prove
    Your precontract, when sh'has confessed it?
LAXTON   Um, sir

Has she confessed it?

GALLIPOT   Sh'has, 'faith, to me, sir,
Upon your letter sending.

MISTRESS GALLIPOT   I have, I have.   225

LAXTON [*aside*] If I let this iron cool, call me slave!
[*To her*] Do you hear, you dame Prudence? Think'st thou, vile
    woman,
I'll take these blows and wink?

MISTRESS GALLIPOT   Upon my knees—

LAXTON Out, impudence!

GALLIPOT   Good sir—

LAXTON   You goatish slaves!
No wild fowl to cut up but mine?°

GALLIPOT   Alas, sir,   230
You make her flesh to tremble. Fright her not.
She shall do reason, and what's fit.

LAXTON I'll have thee, wert thou more common
Than an hospital, and more diseased—

GALLIPOT   But one word, good sir.

LAXTON   So, sir?

GALLIPOT I married her, have lain with her, and got   235
Two children on her body, think but on that.
Have you so beggarly an appetite
When I upon a dainty dish have fed
To dine upon my scraps, my leavings? Ha, sir?
Do I come near you now, sir?

LAXTON   Be lady,° you touch me.   240

GALLIPOT Would not you scorn to wear my clothes, sir?

LAXTON   Right, sir.

GALLIPOT Then pray, sir, wear not her, for she's a garment
So fitting for my body, I'm loath
Another should put it on—you will undo both.
Your letter, as she said, complained you had spent   245
In quest of her, some thirty pound: I'll pay it.
Shall that, sir, stop this gap up 'twixt you two?

LAXTON Well, if I swallow wrong, let her thank you:
The money being paid, sir, I am gone.
Farewell. O, women, happy's he trusts none.   250

MISTRESS GALLIPOT Dispatch him hence, sweet husband.

GALLIPOT   Yes, dear wife—
Pray, sir, come in. [*To her*] Ere Master Laxton part

Thou shalt drink wine to him.

MISTRESS GALLIPOT   With all my heart.

[*Aside to Laxton*] How dost thou like my wit?

LAXTON [*aside to her*]   Rarely!

    Exeunt Master Gallipot and his wife

                                     That wile,

By which the serpent did the first woman beguile,   255

Did ever since all women's bosoms fill:

You're apple-eaters all, deceivers still.

    Exit Laxton

[Scene 7]

    Enter Sir Alexander Wengrave, Sir Davy Dapper, Sir Adam
    Appleton at one door, and Trapdoor at another door

SIR ALEXANDER Out with your tale, Sir Davy, to Sir Adam.

    A knave is in mine eye° deep in my debt.

SIR DAVY Nay, if he be a knave, sir, hold him fast.

    [*Sir Davy and Sir Adam talk apart*]

SIR ALEXANDER Speak softly, what egg is there hatching now?

TRAPDOOR A duck's egg, sir, a duck that has eaten a frog. I have   5

    cracked the shell, and some villainy or other will peep out presently.

    The duck that sits is the bouncing ramp,° that roaring girl, my

    mistress; the drake that must tread is your son, Sebastian.

SIR ALEXANDER Be quick.

TRAPDOOR As the tongue of an oyster-wench.   10

SIR ALEXANDER And see thy news be true.

TRAPDOOR As a barber's every Saturday night.—Mad Moll—

SIR ALEXANDER Ah!

TRAPDOOR Must be let in without knocking at your back gate.

SIR ALEXANDER So.   15

TRAPDOOR Your chamber will be made bawdy.°

SIR ALEXANDER Good.

TRAPDOOR She comes in a shirt of mail.

SIR ALEXANDER How, shirt of mail?

TRAPDOOR Yes, sir, or a male shirt, that's to say, in man's apparel.   20

SIR ALEXANDER To my son?

TRAPDOOR Close to your son: your son and her moon will be in

    conjunction,° if all almanacs lie not. Her black safeguard is turned

into a deep slop, the holes° of her upper body to button-holes, her
waistcoat° to a doublet, her placket to the ancient seat of a codpiece; 25
and you shall take 'em both with standing collars.°

SIR ALEXANDER Art sure of this?

TRAPDOOR As every throng is sure of a pickpocket, as sure as a whore
is of the clients all Michaelmas Term,° and of the pox after the term.

SIR ALEXANDER And the time of their tilting? 30

TRAPDOOR Three.

SIR ALEXANDER The day?

TRAPDOOR This.

SIR ALEXANDER Away, ply it, watch her.

TRAPDOOR As the devil doth for the death of a bawd, I'll watch her; 35
do you catch her.

SIR ALEXANDER She's fast; here weave thou the nets. Hark—

TRAPDOOR They are made.

SIR ALEXANDER [glancing at Sir Adam and Sir Davy] I told them thou
didst owe me money; hold it up, maintain't. 40

TRAPDOOR Stiffly, as a puritan does contention.
[Aloud, as if quarrelling] Fox, I owe thee not the value of a
halfpenny halter!

SIR ALEXANDER Thou shalt be hanged in't ere thou 'scape so!
Varlet, I'll make thee look through a grate!°

TRAPDOOR I'll do't presently—through a tavern grate. Drawer!° Pish! 45
    Exit Trapdoor

SIR ADAM Has the knave vexed you, sir?

SIR ALEXANDER   Asked him my money,
He swears my son received it. O, that boy
Will ne'er leave heaping sorrows on my heart,
Till he has broke it quite.

SIR ADAM   Is he still wild?

SIR ALEXANDER As is a Russian bear.

SIR ADAM   But he has left 50
His old haunt with that baggage?

SIR ALEXANDER   Worse still and worse,
He lays on me his shame, I on him my curse.

SIR DAVY My son, Jack Dapper, then shall run with him
All in one pasture.

SIR ADAM   Proves your son bad too, sir?

SIR DAVY As villainy can make him: your Sebastian 55
Dotes but on one drab, mine on a thousand!
A noise° of fiddlers, tobacco, wine, and a whore,

A mercer that will let him take up° more,
Dice, and a water-spaniel with a duck. O,
Bring him a bed with these. When his purse jingles,   60
Roaring boys follow at's tail, fencers and ningles,
Beasts Adam ne'er gave name to,—these horse-leeches suck
My son,—he being drawn dry, they all live on smoke.

SIR ALEXANDER Tobacco?

SIR DAVY   Right; but I have in my brain
A windmill going that shall grind to dust   65
The follies of my son, and make him wise,
Or stark fool. Pray lend me your advice.

SIR ALEXANDER AND SIR ADAM That shall you, good Sir Davy.

SIR DAVY   Here's the springe
I ha' set to catch this woodcock° in: an action
In a false name, unknown to him, is entered   70
I'th' Counter° to arrest Jack Dapper.

SIR ALEXANDER AND SIR ADAM   Ha, ha, he!

SIR DAVY Think you the Counter cannot break him?

SIR ADAM   Break him?
Yes, and break's heart too, if he lie there long.

SIR DAVY I'll make him sing a counter-tenor,° sure.

SIR ADAM No way to tame him like it. There he shall learn   75
What money is indeed, and how to spend it.

SIR DAVY He's bridled there.

SIR ALEXANDER   Ay, yet knows not how to mend it!
Bedlam cures not more madmen in a year,
Than one of the Counters does; men pay more dear
There for their wit than anywhere. A Counter,   80
Why, 'tis an university, who not sees?
As scholars there, so here men take degrees
And follow the same studies all alike.
Scholars learn first logic and rhetoric,°
So does a prisoner. With fine honeyed speech   85
At's first coming in he doth persuade, beseech,
He may be lodged with one that is not itchy,
To lie in a clean chamber, in sheets not lousy,
But when he has no money, then does he try
By subtle logic and quaint sophistry   90
To make the keepers trust him.

SIR ADAM   Say they do?

SIR ALEXANDER Then he's a graduate!

SIR DAVY   Say they trust him not?
SIR ALEXANDER Then is he held a freshman and a sot,
  And never shall commence° but, being still barred,°
  Be expulsed from the Master's side,° to th' twopenny ward,°   95
  Or else i'th' Hole° be placed.
SIR ADAM   When then, I pray,
  Proceeds° a prisoner?
SIR ALEXANDER   When, money being the theme,
  He can dispute with his hard creditors' hearts,
  And get out clear, he's then a Master of Arts!
  Sir Davy, send your son to Wood Street° College,   100
  A gentleman can nowhere get more knowledge.
SIR DAVY There gallants study hard?
SIR ALEXANDER   True: to get money.
SIR DAVY 'Lies° by th' heels, i'faith. Thanks, thanks; I ha' sent
  For a couple of bears shall paw him.
        Enter Sergeant Curtalax and Yeoman Hanger
SIR ADAM   Who comes yonder?
SIR DAVY They look like puttocks;° these should be they.
SIR ALEXANDER   I know 'em,   105
  They are officers. Sir, we'll leave you.
SIR DAVY   My good knights,
  Leave me. You see I'm haunted now with sprites.
SIR ALEXANDER AND SIR ADAM Fare you well, sir.
        Exeunt [Sir] Alex[ander] and [Sir] Adam
CURTALAX This old muzzle chops should be he by the fellow's
  description. Save you, sir.   110
SIR DAVY Come hither, you mad varlets, did not my man tell you I
  watched here for you?
CURTALAX One in a blue coat,° sir, told us, that in this place an old
  gentleman would watch for us, a thing contrary to our oath, for we
  are to watch for every wicked member in a city.   115
SIR DAVY You'll watch then for ten thousand. What's thy name,
  honesty?°
CURTALAX Sergeant Curtalax I, sir.
SIR DAVY An excellent name for a sergeant, Curtalax.
  Sergeants are indeed weapons of the law: 120
  When prodigal ruffians far in debt are grown,
  Should not you cut them, citizens were o'erthrown.
  Thou dwell'st hereby in Holborn, Curtalax?
CURTALAX That's my circuit, sir, I conjure most in that circle.

SIR DAVY And what young toward° whelp is this?   125
HANGER Of the same litter, his yeoman, sir. My name's Hanger.
SIR DAVY Yeoman Hanger.
　　One pair of shears, sure, cut out both your coats,°
　　You have two names most dangerous to men's throats.
　　You two are villainous loads on gentlemen's backs,   130
　　Dear ware,° this Hanger and this Curtalax.
CURTALAX We are as other men are, sir, I cannot see but he who
　　makes a show of honesty and religion, if his claws can fasten to his
　　liking, he draws blood; all that live in the world are but great fish
　　and little fish, and feed upon one another. Some eat up whole men, 135
　　a sergeant cares but for the shoulder° of a man. They call us knaves
　　and curs, but many times he that sets us on, worries more lambs
　　one year than we do in seven.
SIR DAVY Spoke like a noble Cerberus! Is the action entered?
HANGER His name is entered in the book of unbelievers.   140
SIR DAVY What book's that?
CURTALAX The book where all the prisoners' names stand, and not
　　one amongst forty, when he comes in, believes to come out in haste.
SIR DAVY Be as dogged to him as your office allows you to be.
CURTALAX AND HANGER O, sir!   145
SIR DAVY You know the unthrift Jack Dapper?
CURTALAX Ay, ay, sir, that gull? As well as I know my yeoman.
SIR DAVY And you know his father too, Sir Davy Dapper?
CURTALAX As damned a usurer as ever was among Jews! If he were
　　sure his father's skin would yield him any money, he would, when 150
　　he dies, flay it off and sell it to cover drums for children at
　　Bartholomew Fair!°
SIR DAVY [aside] What toads are these to spit poison on a man to his
　　face?—[To them] Do you see, my honest rascals, yonder Grey-
　　hound is the dog he hunts with? Out of that tavern Jack Dapper   155
　　will sally. Ça, ça!° Give the counter.° On, set upon him!
CURTALAX AND HANGER We'll charge him upo' th' back, sir.
SIR DAVY Take no bail, put mace enough into his caudle.°
　　Double your files! Traverse your ground!°
CURTALAX AND HANGER Brave, sir.   160
SIR DAVY Cry arm, arm, arm!
CURTALAX AND HANGER Thus, sir.
SIR DAVY There boy, there boy, away: look to your prey, my true
　　English wolves,°—and so I vanish.
　　　　Exit S[ir] Davy

CURTALAX Some warden of the sergeants begat this old fellow, upon 165
my life! Stand close.

HANGER Shall the ambuscado lie in one place?

CURTALAX No, nook° thou yonder.

[*Curtalax and Hanger hide at opposite sides of the stage.*]
Enter Moll and Trapdoor

MOLL Ralph.

TRAPDOOR What says my brave captain male and female? 170

MOLL This Holborn is such a wrangling street.

TRAPDOOR That's because lawyers walks to and fro in't.

MOLL Here's such jostling, as if every one we met were drunk and
reeled.

TRAPDOOR [*noticing the sergeants and speaking aside to Moll*] Stand, 175
mistress, do you not smell carrion?

MOLL [*aside to Trapdoor*] Carrion? No, yet I spy ravens.

TRAPDOOR [*aside to Moll*] Some poor wind-shaken gallant will anon
fall into sore labour, and these men-midwives must bring him to
bed i'th' Counter, there all those that are great with child with 180
debts lie in.

MOLL [*aside to Trapdoor*] Stand up.

TRAPDOOR [*aside to Moll*] Like your new maypole.

HANGER [*to Curtalax*] Whist, whew!

CURTALAX [*to Hanger*] Hump, no!° 185

MOLL Peeping? It shall go hard, huntsmen, but I'll spoil your game.
They look for all the world like two infected maltmen° coming muffled up in their cloaks in a frosty morning to London.

TRAPDOOR A course, Captain, a bear comes to the stake.
Enter Jack Dapper and Gull

MOLL It should be so, for the dogs struggle to be let loose. 190

HANGER [*to Curtalax*] Whew!

CURTALAX [*to Hanger*] Hemp!

MOLL Hark, Trapdoor, follow your leader.

JACK DAPPER Gull.

GULL Master? 195

JACK DAPPER Didst ever see such an ass as I am, boy?°

GULL No, by my troth, sir, to lose all your money, yet have false dice
of your own. Why 'tis as I saw a great fellow used t'other day, he
had a fair sword and buckler, and yet a butcher dry-beat him with a
cudgel. 200

[MOLL] [*accosting the sergeant*] Honest sergeant!

[TRAPDOOR] Fly, fly Master Dapper, you'll be arrested else!

JACK DAPPER Run, Gull, and draw!

GULL Run, master! Gull follows you!

Exit Dapper and Gull

CURTALAX [*shaking off Moll and drawing his sword*] I know you well   205
enough, you're but a whore to hang upon any man!

MOLL Whores then are like sergeants, so now hang you! Draw, rogue,
but strike not? [*To Trapdoor*] For a broken pate they'll keep their
beds, and recover twenty marks damages!

CURTALAX You shall pay for this rescue. [*To Hanger*] Run down Shoe   210
Lane° and meet him!

TRAPDOOR Shoo! Is this a rescue,° gentlemen, or no?

[*Exeunt Curtalax and Hanger*]

MOLL Rescue? A pox on 'em, Trapdoor, let's away!
I'm glad I have done perfect one good work to day:
If any gentleman be in scrivener's bands,°
Send but for Moll, she'll bail him by these hands!   215

Exeunt

[Scene 8]

*Enter Sir Alexander Wengrave alone [carrying his watch and
wearing a heavy gold chain and his ruff with its diamond]*

SIR ALEXANDER Unhappy in the follies of a son,
Led against judgement, sense, obedience,
And all powers of nobleness and wit;
O, wretched father.

Enter Trapdoor

Now, Trapdoor, will she come?

TRAPDOOR In man's apparel, sir, I am in her heart now,   5
And share all her secrets.

SIR ALEXANDER   Peace, peace, peace.
Here, take my German watch, hang't up in sight,
That I may see her hang in English for't.

[*He gives Trapdoor the watch*]

TRAPDOOR I warrant you for that now, next Sessions° rids her, sir.
This watch will bring her in better than a hundred constables.   10

SIR ALEXANDER Good Trapdoor, sayst thou so? Thou cheer'st my
heart
After a storm of sorrow.—My gold chain too:

Here, take a hundred marks in yellow links.
> [*He hands Trapdoor the gold chain from around his neck*]

TRAPDOOR That will do well to bring the watch to light, sir.
And worth a thousand of your headborough's lanterns.°   15

SIR ALEXANDER Place that o'th' court cupboard,° let it lie
Full in the view of her thief-whorish eye.
> [*Trapdoor discovers the court cupboard with a viol de gamba
> hanging above. He arranges the watch and chain conspicuously
> on the cupboard*]

TRAPDOOR She cannot miss it, sir, I see't so plain, that I could steal it
myself.

SIR ALEXANDER Perhaps thou shalt too,   20
That or something as weighty. What she leaves,
Thou shalt come closely° in and filch away,
And all the weight upon her back I'll lay.

TRAPDOOR You cannot assure that, sir.

SIR ALEXANDER No? What lets° it?   25

TRAPDOOR Being a stout girl, perhaps she'll desire pressing,°
Then all the weight must lie upon her belly.

SIR ALEXANDER Belly or back, I care not, so I've one.

TRAPDOOR You're of my mind for that, sir.

SIR ALEXANDER Hang up my ruff-band with the diamond at it,   30
It may be she'll like that best.
> [*Hands Trapdoor his ruff-band*]

TRAPDOOR It's well for her, that she must have her choice—[*aside*] he
thinks nothing too good for her! [*Aloud*] If you hold on this mind a
little longer, it shall be the first work I do to turn thief myself;
would do a man good to be hanged when he is so well provided for.   35

SIR ALEXANDER So, well said; all hangs well, would she hung so too,
The sight would please me more than all their glisterings:
O, that my mysteries° to such straits should run,
That I must rob myself to bless my son.
> *Exeunt* [*Sir Alexander and Trapdoor.*] *Enter Sebastian,
> with Mary Fitzallard like a page, and Moll* [*dressed as a
> man*]

SEBASTIAN Thou hast done me a kind office, without touch   40
Either of sin or shame, our loves are honest.

MOLL I'd scorn to make such shift to bring you together else.

SEBASTIAN Now have I time and opportunity
Without all fear to bid thee welcome, love.
> [*Sebastian*] *kiss*[*es Mary*]

MARY Never with more desire and harder venture.   45
MOLL How strange this shows, one man to kiss another.
SEBASTIAN I'd kiss such men to choose,° Moll,
  Methinks a woman's lip tastes well in a doublet.
MOLL Many an old madam has the better fortune then,
  Whose breaths grew stale before the fashion came,°   50
  If that will help'em, as you think 'twill do,
  They'll learn in time to pluck on the hose too.
SEBASTIAN The older they wax, Moll, troth I speak seriously,
  As some have a conceit their drink tastes better
  In an outlandish cup than in our own,   55
  So methinks every kiss she gives me now
  In this strange form, is worth a pair of two.
  Here we are safe, and furthest from the eye
  Of all suspicion, this is my father's chamber
  Upon which floor he never steps till night,   60
  Here he mistrusts me not, nor I his coming.
  At mine own chamber he still pries unto me,
  My freedom is not there at mine own finding,
  Still checked and curbed, here he shall miss his purpose.
MOLL And what's your business, now you have your mind, sir?   65
  At your great suit I promised you to come:
  I pitied her for name's sake, that a Moll
  Should be so crossed in love, when there's so many
  That owes nine lays apiece,° and not so little.
  My tailor fitted her, how like you his work?   70
SEBASTIAN So well, no art can mend° it for this purpose,
  But to thy wit and help we're chief in debt,
  And must live still beholding.
MOLL   Any honest pity
  I'm willing to bestow on poor ring-doves.°
SEBASTIAN I'll offer no worse play.
MOLL [drawing her sword]   Nay, and you should, sir,   75
  I should draw first and prove the quicker man.
SEBASTIAN Hold, there shall need no weapon at this meeting,
  But 'cause thou shalt not loose thy fury idle,°
  Here, take this viol, run upon the guts,°
  And end the quarrel singing.   80
      [Sebastian takes down the viol and offers it to Moll]
MOLL Like a swan above bridge,°
  For look you, here's the bridge, and here am I.

SEBASTIAN Hold on, sweet Moll.

MARY I've heard her much commended, sir, for one that was ne'er
taught.   85

MOLL I'm much beholding to'em. Well, since you needs put us
together, sir, I'll play my part as well as I can: it shall ne'er be said I
came into a gentleman's chamber and let his instrument hang by
the walls.

SEBASTIAN Why, well said Moll, i'faith. It had been shame for that   90
gentleman then, that would have let it hang still, and ne'er offered
thee it.

MOLL There it should have been still then for Moll, for though the
world judge impatiently of me, I ne'er came into that chamber yet
where I took down the instrument myself.   95

SEBASTIAN Pish, let 'em prate abroad. Thou'rt here where thou art
known and loved. There will be a thousand close dames that will
call the viol an unmannerly instrument for a woman,° and therefore
talk broadly of thee, when you shall have them sit wider to a worse
quality.   100

MOLL Push, I ever fall asleep and think not of 'em, sir, and thus I
dream.

SEBASTIAN Prithee, let's hear thy dream, Moll.

MOLL [sings, accompanying herself on the viol]

> *I dream there is a mistress,*
> *And she lays out the money,*   105
> *She goes unto her sisters,*
> *She never comes at any.*

Enter Sir Alexander behind them

> *She says she went to th' Burse° for patterns,*
> *You shall find her at Saint Kathern's°*
> *And comes home with never a penny.*   110

SEBASTIAN That's a free mistress, 'faith.

SIR ALEXANDER [aside] Ay, ay, ay, like her that sings it, one of thine
own choosing.

MOLL But shall I dream again?

[Sings]

> *Here comes a wench will brave ye,*   115
> *Her courage was so great,*
> *She lay with one o'th Navy,*

> *Her husband lying i'th'Fleet.°*
> *Yet if with him she cavilled*
>   *I wonder what she ails*   120
> *Her husband's ship lay gravelled*
>   *When hers could hoise up sails;°*
> *Yet she began like all my foes,*
>   *To call whore first: for so do those,*
> *A pox of all false tails!°*   125

SEBASTIAN Marry, amen I say.

SIR ALEXANDER [*aside*] So say I, too.

MOLL [*handing the viol to Sebastian*] Hang up the viol now, sir: all this
    while I was in a dream.—One shall lie rudely then, but being
    awake, I keep my legs together.   130
        [*Sebastian replaces the viol*]
    A watch?° What's o'clock here?

SIR ALEXANDER [*aside*] Now, now, she's trapped.

MOLL Between one and two; nay then, I care not: a watch and a
    musician are cousin germans° in one thing, they must both keep
    time well, or there's no goodness in 'em, the one else deserves to be   135
    dashed against a wall, and t'other to have his brains knocked out
    with a fiddle case.
    What, a loose chain and a hanging diamond?
    Here were a brave booty for an evening-thief now,
    There's many a younger brother would be glad   140
    To look twice in at a window for't
    And wriggle in and out, like an eel in a sandbag.
    O, if men's secret youthful faults should judge 'em,
    'Twould be the general'st execution
    That e'er was seen in England!   145
    There would be but few left to sing the ballads,° there would be so
    much work: most of our brokers° would be chosen for hangmen, a
    good day for them:—they might renew their wardrobes of free
    cost° then!

SEBASTIAN [*to Mary*] This is the roaring wench must do us good.   150

MARY [*to Sebastian*] No poison, sir, but serves us for some use,
    Which is confirmed in her.

SEBASTIAN   Peace, peace!
    Foot,° I did hear him sure, where'er he be.

MOLL Who did you hear?

SEBASTIAN   My father,
'Twas like a sigh of his,—I must be wary.   155

SIR ALEXANDER [*aside*] No, wilt not be. Am I alone so wretched
That nothing takes? I'll put him to his plunge° for't.
> [*Sir Alexander emerges from his hiding place, pretending to enter the room*]

SEBASTIAN [*aside to Moll and Mary*] Life, here he comes!—[*Aloud to Moll*] Sir, I beseech you take it.
Your way of teaching does so much content me,   160
I'll make it four pound:—here's forty shillings, sir,
I think I name it right,—[*aside*] help me good Moll,
[*Aloud*] Forty in hand.

MOLL   Sir, you shall pardon me,
I have more of the meanest scholar I can teach,
This pays me more than you have offered yet.   165

SEBASTIAN At the next quarter
When I receive the means my father 'lows me,
You shall have t'other forty.

SIR ALEXANDER [*aside*]   This were well now,
Were't to a man, whose sorrows had blind eyes,
But mine behold his follies and his untruths,   170
With two clear glasses.
> [*Sir Alexander comes further forward*]
                How now?

SEBASTIAN   Sir?

SIR ALEXANDER   What's he there?

SEBASTIAN You're come in good time, sir, I have a suit to you:
I'd crave your present kindness.

SIR ALEXANDER   What is he there?

SEBASTIAN A gentleman, a musician, sir, one of excellent fingering.

SIR ALEXANDER Ay, ay, I think so. [*Aside*] I wonder how they 'scaped   175
her?°

SEBASTIAN 'Has the most delicate stroke,° sir.

SIR ALEXANDER A stroke indeed,—[*aside*] I feel it at my heart.

SEBASTIAN Puts down° all your famous musicians.

SIR ALEXANDER Ay? [*Aside*] A whore may put down a hundred of 'em.

SEBASTIAN Forty shillings is the agreement, sir, between us;   180
Now, sir, my present means mounts° but to half on't.

SIR ALEXANDER And he stands upon the whole.

SEBASTIAN Ay, indeed does he, sir.

SIR ALEXANDER And will do still, he'll ne'er be in other tale.°

SEBASTIAN Therefore I'd stop his mouth, sir, an I could.   185
SIR ALEXANDER Hum true. There is no other way indeed.
  [*Aside*] His folly hardens, shame must needs succeed.
  [*To Moll*] Now, sir, I understand you profess music?
MOLL I am a poor servant to that liberal science, sir.
SIR ALEXANDER Where is it you teach?
MOLL   Right against Clifford's Inn.°   190
SIR ALEXANDER Hum, that's a place fit for it. You have many
  scholars?
MOLL And some of worth, whom I may call my masters.
SIR ALEXANDER [*aside*] Ay, true, a company of whoremasters! [*To
  Moll*] You teach to sing,° too?   195
MOLL Marry, do I, sir.
SIR ALEXANDER I think you'll find an apt scholar of my son, especially
  for prick-song.°
MOLL I have much hope of him.
SIR ALEXANDER [*aside*] I am sorry for't, I have the less for that. 200
  [*To Moll*] You can play any lesson?
MOLL   At first sight, sir.
SIR ALEXANDER There's a thing called 'The Witch', can you play that?
MOLL I would be sorry if any one should mend me in't.
SIR ALEXANDER Ay, I believe thee! [*Aside*] Thou hast bewitched my
  son,
  No care will mend the work that thou hast done.   205
  I have bethought myself, since my art fails,
  I'll make her policy the art to trap her.
  Here are four angels marked with holes in them
  Fit for his cracked companions—gold he will give her—
  These will I make induction to her ruin,   210
  And rid shame from my house, grief from my heart.
  [*To Sebastian*] Here son, in what you take content and pleasure,
  Want shall not curb you.
     [*Giving him a purse*]
                Pay the gentleman
  His latter half in gold.
SEBASTIAN   I thank you, sir.
SIR ALEXANDER [*aside*] O, may the operation on't, end three: 215
  In her, life; shame in him; and grief in me.
     Exit [*Sir*] *Alexander*
SEBASTIAN Faith, thou shalt have 'em, 'tis my father's gift,
  Never was man beguiled with better shift.

MOLL He that can take me for a male musician,
    I cannot choose but make him my instrument,   220
    And play upon him.
       Exeunt

[Scene 9]

*Enter Mistress Gallipot and Mistress Openwork [carrying
masks]*

MISTRESS GALLIPOT Is then that bird of yours, Master Goshawk, so
    wild?

MISTRESS OPENWORK A goshawk, a puttock: all for prey. He angles
    for fish, but he loves flesh better.

MISTRESS GALLIPOT Is't possible his smooth face should have   5
    wrinkles in't, and we not see them.

MISTRESS OPENWORK Possible? Why, have not many handsome legs
    in silk stockings villainous splay feet for all their great roses?°

MISTRESS GALLIPOT Troth, sirrah, thou sayst true.

MISTRESS OPENWORK Didst never see an archer, as thou'st walked   10
    by Bunhill,° look asquint when he drew his bow?

MISTRESS GALLIPOT Yes, when his arrows have flown toward Isling-
    ton, his eyes have shot clean contrary towards Pimlico.°

MISTRESS OPENWORK For all the world, so does Master Goshawk
    double with me.   15

MISTRESS GALLIPOT O, fie upon him, if he double once, he's not for
    me!

MISTRESS OPENWORK Because Goshawk goes in a shag-ruff band,
    with a face sticking up in't which shows like an agate set in a
    cramp-ring,° he thinks I'm in love with him.   20

MISTRESS GALLIPOT 'Las, I think he takes his mark amiss in thee.

MISTRESS OPENWORK He has, by often beating into me, made me
    believe that my husband kept a whore.

MISTRESS GALLIPOT Very good.

MISTRESS OPENWORK Swore to me that my husband this very morn-   25
    ing went in a boat with a tilt° over it to the Three Pigeons at Brent-
    ford, and his punk with him under his tilt.

MISTRESS GALLIPOT That were wholesome.

MISTRESS OPENWORK I believed it, fell a-swearing at him, cursing of
    harlots, made me ready to hoise up sail, and be there soon as he.   30

MISTRESS GALLIPOT So, so.

MISTRESS OPENWORK And for that voyage, Goshawk comes hither
   incontinently! But, sirrah, this water-spaniel dives after no duck
   but me.—His hope is having me at Brentford to make me cry quack.

MISTRESS GALLIPOT Art sure of it?   35

MISTRESS OPENWORK Sure of it? My poor, innocent Openwork
   came in as I was poking my ruff;° presently hit I him i'the teeth° with
   the Three Pigeons: he forswore all, I up and opened all, and now
   stands he, in a shop hard by, like a musket on a rest,° to hit Goshawk
   i'the eye when he comes to fetch me to the boat.   40

MISTRESS GALLIPOT Such another lame gelding offered to carry me
   through thick and thin—Laxton, sirrah—but I am rid of him now.

MISTRESS OPENWORK Happy is the woman can be rid of 'em all!
   'Las, what are your whisking gallants to our husbands, weigh 'em
   rightly, man for man?   45

MISTRESS GALLIPOT Troth, mere shallow things.

MISTRESS OPENWORK Idle, simple things, running heads,°—and yet
   let 'em run over us never so fast,—we shopkeepers, when all's
   done, are sure to have 'em in our purse-nets° at length, and when
   they are in, Lord, what simple animals they are! Then they hang   50
   the head—

MISTRESS GALLIPOT Then they droop—

MISTRESS OPENWORK Then they write letters—

MISTRESS GALLIPOT Then they cog—

MISTRESS OPENWORK Then deal they underhand with us, and we   55
   must ingle with° our husbands abed, and we must swear they are our
   cousins, and able to do us a pleasure at Court.

MISTRESS GALLIPOT And yet when we have done our best, all's but
   put into a riven dish, we are but frumped at° and libelled upon.

MISTRESS OPENWORK O, if it were the good Lord's will, there were a   60
   law made, no citizen should trust any of 'em all.

   Enter Goshawk

MISTRESS GALLIPOT Hush, sirrah, Goshawk flutters.

GOSHAWK How now, are you ready?

MISTRESS OPENWORK Nay, are you ready? A little thing, you see,
   makes us ready.   65

GOSHAWK Us? [*Gesturing to Mistress Gallipot*] Why, must she make
   one i'the voyage?

MISTRESS OPENWORK O, by any means: do I know how my husband
   will handle me?

GOSHAWK [*aside*] 'Foot, how shall I find water to keep these two mills   70

going?—[*To them*] Well, since you'll needs be clapped under
hatches, if I sail not with you both till all split,° hang me up at the
main-yard, and duck me.—[*Aside*] It's but liquoring them both
soundly, and then you shall see their cork heels fly up high, like two
swans when their tails are above water, and their long necks under   75
water, diving to catch gudgeons.—[*To them*] Come, come, oars
stand ready, the tide's with us, on with those false faces! Blow
winds, and thou shalt take thy husband, casting out his net to catch
fresh salmon at Brentford.

MISTRESS GALLIPOT I believe you'll eat of a cod's head of your own   80
dressing° before you reach half way thither.
    [*The women start to mask themselves*]

GOSHAWK So, so, follow close, pin° as you go.
    Enter Laxton muffled

LAXTON Do you hear?
    [*Laxton accosts Mistress Gallipot and they talk apart*]

MISTRESS GALLIPOT Yes, I thank my ears.

LAXTON I must have a bout with your 'pothecaryship.   85

MISTRESS GALLIPOT At what weapon?

LAXTON I must speak with you.

MISTRESS GALLIPOT No.

LAXTON No? You shall.

MISTRESS GALLIPOT Shall? Away, soused sturgeon, half fish, half   90
flesh!

LAXTON 'Faith, gib,° are you spitting? I'll cut your tail, puss-cat, for
this!

MISTRESS GALLIPOT 'Las, poor Laxton, I think thy tail's cut° already.
Your worst!   95

LAXTON If I do not—
    Exit Laxton

GOSHAWK [*to Mistress Gallipot*] Come, ha' you done?
    Enter Master Openwork
    [*To Mistress Openwork*] 'Sfoot, Rosamond, your husband!

OPENWORK How now? Sweet Master Goshawk, none more welcome!
I have wanted° your embracements: when friends meet,   100
The music of the spheres sounds not more sweet
Than does their conference. Who is this? Rosamond?
Wife? [*To Mistress Gallipot*] How now, sister?

GOSHAWK   Silence, if you love me.

OPENWORK [*pointing to the masks*] Why masked?

MISTRESS OPENWORK   Does a mask grieve you, sir?

OPENWORK   It does.

MISTRESS OPENWORK Then you're best get you a-mumming.°   105

GOSHAWK 'Sfoot, you'll spoil all!

MISTRESS GALLIPOT May we not cover our bare faces with masks
    As well as you cover your bald heads with hats?

OPENWORK No masks,—why, they're thieves to beauty, that rob eyes
    Of admiration in which true love lies.   110
    Why are masks worn? Why good? Or why desired?—
    Unless by their gay covers wits are fired
    To read the vilest looks. Many bad faces,
    Because rich gems are treasured up in cases,
    Pass by their privilege current,° but as caves   115
    Damn misers' gold, so masks are beauties' graves.
    Men ne'er meet women with such muffled eyes,
    But they curse her that first did masks devise,
    And swear it was some beldame.° Come, off with't!

MISTRESS OPENWORK I will not!   120

OPENWORK Good faces, masked, are jewels kept by sprites:
    Hide none but bad ones, for they poison men's sights,—
    Show them as shopkeepers do their broidered stuff,°
    By owl-light—fine wares cannot be open enough.
    Prithee, sweet Rose, come strike this sail.

MISTRESS OPENWORK   Sail?

OPENWORK   Ha!   125
    Yes, wife, strike sail, for storms are in thine eyes.

MISTRESS OPENWORK They're here, sir, in my brows, if any rise.

OPENWORK Ha, brows? What says she, friend? Pray tell me why
    Your two flags were advanced? The comedy,°
    Come what's the comedy?

MISTRESS [GALLIPOT]   *Westward Ho!*°

OPENWORK   How?   130

MISTRESS OPENWORK 'Tis *Westward Ho!* she says.

GOSHAWK   Are you both mad?

MISTRESS OPENWORK Is't market day at Brentford, and your ware
    Not sent up yet?

OPENWORK   What market day? What ware?

MISTRESS OPENWORK A pie with three pigeons in't,—'tis drawn and
    stays your cutting up.°   135

GOSHAWK As you regard my credit—

OPENWORK Art mad?

MISTRESS OPENWORK Yes, lecherous goat! Baboon!

                    284

OPENWORK Baboon? Then toss me in a blanket.°

MISTRESS OPENWORK [*aside to Mistress Gallipot*] Do I it well? 140

MISTRESS GALLIPOT [*aside to Mistress Openwork*] Rarely.

GOSHAWK Belike, sir, she's not well; best leave her.

OPENWORK   No,
I'll stand the storm now, how fierce soe'er it blow.

MISTRESS OPENWORK Did I for this lose all my friends? Refuse
Rich hopes, and golden fortunes, to be made 145
A stale° to a common whore?

OPENWORK   This does amaze me.

MISTRESS OPENWORK O, God, O, God! Feed at reversion° now?
A strumpet's leaving?

OPENWORK   Rosamond?

GOSHAWK [*aside*] I sweat. Would I lay in Cold Harbour.°

MISTRESS OPENWORK Thou hast struck ten thousand daggers 150
through my heart!

OPENWORK Not I, by heaven, sweet wife.

MISTRESS OPENWORK Go, devil, go! That which thou swearest by,
damns thee.

GOSHAWK [*aside to Mistress Openwork*] 'Sheart, will you undo me?

MISTRESS OPENWORK [*to Openwork*] Why stay you here? The star by
which you sail
Shines yonder above Chelsea; you lose your shore. 155
If this moon light you, seek out your light° whore!

OPENWORK Ha?

MISTRESS GALLIPOT Push, your western pug!°

GOSHAWK [*aside*]   Zounds, now hell roars!

MISTRESS OPENWORK With whom you tilted° in a pair of oars,
This very morning.

OPENWORK   Oars?

MISTRESS OPENWORK   At Brentford, sir.

OPENWORK Rack not my patience. Master Goshawk, 160
Some slave has buzzed this into her, has he not?
I, run a-tilt in Brentford with a woman?
'Tis a lie!
What old bawd tells thee this? 'Sdeath, 'tis a lie.

MISTRESS OPENWORK 'Tis one to thy face shall justify 165
All that I speak.

OPENWORK   Ud' soul, do but name that rascal.

MISTRESS OPENWORK No, sir, I will not.

GOSHAWK [*aside*]   Keep thee there, girl:—[*to them*] then!

OPENWORK [*to Mistress Gallipot*] Sister, know you this varlet?
MISTRESS GALLIPOT   Yes.
OPENWORK   Swear true.
   Is there a rogue so low damned? A second Judas?
   A common hangman? Cutting a man's throat?   170
   Does it to his face? Bite me behind my back?
   A cur dog? Swear if you know this hell-hound!
MISTRESS GALLIPOT In truth, I do.
OPENWORK   His name?
MISTRESS GALLIPOT   Not for the world,
   To have you to stab him.
GOSHAWK [*aside*]   O, brave girls, worth gold.°
OPENWORK A word, honest Master Goshawk.
       Draw[s] out his sword
GOSHAWK   What do you mean, sir? 175
OPENWORK Keep off,° and if the devil can give a name
   To this new fury, holla it through my ear,
   Or wrap it up in some hid character.°
   I'll ride to Oxford, and watch out mine eyes,
   But I'll hear the brazen head° speak, or else   180
   Show me but one hair of his head or beard,
   That I may sample it. If the fiend I meet
   In mine own house, I'll kill him [*stabs with sword*]—the street [*stabs
       again*],
   Or at the church door°—[*stabs again*] there—'cause he seeks to untie
   The knot God fastens, he deserves most to die.   185
MISTRESS OPENWORK My husband titles him!
OPENWORK Master Goshawk, pray sir,
   Swear me that you know him or know him not,
   Who makes me at Brentford to take up a petticoat
   Beside my wife's.
GOSHAWK   By heaven, that man I know not.   190
MISTRESS OPENWORK Come, come, you lie!
GOSHAWK   Will you not have all out?
   By heaven I know no man beneath the moon
   Should do you wrong, but if I had his name
   I'd print it in text letters.°
MISTRESS OPENWORK   Print thine own then.
   Didst not thou swear to me he kept his whore?   195
MISTRESS GALLIPOT And that in sinful Brentford they would
       commit

That which our lips did water at, sir?—Ha?

MISTRESS OPENWORK Thou spider, that hast woven thy cunning
    web
  In mine own house t'ensnare me. Hast not thou
  Sucked nourishment even underneath this roof   200
  And turned it all to poison, spitting it
  On thy friend's face, my husband, he—as 'twere sleeping—
  Only to leave him ugly to mine eyes,
  That they might glance on thee?

MISTRESS GALLIPOT   Speak, are these lies?

GOSHAWK Mine own shame me confounds.

OPENWORK   No more, he's stung.   205
  Who'd think that in one body there could dwell
  Deformity and beauty, heaven and hell?
  Goodness I see is but outside; we all set
  In rings of gold, stones that be counterfeit.
  I thought you none.

GOSHAWK   Pardon me.

OPENWORK   Truth, I do.   210
  This blemish grows in nature, not in you,
  For man's creation stick even moles in scorn
  On fairest cheeks. Wife, nothing is perfect born.

MISTRESS OPENWORK I thought you had been born perfect.

OPENWORK What's this whole world but a gilt rotten pill?   215
  For at the heart lies the old core still.
  I'll tell you, Master Goshawk, ay, in your eye,
  I have seen wanton fire, and then to try
  The soundness of my judgement, I told you
  I kept a whore, made you believe 'twas true,   220
  Only to feel how your pulse beat, but find
  The world can hardly yield a perfect friend.
  Come, come, a trick of youth,° and 'tis forgiven.
  This rub° put by, our love shall run more even.

MISTRESS OPENWORK You'll deal upon men's wives no more?

GOSHAWK   No.—You teach me   225
  A trick° for that!

MISTRESS OPENWORK Troth, do not; they'll o'er-reach thee.

OPENWORK Make my house yours, sir, still.

GOSHAWK   No.

OPENWORK   I say you shall:
  Seeing, thus besieged, it holds out, 'twill never fall.

Enter Master Gallipot, and Greenwit like a summoner;° Laxton
muffled aloof off

ALL How now?

GALLIPOT [*to Greenwit*] With me, sir?   230

GREENWIT [*to Gallipot*] You, sir. I have gone snuffling up and down
   by your door this hour to watch for you.

MISTRESS GALLIPOT What's the matter, husband?

GREENWIT I have caught a cold in my head, sir, by sitting up late in
   the Rose° Tavern, but I hope you understand my speech.   235

GALLIPOT So, sir?

GREENWIT I cite you by the name of Hippocrates Gallipot, and you
   by the name of Prudence Gallipot, to appear upon *crastino*,—
   [*showing a writ*] do you see,—*Crastino Sancti Dunstani*,° this Easter
   Term, in Bow Church.°   240

GALLIPOT Where, sir? What says he?

GREENWIT Bow.—Bow Church, to answer to a libel° of precontract
   on the part and behalf of the said Prudence and another; you're
   best, sir, take a copy of the citation, 'tis but twelvepence.

ALL A citation?   245

GALLIPOT You pocky-nosed rascal, what slave fees you to this?

LAXTON [*coming forward*] Slave? [*Aside to Goshawk*] I ha' nothing to
   do with you, do you hear, sir?

GOSHAWK Laxton, is't not?—What vagary is this?

GALLIPOT Trust me, I thought, sir, this storm long ago   250
   Had been full laid, when—if you be remembered—
   I paid you the last fifteen pound, besides
   The thirty you had first,—for then you swore—

LAXTON Tush, tush, sir, oaths—
   Truth, yet I'm loath to vex you.—Tell you what,   255
   Make up the money I had an hundred pound,
   And take your bellyful of her.

GALLIPOT   An hundred pound?

MISTRESS GALLIPOT What, a hundred pound? He gets none!
   What, a hundred pound?

GALLIPOT Sweet Prue, be calm, the gentleman offers thus: 260
   If I will make the moneys that are passed,
   A hundred pound, he will discharge all courts
   And give his bond never to vex us more.

MISTRESS GALLIPOT A hundred pound? 'Las; take, sir, but
   threescore,
   Do you seek my undoing?

LAXTON   I'll not 'bate one sixpence.   265
   [Aside to Mistress Gallipot] I'll maul you, puss, for spitting.
MISTRESS GALLIPOT *[aside to Laxton]*   Do thy worst!
   [Aloud] Will fourscore stop thy mouth?
LAXTON   No.
MISTRESS GALLIPOT   You're a slave!
   Thou cheat, I'll now tear money from thy throat.
   Husband, lay hold on yonder tawny-coat.°
GREENWIT Nay, gentlemen, seeing your women are so hot,   270
   I must lose my hair° in their company, I see.
      [Removes wig]
MISTRESS OPENWORK His hair sheds off, and yet he speaks not so
    much
   In the nose as he did before.
GOSHAWK   He has had
   The better chirurgeon. Master Greenwit,
   Is your wit so raw as to play no better part   275
   Than a sumner's?
GALLIPOT   I pray, who plays
   A Knack to Know an Honest Man° in this company?
MISTRESS GALLIPOT Dear husband, pardon me, I did dissemble,
   Told thee I was his precontracted wife,
   When letters came from him for thirty pound,   280
   I had no shift° but that.
GALLIPOT   A very clean shift,
   But able to make me lousy. On—
MISTRESS GALLIPOT   Husband, I plucked,
   When he had tempted me to think well of him,
   Get-feathers from thy wings, to make him fly
   More lofty.
GALLIPOT O'the top of you, wife. On—   285
MISTRESS GALLIPOT He, having wasted them, comes now for
    more,
   Using me as a ruffian doth his whore,
   Whose sin keeps him in breath. By heaven, I vow,
   Thy bed he never wronged more than he does now.
GALLIPOT My bed? Ha, ha! Like enough a shop board will serve   290
   To have a cuckold's coat cut out upon:
   Of that we'll talk hereafter.—*[To Laxton]* You're a villain.
LAXTON Hear me speak, sir, you shall find me none.
ALL Pray, sir, be patient and hear him.

GALLIPOT   I am
  Muzzled for biting, sir; use me how you will.   295
LAXTON The first hour that your wife was in my eye,
  Myself with other gentlemen sitting by,
  In your shop, tasting smoke, and speech being used
  That men who have fairest wives are most abused
  And hardly 'scaped the horn,° your wife maintained   300
  That only such spots in City dames were stained
  Justly, but by men's slanders. For her own part,
  She vowed that you had so much of her heart,
  No man by all his wit, by any wile
  Never so fine spun, should yourself beguile,   305
  Of what in her was yours.
GALLIPOT   Yet, Prue, 'tis well.
  Play out your game at Irish,° sir: who wins?
MISTRESS OPENWORK The trial is when she comes to bearing.°
LAXTON I scorned one woman, thus, should brave all men,
  And, which more vexed me, a she-citizen.   310
  Therefore, I laid siege to her, out she held,
  Gave many a brave repulse, and me compelled
  With shame to sound retreat to my hot lust.
  Then seeing all base desires raked up in dust,
  And that to tempt her modest ears, I swore   315
  Ne'er to presume again. She said her eye
  Would ever give me welcome honestly,
  And,—since I was a gentleman,—if it run low,
  She would my state relieve, not to o'erthrow
  Your own and hers; did so; then seeing I wrought   320
  Upon her meekness, me she set at nought.
  And yet to try if I could turn that tide,
  You see what stream I strove with.—But sir, I swear
  By heaven and by those hopes men lay up there,
  I neither have, nor had, a base intent   325
  To wrong your bed. What's done is merriment:
  Your gold I pay back with this interest,
  When I had most power to do't, I wronged you least.
GALLIPOT If this no gullery be, sir—
ALL   No, no, on my life!
GALLIPOT Then, sir, I am beholden,—not to you, wife—   330
  But Master Laxton, to your want of doing ill,
  Which it seems you have not.—Gentlemen,

Tarry and dine here all.
OPENWORK   Brother, we have a jest,
As good as yours to furnish out a feast.
GALLIPOT We'll crown our table with it.—Wife, brag no more,   335
Of holding out: who most brags is most whore.
            Exeunt

[Scene 10]

Enter Jack Dapper, Moll, Sir Beauteous Ganymede, and Sir
Thomas Long

JACK DAPPER But prithee, Master Captain Jack, be plain and perspi-
cacious with me: was it your Meg of Westminster's° courage that
rescued me from the Poultry° puttocks, indeed?
MOLL The valour of my wit, I ensure you, sir, fetched you off bravely
when you were i'the forlorn hope among those desperates. Sir   5
Beauteous Ganymede here, and Sir Thomas Long, heard that
cuckoo, my man Trapdoor, sing the note of your ransom from
captivity.
SIR BEAUTEOUS Uds-so, Moll, where's that Trapdoor?
MOLL Hanged, I think by this time. A justice in this town, that speaks   10
nothing but 'Make a *mittimus*° away with him to Newgate',° used that
rogue like a firework to run upon a line° betwixt him and me.
ALL How, how?
MOLL Marry, to lay trains° of villainy to blow up my life; I smelt the
powder, spied what linstock° gave fire to shoot against the poor   15
captain of the galley-foist,° and away slid I my man, like a shovel-
board shilling.° He struts up and down the suburbs, I think, and eats
up whores, feeds upon a bawd's garbage.
SIR THOMAS Sirrah Jack Dapper—
JACK DAPPER What sayst, Tom Long?   20
SIR THOMAS Thou hadst a sweet-faced boy, hail-fellow with thee to
your little gull: how is he spent?
JACK DAPPER Troth, I whistled the poor little buzzard off° o' my fist
because when he waited upon me at the ordinaries the gallants hit
me i'the teeth still, and said I looked like a painted alderman's   25
tomb,° and the boy at my elbow like a death's head.° Sirrah Jack,
Moll.
MOLL What says my little Dapper?

SIR BEAUTEOUS Come, come, walk and talk, walk and talk.

JACK DAPPER Moll and I'll be i'the midst.   30

MOLL These knights shall have squire's places° belike then. Well,
Dapper, what say you?

JACK DAPPER Sirrah Captain, Mad Mary, the gull, my own father,
Dapper Sir Davy, laid these London boot-halers, the catchpoles, in
ambush to set upon me.   35

ALL Your father? Away, Jack!

JACK DAPPER By the tassels of this handkerchief, 'tis true.—And
what was his warlike stratagem, think you? He thought because a
wicker cage tames a nightingale, a lousy prison could make an ass of
me.   40

ALL A nasty plot!

JACK DAPPER Ay, as though a Counter, which is a park in which all
the wild beasts of the city run head by head, could tame me.

    Enter the Lord Noland

MOLL Yonder comes my Lord Noland.

ALL Save you, my lord.   45

LORD NOLAND Well met, gentlemen all. Good Sir Beauteous
Ganymede, Sir Thomas Long. And how does Master Dapper?

JACK DAPPER Thanks, my lord.

MOLL No tobacco, my lord?

LORD NOLAND No, faith, Jack.   50

JACK DAPPER My Lord Noland, will you go to Pimlico with us? We
are making a boon voyage to that nappy land of spice cakes.°

LORD NOLAND Here's such a merry ging, I could find in my heart to
sail to the world's end with such company. Come gentlemen, let's
on.   55

JACK DAPPER Here's most amorous weather, my lord.

ALL Amorous weather?

    They walk

JACK DAPPER Is not amorous a good word?

    *Enter Trapdoor like a poor soldier with a patch o'er one eye, and
    Tearcat with him, all tatters*

TRAPDOOR Shall we set upon the infantry, these troops of foot?
Zounds! Yonder comes Moll, my whorish master and mistress.   60
Would I had her kidneys between my teeth!

TEARCAT I had rather have a cow-heel.°

TRAPDOOR Zounds, I am so patched up, she cannot discover me:
we'll on.

TEARCAT *Alla corago°* then!   65

TRAPDOOR Good your honours, and worships, enlarge the ears of
  commiseration, and let the sound of hoarse military organ-pipe
  penetrate your pitiful bowels to extract out of them so many small
  drops of silver, as may give a hard straw-bed lodging to a couple of
  maimed soldiers.   70
JACK DAPPER Where are you maimed?
TEARCAT In both our nether limbs.
MOLL Come, come, Dapper, let's give 'em something.—'Las, poor
  men, what money have you? By my troth, I love a soldier with my
  soul.   75
SIR BEAUTEOUS Stay, stay, where have you served?
SIR THOMAS In any part of the Low Countries?
TRAPDOOR Not in any part of the Low Countries, if it please your
  manhood, but in Hungary against the Turk at the siege of
  Belgrade.°   80
LORD NOLAND And who served there with you, sirrah?
TRAPDOOR Many Hungarians, Moldavians, Walachians, and Tran-
  sylvanians, with some Slavonians, and retiring home, sir, the Vene-
  tian galleys took us prisoner, yet freed us, and suffered us to beg up
  and down the country.   85
JACK DAPPER You have ambled all over Italy then?
TRAPDOOR O, sir, from Venice to *Roma*, Vecchio, *Bononia*, Romagna,
  Bologna, Modena, Piacenza, and *Tuscana*, with all her cities, as
  Pistoia, Valteria, Mountepulchiano, Arezzo, with the *Siennois*, and
  diverse others.   90
MOLL Mere rogues, put spurs to 'em once more.
JACK DAPPER Thou lookst like a strange creature, a fat butter-box,°
  yet speakest English. What art thou?
TEARCAT *Ick, mine Here? Ick bin den ruffling Tearcat, den brave sol-
  dado. Ick bin dorick all Dutchlant gueresen. Der shellum das meere ine* 95
  beasa, ine woert gaeb. Ick slaag um stroakes ou tom cop, dastick den
  hundred touzen divell halle, frollick mine Here.°
SIR BEAUTEOUS Here, here, [*offering money*]—let's be rid of their
  jobbering.
MOLL Not a cross,° Sir Beauteous. You base rogues, I have taken   100
  measure of you, better than a tailor can, and I'll fit you, as you—
  monster with one eye°—have fitted me.
TRAPDOOR Your worship will not abuse a soldier!
MOLL Soldier? Thou deservest to be hanged up by that tongue which
  dishonours so noble a profession. Soldier, you skeldering° varlet?   105
  Hold, stand, there should be a Trapdoor hereabouts!

Pull[s] off his patch

TRAPDOOR The balls of these glaziers° of mine, mine eyes, shall be
shot up and down in any hot piece of service for my invincible
mistress.

JACK DAPPER I did not think there had been such knavery in black   110
patches as now I see.

MOLL O, sir, he hath been brought up in the Isle of Dogs,° and can
both fawn like a spaniel, and bite like a mastiff, as he finds occasion.

LORD NOLAND What are you, sirrah? A bird of this feather, too?

TEARCAT A man beaten from the wars, sir.   115

SIR THOMAS I think so, for you never stood to fight.

JACK DAPPER What's thy name, fellow soldier?

TEARCAT I am called by those that have seen my valour, Tearcat.

ALL Tearcat?

MOLL A mere whip-jack,° and that is, in the commonwealth of rogues, 120
a slave that can talk of sea-fight, name all your chief pirates, discover more countries to you, than either the Dutch, Spanish,
French or English ever found out, yet indeed all his service is by
land, and that is to rob a fair, or some such venturous exploit.
Tearcat,—'foot, sirrah, I have your name, now I remember me, in   125
my book of horners, horns for the thumb°—you know how.

TEARCAT No indeed, Captain Moll, for I know you by sight, I am no
such nipping Christian, but a maunderer upon the pad,° I confess,
and meeting with honest Trapdoor here, whom you had cashiered
from bearing arms, out at elbows under your colours, I instructed   130
him in the rudiments of roguery, and by my map made him sail
over any country you can name, so that now he can maunder better
than myself.

JACK DAPPER So then, Trapdoor, thou art turned soldier now?

TRAPDOOR Alas, sir, now there's no wars, 'tis the safest course of life I 135
could take.

MOLL I hope then you can cant,° for by your cudgels, you, sirrah, are
an upright man.

TRAPDOOR As any walks the highway, I assure you.

MOLL And Tearcat, what are you? A wild rogue,° an angler,° or a   140
ruffler?°

TEARCAT Brother to this upright man, flesh and blood, ruffling Tearcat is my name, and a ruffler is my style, my title, my profession.

MOLL Sirrah, where's your doxy? Halt not° with me.

ALL Doxy, Moll, what's that?   145

MOLL His wench.

TRAPDOOR My doxy? I have, by the solomon,° a doxy that carries a
kinchin mort° in her slate at her back, besides my dell and my dainty
wild dell, with all whom I'll tumble this next darkmans in the
strommel, and drink ben booze, and eat a fat gruntling-cheat, a   150
cackling-cheat, and a quacking-cheat.°

JACK DAPPER Here's old cheating.

TRAPDOOR My doxy stays for me in a boozing-ken,° brave captain.

MOLL He says his wench stays for him in an alehouse. [*To Trapdoor
and Tearcat*] You are no pure rogues.   155

TEARCAT Pure rogues? No, we scorn to be pure rogues, but if you
come to our libken, or our stalling-ken,° you shall find neither him
nor me a queer cuffin.°

MOLL So, sir, no churl of you.

TEARCAT No, but a ben cove, a brave cove, a gentry cuffin.°   160

LORD NOLAND Call you this canting?

JACK DAPPER Zounds, I'll give a schoolmaster half a crown a week,
and teach me this pedlar's French.°

TRAPDOOR Do but stroll, sir, half a harvest° with us, sir, and you shall
gabble your bellyful.   165

MOLL Come, you rogue, cant with me.

SIR THOMAS Well said, Moll. [*To Trapdoor*] Cant with her, sirrah, and
you shall have money, else not a penny.

TRAPDOOR I'll have a bout if she please.

MOLL Come on, sirrah.   170

TRAPDOOR Ben mort, shall you and I heave a booth, mill a ken, or nip
a bung, and then we'll couch a hogshead under the ruffmans, and
there you shall wap with me, and I'll niggle° with you.

MOLL Out, you damned impudent rascal!

TRAPDOOR Cut benar whids, and hold your fambles and your stamps!°   175

LORD NOLAND Nay, nay, Moll, why art thou angry? What was his
gibberish?

MOLL Marry, this, my lord, says he: 'Ben mort', good wench, 'shall
you and I heave a booth, mill a ken, or nip a bung?' Shall you and I
rob a house, or cut a purse?   180

ALL Very good.

MOLL 'And then we'll couch a hogshead under the ruffmans.' And
then we'll lie under a hedge.

TRAPDOOR That was my desire, captain, as 'tis fit a soldier should lie.

MOLL 'And there you shall wap with me and I'll niggle with you', and   185
that's all.

SIR BEAUTEOUS Nay, nay, Moll, what's that 'wap'?

JACK DAPPER Nay, teach me what 'niggling' is, I'd fain be niggling.

MOLL 'Wapping' and 'niggling' is all one. The rogue my man can tell
  you.   190

TRAPDOOR 'Tis fadoodling,° if it please you.

SIR BEAUTEOUS This is excellent. One fit more, good Moll.

MOLL Come, you rogue, sing with me.

[MOLL AND TEARCAT] [*singing*]

> A gage of ben Rome booze
> In a boozing ken of Romeville   195
>
> TEARCAT *Is benar than a caster,*
> *Peck, pannam, lap, or poplar,*
> *Which we mill in Deuce-a-ville.*
>
> MOLL, TEARCAT *O, I would lib all the lightmans.*
> *O, I would lib all the darkmans,*   200
> *By the solomon, under the ruffmans,*
> *By the solomon, in the harmans.*
>
> TEARCAT *And scour the queer cramp-ring,*
> *And couch till a palliard docked my dell,*
> *So my boozy nab might skew Rome booze well.*   205
>
> MOLL, TEARCAT *Avast to the pad, let us bing,*
> *Avast to the pad, let us bing.*°

ALL Fine knaves, i'faith.

JACK DAPPER The grating of ten new cartwheels, and the gruntling
  of five hundred hogs coming from Romford market,° cannot make a   210
  worse noise than this canting language does in my ears. Pray, my
  Lord Noland, let's give these soldiers their pay.

SIR BEAUTEOUS Agreed, and let them march.

LORD NOLAND Here, Moll.

MOLL Now I see that you are stalled to° the rogue, and are not   215
  ashamed of your professions. Look you, my Lord Noland here, and
  these gentlemen, bestows upon you two, two bords° and a half, that's
  two shilling sixpence.

TRAPDOOR Thanks to your lordship.

TEARCAT Thanks, heroical captain.   220

MOLL Away.

TRAPDOOR We shall cut ben whids of your masters and mistress-ship,
  wheresoever we come.

MOLL You'll maintain, sirrah, the old justice's plot in his face?

TRAPDOOR Else trine me on the cheats:° hang me!   225

MOLL Be sure you meet me there.

TRAPDOOR Without any more maundering I'll do't. Follow, brave
Tearcat.

TEARCAT I *prae, sequor;*° let us go mouse.

Exeunt [Trapdoor and Tearcat]. The rest [remain]

LORD NOLAND Moll, what was in that canting song?   230

MOLL Troth, my lord, only a praise of good drink, the only milk
which these wild beasts desire to suck, and thus it was:

[*Moll sings*]

> *A rich cup of wine,*
> *O, it is juice divine,*
> *More wholesome for the head,*   235
> *Than meat, drink, or bread.*
> *To fill my drunken pate*
> *With that, I'd sit up late,*
> *By the heels would I lie,*
> *Under a lousy hedge die.*   240
> *Let a slave have a pull*
> *At my whore, so I be full*
> *Of that precious liquor—*

and a parcel of such stuff, my lord, not worth the opening.

Enter a Cutpurse very gallant,° with four or five men after him,
one with a wand

LORD NOLAND What gallant comes yonder?   245

SIR THOMAS Mass, I think I know him, 'tis one of Cumberland.

1ST CUTPURSE Shall we venture to shuffle in amongst yon heap of
gallants, and strike?

2ND CUTPURSE 'Tis a question whether there be any silver shells°
amongst them, for all their satin outsides.   250

ALL [CUTPURSES] Let's try.

MOLL Pox on him, a gallant? Shadow me,° I know him: 'tis one that
cumbers the land, indeed. If he swim near to the shore of any of
your pockets, look to your purses!

ALL [GENTLEMEN] Is't possible?   255

MOLL This brave fellow is no better than a foist.

ALL [GENTLEMEN] Foist, what's that?

MOLL A diver with two fingers—a pick-pocket. All his train study the
figging law, that's to say, cutting of purses and foisting. One of them
is a nip,° I took him once i'the twopenny gallery° at the Fortune; then   260
there's a cloyer, or snap,° that dogs any new brother in that trade,

and snaps will have half in any booty. He with the wand is both a
stale, whose office is to face a man i'the streets, whilst shells are
drawn by another, and then with his black conjuring rod in his
hand, he, by the nimbleness of his eye and juggling stick, will in   265
cheaping° a piece of plate at a goldsmith's stall, make four or five
rings mount from the top of his caduceus° and, as if it were at leap-
frog, they skip into his hand presently.

2ND CUTPURSE Zounds, we are smoked!

ALL [CUTPURSES] Ha?   270

2ND CUTPURSE We are boiled, pox on her! See, Moll, the roaring
drab.

1ST CUTPURSE All the diseases of sixteen hospitals boil° her! Away!

MOLL Bless you, sir.

1ST CUTPURSE And you, good sir.   275

MOLL Dost not ken° me, man?

1ST CUTPURSE No, trust me, sir.

MOLL Heart, there's a knight, to whom I'm bound for many favours,
lost his purse at the last new play i'the Swan,° seven angels in't.
Make it good, you're best; do you see? No more.   280

1ST CUTPURSE A synagogue° shall be called, Mistress Mary. Disgrace
me not; *pacus palabros*,° I will conjure for you. Farewell.
      [*Exeunt Cutpurses*]

MOLL Did not I tell you, my lord?

LORD NOLAND I wonder how thou camest to the knowledge of these
nasty villains.   285

SIR THOMAS And why do the foul mouths of the world call thee Moll
Cutpurse? A name, methinks, damned and odious.

MOLL Dare any step forth to my face and say,
   'I have ta'en thee doing so, Moll'? I must confess
   In younger days, when I was apt to stray,   290
   I have sat amongst such adders; seen their stings—
   As any here might—and in full playhouses
   Watched their quick-diving hands, to bring to shame
   Such rogues, and in that stream met an ill-name.
   When next, my lord, you spy any one of those,   295
   So he be in his art a scholar, question him,
   Tempt him with gold to open the large book
   Of his close villainies, and you yourself shall cant
   Better than poor Moll can, and know more laws
   Of cheaters,° lifters, nips, foists, puggards, curbers,°   300
   Withal the devil's black guard,° than it is fit

298

Should be discovered to a noble wit.
I know they have their orders, offices,
Circuits and circles, unto which they are bound,
To raise their own damnation in.   305
JACK DAPPER How dost thou know it?
MOLL As you do: I show it you, they to me show it.
Suppose, my lord, you were in Venice—
LORD NOLAND   Well.
MOLL If some Italian pander there would tell
All the close tricks of courtesans, would not you   310
Hearken to such a fellow?
LORD NOLAND   Yes.
MOLL   And here,
Being come from Venice, to a friend most dear
That were to travel thither, you would proclaim
Your knowledge in those villainies, to save
Your friend from their quick danger: must you have   315
A black ill name, because ill things you know?
Good troth, my lord, I am made Moll Cutpurse so.
How many are whores in small ruffs and still looks?
How many chaste whose names fill slander's books?
Were all men cuckolds, whom gallants in their scorns   320
Call so, we should not walk for goring horns.
Perhaps for my mad going, some reprove me—
I please myself, and care not else who loves me.
ALL A brave mind, Moll, i'faith.
SIR THOMAS Come, my lord, shall's to the ordinary?   325
LORD NOLAND Ay, 'tis noon, sure.
MOLL Good my lord, let not my name condemn me to you or to the
world. A fencer, I hope, may be called a coward, is he so for that? If
all that have ill names in London were to be whipped, and to pay
but twelve pence apiece to the beadle,° I would rather have his office,   330
than a constable's.
JACK DAPPER So would I, Captain Moll: 'twere a sweet tickling° office,
i'faith.
    Exeunt

[Scene 11]

Enter Sir Alexander Wengrave, Goshawk and Greenwit, and
others

SIR ALEXANDER My son marry a thief, that impudent girl
  Whom all the world stick their worst eyes upon?
GREENWIT How will your care prevent it?
GOSHAWK 'Tis impossible.
  They marry close.° They're gone, but none knows whither.   5
SIR ALEXANDER O, gentlemen, when has a father's heart-strings
  Held out so long from breaking?
    Enter a Servant
                      Now what news, sir?
SERVANT They were met upo' th' water an hour since, sir,
  Putting in towards the Sluice.°
SIR ALEXANDER   The Sluice? Come, gentlemen,
  'Tis Lambeth° works against us.
    [Exit Servant]
GREENWIT   And that Lambeth   10
  Joins more mad matches, than your six wet towns,°
  'Twixt that and Windsor Bridge, where fares lie soaking.
SIR ALEXANDER Delay no time, sweet gentlemen: to Blackfriars!°
  We'll take a pair of oars and make after 'em.
    Enter Trapdoor
TRAPDOOR Your son, and that bold masculine ramp my mistress   15
  Are landed now at Tower.°
SIR ALEXANDER   Hoyda, at Tower?
TRAPDOOR I heard it now reported.
    [Exit Trapdoor]
SIR ALEXANDER Which way, gentlemen, shall I bestow my care?
  I'm drawn in pieces betwixt deceit and shame.
    Enter Sir [Guy] Fitzallard
SIR GUY   Sir Alexander.
  You're well met, and most rightly served: 20
  My daughter was a scorn to you.
SIR ALEXANDER   Say not so, sir.
SIR GUY A very abject she, poor gentlewoman.
  Your house had been 'dishonoured'! Give you joy, sir,
  Of your son's gaskin-bride.° You'll be a grandfather shortly
  To a fine crew of roaring sons and daughters,   25

'Twill help to stock the suburbs passing well, sir.

SIR ALEXANDER O, play not with the miseries of my heart!
Wounds should be dressed and healed, not vexed, or left
Wide open to the anguish of the patient,
And scornful air let in; rather let pity   30
And advise charity help to refresh 'em.

SIR GUY Who'd place his charity so unworthily,
Like one that gives alms to a cursing beggar?
Had I but found one spark of goodness in you
Toward my deserving child, which then grew fond   35
Of your son's virtues, I had eased you now.
But I perceive both fire of youth and goodness,
Are raked up in the ashes of your age,
Else no such shame should have come near your house,
Nor such ignoble sorrow touch your heart.   40

SIR ALEXANDER If not for worth, for pity's sake assist me.

GREENWIT You urge a thing past sense, how can he help you?
All his assistance is as frail as ours,
Full as uncertain, where's the place that holds 'em?
One brings us water-news; then comes another   45
With a full-charged mouth, like a culverin's° voice
And he reports the Tower: whose sounds are truest?

GOSHAWK In vain you flatter him, Sir Alexander.

SIR ALEXANDER I, flatter him? Gentlemen, you wrong me grossly.

GREENWIT He does it well, i'faith.

SIR GUY   Both news are false,   50
Of Tower or water. They took no such way yet.

SIR ALEXANDER O, strange: hear you this gentlemen? Yet more
plunges.°

SIR GUY They're nearer than you think for, yet more close
Than if they were further off.

SIR ALEXANDER   How am I lost
In these distractions?

SIR GUY   For° your speeches, gentlemen,   55
In taxing me for rashness; 'fore you all,
I will engage° my state to half his wealth,
Nay, to his son's revenues, which are less,
And yet nothing at all, till they come from him;
That I could, if my will° stuck to my power,   60
Prevent this marriage yet, nay, banish her
Forever from his thoughts, much more his arms!

SIR ALEXANDER Slack not this goodness, though you heap upon me
    Mountains of malice and revenge hereafter.
    I'd willingly resign up half my state to him,   65
    So he would marry the meanest drudge I hire.
GREENWIT He talks impossibilities, and you believe 'em?
SIR GUY I talk no more than I know how to finish,
    My fortunes else are his that dares stake with me.
    The poor young gentleman I love and pity,   70
    And to keep shame from him, because the spring
    Of his affection was my daughter's first,
    Till his° frown blasted all, do but estate him
    In those possessions, which your love and care
    Once pointed out for him, that he may have room,   75
    To entertain fortunes of noble birth,
    Where now his desperate wants casts him upon her;°
    And if I do not for his own sake chiefly,
    Rid him of this disease, that now grows on him,
    I'll forfeit my whole state, before these gentlemen.   80
GREENWIT Troth, but you shall not undertake such matches,°
    We'll persuade so much with you.
SIR ALEXANDER   Here's my ring.
    He will believe this token. 'Fore these gentlemen
    I will confirm it fully: all those lands
    My first love lotted him, he shall straight possess   85
    In that refusal.°
SIR GUY If I change it not, change me into a beggar.
GREENWIT   Are you mad, sir?
SIR GUY 'Tis done.
GOSHAWK   Will you undo yourself by doing,
    And show a prodigal trick in your old days?
SIR ALEXANDER 'Tis a match, gentlemen.
SIR GUY   Ay, ay, sir, ay.   90
    I ask no favour, trust to you for none—
    My hope rests in the goodness of your son.
       Exit Fitzallard
GREENWIT [*aside to Goshawk*] He holds it up well yet.
GOSHAWK [*aside to Greenwit*]   Of° an old knight, i'faith.
SIR ALEXANDER Cursed be the time, I laid his first love barren,
    Wilfully barren, that before this hour   95
    Had sprung forth fruits of comfort and of honour;
    He loved a virtuous gentlewoman.

Enter Moll [dressed as a man]

GOSHAWK Life, here's Moll.

GREENWIT Jack.

GOSHAWK How dost thou, Jack?

MOLL   How dost thou, gallant?   100

SIR ALEXANDER Impudence, where's my son?

MOLL   Weakness, go look him.

SIR ALEXANDER Is this your wedding gown?

MOLL   The man talks monthly.°

Hot broth and a dark chamber° for the knight,

I see he'll be stark mad at our next meeting.

    Exit Moll

GOSHAWK Why, sir, take comfort now, there's no such matter.   105

No priest will marry her, sir, for a woman,

Whiles that shape's on, and it was never known,

Two men were married and conjoined in one.

Your son hath made some shift to love another.

SIR ALEXANDER Whate'er she be, she has my blessing with her: 110

May they be rich and fruitful, and receive

Like comfort to their issue,° as I take

In them. He's pleased me now, marrying not this,

Through a whole world he could not choose amiss.

GREENWIT Glad you're so penitent for your former sin, sir.   115

GOSHAWK Say he should take a wench with her smock dowry,°

No portion with her but her lips and arms?

SIR ALEXANDER Why? Who thrive better, sir? They have most

    blessing,

Though other have more wealth, and least repent:

Many that want most, know the most content.   120

GREENWIT Say he should marry a kind° youthful sinner?

SIR ALEXANDER Age will quench that.

Any offence but theft and drunkenness,

Nothing but death can wipe away.°

Their sins are green, even when their heads are grey—   125

Nay I despair not now, my heart's cheered, gentlemen,

No face can come unfortunately to me.

    Enter a Servant

Now, sir, what news?

SERVANT   Your son with his fair bride

Is near at hand.

    [Exit Servant]

303

SIR ALEXANDER   Fair may their fortunes be.

GREENWIT Now you're resolved, sir, it was never she?   130

SIR ALEXANDER I find it in the music of my heart.

> *Enter Moll [dressed as a woman] masked, in Sebastian's hand,*
> *and [Sir Guy] Fitzallard*

See where they come.

GOSHAWK   A proper lusty° presence, sir.

SIR ALEXANDER Now has he pleased me right. I always counselled
him

To choose a goodly personable creature.

Just of her pitch° was my first wife, his mother.   135

SEBASTIAN Before I dare discover my offence,

I kneel for pardon.

> *[Kneels]*

SIR ALEXANDER   My heart gave it thee,

Before thy tongue could ask it.

Rise, thou hast raised my joy to greater height

Than to that seat where grief dejected it.   140

Both welcome to my love, and care forever!

Hide not my happiness too long, all's pardoned—

Here are our friends. Salute her, gentlemen!

> *They unmask her*

ALL [GENTLEMEN] Heart, who? This? Moll?

SIR ALEXANDER O, my reviving shame! Is't I must live,   145

To be struck blind? Be it the work of sorrow,

Before age take't in hand.

SIR GUY   Darkness and death!

Have you deceived me thus? Did I engage

My whole estate for this?

SIR ALEXANDER   You asked no favour,

And you shall find as little. Since my comforts,   150

Play false with me, I'll be as cruel to thee

As grief to fathers' hearts.

MOLL   Why, what's the matter with you?

'Less too much joy should make your age forgetful?

Are you too well, too happy?

SIR ALEXANDER   With a vengeance!

MOLL Methinks you should be proud of such a daughter: 155

As good a man, as your son!

SIR ALEXANDER   O, monstrous impudence!

MOLL You had no note° before, an unmarked° knight,

Now all the town will take regard on you,
And all your enemies fear you for my sake.
You may pass where you list, through crowds most thick,   160
And come off bravely with your purse unpicked.
You do not know the benefits I bring with me:
No cheat dares work upon you, with thumb or knife,°
While you've a roaring girl to your son's wife.

SIR ALEXANDER A devil rampant!

SIR GUY   Have you so much charity   165
Yet to release me of my last rash bargain
And I'll give in your pledge?

SIR ALEXANDER   No, sir, I stand to't.
I'll work upon advantage as all mischiefs do
Upon me.

SIR GUY   Content. Bear witness all then,
His are the lands, and so contention ends.   170
Here comes your son's bride twixt two noble friends.

          Enter the Lord Noland, and Sir Beauteous Ganymede, with
          Mary Fitzallard between them, the Citizens and their Wives
          with them

MOLL Now are you gulled as you would be. Thank me for't,
I'd a forefinger in't.°

SEBASTIAN   Forgive me, father:
Though there before your eyes my sorrow feigned,
This still was she, for whom true love complained.   175

SIR ALEXANDER Blessings eternal, and the joys of angels
Begin your peace here, to be signed in heaven!
How short my sleep of sorrow seems now to me,
To this eternity of boundless comforts,
That finds no want but utterance and expression.   180
My lord, your office here appears so honourably,
So full of ancient goodness, grace, and worthiness,
I never took more joy in sight of man
Than in your comfortable° presence now.

LORD NOLAND Nor I more delight in doing grace to virtue   185
Than in this worthy gentlewoman, your son's bride,
Noble Fitzallard's daughter, to whose honour
And modest fame, I am a servant vowed:
So is this knight.

SIR ALEXANDER   Your loves make my joys proud.
[*Calling within*] Bring forth those deeds of land my care laid ready,   190

And which, old knight, thy nobleness may challenge,
Joined with thy daughter's virtues, whom I prize now,
As dearly as that flesh I call mine own.
Forgive me, worthy gentlewoman, 'twas my blindness
When I rejected thee, I saw thee not.   195
Sorrow and wilful rashness grew like films
Over the eyes of judgement, now so clear
I see the brightness of thy worth appear.
          [*Enter Servant with deeds*]
MARY Duty and love may I deserve in those,°
And all my wishes have a perfect close.   200
SIR ALEXANDER That tongue can never err, the sound's so sweet.
[*Handing over deeds*] Here, honest son, receive into thy hands,
The keys of wealth, possession of those lands
Which my first care provided: they're thine own.
Heaven give thee a blessing with 'em! The best joys   205
That can in worldly shapes to man betide
Are fertile lands, and a fair fruitful bride,
Of which I hope thou'rt sped.°
SEBASTIAN   I hope so too, sir.
MOLL Father and son, I ha' done you simple° service here.
SEBASTIAN For which thou shalt not part, Moll, unrequited.   210
SIR ALEXANDER Thou art a mad girl, and yet I cannot now
     Condemn thee.
MOLL   Condemn me? Troth and° you should, sir,
     I'd make you seek out one to hang in my room:
     I'd give you the slip at gallows, and cozen the people.
     Heard you this jest, my lord?
LORD NOLAND   What is it, Jack?   215
MOLL He was in fear his son would marry me,
     But never dreamt that I would ne'er agree!
LORD NOLAND Why? Thou had'st a suitor once, Jack. When wilt
     marry?
MOLL Who, I, my lord? I'll tell you when, i'faith:
     When you shall hear   220
     Gallants void from sergeants' fear,
     Honesty and truth unslandered,
     Woman manned but never pandered,
     Cheats booted but not coached,°
     Vessels° older ere they're broached: 225
     If my mind be then not varied,

Next day following, I'll be married.

LORD NOLAND This sounds like doomsday.

MOLL   Then were marriage best,
    For if I should repent, I were soon at rest.

SIR ALEXANDER In troth, thou'rt a good wench. I'm sorry now   230
    The opinion was so hard I conceived of thee.
    Some wrongs I've done thee.

      Enter Trapdoor

TRAPDOOR   Is the wind there now?
    'Tis time for me to kneel and confess first,
    For fear it come too late and my brains feel it.
    Upon my paws I ask you pardon, mistress.   235

MOLL Pardon? For what, sir? What has your rogueship done now?

TRAPDOOR I have been from time to time hired to confound you
    By this old gentleman.

MOLL   How?

TRAPDOOR   Pray forgive him,
    But may I counsel you, you should ne'er do't.
    Many a snare to entrap your worship's life   240
    Have I laid privily—chains, watches, jewels—
    And when he saw nothing could mount you up,
    Four hollow-hearted° angels he then gave you,
    By which he meant to trap you, I to save you.

SIR ALEXANDER To which shame and grief in me cry guilty.   245
    Forgive me, now I cast the world's eyes from me,
    And look upon thee freely with mine own:
    I see the most of many wrongs before thee
    Cast from the jaws of Envy and her people,
    And nothing foul but that.° I'll never more   250
    Condemn by common voice for that's the whore
    That deceives man's opinions, mocks his trust,
    Cozens his love, and makes his heart unjust.

MOLL Here be the angels, gentlemen. They were given me
    As a musician. I pursue no pity,   255
    Follow the law, and you can cuck me,° spare not.
    Hang up my viol by me, and I care not!

SIR ALEXANDER So far I'm sorry, I'll thrice double 'em
    To make thy wrongs amends.
    Come, worthy friends, my honourable lord,   260
    Sir Beauteous Ganymede, and noble Fitzallard,
    And you kind gentlewoman, whose sparkling presence

Are glories set in marriage, beams of society,
For all your loves give lustre to my joys.
The happiness of this day shall be remembered,   265
At the return of every smiling spring:
In my time now 'tis born, and may no sadness
Sit on the brows of men upon that day, ·
But as I am, so all go pleased away.
      [*Exeunt all except Moll*]

EPILOGUE

[MOLL] A painter having drawn with curious art
    The picture of a woman, every part,
    Limned° to the life, hung out the piece to sell.
    People who passed along viewing it well,
    Gave several verdicts on it: some dispraised   5
    The hair, some said the brows too high were raised,
    Some hit her o'er° the lips, misliked their colour,
    Some wished her nose were shorter, some, the eyes fuller;
    Other said roses on her cheeks should grow,
    Swearing they looked too pale, others cried no.   10
    The workman still as fault was found, did mend it,
    In hope to please all; but, this work being ended
    And hung at open stall, it was so vile,
    So monstrous, and so ugly, all men did smile
    At the poor painter's folly. Such we doubt   15
    Is this our comedy—some perhaps do flout
    The plot, saying 'tis too thin, too weak, too mean;
    Some for the person will revile the scene,
    And wonder that a creature of her being
    Should be the subject of a poet, seeing   20
    In the world's eye, none weighs so light; others look
    For all those base tricks published in a book,
    Foul as his brains they flowed from, of cutpurses,
    Of nips and foists, nasty, obscene discourses,
    As full of lies, as empty of worth or wit,   25
    For any honest ear or eye unfit.
    And thus,
    If we to every brain that's humorous°

Should fashion scenes, we, with the painter, shall
In striving to please all, please none at all.   30
Yet for such faults, as either the writer's wit
Or negligence of the actors do commit,
Both crave your pardons: if what both have done
Cannot full pay your expectation,
The Roaring Girl herself, some few days hence,   35
Shall on this stage, give larger recompense,°—
Which mirth that you may share in, herself does woo you,
And craves this sign: your hands to beckon her to you.
        [*Exit*]

Appendix

[EPISTLE]

TO THE COMIC PLAY-READERS, VENERY° AND LAUGHTER.

The fashion of play-making I can properly compare to nothing so
naturally as the alteration in apparel: for, in the time of your great
crop-doublet,° your huge, bombasted plays, quilted with mighty words   5
to lean purpose, was only then in fashion; and, as the doublet fell,°
neater inventions began to set up. Now in the time of spruceness,° our
plays follow the neatness° of our garments—single plots, quaint conceits, lecherous jests, dressed up in hanging-sleeves,°—and those are fit
for the times and the termers.° Such a kind of light-colour summer   10
stuff, mingled with diverse colours, you shall find this published comedy,—good to keep you in an afternoon from dice at home in your
chambers; and for venery, you shall find enough for sixpence,° but well
couched an you mark it.° For Venus, being a woman, passes through
the play in doublet and breeches, a brave disguise and a safe one, if the   15
statute untie not her codpiece point!° The book I make no question but
is fit for many of your companies, as well as the person itself, and may
be allowed both gallery-room° at the playhouse and chamber-room at
your lodging. Worse things, I must needs confess, the world has taxed
her for than has been written of her;° but 'tis the excellency of a writer   20
to leave things better than he finds 'em—though some obscene fellow,
that cares not what he writes against others, yet keeps a mystical°
bawdy-house himself, and entertains drunkards to make use of their
pockets and vent his private bottle-ale at midnight,°—though such a
one would have ripped up the most nasty vice that ever hell belched   25
forth and presented it to a modest assembly, yet we rather wish in such
discoveries° where reputation lies bleeding, a slackness of truth than
fullness of slander.

Thomas Middleton.

EXPLANATORY NOTES

The *Oxford English Dictionary* (*OED*) has been used as a basis for all simple glosses. All references to Shakespeare cite *The Complete Works: Compact Edition*, ed. Stanley Wells *et al.* (Oxford, 1988). References to Thomas Kyd's *The Spanish Tragedy* are taken from *The Spanish Tragedy*, ed. J. R. Mulryne (London, 1989).

ABBREVIATIONS

Dent   R. W. Dent, *Proverbial Language in English Drama Exclusive of Shakespeare, 1495–1616: An Index* (Berkeley, 1984)

EMI   *Every Man In His Humour*

EH   *Eastward Ho*

F   *The Workes of Ben Jonson* (London, 1616).

H&S   *Ben Jonson*, ed. C. H. Herford and Percy and Evelyn Simpson, 11 vols. (Oxford, 1925–52)

Q   The first published version of the play, in quarto

RG   *The Roaring Girl*

SH   *The Shoemaker's Holiday*

Tilley   Morris Palmer Tilley, *A Dictionary of the Proverbs in England in the Sixteenth and Seventeenth Centuries* (Ann Arbor, 1950)

The Shoemaker's Holiday

THE PERSONS OF THE PLAY

Simon Eyre: a historical figure who became Lord Mayor of London in 1445.

Hodge: a typical name for an English rustic.

journeyman: someone who has served an apprenticeship and become qualified to work at a trade.

Firk: a name which suggests liveliness, cheating, and fucking.

Dodger: the name suggests artfulness in shifts or dodges, but this does not seem to be borne out by the character's brief appearances.

The King: Henry VI at the time of the play's setting, but it is significant that no historical king is named.

[**Scene 1**].5 *cousin*: a loose term for a relative, Lacy is Lincoln's nephew.

6 *affected to*: enamoured with.

11 *mean*: lowly, base-born.

15 *doubt*: worry about.

21 *bills of exchange*: promissory notes.

27 *embezzled*: squandered.

35 *rioting*: dissolute behaviour.

46 *his Grace*: the King.

48 *Mustered*: conscripted.

53 *powers*: forces.

56 *forwardness*: readiness.

58 *Mile End*: the green there, in the north-east of London, was a place for military drills and mustering.

59 *Tothill Fields*: a military training ground in Westminster.

61 *Finsbury*: an area north of Moorfields used for archery practice and military training.

63 *imprest*: conscription pay.
   furniture: munitions of war.

65 *Guildhall*: civic hall of London, centre of local governmental affairs.

66 *brethren*: fellow members of the Guildhall.

67 *approve*: make proof of.

77 *painted*: decorated (with cosmetics), with the implication that citizens try to appear above their station.

85 *start . . . bias*: stray from the proper path, cf. *RG* 6.175.

99 *policies*: schemes.

110 *higher consequence*: more significant endeavours.

114 *jealous*: suspiciously watchful.

116 S.D. *piece*: firearm.

119 *Go to*: a common expression of derision.

122 *cavaliers*: horse-riding soldiers.

124 *pishery-pashery*: a nonce-word, appearing to mean 'contemptible talk'.

127 *mad*: exuberant, madcap.

128 *Tower Street*: the street running east to the Tower of London.

130 *firking*: lively, with a play on 'fucking'.

135 *midriff*: the diaphragm, so that which expels (excessive) air from the lungs.

136 *Cormorant*: a (perhaps intentional) mispronunciation of 'colonel'; a 'cormorant' is a greedy person.

138 *undo*: punning on 'do' as 'have sexual intercourse'.

140 *prick . . . awl*: tools for punching holes in leather, but with bawdy quibbles on prick as 'penis' and awl as 'hole'.

141 *undone*: *done* can also mean 'copulated with'.

143 *occupied*: filled (in the sexual sense).

145 *pressed*: conscripted.

146 *Lord Mayor*: the mayor of London had powers of conscription.

150 *within a year . . . marriage*: referring to Deuteronomy 24.5: 'When a man hath taken a new wife, he shall not go out to war . . . but he shall be free at home one year . . .'.

151 *melancholy*: thoughtful.

153 *stand so stiffly against*: remain so inflexible towards, with a quibble on 'stiffly' as 'with an erection'. The bawdy continues with 'case' (= vaginal canal) and 'newly entered'.

157 *pols . . . edepols*: senseless talk.

158 *Cecily Bumtrinket*: the name of Margery's maid, who may be present on stage, but here it seems to be used as a nickname for Margery.

     your head: i.e. Eyre, the head of the household.

159 *horns*: cuckolds were traditionally held to have 'horns' coming from their brows.

160 *Tawsoone*: be quiet (Welsh).

164 *Hector*: considered the bravest of the Trojan soldiers.

     Termagant: imaginary deity held to be worshiped by Muslims and represented in medieval mystery plays as overbearing and violent.

165 *Lord of Ludgate*: one of Eyre's characteristically elaborate oaths, perhaps referring to the legend that Ludgate (the western entrance to London) was built by King Lud.

175 *for your . . . respect him*: because of your praise, he will be better esteemed than an ordinary recruit.

182 *gimlet*: a boring tool, here meaning 'penis'.

     weak vessels: alluding to 1 Peter 3: 7, which describes the wife as 'the weaker vessel'.

184 *Tower Hill*: the hill upon which the Tower of London sits; Stow calls it 'a royal palace for assemblies'; cf. John Stow, *A Survey of London, written in the year 1598*, ed. Henry Morley (1912; repr. Stroud: Sutton, 1994), 87.

185 *Stays*: waits.

189 *parasite*: servant, the term usually had connotations of obsequiousness and flattery in the period.

197 *hie to your colours*: go quickly to your regiment's standard.

203 *cracked groats*: damaged coins worth fourpence; *groat* was a byword for a nominal sum.

. *mustard tokens*: tokens given to purchasers of mustard which could later be redeemed for a nominal sum.

209 *bombast-cotton-candle-quean*: a mild reproach, suggesting that Jane should spin (or, more generally, do a woman's household chores) while her husband is away. *Bombast* is cotton, which, when spun, was used for candle-wicks.

211 *sixpences*: sixpence was roughly the daily wage of a skilled craftsman like Ralph.

213 *Saint Martin's*: the area around the church of St Martin's-le-Grand, noted as a centre of the shoemaking trade.

Bedlam: Bethlehem Hospital, London's lunatic asylum, hence 'mad knaves'.

214 *Fleet Street . . . Whitechapel*: Fleet Street and Whitechapel were shoe-making areas; Eyre's shop is on Tower Street.

crowns: heads.

219 *sorrow is dry*: proverbial (Dent S656)

baisez-mon-culs: French for 'kiss-my-arses'.

222 *French crowns*: gold coins, upon which the English crowns (worth five shillings) were modelled.

230 *pinked*: pricked (with holes that form a decorative design).

235 *moe*: more.

s.d. *pass over*: walk or march across.

[Scene 2].4 *gillyflowers*: pinks or wallflowers.

5 *coronet*: i.e. the garland she is making.

9 *loured you so at*: did you look so unfavourably upon.

18 *against*: in preparation for when.

Lady of the Harvest: an honorific given to a young woman at harvest time.

22 *Doctors' Commons*: lodgings for the Doctors of the College of Law.

25 *out of cry*: beyond all measure; proverbial (Dent C871.1).

a wore: he wore.

26 *scarf*: a strip of cloth commonly worn as a gift from a lover. All of the objects Sybil names suggest such favours, so she implies that Lacy has been receptive to other women.

28 *Old Ford*: a village beyond Stratford Bow, about 3 miles from London. The reference sets the scene and suggests Rose's seclusion from the City.

29 *Cornhill*: a busy street running to the Exchange and the location of the Oatley town house.

31 *Marry gup*: a common exclamation of derision at snobbery (Dent M699.2).

32 *humorous*: peevish.

35 *gentle as a lamb*: proverbial (Dent L34), and ironic considering his new occupation in 'the gentle craft'.

37 *stamped crabs*: crab-apples crushed to extract their sour juice.

38 *verjuice*: juice of unripe fruit, used in cookery; 'sour as verjuice' was proverbial (Dent V32).

Go thy ways: i.e. 'do what you like (it is of little interest to me)'.

39 *gaskins . . . netherstocks*: breeches and stockings; the phrase suggests outward acquaintance without intimacy.

41 *Go by Hieronimo*: i.e. 'go away' in this context. The phrase is taken from Thomas Kyd's popular play *The Spanish Tragedy*, written about a decade earlier, which was repeatedly quoted and lampooned in the period.

43 *set . . . goose giblets*: i.e. 'consider how much would be lost for so little gain', (*driblets* = petty sums); proverbial (Dent H161).

47 *see*: colloquial for 'saw'.

48 *proper*: fine, handsome; 'he is handsome that handsome does' was proverbial (Dent D402).

49 *snick up*: hang.

53 *Romish*: Italian.

56 *at whose suit*: i.e. 'I'd do it for anyone'.

58 *sweat in purple*: work in clothing not normally had by workers.

59 *o' God's name*: i.e. for free.

60 *have at uptails all*: an expression of high spirits.

jiggy-joggy: with a jolting motion (because going fast).

[Scene 3] S.D. *like . . . a Dutch shoemaker*: the occupation could have been visually indicated on stage by Lacy carrying shoemaking tools; the nationality was perhaps signified by a felt hat and 'great Dutch slop', or baggy breeches (cf. *RG* 4.77n.).

2 *How many . . . loves*: as described most famously in Ovid's *Metamorphoses*, in which the gods adopt disguises in order to seduce human lovers.

6 *only happy presence*: i.e. the only presence which brings my happiness.

11 *bareness*: destitution. The fourth printing of the text reads 'baseness', which may correct an earlier misprint.

[Scene 4] S.D. *Eyre . . . ready*: Eyre has just risen and is finishing getting dressed.

4 *powder-beef*: beef salted for preservation.

4 *Madge Mumblecrust*: a character in Nicholas Udall's *c.*1553 play *Ralph Roister Doister*, here used as a nickname for Margery (*mumble* = chew without teeth).

5 *midriff-swag-belly*: intensifying 'fat' from the previous line.

6 *kennels*: gutters.

7 *shop windows*: shutters served as counters in Elizabethan shops, which were fronted like modern market stalls. Playhouses probably used booths to represent such shops.

9 *speak bandog and bedlam*: speak like a savage dog and a madman.

15 *Let them . . . souse-wife*: a souse-wife prepared pigs' faces for eating; Firk is saying that he has no need for a clean face because his is not going to be eaten.

20 *Here's . . . towards*: i.e. it looks like it will be a fine day.

22 *dry as dust*: proverbial for 'thirsty' (Dent D647).

23 *clowns*: rural labourers.

26 *can . . . rise*: i.e. 'is it light enough for you to get up?'
   Trip and go: i.e. 'get a move on'.

29 *marvel*: wonder.

33 *privy*: secret (with pun on *privy* as 'toilet').

34 *want*: lack (through her negligence).
   swinge her in: beat her with.

35 *dry beating*: a beating which does not draw blood.

41 *Der was . . . mannekin*: 'There was a boor [peasant] from Gelderland, merry they be. He was so drunk he could not stand, pissed [drunk] they all be. Fill up the cannikin [small drinking vessel], drink my fine manikin [little man].' Lacy enhances his disguise by playing on the Dutch reputation for heavy drinking.

43 *Saint Hugh's bones*: shoemaker's tools. Saint Hugh became a shoemaker in order to win his love, Winifred, and was later martyred with her. His bones were used to make tools by other shoemakers. The story is told in Dekker's source, Thomas Deloney's *The Gentle Craft*, ch. 4.

44 *uplandish*: outlandish, foreign.

45 *gibble-gabble*: gibberish.

46 *A hard world*: 'it is a hard world' was proverbial (Dent W877.1); Eyre uses the proverb as an excuse for not helping Lacy.

50 *butter-box*: the Dutch were thought to be great eaters of butter.

61 *prick . . . play*: i.e. put away my tools and do no work.

63 *pudding broth*: water in which pudding (or sausage) has been boiled. The term is directed at Margery, who is presumably about to speak or has been expostulating throughout the exchange.

64 *gallimaufry*: dish made from hashed leftovers (again directed at Margery).

65 *you to him*: you (go) to him.

66 *Goeden . . . auch*: 'Good day master, and you mistress, too.' *Auch* is pronounced 'oak', as its spelling in Q suggests, so Firk calls him 'friend Oak'.

69 *Yaw . . . skomaker*: 'Yes, yes, I am a shoemaker.'

71 *rubbing-pin*: the term suggests a small piece of wood or metal used to smooth and prepare shoe leather. The meanings of most of these terms have been lost, so determining their use involves guesswork.

stopper: a 'stopping-stick', perhaps used to fill crevices.

72 *dresser*: some sort of implement for finishing the shoe.

wax: for rubbing on thread so that it passes through leather smoothly.

73 *hand and thumb-leathers*: for protecting the hand when working with leather.

76 *Yaw . . . klene*: 'Yes, yes, be not worried. I have everything to make shoes large and small.'

79 *mystery*: craft.

80 *Ik . . . niet*: 'I don't understand what you say; I do not understand you.'

82 *Yaw . . . doen*: 'Yes, yes, yes, I can do that well.'

84 *double*: strong.

91 *trullibubs*: a variant of *trillibubs* (entrails), suggesting fatness. The first syllable also suggests *trull* or 'whore'. Cf. 'fat midriff-swag-bellied whore' in line 5.

92 *use thyself*: be.

95 *Gargantua*: a giant in French folklore.

97 *heelblock*: a block used in fastening a heel to a shoe.

99 *O, ik . . . freelick*: 'Oh I understand you: I must pay for half-a-dozen cans. Here, boy, take this shilling, fill up merrily.' *Can* in the period referred to drinking vessels in general, not necessarily those made of metal.

100 *snipper-snapper*: whipper-snapper.

101 *last . . . fives*: a last (or wooden model) for a small, size-five, foot; here it is used to address the boy.

102 *Have*: here's.

103 *mad Greeks*: proverbial for 'lively companions' (Dent G439.11).

104 *Trojans*: merry fellows, boon companions.

109 *Clapper-dudgeon*: beggar.

110 *soused conger*: pickled conger eel.

111 *Hyperboreans*: mythical inhabitants of the extreme north. Hyperbolic references to unusual locations or peoples appear frequently in Eyre's bombast.

[Scene 5].1 *brake*: thicket, registering the change to a rural location.

6 *take soil*: go to a pool of water for refuge.

7 *embossed*: driven to extremity.

9 *trace*: (a) pass over; (b) follow the tracks on.

12 *pale*: fence.

Over he skipped me: over he skipped; *me* is the ethic dative, used here and in the next line for rhetorical effect. The line does not mean 'he skipped over me'.

13 *There boy, there boy*: the hunters' encouragement to their dogs.

[Scene 6] S.D. *Hunting within*: i.e. hunting noises are made offstage.

1 *prove*: become.

2 *Upon some*: an exclamatory phrase used to intensify *no*. It appears often in this scene.

go by: go away.

11 *have . . . you*: rebuke you.

12 *gross*: ignorant (since Sybil is not a lady).

13 *does*: i.e. herself and Sybil.

15 *when . . . tell?*: a proverbial expression of defiance (Dent T88).

21 *Follow your nose*: i.e. go in any direction you choose; proverbial (Dent N230).

his horns . . . right: i.e. 'his [Hammon's] cuckold's horns will lead you to the (horned) deer'.

23 *like*: likely.

27 *Come up*: an expression of contempt.

honey-sops: bread soaked in honey, a response to 'sugar-candy'.

35 *impale me*: (a) put a fence around me; (b) pierce me (in a sexual sense).

42 *hind*: female deer.

43 *luck had horns*: the proverbial phrase (Dent L579.11) refutes Rose's claim that his *hart* could prove a *hind* 'by such luck'.

44 *send luck*: i.e. send horns (as worn by the cuckold).

46 *God's pitikens*: by God's pity (a mild oath).

hands off: Warner is making physical advances towards Sybil.

54 *hunter's feast*: scanty meal.

[Scene 7].1–5 *Ik . . . Hans?*: 'I shall tell you what to say, Hans; this ship that comes from Candy [Crete], is all full, by God's sacrament, of sugar, civet, almonds, cambric, and all things—a thousand, thousand things. Take it, Hans, take it for your master. There are the bills of lading [inventories]. Your master Simon Eyre shall have a good bargain. What say you, Hans?'

6 *Wat . . . slopen*: Firk's mockery of the Skipper.

9 *Mine . . . Hodge*: 'My dear brother Firk, bring Master Eyre to the Sign of the Swan [a tavern]. There you will find this skipper and me. What say you, brother Firk? Do it, Hodge.'

11 *worth the lading of*: with a cargo worth.

12 *two . . . pounds*: this figure is far too great to represent the Elizabethan value for such cargo.

14 *dares . . . head*: the owner appears to be in some sort of legal bind which prevents him from selling the goods himself.

17 *reasonable . . . payment*: fair amount of time until he must pay for the goods.

19 *porpentines*: porcupines; Firk's mistake for *portagues*.

20 *earnest-penny*: down-payment.

22 *Saint Mary Overy's*: the church of Saint Mary Overy was in Southwark on the south bank of the Thames.

25 *Monday's our holiday*: Monday was the traditional day off for shoemakers; Margery's comment indicates that Firk sings the line.

26 *Sir Sauce*: a mock-formal address to Firk for his impudence or sauciness.

    beshrew: curse.

29 *take down*: admonish.

32 *take her down . . . lower*: i.e. I will bring her down a peg (with a play on to *take down* for lovemaking); proverbial (Dent P181).

35 *meddle with*: (a) interfere with; (b) sexually deal with.

36 *Queen of Clubs*: another of Eyre's idiosyncratic insults. 'Clubs' was the traditional cry of apprentices when uniting for (violent) action.

43 *Prince . . . shoemaker*: 'a shoemaker's son is a prince born' was proverbial (Dent S386).

44 *kitchen-stuff*: kitchen refuse.

46 *sort*: group.

48 *venentory*: Firk's mistake for 'inventory'.

52 *more . . . Malkin*: proverbial for the ability to find other servants (Dent M39).

55 *turned to a Turk*: proverbial for an insidious change of character (Dent T609).

56 *Finsbury*: archery practice fields north of Moorgate, where effigies of Turks were used as targets.

59 *Rip*: make haste.

60 *brown-bread Tannikin*: another of Eyre's unusual insults; *brown bread* was considered coarse and *Tannikin* is a familiar form for Anne.

61 *Eastcheap*: a street off Tower Street, known for its butchers.

66 *chitterling*: pig's intestine, especially when prepared as food by frying or boiling.

67 *Boar's Head*: several taverns in London bore this name.

73 *No more ... more*: probably a mock acquiescence to his wife (who may make some sign of protest at his generosity) as an attempt to explain the missing beer.

74 *Well said*: i.e. 'well done', with reference to their drinking.

81 *Yerk*: sew (leather).

85 *earnest*: down-payment.

90 *Skellum ... spreaken*: i.e. the skipper. Firk puts together words that sound like Dutch gibberish to him.

91 *silk ... sugar candy*: Firk confuses the skipper's account of the ship's origins and content.

94 *seal ring ... cassock*: Eyre acquires signs of his alderman's status. *Seal rings* made personalized impressions on wax to seal letters; *guarded* means braided.

98 *proud ... doublet*: proverbial for misplaced pride (Dent D452).

100 *for rearing of*: to prevent raising of.

104 *give ... wall*: allow you to walk near the wall (away from the muck typically in the centre of early modern streets).
come upon: address.

105 *Right Worshipful*: appropriate way to address an alderman.

107 *turned and dressed*: fashioned and adorned.

113 *but only for*: except merely in.

115 *Godden ... nempt it*: 'Good day, master. This is the skipper who owns the ship of merchandise. The commodity is good: take it, master, take it.'

120 *De skip ... copen*: 'The ship is in the river. There are sugar, civet, almonds, cambric, and a thousand thousand things, by God's sacrament! Take it, master, you shall have a good bargain.'

122 *brave*: fine.
meat: food.

125 *have ... drink*: this may be a courteous inquiry, instead of an attempt to intoxicate the skipper.

126 *Yaw ... gedrunk*: 'Yes, yes, I have drunk well.'

128 *countenance*: patronage.

130 *veal*: Firk's mistake for the Dutch *veale*.

137 *feel ... ring on*: i.e. have an erection, being dressed like a bridegroom.

138 *pull him down*: (a) belittle him; (b) make him detumescent.

139 *my worship*: i.e. 'me' (with mock haughtiness befitting her new status).

142 *pass . . . state*: exit in a stately manner.

[Scene 8].2 *eighteen*: eighteenth.

9 *name*: high rank.

10 *Hyam . . . Ardington*: names invented by Dekker.

19 *advised*: certain.

22 *Sent . . . France*: sent me from France to Lacy.

29 *estimate*: value.

42 *credit*: reputation.

44 *to his*: for his.

[Scene 9].2 *wedding knot*: betrothal (not an actual wedding).

15 *If flesh be frail*: 'flesh is frail' was proverbial for how the body is physically (and morally) weak (Dent F363).

16 *brawl*: squabble.

19 *sport*: jest.

20 *square*: quarrel. Oatley's question suggests that he and Scott might be positioned on stage so that they cannot hear the 'lovers' but are able to see their interaction.

22 *strange in fancying*: unwilling to love, unfriendly towards.

24 *to fond my love*: i.e. to dote. 'To fond' means to love foolishly; there is also a play on 'to found'.

25 *quit*: requite.

31 *But . . . said*: Hammon seems to realize that Rose loves someone else, as the normal phrase is 'live and die a maid', i.e. never marry.

39 *to another end*: for another purpose.

44 *spoil*: endeavour.

45 *glove*: traditionally worn by a knight as a favour from his love.
tourney: tournament.

51 *Old Change*: the street of the old Exchange, which was superseded by the new Royal Exchange in 1566.

56 *mammet*: a general term of abuse, used by authority figures to admonish 'impertinent' young women.

57 *coyness*: reluctance.

59 *strait*: strictly.

75 *it likes yourself*: it pleases you.

82 *sheriff*: a high honour, only two were elected annually.

87 *keeps*: resides.

94 *start him*: force him out.

[Scene 10].7 *forswear*: renounce.

8 *Nay, when?*: i.e. Well, when are you going?

compendious: concise; Margery misunderstands the word.

10 *like a new cart-wheel*: squeakily, in an affected manner.

11 *musty ale-bottle*: made of leather, ale 'bottles' were cleaned by being scalded.

15 *dame*: used to address women of lower rank, so Hodge corrects himself.

19 *Me . . . fro*: 'I thank you, madam.'

23 *back friend*: false friend.

25 *Yaw . . . fro*: 'Yes, I will, madam.'

26 *thou knowest . . . foot*: (a) literally, so that a shoe can be made; (b) proverbial (Dent L202), meaning: 'you know how to win my love'.

28 *cork . . . heel*: cork and wood were used to give fashionable added height.

30 *farthingale-maker*: a farthingale was a hooped petticoat.

31 *French-hood-maker*: a French hood was a pleated hood commonly worn by citizens' wives; it may also have been the name of the head-dress worn by women who were punished for sexual misbehaviour.

33 *As a cat out*: i.e. like a whore (looking) out.

35 *all . . . grass*: proverbial for the mortality of the body (Dent F359), but inappropriate in this context.

36 *hair*: hair-piece.

37 *poulterer's*: Hodge mishears Margery's 'hair' as 'hare'. Hare was considered poultry in the period.

Gracious Street: Gracechurch Street was also known as 'Grass' Street; Hodge may pronounce so as to bring out the pun.

42 *fan . . . mask*: accessories for the Elizabethan woman of fashion.

44 *this . . . calling*: i.e. our calling in the world (of fashionable society).

48 *Ik . . . so*: 'I am cheerful; let's see you so.'

49 *drink*: taking tobacco was frequently described as *drinking*.

tobacco: the popularity of tobacco was a contentious issue in contemporary London.

51 *idle*: useless.

baubles: toys, but with a secondary meaning of 'penises'.

55 *tall*: brave.

56 *broder*: brother.

61 *impotent*: unable to use one's limbs.

62 *sunburnt*: the secondary meaning, 'infected with venereal disease', may also apply.

64 *France*: Margery hints at the 'French' disease, syphilis.

79 *stately*: proud.

   checked: rebuked.

81 *ka me, ka thee*: i.e. I'll do for you what you do for me; proverbial (Dent K1).

86 *opened her case*: discussed her plight; there is also a bawdy pun on *case* as 'vagina'.

89 *Yaw . . . fro*: 'Yes, I shall, mistress.'

92 *naked . . . things*: a paraphrase of Job 1: 21.

94 *pull . . . heart*: take heart; 'pluck up your heart' was proverbial (Dent H323).

95 *brave*: finely dressed.

99 *worshipful*: honourable (and pointing to her new status).

104 *smug*: smarten.

105 *condemned*: this could refer to the common reluctance to take up public office, but Firk probably means that the decision is irreversible.

108 *voices*: votes.

109 *fists . . . ears*: hands raised in support (comically stemming from the desire for 'hands' and 'voices' above).

112 *salute*: embrace or kiss (indicative of the stage action).

113 *Yaw . . . shrieve*: 'Yes, my master is the great man, the sheriff.'

120 *rose*: roses were impressed upon some higher-value coins that were otherwise indistinguishable from lower denominations; they were stamped on threepences (but also on three-halfpenny pieces).

124 *'Hodge' . . . mouth*: i.e. as you used to say before you delicately began to call him 'Roger'.

125 *cry twang*: i.e. are so satisfied as to make a twanging sound.

   S.D. *gold chain*: a sign of his new office.

126 *See . . . meester*: 'See, my dear brother, here comes my master.'

132 *flap . . . mutton*: i.e. the French hood.

134 *for twenty*: i.e. for the twenty angels he lent to Eyre.

143 *crotchets*: fanciful entertainments.

144 *gentle*: i.e. gentlemanly, not 'mild'.

[Scene 11].12 *a fig for gravity*: i.e. I scorn gravity; 'a fig for (it)' was proverbial opprobrium (Dent F210).

13 *scarlet*: colour of the ceremonial gown for aldermen and the Lord Mayor.

16 *flip-flap*: i.e. senseless chatter.

21 *pound . . . debt*: proverbial (Dent P518).

22 *sack and sugar*: a common drink for those of 'old age'.

29 *A thousand marks*: a mark was ⅔ of a pound. *A thousand marks* would have been a substantial bonus to a dowry.

31 *ape*: fool.

34 *cockney*: spoilt child.

39 *Wash*: kitchen refuse, as in 'hog-wash'.

41 *marry me*: i.e. you should marry; the *me* is the ethic dative (used for rhetorical emphasis).

44 *pack*: go, be sent away.

46 S.D. *noise . . . pipe*: backstage, a small drum and pipe are played.

58 *represent'st*: resemble; this line may be spoken as an aside and confirm Rose's recognition of Lacy.

60 *Ik . . . frister*: 'I thank you, good maid.'

61 *want*: lack.

67 *Stratford Bow*: a village on the way to London from Old Ford and a frequent stopping-place for travellers.

69 *tickle it*: i.e. enjoy yourself.

[Scene 12] S.D. *sempster's shop*: this could be represented by a booth on stage.

S.D. *muffled*: disguised with some fabric over his face.

7 *still love one*: always love someone.

10 *curious*: cautious, difficult to satisfy.

14 *happy work*: i.e. the needlework is lucky to be held by Jane's hand.

22 *What . . . lack*: the trader's traditional call for customers; cf. *RG* 3.1.

23 *bands*: decorative collars or cuffs.

25 *How*: at what price.

29 *But . . . when*: i.e. that's not likely.

34 *Look how*: just as.

wound this cloth: i.e. by pricking it with the needle.

46 *fray*: (a) timidity; (b) brawl, noise.

55 *myself thine*: me yours.

75 *by wanting*: because of missing.

85 *place*: high rank.

95 *bill*: letter, list.

99 *mourning . . . mourn*: a commonplace idea (Dent D126).

108 *moan*: sorrow.

115 *grow rude*: this suggests that he might grab her hand or arm.

119 *Not . . . present*: i.e. not because you personally are here.

[Scene 13] s.d. *at his shop board*: once again a workplace setting is established, either by bringing a table or booth onstage, or by opening one of
the doors behind the stage to 'reveal' a shop.

  1 *Hey . . . down-derry*: this typical song refrain suggests that one of the
Three-Man's songs (see Additional Passages) could be sung here.

  2 *Well said*: i.e. well done.

  7 *Yaw, meester*: 'yes, master.'

 11 *Forware . . . boots*: 'indeed, Firk, you are a jolly youngster. Hey, master, I
bid you cut me a pair of vamps for Master Jeffrey's boots.' A *vamp* is the
part of the shoe which covers the front of the foot.

 15 *cutting vein*: with a secondary sense of 'insulting mood' (because he called
Firk a 'boy').

 16 *counterfeits*: i.e. vamps just like the ones you are doing for Hans.

     pass current: playing on the idea of currency and counterfeit money.

 19 *aunts*: whores.

 21 *in hand with*: working on.

 23 *doing*: in the sense of 'having sexual intercourse'.

 25 *yerked*: stitched, but Firk equates the word with 'fucked'.

 26 *gear . . . hold*: this won't hold up; *gear* could be a reference to Firk's voice,
the shoe he is working on, or Ralph's sexual ability.

 29 *Oatmeal*: i.e. Oatley.

     meal . . . nature: oatmeal was of such high quality.

 30 *bag-puddings*: puddings made of skin stuffed with meat and oatmeal.

 40 *Syb-whore*: a good-natured jibe.

 44 *that . . . have*: i.e. you shall have more good cheer.

 47 *I . . . first*: in asking after the women first, Firk breaks hierarchical
propriety.

 48 *God's me*: God save me.

 51 *Wat . . . frister*: 'What do you want, what would you, girl?'

 52 *pull on*: fit.

 54 *Ware . . . mistress*: 'Where is your noble lady, where is your mistress?'

55   *Cornwall*: a common name for Cornhill Street.

57   *stand upon needles*: proverbial for impatience (Dent N100).

59   *trick . . . budget*: device in my bag (Dent T518.01); Sybil matches Hodge's bawdy play on *pricking* by suggesting a sexual *trick* and using *budget* in the sense of 'vagina'.

61   *Yaw . . . gane*: 'Yes, yes, I will go with you.'

[Scene 14].1   *sign of the last*: typical sign for a shoemaker's shop.

 5   *against*: in time for.

 9   *at any hand*: in any case.

21   *Golden Ball*: a typical inn name.

     Watling Street: a street known for its drapers, near St Paul's.

30   *Saint Faith's*: a church in the crypt of St Paul's.

39   *countryman*: neighbour.

41   *thing*: slang for male and female genitals.

44   *mere*: complete.

48   *pricked*: punched in the shoe as decoration.

67   *Cripple-gates*: Cripplegate was one of the gates in the City walls; Firk pokes fun at Ralph's lameness.

68   *God . . . fortune*: i.e. those least deserving are the most lucky; proverbial (Dent G220).

70   *wedding . . . destiny*: i.e. getting married or hanged is beyond our control; proverbial (Dent W232).

[Scene 15].2   *cross*: adverse.

 6   *too . . . me*: excessive attention for (my reputation).

25   *want*: lack.

30   *Forware . . . betaelen*: 'Indeed, mistress, 'tis a good shoe, it will do well, or you shall not pay for it.'

33   *Fit . . . well*: with an unintentional suggestion of 'fill her with your penis', which Lacy takes up.

36   *Yaw . . . heer*: 'Yes, yes, I know that well. Indeed, 'tis a good shoe, 'tis made of neat's [cow's] leather, just look, my lord.'

39   *lighted*: arrived.

50   *presently*: immediately.

[Scene 16].7   *given head to*: instigated.

15   *he . . . That*: i.e. the person has wronged him who.

18   *conference . . . of*: i.e. any meetings with, or news of.

40   *as true . . . heaven*: proverbial (Dent G175).

45 *honnikin*: an obscure insult, the only known example of which occurs here.

54 *as fit . . . pudding*: part of the proverb, 'As fit as a pudding for a friar's mouth' (Dent P620).

59 *hoping . . . Firk*: Firk mimics the closure of a formal letter.

62 *knave . . . shoemaker*: implying that Oatley is a knave, while Firk is a shoemaker.

64 *moved . . . stir*: the language suggests anger as well as motion.

67 *Sit . . . merry*: i.e. keep good cheer.

72 *maw . . . gear*: appetite for this stuff. Firk pretends to believe that Oatley is trying to match him with Sybil.

75 *Rogero*: a popular tune.

78 *I have him*: I know him.

81 *shaking . . . sheets*: the title of a song, with proverbial suggestion of sexual activity in bed (Dent S265.11).

82 *diggers*: i.e. questioners.

85 *Canst*: know.

   sadness: seriousness.

90 *feeling*: i.e. having the money in his hand.

91 *aurium tenus . . . genuum tenus*: 'up to the ears' . . . 'up to the knees'. Firk seems to indicate how much of the truth he will reveal for various amounts of money; the gold will buy most of the truth, the silver, only a part.

92 *stretchers*: (a) shoe stretchers; (b) lies.

95 *No point*: not at all.

96 *corporation*: guild of shoemakers.

102 *Pitchers have ears*: proverbial warning against talking in front of potential spies (Dent P363).

104 *gear*: business.

   rush: i.e. something of little value; rushes were used for floor covering at homes and on stages.

108 *London Stone*: a large stone near St Swithin's Church, which was an ancient and well-known landmark.

   Pissing Conduit: a conduit in London named for the narrow stream of water flowing through it.

109 *Mother Bunch*: beer served by a well-known alehouse hostess of that name (Dent D1208.01); Firk implies that the conduit's water resembles it.

113 *swearing church*: i.e. one whose name resembles an oath.

116 *incony*: rare, fine (but with a bawdy suggestion of 'in cunny').

126 *Refrain*: restrain.

128 *what else*: anything you like.

130 *hey pass, and repass*: a conjurer's phrase; Firk is mocking the marriage ceremony.

pindy-pandy: i.e. handy dandy, a game of choosing in which hand an object is hidden.

137 *ban*: curse.

143 *coney-catched*: won with trickery.

146 *chop up the matter*: i.e. exchange vows.

Savoy: a pauper's hospital (with a chapel which could be used for marriages).

151 *the Woolsack*: a tavern.

154 *hold out tack*: hold your own, be a match for (men).

155 *smocks*: i.e. maidenheads.

for this jumbling: because of this muddle.

[Scene 17].9 *Dainty . . . me*: a popular tune.

10 *stand*: act as, with a bawdy hint at 'grow erect'.

14 *cast . . . teeth*: said against me (Dent T429).

15 *Saracen's head*: another of Eyre's unusual insults; Saracens' heads were represented on inn-signs.

17 *red petticoat*: the scarlet gown of the Lord Mayor; cf. 11.12.

22 *buff-jerkin varlets*: i.e. sheriff's officers, who wore buff-coloured jerkins.

23 *brown*: Eyre could be referring to Margery or something she is wearing.

25 *countenance*: witness.

26 *Hamburg*: The comment seems to be another of Eyre's irrelevant geographic terms; cf. 'Cappidoceans' at line 41 and 'Assyrian' at line 46 below.

38 *my new buildings*: Leadenhall; cf. 21.129 ff.

41 *Cappidoceans*: another of Eyre's good-hearted (and meaningless) terms for his companions.

42 *served . . . Conduit*: i.e. gathered water for their masters during apprenticeship.

46 *pancake bell*: the church bell on Shrove Tuesdays.

[Scene 18].2 *bloods*: brotherhood.

4 *king of spades*: setting up the pun on *delve*.

delve in thy close: i.e. copulate with your wife.

5 *sufferance*: consent.

18 *Hammon nor hangman*: alluding to the Haman in the biblical Book of Esther who built a gallows for his enemy, Mordecai, and was hanged on it himself.

20 S.D. *others*: i.e. wedding attendants.

29 *Clubs*: the traditional cry of apprentices when uniting for (violent) action.

33 *bird-spits*: a mocking reference to the slim rapiers worn by gentlemen.

   steel . . . back: proverbial for courageousness (Dent S842).

38 *look not strange*: don't look at him as if he were a stranger.

45 *pack*: take yourself.

57 *affect*: love.

61 *his attire*: i.e. the wedding clothes Hammon bought for Jane.

66 *busk-point*: lace for tying a bodice, i.e. the part of her clothing of the least value.

67 *appurtenances*: rights to the property (that comes with Jane).

70 *Bluecoat*: blue was the traditional colour of servants' livery.

71 *Shrove . . . day*: i.e. turn a traditional day of feasting to 23 April, the day when servants sought new employment, and thus would be in a needy position (and change their livery). This reference reveals why so many apprentices are not working—Shrove Tuesday was a holiday for them.

72 *For*: for the sake of.

73 *sheep's eye*: amorous look; proverbial (Dent S323).

75 *no striving*: no use in resisting.

86 *commodity*: profit.

90 *pelf*: ill-earned money.

101 *mask*: frequently worn by women in the period as protection against the sun.

107 *Mars in Venus*: a bawdy, mock-astrological reference to the affair had by Venus and Mars in classical mythology.

119 *I'll his . . . cure*: Lincoln probably takes away Ralph's crutch or pushes him.

120 *Lie . . . laugh*: i.e. roll over with laughter; proverbial (Dent L92).

121 *Damask*: a variety of rose.

125 *powers*: troops.

143 *base . . . mean*: Firk puns on the musical bass and middle ranges.

146 *laced mutton*: slang for prostitute, but here used for Jane because it sounds like 'Lacy'.

148 *journeyman villain*: i.e. villain who journeys (and is liable to prosecution as a vagrant).

154 *officers*: City officers, those who could enforce the Mayor's authority.

158 *stand*: Firk puns on stand as 'grow erect'.

160 *his Grace*: the King.

168 *lammed . . . flouts*: beat them with insults.

169 *point*: lace holding the codpiece together.

172 *answered*: settled.

175 *Madge*: presumably a servant, and not Eyre's wife.

177 *meat*: food.

184 *Keep in*: lock up.

190 *brave*: fine.

195 *comes*: the singular inflection with a plural subject was common usage in the period.

    dry vats: barrels for dry goods.

197 *scuttles*: dishes.

198 *malt shovels*: large shovels used for malt.

    S.D. *Enter more Prentices*: this indicates that the 'five or six shoemakers' who enter at the beginning of the scene are apprentices.

205 *incomprehensible*: infinite.

208 *year of jubilee*: annual holiday.

[Scene 19] S.D. *pass over the stage*: i.e. walk across the stage.

  6 *state*: position as mayor.

 10 *with child*: in suspense; proverbial (Dent C317).

    huff cap: swash-buckler.

 11 *all my doubt is*: my only apprehension is.

[Scene 20] S.D. *napkins . . . shoulders*: indicating that they are enjoying a meal.

  2 *cannibals*: another of Eyre's flamboyant names for those who serve him.

  4 *livery . . . company*: those wearing the livery of shoemakers.

  9 *lamb-skins*: purses.

 10 *Rip*: make haste.

 14 *Avoid*: move.

 15 *Carouse . . . healths*: i.e. drink deeply.

 18 *meat*: food.

 22 *shambles*: meat-selling stalls.

 23 *chargers*: serving dishes.

 40 *grace*: favour.

46 *Islington whitepot*: a kind of custard or milk-pudding, eaten on excursions to the rural village Islington.

  hopper-arse: large-buttocks.

47 *barley-pudding*: a kind of sausage.

  broiled carbonado: meat that has been scored and grilled.

48 *Mephistophilus*: the devil dramatized in Marlowe's popular *Dr Faustus* (1592).

49 *Mother Miniver-Cap*: presumably Margery is wearing an expensive ermine-trimmed cap.

51 *flews*: flaps.

52 *Sultan Soliman . . . Tamburlaine*: bombastic Middle Eastern conquerers dramatized in the *c.*1590 play *Soliman and Perseda* and Marlowe's 1587 *Tamburlaine the Great*.

55 *free-booters*: pirates (with a shoemaking pun).

[Scene 21].1 *fact*: deed. Desertion was a capital offence.

10 *craft*: guile.

15 *Diocletian*: a Roman (tyrannical) emperor, of the type that Eyre frequently mentions.

  hump: an interjection used throughout the scene; it perhaps indicates some celebratory stage action here, such as having a drink.

17 *merry . . . pie*: 'merry as a (magpie)' was proverbial (Dent P281).

22 *king . . . ransom*: i.e. a king's ransom.

  Tamar Cham's beard: this ruler of China was the subject of a now lost 1596 play; he was probably staged with an unusual beard.

29 *get*: beget.

32 *Apollo*: in classical mythology, the god of music and poetry, and usually associated with the sun. He also represented perfect male beauty.

39 *spend*: give up.

44 *degenerous*: degenerate.

53 *want*: lack.

64 *bands*: bonds.

87 *bride*: spouse, 'bride' was used for both sexes.

102 *love . . . blood*: cf. the proverb 'love has no respect of persons' (Dent L505).

129 *Leaden Hall*: the building was still standing and familiar to Elizabethans as Eyre's most important benefaction to London.

140 *Sometimes*: once.

141 *merry . . . emperor*: 'merry as a king' was proverbial (Dent K54).

163 *banquet*: the word could be used for the dessert at the end of a meal.

169 *I promised*: cf. 17.41–4.

172 *coat . . . back*: proverbial for 'it hasn't hurt me at all' (Dent C472.11).

ADDITIONAL PASSAGES

A. Prologue

4 *goddess*: i.e. the Queen.

8 *strike*: lower.

15 *chastity*: the unmarried Elizabeth was frequently praised for this virtue.

16 *life-breathing*: i.e. 'live-giving.'

B. Songs

The First Three-Man's Song

8 *her breast . . . briar*: nightingales were held to sing in sorrow with a thorn pressed into their breasts.

9 *cuckoo*: a bird traditionally associated with cuckoldry because it lays its eggs in other birds' nests.

The Second Three-Man's Song

1 *latter end*: possibly the latter half of the play, but the precise meaning of this instruction is now lost.

3 *Saint Hugh*: patron saint of shoemakers.

6 *Troll the bowl*: pass the bowl around.

 nut-brown: the colour of ale.

11 S.D. *close . . . tenor boy*: i.e. a young tenor should sing the next two lines on his own.

13 *Ring compass*: i.e. exceed measure.

APPENDIX

2 *professors*: those belonging to the profession.

 Gentle Craft: the traditional name for the shoemaking trade.

5 *conceited*: full of conceits, or entertaining devices.

6 *Lord Admiral's Players*: one of the principal theatrical companies in London performing at the Rose Theatre and at court.

9 *argument*: plot summary.

17 *accidents*: events.

18 *three man's songs*: songs for three male voices.

20 *Mirth . . . life*: 'a merry heart lives long' was proverbial (Dent H320a).

Eastward Ho

THE PERSONS OF THE PLAY

Touchstone: a stone used for determining the quality of gold, by the colour of the streak produced when gold is rubbed against it. Goldsmiths were among the most wealthy of the London artisans.

Quicksilver: mercury, used to treat venereal disease.

Sir Petronel Flash: a *petronel* was a kind of large pistol, and *flash* points to the bright light of ignited gunpowder. The name suggests attracting, through noise and show, a lot of attention to oneself.

Security: property made over to secure a loan.

Sindefy: suggesting either defiant sinfulness or (ironically) the ability to defy sin.

Bramble: a thorny shrub, suggesting legal entanglement.

Poldavy: a coarse canvas cloth used for sails.

Hamlet: alluding to Shakespeare's tragic hero.

Potkin: a small pot.

THE PROLOGUE

5 *That . . . title*: the play *Westward Ho*, by Thomas Dekker and John Webster, was performed in 1604.

8 *God . . . even*: i.e. God give you good evening. This alludes to the uninformative titles of other plays, such as *As You Like It*.

11 *Nor . . . enforced*: i.e. the play's action does not move eastward only.

[1.1] S.D. *several*: separate.

trussed: tied.

discovering: revealing. The 'middle door' probably had a curtain in front of it which could be drawn to reveal an inner recess.

1 *whither . . . you*: i.e. where are you going.

9 *furniture*: provisions, equipment.

12 *Work . . . now*: Touchstone's catchphrase, meaning, 'you better consider that', usually said as an admonishment.

13 *with*: in keeping with.

17 *though . . . alderman*: aldermen had the right to wear honorary cloaks. Quicksilver is not wearing such a cloak, but Touchstone is suggesting that only aldermen should normally be subjected to divestment (when they give up office).

18 *Ruffians' Hall*: a field in Smithfield known as a meeting place for duels.

  racket: (a) tennis racket; (b) uproar (caused by disorderly conduct).

21 *indentures*: contracts of apprenticeship.

23 *quorum*: a higher ranking justice of the peace whose presence was necessary to constitute a bench for ruling.

25 *lid*: eyelid.

  commodity: profit.

29 *fly*: i.e. be sold.

30 *refusal*: initial opportunity to purchase.

32 *humours*: fancies.

34 *cunning secondings*: knowledgeable assistance or companionship.

35 *I am going*: suppose I am going.

  ordinary: tavern.

36 *light gold*: coins of a reduced weight.

45 *as*: like.

46 *keep . . . thee*: i.e. look after your shop, and it will be profitable enough to support you. Proverbial (Dent S392).

47 *Light . . . purses*: i.e. small profit margins lead to greater returns in the long term. Proverbial (Dent G7).

  'Tis . . . wise: proverbial (Dent G324).

48 *horn of suretyship*: an emblem of the period showed a man being forced through a horn and coming bedraggled out of the mouthpiece. This was meant to show the consequences of suretyship, or guaranteeing other people's loans (H&S).

51 *buccal*: mouthpiece of the horn.

52 *bear . . . high*: i.e. am just as important.

53 *bond*: obligation to pay debt (for your indenture).

  lies: is deposited.

54 *in the rear*: in arrears.

57 *socks*: light shoes.

60 *What do ye lack*: the trader's traditional call for customers.

63 *better meaned*: of better (financial) means.

  pump it: i.e. wear pumps.

64 *bavins*: bundles of brushwood used to light fires (and thus, highly transitory). Cf. the proverb, 'The bavin burns bright but it is but a blaze' (Dent B107).

75 *nice*: (a) lascivious; (b) 'refined'.

78 *court-cut . . . tail*: fashionable courtly attire with long trains; *tail* also means 'penis' in this context. 'Cut and longtail' was proverbial for 'of all kinds' (Dent C938), so there is the additional implication that Gertrude will be attracted to *any* man in the court.

ill natured: i.e. opposed.

90 *foh*: an exclamation of disgust.

flatcap: unfashionable round cap with a low, flat crown, as worn by merchants. Cf. 'low-capped' at 1.2.3.

91 *give arms*: deliver my coat of arms (the sign of gentlemanly rank).

96 *goodfellow*: jovial companion, reveller.

97 *let . . . Erebus also*: recalling Pistol in Shakespeare's *2 Henry IV*, 2.4.165–6. *Erebus* is the mythological place of darkness between Earth and Hades.

Don Phoebus: the sun.

100 *Eos*: the goddess of dawn.

102 *bully*: good friend.

103 *satin-belly . . . canvas-backed*: implying that he puts on a showy front to disguise his baseness.

104 *sold gingerbread*: not considered a noble occupation. Cf. Joan Trash, the gingerbread-seller in Jonson's *Bartholomew Fair*.

Christ Church: the parish of Christ Church contained a monastery before the Reformation. It was not a disreputable place.

108 *make . . . shillings*: skip shillings (12 pence coins) across water like stones; proverbial for wasting money (Dent D632).

109 *pate*: head.

110 *penthouse*: shop awning.

bear tankards: apprentices had to carry water (in tankards) from wells to their masters' shops; cf. *SH* 17.42, where Eyre describes how he 'served at the Conduit' as an apprentice.

111 *Be ruled*: i.e. listen to me.

112 *Ta ly . . . re, ro*: Quicksilver sings a little to show his carefree attitude.

Who . . . I am: a line from Thomas Kyd's popular 1587 play, *The Spanish Tragedy*.

118 *in soft terms*: i.e. even put respectfully.

120 *Untruss me*: i.e. let me go.

121 *undo*: ruin, but also punning on *untruss* as 'unfasten'.

122 *shot-clog*: an unwelcome companion tolerated because he pays the shot (buys the round) for the rest.

123 *Moorfields*: fields north of the City, frequented by beggars.

124 *band*: collar.

 doublet . . . buttons: doublets, or close fitting jackets, typically had many buttons in the period.

125 *point*: lace (for tying).

 cudgel: because unable to afford the rapier that he currently wears.

127 *take this . . . all*: if you take this (my sword), you might as well take everything that I have. Losing one's sword was considered a great dishonour to a gentleman.

129 *recover*: mend.

[1.2] S.D. *fair gown . . . attire*: all of these garments suggest social aspiration. A *fair gown* is a 'beautiful' one, a *Scotch farthingale* is a hooped petticoat, a *French fall* is a collar worn flat round the neck, and *French head attire* is some form of fashionable head-dress.

 S.D. *monkey*: monkeys were popular pets.

5 *medam*: 'madam' given a pseudo-sophisticated pronunciation.

7 *cut*: style.

 in any hand: by no means.

 pax: i.e. pox, or syphilis (a mild oath).

9 *Thus . . . sake*: a line from John Dowland's song, 'Sleep Wayward Thoughts' in *First Book of Songs or Airs* (1597).

11 *tire*: attire.

12 *that*: i.e. the trader's lifestyle.

15 *coif . . . licket*: small cap with a ribbon (to tie it) of the London fashion.

16 *stammel . . . guards*: a petticoat made of coarse woollen cloth and having only two pieces of decorative trim.

 buffin: an inexpensive cloth.

 tuftaffety: a (luxurious) taffeta having designs formed by a raised nap.

17 *humours*: whims.

18 *angel*: approximately ten shillings, a dear price at the time.

19 *scarlet*: a rich cloth, often red in colour.

 grogram: grosgrain, a coarse fabric of silk.

20 *pure*: clean.

 smocks: women's undergarments.

22 *niceries*: niceties.

22 *pipkins*: 'small French hats with a large crown pleated into a narrow brim', M. Channing Linthicum, *Costume in the Drama of Shakespeare and His Contemporaries* (Oxford, 1936).

durance: a stout durable cloth.

bodkins: long pins used by women to fasten up hair.

24 *long*: i.e. late.

25 *shout home*: i.e. ejaculate.

longer: (a) with more staying power; (b) with a longer penis.

28 *those . . . wing*: this maxim sounds proverbial, but is not recorded elsewhere.

29 *Bow-bell*: i.e. someone born within the sound of St Mary-le-Bow church bells, in Cheapside, and so a true Londoner. To be 'born within the sound of Bow bell' was proverbial (Dent S671).

35 *Ulysses . . . dogs*: Mildred is mistaken; Ulysses yoked an ass and an ox.

42 *like*: likely.

44 *doubled*: i.e. repeated a line. There is an additional suggestion of sexual coupling.

46 *Lady's*: Our Lady (the Virgin Mary) is.

ape's: fool is.

47 *Scot*: i.e. Scotch farthingale.

48 *clip . . . round*: i.e. fit snugly and keep itself up with fullness.

51 *steel instrument*: (a) needle; (b) penis.

55 *members*: with a suggestion of member as 'penis', as at line 81 below.

go upright: suggesting 'grow erect'.

56 *Light*: nimbly, quickly.

58 *light*: wantonly, unchastely.

59 S.D. *trips about*: moves nimbly around.

61 *false gallop*: canter; the phrase also suggests the artificiality of courtliness.

64 *band*: collar (which has not been put on yet).

74 *country lady*: lady of the landed gentry.

76 *progress*: state procession.

77 *balloon*: a game played with a large leather ball, struck back and forth by a piece of wood attached to the arm.

78 *crowns*: worth five shillings, so four of them made up a pound. This was a large sum to wager, and Sir Petronel is trying to establish his courtliness by mentioning this bet with his titled companions.

79 *baboon*: Gertrude obviously has no idea what 'balloon' is, mishearing it as 'baboon', yet she thinks that it must be the height of courtly sophistication.

337

87 *hundred . . . land*: land worth £100 per annum.

95 *pay . . . fees*: i.e. to buy his knighthood, an objectionable practice in James's reign.

98 *And*: if.

99 *dubbed you*: given you a new title.

103 *place of*: precedence over.

108 *take the wall*: walking nearer to the wall than someone else (to escape the muck of the street) was an assertion of superiority. Gertrude comically applies the distinction to animals.

110 *solemnity*: ceremony.

114 *better-traded*: with established positions in trade.

115 *Body o' truth*: a mild oath.

Chitizens: another example of Gertrude mispronouncing a word in order to sound sophisticated.

117 *Newcastle coal*: coal was brought to London from Newcastle, a place proverbially associated with coal production (Dent C466).

118 *down with me*: i.e. (a) take me to the country; (b) take me down for sex.

121 *The greatest . . . springs*: proverbial: 'Little brooks make great rivers' (Dent B681).

123 *He . . . athirst*: 'ever drunk ever dry' was proverbial (Dent D625).

135 *big*: grand (said ironically).

137 *elephant . . . castle*: punning on the howdahs, or fortifications, carried by elephants in India. Golding suggests that Petronel might own no more than his courtly clothes.

144 *indifferent*: average, middle of the road.

146 *which . . . suspect her*: i.e. because she is only moderately pretty, you will not need to make sure that other men keep away, nor is she so ugly that she will welcome advances from anyone.

towardly: full of promise.

148 *give . . . thine*: joining hands (usually the couple's) in this way constituted a formal betrothal called 'handfasting'.

153 *somewhat to take to*: something to lay hold of (as a means of subsistence).

154 *well-parted*: i.e. with good 'parts', or abilities.

159 *Lip*: kiss.

163 *mean*: modest, lowly.

166 *'tis . . . expense*: i.e. it is a good use of time.

167 *seeming lightness*: apparent whimsicalness.

[2.1] s.d. *Golding ... stall*: the *stall* is probably a small booth or table with goods for sale upon it, possibly brought on stage by Golding and Mildred before they sit down.

3 *Ump*: Quicksilver is drunkenly hiccuping.

5 *familiar addition*: i.e. a Christian or first name as used by acquaintances. Quicksilver answers only to the most formal mode of address, 'Master Quicksilver', without the 'Francis'.

6 *truss ... points*: tie the laces on my clothing.

11 *cause natural*: alluding to the 'Natural' Philosophy of Aristotle, in which everything has four causes, the efficient, formal, material, and final causes.

19 *coming off ... coming on*: suggesting wedding-night sexual intercourse.

21 *coming off ... soldier*: militarily, to 'come off' is to leave the field of combat, often with victory or honour, as Quicksilver suggests here.

25 *the scripture*: Isaiah 5: 11: 'Woe unto them, that rise up early to follow drunkenness, and to them that continue until night, 'til the wine do inflame them.'

27 *o' ... knees*: i.e. drinking healths on their knees.

31 *separated crew*: i.e. separated from the common citizens.

40 *waked*: kept awake.

43 *conduit*: where servants collected water and gossiped.

46 *we lose ... amends for it*: i.e. for all of the time our sensuality loses by not drinking, we make up for it later through intemperance.

47 *see, here*: Touchstone indicates Golding and Mildred.

48 *parcels*: i.e. individuals.

50 *preferred*: advanced.

54 *gowns ... colours*: i.e. the fool's motley.

57 *observation*: honour.

58 *convenience*: suitability.

63 *stay*: rest.

65 *go*: walk.

80 *ill-yoked*: unfastened, dishevelled.

   s.d. *unlaced*: with his clothing unfastened.

81 *Holla ... Asia*: a bombastic line from Christopher Marlowe's *Tamburlaine the Great Part II*.

83 *Pulldo, pulldo*: the meaning of this has not been determined; in any case it primarily serves to indicate Quicksilver's intoxication.

   Showse: i.e. bang.

85 *what a pickle*: i.e. what a sorry plight. 'To be in a pickle' was proverbial (Dent P276).

86 *Pickle . . . throat*: i.e. you lie, from the phrase 'you lie in thy throat'.

87 *Wahahowe*: the falconer's cry to a hawk.

88 *counterbuff*: counter-blow. To be struck and not return the blow was a grave disparagement to the honour of a gentleman. Here the term suggests the sexual exchanges of the newlyweds.

91 *jolthead*: blockhead.

92 *Go to*: a common expression of derision.

96 *credit*: (a) financial assets; (b) reputation.

101 *Hast . . . here*: a line probably originating in George Peele's lost play, *The Turkish Mahamet and Hyrin the Fair Greek* (*c.*1594). *Hiren* came to mean 'a harlot'.

103 *vein's this*: humour or mood is this.

104 *Who . . . you*: a line quoted in other plays in the period, including Jonson's *Poetaster*. It probably comes originally from a work now lost.

111 *what . . . out*: what you lack.

114 *go westward ho*: i.e. to the gallows at Tyburn.

115 *dishonest*: bring disgrace upon.

   stock: (a) possessions; (b) kindred.

116 *licence*: lack of restraint.

121 *Rent*: wages.

122 *Fly . . . mouth*: the phrase refers to money that has been invested and comes back with interest. Quicksilver suggests that he will live by his own means.

126 *change . . . play ends*: i.e. exchange remnants of gold for pieces of plays.

130 *When . . . my name*: Quicksilver slightly misquotes Don Andrea's opening lines from *The Spanish Tragedy*.

142 *portion*: dowry.

153 *states*: persons of high rank or dignity.

   reverent: reverend.

156 *fondling*: fool.

   Sir-reverence: a polite phrase meaning, 'with all respect for', but mocking in this context.

157 *handsel*: inaugurate.

[2.2].2 *bride-bowl*: bride-cup, a bowl of drink passed at wedding celebrations.

   3 *in . . . likeness*: more like a gallant.

5 *vails*: occasional profits in addition to his salary.

6 *in . . . similitude*: i.e. like a prodigal.

10 *indented sheepskin*: contract of apprenticeship. Legal documents were written on vellum, which is made from animal skin. There is also a suggestion of Quicksilver having been a wolf in sheep's clothing.

14 *ka me, ka thee*: i.e. I'll do for you what you do for me; proverbial (Dent K1).

15 *K's*: 'key' and 'Ka' were pronounced 'kay'.

18 *Hob*: a generic name for a rustic.

hobnails: short nails used in the soles of boots.

21 *London . . . thrift*: quickest road to profit.

22 *scrap*: bait.

23 *use . . . thrive simply*: practice virtue for its own sake, live poorly.

24 *Weight . . . cuckolds*: i.e. their time spent in weighing and fashioning gold allows their wives to be with other partners.

26 *bravery*: fine clothes.

27 *trunks*: (a) chests of clothing; (b) pea-shooters (H&S).

30 *Via*: away!

shadowed Borgia: disguised (Cesare) Borgia. The source of this allusion has not been traced. Van Fossen suggests that it points to Borgia's disguising himself as a stable boy to escape from Charles VIII of France. Cf. R. W. Van Fossen (ed.), *Eastward Ho* (Manchester and New York, 1979). Quicksilver probably throws off his apprentice's cloak here, just as he removed his cap during the previous line.

33 *Samson . . . Dalida*: in the Bible Dalida betrays Samson to his enemies by cutting off his hair, the source of his prodigious strength, when he is asleep on her lap (Judges 16). *Dalida* is the form for 'Dalila' in the Greek translation of the Old Testament.

36 *When . . . then*: lines from a popular ballad.

43 *Dad*: i.e. old father.

dressed: groomed.

44 *Cock*: a common tavern name.

45 *dressed . . . breakfast*: punning on *dress* as 'to prepare for use as food', and the sense that the ostler groomed the horse in order to be finished with his duties before breakfast.

51 *all this*: i.e. this lifestyle.

58 *tennis balls*: Quicksilver refers to real tennis, a game played indoors, with rules similar to lawn tennis and in which balls rebound off irregularly shaped walls.

60 *under-line*: under the level of the sea. This probably also refers to the line supporting the net that stretches across a real tennis court.

the house: the penthouse, a sloped roof connecting inner and outer walls of the court. The ball is not out of play if hit *over the house*, but this fits Quicksilver's suggestion of the up and down pitch of a boat on rough seas.

brick-walled: bounced against the wall with unusual spin to be propelled towards an opponent.

61 *guts*: (a) stuffing of a ball; (b) contents of a ship.

62 *hazard*: the walls of real tennis courts have holes called *hazards*. A ball struck into a hazard scores a point, while hitting the area under the hazard forfeits a point.

73 *trencher-bearer*: i.e. waiter. A trencher is a wooden plate.

74 *intelligence*: information gathering.

75 *rules . . . roost*: has control; proverbial (Dent R144).

77 *close stool*: a chamber pot enclosed in a stool or box.

82 *long of*: on account of, owing to.

88 *wooden wall*: i.e. ship's hull.

91 *thirty . . . hundred*: these rates were considered exorbitant usury in the period.

103 *forget themselves*: i.e. rain too heavily.

104 *falls out*: happens to be.

107 *falls . . . joint*: he becomes disordered.

Where: whereas.

111 *so*: so that.

116 *we . . . wings*: proverbial (Dent F407).

117 *scurvy phrases*: despicable sayings.

124 *entire*: containing all that is desirable.

127 *prick*: the pin in the centre of a target.

128 *your farmer*: i.e. the farmer of that land; *your* is used here for rhetorical effect.

138 *out of doors*: i.e. inappropriately. The phrase also literally suggests 'for that which does not belong in my household'.

141 *frame*: scheme, plan.

closely: secretly.

146 *frank*: steady.

148 *competent*: adequate.

150 *seal*: endorse the contract with her seal.

152 *engines*: devices, plots.

156 *toward*: disposed to.

157 *devices*: chat.

163 *fashionable*: (a) stylish; (b) capable of manipulating.

164 *as . . . her*: it's as good if she spoil the lady, or the lady spoil her.

 'tis . . . one: i.e. the odds are three to one.

169 *festination*: haste.

 broken . . . to it: started it. 'To break the ice' was proverbial (Dent I3).

171 *man*: escort.

175 *Cu*: a nick-name for Security.

179 *all . . . do*: make a whinnying sound.

182 *Jew's trump*: another name for a Jew's harp, here meaning 'usurer'.

187 S.D. *wand*: switch, used like a modern riding crop.

190 *ordinaries*: taverns with fixed-price meals.

 blown up: ruined.

 stand: standstill.

191 *houses of hospitality*: inns.

 feather . . . spur: feathered hats and spurs were worn by gallants.

196 *castles . . . air*: 'to build castles in the air' was proverbial (Dent C126).

201 *full butt*: head-first.

209 *approve*: prove.

210 *crupper*: hind-quarters (of a horse).

214 *ability*: resources.

215 *blood*: passion, mood.

 humours: whims.

217 *commodity*: goods (taken on at an inflated value and then sold back to the usurer at a loss).

221 *frail*: (a) transient; (b) packed in fruit baskets called 'frails'.

223 *pound*: pounds sterling.

225 *stomach to*: desire for (with obvious pun).

227 *laid*: set a trap, or watch.

229 *sureties*: bonds given to secure a payment. Quicksilver puns on the additional sense 'conditions of safety or security' (i.e. in prison).

231 *King's Bench . . . Counters*: London prisons.

234 *present money*: ready money.

236 *earnest*: punning on *earnest* as 'money paid as an instalment, especially for securing a bargain or contract'.

239 *There . . . angel*: proverbial (Dent A242).

242 *foisting*: farting.

243 *You . . . ear*: i.e. that's the right way to proceed; proverbial (Dent S684).

245 *long*: Quicksilver develops a pun on women's 'longings' or cravings during pregnancy.

248 *charge . . . humour*: expense and shifting of whims.

249 *tackling*: genitals.

250 *turnspit dog*: dog on a treadmill that turns a spit of roasting meat.

251 *wheel*: i.e. vagina.

257 *cunning women*: women with secret or magical knowledge.

260 *let . . . blood*: blood was let for medicinal purposes.

263 *mark*: worth ⅔ of a pound.

264 *Scotch knight*: shortly after King James of Scotland became King of England in 1603, he created many new knights among his countrymen and so devalued the rank.

265 *never . . . married him*: under certain circumstances, Scottish law recognized as man and wife couples who had not undertaken the formal marriage ceremony.

poinados: small daggers, or poniards (suggesting 'penises').

266 *pull you down*: make you detumescent.

268 *Out of*: i.e. out upon.

269 *large*: generous.

time-fitted: befitting the times.

270 *form*: bench.

271 *painted*: artificial. Students could literally be chained to desks in the period.

272 *ne'er . . . me*: no less remote from my advances (because she is married).

273 *Thereby . . . tale*: proverbial (Dent T48), and punning on *tail* as 'pudendum'.

275 *entertain for*: employ as.

280 *bravery*: fine clothing.

291 *You . . . hat yet*: Gertrude, instead of politely requesting that Security put his hat on (after doffing it in respect), tells him to keep it off.

298 *honest humours*: flighty notions of being chaste.

300 *nun substantive . . . adjective*: i.e. a real nun, or a woman who is like a 'nun' (as in 'prostitute'); *substantive* = noun.

302 *maid . . . order*: (a) a maid who follows commands; (b) a maid who associates with ladies of rank.

306 *hold up . . . head*: Sindefy has been feigning modesty.

313 *draw . . . bow*: place my servants at my power; proverbial (Dent B565).

314 *put me riddles*: put riddles to me.

330 *burr*: in general senses, 'a ring or circle', here meaning 'vagina'.

335 *medicine*: treatment (for any desire to stay married).

339 *In policy . . . sealed*: i.e. it is cunning for Sir Petronel to obey her, until tomorrow when she has signed away her property.

3.1.3 *amends*: reciprocity.

11 *gossip*: godfather.

15 *event*: the outcome.

17 *wedlock*: wife.

Make . . . strange of: do you show distant or cold demeanour towards.

33 *foreright*: straight in the line of the course, favourable.

41 *their . . . dangerous*: suggesting that they are fleeing from the law.

42 *colonel*: used figuratively; Sir Petronel is not a military officer.

45 *Billingsgate*: ward around Billingsgate, a watergate from the Thames situated between London Bridge and the Custom House. It was known for its taverns and as an important departure point for foreign travellers.

47 *expedition*: promptness.

49 *carried closely*: kept secret.

52 *attached*: confiscated.

56 *take . . . vantage*: make the most of the opportunity.

61 *crowns*: gold coins worth ¼ of a pound.

[3.2] S.D. *feeding*: eating.

5 S.D. *tankard-bearer*: water-carrier, cf. Cob in *EMI*.

7 *brush . . . mistress*: i.e. brush Mistress Touchstone's clothes (to clean them).

9 *blue coat*: the servant's uniform.

14 *last day*: yesterday.

23 *come away*: come straightaway.

30 *long*: referring to 'longings', or strong cravings incident to pregnancy.

31 *afore . . . married*: the wedding took place between Acts 1 and 2, yet Gertrude could be suggesting that she has not been married for long enough to experience the longings of a legitimate pregnancy.

34 *prick*: (a) wound; (b) penis.

35 *ancome*: boil; also suggesting the *swell* of an erection.

36 *cases*: punning on *case* as 'vagina'.

41 *higher . . . fire*: misquoted from the song, 'Mistress, Since You So Much Desire', printed in Thomas Campion's *Booke of Ayres* (1601). The lines suggest increasing penetration during sexual intercourse.

44 *gives . . . milk*: has no other use. But *milk* here could be used figuratively for *semen*, making the other servant's employment a sexual one.

48 *ease*: relieve.

60 *in . . . haste*: in all haste.

61 *cold meat . . . table*: like 2.1.150–1, but more directly, an allusion to *Hamlet*, 'The funeral baked meats | Did coldly furnish forth the marriage tables' (1.2.179–80).

74 *clapped what-d'-ye-call-'ts*: i.e. put our genitals together, had intercourse.

82 *God . . . labour*: i.e. God give support to your labour. This and the song before it suggests that Quicksilver has enjoyed, but will have no more, sexual favours from Gertrude.

83 S.D. *rosemary*: associated with wedding ceremonies as an emblem of remembrance.

85 *God's my precious*: from 'by God's precious (blood)', a mild oath.

86 *What-lack-you*: the trader's call for custom.

87 *taffeta hat*: Gertrude had disparaged taffeta 'pipkins' at 1.2.22.

89 *countenance*: favour, patronage.

96 *by heraldry*: by the rules of heraldry.

97 *misproud*: wrongly proud.

108 *Master me*: call me 'master'.

113 *stand . . . gentry*: insist upon your status as a gentleman.

114 *arms*: coat of arms.

124 *natural*: (a) innate, born; (b) fool.

127 *set*: preconceived, not spontaneous.

128 *Cry you mercy*: beg your pardon.

133 *gallantry indeed*: in a true (as opposed to mock) gallant style.

134 *save . . . broth*: 'Save your breath to cool your broth' was proverbial for keeping quiet (Dent W422).

144 *Now . . . move*: more misquoted lines from a song in Dowland's *The First Book of Songs or Airs* (1597).

145 *in capital letters*: prominently.

151 *lie . . . side*: i.e. stem from that feeling.

154 *girdlestead*: waist. Once again there is a suggestion that Gertrude is interested in only the nether regions of men.

162 *hand*: signature.

170 *It . . . chewing*: i.e. she swallowed the explanation easily.

177 *take thee down*: (a) bring you with me; (b) take you down for sexual intercourse.

182 *vagary*: excursion, ramble.

186 *rid . . . coach*: pointing to the illicit sex that coaches facilitated.

195 *compeer*: companion.

207 *secretary*: one entrusted with secrets.

224 *to . . . nerve*: to the best of my ability.

225 *friend*: paramour.

228 *in . . . neighbourhood*: as a gesture of neighbourliness.

241 *enlargement*: release from confinement.

242 *pithy*: vigorous, strong.

244 *point-device*: something coming near the point of perfection.

245 *Draco*: Sir Francis Drake, whose *Golden Hind* had circumnavigated the world in 1580.

247 *compassing . . . world*: any of these senses could apply: (a) embracing the lady; (b) encircling Bramble; (b) circumnavigating the world.
 himself: itself.
 it: i.e. the world.

251 *fork*: suggesting the cuckold's horns.

257 *over-reached*: exceeded, outwitted.
 over-reaching: deception.

259 *watch . . . exit*: discover the exact time to arrive (at Bramble's house) as he is leaving.

265 *outreacheth*: outmatches (in intellect).

266 *rampant*: i.e. that stands tall.
 very quiblin: matchless trick.

267 *pitch . . . lawyers*: use lawyers (as pitchforks) to load carts.

269 *apes*: imitators.

270 *honeyed*: coaxed, delighted.

275 *Upon this sudden*: at this instant.

281 *figent*: restless, volatile.

286 *mutton*: slang for 'prostitute'.

347

291 *Cast . . . away*: i.e. forget your worries. Proverbial (Dent C87.13).

298 *gird*: jest or gibe at.

299 *policy*: a crafty device.

301 *abroad*: (for going) abroad.

302 *a quirk*: a sudden turn.

    firk: cheat.

304 *furnish*: supply.

308 *devil . . . lawyer*: alluding to the medieval story of the devil carrying off a lawyer, because the townspeople really meant it when they said 'Devil take you' to him (H&S).

311 *toy*: whim.

319 *cracked*: damaged, flawed.

321 *fetched*: deceived.

[3.3] S.D. *in the tavern*: i.e. the stage scene represents a tavern location.

    S.D. *Drawer*: tapster, barman.

  1 *neatest hogsheads*: purest barrels.

  9 *pewter coats*: i.e. armour. Drinking vessels were commonly made of pewter.

14 *her maidenhead*: humour based on the first two syllables of Virginia, named after the virgin Queen Elizabeth.

20 *A whole . . . feet*: Seacoal's description is inaccurate, as the earliest English settlers arrived in 1585 and there were no English in Virginia in 1605, after the disappearance of the 1587 colony.

25 *dripping pans*: pans that catch dripping fat from roasting meat.

27 *chain . . . streets*: chains were used as barriers in the period to obstruct streets.

30 *saffron gilt*: saffron-coloured (to resemble gold).

36 *intelligencers*: spies.

44 *preposterously*: perversely.

45 *scavenger*: street cleaner.

49 *indifferent*: fairly.

51 *Cape Finisterre*: at the north-western tip of Spain.

60 *both . . . knee*: with cap off and kneeling (a common way to give a toast).

66 *hit . . . one*: i.e. used Security's favourite phrase.

67 *from . . . forehead*: i.e. from head to toe, with a suggestion of the cuckold's horns that appear on the forehead.

73 *tall*: brave.

78 *prick*: thorn (but also suggesting 'penis').

81 *supporters*: i.e. knees.

notorious: memorable.

90 *mask*: commonly worn by women in the period.

100 *His learning*: i.e. Bramble.

104 *Cuckold's Haven*: undeveloped area on the south bank of the Thames, 1 mile east of London Bridge.

105 *gone round*: i.e. been pledged by everyone.

107 *toward*: promising.

108 *fatally*: unfortunately.

117 *earns*: grieves.

abused: deceived, wronged.

118 *respected*: heeded.

121 *withered*: punning on 'made detumescent'.

123 *watermen*: boatmen who carried passengers on the Thames.

124 *flood . . . hours*: flood tide (on the Thames) for the next three hours.

129 *Blackwall*: busy seaport 4 miles east of St Paul's.

132 *of all*: by all.

135 *aboard . . . ship*: the *Golden Hind* was preserved after its 1579 journey and used as a place of entertainment.

136 *banquets*: dainty dishes.

137 *My . . . me*: i.e. I think.

138 *desert . . . her*: i.e. the empty ribs of the ship.

139 *orgies*: rites.

141 *Rarely conceited*: admirably contrived.

143 S.D. *compass in*: form a circle round.

154 *admiration*: wonder.

159 *Cucullus . . . monachum*: 'the cowl makes not the monk'; proverbial (Dent H583).

168 *charge*: command, order.

170 *proper taking*: good condition.

172 *drunken . . . harm*: proverbial (Dent M94).

[3.4].2 *gadfly*: person who is constantly gadding (wandering) about.

5 *A boat . . . boat*: parodying Shakespeare's *Richard III*, 'A horse! A horse! My kingdom for a horse!' (5.7.7).

[4.1] S.D. *ox horns*: a pair of ox horns situated atop a pillar was a local landmark at Cuckold's Haven. The ox horns were emblematic of the cuckold's horns.

[4.1] S.D. *discovering . . . above*: revealing Cuckold's Haven in an upper gallery of the stage. Upper galleries were used as playing spaces and by the musicians.

3 *butcher*: butchers ensured that the pillar at Cuckold's Haven was kept in good repair.

East Cheap: a street known for its butchers.

4 *in . . . Luke*: the ox was St Luke's emblem, and his saint's day became associated with cuckolds (H&S).

5 *ensigns*: signs.

6 *tree*: pillar. It seems that Slitgut is indicating a stage pillar (either especially erected or a permanent part of the rear stage wall) which is to be taken as the famous pole of Cuckold's Haven.

all . . . leaves: perhaps referring to the 'fruit' of illicit sexual relations.

7 *crest . . . occupation*: the horns of cattle being emblematic of the slaughter and butchery of the trade.

Up then: Slitgut begins to climb at this point.

11 *coil*: tumult.

unjust: dishonest.

12 *curvets*: leaps about (usually said of a horse).

15 *runs against*: i.e. is pointed towards.

20 *recover*: reach.

next: nearest.

24 *wind*: breath.

27 S.D. *band*: collar.

30 *sea-mark*: notable place.

51 *Saint Katherine's*: a hospital just east of the Tower of London, about 1 mile from Cuckold's Haven.

53 *bravely*: handsomely.

54 *taking . . . clothes*: i.e. the lifting up of her skirts before sex.

56 *A pox of*: i.e. curse.

57 *Cry . . . mercy*: give thanks to God.

59 *well said*: i.e. well done.

where . . . fell in: just upriver from St Katherine's. The story that this place alludes to has not been discovered.

63 S.D. *the Drawer . . . before*: the drawer who was in the tavern in 3.3.

66 *fame*: reputation.

82 *shift you*: change your garments.

92 *resolve*: rest assured.

93   *nothing . . . discovery*: i.e. you will be discovered only if you wish it.

96   *hold*: bet.

     a-taking up: coming to shore.

97   *Wapping*: district on the north shore of the Thames just east of Saint Katherine's.

     sort: throng.

98   *gallows*: the gallows at Wapping where sea criminals were hanged at low water and left for the tide to drown.

100 *taken down*: i.e. after hanging.

104 *fatal*: unfortunate.

108 *frame of*: fashioning, contriving.

135 *elevation . . . pole*: angle of the north star, which can be used to determine latitude. (This also has an ironic suggestion of the pole at Cuckold's Haven).

     altitude . . . climate: referring to the idea that climate is determined by latitude.

137 *Englishmen . . . Frenchified*: cf. Jonson's parody of the 'Frenchified' English courtier in 'On English Monsieur': 'Would you beleeve, when you this Movnsievr see, | That his whole body should speak *french*, not he' (H&S viii.56).

145 *Monsieur . . . naufrage*: Sir Petronel's rough French translates to: 'Monsieur, would you please have pity on our great misfortunes? I am a poor English knight, who has suffered the misfortune of a castaway'.

148 *Oui . . . fortune*: 'Yes, monsieur, it is too true, but you know well we are all subject to fortune.'

150 *poor . . . Windsor*: military pensioner residing in the precincts of Windsor Castle.

153 *Isle o' Dogs*: a peninsula on the north bank of the Thames, opposite Greenwich.

157 *ken . . . weel*: know the man well (in a mock-Scottish accent).

158 *thirty-pound knights*: James I was lavish in bestowing titles, and this jibe suggests that knighthoods could be purchased for little money. Officially at this time, titles could not be purchased.

160 *grand day*: possibly a reference to James's ascension to the English throne, when many new knights were created.

     page: i.e. a lowly member of the King's household.

162 *overshot*: (a) mistaken; (b) intoxicated.

171 *shift us*: change our garments.

173 *attached*: confiscated for debts.

179 *Let . . . sink*: if our ship were to sink.

192 *blanch copper*: whiten copper to make it look like silver.

193 *test*: movable hearth of the reverberatory furnace in which silver is separated from base metals.

    malleation: hammering.

194 *ponderosity of Luna*: weight of silver.

    tenacity: cohesiveness.

    friable: reducible to powder.

198 *arsenic . . . realga*: white arsenic, more commonly known as 'ratsbane'.

199 *Sublime*: vaporize and then allow to return to a solid state.

201 *chymia*: chemical analysis.

    decoction natural: maturation by heat for a 'natural' day, or twenty-four hours.

202 *fixed*: solid.

203 *project . . . copper*: cast it upon well-cleansed copper.

204 *et habebis magisterium*: and you will have the philosopher's stone (said to change base metal to gold).

209 *want*: lack.

210 *sal alchyme*: salt without liquid.

215 *sconces*: heads.

221 *colour*: pretence.

239 *sorts this*: has this sorted itself out.

245 *unbelieved*: incredible.

250 *transferred*: carried.

261 *dishonest satire*: parody of infidelity (i.e. the horn).

262 *horn . . . hunger*: dinner horn.

263 *Inns of Court*: the legal societies of London.

    manger: sumptuous meal.

264 *horn of abundance*: cornucopia.

    headsmen: (a) head men; (b) cuckolds.

266 *horn of pleasure*: horn of sport, or hunting, but also suggesting 'penis'.

267 *destiny*: because all married men will become cuckolds.

269 *stone fruit*: fruit with kernels, with a suggestion of *stone* as 'testicle'.

[4.2].1 *can*: know.

  4 *cavallaria*: 'tenure of land held on condition of knightly service' (H&S).

  5 *coloronia*: a farming tenant. Touchstone mocks Sir Petronel's scheme for developing Virginia's land.

6 *crack*: empty, drink.

7 *brown*: round.

Monmouth caps: flat round caps worn by sailors.

10 *Gravesend*: further down the Thames. (The term suggests too that they are likely to end their journey in a grave.)

11 *admiral*: flagship.

12 *remora*: sucking-fish, believed by the ancients to have the power of hindering the progress of any ship to which it is attached.

13 *sconce*: (a) head; (b) small fort.

14 *and*: if.

vie: wrangle.

16 *region*: referring to the different cloud levels in the sky.

20 *found . . . cross*: come back remorsefully; proverbial (Dent W248).

21 *malkin*: servant.

bite . . . bridle: i.e. chew the bit and starve; proverbial (Dent B670).

22 *for William*: as far as I care.

23 *go . . . common*: suggesting that they will have to become 'common' whores.

25 *sprites*: spirits.

26 *Guildhall*: civic hall of London, centre of local governmental affairs.

27 *marvel*: wonder.

29 *i' my thought*: as I was thinking about him.

30 *Aldermen*: chief officers of the wards of London, next in dignity to the mayor.

34 *commoners*: members of the Court of Common Council.

35 *presentation . . . inquest*: report to the Council about an official inquiry.

45 *conspires*: combines.

46 *livery*: distinct group who could wear the livery, or festive garments, of the guild.

freedom: release from apprenticeship.

51 *worship*: distinction.

52 *sufficient*: capable.

54 *expects*: is anticipated for.

59 *opinion*: credit, esteem.

61 *scarlet*: the scarlet gowns of the alderman or mayor.

63 *monuments*: i.e. people commemorated by monuments.

64 *Lady Ramsey*: Lady Mary Ramsay, charitable wife of Sir Thomas Ramsey, Lord Mayor in 1577.

65 *Gresham*: Sir Thomas Gresham, who founded the Royal Exchange in 1566.

Whittington . . . puss: Richard Whittington (d. 1423) was thrice mayor and a generous benefactor of London. His cat supposedly helped him gain his fortune.

66 *posies*: mottos.

69 *get-penny*: i.e. guaranteed money-maker.

78 *false brother*: spying associate.

79 *masterless men*: vagabonds.

82 *lay*: set a trap.

84 *Anchor*: a tavern name.

85 *colour*: pretence.

86 *press*: conscription for military service. Golding will threaten to select them for the draft.

89 *arrested*: confiscated.

92 *first quarter*: beginning of service.

unreflected: without being diverted.

97 *undubbed*: i.e. not 'knighted' through her marriage to Sir Petronel.

98 *foot-pace*: walking pace, i.e. demurely.

102 *fished . . . frog*: proverbial for marrying poorly (Dent F767).

112 *Law*: an exclamation of surprise.

124 *equipage*: regular marching step.

125 *birds . . . feather*: 'birds of a feather flock together' was proverbial (Dent B393).

127 *fist*: fart.

128 *as . . . man*: proverbial (Dent F63).

132 *Hunger . . . nose*: proverbial for stinginess (Dent H813).

133 *fair . . . tongue*: proverbial (Dent W793).

134 *gold-ends*: 'wise' maxims.

138 *no . . . gold*: proverbial (Dent M338).

list not: do not wish to.

my . . . girdle: 'To have one's head under [another's] girdle' was proverbial for inferiority (Dent H248).

139 *As . . . drink*: i.e. she must face the consequences of her actions. Proverbial (Dent B654).

140 *she . . . wedding*: proverbial (Dent W231.11).

141 *It's . . . ladyship*: 'It is but honeymoon with them' was proverbial (Dent H563).

149 *pride . . . after*: proverbial (Dent P576).

150 *Thou . . . calf*: 'many a good cow has an ill calf' was proverbial (Dent C761).

152 *without*: outside.

154 *by . . . means*: by all means.

156 *melancholy*: ill-temper.

161 *foil*: a thin leaf of metal placed under a precious stone to increase its brilliance.

166 *trussed up*: hanged.

170 *You . . . girdle*: i.e. show respect by calling Golding 'master'; proverbial (Dent M1).

174 *Low Countries*: England gave active military support to the Protestant cause against the Spanish in the Low Countries.

175 *Bridewell*: a prison and place for detaining conscripted soldiers.

176 *they*: so that they.

179 *for our discharge*: to take the burden of responsibility away.

188 *see*: saw.

   furniture: apparel, personal belongings.

190 *spurs*: knights commonly wore gilt spurs.

200 *pray . . . covered*: polite way of asking someone to put their hat back on. This is ironic, as the Constable indicated that they no longer have hats.

   biscuit: i.e. the ship's biscuit ration.

202 *a degree . . . southward*: i.e. your journey to Virginia, which has a more southerly latitude than England.

204 *offers*: i.e. attempts to speak for yourselves.

211 *gresco*: a card game, the rules of which are now unknown.

   primero: a card game in which four cards are dealt to each player, and the winner holds the 'prime' or best hand.

212 *bright . . . crimson*: i.e. gaudily dressed gallant.

213 *changeable . . . apparel*: trunks of apparel for changing into.

   at livery: as provisions.

217 *parcels*: small sums of money.

223 *flesh*: (a) meat; (b) a woman's body.

229 *under correction*: i.e. subject to being corrected. Golding is being humble.

231 *gird*: gibe.

233 *flashes*: abortive outbursts.

236 *place*: office.

  wink at: ignore.

242 *proper*: handsome.

243 *God . . . thee*: proverbial for being well-formed (Dent G188).

245 *neat*: refined.

248 *returned*: responded.

254 *outrecuidance*: excessive self-esteem.

265 *forehead*: effrontery.

  chop logic: argue fine points.

273 *boon companion*: good fellow.

276 *pox*: syphilis.

277 *piles*: haemorrhoids.

278 *clew*: ball of string for 'threading' a way through a labyrinth or maze.

279 *cart of calamity*: cart taking criminals to execution.

281 *crocodile*: crocodiles were thought to weep false tears.

286 *security*: bail; Touchstone takes this as 'Security', the usurer.

289 *engineer*: contriver.

[5.1.].3 *cold comfort*: proverbial (Dent C542).

  6 *O, hone . . . nero*: line from an Irish ballad.

22 *Hunger . . . walls*: proverbial (Dent H811).

24 *an*: as if.

25 *Knight . . . Sun*: the hero of Diego Ortunez's *Mirror of Princely Deeds and Knighthood*, translated by Margaret Tiler in 1578.

  Palmerin of England: hero of Francisco Moraes's *Palmerín de Inglaterra*, translated by Anthony Munday.

26 *Sir Lancelot . . . Tristram*: knights of the Round Table in the legend of King Arthur.

34 *still*: ever.

39 *Winchester*: a table supposed to be the Round Table of Arthur's court was kept in Winchester.

40 *hazard*: a dice game.

44 *by . . . salt*: proverbial (Dent B616.11).

46 *beholding*: beholden, indebted.

50 *lay . . . lavender*: 'to lay in lavender' was slang for pawning (Dent L96).

53 *waistcoat*: also worn by women in the period, but considered unfashionable by Gertrude.

    peat: disrespectful girl.

54 *avail*: relief.

55 *turn the lip*: reveal contempt with a movement of the lips.

63 *a pennorth*: a pennyworth, i.e. their money's worth.

64 *worse . . . wearing*: proverbial (Dent W207).

    bate: abate, decrease.

67 *with . . . needles*: in addition to what we would earn by sewing.

68 *fairies*: Gertrude goes on to relate some common superstitions regarding fairies.

72 *soon*: early.

74 *o' the backside*: at the back of the house.

84 *on't*: of it.

85 *laid up*: in prison.

86 *golden shower*: alluding to the myth of Danaë, seduced by Jove in the guise of a shower of gold.

91 *caught a clap*: had a shock.

92 *hap*: fortune.

93 *blow*: suggesting the strokes of intercourse.

107 *Thou . . . leaped*: proverbial (Dent L429).

108 *blow . . . coal*: proverbial for becoming impassioned (Dent C460).

109 *Self do . . . have*: proverbial (Dent S217).

    The hasty . . . woe: proverbial (Dent M159).

111 *A body . . . I*: i.e. someone would have thought that you were the older (and wiser); I just followed your advice.

113 *'Tis . . . living*: proverbial (Dent L18.11); *living* = income.

    cittiner: citizen.

114 *on*: from.

117 *tother*: other.

119 *take up*: rebuke.

121 *dole*: grief.

123 *French-wires*: wires used for fixing hair or ruffs.

124 *cheat-bread*: wheaten bread of the second quality, made of more coarsely sifted flour.

131 *intoxicate*: stupefied.

132 *The leg . . . kite*: proverbial (Dent L186).

357

138 *lady bird*: a term of endearment.

149 *chuck*: a familiar term of endearment.

153 *take order for*: i.e. arrange to pay.

[5.2].3 *find*: know.

5 *packing*: private or underhand arrangement.

10 *blind justice*: justice was traditionally represented as blind (to suggest her impartiality).

18 *kind*: the natural order of things.

23 *that*: so that.

24 *descant*: make remarks.

25 *mortified*: rendered dead to the world (for thinking of heavenly ideals instead).

27 *Papist*: Catholic. It was illegal to practise Catholicism.

28 *Brownist*: puritan followers of Robert Browne's sect, which opposed parish divisions and ordination.

   Anabaptist: a radical Protestant sect originating in Germany.

   Millenary: one who holds that Christ will reign in person over the earth for a period of one thousand years.

   Family o' Love: a sect originating in Holland, which held that religion consisted chiefly in the exercise of love.

29 *Good-fellow*: (1) thief; (2) agreeable companion.

32 *fees*: prisoners had to pay fees to be kept in prison, and they paid higher fees for better accommodation.

37 *Knight's Ward*: the second-best ward. Wolf suggests that Sir Petronel is unwilling to reside in the best ward.

38 *the Hole*: the worst accommodation in prison.

42 *Two-penny Ward*: slightly better accommodation than the Hole.

   take: i.e. carry.

43 *for*: because of.

47 *cut his hair*: as a sign of penitence.

   given: disposed.

48 *Book of Martyrs*: John Foxe's *Acts and Monuments* or *Book of Martyrs* (1563) was a popular collection of Protestant martyr narratives.

49 *Sick-Man's Salve*: Thomas Becon's popular pious book of 1561.

   without book: by heart.

53 *bandog*: dog chained up, either to guard a house, or on account of its ferocity.

56 *intelligencer*: one employed to obtain secret information, an informer. This was a poorly reputed trade, but Wolf suggests that it is better than being a sergeant.

57 *coming*: wavering.

59 *rheum*: cold in the head or the lungs. The word also meant 'tears'.

61 *fish . . . pools*: proverbial (Dent F307).

62 *touched . . . tried*: gold-working terms; *touch* means 'test the fineness (of gold or silver) by rubbing it upon a touchstone', and *try* means 'refine or purify metal by fire'.

   proof: capable of withstanding the test. Touchstone puns on the additional sense of 'a witness in a trial'.

65 *deaf . . . adder*: proverbial (Dent A32).

   blind . . . beetle: proverbial (Dent B219).

68 *recover*: redeem.

71 *this*: i.e. converting Touchstone.

73 *ambitious*: desirous.

[5.3].4 s.d. *the grate*: the prison bars. Presumably these were positioned over a stage door or over an opening in the stage floor.

7 *grafts . . . forehead*: i.e. plants horns on my forehead.

23 *respect*: comparison.

24 *Jubilae*: time of release.

25 *feast . . . new-moon*: the 'horns' of the crescent moon, associated with the cuckold's horns.

39 *play you*: play. The *you* is the ethic dative, used for rhetorical effect.

41 *in a livery*: as servants (dressed in livery).

42 *cloth of silver*: a cloth consisting of threads of silver, generally interwoven with silk or wool.

47 *basket*: alms basket.

53 *wonder*: marvel at.

55 *rug gown*: coarse wool gown (as a sign of penitence).

57 *carted*: rid through the streets in a cart as a humiliating punishment (usually for sexual offences).

58 *lay . . . pounds*: pay a £200 bond to prevent the sentence.

63 *habeas corpus*: legal right of a prisoner to be heard in court. *Habeas corpus* prevented illegal imprisonment by public officials and could be used to challenge an excessive bail set before trial.

64 *sensibly*: so as to impress the feelings.

66 *in terrorem*: to frighten (and thus deter) others.

69 *return*: response.

76 *winding devices*: devious schemes.

90 *estate*: plight.

99 *train*: artifice.

abroad: from his home.

100 *event*: outcome.

[5.4].1 *hear*: be subject to (but punning on the more usual sense).

2 *Ulysses*: in order to pass safely by the island of the Sirens, Ulysses had his crew block their ears with wax. Ulysses did not block his ears, but was tied to the mast so that he could hear the song without danger.

16 *shoemaker's wax*: for waxing thread so that it passes through leather smoothly.

Lethe: in Greek myth, the river of oblivion in the underworld. It was believed that those who drank from the River Lethe would lose all memory of their past existence.

mandragora: a root used to narcotic effect.

31 *voice . . . hyena*: it was thought that hyenas mimicked the human voice in order to lure men as prey.

40 *required*: desired.

[5.5].5 *shrewd*: malicious.

8 *Toby*: probably the first name of the 2nd Prisoner.

9 *curious*: unsociable.

21 *Whitefriars*: precinct below Fleet Street, named for a Carmelite church built in 1241. Criminals could find sanctuary there even after the dissolution of the monasteries.

36 *Mannington's*: George Mannington's *Woeful Ballad* (1576), a pre-execution lament.

39 *I wail . . . pain*: line of a popular tune called 'Labandala Shot'.

47 *black*: alluding to the colour of touchstones.

52 *him*: i.e. Quicksilver.

he: i.e. Touchstone.

55 *False . . . manners*: i.e. imitations of court manners.

65 *the . . . horse*: proverbial (Dent C522).

72 *black . . . foot*: proverbial for affliction (Dent O103).

73 *'longed*: belonged.

74 *touch . . . still*: i.e. continue to use your values to judge me.

75 *current*: true (as in genuine currency).

77 *Stay him*: i.e. stop Touchstone from approaching Quicksilver (and prematurely ending the song).

83 *project*: plan.

95 *conceited*: conceived.

100 *a whole prenticeship*: an entire period of apprenticeship, usually seven years.

102 *Forth*: continue.

108 *drabs*: whores.

109 *French scabs*: sores from syphilis.

111 *cut . . . leather*: proverbial for living within one's means (Dent T229).

113 *Spital*: hospital (for venereal disease).

122 *desperate*: forlorn.

reclaim: reform.

125 *passages*: occurrences.

127 s.d. *A shout*: i.e. from Security.

154 *make . . . at*: i.e. make faces at.

156 *Twierpipe*: a well-known taborer.

171 *yellow*: the colour worn in prison, and symbolic of jealousy.

174 *corrosive*: cause for remorse.

177 *wedlock pain*: alluding to the task of lovemaking.

179 *one . . . race*: because cuckolds have horns like the devils.

182 *resolved*: convinced.

190 *glass*: conflating the ideas of 'mirror' and 'hourglass'.

EPILOGUE

3 *stuck*: tightly packed.

4 *the streets . . . ladies*: Quicksilver looks around the yard and galleries of the playhouse and imagines a street full of people.

pageant: the Lord Mayor's annual election, a day of public procession through the streets.

8 *once a week*: performances at the Blackfriars were held on Saturday.

Every Man In His Humour

THE PERSONS OF THE PLAY

Knowell: reflecting the character's confidence in his own wisdom.
Brainworm: suggestive of madness, and here indicative that the character is 'madcap'.
man: servant.
country gull: a fool from the country (who lacks city refinement).
plain squire: plain-dealing country gentleman.
Cob: a herring. This name is the subject of several jokes in the play.
water-bearer: fresh water was carried from conduits and wells to homes in the period; Cob has one of London's more menial jobs, cf. *SH* 21.170–3.
Tib: a diminutive of Isabel.
Paul's man: someone who socialized and conducted business at St Paul's Cathedral, a gathering place for gallants.

PROLOGUE

4 *Yet . . . age*: i.e. yet this poet, because of poverty, does not so much need a living from the stage as to represent current depravities (to be popular).

9 *child . . . years*: Jonson refers to the violation of the unity of time, a classical dramatic ideal which insists that a play's time-frame should not exceed a single day. This ideal was frequently ignored in the period's drama.

10 *foot . . . words*: unnatural diction (from over-elaborate poetry).

11 *York . . . jars*: the Wars of the Roses; this is the first of many derogatory allusions to Shakespeare's history plays.

12 *tiring-house*: actors' changing rooms, behind the stage at the Globe.

20 *Where . . . come*: Jonson attacks common theatrical devices. The Chorus was used in Shakespeare's *Henry V* to bridge the action between England and France; thrones descending from the stage roof conveyed 'divine' characters; *squibs*, or fireworks, were used in supernatural scenes; and bullets rolled on sheet metal or beating drums signified thunder.

26 *Except . . . ill*: i.e. except when we make follies into crimes by knowing they are wrong and continuing to do them.

30 *monsters*: i.e. the unnatural beings who normally tread the stage.

[1.1].1 *A goodly . . . toward*: i.e. it looks like it will be a fine day.

5 *at his book*: studying.

11 *both . . . universities*: Oxford and Cambridge.

12 *graces*: dispensations which exonerate a person from the formal requirements of a degree (needed for honorary degrees).

14 *fond*: foolish.

19 *professors*: those who make a profession of (poetry).

20 *mistress of*: governing force over. The arts are traditionally personified as feminine.

29 *doubt*: suspect.

30 *an . . . e're a*: if he has any.

33 *wusse*: iwis, certainly.

against: for.

34 *hood . . . bells*: a hood was used to blind an inactive hawk; bells helped pinpoint a bird's location.

35 *to . . . by*: to instruct me how to keep it.

39 *rush*: a straw, proverbial for something of little value (Dent S917).

40 *He . . . no*: he is not fit for.

41 *by God's lid*: i.e. by God's eyelid; this is typical of the elaborate oaths used in the play.

42 *consort . . . humdrum*: companion to every dull fellow.

43 *Hogsden*: Hoxton, a popular recreation ground.

44 *archers of Finsbury*: archery was practised in Finsbury fields. The bow was no longer the weapon of gentlemen, however, and Stephen implies that he does not associate with archers.

45 *a-ducking*: duck hunting, often practised in Hoxton.

Islington ponds: Islington, surrounded by marsh in this period, was a popular duck-hunting locale.

49 *go to*: a common expression of derision.

50 *never . . . me*: don't look at me like that.

54 *kite*: an ill-reputed bird of prey.

58 *on*: of.

64 *brain*: thought.

67 *desert*: merit.

71 *Nor would I*: Nor would I (have it that).

73 *blaze of gentry*: bright show of gentry, but punning on 'blazon of gentry', or those traits which make a gentleman, and thereby pointing to Stephen's lack of qualifications. Sir John Ferne's 1586 *The Blazon of Gentry* reflects similar exclusivity in its subtitle: 'for the instruction of all gentlemen bearers of arms, whom and none other this work concerneth'.

76 *property*: trait.

78 *sail . . . boat*: 'make not your sail too big for the boat' was proverbial (Dent S24).

81 *Nor . . . gentility*: nor insist too much on your being born a gentleman.

85 *Save you*: 'God save you', a common greeting.

88 *thousand . . . land*: i.e. he earns a thousand pounds per annum from his land in Middlesex.

89 *simple*: (a) humble, plain; (b) foolish.

91 *pretty*: considerably large.

   hard by: close by.

92 *In . . . time*: i.e. if things go well. This could be said sincerely or with irony.

96 *were . . . best*: had better not.

104 *saucy companion*: impudent fellow.

105 *mine . . . ground*: where it would be ungentlemanly to fight.

106 *stand . . . gentility*: according to some conduct manuals, gentlemen were not obliged to fight those of lower rank.

110 *peremptory gull*: arrogant fool.

112 *demeans*: humbles.

114 *unseasoned*: out of place.

115 *carriage*: bearing.

125 *Cry . . . mercy*: beg your pardon.

126 *City*: the heart of London, within the old City walls.

129 *remember . . . courts'y*: i.e. put your hat back on.

136 *old Jewry*: a London street formerly inhabited by Jews, running from Cheapside towards Moorgate, a northern gate in the City walls.

147 *answer*: live up to.

151 *yet*: still.

152 *frippery*: a place where old clothing is sold.

153 *change . . . smock*: i.e. change your father's company for that of a healthy woman.

   conceive: imagine.

155 *number over*: count.

159 *coddling . . . fruit*: to coddle is literally to stew, but *cod* suggests *penis* (as in cod-piece); the sense of coddle as *stew* also has bawdy possibilities, as *stew* was a colloquial term for 'bordello'. So *coddling* here roughly means, 'fucking'. (A *codling* is also a type of apple). The phrase, 'kernel of the fruit', has bawdy secondary meaning as 'the core of the reproductive envelope (vagina)'. There is in addition a traditional association of fruit-women with prostitution, fitting the suggestion of bordello in *coddling*.

161 *Turkey Company*: a trading company which gave gifts to the Turkish leader in exchange for trading rights.

162 *your . . . leaven*: i.e. formed from the same poetical materials as you are.

163 *Poet-Mayor*: punning on 'Lord-mayor' and suggesting that position's prominence in public ceremony.

167 *Guildhall verdict*: London juries were known for severity.

168 *viaticum*: travel expense.

169 *Windmill*: a tavern in the Old Jewry.

171 *Spital . . . Pict-hatch*: hospital (for venereal disease) or the prostitution district.

172 *happiest*: most apt, felicitous.

173 *choicest*: most excellent.

182 *Hesperian dragon*: in classical mythology, the dragon, Ladon, that protected Juno's golden apples (received as a wedding present when she married Jove). Stealing these apples was one of the labours of Hercules.

199 *that . . . indeed*: i.e. don't make me laugh; proverbial (Dent J41.1).

201 *stay*: restrain.

204 *generous*: thoroughbred.

205 *ne'er . . . withheld*: i.e. if only a little held back from its prey.

211 *but for that fit*: only for that short time.

1.[2].13 *what-sha'-call-him doublet*: the fashion for doublets was constantly changing (cf. *RG* Epistle 3–8); Stephen doesn't know what the style is called, showing that he, as 'a country gull', is ignorant of London trends.

15 *mind*: inclination.

21 *stayed i'the fields*: i.e. waited at the other (field-facing) side of the house. Duellists used the fields outside of London for fighting.

26 *fine . . . hard*: a common substitute for riding boots.

27 *no boot*: no use.

29 *trussed*: (a) tied up (like a bird) for cooking; (b) hanged.

30 *unbraced*: unfastened.

31 *choler*: anger, punning on 'collar'.

40 *sadness*: seriousness.

49 *familiar epistles*: private correspondence; the expression was used as the title for many collections of letters.

50 *gelt*: castrated, like some Italian and German boys in the period, to sing with a high voice.

troll . . . Trundle: sing for a well-known London ballad seller.

59 *Fortune*: the goddess Fortune was held to be blind.

75 *Moorgate*: a northern gate in the London City walls.

77 *bond*: (a) imprisonment; (b) contractual obligation to pay a debt.

78 *that's . . . 'twere*: i.e. it wouldn't matter if it were.

82 *By my fackins*: by my faith.

86 *turn*: purposes.

90 *wight*: man.

91 *savour*: indication, smell.

94 *again' . . . time*: in preparation for a celebration.

97 *smoky lawn*: smoke-coloured linen.

 black cypress: a transparent material worn by those in mourning.

98 *answered*: excused.

99 *Drake's . . . Deptford*: Francis Drake's ship, the *Golden Hind*, which had circumnavigated the world in 1580, was a popular venue for entertainment in the docks at Deptford.

102 *physiognomy*: face.

106 *melancholy*: surly, in the affected manner of a thoughtful and touchy gentleman.

108 *height*: i.e. high opinion of himself.

109 *suburb-humour*: parochial foolishness. *Humour*, as the title indicates, is an important term in this play. It traditionally suggests the belief in ancient and medieval physiology that four chief fluids in the body (blood, phlegm, choler, and melancholy) determine in their relative proportion the disposition and physical health of a person. In Jonson, the term usually means some distinctive character trait.

 City: i.e. Wellbred's City fool.

110 *play him*: wager Stephen to be the biggest ninny.

112 *go before*: Edward gives Stephen the socially inferior position.

1.[3].3 *gi'*: God give.

10 *Herring . . . Fish*: that herrings were the kings of fish was a proverbial idea (Dent F320).

13 *heralds'*: officials who kept track of the lineage of noble and gentry families.

24 *Roger Bacon*: thirteenth-century scientist-sorcerer, professor at Oxford University. He was dramatised in Robert Greene's 1589 play, *Friar Bacon and Friar Bungay*, in which Bacon is held to have made a Brazen Head that could speak sagaciously and predict the future.

28 *raw*: untutored (continuing the cooking metaphor).

39 *was in't*: was wrong.

42 *as though . . . lost*: i.e. expressionless. Proverbial (Dent L437).

43 *cast*: (a) thrown dice; (b) vomited.

46 *tavern token*: token given as change in a tavern. Cob could hint that Bobadill drank too much or simply offer an excuse for his illness.

49 *carried . . . turns*: i.e. borne two loads of water.

57 *worshipful*: title given to a member of a City company.

60 *invincibly*: strongly.

75 *tunnels*: nostrils.

76 *forty shillings*: a substantial sum to a water-carrier.

78 *Action*: military campaign.

79 *Helter-skelter . . . hangman*: proverbial expressions (cf. Dent C85, C84, and F210.11); all of which are roughly equivalent to 'Oh, well, I mustn't concern myself'.

1.[4] S.D. *discovered*: shown in the recess behind one of the stage entrances, which probably had a curtain in front of it which could be drawn aside to reveal an inner space.

3 *small beer*: inexpensive beer, a typical breakfast beverage.

16 *audacious*: forward (in coming uninvited).

17 *sort*: company.

28 *in any case*: whatever you do.

32 *cabin*: temporary shelter.

35 *conceive*: understand.

38 *thus far*: i.e. letting you visit.

39 *resolve*: believe.

42 *Go by Hieronimo*: a well-known line from Thomas Kyd's play, *The Spanish Tragedy* (1587).

61 *turtle-billing*: nuzzling like turtle doves.

63 S.D. *making . . . ready*: preparing to go out.

64 *Where's this*: i.e. where's this poetry to be found.

75 *pied*: of two highly contrasting colours.

78 *rook*: a general term of disparagement.

81 *holden*: held.

86 *hobnails*: (a) short nails used in the soles of boots; (b) uncouth rustics.

87 *carry . . . manhood*: i.e. win the day with bravado.

98 *dependence*: justification (to issue a challenge).

Caranza: the author of *De la Filosofia de las Armas* (1569), a well-known book on fencing.

102 *mystery*: art.

106 *of divers*: by various (people).

109 *time, distance*: timing and judgement of distance, important principles in duelling theory.

113 *bedstaff*: a long wooden stick used to beat and clean a bed.

115 *point*: (rapier) point.

at any hand: by no means.

116 *poniard*: dagger. Duels were often fought with rapier and dagger, one in each hand.

125 *out of measure*: immeasurably, extremely.

129 *career at*: rapid movement towards.

136 *venue*: bout.

141 *breathe you*: exercise with you.

150 *somewhat . . . least*: i.e. not much.

151 *taste*: flavour.

153 *Corydon*: a shepherd in Virgil, and a generic literary name for a rustic.

2.1.5 *tell over*: count.

6 *pieces of eight*: Spanish silver coins.

8 *Master Lucar*: suggesting 'lucre', or profit.

10 *Exchange*: the Royal Exchange, an important centre of trade.

14 *of*: i.e. as.

16 *bred . . . Hospital*: provided for his upbringing at Christ's Hospital (which looked after orphans).

17 *toward imp*: promising child.

38 *brother*: Wellbred is Kitely's brother-in-law.

56 *stale . . . societies*: lower his dignity through excessive familiarity with the wrong crowds.

63 *leap*: (a) bound about; (b) copulate.

66 *cracked three-farthings*: damaged coin of small value (a common way to express worthlessness); cf. *SH* 1.203. Four farthings made one penny.

67 *It will . . . bone*: i.e. he'll never change; proverbial (Dent F365).

69 *shoulder . . . horse*: proverbial (Dent S399).

70 *'fore George*: I swear before St George.

74 *he has . . . part with't*: a series of proverbs (Dent S685, D376, H80) expressing an unwillingness to give money.

81 *vouchsafe . . . travail in*: agree to work on.

82 *circumstance*: manner.

84 *stomach*: haughtiness, anger.

86 *warrants*: assures.

87 *by . . . seconded*: augmented by your demeanour.

95 *heat of humour*: i.e. choler, one of the four humours, an excess of which was thought to cause anger.

97 *blow . . . familiars*: whisper to his friends.

100 *relieve . . . fable*: assist his storytelling.

103 *flat . . . shoes*: round cap with a low, flat crown and leather shoes worn by London merchants.

110 *as sure as death*: proverbial (Dent D136).

111 *quarrelled*: quarrelled (with).

114 *like*: likely.

125 *How then*: Downright takes offence at being ignored or spurned.

131 *scavenger*: literally 'street-cleaner', but here meaning 'dishonourable person'.

138 *put it up*: i.e. take (the insult).

139 *rankest*: most loathsome.

140 *Fleet Street*: a central thoroughfare, and frequent location of brawls.

141 *madge howlet*: an owl, with a suggestion of domesticity in 'madge'; cf. *SH* 18.176.

143 *'Heart . . . somewhat*: i.e. 'By God's heart, I'll come close to filling your giant trousers (*Gargantua breech*) with something'; by implication the *somewhat* is either blood or faeces.

144 *carry it away*: i.e. 'win the day', but punning on literally carrying the filled breeches.

148 *hangman cut*: fit for the hangman.

151 *as he . . . drink*: proverbial (Dent B654).

152 *tightly*: soundly, well.

153 *reprehension*: rebuke.

158 *labour to reclaim*: struggle to remember.

160 *let . . . for*: trust me to do.

165 *have . . . back*: lay hold of you (in anger).

167 *by the belly*: cf. the proverb, 'The back of a herring . . . the belly of a wench are best' (Tilley B11).

172 *I . . . world*: I try to appear to others.

178 *factious*: conflict-provoking.

180 *make head*: press forward (with a secondary sexual sense).

182 *treat*: negotiate a treaty.

184 *parley*: hold a discussion.

185 *conspiracy*: plot to commit illicit (sexual) acts.

202 *muss*: a term of endearment.

203 *angels*: gold coins worth 10 shillings.

214 *all . . . nothing*: I would wager all the world to nothing; proverbial (Dent W865.1).

217 *air*: Kitely may think that his wife is suggesting 'heir'.

  has . . . wind: has picked up my scent; i.e. she has found me out.

223 *houses . . . brain*: threefold division of the brain into imagination, judgement, and memory.

227 *like*: the same.

234 *erection*: vigour, but also suggesting tumescence.

2.[2].3 *grace*: credible aspect.

  4 *the lie . . . fico*: i.e. calling a soldier a liar is as bad as gesturing offensively with the thumb and forefinger (the *fico*, or 'fig').

  5 *have*: maintain, hold.

  8 *dryfoot*: by following the scent alone.

  9 *match*: contest.

  10 *insinuate*: win favour.

  12 *wear . . . end*: wear a mish-mash of ragged clothing when our contract expires.

  motley: fool's apparel.

  16 *veni, vidi, vici*: Julius Caesar's, 'I came, I saw, I conquered', suggesting a sense of supreme achievement.

  18 *arm here*: sword, or possibly his way of feigning an injured arm.

  31 *jet*: a black stone used to make inexpensive rings.

  37 *The deeper . . . sweeter*: proverbial (Dent D188), and suggesting sexual penetration.

  42 *venture*: take a risk.

  44 *crowns*: gold coins worth five shillings.

  57 *Bohemia . . . Adriatic Gulf*: genuine sixteenth-century battle sites.

  58 *galleys*: Mediterranean ships which used slaves as oarsmen.

  62 *How*: for how much.

  rapier: the rapier, or long thrusting sword, was the preferred weapon of gentleman in the period.

69 *velvet scabbard*: i.e. for ornamentation, not fighting.

71 *flat*: certain.

73 *Toledo*: swords made in Toledo in Spain were noted for their high quality; the next line suggests that Stephen doesn't know that Toledo is in
Spain.

80 *Higgenbottom*: an unidentified character that seems to have been well-
known to theatre audiences. A pun on the name appears in the *c.*1622
play, *Beggars' Bush*: '*Higgen* hath prig'd the prancers in his dayes, And
sold good peny-worthes; we will have a course, The spirit of *Bottom*, is
growne bottomlesse' (in *The Dramatic Works of the Beaumont and Fletcher
Canon*, ed. Fredson Bowers, vol. 3 (Cambridge, 1976), 5.2.3–5).

84 *field rapier*: most pre-arranged duels were fought in fields outside of the
City walls. *Field* as 'battle-ground' may also apply in Stephen's
reasoning.

2.[3].2 *admire*: wonder at.

7 *he . . . head*: i.e. not even one who lived in a brothel would have dared to
consider disrespect towards an elder.

13 *it*: 'fear'.

14 *even*: i.e. even as.

26 *long coat*: smock worn by young children.

27 *like*: likely.

38 *remainder*: i.e. inheritance.

40 *seal*: i.e. bond them to the 'fellowship of vice'.

41 *affection*: *affiction* in F, which could alternatively be emended to
'affliction'.

46 *Venetian courtesans*: Venice was seen as a centre of prostitution.

51 *my lord's letter*: a good reference from an aristocrat.

52 *Dressed . . . curiously*: prepared strange dishes of snails and mushrooms.

54 *Preceding*: i.e. leading the way.

55 *ordinaries*: eating-houses with fixed-price meals.

60 *rape . . . precipice*: carry youth to the edge of danger.

65 *conversing*: i.e. discourse 'with his companions'.

66 *example*: i.e. the poor example given by some fathers.

68 *fleshed . . . well*: i.e. I have tasted the game now and want more, since I
have been so successful.

83 *the edge*: i.e. the blade.

87 *it . . . time*: i.e. it will no longer be 'given' when I pay it back.

88 *sucked*: extracted profit from. Rapiers often featured elaborate hilts.

105 *metal*: stuff, essence, with a play on 'mettle'.

107 *afore me*: i.e. 'I swear'.

116 *purchased*: procured.

119 *Fitzsword*: the son of the sword.

121 *entertain*: employ.

128 *prove*: try, test.

133 *fox in years*: i.e. old fox.

134 *by . . . master*: through me, so will my young master.

139 *musket-rest*: heavy muskets needed shoulder-high rests in the period.

Mile End: the green there, in the north-east of London, was a place for military drills and mustering.

3.1.3 *delivered us*: said to us.

10 *thing . . . saved*: soul.

11 *part*: attribute.

12 *faces about*: i.e. change direction.

15 *rustical cut*: i.e. countrified, unrefined style.

18 *quos . . . Jupiter*: 'those whom equitable Jupiter has loved', from Virgil's *Aeneid*, book VI.

22 *genius*: attendant spirit.

Apollo . . . girls: Apollo, the sun god of the Greeks and Romans, was patron of music and poetry; *Thespian* refers to Thespis, the traditional father of Greek tragedy, but *Thespian girls* here more broadly means the muses, divine inspirers of the arts.

23 *fury*: avenging or tormenting infernal spirit.

27 *rare*: excellent (with irony).

29 *Pliny*: Roman writer of the first century AD known for his literary letters.

Symmachus: Roman politician whose epistolary style was modelled on Pliny.

30 *burned . . . rogue*: branding was a typical punishment for criminals.

vein: strain of talent or genius.

31 *camel*: i.e. beast of burden.

32 *ordinary*: customary, regular.

41 *flourishing*: highly embellished.

52 *wind*: the noun 'wind' was pronounced like the verb, leading to this pun.

53 *sign . . . Dumb Man*: Wellbred compares Stephen to an alehouse sign representing a silent man.

59 *take . . . so*: understand him, so be it.

69 *general man*: man of common acquaintance.

74 *melancholy*: habitual sadness, one of the four humours and a fashionable stance for a young gentleman.

75 *only fine*: finest.

79 *utters*: (a) speaks; (b) sells.

  by the gross: in large quantities, but *gross* here also suggests ignorance or a lack of culture.

80 *out . . . measure*: beyond limits, excessively.

81 *better . . . measure*: i.e. better than you could love them according to their poetic metre (which you don't understand).

96 *Saint Mark's Day*: 25 April.

99 *Strigonium*: Esztergom, Hungary, was taken from the Turks in 1595.

101 *breach*: gap in a fortification made by a battery assault.

104 *Genoese*: no such battle is known.

105 *ranged*: placed.

108 *'So . . . gentleman*: i.e. by God's soul, as much as having a ten-shilling coin I would like to be able to swear like that gentleman.

109 *servitor*: soldier.

120 *rack*: instrument of torture upon which victims were stretched to force them to 'confess' a crime.

121 *planted me*: i.e. planted. The *me* is the ethic dative used for rhetorical effect.

123 *give on*: attack.

126 *single*: solitary, pertaining to one person only.

127 *ordnance*: cannons.

129 *sword . . . rapier*: swords were short and sturdy, used for heavy cutting. Rapiers, longer and thinner, were primarily thrusting weapons. There were contentious debates in the period about which weapon was superior, and Bobadill's switch suggests that he is lying (as Wellbred hints).

132 *impeach*: damage.

135 *Morglay . . . Durindana*: the legendary swords of Bevis of Hampton, King Arthur, and Orlando.

144 *Fleming*: a cheap Flemish sword.

  guilder: a Dutch coin worth about 20 pence.

150 *provant*: part of a soldier's allowance, and, thus, of common quality.

152 *Put it up*: put it away (in its sheath).

158 *ostrich stomach*: ostriches were proverbially able to digest iron (Dent I97).

160 *stomach*: spirit, courage.

162 *as 'tis*: i.e. that we don't see your 'stomach'.

178 *under favour*: if he agrees to it.

182 *make . . . him*: i.e. use him well (to see what further drollery he speaks).

  happily: suitably.

188 *conceited*: witty, amusing.

191 *catechism*: the Anglican catechism began by asking the child's name.

192 *that coat*: i.e. a clergyman's coat.

194 *servant . . . extraordinary*: soldier used to augment the regular troop, but punning on the sense of *extraordinary* as 'of a kind not usually met with'.

209 *but stays*: waits only for.

213 *device*: stratagem.

218 *prorogue . . . expectation*: extend his waiting.

222 *porters*: known for weak brains, cf. *RG* 4.26.

223 *Thames . . . Quay*: routes busy with moving goods to and from the Thames.

224 *civil . . . carmen*: porters and carmen (who carried good in carts) competed for business along the busy Thames.

3.[2].20 *fruit . . . eyes*: referring to the Hesperian dragon, cf. 1.1.182 n.

25 *jet*: a hard, black stone able to attract light objects when electrified by rubbing; 'as a jet draws straws' was proverbial (Dent J49.00).

26 *Put . . . ice*: proverbial phrases for the impossible (Dent S879, F284).

27 *leap*: in addition to the literal sense, *leap* here suggests a sexual mounting.

31 *or time*: either time.

34 *most . . . attractive*: powerful lure.

  heads: leaders, but also suggesting the literal site of cuckold's horns.

37 *straight*: straightaway.

38 *three-piled acorns*: hats shaped like an acorn's cup and made out of velvet with a very dense, or *three-piled*, nap.

  my horns: the horns of a cuckold.

44 *Exchange time*: time at which the Exchange opens, around 10 or 11 a.m.

52 *stay upon*: wait for.

53 *put in act*: start acting upon.

54 *build upon*: i.e. trust.

58 *there's . . . him*: there's no telling him.

59 *there . . . Thomas*: i.e. Thomas would be the best person on earth to tell.

61 *chink*: crack.

76 *private*: personal affairs.

77 *crest*: a family's heraldic device worn on a knight's helmet, here signifying Kitely's reputation; but the suggestion of crest as the location of cuckold's horns is also made.

83 *disclaim*: renounce.

88 *precisian*: one who is rigidly precise or punctilious in the observance of rules or forms, often synonymous with 'Puritan'.

90 *fayles . . . tick-tack*: forms of backgammon. Such games were opposed by Puritans and Catholics alike, as was swearing.

98 *protest*: affirm, assert in formal or solemn terms.

101 *need not*: are not needed.

108 *Say you?*: What do you say?

120 *out . . . way*: away from here.

133 *when I meant*: i.e. when I before spoke of.

137 *midnight*: i.e. darkly.

here: Kitely probably indicates Cash's bosom.

140 *take head*: have its origin (like a *flood* or river).

141 *running humour*: hasty mood; *running* also means (of a vessel) 'leaking', continuing the metaphor.

146 *Fasting days*: days on which no meat could be eaten, including Fridays, Saturdays, and other appointed seasons, so fish was eaten instead.

147 *on a light fire*: in a blaze.

148 *ember weeks*: four periods of fasting and prayer appointed by the Church to be observed in the four seasons of the year; the Wednesdays, Fridays, and Saturdays of these weeks were days of fasting.

152 *ride*: oppress.

154 *show . . . trick*: act like an ill-tempered horse; proverbial (Dent J29.1).

157 *rheum*: a term applied to any bodily fluid that was thought to be harmful; Cob uses it here for 'choler'.

160 *Mack*: an oath, suggesting 'by the Mass'.

166 *Feed . . . humour*: minister to the demands of my disposition; proverbial (Dent H806.1).

168 *make . . . monstership*: i.e. cater for your monstrousness.

170 *rascally*: miserable.

174 *stomach*: resent.

175 *I have . . . 'em*: i.e. I have an appetite (*maw*) now, huge enough even for Sir Bevis's horse, against them. The story of Sir Bevis of Hampton was told in a popular verse romance of the fourteenth century; his sword is mentioned at 3.1.135.

179 *an . . . know*: i.e. if you must know.

180 *Flemish*: the people of Flanders were thought to be great eaters of butter.

    ravin up: devour.

186 *generation*: breed (i.e. of herrings).

188 *martyrs . . . passion*: early and late Christian martyrs were often killed by fire; (*passion* = 'the sufferings of martyrdom').

189 *Hannibal*: legendary Carthaginian general; Cob's mistake for 'cannibal'.

192 *King Cophetua*: famous African monarch who became a byword for extreme wealth.

194 *almanacs*: popular calendars of months and days, which gave astronomical data and calculations, ecclesiastical and other anniversaries, and astrological and meteorological forecasts.

197 *utter*: sell.

202 *Beshrew . . . was*: i.e. curse me if it wasn't.

203 *carried*: carried off.

208 *an . . . masters*: i.e. even if I might have been given letters patent (an open letter of authorization) to take office alongside the seven wise masters (the seven philosophers who tutored Diocletian's son and saved him from a plot devised by his stepmother).

209 *habit*: attire.

210 *gentlemen . . . round*: members of a military watch who go round a city patrolling its outskirts.

211 *provost*: officer charged with the apprehension, custody, and punishment of offenders.

212 *halberdiers*: guards armed with halberds, or weapons consisting of sharp-edged blades and spear heads mounted on wooden handles five to seven feet long.

213 *hackney-pace*: slow pace of a hired horse.

214 *shove-groat shilling*: a shilling used to play 'shove-groat', a table-game similar to the modern-day shuffleboard.

215 *reformados*: officers left without command (owing to the 're-forming' or disbanding of their companies).

222 *artificer*: artful or wily person, trickster.

225 *for the clothing of it*: i.e. to create a believable justification for his begging.

227 *Houndsditch*: a trading-centre for old-clothes brokers.

233 *shifts*: (a) evasive stratagems; (b) shirts.

235 *Francis! Martin!*: Cash is calling for household servants.

    a spite's: an irritation is.

245 *only mad*: most madcap.

250 *taking . . . wall*: walking nearer to the wall, away from the muck of the street.

255 *match*: a piece of cord, cloth, paper, etc. dipped in melted sulphur, so as to be readily ignited by the use of a tinder-box.

256 *Fire on*: i.e. to hell with.

259 *Here's . . . seven-night*: i.e. here's all that's left of seven pounds of tobacco that I bought eight days ago.

260 *Trinidado*: tobacco from Trinidad.

266 *reprove*: disprove.

269 *simple*: medicine composed of only one ingredient.

271 *in the nature*: in its natural state.

272 *Italy*: murder by poison was thought to be common in Italy.

273 *green*: fresh, unhealed.

275 *Nicotian*: a generic term for tobacco, after Jacques Nicot, thought to have introduced tobacco into France. Bobadill mistakenly believes that *Nicotian* is a specific type of tobacco.

277 *rheums*: mucus caused by head or chest colds.

crudities: imperfectly 'concocted' humours, arising from poor digestion.

288 *San Domingo*: Santo Domingo. The island was a noted centre of tobacco cultivation.

290 *By God's . . . tobacco*: exhortations against tobacco were common in the period, and its popularity was a contentious issue in contemporary London.

292 *bell*: death knell.

294 *voided*: discharged (through a bodily orifice).

295 *present*: immediate.

303 *meddle . . . match*: fight with his equal; proverbial (Dent M747) and playing on the literal *match* that Cash holds.

319 *drunk*: taking tobacco was often described as *drinking*.

322 S.D. *practising . . . post*: Stephen is probably practising fencing moves, using one of the pillars supporting the stage roof as his 'opponent'.

324 *glance*: i.e. look at Stephen.

332 *Artillery Garden*: fields near Bishopsgate, where the City Trainband (formed in 1585 to protect against Spanish attack) performed military drills.

338 *soft*: wait a minute.

347 *drawn out*: protracted, extended.

349 *larded*: in cooking (especially French), to *lard* is to insert strips of fat into meat to help preserve moistness.

3.[3].10 *they sting . . . large*: i.e. they sting Kitely's head by making him grow cuckold's horns.

16 *Bane*: an agent or instrument of ruin or woe. Kitely also puns on *banns*, or the proclamation of marriage, which was pronounced 'banes' and could be singular in the period.

17 *ranked*: placed, arranged.

22 *store*: i.e. of gallants.

24 *cornucopiae*: horns of plenty, alluding to the cuckold's horns.

25 *entertainment*: welcome.

30 *motion*: inward prompting or impulse.

state: original, proper, or normal condition.

faculty: inherent power or property.

36 *Bridewell*: a house of correction for those unable to pay debts.

38 *kissed the post*: been shut out or disappointed; proverbial (Dent P494).

39 *with a pox*: i.e. wishing a pox (disease) upon them.

43 *Nay . . . spit*: i.e. no, proceed slowly, I have other business at hand; proverbial (Dent E86). *Eggs on the spit* refers to eggs roasted on the fire.

46 *three . . . mustard, revenge*: Cob's speech is a parody of the rhetorical excesses of earlier stage avengers and their desire for 'sharp revenge'.

50 *bands*: circular frills around the sleeve or neck of a garment.

52 *host*: army, multitude of angels.

63 *sign . . . water-tankard*: 'the sign of . . . ' was a standard phrase used to describe a particular inn; Cob adapts this formula to indicate his house.

64 *Green Lattice*: latticed windows or painted imitations were commonly found on alehouses.

scot . . . lot: an equal share in the tax burden.

70 *crave the peace*: i.e. ask you to use your authority to restrain (Bobadill).

76 *compass it*: achieve it.

78 *far . . . about*: i.e. in a circuitous way, like a 'compass'.

81 *twelve-month . . . day*: if a victim died within a year and a day of an assault, charges for murder could be brought.

84 *colour*: reason, ground.

91 *bob*: pommel.

95 *vagrant*: belonging to a vagrant or wandering beggar.

105 *God's precious*: 'by God's precious (blood)', a mild oath.

106 *tankards*: (a) tankard-bearers, water-carriers; (b) tall, wooden drinking vessels, used chiefly for beer.

106 *I . . . done*: i.e. I give up.

109 *Sweet Oliver*: common name for a romantic hero (Dent O40). Knowell uses it comically to highlight Cob's plight.

112 *piss-pot metal*: pewter, used for chamber pots and cheap drinking vessels.

121 *fear*: scare, frighten.

122 *Do . . . stink*: i.e. don't be so frightened that you shit yourself.

126 *In dumps*: melancholy.

132 *staid*: of grave and sedate deportment, dignified.

   unthrift: spendthrift, prodigal.

136 *muse*: wonder (that).

   parcel: small piece; Clement suggests that Brainworm is not much of a soldier.

4.1.6 *sprites*: spirits.

  8 *a . . . devil*: i.e. it wouldn't take much to get me to cause havoc.

 13 *parboiled*: thoroughly boiled.

 15 *God's . . . life*: a mild oath.

 20 *Servant*: in the sense of a 'professed lover'.

 24 *Hey-day*: an interjection denoting surprise or wonder.

   stuff: worthless discourse or writing, rubbish.

 25 *stand close*: i.e. stay hidden (spoken to Edward).

 28 *odd toy*: ephemeral composition.

 29 *mock an ape*: deceive a fool. 'A toy to mock an ape' was proverbial (Dent T456).

 32 *rhyme-given*: i.e. given to rhyme.

 35 *foppery*: foolishness (ironic).

   Death: by God's death (an oath).

 38 *hold . . . water*: prevent himself from urinating.

 40 *cheese . . . bagpipe*: both were supposed to cause a need to urinate.

   mark . . . protestation: i.e. listen, or you'll miss Matthew's excuses (for his verse).

 41 *how it is*: i.e. how (good) it is.

 47 *forswear himself*: break his oath.

 50 *incipere dulce*: to begin is sweet (Latin).

 51 *Insipere*: to be a fool; cf. the proverb 'in knowing nothing is the sweetest life' (Dent K188).

 55 *mot*: word, motto.

 57 *benchers' . . . verba*: Benchers could be: (a) those who sit on benches in

379

taverns; (b) judges. *Pauca verba* means 'few words', implying in the ale-house, 'drink more, and talk less' (H&S).

62 *Hero and Leander*: Matthew's verse loosely quotes Christopher Marlowe's narrative poem of this title.

69 *catastrophe*: denouement.

73 *free . . . brokers*: i.e. a freeman (member) of a 'guild' of traders in second-hand writing.

75 *Hang him*: stealing was a capital offence in the period.

76 *the dead*: Marlowe died in 1593.

80 *good . . . morning*: Matthew suggests that literary output could grow stale within a few hours.

84 *Star*: a tavern's name.

88 *his . . . already*: i.e. Matthew and his stars are even, because his stars (or destiny) have already cursed him with a poor fate.

94 *ne'er . . . me*: none of my bones.

95 *build . . . breed*: i.e. stay permanently.

97 *encomions*: the Greek form of encomium, a formal or high-flown expression of praise.

102 *do tricks*: i.e. (a) write verses; (b) perform sexual favours (the sense understood by Downright).

108 *vied . . . revied*: hazarded as a sum and then raised by another bid (from card-playing).

monkeys: i.e. those who mimic like monkeys.

112 *lamp . . . virginity*: symbol of female chastity (Dent L44.11).

take . . . snuff: take it in scorn or with contempt; proverbial (Dent S598), and with a suggestion of 'extinguish'.

113 *poetical fury*: the inspiration of the poet, *furor poeticus*.

114 *concealment*: in an earlier part of Elizabeth's reign, anyone discovering property that was confiscated from the monasteries by Henry VIII yet was never received by the crown, would receive a reward. The legislation was frequently abused, so Wellbred suggests that Matthew, in using Marlowe's verse, is attempting to falsely claim the poetic 'property'.

116 *teston*: sixpence, the price of an ordinary printed play.

119 *I wusse*: I know, i.e. without a doubt.

121 *Whose . . . calved*: i.e. what's the matter; proverbial (Dent C756).

123 *I'll . . . of it*: i.e. I'll show you (by beating or arguing).

124 *companions*: used as a term of contempt.

128 *soldados . . . foolados*: soldiers (Spanish) and fools (mock Spanish).

130 *slops*: i.e. Bobadill, who is wearing *slops*, or wide, baggy breeches.

134 *Cut a whetstone*: i.e. you would as well to try and cut a whetstone; proverbial (Dent W296.11). This alludes to the myth of Accius Naevius, who cut a whetstone with a razor.

141 *Holofernes*: in the apocryphal biblical book of Judith, Holofernes is Nebuchadnezzar's avenging general, whom Judith murders when he is drunk. He was a stock ranting villain in medieval drama.

142 *pink*: pierce, stab.

143 S.D. *offers*: makes an attempt.

155 *ancient*: long-established, customary.

160 *mar*: cause bodily harm to.

161 *shapes*: fashions. Downright finds Bobadill's clothing fantastical.

162 *songs-and-sonnets*: i.e. Matthew. 'Songs and sonnets' was a popular title for verse collections.

166 *chiefly*: and most of all.

173 *demeaned*: behaved, conducted.

176 *portion*: dowry.

179 *minion*: lover.

182 *parts*: personal qualities or attributes. Kitely takes this to mean 'genitalia'.

195 *I'll . . . have*: i.e. I wager my life that they have.

4.2.5 *will . . . me*: i.e. will be permanent like the horns of a cuckold.

7 *list*: choose.

9 *lie . . . throat*: a formal accusation in the period, which, as a grave insult, frequently provoked duels.

13 *stabbed*: Cob now takes the word to mean 'penetrated (by a penis)'.
   Mass: by the Mass (a mild oath).

14 *foist*: pickpocket.

15 *Burgullian*: Burgonian or Burgundian, used generically for 'bully' or 'braggadocio'. This refers to John Barrose, a Burgonian who came to London and challenged English fencers; he was later hanged for murdering a City officer (H&S).
   tickle: beat, chastize.

17 *basted*: thrashed.

18 *black and white*: i.e. the written warrant to restrain Bobadill.

19 *Trojan*: merry fellow.

22 *smoked*: stupefied, made uncomfortable.

23 *his good . . . guest*: i.e. Bobadill, whom Cob makes a demon of Satan.
   wife . . . Tib: 'tib' was slang for strumpet, so Cob is making a distinction between a faithful wife and a whore.

24 *let . . . to you*: there is a secondary sexual meaning to Cob's instructions.

4.[3].5 *to start him*: i.e. to make him react.

  7 *fancy*: creative imagination.

  8 *possessed . . . withal*: informed me about.

13 *howsoever*: howsoever (it works out).

16 *ingenuously*: frankly.

    affect: love.

17 *pretendest*: profess or claim.

20 *ornament*: qualities conferring beauty, grace, or honour.

    except I conceived: unless I thought.

27 *'Point*: appoint.

4.[4].3 *Moorfields*: the fields outside of Moorgate, used for military training and duelling.

  6 *peace . . . comfort*: i.e. the thought of death is my only comfort.

  7 *comfort of*: comfort from (performing).

  9 *entertainment*: employment.

14 *discovered*: revealed.

19 *black art . . . scholar*: scholars were traditionally held to have skill in black magic.

29 *seemed men*: acted aggressively.

34 *an anatomy*: a dissected body.

36 *a light heart*: one or more of the following may apply: (a) a clear conscience; (b) a frivolous, unthinking spirit; (c) a lightweight core (i.e. body).

37 *bottom of pack-thread*: ball of stout thread or twine.

42 *wall*: the City wall of London.

45 *match*: appointment.

46 *Justice Clement's man*: Formal has been standing by silently.

49 *Much wench . . . son*: said sarcastically, as Knowell will find neither.

52 *the sport . . . durst*: i.e. how I would laugh to see him there, if I dared.

55 *to light . . . novice*: to find a fool, now, in this Justice's clerk.

61 *pottle*: two–quart drinking vessel.

66 *Roman histories*: Roman histories of warfare, such as those of Julius Caesar, were still seen as instructive in military matters.

71 *neat grist*: undiluted (*neat*), strong beer made from crushed malt.

73 *make . . . you*: i.e. use you for my gain.

4.[5].1 *taste . . . him*: see such a rustic as Downright.

7 *prevention*: defence.

8 *generously*: gentlemanly, bravely.

13 *hai*: a fencing expression meaning 'you have [it]' (Italian), said when an opponent is hit.

16 *punto*: (a) instant; (b) sword-thrust.

17 *prove . . . upon*: test yourself against.

18 *masters of defence*: fencing instructors.

21 *travail*: (a) labour; (b) travel.

   mystery: craft, art.

26 *out . . . measure*: beyond measure.

35 *credit*: reputation.

39 *a more*: another.

   preposterous: perverse.

41 *skirts*: outskirts.

42 *Turnbull . . . Shoreditch*: suburbs of London with cheap accommodation.

43 *ordinary*: tavern serving fixed-price meals.

47 *spurn abroad*: kick apart.

52 *conceit*: opinion.

54 *peculiar*: single.

57 *by . . . seal*: i.e. privately, and not to be disclosed.

69 *character*: distinctive trait, characteristic.

70 *Reverso*: back-blow.

   Imbroccata: a sword thrust given over a dagger (which was often held in the weaker hand by duellists).

71 *Montanto*: upward thrust.

79 *twenty score, that's two hundred*: Bobadill miscalculates, *twenty score* is four hundred.

87 *in Downright's state*: i.e. in Downright's shoes.

91 *his mind*: as he likes.

100 *keep . . . good*: save your hanging.

106 *Pharaoh's foot*: Downright mocks Bobadill for swearing 'by the foot of Pharaoh'.

107 *tools*: rapier and dagger.

    gipsy: cunning rogue.

110 *Tall*: brave.

115 *Prate . . . this*: i.e. speak nonsense again, if you want another beating like this one.

116 *control the point*: manage the point of a sword. This is Bobadill's own phrase for his fencing skill, cf. 1.4.115.

123 *construction . . . sort*: interpretation of my conduct, in a fair manner.

125 *struck . . . planet*: stricken by the supposed malign influence of an adverse planet; proverbial (Dent P389).

127 *under a planet*: Edward puns on *planet* as a chasuble, or large loose mantle covering the entire body.

136 *challenge*: claim.

4.[6].5 *where . . . war*: i.e. where there is already cause for concern about impending household conflict.

adjection: addition.

6 *occasion*: giving occasion (for conflict).

9 *his own man*: truly himself.

13 *fall in with*: agree with.

16 *clothes . . . poisoned*: poison administered through clothing was a common trope in the period.

21 *suffer murder*: permit murder to remain.

24 *sick at heart*: (a) feeling pain in the chest; (b) depressed.

26 *My . . . has*: my very words have.

29 *conceits*: fantasies.

31 *toy*: whim. The phrase 'to have a toy in one's head' was proverbial (Dent T456.1).

48 *bestow . . . me*: i.e. buy drinks for me.

49 *marshalled*: led, guided (with a suggestion of deploying troops).

50 *too much heat*: i.e. his blood was warmed by the alcohol and/or the discussion of military affairs.

53 *bill*: halberd, a weapon consisting of a sharp-edged blade and spearhead mounted on a wooden handle five to seven feet long. They were often used by the watch.

59 *the Tower*: the Tower of London was not subject to City authority or part of any ecclesiastical parish, so couples could be married without the usual waiting period for reading the banns (H&S).

61 *stand upright*: act honourably. Here the phrase also suggests 'achieve an erection'.

committed to: consigned to. The additional sense, 'incarcerated in', is suggested by *prison*.

63 *liberty*: (a) freedom; (b) status as a *liberty*, or a place free from City authority. The *liberty of the prison*, or the outside area within which prisoners were sometimes permitted to reside, may also be suggested.

65 *lay . . . ears*: give your ears to, listen.

70 *show . . . rooms*: i.e. show him around the house, with an additional sexual significance brought out in the proverb, 'she lies backward and lets out her forerooms' (Dent F594).

the jest is stale both because of its proverbial status and because *stale* is slang for 'whore'.

72 *hang . . . after*: i.e. remain with him, and do not let him follow her within.

74 *toy*: trifle. Small pieces of clothing often had significance in the period's customs of sexual exchange.

75 *But*: if she only.

80 *bear . . . out*: back you up, be responsible for your actions.

81 *As . . . self*: 'it is as true as truth itself' was proverbial (Dent T565).

90 *fair . . . hearts*: cf. the proverb, 'fair face foul heart' (Dent F3).

95 *I would . . . there*: i.e. I hope I am fortunate enough to catch him there.

I'd return . . . own: i.e. I'd give him a dose of his own medicine.

99 *touches . . . me*: does not apply to me.

103 *abide the touch*: (a) permit physical contact (by both men and the application of cosmetics); (b) prove worthy (in the sense of a touchstone being used to test the quality of gold or silver).

104 *of all ceruse*: on all white lead (used as a cosmetic).

in the—: Wellbred omits to say 'whole', because it sounds like 'hole', which might be carrying his ribald jokes too far. An actor would need to convey this omission to the audience, perhaps by coughing.

107 *bonfires*: *bone-fires* in F, suggesting the 'bone-ache' as syphilis was known.

110 *exception against*: objection to.

116 *savours of*: seems like.

119 *squire*: a 'knight-adventurer's servant', but also an 'apple-squire' or pimp; cf. 4.8.58.

128 *dors*: makes a fool of.

129 *discovered*: revealed.

4.[7].4 *respectful . . . lineaments*: i.e. cautious about his own physical well-being.

7 *part*: act.

soft wood: i.e. as opposed to the hard steel of a rapier.

11 *Nobilis*: nobles (Latin).

12 *Gentilezza*: gentlemen (Italian).

13 *retricato*: this word is unknown, but it suggests 'retreating' or drawing back, which fits with the probable stage action. In rapier duelling, the

defensive stance for a right-handed swordsman places the left leg foremost. For attack, the left leg would be drawn back and the right leg shot forward with the thrust. Cf. 'Of the Agreement of the Foot and Hand', in Giacomo DiGrassi's *His True Art of Defence* (1594).

13 *his*: its.

14 *assalto*: assault.

15 *base wood*: this and the 'soft wood' in line 7 may suggest that Downright beat Bobadill with a cudgel, or a short stick.

16 *fascinated*: under a spell.

29 *my service . . . living*: my service (to Justice Clement) is my livelihood.

30 *his . . . preferment*: the only income that he gives to me.

34 *account*: importance in the eyes of others.

35 *brace of angels*: a pair of gold coins worth 10 shillings (or 50p) each. This would be an unusually large fee.

38 *cross*: crosses were stamped on the reverse side of the English penny and halfpenny.

58 *russet*: (a) a reddish-brown colour; (b) roughly spun fabric.

66 *varlets*: sergeants who made arrests and delivered summons.

4.[8].9 *O' God's name*: i.e. what are you trying to do? This may be a response to an attempt by Knowell to barge in.

16 *copesmate*: paramour.

20 *get something*: are paid (as a bawd).

23 *tried*: select, excellent (said ironically).

24 *tried*: (a) judicially examined; (b) sexually solicited.

27 *device*: stratagem.

28 *Soft*: wait a minute.

29 *forestalled . . . market*: intercepted goods before they reached your honest market. 'Honest' is ironic because the market is illicit sex.

30 *close*: secret.

31 *smoked you*: forced you from your hiding place (as if by smoking you out). Proverbial (Dent S577).

33 *hussy*: here, a woman of loose morals.

38 *twice sod*: twice boiled, unpalatable.
   treacher: deceiver.

41 *Steal'st thou*: do you sneak.

43 *goat*: goats were proverbially lecherous (Dent G167).

45 *With . . . jest*: by using this old whore's trick.

46 *incontinent*: one unable to restrain a sexual appetite.

48 *When . . . so hot*: i.e. when you are no longer able to perform lecherous acts, to still desire them.

53 *hear you*: listen.

57 *hoddy-doddy*: a small snail with a shell; it is used here to mean 'cuckold' because snails have horns.

58 *apple-squire*: pimp.

73 *preferred thither*: promoted there (i.e. to the status of 'bawd').

74 *Is'bel*: i.e. Jezebel, or whore.

75 S.D. *falls upon*: rushes upon, assaults.

81 *hemp*: hemp was beaten before being worked into rope.

83 *quean*: whore.

4.[9].3 *'rests*: arrests.

5 *mace*: (a) staff of office (carried by sergeants); (b) sceptre of sovereignty; (c) spice, consisting of the nutmeg's outer casing.

made like: i.e. resembling.

19 *Bear back*: i.e. stand back.

24 *bonds . . . books*: i.e. contracts or accounts (promising to repay a debt).

29 *gull*: fool.

40 *let's . . . Justice*: let's go ahead and make for the Justice (to plead our case).

41 *The varlet's*: i.e. Brainworm's.

tall: brave.

53 *answer it*: answer (for) it.

55 *for his appearance*: that he will appear (before Justice Clement).

59 *swinge*: strike.

66 *mash*: muddle.

70 *I . . . behind*: i.e. I do not like having someone with your despondent look behind me.

5.1.21 *used thither*: i.e. frequented there.

22 *used*: conducted.

39 *worthily*: justly.

so: i.e. that she has been a whore.

40 *like . . . sentence*: likely, and a bit of a maxim. Cob had literally said that an action is worthy, if it proves worthy, which sounds like an aphorism.

47 *when*: i.e. hurry up.

49 *gorget*: a piece of armour that protects the throat.

49 *A soldier . . . my sword*: a story of a similar instance of comic overreaction circulated in Antony Copley's 1595 *Wits, Fits, and Fancies* (H&S).

64 *laid me along*: knocked me down.

68 *put up*: put up with, not offer resistance to.

77 *Set . . . picture*: i.e. let the claims of this picture (i.e. Bobadill, who has the appearance, but not the qualities, of a soldier) rest for a moment.

79 *Freshwater's*: a 'freshwater soldier' has seen no military action.

80 *suit*: punning on the fact that Stephen is wearing Downright's clothing.

87 *would . . . find it*: i.e. I swear by my life that I found it; proverbial (Dent S861).

89 *erewhile*: just a while ago.

92 *breathe*: rest.

96 *Nay . . . passion*: ironic; Clement again mocks Bobadill for his meekness.

99 *my hand not at*: my signature not on.

101 *discharge*: release, exoneration.

109 *help me off*: help me take off some of this bulky clothing.

131 *I will . . . certain*: i.e. I will not lose, I swear by all my hard work, any part of my assured fame (for the other clever tricks that are not yet known).

139 *sword . . . balance*: traditionally representative of the strength and fairness of justice.

141 *bespeak*: request.

146 *shrewdly*: grievously, immensely.

148 *retained me*: paid for my services.

162 *sure*: married.

165 *prevent 'em*: meet them beforehand.

174 *shirt*: i.e. underclothing.

   vein: state.

180 *Pledge me*: i.e. have a drink with me.

182 *suspect . . . ingine*: doubt his mother wit.

193 *what . . . armour*: i.e. what does this have to do with you wearing armour.

195 *drawers*: tapsters, barmen.

196 *penance . . . shirt*: being forced through the streets semi-naked was a common form of punishment.

203 *bound*: obliged.

208 *place*: position, capacity.

209 *Of her delight*: for her delight, with a suggestion of sexual pleasing.

   below the stairs: i.e. as a servant, but also punning on 'downstairs' anatomically.

213 *Phlegon*: one of the horses of the sun's chariot, and hence 'most highly aspiring'.

214 *Saturn*: the Roman god who ruled until he was defeated by his son, Jupiter.

    ebon: black.

215 *podex*: rear end.

    white as ivory: proverbial (Dent I109).

216 *thundered*: i.e. farted.

220 *taste . . . vein*: example of his approach, or method.

221 *the Queen's Justice*: i.e. a search in the name of the Queen's Justice.

222 *under . . . rebellion*: or you would face charges for disobeying a legal summons.

224 *realm*: punning on the similarity at the time of pronouncing 'realm' and 'ream', or 480 sheets of paper.

225 *subjects*: (a) poetic subjects; (b) people of his 'commonwealth'.

227 *Unto . . . eyes*: absurdly corrupted opening lines of Samuel Daniel's sonnet sequence *Delia* (1592).

231 *batch*: sort, assemblage.

233 *infected*: Clement compares the stolen verses to disease, which was combated in the period with cleansing fire.

237 *Sic transit gloria mundi*: 'so passes the glory of this world'; cf. the English proverb, 'all worldly glory is transitory' (Dent G141.11).

238 *emblem*: picture expressing a moral fable.

240 *profess it worthily*: i.e. are good at (poetry).

244 *out . . . year*: i.e. after his one-year term has finished.

246 *with the fact*: i.e. in the very act of writing such bad verse.

251 *sign . . . midnight*: Clement compares Bobadill and Matthew to inn signs (cf. 3.3.64n.), who do not truly live up to what they represent, and suggests that their company embarrasses him so much that he would not like to be connected with them until midnight, when no one would be around to see them.

252 *court, without*: courtyard, outside.

254 *forgive . . . forget*: 'forgive and forget' was proverbial (Dent F597).

255 *a third*: i.e. Formal.

    tender: care for.

256 *provided . . . purpose*: dressed appropriately (in armour, like a watchman).

260 *buttery*: larder or pantry, where the servants eat.

266 *mortal*: fatal, perhaps a mistake for 'moral', but suggesting 'till death us do part'.

268   *complement*: (a) completion, consummation; (b) courtesy.

272   *while that is fed*: while jealousy is sustained.

275   *drove*: flock.

284   *everyone, a fellow*: i.e. every one exit with a companion.

285   *To whom . . . reference*: i.e. who will be the reference point of all of my courtship. Clement chooses Brainworm as his partner in the traditional coupling at the close of Renaissance comedy.

288   *applause*: the metatheatricality that was introduced with Kitely's claim to have learned from 'a jealous man's part in a play' here serves to invite the audience's applause.

APPENDIX

5   *Camden, Clarenceux*: William Camden was Jonson's teacher at Westminster school and a noted scholar. The *Clarenceux*, which Camden became in 1597, was one of the heads of the Heralds' College, which traced ancestral lineage and issued titles.

8   *in this kind*: i.e. dedications.

10   *the authority . . . poetry*: i.e. no other authority than their ignorance for attacking poetry.

     professors: i.e. poets.

     my gratitude . . . leave: i.e. my expression of thanks in this dedication must not be interrupted.

11   *none*: not one.

16   *had . . . the first*: i.e. had I been lucky enough and disposed to produce other or better works, you would still have received my tribute first. *EMI* was the first play printed in Jonson's 1616 *Works*.

17   *confession*: display.

19   *for the profession . . . thankfulness*: i.e. because of this dedication.

     it: i.e. the play.

The Roaring Girl

THE PERSONS OF THE PLAY

Jack Dapper: an inversion of 'dapper Jack', an upstart.

Sir Beauteous Ganymede: Ganymede was Jove's cupbearer and lover, noted for his beauty.

Laxton: implying a lack of 'stones' or testicles.

Goshawk: a large, short-winged hawk.

Greenwit: unripe mental faculties or judgement.

[*Hippocrates*] *Gallipot*: Hippocrates was one of the greatest classical physicians; a 'gallipot' is a glazed earthen pot used by apothecaries.

Openwork: a fabric with patterned openings.

Tiltyard: a place for tilting or jousting. To 'tilt' suggests amorous play, as at 9.158, and 'yard' meant 'penis' as well as the unit of measure.

Trapdoor: an entrance in the floor of the stage, used symbolically by infernal characters.

Tearcat: a ranter or swaggerer.

Curtalax: a heavy, slashing sword.

Hanger: (a) a loop from which a sword is hung; (b) a hangman, or someone who causes someone else's hanging.

PROLOGUE

6 *mews*: cries 'mew' derisively. The word is associated with play audiences in the Prologue to *The Isle of Gulls* (1606) and the Induction to *Every Man Out of His Humour* (1599).

9 *A roaring girl . . . were*: a riotous girl, whose characteristics until this age have not been seen. The term 'roaring girl' follows that of 'roaring boy', a type of boisterous masculinity emerging late in Elizabeth's reign.

17 *bowls*: broad, shallow drinking vessels.

18 *the watch*: guard.

19 *gives braves*: acts defiantly.

21 *suburb-roarers*: the suburbs, as places escaping City authority, were known for criminality.

24 *through an iron grate*: in prison.

26 *character*: a literary genre which succinctly describes certain categories of people (courtiers, lawyers, etc.); lines 16–24 give a 'character' of roaring girls. Dekker wrote characters for Thomas Overbury's 1613 collection, *A Wife*. There is also a pun on 'character' as a printed letter, suggesting that printed stories about Mary Frith (Moll Cutpurse) are superseded by the spoken words of the play.

28 *Is better . . . express*: expresses the person better than (characters). The insufficiency of generalizations about Moll, a recurrent theme in the play, is highlighted here.

[Scene 1] S.D. *sempster*: seamstress.

S.D. *bands*: decorative collars. The word is also used throughout the scene to mean a bond, or promise, to marry.

3 *transcendent*: permitted to address the 'young gentleman', so figuratively

391

rising to his level. Neatfoot uses pretentiously 'formal' (35–6) language throughout this exchange.

5 *fructify in*: (a) receive; (b) grow pregnant by. Bawdy puns continue with 'pleasure' and 'erected', and probably also with 'come' as 'achieve orgasm'.

7 *tree of generation*: stemming from 'fructify' in its sense of 'bearing fruit'.

14 *falling bands*: (a) flat collars; (b) vows (bonds) that are being forgotten (have fallen).

16 *curl-pated*: curly headed.

21 *Orleans*: wine from Orleans.

27 *ape*: i.e. mimic.

33 S.D. *Enter Sebastian*: Sebastian's meal is being interrupted, and he may enter with signs of coming 'from table'.

35 *viva voce*: 'living voice', orally (Latin). Neatfoot uses the phrase to mean 'in person'.

41 *upon rising*: about to leave the table.

46 *needlewoman*: (a) seamstress; (b) whore, because 'needle' = penis.

51 *oaths*: Sebastian and Mary have a *de futuro* marriage contract because they have sworn to marry. Such contracts were legally binding.

59 *the wolf's at door*: danger is near.

65 *Moll*: diminutive for 'Mary'.

68 *As a horse . . . still*: mill horses were made 'blind' (had their eyes covered) and walked in a circle to turn the grindstone. Sebastian goes 'out every step' through his circuitous path (by pursuing 'another Moll'), yet that pursuit actually allows him to preserve his constancy, or 'keep . . . one path still'.

84 *five thousand marks*: £3,333; a substantial amount of money, compare Gertrude's £100 per annum dowry in *Eastward Ho* 1.2.87.

[Scene 2].9 *the prospect*: that which is seen, i.e. 'the spectacle'.

13 *good . . . most dear*: when goods are highly esteemed, any cost seems reasonable.

14 *look . . . galleries . . .*: Sir Alexander's examination of his well-furnished chamber also considers the nature of the theatre audience, immediate and visible in the Fortune Theatre, where the play was first performed.

15 *trimmed up*: decorated, furnished.

19 *a thousand heads*: Sir Alexander describes a painting or tapestry of a crowd scene, but his description also suggests the living theatre audience, which, in public theatres like the Fortune, could easily exceed 1,000 people.

24 *plaudities*: applause.

34 *comical*: like the conclusion of a comedy, happy.

47 *an easy gift*: (a) a gift of little value; (b) a comforting, or *ease*-bringing gift.

50 *back friend*: (a) a chair with a back, as opposed to a stool without one; (b) a false friend; (c) a supportive friend or backer.

52 *Pray . . . your perch*: chairs were luxurious items in this period, and there is a strong sense of social hierarchy in Sir Alexander's arrangement of his friends. Sir Davy and Sir Adam, being knights, are given more comfortable chairs and are offered them politely. Sir Alexander speaks with less respect to Goshawk; punning on his name by asking him to 'perch' on a stool.

53 *stoop . . . lure*: a phrase from falconry for when a hawk returns to the falconer (stoops) for a decorated piece of flesh (lure). Here, Goshawk accepts the stool and sits down.

56 *what . . . a stone*: punning on Laxton's name by suggesting that he has no testicles.

57 *I had rather stand*: Laxton affirms his masculinity by using 'stand' as 'have an erection'; thus, on stage he could sit down nonetheless.

59 *a mess*: four, suggesting that Sebastian and Greenwit are positioned away from the others. Cf. lines 53–4.

60 *Because . . . long*: so that time will not pass slowly.

66 *upon . . . grave*: i.e. whose wrinkles suggest that he is my age.

76 *her wheel . . . threads*: Fortune's wheel signifies the vicissitudes of luck. It was not a spinning wheel, however; Sir Alexander may be confusing Fortune and the Fates, who, in classical mythology, spin and cut the thread of an individual's life. There may also be a play on the 'wheel'-shaped Fortune Theatre.

93 *read . . . cards*: consider his fate.

106 *smell a fox*: become suspicious, 'smell a rat'.

108 *mellow in years*: old.

117 *Adam Bell*: a legendary archer.

124 *flesh-fly*: a fly which deposits eggs on dead flesh; thus, a vile form of reproduction.

126 *he*: his son.

130 *made*: with a pun on 'maid'.

132 *two shadows*: one for a man and one for a woman.

134 *blazing star*: meteor.

    A creature . . . eyes after it: the division of the sexes was, in theory, inviolable in the early modern period, making Moll's manliness particularly transgressive.

136 *bristle*: show aggravation.

137 *naughty pack*: a worthless or vicious person.

140 *sticks ... villain*: i.e. belongs to a liar. This insult was considered an outright provocation to duel.

157 *nought*: (a) nothing; (b) illicit sexual (naughty) acts.

169 *baffle*: deceive, disgrace.

181 *wash a negro*: i.e. labour fruitlessly; proverbial (Dent E186). Fairness of skin was the standard for beauty in early modern England.

185 *turn thee*: divert you to the opposite direction, thus reducing the distance between the 'buck' and the hunter.

186 *ape's tricks*: absurd mimicry (of courtly behaviour); cf. 1.20–1. Trapdoor may bow elaborately.

188 *prefer*: recommend.

190 *To be ... trencher*: to eat from your dish.

203 *Simon and Jude's day*: 28 October, a proverbially wet holiday.

205 *watermen*: boatmen who carried passengers on the Thames.

Bankside: the area on the Southwark bank of the Thames, notorious for its brothels.

207 *burnt*: branded, a punishment for criminals who had committed a felony, but who escaped more severe punishment because they claimed the benefit of clergy.

214 *mermaid*: mermaids were purported to be sinister temptresses of sailors.

216 *cut her comb*: i.e. humiliate her; the rooster's crest is a traditional emblem of pride, and mermaids were traditionally depicted combing their hair.

221 *jingling ... bells*: (a) the bells of the morris dancer; (b) noise of gold coins.

222 *hobby-horse*: (a) in the morris dance, a horse costume; (b) a stick with a horse's head, bestrid by children as a toy (here, suggesting an erect penis).

225 *follow*: obey (with the implication that a woman should be led by a man).

226 *Beat ... brains*: strain your wits; proverbial (Dent B602).

228 *till butter comes*: with a pun on 'until orgasm'.

233 *worshipful bencher*: judge. 'Worshipful' was a title of respect for London City and guild officials.

238 *entertain thee*: maintain you (as a servant).

240 *Ralph*: pronounced 'Rafe'.

[Scene 3] S.D. *three shops ... in a rank*: three booths (like modern market stalls) were probably brought on stage to represent the shops. The action throughout the scene moves from shop to shop, as indicated by the stage directions; those shops not part of the dramatic focus at any given moment may become less significant through inactivity or silence, but nonetheless remain on stage for the entire scene.

s.d. *feather shop*: feathers were fashionable accessories in the period.

1 *what . . . lack?*: the trader's traditional call for customers; cf. *SH* 12.22.

2 *lawns . . . cambrics*: types of white linen.

9 *pot-herbs*: culinary herbs; not necessarily inappropriate, as tobacco (grown in North America, hence 'Indian') was seen as a type of nourishment.

11 *pipes*: (a) tobacco pipes; (b) penises.

13 *raising . . . head*: i.e. a woman lifting her skirts gives a man an erection.

15 *grope*: understand; but also continuing the bawdy banter.

17 *ditch*: quibble on 'vaginal canal'.

18 *mystical*: hidden.

21 *ell . . . smock*: a length of a woman's underskirt.

22 *closest striker*: most hidden fornicator.

23 *smockster*: one who deals in smocks, or a pimp.

25 *naked . . . vial*: i.e. a helpless creature subjected to public view. This phrase possibly has some other, unknown, contemporary relevance.

29 *a farmer's son . . . feather*: a country boy making his first attempt at being fashionable (by wearing a feather).

   hangings: tapestries, hung on walls or over beds.

38 *almanac*: almanacs, or calendars with astrological and weather forecasts, were calculated for specific longitudes yet adjusted to cover entire countries.

41 s.d. *puts . . . fire*: lights it; pipes were lit using wicks or hot coals held with tongs.

42 *I . . . so*: continuing the play on 'pipe' as 'penis'.

43 *used . . . fashion*: i.e. burned.

44 *French*: syphilis, the 'French' disease, known for its burning effect.

45 *I pray be covered*: this instruction may be indicative of some unknown stage business. Laxton could be telling Goshawk to 'put on your hat'.

   Jack: a generic name for a man, here directed at Goshawk.

47 *To me*: Greenwit is requesting a pipe or a light; in line 53 he shows appreciation for the tobacco.

49 *strange*: unfamiliar (with me).

51 *Push*: an interjection, meaning roughly 'don't worry about that'.

395

62 *form*: (a) manners; (b) bench; this leads to the following pun on 'stool'.

He's . . . chamber: (a) the chamber is furnished with chairs; (b) he empties his chamber pot frequently.

67 *Pooh, pooh*: the sound Laxton makes while 'he blows tobacco in their faces'.

68 *O, pooh! Ho, ho!*: the sound of their coughing.

75 *Though . . . hands*: a mild reproach to him for not pleasuring her.

79 *bear her in hand*: deceive her; proverbial (Dent H94).

84 *strangle him*: stifle him (with smoke).

95 *drink*: taking tobacco was often described as *drinking*.

101 *Faith*: by my faith.

106 *ordinary*: a fixed-price meal at an eating house or tavern.

Paul's: St Paul's Cathedral, a popular meeting place for those conducting business.

108 *ha'p'orth*: halfpenny-worth.

113 *eggs*: progeny, remainder.

120 *naked picture*: picture of a naked person.

122 *puny*: novice.

128 *Draw . . . man*: i.e. can I share your pipe?

132 *beaver gallants*: men with expensive beaver-fur hats.

stone-riders: riders of stallions, horses with 'stones' (testicles).

133 *private stage's . . . gentlemen*: 'private', indoor theatres charged more than public ones (like the Fortune); a 'twelvepenny-stool', or an especially good seat, cost the equivalent of an artisan's daily wage.

140 *hench-boy*: boy attendant.

146 *snail*: a jibe at his being a cuckold, because snails have 'horns', the traditional emblem of cuckolds.

148 *I hold . . . yourself*: continuing the insult, she suggests that she has better sex there than with her husband.

154 *yard*: suggesting 'penis'.

shepherd's holland: coarse linen.

157 *arrantest*: most thorough.

s.d. *frieze jerkin*: a coarse woollen, close-fitting jacket worn by men.

safeguard: an outer skirt worn to protect clothing when riding.

172 *get*: beget.

173 *Mile End milksops*: citizens performed military drills on the green at Mile End. Their inadequacy was often subject to derision.

174 *marrowbone . . . Italian*: bone marrow was considered an aphrodisiac, and Italians were seen as particularly lecherous.

175 *bona-roba*: 'good stuff' (Italian), applied to an attractive woman.

180 *how . . . ounce?*: Moll suggests that he praises it as if he were selling it.

183 *shag ruff*: ruffled collar made of 'shag', a material with a velvet nap.

188 *fat eel . . . fingers*: eels were proverbially slippery and considered a favourite food of the Dutch.

190 *both man and woman*: a hermaphrodite.

206 *Low Countries*: female genitals (with a play on 'cunt' for 'countries').

209 *I'm served . . . nothing*: i.e. I'm given a poor lover by a trick (his unfaithfulness), that makes his penis lie limp in my hands! I might as well keep my vagina closed, because nothing ever enters it.

210 *a-ringing*: i.e. making as much noise as a bell.

214 *warn ye*: bar you from.

217 *sews . . . skin-coat*: arranges erotic encounters; 'skin-coat' = skin. A 'bawdy skin-coat' could possibly also mean a condom, which, although rare, were made of linen in the period.

218 *shirt and smock*: i.e. man and woman.

220 *shapes*: (a) costumes; (b) genitals.

235 *Had I . . . nobody by*: this is a cowardly parody of Baldassaro Castiglione's famous instruction for men of valour in *The Courtier* that they should fight 'in the sight of noble men that be of most estimation'; cf. *The Book of the Courtier*, trans. Sir Thomas Hoby, 1581 (London and Toronto, 1928), 95–6.

236 *tread . . . turn tail*: even the most meagre creature will react when provoked.

243 *London measure*: London mercers allowed slightly more cloth than the standard yard.

245 *stone-horse*: cf. line 132; but also, a 'man'.

250 *Tyburn*: a place of public execution.

253 *Brentford, Staines, or Ware*: towns frequently visited on day trips from London, especially for amorous encounters.

268 *Holborn*: a busy road leading west from London.

269 *Gray's Inn Fields*: fields north of Gray's Inn, used for archery practice.

274 s.d. *Fall from them*: Moll and Laxton withdraw, and the other group (who have been on stage throughout) come back into prominence.

277 *Saint Antling's*: a church in Watling Street, whose bell rang at 5 a.m.

278 *freeman*: a citizen of London.

279 *liberties*: districts extending beyond the City yet which were under its control. The *suburbs* escaped London jurisdiction.

288 *nobleman's bedpost*: rich, brightly coloured hangings adorned the beds of the wealthy.

289 *like Kent unconquered*: it was believed that Kent had never been successfully invaded.

302 *Spital dealing*: dealing with those who belong in hospitals, or *Spitals* (because they have venereal disease).

303 *arms*: coat of arms; the formal qualification for gentility.

309 *Hark . . . ear*: Goshawk offers to whisper to Mistress Openwork. Here the whispering suggests lascivious familiarity, cf. *Troilus and Cressida*, 5.2.8, 33.

312 *burr*: a broad iron ring on a tilting spear. Moll suggests that she has only a burr (vagina) when a lance (penis) is needed to test chastity.

324 *put case*: suppose; there may be a pun on 'case' as 'vagina'.

327 *stand*: (a) remain steadfast; (b) grow erect.

336 *the high German's size*: a tall German fencer visited London at this time and had repeated successes against English swordsmen.

342 *kept*: defended.

357 *same wine*: i.e. 'bastard', a sweet Spanish wine.

   s.d. *The bell*: possibly of the Exchange or a local church.

360 *Parker's Ordinary*: Parker's tavern or eating house.

364 s.d. *with . . . duck*: indicating that they are going duck-hunting, a popular pursuit for citizens, cf. *EMI* 1.1.45. It was fairly unusual to employ live animals on the early modern stage.

367 *Pooh . . . pist*: Gallipot appears to be calling the dogs.

369 *Hogsden*: a popular duck-hunting locale; cf. *EMI* 1.1.43–5.

372 s.d. *spits . . . dog's mouth*: a common way of showing affection to dogs.

373 *Hum . . . pist*: Tiltyard is either calling a dog or spitting into its mouth.

377 *Parlous Pond*: a popular swimming hole in Hoxton, where citizens also hunted for ducks.

   Trug: the dog's name.

[Scene 4].10 *two-leaved*: forked.

 19 *made match*: pre-arranged meeting.

 22 *Fiddle . . . hog-rubber*: The viol was considered a more refined instrument than the more rustic fiddle. Moll may also object to the use of 'fiddle' as 'sexual dealings'. 'Hog-rubber' = menial, one who cleans or associates with hogs.

 26 *pageant-bearer*: someone who carries a portable stage (pageant) for street performances. Possibly, they have 'the worst memories' of an acting

company and must serve as stagehands. This may be a metatheatrical joke at the expense of the person playing the Porter, the smallest part in the play.

40 *at first*: to begin with.

41 *chopping and changing*: exchange of one thing for another.

42 *one head*: her maidenhead.

54 *out at heels*: in distress.

57 *younger . . . widows*: younger brothers, who under primogeniture could expect little inheritance, notoriously sought their fortunes by marrying widows, who by law would have inherited at least a third of their previous husband's estate. Here the widows are 'cozening' because they forfeit that estate so that a new husband would not be able to control it.

64 *as if . . . Virginia*: the implication is that one would marry hastily before undertaking a long sea voyage.

67 *So ho ho, so ho*: a falconer's call, hence 'a-hawking' in the next line.

68 *There boy, there boy*: a hunter's cry of encouragement to dogs. Cf. the phrase's use in a hunting context in *SH* 5.13–14.

69 *clout*: a strip of cloth, possibly a pincushion or measure, but punning on the brightly clad flesh used by falconers to lure a hawk.

72 *monster . . . trinkets*: hermaphrodite, 'trinkets' = sexual organs.

74 *fiddling's*: trick is.

77 *great Dutch slop*: wide, baggy breeches.

100 *He that . . . clock*: i.e. the young should not take advice from those past their prime.

102 *By . . . Ludgate*: Sebastian backs down from a direct challenge by swearing by a real clock near Ludgate.

104 *that insensible work*: the invisible clock works.

105 *lets*: it lets.

108 *Beats by all stops*: stops in the works of a clock prevent the action from moving too quickly, so Sir Alexander implies that Sebastian's judgement is over-hasty.

111 *a short prayer*: insufficient penance.

139 *Keep . . . still*: keep to your perverse path.

160 *of the devil's*: those of the devil's party.

162 *o'th good man's*: of God's party. 'God is a good man' was proverbial (Dent G195).

174 *give but aim*: only point the way.

[Scene 5].3 *tester*: sixpence.

5 *Marylebone Park*: Marylebone Park (now part of Regent's Park) was known as a place of assignation.

11 *Smithfield*: a field north-west of the City; its market was notorious for selling inferior horses.

12 *coached*: i.e. within a coach, also a play on couched, or embroidered with gold.

13 *tuftaffety*: a (luxurious) taffeta having designs formed by a raised nap.

15 *My life for yours*: i.e. 'on my life'.

36 *no bankrupt . . . sergeant's place*: because sergeants would have no debtors to arrest.

37 *catchpole rightly derived*: the pedigree of a sheriff's officer ('catchpole') correctly traced.

49 *You're . . . your eyes*: Moll suggests that venereal disease has led to his 'blindness'.

51 *Three Pigeons*: an inn in Brentford.

54 *No, not here*: Laxton takes Moll's 'know' in the sense of 'have sexual relations with'.

57 *untruss a point*: unfasten the laces of your clothing.

here's the point: i.e. her sword.

58 *tag*: punning on the point of metal at the end of a lace, but literally Moll's metal sword-point.

60 *pace*: movement.

61 *racks*: rides (at a walking pace), but punning also on the pain caused by torture on the rack.

63 *Win 'em and wear 'em*: win them and keep them; proverbial (Dent W408).

64 *serve an execution*: carry into effect a writ or judgement (in this case, capital punishment).

75 *her monkey*: monkeys were popular pets in the period, cf. *EH* 1.2 S.D.

79 *beyond cup and lip*: i.e. except for drinking from the betrothal cup.

85 *if it lay ledger*: if it were recorded (as in a ledger) there.

95 *poor shifting sisters*: (a) women who must earn their own living; (b) women who have no permanent abode.

115 *a rope*: hanging.

121 *familiar*: familiar spirit, a demon in someone's service.

138 *umbles*: inner parts; but Moll seems to mean his outer form.

139 *stand to't stiffly*: face an opponent resolutely, but with a suggestion of the stiffness of an erection.

160 *Temple*: a member of the Middle or Inner Temple, two legal societies controlling admittance to the bar.

S.D. *Fillips him*: strikes him, either with a flick of the finger or a full blow.

162 *Chick Lane*: an area known for its criminals.

183 *wide straddle*: a habit of standing or walking with feet wide apart.

186 *entertainment*: maintenance (for your service); cf. 2.238.

192 *Saint Thomas Apostles*: a church with clothiers in its vicinity.

[Scene 6].2 *pru-ing*: i.e. repetition of 'Prue'.

3 *kyes*: baby talk for 'cries'.

9 *up and ride*: i.e. copulate.

14 *You're best . . . physician*: i.e. you have too dispassionate a view of female sexuality.

22 *teeth*: i.e. mouth.

25 *so cookish*: like a cook, perhaps 'too delicate', but also cf. 'cotqueans' at line 32.

28 *fool's head*: head void of sense or intelligence.

34 *breeds*: is pregnant.

37 *milch kine*: milk-cows.

44 *scurvy-grass*: a plant used as a medicine for scurvy.

55 *Demophon . . . Phyllis*: Demophon, son of Theseus and Phaedra, promised his wife, Phyllis, that he would journey to Athens and return at a certain time. When he did not return, Phyllis hanged herself.

56 *Pan-da-rus . . . Cres-sida*: Pandarus, from whose name the word pander derives, brought Cressida and Troilus together. Laxton, thus, suggests that he will be her pimp, not her lover.

Aeneas . . . Dido: Aeneas left his lover Dido, Queen of Carthage, and she committed suicide.

die: punning on the sense, 'to have an orgasm'.

67 *childbed linen*: linen used for childbirth.

68 *mark*: identifying mark on the linen.

74 *smell a goose*: smell a rat; cf. 2.106.

76 *Steal, steal*: Gallipot attempts to sneak up on his wife and read the letter.

90 *Bedlam*: St Mary of Bethlehem, a hospital for lunatics.

94 *Hockley Hole*: a village above Clerkenwell Green.

96 *factor*: mercantile agent.

the Jonas: the name of a ship, inappropriately recalling the Biblical Jonah, who was cast overboard and swallowed by a whale.

121 *I swore*: such an exchange of vows could be legally binding.

133 *no odd sleight*: no unusual stratagem (will prevent his claim).

158 *sirrah*: a form of address to a man or woman.

158 *sister*: a general mode of address to a woman, not necessarily implying kinship.

165 *sadness*: seriousness.

174 *rubbers*: a set of games in bowls, with a pun on sexual rubbing.

175 *wrong bias*: bowls are counterweighted so that they can swerve along a bias; Goshawk suggests that Openwork does not follow a true course.

179 *rack and manger*: feeding (his sexual appetite) in the stable; 'rack' also means a neck of mutton, continuing Mistress Openwork's metaphor.

193 *because*: so that.

201 *tread*: copulate with.

206 *pudding-tobacco*: compressed tobacco, made into rolls resembling a pudding or sausage.

230 *No wild . . . but mine*: i.e. no woman to copulate with but mine.

240 *Be lady*: 'By our Lady'.

[Scene 7].2 *eye*: sight.

7 *bouncing ramp*: loud, vulgar woman.

16 *made bawdy*: used like a brothel.

23 *in conjunction*: lined up, an astrological term which here suggests copulation.

24 *holes*: perhaps 'nipples' or holes for the laces of a bodice.

25 *waistcoat*: also worn by women in the period.

26 *standing collars*: with a pun on clitoral and penile tumescence.

29 *Michaelmas Term*: the first term of the year, when more money was available because there had been little time to spend it.

44 *a grate*: i.e. prison bars.

45 *Drawer!*: Trapdoor calls out for a tavern drawer.

57 *noise*: band of musicians.

58 *take up*: borrow.

69 *springe . . . woodcock*: trap to catch this fool; proverbial (Dent S788).

71 *Counter*: court attached to a 'counter', one of the two London prisons of this name.

74 *counter-tenor*: a singing voice between tenor and alto; it was frequently sung by castrati (in Italy and the southern German states), so Sir Davy threatens to geld his son.

84 *logic and rhetoric*: key components of university education in the period.

94 *commence*: to take a higher degree.

   barred: (a) prevented from graduating; (b) behind prison bars.

95 *the Master's side*: the most expensive accommodation in a prison.

twopenny ward: cheaper prison accommodation.

96 *th' Hole*: the worst cells, for the destitute.

97 *Proceeds*: advances to a higher degree.

100 *Wood Street*: location of one of London's 'counters'.

103 *'Lies*: (Jack) lies.

105 *puttocks*: kites, applied contemptuously to officers who arrest for debt.

113 *One . . . coat*: i.e. a servant; blue coats were their traditional uniforms.

117 *honesty*: i.e. honest man.

125 *toward*: promising.

128 *One pair . . . coats*: i.e. you are two of a kind.

131 *Dear ware*: costly goods.

136 *cares . . . shoulder*: because shoulders are grabbed when making arrests.

152 *Bartholomew Fair*: the great London fair held on 23 August.

156 *Ça, ça*: a hunting signal meaning 'pay attention'.

   Give the counter: in hunting, to go in the opposite direction to the game; in this sense, 'wait where the quarry will double back on its trail'.

158 *mace . . . caudle*: a play on mace as a sergeant's weapon and a spice; 'caudle' is a warm, thin gruel.

159 *Double . . . ground*: military drill commands, 'make the files longer (by decreasing the rank), cover ground from side to side'.

164 *true English wolves*: wolves were extinct in England at this time, so Sir Davy implies that sergeants take up their lost role.

168 *nook*: hide in that nook.

185 *Whist . . . no*: Hanger and Curtilax signal to one another; on stage, they are probably hiding separately.

187 *infected maltmen*: malt-makers (who brought their product to London) with the plague.

196 *boy*: often applied to a servant who is not literally a 'boy' in age.

211 *Shoe Lane*: running from Holborn to Fleet Street.

212 *Is this a rescue*: rescuing a prisoner was a serious offence; Trapdoor wants to avoid being accused of the crime.

214 *scrivener's bands*: (a) documents which legally bind to a debt (made official by a scrivener, or notary); (b) bonds of debt owed to scriveners (who also lent money for interest).

[Scene 8].9 *Sessions*: periodical sittings of the justices of the peace.

15 *headborough's lanterns*: constable's lanterns.

16 *court cupboard*: a sideboard used for display.

22 *closely*: secretly.

25 *lets*: prevents.

26 *pressing*: (a) crushing with weights as a form of legal torture (designed to force a confession); (b) sexual intercourse.

38 *mysteries*: craft.

47 *to choose*: by choice.

50 *Many . . . came*: Moll implies that if such a simple change makes women more attractive, it will especially benefit the unattractive.

69 *owes . . . apiece*: the meaning here is obscure, but Moll seems to suggest that many women are so uninterested in true love that they have made sexual promises (for 'lays') to nine different suitors.

71 *mend*: better.

74 *ring-doves*: wood pigeons, with a pun on human 'love birds' who have exchanged rings.

78 *loose . . . idle*: i.e. vent your passion to no purpose.

79 *run . . . guts*: play the catgut strings, with a pun on piercing the guts of a fencing opponent.

81 *above bridge*: west of the London Bridge, with a pun on the bridge of the viol.

98 *unmannerly . . . woman*: because it is positioned between widely spread legs.

108 *Burse*: an exchange, where large quantities of goods were bought and sold.

109 *Saint Kathern's*: in the area of St Katherine's hospital, adjacent to the Tower. It was a disreputable area.

118 *Fleet*: a very polluted river running into the Thames west of St Paul's.

122 *hoise up sails*: suggesting the lifting of a woman's skirts.

125 *tails*: sexual organs, with a play on 'tales'.

131 *A watch*: Moll sees the watch Sir Alexander has placed to entrap her.

134 *cousin germans*: first cousins, punning on the origin of the German watch.

146 *ballads*: here, those in commemoration of the dead.

147 *brokers*: pawnbrokers.

149 *of free cost*: hangmen received the clothes of their victims.

153 *Foot*: i.e. 'by God's foot'.

157 *to his plunge*: over his head (in difficulties).

175 *they 'scaped her*: i.e. the watch and chain escaped her (fingers).

176 *stroke*: suggesting the strokes of sexual intercourse.

178 *Puts down*: excels. Sir Alexander uses the sense 'puts down (for sex)' in the next line.

181 *mounts*: throughout this exchange, words have a second, sexual significance. *Mounts* suggests sexual mounting; 'stands upon the whole' suggests 'growing erect in front of the hole (vagina)'; 'stop his mouth' suggests kissing.

184 *in other tale*: (a) with any other opportunity (for payment); (b) in another pudendum.

190 *Clifford's Inn*: one of the Inns of Chancery, on Fleet Street.

195 *sing*: with a second meaning of 'copulate'.

198 *prick-song*: music played from written notes as opposed to by ear (with bawdy pun).

[Scene 9].8 *great roses*: referring to the fashion for ornamental roses of ribbon on shoes.

11 *Bunhill*: an artillery ground above Moorfields.

13 *Pimlico*: formerly a part of Hoxton, not the present-day Pimlico near Victoria.

20 *cramp-ring*: a ring held to prevent cramp and similar ailments, but of little material value.

26 *tilt*: awning.

37 *poking my ruff*: crimping folds in the ruff with a 'poking-stick'.
    hit . . . teeth: challenged or mocked him; proverbial (Dent T429).

39 *musket on a rest*: muskets were heavy enough to need shoulder-high rests in the period.

47 *running heads*: (a) giddy brains; (b) the heads of running sores (from venereal disease).

49 *purse-nets*: bag-shaped nets used for catching rabbits, or cony-catching.

56 *ingle with*: coax.

59 *frumped at*: mocked, snubbed.

72 *split*: shipwreck; 'to make all split' was proverbial (Dent A205.1).

81 *eat . . . dressing*: i.e. make a fool ('cod's head') of yourself. Cod's heads were eaten in the period.

82 *pin*: fasten (your clothes).

92 *gib*: a familiar name for a cat.

94 *thy tail's cut*: i.e. you lack sexual organs.

100 *wanted*: missed.

105 *get . . . a-mumming*: (a) disguise yourself (i.e. 'find your own mask'); (b) play in a dumb show, keep quiet.

115 *Pass by . . . current*: are accepted, because of masks, as genuinely beautiful.

405

119 *beldame*: witch.

123 *broidered stuff*: ordinary goods that have been embellished.

129 *two flags . . . comedy*: flags on playhouses signalled that a play was being performed; 'flag' also means apron, here describing the two women's preparations for travel.

130 *Westward Ho!*: call by boatmen to announce that they are going west; it is also the name of a 1604 comedy by Webster and Dekker.

135 *cutting up*: slang for sexual activity, as at 6.229.

139 *toss . . . blanket*: a rough form of punishment in which a person is literally thrown trampoline-like in a blanket.

146 *stale*: (a) a mistress whose devotion is ridiculed by her lover to amuse another mistress; (b) the lowest form of prostitute, used as a decoy by criminals.

147 *Feed at reversion*: eat leftovers.

149 *Cold Harbour*: tenements associated with debtors and others in despair, with a pun on Laxton's desire to cool down.

156 *light*: lascivious.

157 *pug*: (a) harlot; (b) bargeman (carrying passengers west).

158 *tilted*: (a) jostled; (b) played with sexually.

174 *worth gold*: 'a girl worth gold' was proverbial (Dent G117.11).

176 *Keep off*: stay back.

178 *hid character*: code, language of sorcery.

180 *brazen head*: a head of brass, built by Roger Bacon (thirteenth-century scientist-sorcerer, professor at Oxford University), to predict the future.

184 *In mine . . . church door*: violating the law of hospitality, civil law, and Christian doctrine.

194 *text letters*: large or capital letters.

223 *a trick of youth*: i.e. blame it on inexperience; proverbial (Dent T519.11).

224 *rub*: obstacle, suggesting an obstruction in bowls, cf. 6.175.

226 *trick*: clever contrivance (serving as a lesson).

228 s.d. *summoner*: official who summons people to appear at court.

235 *Rose*: a common tavern name.

239 *Crastino Sancti Dunstani*: the day after St Dunstan's Day (19 May).

240 *Bow Church*: church east of the City, which served as an ecclesiastical court.

242 *libel*: written declaration of charges.

269 *tawny-coat*: servants of the courts wore tawny livery.

271 *lose my hair*: an effect of syphilis.

277 *who plays ... Honest Man*: a common phrase meaning 'who can spot an honest man' (Dent K117.11).

281 *shift*: Gallipot puns on *shift* as underclothing.

300 *horn*: cuckolds were supposed to have horns growing from their forehead which everyone could see but themselves.

307 *Irish*: a game resembling backgammon.

308 *bearing*: (a) in backgammon, removing a piece at the end of a game; (b) giving birth (to a child of questionable parentage).

[Scene 10].2 *Meg of Westminster*: another, earlier London woman famous for her fencing skills.

3 *Poultry*: one of the London prisons.

11 *mittimus*: warrant to hold someone prisoner until they are delivered to court.

Newgate: the prison at Newgate.

12 *firework ... line*: fireworks were often guided by attaching them to lines. Moll suggests that Trapdoor served as the path for dangerous plots against her.

14 *trains*: trails of gunpowder which carry fire to a charge.

15 *linstock*: staff which holds a match to light munitions.

16 *galley-foist*: state barge. The point is that the target is an inappropriate one.

17 *shovel-board shilling*: a shilling used to play 'shovel-board', a table-game similar to modern-day shuffleboard.

23 *whistled ... off*: a falconry term, meaning 'to cast off by whistling'.

26 *alderman's tomb*: tombs for the wealthy were often decorated in gaudy colours.

death's head: skull (accompanying tombs as an emblem of mortality).

31 *have squire's places*: i.e. be subordinate attendants (when they are actually knights).

52 *nappy ... spice cakes*: 'nappy' = intoxicating. Spice cakes could be had at the Pimlico Inn in Hoxton.

62 *cow-heel*: jelly made from the foot of a cow or ox.

65 *Alla corago*: in a courageous manner.

80 *siege of Belgrade*: not subject to siege since 1456.

92 *butter-box*: contemptuous designation for a Dutchman.

97 *Ick, mine ... Here*: this passage, in a corrupt form of Dutch, expounds on Tearcat's military exploits, but the dramatic point is that it is 'jobbering' or jabbering; a rough translation is: 'I, sir? I am the swaggering Tearcat, the brave soldier, I have been throughout Holland: the rascal who gave

more than a kiss and a word. I beat him with strokes on the head; pulled out thence a hundred-thousand devils, cheerfully, sir.'

100 *cross*: many coins had crosses on the reverse. Sir Beauteous tries to get rid of them by giving money.

102 *monster . . . eye*: because Trapdoor is wearing an eye-patch.

105 *skeldering*: passing oneself off as a wounded soldier.

107 *glaziers*: eyes.

112 *Isle of Dogs*: Thames peninsula east of London, near Greenwich.

120 *whip-jack*: a beggar who pretends to be a disbanded soldier.

126 *horns . . . thumb*: a thumb protected by a thimble of horn to aid in cutting purses.

128 *maunderer . . . pad*: beggar on the road.

137 *cant*: speak cant, the jargon of vagabonds and thieves.

140 *wild rogue*: born criminal.

   angler: someone who uses a hook to steal through windows.

141 *ruffler*: someone who seeks service by pretending to be a former soldier.

144 *Halt not*: do not hesitate.

147 *by the solomon*: an oath.

148 *kinchin mort*: infant girl.

151 *I'll tumble . . . quacking cheat*: I'll tumble tonight in the straw, and drink good booze, and eat a fat pig, a capon, and a duck.

153 *My . . . boozing-ken*: Moll translates in the next line.

157 *libken . . . stalling-ken*: sleeping house, or our house for keeping stolen goods.

158 *queer cuffin*: naughty man.

160 *a ben cove . . . gentry cuffin*: a good fellow, a brave fellow, and a gentleman.

163 *pedlar's French*: proverbial for canting jargon (Dent P175).

164 *half a harvest*: for one half of their harvest (stealing) season.

173 *Ben mort . . . niggle*: Moll and Trapdoor translate in the next lines.

175 *Cut benar . . . stamps*: speak better words and hold your hands and feet. Trapdoor reacts to Moll's violence.

191 *fadoodling*: i.e. fucking.

207 *A gage . . . us bing*: Moll roughly translates at lines 233–43.

210 *Romford market*: Romford, in Essex, had a famous hog market.

215 *stalled to*: stuck with.

217 *bords*: i.e. 'shovel-board shillings', coins worth twelve pence.

225 *trine me . . . cheats*: hang me on the gallows.

229 *I prae, sequor*: go before, I follow (Latin).

244 s.d. *gallant*: finely dressed.

249 *shells*: money.

252 *Shadow me*: stay close to me.

260 *nip*: one who cuts the purse or picks the pocket.

twopenny gallery: the least expensive gallery, still costing twice as much as entry into the yard.

261 *cloyer, or snap*: one who claims a share of the profits from new thieves.

266 *cheaping*: bargaining for.

267 *caduceus*: fabled wand carried by Mercury, messenger of the gods and known for his thievery and swiftness.

273 *boil*: give boils to.

276 *ken*: know.

279 *Swan*: a theatre on the south bank of the Thames.

281 *synagogue*: assembly.

282 *pacus palabros*: 'few words' (corrupt Spanish). This also suggests 'hocus pocus', which leads to the mention of 'conjure'.

300 *cheators*: those who gamble with false dice.

lifters ... curbers: thieves. In more specific senses, 'nips' cut purses, 'foists' pick pockets, and 'curbers' catch goods with hooks.

301 *black guard*: guard of attendants, black in appearance or character.

330 *beadle*: a warrant officer (with less authority than a constable) who whipped miscreants.

332 *tickling*: gratifying.

[Scene 11].5 *close*: in secret.

9 *Sluice*: landing-point on the south bank of the Thames.

10 *Lambeth*: area on the south bank of the Thames opposite the City.

11 *wet towns*: riverside towns. There were more than six towns between Lambeth and Windsor Bridge; the first were Chelsea, Battersea, Wandsworth, Fulham, Hammersmith, and Putney.

13 *Blackfriars*: stairs on the north bank of the Thames leading down to the water.

16 *Tower*: on the north bank of the Thames, at the east end of the City.

24 *gaskin-bride*: a bride wearing wide breeches.

46 *culverin's*: of a large cannon.

52 *plunges*: dilemmas.

55 *For*: despite.

57 *engage*: wager.

60 *will*: desire.

73 *his*: i.e. Sir Alexander's.

77 *her*: i.e. Moll.

81 *matches*: bargains.

86 *that refusal*: i.e. Sebastian's refusal of Moll.

93 *Of*: like.

102 *monthly*: in madness (as if deranged by the moon's influence).

103 *Hot broth . . . chamber*: treatments for madness.

112 *to their issue*: as to their children.

116 *smock dowry*: i.e. with only a smock for a dowry.

121 *kind*: affectionate.

124 *can wipe away*: can wipe (those) away. The passage appears to be corrupt, but the general sense is apparent.

132 *lusty*: (a) joyful; (b) sexually enamoured.

135 *pitch*: height.

137 *note*: distinction.

unmarked: unknown.

163 *thumb or knife*: to snip the strings of a purse.

173 *a forefinger in't*: a part in it.

184 *comfortable*: cheering.

199 *those*: i.e. the eyes of line 197.

208 *sped*: provided.

209 *simple*: straightforward, honest, plain.

212 *and*: if.

224 *coached*: furnished with coaches.

225 *Vessels*: i.e. maidenheads.

243 *hollow-hearted*: hollowed out.

250 *that*: i.e. Envy's mistaken gossip.

256 *cuck me*: set me in a cucking stool (a chair in which disorderly women were tied and ducked in a pond or river).

EPILOGUE

Possibly spoken by Moll, in keeping with the measure of control that she enjoys in the play itself.

3 *Limned*: depicted.

7 *hit her o'er*: disparaged.

28 *humorous*: full of fancies.

36 *The Roaring Girl . . . recompense*: the real Mary Frith did appear (possibly in this play) on the Fortune stage in 1611.

APPENDIX

2 *Venery*: (a) good hunting; (b) amorous pursuit.

5 *great crop-doublet*: short jacket stuffed with 'bombast' or cotton.

6 *fell*: lengthened.

7 *spruceness*: neatness.

8 *neatness*: refinement.

9 *hanging-sleeves*: long, open sleeves.

10 *the termers*: those who visit London in term time, when the courts are active.

13 *sixpence*: roughly the price of a printed play.

14 *well couched . . . mark it*: (a) richly contrived if you read carefully, i.e. venery is not included for its own sake; (b) well hidden if you look for it.

16 *For Venus . . . codpiece point*: women were not allowed to perform on stage in England. The passage draws a parallel between this prohibition and one against lewdness, to suggest that lust is disguised (by *double entendre*) in the play, and so is permissible if the censors do not detect it; 'untie not her codpiece point' means 'do not unlace the tags of her breeches (and discover her true nature)'.

18 *gallery-room*: the galleries around the stage had higher entrance fees than the standing room available to 'groundlings'; the implication is that the play (and book) is suitable for the better taste of such patrons.

20 *written of her*: i.e. in this play.

22 *mystical*: secret.

24 *vent . . . midnight*: discharge his inferior beer when they are too drunk to notice.

27 *discoveries*: manifestations, i.e. plays.

GLOSSARY

a the unstressed form of 'he'
ambuscado ambush
an if
angel gold coin (stamped with St Michael) worth 10 shillings
anon 'in a while', or shortly
apace quickly
aquafortis nitric acid
artificer artisan
avaunt be gone
Bacchus Greek god of wine
baffle mock, disgrace
balked prevented
balsamum aromatic medicinal preparation for healing wounds and soothing pain
bastinado cudgelling, beating with a stick
bauble toy
be-Lady 'by our Lady'
beshrew curse
betimes early, in good time
blear dim
blue-waiters i.e. servants, those who attend in blue livery
bob make sport of, deceive
boon goodly, prosperous
boon companion good fellow
boot-haler highwayman
brace pair
brewis broth
brisk spruce
bully good fellow, friend
buttery a room for (kitchen) provisions
by-blows blows from the side
calico cotton cloth
cambric fine white linen
caract caret
carouse full draught, cupful
cassock long coat worn by soldiers
catchpole petty officer of justice
Cavaliero swaggering fellow
Cerberus the mythological three-headed dog guarding the gates of hell

chartel formal challenge to duel
chincough whooping cough
chirurgeons surgeons
churl base fellow
civet musky perfume
cloak-bag a portmanteau or valise for carrying a cloak or other clothes
clouts rags
cock-horse toy, usually a stick with a horse's head, upon which children pretend to ride
codpiece cover for the crotch of a man's breeches
cog cheat
coistril base fellow, varlet
collops bacon
comely (a) attractive; (b) appropriate
conger salt-water eel
cony-catching cheating, swindling
cordwainers shoemakers
costermonger fruit-seller, also used as a term of abuse
cotqueans men who act like housewives
Counters London debtor's prisons
coxcomb fool
coz cousin, kinsman
cozen cheat
credit (a) reputation; (b) belief in ability to pay
cudgel club
cullion (a) testicle; (b) base fellow
cutpurse thief
dankish damp
dell young girl
demi-culverins small cannons
dilling darling
doublet close-fitting man's jacket
doxy thief's mistress
drab (a) whore; (b) slatternly woman
dry-beat thrash so that no blood is drawn
ell 45 inches
engross buy up to sell for a profit

enjoined forced
enow enough
Eos the goddess of dawn
ergo therefore
fackins faith
farthingale hooped petticoat
firkin small keg
fleering sneering
flout mock, insult
fond foolish
footboy page, boy-attendant
forseek seek (through)
forsooth in truth, surely
frampold spirited
gallant fashionable man
gamesters gamblers
gelding castrated horse
ging company
glister clyster, or enema
goatish lascivious
godamercy 'God have mercy'; (a) an
   oath; (b) an expression of thanks
God's me 'God save me'
God-so 'by God's soul'
God's so 'by God's soul'
goll hand
goodman male head of household, used
   as a title of respect
gramercy thank you
groat silver coin worth four pence
grogans coarse fabrics
groom (a) fellow (implying baseness);
   (b) servant
gudgeons small, freshwater fish
gull dupe, fool, trick
gullery deception
hackney (a) hired horse; (b) prostitute
hail-fellow intimate
handkercher handkerchief
hang-bys hangers-on
hanger loop from which a sword is hung
hap chance, fortune
'heart 'by God's heart'
hobby-horse a stick with a horse's head,
   upon which children pretend to ride
importunate burdensome
interlude old-fashioned name for a play
iwis certainly, truly
jade (a) inferior horse; (b) whore
journeyman one who has served an

apprenticeship and is qualified to work
   for wages
lance-knights foot soldiers armed with
   lances
lawn fine linen
laystalls rubbish-heaps
leaguer siege
legiblest most legibly
linstock staff with a wick at its end, used
   to fire cannons
lubber lout
lurch lurk
marchpane marzipan
mar'l marvel, wonder
marry indeed (from 'by Mary')
Mass 'by the Mass'
mess a group (usually four), especially
   when gathered for a meal
milliner seller of fine clothing
minion hussy
mithridate a supposed antidote against
   poison
morrow morning
mun must
murrain plagues
'nails 'by God's nails'
ningles catamites, or young male
   lovers
nipping stealing
noisome ill-smelling
'odso 'by God's soul'
ordinary *sb.* eating-house with fixed-
   price meals
pannier large provision basket
partlets collars, ruffs
passada a forward thrust with the
   sword, with the weaker foot advanced
   at the same time
pate head
pell-mell incessantly
perdie 'by God', indeed
pestiferous pestilent, harmful
peterman fisherman
petronel petronel, a large pistol or
   carbine
pickthank sycophantic
pieces of eight Spanish silver dollars
pigsney 'pig's eye', a term of affection
pinnace small, light vessel
pismire ant

413

placket opening in the top of a petticoat or skirt

polity policy

portague Portuguese gold coin, worth up to £4½

posy verse motto inscribed within a ring

potlings tipplers, drinkers

pox disease (syphilis)

prate talk, blab

presently immediately

prithee 'I pray (beseech) thee'

privy (a) secret; (b) intimate

puling whining, crying like a child

punk whore

purblind completely sightless

quacksalver ignorant person who pretends to a knowledge of medicine or miraculous remedies

quean whore, wench

quotha say you (says he or she)

rakehell rascal, scoundrel

rapier long, thin thrusting sword

ratsbane poison (white arsenic)

reverso back-blow

riven split

rosaker realgar, a form of arsenic

rosewater water infused with rose petals

runagate vagrant

sack Spanish white wine

St John's wort a type of hypericum, used for a variety of medicinal purposes

'save 'God save'

'sblood 'by God's blood'

scanderbag rascally

scrivener notary

scroyles scoundrel, wretch

scud run hurriedly

scurvy worthless, contemptible

'sdeath 'by God's death'

'sdeynes 'by God's dignity'

sergeant an officer who makes arrests and issues summons

sessions house court house

'sfoot 'by God's foot'

sirrah a contemptuous form of address, an address to servants

sith since

'slid 'by God's eyelid'

'slight 'by God's light'

slops wide, baggy breeches

'slud 'by God's blood'

small beer cheap, poor quality beer

snaffle bridle bit

'snails 'by God's nails'

somewhat something

spleen envy

sprites spirits

stews brothel

stoccata a thrust with a rapier

stock-fish dried cod that is beaten before cooking

stomacher an ornamental covering for the chest

stopple stopper for a water tankard

stuffs goods

sundry several

swinge beat

tarry stay, wait

tenement house

teston sixpence

trencher wooden dish

toil *sb.* trap, snare

trow believe; (do you) believe

truss tie up the laces that fasten clothing

ud'so 'by God's soul'

ud'soul 'by God's soul'

unthrift spendthrift

upsolve resolve

varlet (a) servant; (b) rascal

viands provisions

vild abhorrent

vouchsafe concede, grant

wanion vengeance

weasand throat

weeds clothes

welkin sky, heaven

whitemeat foods prepared from milk

wisking brisk, lively

wonted usual

worshipful an honorific to denote distinguished rank or importance

wot know

'wounds 'by God's wounds'

writhen contorted

yard (a) unit of measure; (b) yard stick; (c) penis

yawling yelling

younker youngster

zounds 'by God's wounds'

American Literature

British and Irish Literature

Children's Literature

Classics and Ancient Literature

Colonial Literature

Eastern Literature

European Literature

Gothic Literature

History

Medieval Literature

Oxford English Drama

Poetry

Philosophy

Politics

Religion

The Oxford Shakespeare

A complete list of Oxford World's Classics, including Authors in Context, Oxford English Drama, and the Oxford Shakespeare, is available in the UK from the Marketing Services Department, Oxford University Press, Great Clarendon Street, Oxford OX2 6DP, or visit the website at www.oup.com/uk/worldsclassics.

In the USA, visit www.oup.com/us/owc for a complete title list.

Oxford World's Classics are available from all good bookshops. In case of difficulty, customers in the UK should contact Oxford University Press Bookshop, 116 High Street, Oxford OX1 4BR.